To the
Library of the
University of Colorado
from
Mrs Roswell Skeel. Jr.

Day of Publication
January 15. 1929

# MASON LOCKE WEEMS

## BIBLIOGRAPHY

1791–1927

OF THIS VOLUME

*Two Hundred Copies*

*have been printed*

THIS IS NUMBER

195

PAUL LEICESTER FORD

Painted by Lillie V. O'Ryan, about 1898

# *Mason Locke Weems*

## His *Works and* Ways

*IN THREE VOLUMES*

A BIBLIOGRAPHY

*Left Unfinished By*

PAUL LEICESTER FORD

*Edited By*

EMILY ELLSWORTH FORD SKEEL

VOLUME I

NEW YORK MCMXXIX

*Printed in the United States of America*

IN MEMORIAM

**Paul Leicester Ford**

*FRATER AVE ATQUE VALE*

# PREFACE

AS my brother Paul approached the threshold of early manhood it seemed as if every avenue of activity had been closed to him. After an accident in infancy, his had been a childhood of almost constant physical suffering, with interludes of acute inflammation and fever, from which he would emerge spent and broken of body, but undaunted of spirit. Of schooling he had scarcely any, a few desultory months having proved his insuperable frailty. Somewhat later he shared three winters of history-study with the two sisters next above and below him in the family ladder. This home-made tuition, imparted by a third — our sister Rosalie — led gaily through a course of English, French, Greek and American history, the last two, it must be admitted, being considerably scanted by the young teacher's falling in love and preparing for marriage. But by her admirable thoroughness and enthusiasm, as well as by her rare gentleness and charm, the two earlier seasons had been made a joy, in which Paul could share through recumbent study and recitation. Two of her pupils never lost the interest in history, then implanted by her.

These, with a few scattering lessons in arithmetic and French given later to my brother by his elder fellow-student, turned teacher, formed the Alpha and Omega of his brief studies. From that time, as indeed before, his ardent, facile mind trained itself solely by books or in the school of life, and of both was always avid.

None the less, at seventeen a delicate physique — which gave no presage of its later endurance of work and fatigue far outdoing many a strong man — and an utter lack of training in any direction, technical or otherwise, boded ill for his happiness or usefulness in life. Small wonder that he passed through a period of profound depression, known to his family chum only by his subsequent confession. But it is not plausible — save on the assumption of that inscrutable reserve which often screens the deepest experiences from family or friend — that my father remained wholly unconscious of what was then in Paul's mind. The tie between the two was always so intimate and understanding, and from the first the elder had so bent his energies toward encouraging and developing the Benjamin of his sons — cruelly handicapped from babyhood — that he may well have divined the despondency through which Paul was passing.

As the first sign of dawn my brother wrote two little articles of mildly antiquarian content, which were accepted by *The Evening Post.* Well I remember my father's interest and participation, as well as his pride, so pleasant to see, in that first public recognition.

Soon after, Paul's pursuits in bibliography brought back his innate zest for life and work, and trained, if they did not actually create, that delving, painstaking accuracy which ever seemed the most inconsistent complement to his native adventurousness of temperament and mind. To this study he added history, and later turned for recreation to fiction, thus reversing the usual process of individual evolution, where imagination is generally more assertive and exuberant in youth.

*

* *

One evening in the late 'nineties, as Paul and I had nearly finished dining, a card was brought to him which sent him swiftly to welcome a visitor. After a few moments I saw two oddly dissimilar silhouettes pass through the room toward the library, and a faint memory was stirred within me by that of the guest, whose massive head and tall frame were of a slightly uncouth yet unmistakable distinction.

Some hours later Paul rejoined me by the fireside and told me with a saddened gravity that he had been asked to finish and issue a book upon which the other had worked for several years but which he — foredoomed to blindness — knew he could never complete. Paul added that a pledge had been demanded that only *his* name should appear in the finished volumes, without even so much as a hint of their inceptor's. When I cried out against such unmeasured generosity, he stated that the stipulation had been made absolute, and that all the notes for the work were to be destroyed unless he acceded unreservedly to this condition. We were both silent — I overcome by the fineness of such chivalry from an older to a younger man; he perhaps realizing, as I did not, that amongst other colleagues his action might well be misconstrued and be misread as a selfish appropriation of the guerdon due another. In the end he consented, with the understanding that he should defer his part of the book until free from prior tasks.

His friend, unhappily, did not live to see their joint work in print. Paul outlived that moment only briefly. But however strong the urge must have been to name his collaborator, he fulfilled his pledge as scrupulously to the dead as to the living. I hope I may be forgiven for touching on this episode, so honorable alike to him who gave and to him who received. Such instances of mutual trust, generosity and loyalty seem to belong to a common spiritual fund upon which all human hearts may draw.

I, more fortunate than Paul, am free to link my name to his in the following volumes and so to perpetuate a tie which has outlasted time and death. This work on Mason Locke Weems, begun, continued, but alas! not ended by my brother, represents an interest on his part extending over many years. For Weems' vestiges he was constantly on the alert during some fifteen years, and since his death several of his discoveries have been published by others. He purposed to take up the quaint old peddler-divine for his next work, immediately following that issued but a few days before his death, and he had already collected much material. It is noteworthy to contrast his first earlier drafts of articles upon Weems — wherein he roundly scored him as a fabricator and sensation-monger — with his later estimates which showed a larger toleration and understanding born of sympathy and wider knowledge.

It is a source of poignant regret that so picturesque a figure should not have been dealt with in its entirety by my brother's witty, trenchant yet most kindly pen. Such faults as are discoverable in the following pages should, in fairness, be attributed to the editor who has brought to her task only an abiding love for her precursor.

The dedication to my father of the succeeding volumes of *Letters*, is intended to express, in a measure, both Paul's and my recognition of the potent influence which his never-failing stimulus wrought upon this son's character. Coupled with a rare personal self-effacement, his was a constant incitement to his children to make the most of their opportunities or powers, and so to serve their time within the limitations of their capacity.

# PREFACE

After more than half a century of observing men and manners, I count myself blest in my intimacy with two natures so endowed with energy, earnestness, high-mindedness, courage and truth. My voiceless companionship with both, during the preparation of these volumes, has been my all-sufficing reward.

E. E. F. S.

EBBTIDES
SEVEN GATES FARM
September 28, 1925

# CONTENTS

## Volume I



[1] Throughout this *Bibliography* an * signifies that the item so marked has not been seen by the editor. The sign ⋮ indicates that at that point the title is broken into two columns of type, the second column being indicated by ⋮| This procedure follows notes already made by Paul Leicester Ford.

CONTENTS

## CONTENTS

*Frontispiece*

PAUL LEICESTER FORD

1865–1902

From an oil portrait painted in 1898 by
Lillie V. O'Ryan

# LIST OF ILLUSTRATIONS

## LIST OF ILLUSTRATIONS

Facsimile of the [illegible]

Facsimile [illegible] Title Page [illegible]

Facsimile [illegible]

[illegible]

[illegible]

[illegible]

[illegible]

[illegible]

[illegible]

[illegible]

[illegible]

[illegible]

[illegible]

[illegible]

# LIBRARIES AND COLLECTIONS CONSULTED

Bibliographers, like Lazarus, rarely get a full meal at any time. Rather do they gather up the crumbs which fall from the libraries' rich tables, as they go from one to another on their quest. Fortunately the dispensers are of a generous habit, and rarely is a beggar turned away. I have knocked only too often at many a solemn portal, always with a plea to prefer rather than a service to proffer, yet to only one precinct have I been denied access. The obstacles placed in my way, tantamount to a refusal, by the Virginia Historical Society have been crippling to my work. This I deplore, because, amongst their files of Virginia newspapers, I believe that there must be items of interest concerning Weems — a self-elected citizen of the Old Dominion. But in all other libraries mentioned in these volumes I have found not only a welcome but unstinted help. Whether in person or by correspondence, I have never asked in vain, either from a state, public, proprietary or private collection. To each and all I offer my thanks.

But my most earnest tender of appreciation is made explicitly to those who out of affection for my forerunner in this task, or disinterested zeal in the cause of bibliography, have kept my needs unfailingly in mind. To Dr. Wilberforce Eames, and the staff which was formerly his, in the New York Public Library, to Mr. Clarence S. Brigham and the staff of the American Antiquarian Society, to the staff of the Library of Congress, and to my brother, Worthington Chauncey Ford of the Massachusetts Historical Society, I am indebted far beyond my ability to express.

## ABBREVIATIONS

| | |
|---|---|
| AAS. | American Antiquarian Society. |
| APhS. | American Philosophical Society. |
| AugChronOf. | *Augusta Chronicle* Office. |
| BA. | Boston Athenaeum. |
| BM. | British Museum. |
| BPL. | Boston Public Library. |
| CinPL. | Cincinnati Public Library. |
| ClPL. | Cleveland Public Library. |

# ABBREVIATIONS OF LIBRARIES CONSULTED

| | |
|---|---|
| CLS. | Charleston Library Society. |
| ConnHS. | Connecticut Historical Society. |
| CrozTS. | Crozier Theological Seminary. |
| DeR. | De Renne Library. |
| DHS. | Delaware Historical Society. |
| EI. | Essex Institute Library. |
| EPFL. | Enoch Pratt Free Library. |
| ESPCol. | Edwin S. Phelps Collection. |
| FROf. | *Franklin Repository* Office. |
| GaHS. | Georgia Historical Society. |
| GTOf. | *Gettysburg Times* Office. |
| HHL. | Henry Huntington Library. |
| HL. | Hamilton Library. |
| HSDC. | Historical Society of Dauphin County. |
| HSP. | Historical Society of Pennsylvania. |
| HU. | Harvard University Library. |
| IndPL. | Indianapolis Public Library. |
| JCB. | John Carter Brown Library. |
| JHL. | Johns Hopkins Library. |
| LC. | Library of Congress. |
| LCHS. | Lancaster County Historical Society. |
| LCPhil. | Library Company of Philadelphia. |
| LIOf. | *Lancaster Intelligencer* Office. |
| L.&F. | Letter files of Mathew Carey in the possession of Messrs. Lea and Febiger.[1] |
| MdDio'nL. | Maryland Diocesan Library. |
| MdHS. | Maryland Historical Society. |
| MdStL. | Maryland State Library. |
| MHS. | Massachusetts Historical Society. |
| MLCin. | Mercantile Library of Cincinnati. |
| MLPhil. | Mercantile Library of Philadelphia. |
| MStL. | Massachusetts State Library. |
| NCStL. | North Carolina State Library. |
| NJHS. | New Jersey Historical Society. |
| NJStL. | New Jersey State Library. |
| NoHPL. | Northampton Public Library. |
| NorPL. | Norfolk Public Library. |
| NYHS. | New York Historical Society. |
| NYPL. | New York Public Library. |
| N'yptPL. | Newburyport Public Library. |
| NYSocL. | New York Society Library. |
| NYStL. | New York State Library. |

[1]These files are now in the collection of the Historical Society of Pennsylvania.

## ABBREVIATIONS OF LIBRARIES CONSULTED

| | |
|---|---|
| PIL | Peabody Institute Library. |
| Presb'nHS. | Presbyterian Historical Society. |
| PStL. | Pennsylvania State Library. |
| RutgersCL. | Rutgers College Library. |
| SavNewsOf. | *Savannah News* Office. |
| SCHS. | South Carolina Historical Society. |
| Un'yGa. | University of Georgia. |
| Un'yM. | University of Michigan. |
| Un'yNC. | University of North Carolina. |
| UTS. | Union Theological Seminary. |
| VStL. | Virginia State Library. |
| WIFL. | Wilmington Institute Free Library. |
| WIL. | Watkinson Institute Library. |
| WisHS. | Wisconsin Historical Society. |
| YU. | Yale University Library. |

IN THESE OLD TOMES
LIVE THE OLD TIMES.

A SCOTCH CLERGYMAN, ON MOUNTING HIS PULPIT ONE SUNDAY MORNING, AFTER SEARCHING ALL HIS POCKETS THUS ADDRESSED HIS CONGREGATION: 'MA FREENDS, AH FIND A'VE FORGOTTEN MA NOTES, AND SHALL THEREFORE BE CONSTRAINED TO ADDRESS YE THIS MORNIN' IN THE WORDS THE LORD MAY PUT INTO MA MOUTH. IN THE AFTERNOON A'LL HOPE TO COME BETTER PROVIDED.'

IF YOU WANT TO WRITE A BOOK, REFLECT THAT IT MUST BE USEFUL AND NEW, OR AT LEAST INFINITELY AGREEABLE. — *Voltaire.*

7

A
History
of the Life and Death, Virtues
and Exploits,
of
General George Washington;
Dedicated
To
Mrs. Washington;
And containing a great many curious and valuable Anecdotes,
tending to throw much light on the private as
well as the public life and character, of
That very extraordinary Man:
The Whole
Happily calculated to furnish a feast of true
Washingtonian Entertainment and
Improvement
Both to ourselves and our children.

FACSIMILE OF THE HANDWRITING OF
PAUL LEICESTER FORD

# BIBLIOGRAPHY

## FOREWORD

SOME years before his death in 1902, my brother Paul wrote as follows: 'On Washington's death some four hundred biographical sketches, funeral sermons, memorial addresses, & society resolutions came from the press to commemorate and express the feeling of the age at this loss. . . . A little brown pamphlet of some 82 pages only, was being sold by the "penny hawkers" in the streets of our principal cities for the consideration of "2s. 3d. only."' This clearly refers to the signed edition of Weems' *Life*, hitherto considered the first one by him.

Baker made the statement, with which Hough agreed, that Weems had issued this *before* the General's death. Like many others, my brother was undoubtedly on the watch for such an issue, which if ever found, must be left to some more fortunate gleaner than I. In attempting to disprove the legend or finally to discover its source, I retraced my brother's steps which had led him far from his comment above.

Among his papers I found complete photographic prints — lacking only pages 33–36 — of the anonymous *Life of Washington* printed by Matthias Bartgis in 1801. Although this bore no likeness to the accredited book signed by Weems, yet knowing my brother's bibliographic *flair*, amounting to a fine instinct surcharged with imagination, I attached significance to the prints. Later, in going over the unique collection of *Lives* of our first President made by Mr. Walter U. Lewisson of Boston, which has since been added to the Henry Huntington Library, I discovered the Keatinge smaller edition of practically the same text. After this I made a more extended search and discovered the similarity of both to the Bartgis 1809 edition in German. This last, though anonymous, has been attributed to Weems universally, and despite its differences, so many passages are like the acknowledged editions that, ruling out the possibility of wholesale plagiarism, it seems a clear case of two works by the same hand. Further evidence of this contention is to be found in note 2 to title 1.

There can be no doubt that my brother was on this trail and may even have gone so far as to establish the identity of Bartgis' editions of 1801 and 1809, the latter in German. Else why should he have taken all the pains of having the former photographed complete?

To him, therefore, all the credit is due for the final running to earth of the oft-reputed first edition which follows.

# BIOGRAPHIES

NUMBER I 1800?

THE | LIFE | AND | Memorable Actions | OF | GEORGE WASHINGTON | GENERAL AND COMMANDER | *of the* | ARMIES | OF | AMERICA |

Printed by and for GEORGE KEATINGE. | No, 207 Market-street. | [*n.d. 1800?*] 24mo. pp. (5), 2, (1), 1, 5–10, (1), 5, 18–96. *Front.port.* HHL. [*imp.*], HSP., LC. [*imp.*]

1. The portrait is a rude woodcut, profile to left, bust length, set in an oval medallion of one plain-lined border, suspended from the beak of an eagle with wings outstretched in flight; below, following and outside the oval line of the border, is the inscription 'IMMORTAL WASHINGTON'; the unsigned Preface, of thirteen paragraphs, begins: 'THE compiler of this little work . . .' and ends: '. . . let us learn to imitate his virtues.'; CONTENTS, giving synopses of Chapters I–XIII identical with chapter headings throughout the book; the text is markedly different from the hitherto accredited editions, although there are many passages in common [see Bioren's second edition, title 3, pp. 33–34, 35–39, 40–41, 44–45, 46–47, 48, 50, 65, etc. — that edition, rather than the one of Green & English, being selected for comparison because it has, in gen-

THE

LIFE

AND

Memorable Actions

OF

*GEORGE WASHINGTON*

GENERAL AND COMMANDER

*of the*

ARMIES

OF

AMERICA

Printed by and for GEORGE KEATINGE,

No. 207 Market-street.

1800?

Facsimile Frontispiece and Title Page of the Keatinge Edition of *The Life of Washington*

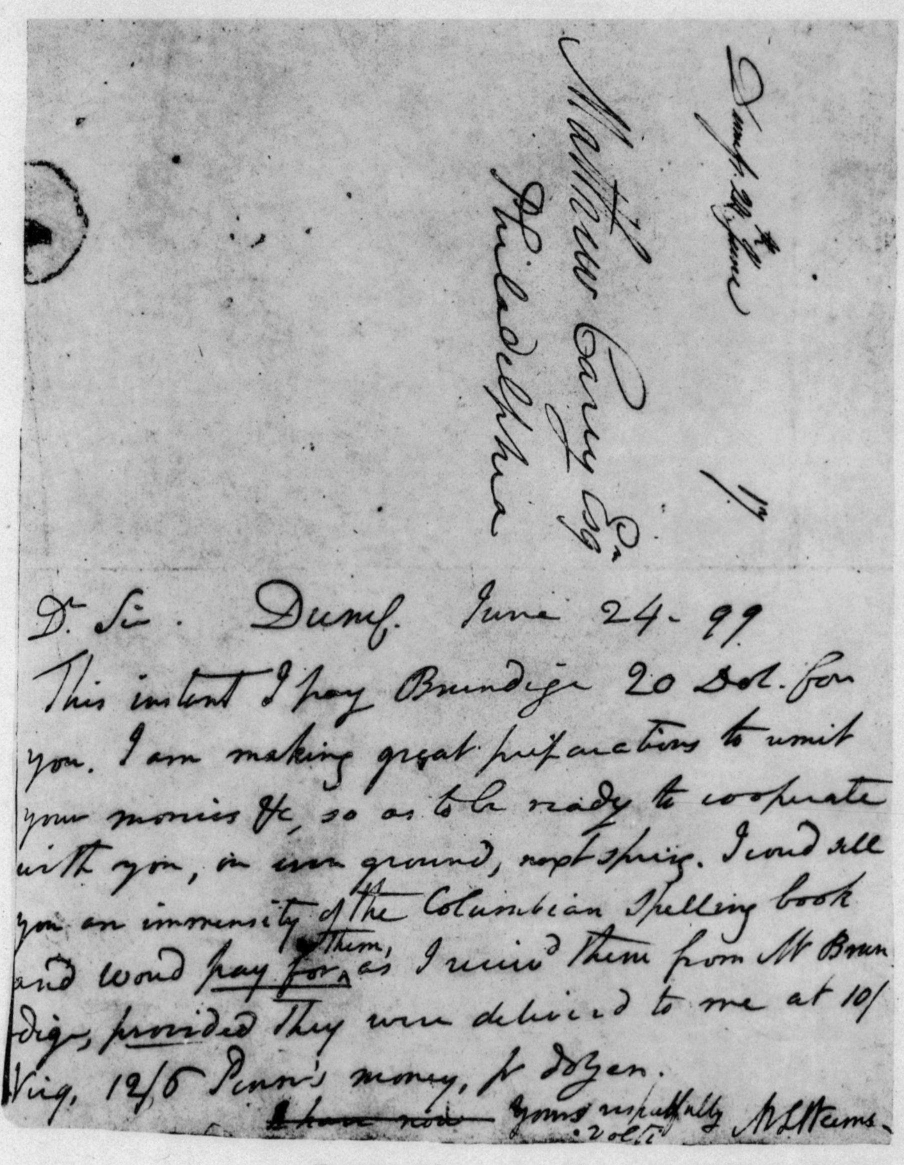

Dumfs 24th June

Matthew Carey Esq.
Philadelphia

1/

Dr. Sir. Dumf. June 24-99.
This instant I pay Brundige 20 Dol. for
you. I am making great preparations to remit
your monies &c, so as to be ready to cooperate
with you, in new ground, next spring. I coud sell
you an immensity of the Columbian Spelling book
and woud pay for them, as I recieved them from Mr Brundige, provided they were delivered to me at 10/
Virg. 12/6 Penn's money, p. dozen.
~~I have now~~ Yours respectfully M L Weems.
2 vol.

Facsimile Letter of Mason Locke Weems First

I have nearly ready for the press 8773 piece christened, or to be christened, "The Beauties of Washington." 'tis artfully drawn up, enlivened with anecdotes, and in my humble opinion, marvellously fitted "ad captandum—gustum populi Americani!!! What say you to printing it for me and ordering a copper plate Frontispiece of that HERO, something in this way.

George Washington Esqr.

"The Guardian Angel of his Country

"Go thy way old George. Die when thou wilt we shall never look upon thy like again"

M. Carey in von. &c.

NB. The whole will make but four sheets and sell like flax seed at quarter of a dollar. I could make you a world of pence and popularity by it

Mentioning a Projected Book on Washington

eral, more passages in common with the Keatinge edition, and, moreover, the changes made in Bioren's second from the Green & English edition were, on the whole, more generally followed in all the subsequent issues of the text up to the fifth edition, 1806; for comparisons between this Keatinge and the Green & English editions, see note 1 to the latter; see also titles 5 and 7]; the note on '*Bon repos*' is on p. 21, the anecdote of Mr. William Payne[1] on pp. 26–34; the style is unmistakably Weems' after the first lines taken from Bell's *Sketch* [see note 3 below]; Bartgis' edition of 1801 is not only copied from this one, but it is almost identical, save the title, even to the ungrammatical *bore* instead of *borne* in the first paragraph of the Preface; Bartgis does not give CONTENTS, and omits the descriptive heading to Chapter I, his German edition of 1809 continuing the same changes. [See also title 5, last item of note 4. Neither the LC. nor the HHL. copy is complete, although they largely supplement each other. The HSP. copy, discovered later, is perfect.

2. Weems' authorship of this early edition is attested by his correspondence with Carey at that time. On June 24, 1799 he wrote to Carey, offering him 'a piece . . . nearly ready for the press . . . to be christened "The Beauties of Washington"' [see facsimiles opposite this page]. To this proposal Carey had not responded as late as Jan. 12, 1800 despite the favorable condition of the market for such a work created by Washington's death a few weeks before. Accordingly Weems wrote on that date that he would be willing to send on half of the work for Carey's inspection. This clearly shows that he was already prepared with material which he could hardly have worked up so soon after Washington's death and that, indeed, he was even revising it. So keen a bookseller as he would have known that a large sale awaited a prompt issue of any book on the dead leader. To have delayed until Carey could make up his mind to print it for him would have lost this immediate market. What more natural to him, then, than to make some changes in his manuscript from the present to the past tense, add an account of the funeral and a few other facts germane to Washington's death, and rush his work into print? Indeed, on Feb. 2, 1800, he wrote to Carey that he had 'resolved to strike off' a few on his own account. [Note his comments upon the Dedication and title page in the same letter, and also that it was not until April 19 that he gave the title as it has hitherto been known to us.] As he was in or near Dumfries during those early weeks of the year, it was natural that he should select Baltimore and Georgetown printers for his first

[1] Widely reprinted throughout the press: see *New Jersey Journal*, Dec. 16, 1800, NJHS.; *South Carolina State Gazette*, Dec. 18, 1800, CLS.; *General Library*, Dec. 25, 1800, NJHS.; *Boston Gazette*, Dec. 26, 1800, NYPL., being those which I have happened to see of that year alone. Quoted, abbreviated, in *Historical Collections of Virginia*, Henry Howe, 1845, pp. 543–544, LC.

and second ventures. [This helps to prove that the Green & English issue *was* earlier than Bioren's second edition. His description of the former as contained in his letter of Jan. 12 and as finally projected, reads quite other than his original plan of June, 1799. These letters are more fully quoted in title 2, note 4.] That he should plan a larger work immediately after the Keatinge edition fits in with his energy of mind and body. This smaller *Life* is less hortatory and discursive than the accredited one issued between 1800 and the fifth edition of Georgia, 1806, when the text was entirely rewritten. Thus we have, between those years, three differing texts, yet with many points in common, and each written after Weems' own manner. Circumstantial evidence of Weems' authorship of the Keatinge and Bartgis version is found in his close relations with Bartgis during this period, for, besides the advertisements of *Washington* in note 3 to title 5, other issues of Weems were advertised in *Bartgis's Federal Gazette* in May and September, 1796 [title 226] and in *Bartgis's Republican Gazette* in November, 1802 [titles 227 and 233] and in July, 1803 [titles 171A and 173].

3. The origin of the first paragraph of both the Keatinge and Bartgis editions [up to the words 'Stafford County,' where changes begin] is manifestly *A Short Sketch of George Washington's Life and Character*, by a Gentleman of Maryland. This was 'reprinted' in London, 1780, for the benefit of the American prisoners (from an as yet undiscovered Annapolis 1779 issue), with *A Poetical Epistle to . . . George Washington* [by Charles Henry Wharton]. The *Sketch* was reprinted many times and gradually its authorship was inscribed by 'John Bell, Esq., of Maryland.'[1] Condie also drew on it for some of his facts, *Philadelphia Monthly Magazine*, 1798, and in his *Life*, 1800. By changing tenses from present to past, altering dates from Old Style to New, giving counties their new names after the Revolution had expunged many of the distinctively royal ones, Weems, as had others before him, took his bare statistics from this well-known sketch, which had been announced as written by one who was 'connected and intimate in the family of' Washington. I

[1] The name John Bell first appeared in a reprint of the *Sketch* in the *Westminster Magazine*, Jan. 1784. For other reprints see: *Biography of Gen. George Washington, and The Liverpool Tragedy* . . . Printed by Edward Gray, For the Compiler, CHS.; *London Chronicle*, July, 1780; *Westminster Magazine*, Aug. 1780; *New Annual Register*, 1780; *Pennsylvania Gazette*, Nov. 28, 1781; *The New-England Almanack*, Nathan Daboll, New London, 1781, T. Green [Evans No. 17131]; *Massachusetts Magazine*, Vol. III, March, 1791, pp. 139–143, AAS.; *Washington Spy* [Hagerstown], July 6, 13, 20, 1796, MDHS.; *Universal Magazine* [London], May, 1800, Vol. 106, pp. 338–344, LC.; New York facsimile reprint 1865 of Annapolis reprint of Dilly's edition of 1780. See also *Early Sketches of George Washington*, William Spohn Baker, 1894, HSP.

have tried to trace John Bell, but ineffectually, for the name, in different forms, is legion in Maryland.

4. The earliest printed mentions which I have found of George Keatinge are advertisements of his bookstore in the *Maryland Journal*, June 6, 1794, and of an edition of the *Pelew Islands* published by him, *Edwards's Balt. D. Adv.*, Apr. 22, 1794, AAS. There are others in the *Telegraphe* of Baltimore, Sept. 22, 1797, PIL. As early as Jan. 1, 1794 he was writing to Mathew Carey from Baltimore, declining a certain exchange of books, but having no objection to opening an account and letting him have 'such books as I am extensively assorted with.' He also writes, on Feb. 2, 1794, from Baltimore, that he has 'lately commenced business in this town in the Bookselling, Bookbinding & Stationary Line, being regularly bred to it in Dublin (Ireland). . . . Has at Press here a small edition (for Children) of Robinson Crusoe, and a Song Book which will be the newest and best on the Continent.' Oct. 26, 1794, he has ready the 'Age of Reason 3 Vols. . . . Ditto 1 Vol. Folly of Reason. . . . Examination of Age of Reason by Wakefield, Democratic Songster, Steuben's Military Discipline, Rowan's Trial and Fille de Chambre.' Jan. 26, 1795 he writes that 'his Edition of the Age of Reason is nearly out of Print.' He writes again in August, and then, on Dec. 31, 1795: 'I will thank you to send me a few Copies of any new Book you may print on your own acc^t^. and place the same to acc^t^. which I shall settle with you every spring & fall.' Jan. 5, 1796 he writes of his proposals in the Baltimore paper 'for a Magazine which [*I have*] at press here' and asks Mathew Carey for his interest in the procuring of plates. 'The first N°, will be published on the 1st of Feb^y^ with an engraved Likeness of the President the plate I purchased from M^r^. Smith of New York & it is the one he has in the political magazine.' Mathew Carey had written to Keatinge on Jan. 2, 1796, and wrote several times thereafter in that year and 1797. [L.&F.] The *Baltimore Directories* between 1796 and 1807 give George Keatinge, describing him variously as bookbinder, book seller and stationer, at different addresses. Sabin states that he was the compiler of a book of Free Masonry in 1797 [G. No. 37138]. *Bannaker's Virginia, Pennsylvania, Delaware, Maryland, Kentucky Almanac* for 1797 [VStL.] was printed by Christopher Jackson for George Keatinge's bookstore. He also published various other almanacs: *Poor Robin's Almanac or Starry Observer*, Baltimore, 1805 [LC]; and numerous editions of *The Washington Almanack* and *Keatinge's Jefferson Almanac*.[1] With this *Jefferson Almanac*, the 1802 edition

[1] *Ad.* 'Almanacs . . . six Cents single. . . . Just Published, and for Sale, At George Keatinge's, . . . The Washington Almanac, For 1803, Being the third Annual Tribute to the Memory of George Washington. It contains, besides every necessary in an Almanac, a number

of which I examined at AAS., it is just possible that Weems had some connection, though there is no direct evidence of it. But his touch is strongly suggested, both in subject and treatment, in one of the 'entertaining stories' on the last page: 'ANECDOTE of *General* WASHINGTON at the Battle of Monmouth' where he reproved Lee who stated that 'your troops will not fight British Grenadiers' by retorting: 'Sir, *you* never tried it [']. Following this is 'Original EPITAPH on a DRUNKARD. | *Pray who* lies here? Why don't you know, | 'Tis stammering, staggering, boozy Joe: | What dead at last! I thought that death | Could never stop his long long breath, | True death ne'er trew [*sic*] his dart at him, | But kill'd like David, with a SLING: | Wheither [*sic*] he's gone we do not know, | But if he former taste inherits, | He's quaffing in a world of SPIRITS.' [The first printing of this doggerel which I have found was in the *Philadelphia Minerva*, July 22, 1797, HU.] Keatinge was still printing in Bath in 1807 — see *Authentic Account of the Appearance of a Ghost in Queen Ann's County, Maryland*, NYPL. See also title 5, note 4.

NUMBER 2 1800?

A | HISTORY, | OF THE LIFE AND DEATH, VIRTUES | AND EXPLOITS. | OF | GENERAL GEORGE WASHINGTON; | DEDICATED | TO | MRS. WASHINGTON; | And containing a great many curious and valuable ANECDOTES, | tending to throw much light on the *private* as | well as *public* life and character, of | THAT VERY EXTRAORDINARY MAN: | THE WHOLE | HAPPILY CALCULATED TO FURNISH A FEAST OF TRUE |

of interesting particulars of the life of Washington and several curious stories. Such persons as wish to give this Almanac a preference, will remark that in the title of each [*sic*] is represented Columbia weeping over the tomb of Washington. In a few days will be published the Jefferson Almanac at the usual price.' *American & Daily Advertiser*, Nov. 22, 1802 *et seq.*, AAS. See also *Republican* (Baltimore), Jan. 4, 1802 *et seq.*, AAS., NYHS.; *American & Baltimore Gazette*, Nov. 1, 1805 *et seq.*, HU.

A

# HISTORY,

OF THE LIFE AND DEATH, VIRTUES, AND EXPLOITS,

*OF*

*GENERAL GEORGE WASHINGTON;*

DEDICATED

*To*

*MRS. WASHINGTON;*

And containing a great many curious and valuable ANECDOTES, tending to throw much light on the *private* as well as *public* life and character, of

*THAT VERY EXTRAORDINARY MAN:*

THE WHOLE

HAPPILY CALCULATED TO FURNISH A FEAST OF TRUE *WASHINGTONIAN ENTERTAINMENT AND IMPROVEMENT*, BOTH TO OURSELVES AND OUR CHILDREN.

---

A wit's a feather, and a chief's a rod;
An honeſt man's the nobleſt work of God.

Who *noble ends* by *noble means* obtains,
Or failing, ſmiles in exile or in chains;
Like good Aurelius let him reign, or bleed
Like Socrates, that man is *great* indeed.

---

PRINTED FOR THE REV. M. L. WEEMS,
*Of Lodge No. 50, Dumfries,*
*BY*
*GREEN & ENGLISH,* GEORGE-TOWN.
*(Price 2s. 3d. only.)*

FACSIMILE TITLE PAGE OF THE GREEN & ENGLISH EDITION OF *THE LIFE OF WASHINGTON*

WASHINGTON ENTERTAINMENT AND IMPROVEMENT, | BOTH TO OURSELVES AND OUR CHILDREN. | A wit's a feather, and a chief's a rod; | An honest man's the noblest work of God. | Who *noble ends* by *noble means* obtains | Or, failing, smiles in exile or in chains; | Like good Aurelius let him reign, or bleed | Like Socrates, that man is great indeed. |

PRINTED FOR THE REV. M. L. WEEMS, | *Of Lodge No. 50, Dumfries,* | BY | GREEN & ENGLISH, GEORGE-TOWN. | (*Price 2s 3d. only*) | [*n.d. 1800?*] 8vo. pp. 1, (1), 1, (1), 1–3, (1), 5–80.
BA., HSP., JCB., NYPL.

1. Dedication to Mrs. Washington, dated Feb. 22, 1800, follows the title sheet; the Preface, unsigned, undated, of eight paragraphs, is entirely different from that in the Keatinge 1800 and Bartgis 1801 issues; it begins 'To promote the love of virtue . . .' and ends with the words 'AMERICAN GLORY to commence.'; the text begins like the Keatinge edition after the *Sketch* of John Bell, 'This truly great man, the third son . . .' and is not divided into chapters, but into sections on 'His Patriotism,' 'His Justice,' etc.; it has many similarities throughout, both in matter and manner, with the Keatinge and Bartgis editions, such as the anecdote of Payne [Keatinge, pp. 26–34, Green & English, pp. 38–42], the note about *bon repos* [Keatinge, p. 12, Green & English, p. 31], the note about whiskey [Keatinge, p. 28, Green & English, p. 20]; up to p. 46 of Keatinge and p. 10 of Green & English, the matter is nearly identical. After that the resemblance ceases, for the Green & English introduces diatribes against gambling, etc., while the Keatinge gives much space to an account of the Revolution and Washington's part in it. The HSP. and NYPL. copies show a different paper for the title and the dedication sheets; as the Preface in these copies has a caption title reading 'A HISTORY | of the Life, Death, Glorious Deeds, &c. | &c. &c. of | GEORGE WASHINGTON, Esq. | , and as the signatures are complete without these, I believe that the book was first printed without a title page or dedication, which were added later. See Weems' letter of Feb. 2, 1800, note 4 below. His letter of Apr. 19, 1800, is the first mention I have found of the title as given in this edition. The note 'abc' on Lakes, Rivers and Mountains, on p. 70 of this edition, and that on Hume, on pp. 65–66, are lacking in Bioren's third edition.

2. Dr. Wilberforce Eames makes this the first 1800 edition of those hitherto accredited. [See his notes written in Bioren's second edition, 1800, NYPL.] I too

believe that only the George Keatinge text is earlier. Whether or not the Green & English be the first issue of this text, it fits well into Weems' own description of his projected book in his letter of Jan. 12, 1800; moreover, his letter of Feb. 2, 1800, shows that one edition had been already printed. As he had remained near Dumfries during that period, it is likely that Georgetown issued it before Philadelphia. Besides, he desired a portrait to be made, and Bioren's edition has one while Green & English's has not. Above all, Bioren's title, *second edition*, states that it is *reprinted*. [See also letter of July 12, title 3, note 3.]

3. Alibone's *Dictionary of American Authors*. *Bibliotheca Washingtoniana*, William Spohn Baker, No 32. 'With a dedication to Mrs. Washington, dated February 22, 1800. Two editions of this book were printed before Washington's death, and many afterwards.' *Washingtoniana*, Franklin B. Hough, Vol. II, p. 274, LC.[1] [In opposition to Baker's and Hough's statements I question whether Weems issued this or any other work on Washington before the latter's death. How could the '. . . *death*' be written, even by so cheerful a romancer as Weems is generally considered, before Washington had lent a slight plausibility to that event?] 'Five years earlier [1800] had appeared the most successful historical book of the day, Weems's Life of Washington. . . .' *Writers on American History, 1783–1850*, John Spencer Bassett, in *Cambridge History of American Literature*, 1918, Vol. II, p. 104, NYPL. [Reference is there made to Weems' 'announcing himself as "Formerly Rector of Mt. Vernon Parish,"' which it will be noted did not appear until the Cochran 1808 sixth edition, save in the newspapers; see titles 11 and 249, notes 5.]

4. Weems wrote to Carey, Jan. 12, 1800: '6 months ago I set myself to collect anecdotes about him [*Washington*] . . . . My plan! I give his history, sufficiently minute — I accompany him from his start, thro the French & Indian & British or Revolutionary wars, to the Presidents [*sic*] chair, to the throne in the hearts of 5,000000 of People. I then go on to show that his unparrelled [*sic*] rise & elevation were owing to his Great Virtues. 1 his Veneration for the Diety [*sic*] or Religious Principles. 2 His Patriotism. 3[d] his Magnanimity. 4 his Industry. 5. his Temperance & Sobriety. 6 his Justice, &[c]. &[c]. . . . All this I have lin[d] and enliven[d] with *Anecdotes apropos interesting* and *Entertaining*. . . . It will not exceed 3 royal sheets on long primer. We may sell it with great rapidity . . . it will be the first. I can send it on, half of it, immediately.' [From this it is clear that Weems was already enlarging

[1] Queries, asking what proof there is of Hough's statement that 'two editions [*of Weems' Washington*] were printed in the lifetime of Washington' are found in *Magazine of American History, Notes & Queries*, Vol. IV, 1880, p. 222, LC. To this inquiry no replies found.

his first work, which I believe was being printed locally, and that the revision being still unfinished he could offer only half of it for Carey's inspection.] Feb. 2, 1800: 'I sent you on a sample of [*the*] History of Washington. In consequence of not hearing from you I resolv[d] to strike off a few on my own acc[t]. . . . Our book will not make more than 4 sheets Royal, small pica Type. . . . The title page, Dedication, (which I have thought of turning to M[rs]. Washington) and Preface, are yet a corps de reserve.' [As the Green & English edition issued over Weems' name has a Preface entirely different from that in the Keatinge book, this fact would again fit the theory of his issuing an earlier work which lacked his revisions.] By Apr. 19, 1800, he was sufficiently advanced in the work to have evolved the title as known hitherto, for he asks Carey: 'For what will you print me 6,000 Copies of a 4 sheet (Royal) Pamphlet? I mean "A history of the Life, Death, Virtues & Exploits of our great & good old Countryman, Gen. Geo. Washington." 4 Sheets of Royal paper, colour & quality of that on w[h] you have printed the Columbian Spell[g] book. No Engravings — No Binding — no anything, save plain fold & stitch. Duoform & long primer type.' May 21, 1800, he again urged Carey to the printing of it: 'Well, go to, and print me 5,000 of my history of Washington, and I will pay you a good price and pay you the *moment I get to Philadelphia.* I send you herewith one half of the work, that you may put it to press *instantly*. . . . — I have some notion (and my heart is not altogether still at the thought) that I shall yet do some great things for you. I say put this moiety to the press instantly, and you shall have the pay of 5,000 Copies the moment I come up. I can sell 10,000 Copies in *Virginia alone!* Let the paper be *fair* & *thick*, like that of the Columbian Spell[g] book. . . . Next week as I come along I shall send you the last sheet. The first Sheet of 24 pages I shall bring up with me, I want the work [*of*] what I send you in readiness at my arrival. The same size as to page & type, but better paper than the copy sent you. I trust you will see that it be correct.'

5. For notes on Green & English see *Maryland and Virginia Almanac*, title 236, note 4.

6. Weems in this edition first quotes Rev. Samuel Davies' prophecy about 'that heroic youth, Col. Washington,' [p. 9] and this has been retained in all subsequent editions (except those of or taken from Bartgis) including the Mt. Vernon edition of 1918 [p. 60]. 'As a remarkable Instance of this [*martial fire*], I may point out to the Public that heroic Youth Col. *Washington*, whom I cannot but hope Providence has hitherto preserved in so signal a manner, for some important Service to his Country.' This was in a Sermon preached a few weeks after Braddock's defeat, entitled 'RELIGION | AND |

PATRIOTISM | The Constituents of a Good SOLDIER | A SERMON | Preached . . . 1755. | *By* SAMUEL DAVIES.' See *General Washington, Prediction*, Samuel A. Green, *MHSProc.*, June, 1892, pp. 454–455, LC. It would be of interest to learn if this early eulogizer of Washington were the subject of the following entry in Rev. William Duke's *Diary* in 1794: 'Oct. 5th, Sunday Went to the Presbiterian [*sic*] meeting and heard Doctr Davidson Preach a political Sermon, recommendatory of order & good government: and the excellence of that of the United States.' For further data see *Davies' Sermons*, title 239.

7. A footnote in praise of Hume on pp. 65–66 calls him 'that ornament of Scotland.' This comment shows Weems' open-mindedness even so early as 1800. In his day it was the fashion for the orthodox to hold Hume in abhorrence. — Weems himself being a mason explains the following squib on p. 48: 'Socrates slipped one day into a large store, something, I suppose like what the *New-Englanders* call a Variety Store . . . he was a master mason.'

8. 'His books, especially his "Life of Washington," had an enormous sale and went through over forty editions. They were necessarily histories of the Revolution. His ideas on that event reached every corner of the country, and every class of life. . . . Reckless in statement, indifferent to facts and research, his books are full of popular heroism, religion and morality, which you at first call trash and cant and then, finding it extremely entertaining, you declare with a laugh, as you lay down the book, what a clever rogue. . . . It is impossible to refrain from quoting from him. He is the most delightful mixture of the Scriptures, Homer, Virgil and the back woods. Everything rages and storms, slashes and tears. At the passage of the stamp act "the passion of the people flew up 500 degrees above blood heat." . . . It is in vain that the historians, the exhaustive investigators, the learned and the accurate rail at or ignore him. He is inimitable. He will live forever. . . . [*He*] captured the American people. He was the first to catch their ear. He said exactly what they wanted to hear. He has been read a hundred times more than all the other historians and biographers of the Revolution put together. . . . [*He*] was a myth-maker of the highest rank and skill and the greatest practical success.' *The Legendary and Myth-making Process in Histories of the American Revolution*, Sydney G. Fisher, reprinted from *AmPhSTrans.*, Vol. LI, April–June, 1912, pp. 65–66, NYPL.

NUMBER 3　1800?

A | HISTORY | OF | THE LIFE AND DEATH, | VIRTUES AND EXPLOITS, | OF | General George Washington. | FAITHFULLY TAKEN | FROM | AUTHENTIC DOCUMENTS, | AND, NOW, IN | A SECOND EDITION IMPROVED, | RESPECTFULLY OFFERED TO THE PERUSAL OF HIS COUN- | TRYMEN; AS ALSO, ALL OTHERS WHO WISH TO SEE | HUMAN NATURE IN ITS MOST FINISHED FORM. | *Price, 25 Cents.* | *A life, how glorious, to his country led!* | *Belov'd while living, as rever'd now dead.* | *May his example, virtuous deeds inspire!* | *Let future ages read it, and admire!* | BY THE REV. M. L. WEEMS, | OF LODGE NO. 50 — DUMFRIES. | Philadelphia: |

RE-PRINTED BY JOHN BIOREN, N°. 83 CHESNUT STREET, | FOR THE AUTHOR. | (*Entered according to Law.*) | [*n.d. 1800?*] 12mo. [*in 8's*] pp. (1), 4, 2–82. *Front.port.*

AAS., APhS., EI. [*lacks port.*], HHL., HSP. [*lacks port.*], LC. [*lacks port.*], NYHS., NYPL. [*lacks port.*], YU.

1. Portrait, bust, signed '*Tanner, sc.*',[1] face 3/4 right in an oval [height 4.5 c., width 3.8] set in an upright rectangle [height 11.9 c., sub height 8.2, width 6.1] of wavy horizontal lines, with inscription inserted 'G. WASHINGTON.' in open letter; below the rectangle the artist's name and still further below '*Engraved for the Rev^d. M. L. Weems.*'; on reverse of title dedication to Mrs. Washington, with slight changes from the Green & English edition; no Preface; there are additions to the Green & English text on pp. 6–23; pp. 59–72, 73–82 rewritten. Note about the offer of supreme power being made by Congress to Washington is on p. 40 of this Bioren edition, omitted from his

[1] As early as Dec. 13, 1793, Alexander Tiebout, writing to Mathew Carey from New York, recommends M^rs. [*sic for Messrs.*] Tisdale & Tanner & doubts 'not they will do them [*the plates*] to satisfaction.' L. & F. — 'B. Tanner, born, as I believe, in New-York, was a pupil of Cornelius Tiebout. He did much work for publishers, and published maps.' *History of the Rise and Progress of the Arts of Design in America*, William Dunlap, New York, 1834, Vol. II, p. 47, LC. — An account of Benjamin Tanner, including this comment: 'As an engraver Tanner worked both in line and stipple.' *American Engravers upon Copper and Steel*, David McNeely Stauffer, 1907, Vol. I, Part I, pp. 263, 264, NYPL.

third and Webster's third editions, but is found in Kollock's 1802 edition on p. 31. This would make Kollock's copy to have followed Bioren's second, yet a note on p. 5 of Bioren's third, and of Kollock's editions, is wanting in Bioren's second, and the note about Braddock in Bioren's third on p. 6, and in Kollock's on p. 5 is wanting in Bioren's second. In the AAS. copy the signatures A to F inclusive are complete, and on one quality of paper, while the five leaves of the signature G and the title leaf are of a different tint and texture, and the portrait leaf is of still another.

2. Alibone's *Dictionary*. Brinley No. 4257. Baker's *Bibliotheca Washingtoniana* No. 33; *Engraved Portraits of Washington* No. 338. Charles Henry Hart's *Engraved Portraits of Washington* No. 524.

3. With Bioren Weems evidently clashed, because in writing to Carey as early as July 10, 1800, he calls him 'alias Black-Beard.' July 12, 1800, he wrote: '. . . the sooner you can *dispose* of the present (the 2$^{d}$) edition of Washington's life the *better*. Hang *me*, if I am not *dog-sick*, on looking at it. And nothing but *necessity* cou'd make me lug it out even on journeymen Hatters & Blacksmiths. . . . [*I*] must have a capital edition this Fall.' Aug. 2, 1800, he asks Carey not to 'put Washington to the press till further communications,' and he repeats this request on Aug. 4. Aug. 9, 1800: 'Thank God, the Bible still goes well, better, I think, than Washington. You may thank Washington & the Bachelor for most of the remittances made you.' Aug. 22, 1800, from New York: 'If you have not already done it, 'twere well to put to press an edition of the Life of Washington in *Duod*$^{o}$. The Likeness, in small, first done by Tiebout will be excellent. Begin at line 8$^{th}$ of 25$^{th}$ page Octavo edition.' Aug. 25, 1800: 'As to the life of Washington, I wanted it in Duod$^{o}$. that it might be bound on *our plan;* & sold as a School book. Wou'd God I cou$^{d}$ have some to take with me down thro Maryland &c. . . . I send you an engraving. May it not do well to get this engrav'd for edition of Washington, alter'd for the Gallant Mercer [?].' [1] Carey wrote to Weems, Sept. 15, 1800: 'I paid 120 Dollars last week for paper purchased for your Books, i.e. Washington &$^{c}$. and I had to give Bioren a note for 109, for his part of the printing. Adams's note will soon be due.' Weems to Carey, Oct. 17, 1800: 'To *me* you have been generous *indeed* — In the 2 edit. of Washington & the Bachelor, your liberality was most Noble.' Carey to Weems, Nov. 15, 1800: 'After all the

[1] Mr. Charles Henry Hart gave an illuminating talk, with illustrations, at a meeting of the American Historical Association at Charleston, on the duplication with different titles of many so-called portraits. Here is a red-handed case of substitution after slight alterations. — 'The custom of making one cut do duty in several representations was . . . well understood.' *Forgotten Books of the American Nursery*, Rosalie V. Halsey, p. 93.

money I advanced for your works, the two notes [*in*] favour of Adams, and the engagements I have entered into for your binding, &c. your remittances do not amount to 12 Dollars per day.'

4. 'Oct. 15, 1800. . . . Read the Life of Gen[l]. Washington by Weems. . . .' *Ms. Diary of the Rev. William Duke.* Owned by MDDIO'NL. in PIL.

5. 'It is hardly exaggerated to say that Washington was pious as Numa; just as Aristides; temperate as Epictetus . . . [*to*] where Washington was born?' Two paragraphs of quotation, followed by a sketch of Weems, with a few inaccurate statements. *Character Portraits of Washington*, William Spohn Baker, Philadelphia, 1887, pp. 120–122, LC.

NUMBER 4    1800?

A | HISTORY | OF | THE LIFE AND DEATH, | VIRTUES AND EXPLOITS, | OF | General George Washington. | FAITHFULLY TAKEN | FROM | AUTHENTIC DOCUMENTS, | AND, NOW, IN | A THIRD EDITION IMPROVED, | RESPECTFULLY OFFERED TO THE PERUSAL OF HIS COUN- | TRYMEN; AS ALSO, OF ALL OTHERS WHO WISH TO SEE | HUMAN NATURE IN ITS MOST FINISHED FORM. | *Price 37½ Cents.* | *A life, how glorious, to his country led!* | *Belov'd while living, as rever'd now dead.* | *May his example, virtuous deeds inspire!* | *Let future ages read it, and admire!* | BY THE REV. M. L. WEEMS, | OF LODGE NO. 50 — DUMFRIES. | Philadelphia: |

RE-PRINTED BY JOHN BIOREN, N°. 83 CHESNUT STREET, | FOR THE AUTHOR. | (*Entered according to Law.*) | [*n.d. 1800?*] 8vo. pp. (1), 4, 4–84, (2). *Front.port.*

AAS., APhS., BA., EI., HSP., HU., LC., MdHS. [*lacks port.*], *NYHS., NYPL.

1. Portrait, after Stuart, engraved, stippled, bust, face ¾ right, oval in a stippled border within which is the engraver's signature '*B. Tanner, Sc.*', oval height 12.3 c., width 10.3, inscription below border 'G. WASHINGTON.' in open letter; the title page arrangement is after Bioren's second edition but is more widely spaced; no Preface; on reverse of title, dedication to Mrs.

Washington with 'stile' in Bioren's second edition changed to 'style'; both type and page are larger in this text than in Bioren's second edition, and there are footnotes added at pp. 5, 6, and 36, as well as eleven lines on p. 66, 'O Columbia! . . . emulate his fame.' The NYPL. has a second copy without portrait, in which Dr. Wilberforce Eames has written: 'This is one of a very few copies accompanied by the portrait engraved by Tanner. Copy B is without the portrait, and was probably so issued. Some new notes appear in this edition.' The AAS. copy has a portrait taken from the *European Magazine.*

2. Alibone's *Dictionary.* Brinley No. 4258. Hart's *Engraved Portraits of Washington* No. 523. Baker's *Bibliotheca Washingtoniana* No. 34; *Portraits of Washington* No. 340. Baker also in *Phil. Inq.*, Feb. 18, 1894. *Cooke's Catalogue*, Part III, No. 2680. Hough's *Washingtoniana*, Vol. II, p. 274.

3. *Reviewed:* 'We should be prompted to laugh at the freaks of this harmless *oddity*, if it were possible to be amused by the strange combinations of any literary *antick*, when connected with the venerable name of *Washington*. . . . Our readers would be greatly diverted by the style of this writer, were we to indulge in quotations, but we shall no farther extend our notice of this whimsical production, than by assuring them, that the very singular *title page* is followed by a more singular *dedication*, which is succeeded by *eighty* pages of as entertaining and edifying matter as can be found in the annals of fanaticism and absurdity. The whole of this heterogeneous compound is concluded by an *epitaph* on the *living* and the *dead*, the language of which has been taken from some country church yard.' [*Anon.*] *Monthly Magazine and American Review*, Vol. III, Sept. 1800, p. 210, BPL. *Ad.* [*M.L.W.?*] 'Third Edition Improved. THE LIFE OF WASHINGTON, *Faithfully taken from authentic Documents, in the Neighbourhood of Mount-Vernon,* [*w*]*here its Hero lived and die*[*d*] EXHIBITING that greatest and best of men . . . *birth — education* . . . part in the great American war . . . as President . . . interesting view of him in private life . . . religion . . . patriotism — honor — economy — generosity — business — . . . with a great number of private and *precious* anecdotes . . . furnishing a feast of the sublimest entertainment and instruction . . . with an elegant Likeness — Price 37½ cents.' *Va. Arg.*, Dec. 26, 1800 *et seq.*, LC., VSTL. 'Washington. A few Copies of the Life of Washington, may be had at the Book and Stationery Store of Edward Mirick, Main-Street. "To the public. To render homage to that Character which forms the subject of the present Work, is the pride and ambition of every true American . . . this Volume, which is intended as a tribute of respect to the Memory of the Father of our Country, will be found to contain a copious variety of matter, highly interesting and valuable." . . . March 20.' *Ep. of the Times*, Mar. 31, 1801, HU.

'EXTRACTS *From the Rev. M. L. Weem's* [*sic*] *History of the Life of* GEORGE WASHINGTON.' *Fred'kt'n Her.*, Jan. 8, 1803, AAS. [With changes in spelling and typography, but evidently taken from Bioren's third edition, first paragraph on p. 36, second paragraph on p. 41, third paragraph on pp. 42–43, and last two paragraphs on pp. 68–69.]

4. Weems wrote to Carey, Oct. 14, 1800: 'Having no books, Almcs & Life of Washington excepted I sold very little,' and he asked for subscription papers for *Washington* & *Mentor* to be sent, stating where they might be found. He also suggested that some few copies of 'the Battle of Lexington' be added. Nov. 8, 1800, from Annapolis: 'I brought with me the last of the 3^d^ edition of Washington. I sold them all in 20 minutes, very sorry am I that we have not a 4^th^ edition.' Dec. 11, 1800: 'These *last ten* were raised from the sale of Washington & Bachelor.' On the same date Carey wrote to Weems that of Washington 'there were a few in the hands of M^rs^. Smith, which I have kept, & credited you for.' Dec. 29, 1800, immediately after a letter of Dec. 17, setting out his grievances, Weems wrote to Carey: 'I shall very cheerfully give any pledge that's reasonable as to the books & monies for which I owe you.' March 10, 1801: 'Washington is gone — the people are tearing me to pieces. Pleasant has sold all — he begs I w^d^ get out another edition — & promises it will outsell any book in America. Can you print me speedily a Neat edition of 1600, on [*sic*] Octavo size, with my large plate of Washington . . . only 100 pages for 4.00 Dol? I'll wholesale [*them*] like fury, and send you the money (Deo Vol.) very soon.' March 24, 1801: 'You saw what I did with the Life of Washington & the Bachelor, of which I have sold between 7 and 8,000 in less than a twelvemonth — Merely because these books suited the taste of the People.' May 8, 1801: 'Now, I beg your advice . . . you know I let my Washingtons escape me 50 pr Cent shorn of their retail fleeces, . . . If you approve my plan of bind'^g^ my books (which are *now useless*) & of exchanging & turn'^g^ them speedily into a stout sum, let me know, and also be so good as to set Robertson about them as far at least as 200 Dol. will bind.' Dec. 3, 1801: 'Have already had application to print my book in this place [*Trenton*]. May God Almighty make me very useful, is my Constant Prayer. But I must turn Democrat & shake the bell under Carroll's[1] cassock, e'er I can hope for your very hearty Co-operation.'

[1] Carey being a Roman Catholic, this pleasantry alludes to that fact, and to Archbishop Carroll of Maryland.

NUMBER 5 1801

THE | LIFE | AND | MEMORABLE ACTIONS | OF | *George Washington*, | GENERAL AND COMMANDER | OF THE | ARMIES | OF | AMERICA. | A New Edition Corrected. | FREDERICK-TOWN, |

Printed by M. BARTGIS. | 1801. | 12mo. pp. (1), 1, (2), 1, (1), 1, 6–8, 1, 10–68. *Front.port.*

HHL., HSP. [*imp., lacks pp. 33–36.*]

1. Portrait, unsigned, is a rude woodcut, of a circle with a plain two-line border, with horizontal lines surrounding the face, bust, face slightly to right; inscription below '*George Washington* [*in script*], | *Died Dec.* 14*th* 1799 *Aged* 68.'; the text is very like the Keatinge edition, with the same Preface, but lacks 'CONTENTS' and Chapter I's heading, and has additions to the heading of Chapter XIII; minor changes in text occur, such as Washington's fixing his 'quarters at the white plains,' or, on p. 43, 'June 1782' instead of '1780,' the ship 'vigilant' [p. 59 of Keatinge] corrected to 'Vigilant' [p. 40 of Bartgis]; the note on '*Bon repos*' is on p. 12, the anecdote of Mr. William Payne on pp. 16–21; a comparison of this Bartgis edition and the Keatinge edition shows the following typographical differences between the two: exactly the same types were used through p. 49 of Keatinge and p. 32 of Bartgis, though they were reset for a larger page in Bartgis, and the same imperfections occur, except that the word 'extolling,' which appears thus in Keatinge, has its second 'l' dropped on pp. 15–16 in Bartgis; the HSP. copy of the Bartgis edition, which is the only one which I have compared with the Keatinge — for at the time I examined the imperfect HHL. copy while still in the collection of Mr. Walter U. Lewisson I had not established its practical identity with that of Keatinge — lacks pp. 33–36 inclusive, corresponding to pp. 50–55 in Keatinge, being parts of Chapters VI and VII; from p. 55 of Keatinge and p. 37 of Bartgis on, the same

George Washington,

Died Dec. 14th 1799 Aged 68.

THE

# LIFE

AND

MEMORABLE ACTIONS

OF

*George Washington,*

GENERAL AND COMMANDER

OF THE

ARMIES

OF

AMERICA.

A New Edition Corrected.

FREDERICK-TOWN,
Printed by M. Eartgis.
1801.

Facsimile Frontispiece and Title Page of the Bartgis 1801 Edition of
*The Life of Washington*

type is used, but is diminished in size in Keatinge in several instances, as on pp. 62–68, 74–75, 79, 80, 88–92, 94, 96; the Keatinge edition also uses italics in inappropriate places on pp. 73 and 80, as though running out of type; the diagrams of Washington's funeral procession differ, both as to type and shape of casket, the larger end of the diamond being uppermost in Keatinge, and *vice versa* in Bartgis; the Keatinge edition lacks the tail-piece of roses which appears in Bartgis before 'FINIS.' The Bartgis edition in general suggests a less careless or hurried issue than the Keatinge edition, thus diminishing the chance of its being prior to that. For further minor changes in the Bartgis German edition of 1809, see notes to title 18.

2. Rice Catalogue No. 2457, where the printer's name is erroneously spelled 'Bartges.'

3. Advertised in *Bartgis's Repub. Gaz.*, Apr. 8, 1801, Feb. 17, 1802 *et seq.*, MDHS.; Nov. 5, 1802 *et seq.*, HU.; Jan. 21, 1803 *et seq.*, AAS.

4. Matthias Bartgis published the *Maryland Chronicle*, established in 1786. In the issue of Jan. 18, 1786, he announced his intention of establishing a post to carry 'my English and German News-papers' to nearby towns. Another advertisement in the same paper, dated June 4, 1787, advertises for a partner to take the management of the 'Printing-Office in the English and German language, and two public papers in this town.' Bartgis was already then preparing to establish printing offices at Winchester, Va., and York, Penn. [At Winchester he published *The Virginia Gazette and Winchester Advertiser*, 1787.] At Fredericktown also he published *Bartgis's Maryland Gazette*, 1792–1794, *Bartgis's Federal Gazette*, 1794–1800, *Bartgis's Republican Gazette*, 1800–1820+, *The Hornet*, 1802–1814; and at Rockville, Md., *The Maryland Register*. See *Bibliography of American Newspapers*, Clarence S. Brigham, *ProcAAS.*, Vol. XXV, Part I, April, 1915, pp. 182, 183, 185, 187 and 192. 'Bartgis's Federal Gazette, is published punctually every Wednesday; . . . Advertissements for the English and German newspapers will be thankfully received with the Cash. . . .' *The Key*, 1798, p. 213, LC. The *Maryland, Virginia and Kentucky Almanack For the Year of our Lord 1798.* . . . Printed for G. Keatinge's Wholesale Book-Store [MDHS.] bears, on reverse of title: 'For Sale at George Keatinge's, A general and extensive assortment of English and German Books'. This points to an early association of Keatinge with German publishers, and so with Bartgis, and these two printers' editions of Weems' first *Life of Washington.*

5. This Bartgis edition of 1801 is noted, and data on it requested by Jos. Henry Dubb, in *Notes & Queries*, *Mag. Am. Hist.*, Aug. 1881, p. 146, but I have not been able to find any reply.

NUMBER 6 1802?

A | HISTORY | OF THE | LIFE AND DEATH, | VIRTUES AND EXPLOITS, | OF | General George Washington. | FAITHFULLY TAKEN | FROM | AUTHENTIC DOCUMENTS, | AND NOW, IN | A THIRD EDITION, IMPROVED, | RESPECTFULLY OFFERED TO THE PERUSAL OF HIS COUNTRY- | MEN; AS ALSO, OF ALL OTHERS WHO WISH TO SEE HUMAN | NATURE IN ITS MOST FINISHED FORM. | *A life, how glorious, to his country led!* | *Belov'd while living, as rever'd now dead.* | *May his example virtuous deeds inspire!* | *Let future ages read it, and admire!* | BY THE REV. M. L. WEEMS, OF LODGE NO. 50, DUMFRIES. | ELIZABETH-TOWN: |

Printed by SHEPARD KOLLOCK, for the author. | [*Entered according to Law.*] | [*n.d. 1802?*] 8vo. pp. (1), 4, 4, 4–61, (1). *Front.port.*
AAS., APhS., BA., EI., HSP., HU., LC., MdHS. [*lacks port.*], NYHS., NYPL.

1. Portrait by Tanner, after Stuart, engraved. stippled, oval, with inscription 'G. WASHINGTON.' in open letter like that in title 4; on reverse of title, Dedication to Mrs. Washington in italics; no Preface; printed after Bioren's third edition, with slight changes from that and his second, being in a smaller type; the paging is therefore different, and there are slight changes or additions on pp. 47, 48, 49 and 59; with differences also from Bioren's second edition on pp. 4, 5, 18 and 27, and alterations in spelling; contains the notes and the additions, pp. 48–49, of Bioren's third edition. See also notes to Webster's Albany third edition [*1802–1803?*], title 7.

2. Brinley No. 4259. Baker's *Portraits of Washington* No. 340; *Bibliotheca Washingtoniana* No. 35.

3. *Ad.* [*?*] '. . . S. Pleasants . . . Eulogies and Orations on the life and death of Gen. George Washington. . . .' *Va. Arg.*, Aug. 7, 1802, VSTL.

'Books for Sale . . . Washington's Life. . . .' *Md. Gaz.*, Oct. 14, 1802 *et seq.*, MDSTL. 'Life of Washington, with biographical anecdotes of the most eminent men who effected the American revolution, 75 c.' *Oracle Dauph.*, May 2, 1803 *et seq.*, LC. 'Weem's [*sic*] History of Washington, extracts from,' Index to Vol. I, *Fred'kt'n Her.*, ending June 11, 1803, AAS.

4. Weems wrote to Carey from New Hope, N. J.: 'Feb. last day! [*1802*] . . . Mr. Kollock has the Life of Washington nearly ready for me, in 8°. which likeness of Washington will best frontispiece it?' Mar. 27, 1802: 'You told me you w[d] charge yourself with the plate of Washington — the larger w[d] be the more profitable to you because the more productive to . . . Yours' Apr. 28, 1802: 'Duyckin[*c*]k wants to buy permission to print my life of Washington. 'Twere imprudent to grant it. I may do good things with that book by & by.' May 24, 1802: 'Mr. Shepperd [*sic*] Kollock. Please to deliver to M[r]. Carey or order Six hundred and twenty one of my Life of Washington, left with you & oblige' To Carey, from Wilmington, Nov. 19, 1802: 'I hasten to Mount Vernon. Thence shall hasten back to Baltimore where I hope to commence with your Bibles & the Washingtoniad in 12 days from this date.' From Dumfries, Dec. 7, 1803: 'I will not be possitive, but tis very possible I shall lose much more than you are aware of, and very much more than, I know, you w[d] like that I sh[d] lose. I have greatly offended the Mount Vernon Family.'

5. 'Shepard Kollock was born at Lewes, Delaware, 1751, and probably learned his trade with James Adams at Wilmington. . . . Did some excellent work as a printer . . . at Chatham, New Brunswick [*New York*] while his Elizabethtown press turned out at least fifty different works. . . . Issued several newspapers [*New Jersey Journal* (*Chatham*), *1782–1783; Political Intelligencer* (*New Brunswick*), *1784; New Jersey Gazetteer, 1784–1786; New Jersey Journal* (*Elizabeth-town*), *1789–1799*], for which he wielded a trenchant pen . . . retired from printing in 1818, was Postmaster . . . 1820–1829, and died in 1839. . . . Nor should it be forgotten that one of the earliest editions of that delightful classic, Weems' "Life of Washington" was printed by Kollock in 180 [*sic*].' *New Jersey Printers of the 18th Century*, William Nelson, *ProcAAS.*, *New Series*, Vol. XXI, April–Oct., 1911, pp. 32–33. 'Kollock Shepard, printer and bookseller, corner of Wall and Water streets.' *The New York Directory for 1786* [Fac-Simile Reprint thereof], LC. Biographical sketch of Shepard Kollock in *American Dictionary of Printing and Bookmaking*, New York, 1894, p. 317, LC. Shepherd Kollock, postmaster, Georgetown, Del., Oct. 1, 1804 [first return] – 1805. See *P.O.Rec.Bk.No.1*, p. 216, P.O. Bldg., Washington, D. C.

NUMBER 7 1802–1803?

A | HISTORY | OF THE | LIFE AND DEATH, VIRTUES AND EXPLOITS, | OF | *General* GEORGE WASHINGTON, | FAITHFULLY TAKEN | FROM | AUTHENTIC DOCUMENTS, | AND, NOW, IN | A THIRD EDITION IMPROVED, | RESPECTFULLY OFFERED TO THE PERUSAL OF HIS | COUN- | TRYMEN; AS ALSO, ALL OTHERS WHO WISH TO SEE | HUMAN NATURE IN ITS MOST FINISHED FORM. | *Price, 25 Cents,* | *A life, how glorious to his country led!* | *Belov'd while living, as rever'd now dead.* | *May his example, virtuous deeds inspire!* | *Let future ages read it, and admire!* | By the Rev. M. L. WEEMS, | OF LODGE NO. 50 — DUMFRIES, VIRGINIA. | ALBANY: |

PRINTED BY CHARLES R. AND GEORGE WEBSTER, | At their Bookstore, corner of State & Pearl-streets. | (ENTERED ACCORDING TO LAW.) | [*n.d. 1802–1803?*] 16mo. pp. 3, 4–83, 1, (2).
AAS.

1. With the Dedication; this Albany edition is word for word like the second edition of Bioren, the earlier pages even matching in many instances in their first and final words, the only differences being slight ones, as follows: 'candour' in Bioren, p. 1 *et seq.*, is spelled without a 'u' in Webster, p. 3; 'brought' in Bioren, p. 45, is printed 'Brot' in Webster, p. 47; the 'u' in 'favoured' in the Dedication of both Bioren editions is omitted in Webster, and 'stile' is spelt thus, like Bioren's second but not third edition; 'chearfully' in Bioren, p. 57, is correct in Webster, p. 58; Webster introduces a dash on p. 72 before 'in the foregoing pages'; 'bing' in Bioren, p. 75, is printed correctly as 'being' in Webster, p. 76; 'now' in Bioren, p. 79, is omitted in Webster, p. 80; a misprint in Webster, p. 81, results in 'the tears of joy' rolling down from 'Angles' rather than from the orthodox inhabitants of Heaven; notes on pp. 5 and 6 of Bioren's third are lacking in Bioren's second and in Webster's third editions. In view of this marked similarity, it seems that this book is almost certainly taken from the second edition of Bioren. As to its date: on the reverse of the last page are publishers' advertisements: 'This Day Printed . . . The Clerks Magazine . . . Also Just Printed . . . Watts' Psalms and Hymns . . .

Also, The Statute Laws of the State of New-York, complete to the 1st January, 1800 in three volumes — price £3.' This last had been advertised as follows: 'Proposals of Charles R. and George Webster and Thomas, Andrews and Penniman, of the City of Albany, for printing by subscription The Revised Laws of the State of New-York. . . . The work will be put to press in the month of August next, and completed with all possible expedition . . . Albany, June 14, 1801.' *Alb. Reg.*, July 3, 1801 *et seq.*, AAS. This *three volume* edition of the Laws of the State of New York is actually dated 1804; but the above advertisements, and the Websters' use of Bioren's second edition as a model, as well as their evident ignorance of there being two third editions already in existence by 1802, coupled with the fact that the publishers probably expected to get out this particular edition of the Laws of the State of New York much earlier than 1804 and hence might have inserted an advertisement for it in a book issued before then, all lead me to ascribe this Albany edition to 1802 or 1803. Moreover, Websters' undated *fourth* edition, of Albany, follows the text of Bioren's third rather than his second edition, which seems added evidence as to the date of *this* earlier one possibly being prior to 1804. From the numbering of this edition as third, when there were already two others thus described, as well as from a letter from Weems to the Websters, dated Mar. 31, 1814 [see note 2 to 1813 edition of *The Drunkard's Looking Glass*, title 198], it seems probable that he had not been consulted about this one. In the earlier years of his printing books, he did not lay much stress upon correctly numbering editions, but after some of his writings had proved to be such good sellers, his letters show that he began to emphasize this point. Knowing his successful methods of publicity, both for Carey's and Wayne's works, as well as his own, it seems to me that had he known of the third and fourth editions of Webster, he would have been likely to advertise the vogue of the *Life of Washington* by numbering the edition which was printed under his supervision in Georgia in 1806, instead of the fifth, the seventh, or possibly even the eighth. It would not have been a misnomer, even though the fifth, sixth and seventh editions had thus been made non-existent, because, had he known of the three third and possibly two fourth editions — assuming that the Albany latter was issued before 1806 — he would have been justified in thus numbering the Georgia edition the seventh or eighth. The great confusion in the numbering of the editions through 1808, 1809 and 1810 may be explained by the fact that the rights of the book were relinquished by Weems in the earliest of these years to Carey, and from that moment he was given less authority and supervision, if any at all, over his book

2. 'ANECDOTE. Of General Wayne. *Bon Repos* is the French term for *good night*. Washington drank it for a signal to break up; for the moment the

company had swallowed the General's *bon repos*, it was take hats and retire. . . . "Well then a fig for *bon repos*, and take your seats again; for by the life of Washington, you shall not stir a peg, till we have started every drop of our drink!"' [*Anon.*] *Ral. Reg.*, July 2, 1804, NCStL. [See letter of July 11, 1816, note 4 to seventeenth edition, 1816, title 29.]

NUMBER 8 1803?

[*M.L.W.?*] ALSO — An HISTORY (4th edition *greatly improved*) of | THE LIFE AND DEATH OF | Gen. George Washington: | Carefully collected, in the neighbourhood of Mount Vernon, from the most | authentic Documents: Exhibiting his very extraordinary Character, not on- | ly as a Soldier and a Statesman, but as a Man; And a man of that early | prudence — admirable fortitude — rigid temperance — unwearied industry — | honor unblemish'd, and uncorrupted patriotism, which rendered *him* the | glory of human nature and admiration of the world, and *this his History* | well worthy the perusal of every Young Man who wishes, like Washington, | to *live*, greatly useful and happy; and to *die*, universally lamented and beloved. | With an elegant copper-plate likeness of him. *Price* 37 1–2 cents. |

(R. COCHRAN, Printer.) | [*n.d. 1803?*]
HSP.

1. This hand-bill, reading as if by Weems, may have been merely one of his plans projected before the work was ready to be given out. Still, Cochran actually printed the sixth editions of 1808, titles 11 and 12. The following verses, found in an unsigned letter to the Charleston *Times*, Feb. 24, 1804, are so different from the usual versions that it seems possible that they were used on the title page of this Cochran as yet undiscovered fourth edition: [*M.L.W.?*] 'A life how glorious! to his Country dear, Her first in council and her first in war. May his example, all our sons inspire! And from their father's history catch his fire.' For other verses see title 15, note 3.

2. 'No copy of the Fourth Edition is known, the above title being taken from a hand-bill in the possession of the writer, issued in 1803.' Baker's *Bibliotheca Washingtoniana* No. 52.

3. Queries, signed 'Biblios', were printed concerning the fourth, fifth and sixth editions of Weems' *Washington*, in *Magazine of American History, Notes & Queries*, Vol. IV, 1880, p. 222, LC. To these inquiries I have not been able to find any replies.

4. [?] *Ad.* 'John Wyeth has now on hand, for sale . . . Life of Washington, with biographical anecdotes of the most eminent men who effected the American revolution, 75 cts. . . .' *Oracle Dauph.*, Jan. 19, 1805, NYHS. [?] Also advertised in *Repub. Arg. & County Adv.*, May 18, 1804, HU.

NUMBER 9 1805–1806?

A | HISTORY | OF THE | LIFE AND DEATH, VIRTUES AND EXPLOITS | OF | GENERAL | GEORGE WASHINGTON, | FAITHFULLY TAKEN | FROM | AUTHENTIC DOCUMENTS, | AND, NOW IN | A FOURTH EDITION IMPROVED, | RESPECTFULLY OFFERED TO THE PERUSAL OF HIS | COUNTRY-MEN; AS ALSO, ALL OTHERS WHO | WISH TO SEE HUMAN NATURE IN ITS | MOST FINISHED FORM | *A life how glorious to his country led!* | *Belov'd while living, as rever'd now dead:* | *May his example, virtuous deeds inspire!* | *Let future ages read it, and admire!* | By the Rev. M. L. WEEMS, | OF LODGE NO. 50 — DUMFRIES, VIRGINIA. | ALBANY: |

PRINTED | BY CHARLES R. AND GEORGE WEBSTER, | At their Bookstore, corner of State Pearl-streets. | (ENTERED ACCORDING TO LAW.) | [*n.d. 1805–1806?*] 16mo. pp. (6), 3, 4–152.
ConnHS.

1. On reverse of title is the Dedication; the text, like Bioren's third edition, contains no chapters, but on p. 64, after 'due to his God', begin: 'WASHINGTON'S PATRIOTISM'; on p. 73, '. . . INDUSTRY'; on p. 88, '. . . BENEVOLENCE'; on p. 103, '. . . JUSTICE'; on p. 134, 'DEATH . . .'; some footnotes are like those in Bioren's third edition, i.e., eulogizing the New Englanders on p. 17 [Bioren, p. 11]; Colonel Scammel, p. 42 [Bioren, pp. 24–25]; whiskey and water, p. 70 [Bioren, p. 40]; supreme power conferred by Congress on Washington, p. 73 [Bioren, p. 42]; Jack B., p. 76 [Bioren, p. 44]; Bon Repos, p. 78

[Bioren, p. 45]; Walpole, p. 104 [Bioren, p. 60]; and final illness, p. 110 [Bioren, p. 64]; the note on Poole, p. 36, is lacking in Bioren, while that does contain the following notes not found in this edition: on Williamsburgh, p. 4; Indians, p. 5; Braddock, p. 6; Donop's wound, p. 18, and Paoli, p. 21; in this fourth Albany edition, there is this quotation not found in other editions: 'CHARACTER OF WASHINGTON, WRITTEN IN 1798. BY AN AMERICAN. "Does the prostitute page of history glow with the enthusiastic eulogia on the characters of tyrants, who have only revelled in a court . . . throne of empire. (2) Washington is equally majestic in mein [*sic*] . . . intercourse delightful. (3) Though he dart not from his eye the vengeful fire . . . laurels of glory. (4) Though his features . . . be forgotten. (5) Though the elegance of our Hero neither electricates [*sic*] by the divine fire of *Demosthenes* . . . dignity. (6) Whatever be the subject . . . truth and justice. (7) In his wise and happy choice . . . Cabinet. (8) In his investigation . . . irresistable [*sic*] genius. (9) To the foregoing . . . universe. (10) In this amiable . . . capricious irregularities. (11) To conclude . . . admiration of the world."' This reference not identified.

2. As in May, 1806, Charles R. and George Webster took their nephew, Elisha W. Skinner, as partner, and the firm became Websters and Skinner, this book was probably issued before, or in the early part of, that year. In 1811, Elisha's brothers, Hezekiah and Daniel, were admitted, and the firm name became Websters & Skinners. See *Bibliography of American Newspapers*, Clarence S. Brigham, *ProcAAS.*, Vol. XXVII, April, 1917, p. 186. Mr. Walter U. Lewisson, whose unique collection of Washingtoniana has since been added to the Henry Huntington Library, copied a title so like this edition, the differences being negligible, that I assume it is the same. This he took from a copy to be sold by Merwin Clayton. He ascribed this edition, which was also called the fourth edition improved, to 1810, but my judgment, in view of the change of the Webster partnership above, is to give it the earlier date.

3. On March 31, 1814, Weems wrote to Websters & Skinners, expressing his appreciation of their sending him $50 through Jacob Johnson of Philadelphia 'as the Author of the little pamphlet "The Life of Washington."' See note 2 to 1813 edition of *The Drunkard's Looking-Glass*, title 198.

4. See title 8, note 3.

NUMBER 10 1806

THE LIFE | OF | WASHINGTON THE GREAT. | ENRICHED WITH A NUMBER OF VERY | CURIOUS ANECDOTES, | PERFECTLY IN CHARACTER, AND EQUALLY | HONORABLE TO HIMSELF, AND EXEMPLARY TO HIS | YOUNG COUNTRYMEN. | *A life how useful to his country led!* | *How* LOV'D! *while* LIVING . . . [*sic*] *how* REVER'D! *now* DEAD! | *Lisp! lisp! his name, ye children yet unborn!* | *And make your Father's virtues all your own!* | THE FIFTH EDITION. . . . [*sic*] GREATLY IMPROVED. | PRICE 50 CENTS. | BY M. L. WEEMS. | OF LODGE NO. 50. . . . [*sic*] DUMFRIES. | AUGUSTA: | RE-PRINTED BY GEO. F. RANDOLPH. | 1806. | COPY RIGHT SECURED | 8vo. pp. 1, (1), 1, 4–80.
NYPL.

1. No portrait, dedication nor Preface; the text, entirely rewritten from former editions, is divided into Chapters I–VII, with verses heading I, II and IV, and begins 'Oh! as along . . . [*which are the first words of four lines of verse as chapter heading*] "Ah! gentlemen!" exclaimed Buonaparte—" . . .'; it includes for the first time the story of the little hatchet and cherry tree, p. 9 ['little' printed in no later edition—see note 2 below]; first introduced into this edition also is the story of Governor Johnson of Maryland on pp. 64–65 [for an earlier printing in the newspapers see note 4 below], which had been used before by Weems as a 'puff' for Wayne's *Washington* by Marshall [see note 4

to that title, 249] and was again repeated in his *God's Revenge against Duelling* [title 214]; also the anecdote of 'the seeds which grew up to form the letters of Washington's name . . . taken from the Life of James Hay Beattie by his father James Beattie, the famous Scotch philosopher.' See '*George Washington's "Billy Sunday."*' [*Anon., Walter B. Norris?*], *Boston Transcript*, Feb. 21, 1917. Though entirely rewritten, this edition retains Davies' prophecy, p. 22, and the anecdotes of 'Col' Washington at Charleston, 'making his mark,' and at Cowpens,[1] pp. 44–47, and of Payne, pp. 58–62; the anecdote of 'poor Donop' appears on pp. 35–36, and of Col. Scammel on pp. 46–47; the text ends with John Dickinson's epitaph: 'TRAVELLER stop! the dust that sleeps below, | was once nam'd WASHINGTON . . . reflect . . . now go. | FINIS.' The book as thus issued was an amplified and lengthened sermon, even to its epilogue or summing up from p. 72 to p. 80.

2. 'This is perhaps the rarest of the early editions, as but one known copy is in existence, belonging to Mr. Ford, of New York.' Article [*Anon.*] quoting William S. Baker, *Phil. Inquirer*, Feb. 18, 1894, LC. This copy, now in the NYPL., is supposed to be unique. On the fly leaf is written in the handwriting of Paul L. Ford, whose widow gave it to the library: 'Unknown to all bibliographers. This rare southern edition is the first "Weems" of popular fame. The first four editions [*writing before 1902*] were merely a biography, but after this issue the author rewrote the work, inventing the hatchet story (p. 9,) and all the other things that makes [*sic*] Weems famous, and which have led to the seventy editions of the book. Weems posed as the pastor of Washington, and as such has figured even in works of historical importance, but the claim was only one more of his lies [*see title 11, note 5, and title 16, note 3*] as I have a letter of his to Washington,[2] stating distinctly that they had never met, and this is reinforced by his dedication of the first edition to Mrs. Washington where he speaks of himself as "her unknown friend."' [See also *Appendix XIX*, Vol. III.] This account of the far-famed cherry-tree tale seems to me unduly scathing. Moreover, Mr. R. T. Haines Halsey has pointed out in the Appendix to *Pictures of Early New York on Dark Blue Staffordshire Pottery*, that a German mug has, on its lower edge, 'as was the custom upon this special class of wares, . . . the date 1776, which unmistakably stamp this piece as made in this year, and the inscription, above "G.W.1776."' [See frontispiece to *Letters*, Vol. II, and an article by Carrington Weems in the *Sun* (N.Y.), Mar. 17, 1912,

[1] Mentioned in *Washington's Southern Tour, 1791*, Archibald Henderson, 1923, pp. 76–77.

[2] I have found no such letter so I surmise that my brother was alluding to Washington's reply to Weems' dedication to him of *The Philanthropist*, 1799, but a few months before Washington's death. See title 156.

Pottery Mug, probably made in Germany, with the Initials *G. W.* and the Date *1776*

giving illustrations and more details of the mug.] Without this expert testimony, I like to believe that my brother, as he worked more and more into Weems' material, would have suspended judgment in some cases, where he lacked evidence which has since come to light. Amongst his papers concerning Weems I find the following light touch: 'One hundred years ago Washington and his "little hatchet" were joined together by an episcopal clergyman, and though many a learned historian has since sat in judgment upon the union, the jury of public opinion has steadily refused to bring in a decree of divorce. Like Christopher Columbus' egg, or William Tell's apple, there is an appropriateness — an atmosphere of verisimilitude — about it which overcomes all higher criticism and skepticism. Recently I asked an old New Englander, who had been trained with the New England Primer, if he really believed that the burning of John Rogers was witnessed "by his wife, with nine small children and one at her breast," and received the prompt response: "I suppose not, but it ought to have been."'[1] The same thought has been more recently so well expressed in the following: 'I think we may safely assume that, in order to gain currency, a new idea must seem "good," and mayhap, noble, beautiful and useful, and that it must fit in pretty well with existing notions; or at least must not threaten violently to dislocate the accepted scheme of things. . . . Ideas like kisses go by favor. . . . It is not the precise truth of an idea . . . that leads to its wide acceptance, but its appeal — its congeniality to a being with the nature and setting of man.' *The Humanising of Knowledge*, James H. Robinson, p. 19. See also title 2, note 8. For some mentions of the cherry-tree story see the lists of works consulted appended to this volume.

3. Baker's *Bibliotheca Washingtoniana* No. 58. Baker's note to the sixth edition [*Washingtoniana* No. 69] as to its being rewritten applies rather more to this issue, of which he had never seen a copy.

4. [*M.L.W.*] 'From the Charleston Times. Anecdote of Washington. The following . . . was related to me by his excellency governor Johnson . . . syllable of it to anybody."' *Guard.*, July 17, 1806, RUTGERSCL.; 'From a Charleston paper.' *Com. Adv.* (N.Y.) in the *Spectator*, Sept. 24, 1806, NYHS. *Ad.* [*M.L.W.*] '"A wit's a feather, and a chief a rod, An honest man's the noblest work of God!" JUST PUBLISHED, *And For Sale at this Office* THE REV. MR. WEEMS'S FIFTH EDITION OF THE Life OF Washington, CHIEFLY his PRIVATE *life*, enriched with a number of VALUABLE ANECDOTES, perfectly characteristic of Washington, and highly interesting to readers of every age. — The shool [*sic*] - boy, the surveyor, the soldier, the statesman, and farmer, whether rich

[1] It is my impression that this was said by the late Lindsay Swift, of the Boston Public Library.

or poor, prosperous or unfortunate, may here find examples greatly honorable to Washington, and highly instructive to themselves. PRICE ONLY 50 CENTS.' *Col. Cent.* (Aug., Ga.), Dec. 13, 1806, UNY'GA. 'Mr. Weems has just published a *new Life of Washington*, which he calls *his private life.*' *Ral. Reg.*, Jan. 19, 1807, NCStL. [*M.L.W.*] 'ALSO, JUST PUBLISHED BY M. L. WEEMS, AND FOR SALE AT THIS OFFICE, WEEMS'S FIFTH EDITION, GREATLY IMPROVED OF THE LIFE OF WASHINGTON THE GREAT. His birth — parentage — curious Anecdotes about his family — Plan of his Education — Memorable instructions given him when a child — At the age of 10 loses his Father — Extraordinary behaviour to his Mother — His character At school — At 16 appointed a Surveyor — Exemplary diligence and neat drawings — At 19 appointed Major and Adjutant General of the Virginia troops — At 21 Commissioned by Gov. Dinwiddie on [*sic*] embassy to the French — Providential escapes — Gallant behaviour in the wars of Braddock — In 57 marries — Interesting view of him as a farmer till 74 — Chosen a member of the first Congress — In 75 appointed Generalissimo of the American armies — Concise and animated history of him during the war — Grand battles of Trenton, Princeton, Sullivan's Island, Saratoga, Cowpens, &c. &c. till 83 — Returns to Congress his Sword and Commission — Returns to private life — In 86 [*sic*] made President of the United States — In 94 [*sic*] resigns — Dies in 99 — Striking display of his character in the *private walks* of life, enriched and enlarged with a number of Curious and Valuable Anecdotes, forming an admirable example for YOUTH, and shewing them as in a *variety of lights*, what it is that makes THE TRULY GREAT AND HAPPY MAN. (*Price only 50 Cents.*) Savannah, February 13.' *Ga. Rep.*, Feb. 17, 1807 *et seq.*, GAHS. 'Anecdotes of Washington The following . . . are . . . on the authority of the Monthly Register, a N.Y. Periodical . . . While a Colonel, Washington . . . Col. Payne . . . lovelier than ever.' *Poulson's Amer. D. Adv.*, Aug. 17, 1807, LC. 'This Book evinces the Mind of a Man of Genius; is replete with original Reflections, and holds up, from the most captivating Points of view, the Charms and Rewards of Virtue, Bravery, and Patriotism. In almost the compass of a page, and with the same happy facility, the Writer makes us alternately weep and laugh; transfuses into our Bosoms the Enthusiasm which distinguished our revolutionary Heroes; and bows us with Adoration, before that Omnipotent Being who conducted these U. S. to Independence and Glory, through the Instrumentality of *Washington* and his illustrious Compatriots. His Battles are drawn in new and animated Colors. I think, at the moment of reading them, I hear the Clash of Bayonets, with all the Horrors of the Battle. I fancy myself on the Scene of Action, giving the Shout of Victory with my brave Countrymen; or, joining their Lamentations over the bloody Corses of their fallen Heroes.

There is a kind of poetic fire running through every sentence of this History, that irresistibly fixes the Attention, warms the Heart, and brings to the Eyes those delicious Waters which flow from Piety, Love, and Admiration. If my feeble voice could have any weight with my young Countrymen, I would raise it to recommend this Life of Washington to their frequent and attentive Perusal.' *Intel.*, Jan. 31, 1809 *et seq.*, LIOF. [Criticism on the '5th Edition' of this Work, signed by Thos. U. P. Charlton, Esq. Attorney General of the State of Georgia, dated 'Savanna', June 17, 1807, following an advertisement of the eighth edition, see title 15, note 3.] Also advertised in: *Col. Cent.* (Aug., Ga.), Jan. 31, 1807, UN'YGA. *Ga. Rep.*, Feb. 13, 20, Mar. 21, 1807, HU., UN'YGA. *Louisv'l. Gaz.*, Mar. 20, 1807, HU.; May 15, 1807 *et seq.*, AAS.

5. Weems wrote to Wayne, May 16, 1805: 'Why wont you send me on my Washington's life. . . .' Aug. 17, 1806: 'I begg[d] you to strike off & send me with all possible dispatch 1500 of my large likeness of Washington — tis for a little pamphlet of the private & moral sort, supplementary to your large work — I told you & now tell you again that it is my wish that you shou'd participate in the profits of that & of every other little or big work that you [*or*] others print [*for me?*] while our Washington Connexion continues.' Oct. 11, 1806: 'I wrote to you, requesting as a very great favor that you w[d] instantly get from M[r]. Carey my plate of the large likeness of Washington and retouch[d] if necessary, and strike off 1500 Copies & send them on immediately by *water*, if you can't send them very cheap by mail.' Though on May 24, 1807, Weems again requested Wayne to obtain the plate from Carey, and to strike off 1500 impressions for this edition, he was probably unsuccessful, as this unique copy has none. Mar. 31, 1808: 'In May, 1806 . . . Having but little to do & vast expenses incurring, . . . I told you I was going to print a little *80 pag[d]* pamphlet, (Life of Wash.) You know you sent me some *likenesses for it.*'

6. George F. Randolph was the publisher of the *Columbian Centinel*, of Augusta, Georgia. See *Bibliography of American Newspapers*, Clarence S. Brigham, *ProcAAS*.

7. See title 8, note 3.

8. Weems very often used the same material in various ways, sometimes working it over. A case of this kind is shown in the following verses, in which he evidently liked the 'zip' at the end of each line and used these terminations for two different editions. In this 1806 edition, at p. 33, appears: 'God save the King, the British heroes cry'd, And God for Washington! Columbia's sons reply'd.'; in the 1808 edition [*title 11*], at p. 89: '*All hands unmoor!* the stamping boatswain cry'd, *All hands unmoor!* the joyous crews reply'd.'

NUMBER 11 1808

THE LIFE | OF | *George Washington;* | WITH | CURIOUS ANECDOTES, | EQUALLY HONORABLE TO HIMSELF, | AND EXEMPLARY TO HIS | YOUNG COUNTRYMEN. | *A life how useful to his country led!* | *How* LOV'D! *while* LIVING . . . *how* REVER'D! *now* DEAD! | *Lisp! lisp! his name, ye children yet unborn!* | *And with* like-deeds *your own great names adorn.* | SIXTH EDITION . . . . . [*sic*] GREATLY IMPROVED. | BY M. L. WEEMS, | FORMERLY RECTOR OF MOUNT-VERNON PARISH. | PHILADELPHIA: |

PRINTED FOR THE AUTHOR, | BY R. COCHRAN. | 1808. | COPYRIGHT SECURED. | 12mo. pp. (3), 2, (1), 1, 4–216, (2). *Front.port.* HSP., NYPL.

1. This is the first edition found in which Weems claims to be the Rector of Mt. Vernon parish [see note 5 below]; there is no Dedication nor Preface; portrait unsigned, stippled, bust, face to left, in circle, with a border, in a rectangle engraved to represent brickwork, with a black line border, inscription on tablet below circle within rectangle 'G. WASHINGTON. | Who departed this Life Dec[r]. 14, 1799 Aged 68. | Sold by W. Spotswood'; inside the border and above the inscription is 'T. Clarke. Sc.'; height 6.7 c., width 6, diameter 4.9; issued in XV chapters entirely rearranged from the 1806 edition except the first two, which are headed by the same verses; thereafter all have new headings in prose, save those from XII to XV, which have verses; last words on p. [*3*] are 'not a thou-' and on p. 76 'order, but'; the anecdote of 'poor Donop' appears on pp. 92–93; that of Colonel Washington, the kinsman of George Washington, making his mark on pp. 113–114, and of Colonel Scammel

on pp. 114–115; changes from the fifth edition on pp. 7–8, and 14 [where the word 'little' is deleted from the hatchet tale in this and all subsequent editions], while pp. 21–29, 34, 36–84, 96–99, 103, 106–108, 112, 115, 143–161 [containing 'Washington's Last Words,' here included for the first time], 166, 168, 170, 171–216 are entirely changed. Some of these alterations seem to be for the sake of accuracy or less redundancy, such as, on p. 21, Washington's leaving school *five* instead of *two* years after his father's death; other changes seem to be questions of taste, such as, on p. 36, George III's pages shrinking from 'his presence' instead of 'each into his augur hole,' and, on the same page, Washington having now become Virginia's 'favourite' instead of her 'darling.' First introduced in this edition are the verses on pp. 27–28: [*M.L.W.?*] 'Then up rose Joe, all at the word, | And took his master's arm, | And to his bed he softly led, | The Lord of Greenwood farm. | There oft he call'd on Britain's name, | And oft he wept full sore. — | Then sigh'd — thy will, O Lord, be done — | And word spake never more.'; also the dream of Washington's mother on pp. 56–58 and the oft-questioned episode of Potts finding Washington at prayer at Valley Forge, on pp. 183–184 [see note 3 below].

2. 'What is called the sixth edition, Phil. 1808 is practically a new work with title.' LC.CATALOGUE. [This note properly applies instead to the hitherto uncollated fifth edition, Georgia, 1806, title 10.] Baker's *Portraits of Washington* No. 195. Hart No. 280.

3. The first printing which I have found of the anecdote of Potts' discovering Washington in prayer is in the *Washington Federalist* of Mar. 12, 1804 [NYHS.], reprinted in the *Petersburg Intelligencer* of Aug. 10, 1804 [CLS.], and stated to have been taken from the *Charleston City Gazette*. The anecdote is preceded by the following dissertation on *The importance of Religion.* [*M.L.W.*] '*The importance of Religion.* Tis said by the wise that "There was never a truly great man without religion." And tho' to such as are about to step out of it, the ferry over life may seem but little wider than that from Haddril's Point to Charleston; yet is this narrow Navigation beset with so many dangers — here, a gust of passion — there, a Mermaid of pleasure — on this side, a Scylla of poverty on that a Charybdis of dissipation. — In short so many villainous ups and downs; so many piratical rocks, shelves, and lee-shores, all at daggers drawn with human virtue, and consequently with human greatness; that no youth of sensibility can cast his eye over the chart, without fervently imploring some angel-pilot to guide him through the scene. But that angel-pilot is no other than religion. She, and she alone, gives the telescope of faith to view those blissful worlds, which first rouse the soul to spread her sails for the voyage; she inspires that heroic hope which alone can ballast the heaven steering bark;

she puts on board all the saving virtues — her Minerva of wisdom, to direct the eventful course — her Palinurus of prudence, to clew up the sails when the stormy passions rise — her Ulysses of fortitude, to stop the ears when the syren pleasures sing — and, above all, she weathers the rich gales of love; [*of?*] divine and social life, that sweetly bear the soul along through the golden tide of duty, of every duty that can dignify the man. In short, religion stands for everything truly and permanently great in the human character. And a more candid proof of this important fact was never, perhaps, afforded than in the life of our illustrious Washington. That he was so unweariedly industrious; so systematically frugal; so elegantly temperate; so sacredly punctual; so unambitious of power; so evincible [*sic*] by pleasure; so incorruptible by gold; so unconquerable by danger: — And that, from comparative poverty, he arose to incomparable wealth; and from the vale of obscurity, to the utmost height of human glory, is entirely to be ascribed to religion; to his early acquaintance with the *infinite being*, an habitual contemplation of whom naturally begets that greatness of soul, which as naturally leads to the sublime and beautiful of action. In 1777, while the American army lay at Valley Forge, a good old quaker by the name of Potts, . . . "some great thing for this country."' This reads so exactly after Weems' style that I feel no slightest hesitation in ascribing it to him. (Indeed, it seems a fair assumption that this newspaper article was taken from his sermon, announced in the *Petersburg Intel.* between July 27 and Aug. 10, 1804.) He used the anecdote thus as an advertisement for Marshall's *Washington* [title 249, note 4] when pushing the sale of that work, but did not include it in the sheaf of tales in his own *Washington* before this edition of 1808, after which it always formed a part of the book, and has thus become an accepted tradition.[1] Given an immortality of sorts, in stone, on the Sub-Treasury building of New York, its removal from that prominent position is the one clear gain in the demolition of that stately old structure. The anecdote of Mrs. Washington's dream was used in similar fashion: [*M.L.W.*] 'COMMUNICATION. CURIOUS DREAM OF MRS. MARY WASHINGTON, (THE HONORED MOTHER OF THE ILLUSTRIOUS GEORGE.) When a man begins to make a noise in the world, his relatives (the Father *sometimes*, but, always that tenderer parent the *Mother*) are sure to recollect certain mighty odd dreams, which they had of him when he was a child. . . . Mrs. Washington also had her dream, which an excellent old Lady of Fredericksburg, Virginia, assur'd me she had often heard her relate, with great satisfaction, and for the last time but a few weeks before her death. . . . "I dreamt," said the Mother of Washington . . . "*Well Ma! now if you and the family will but consent . . . better roof* . . . worse than it

[1] The anecdote was frequently quoted in the newspapers. See title 22, note 3.

was before." This tho' certainly a very curious dream, needs no Daniel to interpret it, especially if we take Mrs. Washington's *new house*, for the Colony Government — the fire on its east side, for the North's Civil war — the gourd which Washington first employ'd, for the American 3 and 6 months enlistments — the old Man with his cap and iron rod, for Doctor Franklin — the *Shoe like* vessel which he reached to Washington, for the Sabboo [*sic*] or wooden shoed nation, the French, whom Franklin courted a long time for America — and the new roof propos'd by Washington, for a staunch Republic. This little dream tho' presenting Washington but as *in crayons*, and dimly seen like Ossian's "Half viewless Heroes," bending forward from their clouds, yet does it surprisingly mark the characteristic features of that unequall'd man; his *active* mind never at rest but in motion — his early passion for labor, the glorious labors of the plow — his quick sensibility to filial duty — his fervent love of his Mother (his Country) — his readiness to fly to the sacred sound of her voice; his undauntedness to meet her dangers — his unconquerable perseverance in her defence — his generous melting over the miseries of his countrymen — and, above all, his ceaseless solicitude for that "*equal government*," which by guarding alike the welfare of all, ought by all to be so heartily beloved as to *indure* [*sic*] *forever*. God grant it!!! A complete and elegant history of this great man, compiled from his own papers, by Chief Justice Marshall, five volumes in calf and gilt, with an atlas of military charts, are now for sale at DR. GEORGE HARRAL's at 20 dollars to subscribers, and 21 to non-subscribers. M. L. Weems tenders his best thanks to those of his numerous *subscribers* whom he has had the honor to see, for the truly filial cheerfulness with which they have generally receiv'd the History of their POLITICAL FATHER. But as the characteristic industry of the Savannah Gentlemen forbids the hope of finding them at all times at home, M.L.W. begs they will be so good as to stop their carriages a moment at Dr. Harral's and *choose their books;* or leave orders, at home, that they may be received and paid for when presented; and for favors of such magnitude in this scalding weather, the Subscriber, as in duty bound, shall most heartily pray that they may be preserved from all perils and dangers of Agues and Fevers, Thunder and Lightning, Caterpillars and Tornado.' *Col. Mus. & Sav. Adv.*, June 12, 1807, GAHS. This anecdote, first included in the above edition, was contained in all editions thereafter except the German editions of 1809, 1810, 1817 [*1824, 1833* or *1841?*] and 1838. Apparently in several instances Weems used some tale which hit his fancy — whether true or fictional — as an advertisement, later incorporating it in his *Life*, and thus building up a body of anecdote which, by experiment, he knew would hit the popular taste.

4. Weems wrote to Wayne, Mar. 31, 1808: 'As to Carey's books, or my own Life of Wash[n]. you know it was agreed that a moiety of *all* books run in Conjunction with your Life of Washington, sh [*be*] yours: and to this engagement I consider myself sacredly bound.' To Carey, Oct. 7, 1808: 'For fear of fire, which w[d] utterly incapacitate me to create an immediate substitute, *pray* get M[r]. Cochran to send you a copy of the Life of Washington as far as he has gone with it. I don't wish you to read it — it is not, qualis sit, — I beg it for *safety's sake*. Did Capt[n] Bush bring you some copy for Cochran?' Mar. 20, 1809: 'My 6th ed. Life of Washington *with a cut*, and one hundred pages more than the Italian Nun, has sold at 62½ only!! In a word, we shall *assuredly prosper*, if we get a good name.' [The price given here was later raised to $1.00; see title 15, note 3, and Carey's Catalogue, 1816.]

5. Although this is the first edition found in which Weems styles himself the Rector of Mount-Vernon Parish, he had already used the phrase in 1804 in announcements of his conducting Sunday services in two newspapers of Georgia — see items between letters of Apr. 12 and May 14, 1804, in Vol. II. See also title 249, note 4. This claim, placed four years later on a title page, is technically not a misstatement, though it smacks clearly of an advertising dodge. Rev. Phillip Slaughter, D.D., mentions Weems' incumbency 'towards the close of the century, some say in 1798,' at Pohick Church, in *History of Truro Parish*, 1908, pp. 100–102, NYPL. He did preach, at various times, on short period engagements, at Pohick Church, in Truro Parish, near Mt. Vernon. In a letter to Carey, written from Dumfries in August, 1802, he himself refers to one such 'supply' period: 'I hope I shall make you out, weekly, an equal remittance, tho' I am somewhat confined in my Operations. In consequence of your long delay in sending me on the Bibles, I went, in a fit of passion (of the self-preservative kind) and engaged with a parish or rather, yielded to the importunities of my Old Mount Vernon Parishoners [*sic*], to preach for them, once a fortnight, till the first *day of December*.' And again, on Nov. 1, 1802: 'I told you many months ago, that after the long waiting in vain for the Bibles, and seeing my precious days running down to waste I had, in a fit of dispair, engag[d] to preach in the Mount Vernon Church once a fortnight, till now.' It is possible, too, that Weems did preach in this church at times before those noted in these letters — the more so as his residence at Dumfries brought him so close. Rev. Ethan Allen, in his *Ms. Report as Historiographer of the Diocess* [*sic*] [MDDIO'NL. in PIL.], says of him, 'After leaving All Hallow' [*1789*] went to V[a]. and had Poheek Ch[*urch*]. settled and lived in Dumfries.' At any rate, it is noteworthy that not until some years after these dates did he coin and use the phrase 'Rector of Mount Vernon Parish.' Also, it evidently became,

with time, a matter of self-deception rather than wilful deceiving of others, for on July 10, 1816, he wrote to Carey from New Holland, Pa.: ''Tis 11 o'clock P.M. and I have just finish$^{d}$ a Sermon to a host of good Dutch People, who are mightily taken with me for having been Chaplain to the Great Gen$^{l}$ Washington, and the writer of his wonderful Life.' It is admitted that Washington attended Pohick Church early in life [1] and even drew the plans which were followed in building a new edifice, as well as selecting the site for it. There are many allusions to this connection in his personal records. On July 16, 1768, he notes: 'Went by Muddy Hole & Doeg Run to the Vestry [*meeting*] at Pohick Church — stayed there till half after 3 oClock & only 4 Members coming returned by Capt$^{n}$. M$^{c}$Carty's & dined there.'; Sept. 9, 1768: 'proceeded to the Meeting of our Vestry at the New Church.' See his *Where and how my life is spent*, LC. In 1770 he recorded the payment by Mr. Wm. Adam 'for my subscription towards decorating the Falls [*Pohick*] church. 1.0.0' while on Aug. 15, 1774, he paid 'by Willm Copan — putt$^{g}$ my Cypher on my Pew in Pohick Church 10.0' *Ledger B*, LC. In 1775, Apr. 20, he 'allow$^{d}$ ditto [*Mr. Alexander Henderson*] for rais$^{g}$ Pews in Pohick Church . . . 3.7.6.' and 'Charge Col$^{o}$. Fairfax with the Rais$^{g}$ his Pew in Pohick Church pr Mr. Henderson . . . 1.2.6.' *Cash Memorandum.* The following entries were made in his *Diary* [LC.], Oct. 2, 1785: 'Went with Fanny Bassett, Burwell Bassett, Doct$^{r}$. Stuart, G. A. Washington, M$^{r}$. Shaw & Nelly Custis to Pohick Church; to hear a M$^{r}$. Thompson preach, who returned with us to dinner.'; Oct. 15, 1786: 'At Pohick Church. Accompanied by Majr Washington his wife — Mr. Lear & the two childn Nelly & Washington Custis — went to Pohick Church & returned to Dinner.'; Oct. 28, 1787: 'Went to Pohick Church Mr. Lear & Washington Custis in the Carriage with me.'; Oct. 26, 1788: 'At Pohick Church. Went to Pohick Church and returned home to dinner — found Dr. Stuart at M$^{t}$. Vernon who dined there & returned home afterwards.' There is no record of his having attended Pohick after this last entry and all the evidence is that before that date he had already transferred his interests to Christ Church, Alexandria. In fact, as early as 1773 there is a record of '[*Almanac of*] Sales of the Pews in Alexandria Church to whom &c. . . . George Washington.' [2] But during the earlier years there are very few mentions of his having attended church elsewhere than at Pohick. The following entry in

[1] 'On Sundays the family [*of Mt. Vernon*] drove to Pohick Church in a chariot and four, handsomely trapped and well cared-for, with negro postillions in livery.' *Georgian Period*, William Rotch Ware, New York, 1923, Vol. I, p. 80, LC. See also *Pohick Church* in *Colonial Churches in the original colony of Virginia*, Rev. Samuel A. Wallis, Richmond, 1908, LC.

[2] *Note* of Paul L. Ford. Reference not found, nor clarified.

*Washington's Diary*, Mar. 3, 1787, has led to misunderstanding: 'The Revd. Mr. Weems, and ye Doctor Craik, who came here yesterday in the afternoon, left this about noon for Port Tob[*acco*].' It seems clear, however, that this does not refer to Mason Locke Weems but to his cousin, the Rev. John, who was for nearly thirty-five years [1787–1821], Rector of Port Tobacco Parish, Maryland, which is only a short distance from the Potomac River, nearly opposite Mt. Vernon. It should be noted also that Weems' letter of dedication to Mrs. Washington in the Green & English and Bioren editions distinctly calls himself her unknown friend, which he would scarcely have done had this item in the diary applied to him. Moreover, he alludes but thrice in his letters to possible visits to Mt. Vernon, some years after Washington's death, when he had relations with Judge Washington in connection with Marshall's *Life*. [See title 249, note 5.] Writing to Wayne, June 16, 1804, he said: 'I shall push on to Mount Vernon unless your orders sh[d] turn my direction — shall I begin at Balt[o]. & thence to the South?' [See *Letters*, Vol. II, Dec. 7, 1803, Aug. 3, Sept. 24, 1805.] Furthermore, Washington's letter to Weems dated July 3, 1799 [see title 220, note 1] was merely such an acknowledgment of a gift as would be made to a stranger. Finally, Weems' letter to Washington presenting and dedicating *The Philanthropist* to him, and the General's reply of acknowledgment and thanks, were both couched in such general terms of civility as prevailed in that more formal day. There is no suggestion in either of the slightest previous acquaintance between them. It is extremely unlikely that a meeting took place during the four months that elapsed before Washington's death. Weems would almost certainly have mentioned such an event at some time in his letters to Carey. Nor is it likely that he would not have boasted, or at least mentioned such an acquaintance with the Chief in his later advertisements, where he merely claimed that he had obtained anecdotes from the playmates, friends, companions or neighbors of Washington. [See title 13, note 3.] Weems' earliest approach to an official connection with Washington's church in Alexandria is recorded by Walter B. Norris, in an article on the *Historian of the Cherry Tree*, in the *National Magazine*, Feb. 1910, Vol. XXXI, p. 496: 'About 1790, also, the vestry of Christ Church, Alexandria, of which Washington was a vestryman, voted to authorize the rector, Rev. Bryan Fairfax, to employ as an assistant the Rev. Mason L. Weems, or any other man he chose.' Although he failed to secure this position, the incident goes to show that his peccadilloes in his Maryland parishes had not been so serious as to be widely known over the state line.

6. Query, signed '*Biblios.*', for Weems' *Washington*, fourth, fifth and sixth editions, in *Magazine of American History, Notes & Queries*, Vol. IV, 1880,

p. 222, LC. No replies found. 'Parson Weems for nearly a century and a quarter has never failed to satisfy his public. . . .' Notice of the Mt. Vernon edition of *Washington,* with a citation from it, in an article in the *Nation* (N.Y.), [*Anon.*], Apr. 18, 1918.

NUMBER 12 1808

THE LIFE | OF | GEORGE WASHINGTON; | WITH | CURIOUS ANECDOTES, | EQUALLY HONORABLE TO HIMSELF, | AND EXEMPLARY TO HIS | YOUNG COUNTRYMEN. | *A life how useful to his country led!* | *How* LOV'D! *while* LIVING! . . . [*sic*] *how* REVER'D! *now* DEAD! | *Lisp! lisp! his name, ye children yet unborn!* | *And with* like-deeds *your own great names adorn.* | SIXTH EDITION — GREATLY IMPROVED. | BY M. L. WEEMS, | FORMERLY RECTOR OF MOUNT-VERNON PARISH. | PHILADELPHIA: |

PRINTED FOR THE AUTHOR, | BY R. COCHRAN. | 1808. | COPY RIGHT SECURED. | 12mo. pp. (3), 2, (1), 1, 4–228, (2). *Front.port.* HSP.

1. This, with the other, and probably earlier, Cochran sixth edition, is the last where 'honorable' is spelled without a 'u,' except in a few 'sport' issues; I place it later than its sister edition of this year because the portrait, though identical, shows great wear, while the text has the following additional material after p. 216, which is included in all subsequent editions: 'CHAP. XVI. WASHINGTON'S CHARACTER — CONTINUED. HIS PATRIOTISM,' on pp. 217–227; 'CONCLUSION. WASHINGTON'S WILL,' on pp. 227–228, without verse-headings; last words on p. [*3*] are 'Have not a thou—'; on p. 27 'Joe' in the verses is printed 'Jue.'

2. 'Quite a different production from title 32 [*Green & English edition, 1800?*] being almost re-written, yet retaining all its quaintness and originality. It is also divided into chapters, and possesses some claims to the dignity of a biography (*sui generis*), being fuller in detail and more consecutive in narrative. Very little of the original sketch has been used, although here and there entire sentences and paragraphs occur. . . . This edition was copy-righted at Philadelphia, September 20th, 1808, as the *Sixth,* but it is really the *First* of the popular "Weems' Washington," as the well known "curious anecdotes," promised on the

title page, such as — *the hatchet story,* — *the cabbage-seed story,* — *the dream of his mother,* etc., etc., appear in this volume for the first time.' Baker's *Bibliotheca Washingtoniana* No. 69. [In this last statement Baker is in error, except concerning the mother's dream. See notes to the Georgia 1806 edition (title 10) which he had not seen. See also a Ms. volume by Baker at HSP. entitled *The Opening Paragraphs To some Biographies and Biographical Sketches of George Washington,* in which he quotes the commencement of the 1808 edition, to show the changes, some of which actually were first made in 1806.] Baker's *Portraits of Washington* No. 195. [See also Article (*Anon.*) quoting William S. Baker in *Phil. Inquirer,* Feb. 18, 1894.] Hart No. 280. Henry Whelen Catalogue No. 227.

3. *Ad.* '*A New Work.* The Private Life of Washington, enlivened and enriched with a great number of very valuable Anecdotes of that illustrious American, from his cradle to his grave. *The sixth Edition, improved* — Price, 5/3 BY M. L. WEEMS, Ci-devent [*sic*] Rector. . . . *Criticism on this Work, from a Baltimore Paper.* "The Author has treated this great subject . . . virtue only can lead to TRUE GREATNESS." [*Anon., By Maj. Gen. H. Lee,* see note 4 to seventh edition, 1808, title 13.] For Sale at Adam Cooke's — Fred'g.' *Va. Her.,* May 10, 1809, LC.

NUMBER 13 1808

THE LIFE | OF | GEORGE WASHINGTON; | WITH | CURIOUS ANECDOTES, | EQUALLY HONOURABLE TO HIMSELF AND EXEMPLARY | TO HIS YOUNG COUNTRYMEN. | A life how useful to his country led! | How loved! while living! — how revered! now dead! | Lisp! lisp! his name, ye children yet unborn! | And with like deeds your own great names adorn. | SEVENTH EDITION — GREATLY IMPROVED. | BY M. L. WEEMS, | FORMERLY RECTOR OF MOUNT-VERNON PARISH. | PHILADELPHIA: |

PRINTED FOR THE AUTHOR. | 1808. | 12mo. pp. (1), 4, 4–228, (2). *Front.port.*

AAS., HSP., MdDio'nL., NYPL., WL.

1. Portrait, unsigned, after Stuart, stippled, bust, 3/4 face to right, in oval, height 4 c., width 3.4, with stippled border in a rectangle of wavy horizontal lines, 3 buttons plainly visible on coat, no inscription; on reverse of title is

copyright notice for the District of Penn. to M. L. Weems, dated 1808; the typography is entirely changed from the earlier 1808 editions; the text follows the longer of those two, title 12.

2. 'A reprint of the preceding number with slight variations . . . in the text.' Baker's *Bibliotheca Washingtoniana* No. 70. [He had evidently not then seen or noted the varying editions of Cochran, 1808, titles 11 and 12.] Baker's *Portraits of Washington* No. 328 states that the head is to left. [Inaccurate, so far as I have seen. This description would seem to apply rather to one of the portraits used in the tenth edition of 1810 — see notes to that, title 19.] 'Artist unknown.' Hart No. 526.

3. *Ad.* 'A New Work. JUST RECEIVED, AND FOR SALE AT THIS OFFICE, *Price, single,* 62½ *cents; and a large allowance to those who buy a quantity.* The Private Life of Washington, Illustrated and enlivened with original and valuable anecdotes. BY M. L. WEEMS, Formerly minister of Washington's Parish.' *Lanc. Jour.*, Feb. 10, 1809 *et seq.*, LIOF. '*A New Work* The private life of . . . With a great number of original anecdotes, BY M. L. WEEMS, Ci-devant Rector of Mount Vernon Parish, and, for fifteen years, the intimate of the grey-hair'd veterans of the last century, who were the neighbors and companions of Washington. Criticism by Judge Brackenridge. . . .' *Mus. & George'n Adv.*, Mar. 8, 1809 *et seq.*; abbreviated June 20, 'Price 87½ cts.,' LC. '(Price fine copy 87½ *cts*, coarse 62½.) THE PRIVATE LIFE OF . . . with a great number of original anecdotes, by *M. L. Weems* . . . Seventh Edition.' *Library*, March, 1809, NYHS. '. . . Private Life of Washington. . . .' *Museum*, Mar. 8, 1809 *et seq.*, LC. *Reviewed.* 'A GOOD OLD BOOK. The Original Record of Washington's Little Hatchet. Few and pitiably ignorant must be those citizens of the United States who have never heard the story of George Washington and his little hatchet. . . . It could have been written by no man that ever lived save its author. . . . We transcribe the title page in full. . . . Seventh edition. . . . 1808. . . .' [*Anon.*] *The Sun* (N. Y.), Jan. 8, 1874, NYPL.

4. Weems wrote to Carey, Jan. 15, 1809: 'Will it not be right to push off a great many first of this edition [*Life of Washington*] [?]' To Jefferson: 'Navy Yard — Doctr. Ewells. Feb[y]. 1. 1809 Sir — The Multitude adore the rising sun: — for me, I honor the steps of his departure. My thoughts return with pleasure to the fields that were bright with his beams where the Olive gladden[d] in her labours and the vine shook her green leaf with joy to the flattering ray that fill[d] her clusters with nectar. Self descending your Excellency sets in glory — and soon to rise in multiplied radiance on all the political stars that are to shine by your absence. I beg your Excellency's acceptance of a copy of a New Work — The Private Life of the man whom, you, of all others most rever'd,

and whom with such peculiar felicity you styled "Columbia's First & Greatest Son." This is the Seventh edition — 10,000 copies have been sold — and some flattering things said — But if, on perusing this private Life of Washington your Excellency should be pleas'd to find that I have not, like *some* of his Eulogists, set him up as a Common Hero for military ambition to idolize & imitate — Nor an Aristocrat, like *others*, to mislead & enslave the nation, but a pure Republican whom all our youth should know, that they may love & imitate his Virtues, and thereby immortalize "the *last Republic now on earth*" I shall heartily thank you for a line or two in favor of it — as a school book. That from the top of your own heaven-kissing hill you may long long look around with a Parents joy on the continuing Peace, Prosperity & Universal blessings of America, is the sincerest wish of your Excellency's greatly oblig'd & most aff. friend M. L. Weems.' [LC.] To Carey, from Dumfries, Mar. 22, 1809: 'I wonder who put that criticism on your Life of Washington in the Balt°. North American of the 18 Your M. L. Weems.' [Alluding to an unsigned 'extract of a letter from a friend' dated 'Mar. 9, 1809. *Rev. Mr. Weems's "Life of Washington."* . . . It has reached its seventh edition, and yet I never saw it before. The author has treated . . . true greatness.' *N. Amer.*, Mar. 18, 1809, LC. By Major Gen. H. Lee. It was printed on the title page either in full, as in the ninth edition, 1809, title 17, or abbreviated as thereafter. See also note 3 to the later sixth edition, Cochran, 1808, title 12.]

NUMBER 14 1809

THE LIFE | OF | GEORGE WASHINGTON; | WITH | CURIOUS ANECDOTES, | EQUALLY HONOURABLE TO HIMSELF AND | EXEMPLARY TO HIS YOUNG COUNTRYMEN. | A life how useful to his country led! | How loved! while living! — How revered! now dead! | Lisp! lisp! his name, ye children yet unborn! | And with like deeds your own great names adorn. | EIGHTH EDITION — GREATLY IMPROVED. | BY M. L. WEEMS. | FORMERLY RECTOR OF MOUNT-VERNON PARISH. | PHILADELPHIA: |

PRINTED FOR THE AUTHOR. | 1809. | 12mo. pp. (2), 3, (2), 4, 4–228. *Front.plate.*

VStL. [*imp., lacks pp. 101–104.*]

1. The three front fly leaves contain 'CRITICISM ON WEEMS'S LIFE OF WASHINGTON.' [the first three words in italic capitals] signed 'NICHOLAS COLLIN, *Minister of the Swedes' Church, Philadelphia,*' [1] 'HENRY MUHLENBERG, *Minister of the Lutheran Church, Lancaster.*', 'JACOB RUSH, *Judge of the Court of Common Pleas, Pennsylvania.*', and 'H. H. BRACKENRIDGE.'; [2] the word 'history,' in the first paragraph of these criticisms, which appears thus in the NYPL. eighth edition of this year, is in the plural in this and all the other eighth editions following, the NYPL. copy also lacking the word 'be' in the expression 'I do not know a better to be put into the hands of young persons,' which appears in the last paragraph of these criticisms in all other copies; no portrait, but a frontispiece, unsigned, '*Surrender of Lord Cornwallis,*' '*Page 114.*', at top right; no other plates; the title, unlike the editions of this year following, does not contain the words 'EMBELLISHED WITH SEVEN ENGRAVINGS'; on reverse of title, Penn. copyright dated 1808, Sixth edition; the word 'WASHINGTON' in the heading to Chapter I, is in italic capitals; the last words on the first page [*3*] of the text are 'have not a thousand,' and on p. 76, 'in tolerable order'; p. 226 is incorrectly numbered 204.

2. Since this is a unique copy, so far as I have found, in not having the announcement on the title page of the seven engravings, it would seem to me that it must have been the first issued of the three eighth editions of this year, and that a comparatively small number were printed. Then came the second of this year, which is now in a number of libraries, followed by the third, of which HSP. only has a copy. It is very unlikely that Weems would have made the announcement of engravings and then withdrawn it in the same year.

3. For advertisements possibly applying to this issue see title 15, note 3.

4. For letters possibly applying to this issue see title 17, note 4.

[1] Dr. Nicholas Collin, author of *Climate of the Country about the Delaware, AmPhSTrans.*, Vol. I, 1818.

[2] 'The . . . Philadelphia editor . . . the eccentric social wit, Hugh Henry Brackenridge, the author of the capital political satire, "Modern Chivalry," (1792), the first satirical novel written in America. A native of Scotland, born in 1748, but was only five years of age when his father settled in York County, Pennsylvania . . . graduated from Princeton college in 1771.' *Philadelphia Magazines*, Albert Henry Smyth, p. 53. — It was through the influence and encouragement of H. H. Brackenridge that the first printing press in Pittsburgh was established; he became a judge of the Supreme Court of Pennsylvania and edited the *United States Magazine*. 'A Narrative, worth reading, of his success, may be seen in his "Gazette Publications."' *McCulloch's Additions to Thomas's History of Printing, ProcAAS.*, Vol. XXXI, Apr. 1921, pp. 95, 98, LC.

NUMBER 15 1809

THE LIFE | OF | GEORGE WASHINGTON; | WITH | CURIOUS ANECDOTES, | EQUALLY HONOURABLE TO HIMSELF AND | EXEMPLARY TO HIS YOUNG COUNTRYMEN. | A life how useful to his country led! | How loved! while living! — how revered! now dead! | Lisp! lisp! his name, ye children yet unborn! | And with like deeds your own great names adorn. | EIGHTH EDITION — GREATLY IMPROVED. | EMBELLISHED WITH SEVEN ENGRAVINGS. | BY M. L. WEEMS, | FORMERLY RECTOR OF MOUNT-VERNON PARISH. | PHILADELPHIA:|

PRINTED FOR THE AUTHOR. | 1809. | 12mo. pp. (1), 3, (1), 2, 4–228, 3, (1). *Front., Port., Plates.*

AAS., HSP., LC. [*imp., lacks after p. 224*], NYHS., NYPL., *NYStL.

1. On reverse of title, copyright notice for Penn. district, Sixth edition, dated 1808; on the third page after title is portrait, unsigned, after Stuart, stippled, in oval, height 4 c., width 3.4, with stippled border in a rectangle of wavy horizontal lines, head to right, three buttons visible on the coat, no inscription; Washington's name at the heading of Chapter I is printed in italic capitals; the last words on the first page of the text are 'Have not a thousand'; this and the succeeding are the first editions seen by me with the unsigned plates as follow: '*Death of Gen*[l]. *Montgomery*' and above '*Frontispiece*'; '*Defeat of Gen*[l]. *Braddock.*' and above '*Page* 40'; '*Battle of Lexington.*' and above '*Page* 70'; '*Battle of Bunker's Hill & Death of Gen. Warren,*' and above '*Page* 77'; '*Capture of Major André.*' and above '*Page* 105'; and '*Surrender of Lord Cornwallis,*' and above '*Page* 114'; the text is the same as the HSP. copy of this year, following, but p. 226 is incorrectly numbered 204 like the VSTL. copy preceding; contains on fly leaves, either first or last, the four signed commendations entitled 'CRITICISMS' [lacks final 'S.' in AAS. copy] noted in preceding title. In the first paragraph of these commendations the word 'history' is printed thus in the NYPL. copy, but in the plural in the others; also, the NYPL. copy differs in that the expressions in the last paragraph of commendations 'to be put into the hands of young persons' and 'painting with interests' in the other copies appear 'to put into the hands of young persons' and 'painting which interests'. For probable date of issue see note 2 to title 14.

2. Baker's *Portraits of Washington* No. 339.

3. *Ad.* 'A new Work. *Just received*, at this Office, The private Life of Washington, illustrated and enlivened with original and valuable Anecdotes. BY M. L. WEEMS, Formerly Minister of Gen. Washington's Parish. *The following Criticism and Commendation are by two learned and pious* Divines: . . . NICHOLAS COLLIN . . . HENRY MUELLENBURG . . .' *Intel.*, Jan. 3, 1809; reprinted, Jan. 31, 1809, without the above commendations, but with a criticism of the 5th edition by Thomas U. P. Charlton, Att'y-Gen'l of Georgia [see title 10, note 4]; abbreviated, Mar. 14, 1809, LIOF. 'Just Received, and for Sale at Samuel Pleasants' Printing Office and Book Store, Life of Washington, by the Rev. M. L. Weems. . . .' *Va. Arg.*, Jan. 31, 1809 *et seq.*, LC.; Feb. 17, 1809, AAS. 'Mr. Weems has just published a *New Life of Washington*, which he calls *his private life*.' *Col. Cent.* (Aug., Ga.), Feb. 4, 1809, UN'YGA. 'New Publications. . . . The Private Life of Washington. By M. L. Weems; some time rector of Mount Vernon Parish, Washington; R. C. Weightman. Price 87½ cents.' *Monthly Anthology*, Vol. VI, March, 1809, p. 215, LC., MHS. 'Mason L. Weems has lately published the Private Life of Washington — price 87½ cents — Judge Brackenridge, in a commendatory note, says it abounds with both the pathetic and the comic.' *Star*, Mar. 16, 1809, NCSTL. 'Just received and for sale at the office of the Watchman. . . . exemplary to his young countrymen. [*Four lines of verse*] Eighth Edition Greatly Improved. Embellished with seven Engravings. By M. L. Weems. Formerly Rector of Mount Vernon Parish.' *Amer. Watch.*, Sept. 13, 1809, AAS. [*M.L.W.*] 'JUST PUBLISHED, And for sale at this Office the eight [*sic*] edition, making near twenty thousand copies already sold, of the Life of George Washington. A Life how useful to his country led! How lov'd while living! — how rever'd now dead! Ye loving Sires! with pleasure all attend, And read the history of your Glorious Friend. Lisp! lisp! his name, ye Children yet unborn! And with like deeds, your own bright lives adorn! [*For other variants of these verses see title 8, note 1.*] BY THE REV. M. L. WEEMS, Formerly Clergyman of Mount Vernon Parish, and intimate with the grey-hair'd veterans of the last century, who were the playmates and companions of the great Washington from his childhood. RECOMMENDATIONS by eminent divines, judges and generals. . . . [*Nicholas Collin, Jacob Rush, H. H. Brackenridge, H. Lee.*] Price one dollar.' *Va. Arg.*, Oct. 17, 24, 1809; abbreviated, Nov. 3, 1809, LC., also Feb. 6 *et seq.*, Sept. 4 *et seq.*, 1810, AAS.; Feb. 16, 1810 *et seq.*, NYPL.; *Ral. Reg.*, Nov. 30, 1809 *et seq.*, NCSTL. Reviewed in *Panoplist & Missionary Magazine* [*Anon.*], Vol. II, April, 1810, pp. 525–532, NYPL.

4. For letters possibly referring to these issues see title 17, note 4.

NUMBER 16 1809

THE LIFE | OF | GEORGE WASHINGTON; | WITH | CURIOUS ANECDOTES, | EQUALLY HONOURABLE TO HIMSELF AND | EXEMPLARY TO HIS YOUNG COUNTRYMEN. | A life how useful to his country led! | How loved! while living! — how revered! now dead! | Lisp! lisp! his name, ye children yet unborn! | And with like deeds your own great names adorn. | EIGHTH EDITION — GREATLY IMPROVED. | EMBELLISHED WITH SEVEN ENGRAVINGS. | BY M. L. WEEMS, | FORMERLY RECTOR OF MOUNT-VERNON PARISH. | PHILADELPHIA; |

PRINTED FOR THE AUTHOR. | 1809. | 12mo. pp. (1), 1, (1), 4, 4–228, (3). *Two fronts.*, *Plates.*
HSP.

1. This edition differs from the preceding eighth of 1809, in lacking a portrait and commendations, in its heading to Chapter I, where the name of Washington is in capitals, but not, as heretofore, in italics, in the last words on p. 76, which in this issue are 'order, but,' while in the other they are 'tolerable order', in having no error in the numbering at p. 226, and in its plates, which have many differences [this HSP. copy was evidently extra-illustrated by Mr. Baker, for there are two plates for every one]; they vary from each other, though not often radically, in inscriptions — as in the two frontispieces, on one of which the word FRONTISPIECE is inscribed thus, in capitals, in the other appears in italics — and in general design, but one set does not often differ from those in the preceding eighth edition, which I have placed earlier because its plates show far less wear; certain differences, however, between the extra set of plates and the usual one used in this and following editions may be noted: in the '*Defeat of Gen[l]. Braddock.*' in this copy [and in AAS. and both NYPL. copies of the other issue] Braddock is at right, facing left, with his legs to left, and the figures are much larger than in any other print of this plate seen [see title 17, note 4], and it is inscribed above '*Page 40*'; '*Battle of Lexington.*' is inscribed above '*P. 71*' instead of 'Page 70'; '*Battle of Bunker's Hill . . .*' '*P. 76*' instead of 'Page 77'; '*Capture of Major Andre,*' '*P. 104*' instead of 'Page 105'; '*Surrender of Lord Cornwallis.*', '*P. 114*' instead of 'Page 114'. Last words of the first page of the text are like those in the preceding edition.

2. Baker's *Bibliotheca Washingtoniana* No. 77 states that this was a reprint of the Sixth Edition, and the last one printed for the author, as the copyright was then sold to Mathew Carey for the sum of one thousand dollars. Note, however, the following, dated five years later: 'In 1809 a reprint of the seventh edition was published, and this edition was the last one printed for the author, as Weems then sold the copyright for a thousand dollars, a very large sum in those early days, and well attesting to the popularity of the work, to Mathew Carey, the well-known publisher and philanthropist. Besides the portrait of Washington, this book was accompanied by six copperplate illustrations exceptionally crude in execution, that are as follows: "Death of General Montgomery." "Defeat of General Braddock." "Battle of Lexington." "Battle of Bunker's Hill and Death of General Warren." "Capture of Major Andre" and "Surrender of Lord Cornwallis."' Article [*Anon.*] quoting William S. Baker in *Phila. Inquirer*, Feb. 18, 1894, LC. See letter of Weems to Benjamin Warner, Richmond, May 26, 1820, in *Letters*, Vol. III.

3. For advertisements possibly applying to this issue see title 15, note 3.

4. For letters possibly referring to this issue see title 17, note 4.

NUMBER 17 1809

THE LIFE | OF | GEORGE WASHINGTON; | WITH | CURIOUS ANECDOTES, | EQUALLY HONOURABLE TO HIMSELF | AND | EXEMPLARY TO HIS YOUNG COUNTRYMEN. | A life how useful to his country led! | How loved! while living! . . . . . [*sic*] how revered! now dead! | Lisp! lisp! his name, ye children yet unborn! | And with like deeds your own great names adorn. | NINTH EDITION. . . . [*sic*] GREATLY IMPROVED. | EMBELLISHED WITH SEVEN ENGRAVINGS. | BY M. L. WEEMS, | FORMERLY RECTOR OF MOUNT-VERNON PARISH. | "The author has treated this great subject with admirable suc- | "cess in a new way. He turns all the actions of Washington to the | "encouragement of virtue, by a careful application of numerous | "exemplifications drawn from the conduct of the founder of our | "republic from his earliest life. No Biographer deserves more | "applause than he whose chief purpose is to entice the young | "mind to the affectionate love of virtue, by personifying it in the | "character most dear to these states." | *H. Lee, Major General Army U. S.* | PHILADELPHIA: |

PRINTED FOR MATHEW CAREY. | 1809. | 12mo. pp. 1, 2–12, (1), 3, (1), 2, 4–228, (2). *Front.port., Plates.*
AAS., BPL. [*lacks port.*], HSP., LC. [*lacks port.*], NoHPL., NYHS., NYPL., *NYStL., YU.

1. These copies differ slightly in pagination; in some the six front fly leaves consist of publisher's advertisements, including Weems' *Washington*, '(PRICE ONE DOLLAR,) WITH A PORTRAIT, AND SIX HISTORICAL ENGRAVINGS.' with four signed 'Criticisms . . .'; in some, these are lacking; this is the first edition found giving Lee's commendation on the title page [first printed in *N. Amer.*, Mar. 18, 1809, see title 13, note 4]; on reverse of title, Penn. copyright notice, with three signed commendations, abbreviated; portrait, unsigned, after Stuart, stippled, bust, 3/4 face to right, oval height 6.4 c., width 3.4, with a border line, in a rectangle of wavy horizontal lines, no buttons visible on the coat, inscription below lines [*lacking in* HSP. *and one* NYPL. *copy; see Hart No. 527a*] 'GL. WASHINGTON.' in shaded letter; there are many discrepancies in the plates, and their inscriptions are sometimes above, sometimes below, some plates are lacking, and some are reversed in the printing; the last words on p. [*3*] are 'Have not a,' and on p. 76, 'tolerable order.' One NYPL. copy has portrait, engraved, profile to right, bust, epaulets and five buttons visible on coat, in an oval background of criss-crossed lines, no border, no inscription.

2. Baker's *Bibliotheca Washingtoniana* No. 78 says: 'The illustrations are the same [*as the 8th ed.*], but from another set of plates; the "Defeat of General Braddock," however, is an entirely different design.' [See letter of Oct. 20, 1809, in note 4 below.] I have not found enough similarity between *all* the above copies to agree with this opinion. It appears to me that in the LC. and one of the NYPL. copies, Carey used for the plates or portraits whatever Weems happened to have on hand. [See title 19, note 2.] *Portraits of Washington* No. 339. Hart Nos. 527, 527a. There is also inserted in one copy of this edition another 'portrait of Washington, profile, face to right, after the dry-point etching by Joseph Wright', — see *Washington's Southern Tour, 1791*, Archibald Henderson, p. 68.

3. *Ad.* 'NEW PUBLICATIONS. JUST RECEIVED *And for Sale at Somervell & Conrad's Book-Store*, THE FOLLOWING NEW WORKS: THE Private life of Gen.

GEORGE WASHINGTON, *ninth edition*, with valuable anecdotes, and six historical engravings. The reader may see, prefixed to the work, some criticisms on it by eminent judges, &c. to which we give the following, by the late governor of Virginia: "I have perused the Life of Washington by Mr. M. L. Weems, formerly rector of Mount Vernon parish. . . ."' [Lee's commendation follows as on title page.] *Republican* (Petersburg, Va.), Apr. 9, 1810; abbreviated, July 5, 1810, AAS. Also advertised in: *Louisv'l. Gaz.*, May 4, 1810, AAS. *Va. Arg.*, July 6, 1810, AAS. *Ga. Jour.*, Nov. 14, 1810, AAS. For other advertisements possibly referring to this issue see title 15, note 3, second eighth edition of 1809. *Reprint:* 'While in North-Carolina, a British officer, Tarleton, dining in a large company, an American lady being one of the company, who chiefly were whigs, . . . looked at his crippled fingers and bit his lips with rage.' Anecdote concerning Colonel Washington making his *mark*, if not able to write his name [pp. 113–114 in this edition]; *Va. Arg.*, Sept. 11, 1810, AAS.

4. Weems wrote to Carey, Jan. 7, 1809: 'I wish that you [*would*] give to M[r]. John Adams the printing of your spring edition of the Life of Washington for Petersburg, Norfolk, Halifax, Edinton — Tarboro, Washington, Newburn, Fayette, Wilmington, Geo. Town, Charleston &[c]. . . . By giving the printing of 5000 of this work to this Family you will feel sometimes stealing across your thoughts the Joy of having thrown a *tow rope* to those who have not been so fortunate as yourself in the tempestuous navigation of life. . . . M[r]. Adams says that in ten weeks he can print 5000 — cost, in printing, paper, copper *plates*, binding, &[c]. . . . [*1450 Doll[s] or thereabouts.*]' From Carey, Jan. 10, 1809: 'I shall put to press a new Edition of Washington, in a week or ten days. I shall print [*illegible*] 5000, and have it out as soon as possible, probably within five or six weeks. I shall have a full supply in every place you choose in the Spring. . . .' To Carey, Jan. 13, 1809: 'I wish you w[d] make great exertions — but why need I make any wish that you sh[d] do all in your power to expedite the sale of what of Washington remains on hand? You have a great deal of money lying in the bones of old George if you will but exert yourself to extract it — Let Henry [*Carey*] make a leg (with his Washington & advertisements) at all the genteel Hotels about the City — And perhaps some good fluent Hawker w[d] aid as much.' Jan. 15, 1809: 'I wish you not to be in too great a hurry about this next edition of Washington. Will it not be right to push off a great many first of this edition.[?]' Jan. 19, 1809: 'The truth is Washington will, if you will but let me lead off the dance for you, do more for you than any *one* book of the *same size*, you ever had anything to do with — Believe me I sometimes mourn that I ever let it go out of my hand, — but *chiefly* because it is not *half finished*, not *half* finish[d]. Several *most valuable* chapters,

chapters *entire*, ought still to be added. And in the work, as it now stands, there are many passages that are capable of being wrought up to a far *more interesting height*, but which can hardly be done except by a mind peculiarly prone to the thing like mine, and enthusiastically heated. However so great [*is*] the interest I take in setting Washington before the youth of our Country, that tho' he is now, mainly your Property; yet will I for some trifling douceur, *left to yourself*, cheerfully undertake to labour on this Work both in adding & polishing, untill it shall be fit for you to set up in metal *perenias are* [*?*] We may do great & good things together by & by if you can but be patient a little.' Jan. 25, 1809: 'You talk[d] of writing to me about Washington, emendated, &[c].' Feb. 22, 1809: 'I thank you for the offer to return me the copyright of my Life of Washington — shall be oblig[d] to you to transmit, as you promise, the bill of sale by mail & I will return your *receipt*. The $450 in question, were offer'd to me long before you thought of purchasing the Life of Washington — They were, as I consider'd the matter, *generously* tender'd to pay for my house — and I had no idea that you wou'd take them back.' Carey to Weems, Feb. 28, 1809: 'I retain the Contract. It is too childish to [*illegible*] break bargains in this way. You will make more in my hands than in your own. I have engaged five engravings, Braddock's defeat, Battle of Bunker's Hill, the Garden [*obliterated*] Capture of Andre, Cudjo's measuring the Atlantic. . . . You shall have 10.000.' Weems to Carey, Mar. 12, 1809: 'But it grieves me to think that the book is turning out, on a large scale, into the world, and in so unfinish[d] & imperfect a state. It is, as you well know, capable of great improvement, not only of polish & melody in the numbers, but in accession of most interesting anecdotes and valuable sentiments. Such is the interest I take in this book that I mean to prepare [*additions?*] for the next edition — leav[g] it to yourself to make me some allowance therefor. . . .' Mar. 15, 1809: 'Judge Johnson who was with me this morning, . . . blames me much for having sold you the Life of Washington, and says that if you play your cards well you may do well with it. So great is my solicitude to have it compleated [*sic*] to my mind & to your profit as well as my own, that I am willing to continue to *collect*, *incorporate*, *retouch*, *amplify*, and so and so on and go thro all the cities & towns of the United States inoculating the work in my *new way*, if you'll allow me but one cent for all that you shall print, while I am with you.' Mar. 20, 1809: 'I beg you to understand one thing, when I sold you my Washington I reserv[d] an interest in it. I never dream'd that you meant to give any person South of the Delaware an interest in it injurious to mine.' Mar. 25, 1809: 'You advanc'd for me, for Mary Findley,[1] Washington &[c] &[c] upwards of a 1000

[1] This alludes to his *God's Revenge against Murder*, title 177 *et seq.*

Doll[s]. This you did from motives disinterested (except on Washington's Life on which I pay you 4 cents pr. book) and waiting to be paid out *of the sales*. For this I thank'd you, for you coud have made more than four cents pr. book on your money — barring your trouble. . . .' Again May 4, 1809: 'As to Washington, I am glad you have got it finished and will soon be ready to furnish *any quantity*.' Sept. 6, 1809: 'I do not forget the generosity that advanc'd so much money to print my little books, last autumn, nor the confidence repos'd in me, of thousands of Doll[s] worth of Books.' Oct. 20, 1809: '. . . rather than live in fear [*of theft*] with all your books, I w[d] give them up, take my chance with Marion[,] Mary Findley & my 30 pr Cent on Old Washington. By them I can live & bring up my children. . . . While this edition of Washington is working off let your Designer improve "The Defeat of Braddock.["] Done con expressione it w[d] produce a fine effect.' Nov. 7, 1809: 'I am to give Sam[l] Pleasants 10$ for the year for advertising your Wash. & to the Printer in Lynchburg, 5$ for advertising the same. This will greatly aid the sales. But if you approve it not, I will advertise no *more* except in *Charleston*, where I think I certainly ought to advertise. . . . You charge me very wrongly about selling my own little Wash. & Findley. *You* know I came loaded with them from your house, & *had them to sell;* & from the sales I have sent you a good deal of money — & paid a great deal for you. And besides I have told you repeatedly I was ready to sell all my own little scribblings to you & thus lose them in the general stock . . . without meaning or hinting at repentance for sell[g] Wash. I declare solemnly, I cou'd maintain my family handsomely on that single book. But still I believe that if you w[d] but aid it with elegant expressive engravings, & wait a little untill we can *work things into a proper train*, we shall yet do admirably.' Nov. 18, 1809: 'M[r]. Pleasants [*sic*] sales of Washington, since he advertized it are such as to lead him to wish you w[d] send him 50 more.' Nov. 27, 1809: 'The 500 Washington were safely come to Grammar. We shall be ruin[d] from your inattention to my earnest & reiterated intreaties. Why were not Elegant Advertisem[ts] of this work, with the letters critical & commendatory by Lee &c &c printed on colour'd paper, sent in the box? . . . I have given you up my Life of Washington at 1000. . . .' Dec. 13, 1809: 'I say had I not fully counted to have had to establish from 2 to 300 *illuminating*, moralizing book stores I w[d] never have sold my Life of Washington. And let me tell you, *once for all* that if you are tired of the connexion I shall never use an argument to bind you to it. Give me back my little book, or as Nathan w[d] say, my little ewe-lamb and take all your thousands of gigantic authors to *yourself*.' Dec. 18, 1809: 'Did you not agree to give me near 1300 Doll[s] for Washington, with the addition.[?] . . .

Have I not subsisted my family & myself by the sales of Washington [?]' From Augusta, Feb. 14, 1810: 'Washington outsells anything I have, no comparison.' Feb. 28, 1810: 'You saw with your own eyes, & heard with your own ears, the rapid sales of Washington & Mary Findley. And here now in this very Country [*Augusta*] where two years ago I sold a great part of *one edition* of Washington & *two* of M. Findley, I still sell more of them than of any, even *the best school books* that you have sent me. . . .'

NUMBER 18 1809

Die | Lebensbeschreibung | und merkwŭrdige Handlungen | von | Georg Waschington, | General und Befehlshaber der | Armeen von Nord-America [*sic*]. | Nebst der | Erklărung der Unabhăngigkeit, | und der | Constitution | der | Vereinigten Staaten. | Aus dem Englischen übersetzt. | Friederichstadt, |

Gedruckt bey M. Bărtgis. | 1809. | 12mo. pp. (30), 7, 6–176. *Front.port.* HHL. [*imp., lacks after p. 117*], HSP.

1. The portrait is a rude woodcut, unsigned, bust, face slightly to right, in an oval of horizontal lines, in a single line border, surrounded by a foliated border identical with the portrait in the Bartgis 1801 edition except that it lacks the inscription and has the foliated instead of the two-lined border; on reverse of title there are two commendations signed 'David F. Schăffer, A.M. Prediger'[1] and 'Daniel Wagner, Prediger'; the text is after the George Keatinge [*1800?*] edition, title 1, and the English Bartgis edition of 1801, title 5 (except that, like its title, it is printed in German characters throughout); with the following changes: the Preface of seven paragraphs,

[1] 'Married, on the 1st instant, by the Rev. David F. Schaeffer, Mr. John Feagler to the amiable and agreeable Miss Susanna Cutler.' *Bartgis's Republican Gazette*, Apr. 10, 1813, AAS.— 'Married. On Tuesday evening last, by the Rev. David F. Schaeffer, Mr. David Barr, of Hagerstown to the amiable Miss Christina Mantz . . .' *Plaindealer*, Aug. 19, 1813, AAS.

Die

Lebensbeschreibung

und merkwürdige Handlungen

von

Georg Waschington,

General und Befehlshaber der

Armeen von Nord-America.

Nebst der

Erklärung der Unabhängigkeit,

und der

Constitution

der

Vereinigten Staaten.

Aus dem Englischen übersetzt.

Friederichstadt,

Gedruckt bey M. Bärtgis.

1809.

Facsimile Frontispiece and Title Page of the Bartgis 1809 Edition in German of *The Life of Washington*

signed 'Der Verfasser,' is abbreviated from these editions [copyright notice, in English, on reverse of last page of Preface]; Chapter I ('*Erstes Capitel*') has no heading of Contents; there are additional items listed in the headings to Chapters VII, VIII, X, and XII, new paragraphs have been added to the text of Chapters VIII and X, and certain paragraphs in the Keatinge and the earlier Bartgis editions are here omitted, i.e., the last paragraph of Chapter X, the last half of the ninth paragraph of Chapter XII, and the first paragraph on p. 67 of Bartgis 1801 and p. 94 of Keatinge; minor textual changes occur, as in Chapter IX, which opens with '*Am 24sten September*, 1780' instead of the '14th of September'; Chapter XI, ninth paragraph, where the date is given '*3ten May 1789*' instead of the '3d of March, 1789,' etc.; Washington's Farewell Address ('*Abschieds-Addresse an das Volk der Vereinigten Staaten.*') is added on pp. 84–119; the Declaration of Independence and the Constitution occupy pp. 127–176; in the funeral procession, p. 123, there is no cut of the coffin, merely the word '*Leiche*' in two pairs of brackets printed vertically. See also notes to the Keatinge and Bartgis editions, titles 1 and 5.

2. For Weems' authorship, as the book was issued anonymously like its two preceding editions, see notes to titles 1 and 5.

3. Baker's *Bibliotheca Washingtoniana* No. 72. *First Century of German Printing in America*, Oswald Seidenstucker, p. 175, AAS.

4. *Ad.* 'District of Maryland, to wit: Be it remembered, that on the first day of July, in the thirty-third year . . . Mathias Bartgis, hath deposited . . . the right whereof . . . to wit: "Die Lebensbeschreibung . . . Georg Waschington. . . ." In conformity to the . . . "act for the encouragement. . . ."' *Bartgis's Repub. Gaz.*, Sept. 23, 1809, MDHS. 'Hat soeben die Presse verlassen und ist zu haben bey dem Herausgeber dieser Zeitung, fur den geringen Preiss von 75 Cents das einzelne Stück, beym Dutzend 7 Thaler und 50 Cents, und in Bogen fur 6 Thaler das Dutzend, das Vortrefliche Werk, welches jeder gute [*sic*] Americaner [*sic*] in seinem Hause haben sollte, nemlich, [*sic*] Die Lebensbeschreibung und Merkwürdige Handlungen von Georg Waschington, General und Befehlshaber der Armeen von Nord-Amerika. Nebst der Erklärung der Unabhängigkeit und der Constitution der Ver. Staaten. Aus dem Englischen übersetzt. (*Copy right secured according to Law.*) Inhalt dieses Buchs: 1. Cap . . . 13. Cap . . . Nebst der Erklärung . . . Dieses Werk ist mit einem Kupferstich des Generals geziert. Empfehlungen . . . Schäffer . . . Wagner . . . Obiges Werk ist auch zu haben in Philadelphia, Lancaster, Reading, Harrisburg, Carleil, Chambersburg, Pittsburgh und verschiedenen andern Orten in Pennsylvanien. Diejenigen welche für dieses Werk unterschrieben haben, werden belieben für ihre Ex-

emplare anzusprechen. Zu Haben bey dem Herausgeber dieser Zeitung.' *Hornet*, Jan. 17, 1810, AAS. 'For sale at this office, The Life of General George Washi-gton-[*sic*] Containing a concise and impartial account of the principal events of his life, his death and a schedule of his property, including a succinct and impartial history of the principal occurences of the revolutionary war. (Price 25 cents.)' *Hornet*, Jan. 17, 1810, AAS. 'Just Published, and for Sale, by M. Bartgis, Printer, Frederick-town, in the German language, the life and memorable actions of George Washington, . . . Declaration of Independence, and the Constitution. . . . It is printed on fine paper . . . embellished . . . a likeness . . . Price 75 cents . . . Subscribers . . . may call . . .' *Bartgis's Repub. Gaz*, Jan. 27, 1810 *et seq*, MDHS. 'Proposals by M. Bartgis, Printer, *Frederick-town*, for Publishing by subscription, the Life and memorable actions of George Washington, Late General & Commander in Chief of the Armies of America. Including the most remarkable Occurences during the Revolutionary War with Great-Britain. To which will be annexed, the Declaration of Independence, and the Constitution of the United States. Dedicated to the Youth of America. (*Copy right secured according to law.*) Conditions. 1. It shall be printed on good paper and a new type, neatly bound in leather, and to contain about 400 pages duodecimo. 2. The price to subscribers will be one dollar per copy, to be paid on delivery of the work; to non-subscribers the price will be enhanced. 3. Any person subscribing for twelve copies and becoming responsible for the payment, shall be entitled to the thirteenth copy gratis. 4. As soon as 400 subscribers are obtained, the work will be put to press. This work will contain, besides a concise history of the life of Washington, a faithful and impartial detail of the most remarkable Battles fought during the revolutionary war, together with other interesting transactions and occurences which happened during that period. To it will be annexed, the Declaration of Independence, and the Constitution of the United States. — From the well-known attachment of the United States to the memory of the departed father of our country, it is hoped on the part of the publisher that this work will meet with a favorable reception. It could likewise be used to much advantage in schools, and teachers would do well to have it introduced, in order to impress on the mind of the youth the shining virtues and noble qualities of the immortal Washington.' *Hornet*, July 4, 1810, AAS. 'Bucher und Schreibmaterialen . . . Weems Waschingtons Lebensbeschreibung, in deutsch, soeben erhalten. William Graydon . . .' [in German text]. *Morg.*, July 14, 1810 *et seq.*, PSTL.

5. Weems wrote to Carey, from Fredericktown, Jan. 25, 1809: '. . . There is a young German Divine in this place who is willing to translate Washington

into Dutch.[1] I mention this that you may revolve it in your mind, whether you w^d^ approve the idea of translating or not — and by whom &c. &c. . . .'

6. 'Printing, in the English and German languages, is performed, with accuracy and despatch, by Matthias Bartgis, at his printing-office in Frederick-town, in Maryland . . . begs leave to . . . informs them that he has established two newspapers, one in English and the other in the German language . . . a large circulation, in the different counties of this state, as Baltimore, Montgomery, Washington, &c. Likewise in the following states, Viz, Pennsylvania, through Philadelphia, Lancaster, York, Cumberland and Franklin counties: Virginia through Loudon, Berkley [*sic*] Frederick, Woodstock, and Augusta counties; North Carolina, Salisbury, and Washington counties. . . . Advertisements for insertion in either of the above papers, are translated gratis, by their humble servant, Matthias Bartgis . . . May 2, 1793.' *Balt. Repos.*, May 23, 1793, AAS. For further notes on Bartgis, see title 5, note 4.

NUMBER 19 1810

THE LIFE | OF | GEORGE WASHINGTON; | WITH | CURIOUS ANECDOTES, | EQUALLY HONOURABLE TO HIMSELF AND | EXEMPLARY TO HIS YOUNG COUNTRYMEN. | *A life how useful to his country led!* | *How loved! while living! . . .* [*sic*] *how revered! now dead!* | *Lisp! lisp! his name, ye children yet unborn!* | *And with like deeds your own great names adorn.* | TENTH EDITION. . . . [*sic*] GREATLY IMPROVED. | EMBELLISHED WITH SEVEN ENGRAVINGS. | BY M. L. WEEMS. | FORMERLY RECTOR OF MOUNT-VERNON PARISH. |

[1] Not identified, unless it be either D. F. Schäffer or D. Wagner mentioned in note 1 preceding.

'The author has treated this great subject with admi- | 'rable success in a new way. He turns all the actions | 'of Washington to the encouragement of virtue, by a | 'careful application of numerous exemplifications | 'drawn from the conduct of the founder of our re- | 'public from his earliest life.' | *H. Lee, Major-General Army U. S.* | PHILADELPHIA: |

PRINTED FOR MATHEW CAREY | 1810. | 12mo. pp. (3), 3, (1), 2, 4–228, (2). *Front., Port., Plates, Map.*
AAS. [*lacks map*], BM., CHS., HSP. [*lacks map*], LC., *N'yptPL., NYPL., *UNC., WL.

1. A different title from the ninth edition, with Lee's commendation abbreviated; portrait, unsigned, after Stuart, stippled, head to right, no buttons visible, oval in a rectangle of horizontal wavy lines, inscription, stippled, below lines 'G[l]. WASHINGTON.', in shaded letter, the plate much worn; plates and inscriptions in this issue vary greatly, though most are *after* the ninth edition 1809; in one copy the 'Defeat of Gen. Braddock' is entirely different from that in the ninth edition [see letter of Oct. 20, 1809, title 17, note 4]; last words on p. [*3*] are 'Have not a,' and on p. 76, 'tolerable order,'. The AAS. and NYPL. copies have back fly leaves, pp. [*1*]–35, of publisher's advertisements, including some of Weems' own publications. All these libraries' copies vary greatly as to their portraits, maps, etc.; HSP. and NYPL. each have one, for example, with title like that given above but with different plates and with map, engraved, signed 'W. Barker,' being the same as that in the earliest editions of *Carey's Pocket Atlas;* a different printing, for on p. 76 the last words are 'tolerable order but'; the portrait is unsigned, stippled, face to left, in oval with inscription below: 'Gen[l]. Washington. [*in script*] Born Feb[r]. 22. 1732. Died Dec[r]. 14. 1799. | *Published by M. Carey.*' Concerning the confusion of issues during this period, see letter of Weems, Dec. 23, 1815, title 27, note 3.

2. 'With the exception of the abbreviation of the quotation from General Lee on the title page, this is a reprint of title 78 [*ninth edition 1809, title 17*] and the title as above given is retained in *all* subsequent editions, of which so many have appeared. The Twenty-sixth, in 1824, seems to have been the last one issued by Carey, who about that time sold the plates — stereotyped in 1818 — to Joseph Allen, of Frankford, near Philadelphia, whose family, it is said, still derive some revenue from them. At the time of the transfer to Allen, the illustrations were from other copper-plates than the originals, of which several

sets had been executed [*see title 17, note 2, and title 27, note 3*]; the new set, — upright in shape — being much better both in design and workmanship. The Twenty-ninth edition, 1826, appears to have been the last numbered one. In 1828 wood-cuts replaced the copper-plates, and subsequently, about 1840, new stereotype-plates were cast, pp. 244, which are still used by the present publishers, Lippincott & Co., the last printing bearing date 1882.' Baker's *Bibliotheca Washingtoniana* No. 86. *Portraits of Washington* Nos. 328 [*Scoles*], 339 [*Tanner*]. Hart No. 447 says of the portrait in this edition, 'Ascribed by Baker to Scoles,[1] but it is executed much better than any work by Scoles that I know.' See also Article [*Anon.*] quoting William S. Baker in the *Philadelphia Inquirer*, Feb. 18, 1894, LC.

3. Through all the changes and chances of these varying editions up to 1820, certain salient features remain, to wit: there is always a kneeling female in the illustration of the Battle of Bunker Hill; Andre at the moment of his capture seems, to judge from his attire, as well as his unsoldierly attitude, to be suffering acutely from stiff neck — in fact, he is more of a lackadaisical Bunthorne than the trig and handsome young blood whom we have generally supposed him to be. Then, too, Gen. Montgomery shows as great a variety of death scenes as the many famous *Camilles* of our day, while Braddock suffers defeat with amazing equanimity, sometimes in a dump-cart and equally well when he has been promoted to a vehicle which strongly resembles a jinricksha.

4. *Ad.* '*The Life of Gen. Washington* . . . BY THE REV. MASON L. WEEMS, . . . A PORTRAIT, AND SIX HISTORICAL ENGRAVINGS.' [Followed by four signed *Criticisms.*] Front leaves of *Carey's Franklin Almanack for 1810*. 'Weems's Life of Washington [*was assigned*] to Dr. Bigelow. . . . Dr. Bigelow read his review of Weems' Life of Washington, which was accepted.' *Journal of the Anthology Society*, Dec. 11, 1810, M. A. DeWolfe Howe, p. 244, MHS. Review follows: '. . . The reverend author of this book before us, which we are at a loss whether to denominate a biography, or a novel, founded on fact, has presented a specimen of writing, which for variety and oddity is almost an unique in the annals of literature. With a style of rotundity and bombast which may distance Macpherson himself, he has intermingled the ludicrous quaintness of Joe Miller; and he often transports us from a strain of religious moralizing, more than commonly exalted, to the low cant and balderdash of the ranks and drinking table . . . from the general tenor of the work one cannot avoid suspecting the author of adopting the plan of Voltaire

[1] John Scoles, an account. '. . . Worked in both line and stipple, but with indifferent success.' *American Engravers upon Copper and Steel*, David McNeely Stauffer, 1907, Vol. I, Part I, pp. 242, 243, LC.

in his Henriade, who, after invoking truth for his guide, does not hesitate to conclude that her appearance may be much improved by the alliance and assistance of fiction. . . . We have questioned whether the book before us may not be termed a novel founded on fact. Second thoughts would induce us to style it rather an epick poem; for, besides, its figures, characters, battles, and episodes, it is duly provided with a suitable quantity of preternatural machinery. The exploits and future greatness of Washington are early foretold by a wonderful dream, two pages in length, which happened to his mother while he was a boy. . . .' [*Anon.*] *Monthly Anthology*, Vol. IX, 1810, pp. 414–419, AAS. Also advertised in: *Bartgis's Repub. Gaz.*, Mar. 17, 1810, MDHS. *Col. Mus. & Sav. Adv.*, Nov. 5, 1810, GAHS. *Ga. Jour.*, Nov. 14, 1810, UN'YGA. *Ga. Express.*, Dec. 8, 1810 *et seq.*, UN'YGA. *Ga. Arg.*, Jan. 16, 1811, HU.

5. Weems wrote to Carey, Feb. 28, 1810: 'You sent me to this place, [*Augusta*] I believe about 300 Life of Washington. Of these, tho' I have been but to two Courts, I find that *one-half is sold.* There are in this State 36 Counties, and each County w[d], to a moral certainty, take from 1 to 2 or 300 of that work. For one County that w[d] take but 100, there are others, richer & more populous, that w[d] take 500. . . . I digress[d] from my first point in this letter which was to tell you that if you coud instantly send off 500 copies of Washington to Charleston to Hoff, and 500 to Augusta, via Savanna I expect to be able to sell them all pretty soon. . . . Inclose 50 Grand folio advertisements in *each Box.*'

NUMBER 20 1810

Das Leben | des | Georg Waschington, | mit | Sonderbaren Anecdoten, | Sowohl ehrenvoll für ihn selbst, | als auch | Nachahmungswürdig für seine junge Landsleute. | Ein Leben wie nützlich seinem Lande geführt! | Wie beliebt, da er lebte! . . . . . [*sic*] wie geehrt, im Tode! | Lispelt! Lispelt seinen Namen, ihr noch ungeborne Kinder! | Und schmücket eure Namen mit ähnlichen Thaten. | Von M. L. Weems, | Ehemaligem Prediger der Mount=Vernon Kirche. | — Aus dem Englischen übersetzt — | Nach der neunten sehr verbesserten Auflage. | Libanon, (Penn.) |

Gedruckt bey J. Schnee, für M. Carey in Philadelphia. | 1810. | 12mo. pp. (3), 6, (2), 2, 8–240, (2). *Front., Port., Plates.*
AAS., BA., HSP., LC., NYPL., PStL., VStL.

1. On reverse of title, Penn. copyright, 1808, in English text, with title in German text; three pages of commendations follow, translated into German from English [in this edition 'Brackenridge' is spelled 'Breckenridge']; portrait, unsigned, after Stuart, stippled, bust, face to right, oval in a rectangle of horizontal lines, inscription below 'GL. WASHINGTON.', like Carey's ninth edition, title 17; the plates, unsigned, and variously placed in the different copies, are identical with those in the ninth edition, but have German inscriptions added below the English ones: 'Tod des Generals Montgomery.', 'Die Niederlage des Generals Braddock.', 'Gefecht zu Lexington.', 'Gefecht auf Bunker's Hill, und Tod des Gen. Warren.', 'Gefangennehmung des Majors Andre.', 'Die Uebergabe des Cornwallis.'; these plates are also identical with those in that one of the tenth editions of 1810 which were not repeated in the twelfth 1812, and tenth 1813 editions; title and text printed in German characters and it may be noted that the sign ˘ used normally only in German *writing* is used throughout the book instead of the correct diæresis ¨, thus exhibiting the speedy change which comes to any language when transplanted. The LC. copy has cover imprint 'Waschington's Leben,' followed by the verses of the title page. This is the first German edition found of the accredited text.

2. Carey's Catalogue, 1816, p. 49. Baker's *Bibliotheca Washingtoniana* No. 85; *Portraits of Washington* No. 339. 'In 1810 a German translation of the ninth edition was printed by Carey. The illustrations are the same, with additional titles in German.' *Article* [*Anon.*] quoting William S. Baker, in *Philadelphia Inquirer*, Feb. 18, 1894. Seidenstucker, p. 179, '1809, 1810.'

NUMBER 21 1811

THE LIFE | OF | GEORGE WASHINGTON; | WITH | CURIOUS ANECDOTES, | EQUALLY HONOURABLE TO HIMSELF AND | EXEMPLARY TO HIS YOUNG COUNTRYMEN. | [*Four lines of verse, not in italics*] | ELEVENTH EDITION. | EMBELLISHED WITH A MAP OF THE UNITED STATES | AND SEVEN OTHER ENGRAVINGS. | BY M. L. WEEMS, | FORMERLY RECTOR OF MOUNT-VERNON PARISH. | [*Six lines*] | PHILADELPHIA: |

PRINTED FOR M. CAREY. | 1811. | 12mo. pp. 228. *Front.*, *Port.*, *Plates.*
*CrozTS., HSP., NYPL.

1. Different title page from the tenth edition, title 19, except that the quotation from Lee is abbreviated as in that edition; on reverse of title page, copyright notice, followed by three signed commendations; the HSP. copy has portrait, unsigned, oval, stippled, set in rectangle of wavy horizontal lines, with inscription below 'G$^{l}$. Washington' in open letter; the NYPL. copy has portrait, unsigned, after Stuart, stippled, oval, bust, 3/4 face to left, with stippled border line, height to border 7.2 c., width 5.6, inscription below 'Gen$^{l}$. Washington [*in script*]. | Born Feb$^{r}$. 22. 1732. Died Dec$^{r}$. 14. 1799. | *Published by M. Carey.*'; the plates are after the tenth edition 1810 but are not identical; last words on p. [*3*] are 'Have not a,' and on p. 76, 'order but.' Of the two copies seen by me, neither has a map.

2. Alibone's *Dictionary*. Baker's *Bibliotheca Washingtoniana* No. 94; *Portraits of Washington* Nos. 328, 339, which latter refers to the HSP. portrait only.

3. Advertised in: *Aug. Chron.*, Mar. 8, 1811 *et seq.*, UN'YGA. *Times*, Apr. 1, 1811 *et seq.*, CLS. *Star*, Aug. 30, 1811, NCSTL. *Va. Gaz.*, Oct. 7, 1811, VSTL.

NUMBER 22 1812

THE LIFE | OF | GEORGE WASHINGTON; | WITH | CURIOUS ANECDOTES, | EQUALLY HONOURABLE TO HIMSELF | AND EXEMPLARY | TO HIS YOUNG COUNTRYMEN. | [*Four lines of verse, not in italics*] | TWELFTH EDITION, GREATLY IMPROVED. | EMBELLISHED WITH SEVEN ENGRAVINGS. | BY M. L. WEEMS. | FORMERLY RECTOR OF MOUNT-VERNON PARISH. | [*Six lines*] | PHILADELPHIA: |

PRINTED FOR MATHEW CAREY. | 1812. | 12mo. pp. (1), 3, (1), 2, 4–228. *Front.*, *Port.*, *Plates*, *Map.*
AAS., HSP. [*lacks map*], LC., NYHS., NYPL.

1. Title page differs from the preceding edition, eleventh, 1811, title 21; on reverse of title, Penn. copyright to Weems, 1808; portrait, unsigned, after Stuart, stippled, bust, 3/4 face to left, in oval, with inscription below, giving

birth and death dates like that in the NYPL. copy of the eleventh edition 1811; plates, unsigned, engraved, like those in the tenth edition 1810, title 19, and identical with the eleventh edition, only facing differently as to pages; larger map unsigned, and this and the portrait sometimes lacking; the AAS. copy lacks portrait, but its impression on the opposite page shows that it was the larger oval, like the NYPL. copy of title 21, without horizontal lines, and was much smaller than the rectangle in the editions which follow this one; last words on p. [*3*] are 'Have not a.'

2. Baker's *Bibliotheca Washingtoniana* No. 100; *Portraits of Washington* No. 328, 'by Scoles'.

3. [*M.L.W.*] 'Tales of Old Times, or Truths well worth recording once a year. The Beginning. "'Twas the celebrated Samuel Chase, the Demosthenes of Maryland, who first taught the startled vaults of Congress to re-echo the name of independence. . . . His swelling soul was fixed on George the Third. . . . That most amiable of men, Governor Thomas Johnson, . . . used to say . . . do we pay as much . . . as for . . . the dog-kennels of the prince of Wales?"' *Repub.* (Sav'a), July 4, 1811, LC. [This was a longer version of the anecdote which first appeared in the Georgia edition of 1806 and which in this twelfth edition is printed on p. 80.] 'From Weems' Life of Washington. In 1777, while the American army lay at Valley Forge . . . some great thing for the country.' *Va. Arg.*, Oct. 29, 1812, LC. [Giving the much-discussed episode of Potts finding Washington on his knees at prayer, first found in the edition of 1808. See title 11, note 3.] Also advertised in *Va. Her.*, June 6, 1812 *et seq.*, LC.

4. Weems wrote to Carey, Feb. 21, 1812: 'I wish you cou'd make some arrangement by diminish$^{g}$ my profits on the pamphlets, Franklin & Marion [1] to raise that on Washington.' June 27, 1812 Weems asked if it would not be 'well, admirably well, to send me, SPEEDILY before the war begins, . . . about 6,000$ worth chiefly of cheap Family Bibles, Washington, Webster's spell$^{g}$ [*books*] and a *few varieties* as I shall advise?' July 15, 1812: 'I am *morally certain*, that if the maps were all happily dispos$^{d}$ off [*sic*] I cou'd make a good living by the bible & Washington alone.'

[1] Titles 131 *et seq.* and 85 *et seq.*

NUMBER 23 1812?

*The Life of George Washington; with Curious Anecdotes, equally Honorable to Himself, and Exemplary to his Young Countrymen. [*Four lines*] Embellished with Six Engravings. By M. L. Weems, formerly Rector of Mount Vernon Parish [*Six lines*] Philadelphia: |

Printed by Joseph Allen. [*1812?*] 12mo. pp. 228.

1. Baker's *Bibliotheca Washingtoniana* No. 101. Rice Catalogue, 1870, No. 2520. [I question its accuracy in spelling 'Honorable' without a 'u.']

NUMBER 24 1813

THE LIFE | OF | GEORGE WASHINGTON; | WITH | CURIOUS ANECDOTES, | EQUALLY HONOURABLE TO HIMSELF, | AND | EXEMPLARY TO HIS YOUNG COUNTRYMEN, | [*Four lines of verse, not in italics*] | TENTH EDITION. . . . [*sic*] GREATLY IMPROVED. | EMBELLISHED WITH EIGHT ENGRAVINGS. | BY M. L. WEEMS, | FORMERLY RECTOR OF MOUNT VERNON PARISH. | 'The Author has treated this great subject with admirable | 'success in a new way. He turns all the actions of Washing- | 'ton to the encouragement of virtue, by a careful application of | 'numerous exemplifications drawn from the conduct of the | 'founder of our republic from his earliest life.' | *H. Lee, Major-General, Army U. S.* | PHILADELPHIA: |

PRINTED BY MATHEW CAREY. | 1813. | 12mo. pp. (1), 3, (1), 2, 4–228, (4). *Front., Port., Plates, Map.*
AAS. [*lacks map*], HHL., LC.

1. Portrait, unsigned, after Stuart, stippled, bust, 3/4 face to left, in rectangle without border, height 12.1 c., width 8.2, dark shadow across the upper left of background, inscription below 'G. WASHINGTON.' in open letter; the map is identical with that in the tenth edition 1810; six plates, unsigned,

identical with those in one of the copies of the tenth edition, 1810, title 19, and in the twelfth edition 1812, title 22; the word 'WASHINGTON' on the first page is not in italics; last words on page [*3*] are 'Have not a,' and on p. 76, 'order, but'; on p. 118 'cotton' is misprinted 'cotten.'

2. Baker's *Bibliotheca Washingtoniana* No. 108. Hart No. 474. [See title 26, note 2.]

3. Advertised in *Alex'a Gaz.*, Apr. 16, 1813 *et seq.*, AAS.

4. Weems wrote to Carey, Sept. 2, 1813: '. . . let me have back my Life of Washington — or let me have what I may want, giving you a fair premium for y[r] trouble & expence of editing them.'

NUMBER 25 1814

THE LIFE | OF | GEORGE WASHINGTON; | WITH | CURIOUS ANECDOTES, | EQUALLY HONOURABLE TO HIMSELF, | AND | EXEMPLARY TO HIS YOUNG COUNTRYMEN, | [*Four lines of verse*] | TENTH EDITION. . . . [*sic*] GREATLY IMPROVED. | EMBELLISHED WITH EIGHT ENGRAVINGS. | BY M. L. WEEMS, | FORMERLY RECTOR OF MOUNT VERNON PARISH. | [*Six lines*] | PHILADELPHIA: |

PRINTED BY MATHEW CAREY. | 1814. | 12mo. pp. (1), 3, (1), 2, 4–228, (2). *Front., Port., Plates, Map.*

AAS., BA., HSP., LC., NYPL. [*lacks map and plates.*]

1. The quotation from Lee on title page is printed like that of the tenth edition 1813, title 24; copyright notice is like that in the twelfth edition 1812, title 22; portrait, unsigned, after Stuart, stippled, bust, 3/4 face to left, in rectangle, with stippled edge but no border, height 11.9 c., width 7.9; inscription below 'G. WASHINGTON.' in open letter; the map, signed '*Bower, Sc.*', is greatly reduced in size, and is the same as that used in Carey's later editions of the *Pocket Atlas;* sometimes it is an unsigned one, identical with that of the tenth editions 1810 and 1813, titles 19 and 24; the plates, signed '*Robinson sc.*' below their margins on the right, are after, but not the same as in the twelfth 1812 and the tenth 1813 editions, titles 22 and 24; last words on pp. [*3*] and 76 are like those in the tenth edition 1813, title 24; on p. 118, 'cotton' misprinted 'cotten'; p. 206 printed '106' in error. The AAS. copy has the larger map, unsigned.

2. Baker's *Bibliotheca Washingtoniana* No. 111. Hart No. 474. [See title 26, note 2.]

3. *Ad.* 'The Life of George Washington; . . . [*Four lines of verse*] Tenth Edition — Greatly Improved — Embellished with Eight Engravings. By the Rev. M. L. Weems, of Virginia. [*Five lines from Lee*]' Back fly leaves of *Webster's Calendar: or, the Albany Almanack*, 1815, Websters' and Skinners', LCPHIL.

4. Weems wrote to Carey, Mar. 4, 1814: 'If I had my little book back again, that, with the additions which I can make to it, & my other scribblings w[d] support my Family whose circumstances are very little, perhaps not one dollar better than they were when you first engaged me in this disastrous business.' [*Postmarked Mar. 19*] 1814: 'As to my Life of Washington, you offer me 33 1/3 pr cent. For *cash* if I had it I can get 40 & even 45 pr Cent on books. 33 1/3 therefore must seem a scanty allowance indeed. . . . I am willing you shou'd keep it & continue to distribute those large quantities which y[r] situation & wealth enable you to do, provided while your types are set you will strike off what I may want; and for so doing I will allow you three times the interest which the Law allows. I have some noble anecdotes to add to it.' Mar. 31, 1814: '. . . you say you gave me a 1000$ for Washington & now "*I am goading you to death to make me a present of it.*" I never ask[d] you to make me a *present of it.* How barbarous to sport thus with one's feelings. So far from asking a present I was willing & told you so time after time, to make you a most liberal allowance for y[r] trouble in letting me have as many copies as I sh[d] want. . . . I dare say you will agree that had it not been for the circumstances of going into *large* business with you 5 years ago I sh[d] never have sold the book to you. And you will I know agree also that now that the business is broken off thro y[r] *own wish* (I don't say anything worse) you ought to return my little book but not as a *present*, but for 500$ as you stated in the Articles. As I have not 500$ now I am willing you sh[d] do all you can with it; & while printing for yourself you will oblige by printing some for me on a liberal allowance to you as aforesaid.'

For the blanks where the eleventh, thirteenth and fifteenth editions are lacking, see insertion preceding title 30.

NUMBER 26 1814

THE LIFE | OF | GEORGE WASHINGTON; | WITH | CURIOUS ANECDOTES, | EQUALLY HONOURABLE TO HIMSELF, | AND | EXEMPLARY TO HIS YOUNG COUNTRYMEN, | [*Four lines of verse*] | Twelfth Edition. . . . . [*sic*] Greatly improved. | EMBELLISHED WITH EIGHT ENGRAVINGS. | BY M. L. WEEMS, | FORMERLY RECTOR OF MOUNT VERNON PARISH. | [*Six lines*] | PHILADELPHIA: |

PRINTED BY MATHEW CAREY. | 1814. | 12mo. pp. 2, (1), 2, 4–228. *Front., Port., Plates, Map.*

AAS. [*lacks map*], BA., HSP., HU., NYSocL.

1. Different title page from the twelfth edition 1812; portrait, unsigned, after Stuart, stippled, bust, 3/4 face to left, in rectangle, without border, inscription below 'G. WASHINGTON.' in open letter, like that in the tenth edition 1814, title 25, but much worn; plates are signed '*Robinson sc.*', exactly the same as those of the tenth edition 1814, title 25, facing title page and pp. 40, 71, 76, 104, 114; last words on p. [3] are 'Have not a,' and on p. 76, 'order but'; on p. 118 'cotton' misprinted 'cotten'; p. 206 printed '106' in error.

2. Baker's *Bibliotheca Washingtoniana* No. 112. 'There would seem to be more than one of these very crude plates nearly alike with the title in open letter.' Hart No. 474.

NUMBER 27 1815

THE LIFE | OF | GEORGE WASHINGTON; | WITH | CURIOUS ANECDOTES, | EQUALLY HONOURABLE TO HIMSELF, | AND | EXEMPLARY TO HIS YOUNG COUNTRYMEN, | [*Four lines of verse*] | Fourteenth Edition. . . . [*sic*] Greatly improved. | EMBELLISHED WITH EIGHT ENGRAVINGS. | BY M. L. WEEMS, | FORMERLY RECTOR OF MOUNT VERNON PARISH. | [*Six lines*] | PHILADELPHIA: |

PRINTED BY MATHEW CAREY. | 1815. | 12mo. pp. (1), 4, (1), 1, 4–228, 6. *Front., Port., Plates, Map.*

AAS., LC., NYPL. [*lacks port.*]

1. Portrait, unsigned, stippled, bust, identical with the tenth edition 1813, title 24, with inscription below 'G. WASHINGTON.' in open letter; map is of the smaller size, signed '*Bower, Sc.*'; plates, signed '*Robinson Sc.*', are the same as those in the tenth edition 1814, title 25, but much worn; on p. 118 'cotton' misprinted 'cotten'; p. 206 printed '106' in error.

2. Carey's Catalogue, 1816, p. 49. Hart No. 474.

3. Weems wrote to Dr. James Ewell, in a letter of introduction to Mathew Carey, June 28, 1815: 'I once thought it impossible that I shou'd ever sell my Life of Washington. I sold it, however, to M[r]. Carey who has distributed, probably 4 times as many of that work as I shoud ever have circulated myself. You feel an equal terror at the thought of parting with a book that you fondly hope will raise you hereafter to the rank of Hipocrates, besides even now putting into your hand the Gold making Secret of the Alchymist. You have had that dream for 7 years. Now were you to follow my past course & present counsel, viz, let M[r] Carey have *some interest* in y[r] book, for he does not want the copyright, 'tis likely that with his *Capital*, his *Connections* & the unbounded range that these & other advantages give him he w[d] easily distribute 5 times as many books, do 5 times as much good to the world, & bring you at least twice as much money as you will ever derive from it in the hobbling way you have heretofore gone on with it.' To Carey, Sept. 28, 1815: 'As to the Life of Washington I shall want a great many.' Dec. 11, 1815: 'Those [*of the Life of Washington*] you gave me were thro' my USUAL Incogitancy put into the box for Alexandria, & now as I go around subscriptioneering I am every hour call[d] on for Washington. Wou'd it not be well to be looking around you for fit *designs* &c &c &c for y[r] 3 Doll edition of Washington? 2 or 3 ad Captandum engravings ought to be exhibited with the prospectus.' Dec. 23, 1815: 'You are not aware of the serious state of things. I had it yesterday from good authority that there are now in existence at least three sets of the stereotype plates [*of the Life of Washington*] if not 4 sets, one of which was lately offer[d] for sale here [*Balto.*] at a cheap rate, and some talk among the Booksellers of taking it.' [See title 19, note 2.] Jan. 4, 1816: 'I have been buying up all y[r] Life of Washington that I can find here. . . . I wish you w[d] instantly give me orders to finish Washington. It cries aloud for 60 or 70 pages more, for it is much clamour[d] against as far too small for a dollar book. Ramsay's is nearly *twice the size*, & better plates, & yet Cushing says he prints it for 40 cents. Yours may in a short time be made exceedingly more popular & useful, were you & I both to set about it.'

For a possible fifteenth edition, see insertion preceding title 30. I have also heard of a Boston edition of 1815, but I have never found a copy.

NUMBER 28 1816

THE LIFE | OF | GEORGE WASHINGTON; | WITH | CURIOUS ANECDOTES, | EQUALLY HONOURABLE TO HIMSELF, | AND | EXEMPLARY TO HIS YOUNG COUNTRYMEN, | [*Four lines of verse*] | Sixteenth Edition. . . . [*sic*] Greatly improved. | EMBELLISHED WITH EIGHT ENGRAVINGS. | BY M. L. WEEMS, | FORMERLY RECTOR OF MOUNT VERNON PARISH. | [*Six lines*] | PHILADELPHIA: |

PRINTED BY MATHEW CAREY. | 1816. | 12mo. pp. (5), 7, (1), 2, 4–228, (2). *Front., Port., Plates, Map.*
HHL.

1. Portrait after, but not identical with, the fourteenth edition 1815, title 27; plates, unsigned, ditto.

2. Carey's Catalogue, 1816, No. 27. Baker's *Bibliotheca Washingtoniana* No. 123. Hart No. 474.

NUMBER 29 1816

THE LIFE | OF | GEORGE WASHINGTON; | WITH | CURIOUS ANECDOTES, | EQUALLY HONOURABLE TO HIMSELF, | AND | EXEMPLARY TO HIS YOUNG COUNTRYMEN, | [*Four lines of verse*] | Seventeenth Edition. . . . [*sic*] Greatly improved. | EMBELLISHED WITH EIGHT ENGRAVINGS. | BY M. L. WEEMS, | FORMERLY RECTOR OF MOUNT VERNON PARISH. | [*Six lines*] | PHILADELPHIA: |

PRINTED BY MATHEW CAREY. | 1816. | 12mo. pp. (3), 3, (1), 2, 4–228, (2). *Front., Port., Plates, Map.*
AAS. [*lacks map*], BPL., CHS. [*lacks port. and map*], HSP. [*lacks map*], HU. [*lacks port.*], PStL.

1. Title is like the twelfth edition 1814, title 26; no commendations follow copyright notice; portrait, unsigned, identical with those in the tenth edition 1813 and the fourteenth edition 1815, titles 24 and 27; plates unsigned,

after but not the same as those in the tenth edition 1813; the map is the smaller one, signed '*Bower, Sc.*'; on p. 118 'cotton' misprinted 'cotten'; page 206 printed '106' in error.

2. 'Weems's (Rev. Mason L.) Life of Washington, with curious Anecdotes equally honorable to himself, and exemplary to his Young Countrymen. Seventeenth edition. Embellished with a Portrait, a Map of the United States, and six Historical Engravings, $1 Philad. 1817 [*error for 1816?*]'. [With two paragraphs quoted from *Panoplist:* '"This little volume . . . by the example of Washington."'] Carey's Catalogue, 1818, No. 651. Baker's *Bibliotheca Washingtoniana* No. 124. Hart No. 474.

3. Advertised in *Alex'a Her.*, Sept. 11, 1816 *et seq.*, LC.

4. Weems wrote to Carey, Feb. 2, 1816: 'Tell [*me*] when you mean to begin the elegant *edition of Washington* at 4 Dolls. — What subjects you mean to select for prints.' Feb. 3, 1816: 'Think of the Elegant edition of y[r] Washington — Instead of 12 plates at 60$ get 8 plates @ 100 or 125 & set me to work without loss of time.' Feb. 14, 1816: 'The binding of Washington is also dreadfully faulted.' Apr. 4, 1816: 'What about Elegant editions of Washington?' May 2, 1816: 'I wish you cou'd make some arrangement by diminish[g] my profits on the pamphlets, Franklin & Marion to raise that on Washington.' May 31, 1816: 'Here is a good idea. If you were to put on a sheet or half sheet one of your good portraits of Washington, and then under it some popular remembrances of his Virtues, Services &c, with a few striking Commendations of y[r] Life of Wash, & the No. of *editions*, *translations*, copies sold &c as best to stimulate Lethargy & spring Curiosity, — have these pasted on bits of pasteboard & sent with 10 or 20 of the books with every box of Bibles that I shall order, you w[d]. in this way augment y[r] sales greatly. The above is merely a hint. You can give it the proper shape.' July 11, 1816: 'Gen[l] Wayne says his father never committed that blunder about Old Bon Repos. He is displeas[d] — and I wish you w[d] put some other name. By the Bye he did commit it.' I do not find that Carey ever complied with this request, nor with the following, made in the same letter: 'I beg you to change Arnold, in the affair of killing Gen[l] Frazer, to Morgan as it stood at first. Persons are now living who have heard Morgan tell it 1000 times, sorrow[g].' ['Morgan' had been printed in the seventh edition 1808, title 13, 'Arnold' in the eighth edition 1809, title 14, and thereafter.]

That there were eleventh, thirteenth and fifteenth editions between Mathew Carey's tenth of 1814 and his sixteenth of 1816, titles 25 and 28, would seem not only likely, but also almost certain from the following advertisement: 'The Life of Washington . . . by the Rev. Mason L. Weems, Embellished with a Portrait, a Map of the United States, and six Historical Engravings. In 12mo. Price 1 dollar bound. "This little volume is designed . . . It has indeed already, *in less than two years, passed through eight editions* . . . the Revolution. It has been a subject of just complaint . . . private walks of life . . . the example of Washington." *Panoplist.*' Carey's Catalogue, 1816, pp. 19–20. 'The Life of George Washington . . . Fifteenth Edition. Embellished with Eight Engravings. By M. L. Weems, . . . *Philadelphia: Printed by Mathew Carey. 1816.* 12mo, pp. 228. Portrait.' Baker's *Bibliotheca Washingtoniana* No. 122. 'In several years two editions were printed, and in 1816 there appeared the fifteenth, sixteenth, and seventeenth.' *Washington after the Revolution*, William Spohn Baker, p. 70.

The fifteenth edition not found, see also announcement preceding title 28. The italics are mine.

NUMBER 30 1817

THE LIFE | OF | GEORGE WASHINGTON; | WITH | CURIOUS ANECDOTES, | EQUALLY HONOURABLE TO HIMSELF, | AND | EXEMPLARY TO HIS YOUNG COUNTRYMEN, | [*Four lines of verse*] | Eighteenth Edition. . . . [*sic*] Greatly improved. | EMBELLISHED WITH EIGHT ENGRAVINGS. | BY M. L. WEEMS, | FORMERLY RECTOR OF MOUNT VERNON PARISH. | [*Six lines*] | PHILADELPHIA: |

PRINTED BY MATHEW CAREY. | 1817. | 12mo. pp. (3), 1, (1), 3, (1), 2, 4–228. *Front., Port., Plates, Map.*
AAS., LC. [*imp.*]

1. Title slightly different from the fourteenth edition 1815, title 27; on reverse of title is Penn. copyright; portrait is identical with that in the seventeenth edition 1816, title 29, and the plates are after but not identical with those in the 1814 and 1815 editions, titles 25, 26 and 27; last words on p. 76 are 'order, but'; on p. 118, 'cotten' misprinted thus; p. 206 printed '106' in error.

2. Baker's *Bibliotheca Washingtoniana* No. 128. Hart No. 474.

3. *Reviewed:* 'New Edition, Philadelphia, 1817, [*Anon.*]' in *Analectic*

*Magazine*, Vol. IX, May, 1817, pp. 389–391, AAS. *Ad.* [*M.L.W.*] 'PROPOSALS OF M. L. WEEMS, FOR PRINTING BY SUBSCRIPTION THE LIVES OF *George Washington. Doctor Franklin,* AND *General Marion.* That GLORIOUS TRIO of AMERICAN WORTHIES, whose heroic labours contributed so largely to the LIBERTIES of their country, and whose GREAT EXAMPLES ought forever to be held up for the encouragement of similar VIRTUES in the rising generation. The LIVES of these three NOBLE PATRIOTS, in three separate volumes, of between two and three hundred pages, neatly printed and bound; and ornamented with a number of handsome copper plate engravings, will be delivered to subscribers for one dollar each. "There is no reading so proper for AMERICAN YOUTH as the LIVES OF AMERICAN WORTHIES." *Geo. Washington. Subscriptions received at this office.*' *Martinsb'g Gaz.*, July 10, 1817, AAS. [Despite the above I have found no proof of any such plan having been executed.] Also advertised in *Frank. Repos.*, Nov. 25, 1817, FROF.

4. Weems wrote to Carey, Jan. 31, 1817: 'Had you printed my Life of Washington on the poor profit of *shares*, I suspect it might not have turn[d] out to such advantages as it has. Now you see by making it your own you have push[d] it with a spirit that has and will all y[r] life make you good returns.' Mar. 6, 1817: 'As to the "proposal for Washington" w[d] it *not be better* for you to send me y[r] best thoughts on the subject & allow me to add *mine* & then send back to you? . . . By all means give me 3 or 4 Ad Captandum Designs with strong expressions & all the Et. Cœtera necessary to insure success. I speak of *Washington* now, having already said enough of this sort about Hunter.' Apr. 30, 1817: 'As we now heartily concur that when on the Cruising ground we may as well try a shot at 2 Galleons as one, you will do well to have [*made for?*] me a handsome Subscription book, in Quarto, with port holes for several pieces of heavy artillery, Washington, Franklin, & Marion may do on the poop as Grasshoppers.' Aug. 15, 1817: 'From the extent of my acquaintance & the good will of the million on account of my writing the Life of their Washington, Marion, &c &c I cou'd in a little time obtain several hundred Doll[ars]. of good orders *every week.*'

NUMBER 31 1817

Das Leben | des | Georg Waschington, | mit | Sonderbaren Anecdoten | Sowohl ehrenvoll für ihn selbst | als auch | Nachahmungswürdig fur seine jungen Landsleute. | Ein Leben, wie nützlich seinem Lande geführt! | Wie beliebt, da er lebte! —

wie geehrt, im Tode! | Lispelt! Lispelt seinen Namen, ihr noch ungeborne Kinder! | Und schmücket eure Namen mit ähnlichen Thaten. | Von | M. L. Weems, | ehemaligem Prediger der Mount=Vernon Kirche. | Aus dem Englischen übersezt | Nach der neunten sehr verbesserten Auflage. |

Baltimore, | Gedruckt und verlegt bey Schäffer und Maund, für sich | selbst, und M. Carey und Sohn, in Philadelphia. | 1817. | 12mo. pp. (1), 7, (1), 2, 8–240, (2). *Front., Port., Plates, Map.*

AAS., BA., BPL., HSP. [*lacks map*], LC., LCPhil., MdHS., MHS., NYPL., PIL.

1. On reverse of title is 1808 copyright in English with title in German; Lee's and four other commendations follow, printed like the title and text throughout in German characters; portrait unsigned, after Stuart, stippled, bust, 3/4 face to left, in rectangle, no border, height 11.9 c., width 7.9, inscription 'G. WASHINGTON.' in open letter; plates after, but not identical with, those of the seventeenth edition 1816, title 29, although the 'Death of Gen. Braddock' is reversed from right to left in impression; they have mixed inscriptions, partly in English, partly German script, the names being always printed in English, thus: 'Tode der [*German script*] *Gen*[l]. *Montgomery* [English script].'; smaller map, unsigned, engraved 'Philad. Published by M. Carey & Son, 1820 [*sic*].' The HSP. has two copies of this issue. One has plates as described above, with the page number given in English in the upper right hand corner; in the second copy the frontispiece, the 'Battle of Bunkers Hill & Death of Gen[l]. Warren.', and the 'Battle of Lexington' are all after rather than identical with those in the first copy, while the inscriptions of the first two differ in that they are given in English, with translation below into German text; the portrait in this second copy is after Stuart, bust, face to right, in oval, with stippled border line, encampment in left background, inscription below border 'Gen[l]. George Washington' in script.

2. Carey's Catalogue, 1818, No. 4055. 'A German translation of the ninth edition of the Life by Weems, No. 78.' Baker's *Bibliotheca Washingtoniana* No. 129; *Portraits of Washington* No. 364. Hart Nos. 474, 545.

3. *Ad.* 'Schäffer und Maund, haben neulich gedruckt, Das Leben des berühmten Waschingtons, mit acht Kupfern; 1. Sein Bildniss —— 2. Tod des General Montgomery —— 3. Karte der vereinigten Staaten —— 4. Niederlage des Gen. Braddock —— 5. Schlacht zu Lexington —— 6. Schlacht zu Bunkers-Hill —— 7. Gefangennehmung des Major Andre —— 8. Ueber-

gabe des Cornwallis, &c. Diese Auflage ist die schönste die in diesem Lande noch gedruckt worden, und der Preis ist nur 1 Thaler.' *Amer. Staats.*, Mar. 18, 1818, NYHS.

4. Schaeffer & Maund (Frederick G. Schaeffer and Thomas Maund) printed and published the *Morning Chronicle* (Baltimore), 1819–1820. *See Bibliography of American Newspapers*, Clarence S. Brigham, *ProcAAS.*, Vol. XXV, April, 1915, p. 165.

NUMBER 32 1818

THE LIFE | OF | GEORGE WASHINGTON; | WITH | CURIOUS ANECDOTES, | EQUALLY HONOURABLE TO HIMSELF, | AND | EXEMPLARY TO HIS YOUNG COUNTRYMEN, | [*Four lines of verse*] | Nineteenth Edition. . . . [*sic*] Greatly improved. | EMBELLISHED WITH EIGHT ENGRAVINGS. | BY M. L. WEEMS, | FORMERLY RECTOR OF MOUNT VERNON PARISH. | [*Six lines*] | PHILADELPHIA: |

PRINTED BY M. CAREY & SON. | 1818. | 12mo. pp. (3), 3, (1), 2, 4–228, (2). *Front., Port., Plates, Map.*

AAS., BPL. [*t.p. mut., lacks port.*]

1. Portrait after Stuart; plates and map identical with the seventeenth 1816 and the eighteenth 1817 editions, titles 29 and 30; last words on p. [*3*] of text are 'Have not a,' and on p. 76, 'order, but'; on p. 118, 'cotten' misprinted thus; p. 206 printed '106' in error.

2. Hart No. 474.

3. Weems wrote to Carey, May 15, 1818: 'But that it is too late now to trouble myself or you with complaints, I w$^{d}$. indulge a strain of deepest regret that Wash. the 19 & Marion the 5 Ed$^{s}$. are so well calculated to fill me with fear & trembling in the presence of my sub$^{s}$. so dark a paper & vol$^{s}$. so compress$^{d}$ & thin, and the latter Vol especially so badly bound were hardly ever yet offer$^{d}$ for one Dollar.'

NUMBER 33 1818

THE LIFE | OF | GEORGE WASHINGTON; | WITH | CURIOUS ANECDOTES, | EQUALLY HONOURABLE TO HIMSELF, | AND | EXEMPLARY TO HIS YOUNG COUNTRYMEN, | [*Four lines of verse*] | Twentieth Edition. . . . [*sic*] Greatly improved. | EMBELLISHED WITH EIGHT ENGRAVINGS. | BY M. L. WEEMS, | FORMERLY RECTOR OF MOUNT VERNON PARISH. | [*Six lines*] | PHILADELPHIA: |

PRINTED BY M. CAREY & SON. | 1818. | 12mo. pp. (1), 2, (1), 2, 4–228, (2). *Front., Port., Plates, Map.*

AAS., NYPL.

1. Portrait like, but not identical with that in eighteenth edition, 1817, title 30; plates identical; the smaller map, unsigned; last words on p. 76 are 'order, but'; p. 118, 'cotten' misprinted thus. In the AAS. copy p. 206 is numbered '106' in error; in the NYPL. copy it is correctly numbered. This would seem to show that the AAS. copy had a new title page but with the printing of the text of the nineteenth edition 1818, title 32, while the NYPL. copy was a new issue.

2. Baker's *Bibliotheca Washingtoniana* No. 132. Hart No. 474.

NUMBER 34 1818

THE LIFE | OF | GEORGE WASHINGTON; | WITH | CURIOUS ANECDOTES, | EQUALLY HONOURABLE TO HIMSELF, | AND | EXEMPLARY TO HIS YOUNG COUNTRYMEN, | [*Four lines of verse*] | Twenty-first Edition. . . . [*sic*] Greatly improved, | EMBELLISHED WITH EIGHT ENGRAVINGS. | BY M. L. WEEMS, | FORMERLY RECTOR OF MOUNT VERNON PARISH. | [*Six lines*] | PHILADELPHIA: |

PRINTED BY M. CAREY & SON. | 1818. | 12mo. pp. (2), 3, 4–228, (2). *Front., Port., Plates, Map.*

AAS. [*lacks port., plates and map*], HSP., MdHS.

1. Title page identical with that of the seventeenth edition 1816, title 29; portrait after, but not identical with that edition; plates appear to have been touched up since that issue; larger map unsigned; last words on p. [*3*] of text are 'Have not a,' and on p. 76, 'order but.'

2. 'Printed from the first set of stereotype-plates. . . . typographical error will be noticed on p. 118 consisting of the transposition of the second t in the word cotton, making it read *cototn*. This error was not corrected, and the word thus printed will be found in all subsequent re-issues from these plates, down to 1840, when new plates were prepared.' Baker's *Bibliotheca Washingtoniana* No. 133. [This had been a stumbling-block to the printers from 1813 on, for evidently in trying to change the misprinting of 'cotten,' they made this second mistake.] Hart No. 474.

3. Weems wrote to James Madison, Jan. 22, 1819: 'My Life of Washington . . . is now in the 21[st] edition.'

NUMBER 35 1819

THE LIFE | OF | GEORGE WASHINGTON; | [*Nine lines*] | Twenty-second Edition Greatly improved. | EMBELLISHED WITH EIGHT ENGRAVINGS. | BY M. L. WEEMS, | [*Seven lines*] | PHILADELPHIA: |

PRINTED BY M. CAREY & SON. | 1819. | 12mo. pp. (1), 4, 4–228, (2). *Front.*, *Port.*, *Plates*, *Map.*

AAS. [*lacks port. and map*], HSP. [*lacks map*], JHL., MLPhil., NYHS., NYPL.

1. The title page is after but not identical with the twenty-first edition stereotyped 1818, title 34; portrait after but not identical with the twentieth edition 1818, title 33; plates, unsigned, identical with those in the nineteenth edition 1818; the smallest map, unsigned; 'cototn' misprinted thus on p. 118.

2. Baker's *Bibliotheca Washingtoniana* No. 138. Hart No. 474.

3. The statements in Weems' *Life of Washington* were questioned in the following: 'To the Editor . . . General Wayne . . . Indian prisoners bayonetted . . . [*signed*] A Friend to Justice.' *Enquirer*, Feb. 13, 1819, VStL.; corroborated, signed 'Philanthropos', *Ibid.*, Mar. 9, 1819, VStL.

NUMBER 36 1820

THE LIFE | OF | GEORGE WASHINGTON; | [*Nine lines*] | Twenty-third Edition greatly improved. | EMBELLISHED WITH EIGHT ENGRAVINGS. | BY M. L. WEEMS, | [*Seven lines*] | PHILADELPHIA: |

M. CAREY & SON. | 1820. | 12mo. pp. 1, (1), 3, (1), 2, 4–228, (4). *Front., Port., Plates, Map.*
AAS., BA., LC.

1. Portrait, unsigned, stippled, oval, bust, stippled border, oval height 8.6 c., width 7.2, inscription 'Genl. George Washington' in script; plates are the same as those in Carey's twenty-second edition 1819; map engraved, signed 'J. G. Melish Del.', different from those in Carey's editions of 1810, 1812, and 1814, titles 19, 22 and 25, and larger than those in the 1815 and 1818 editions, titles 27 and 33.

2. 'With this edition and down to 1828, the illustrations are from different copper-plates to those preceding, being upright in shape and better both in design and execution. They, however, represent the same historical scenes, with the exception of the frontispiece, the "Death of Gen'l Montgomery," which is omitted.' Baker's *Bibliotheca Washingtoniana* No. 142. [In this I believe Baker to be in error, because in the copies of this twenty-third edition which I have seen the plates are identical with those in the preceding editions, including that of 'Genl. Montgomery'. The new and upright plates do not appear until the 1823 edition, title 37.] Baker's *Portraits of Washington* No. 364.

3. *Ad.* [*M.L.W.?*] '. . . Where also may be had, the Biographies of the three NOBLEST FOUNDERS of our LIBERTIES; — WASHINGTON, — . . . of whom not even admiring strangers speak without exclaiming — "FAVOR'D, HAPPY AMERICA! The Lightnings of Heaven bowed to thy Franklin! The Temptations of Earth could not seduce thy Washington! The Demons of Hell were vanquish'd by thy Marion!" N.B. — A liberal part of the profit will be given to the Sunday Schools of Newbern.' *Car. Cent.*, June 16, 1821, NYHS. Also advertised in: *Georgian*, May 15, and, over his own signature, May 18, 1821 [see title 92, note 3], Apr. 18, 1822, GAHS. *Charles. Cour.*, Feb. 16, 1822, CLS.

4. Weems wrote to Carey, May 8, 1820, that printing Washington 'especially on [*sic*] a large edition, for, perhaps 30 cents — & sellg it for 100, shou'd induce you to keep me well supplied.' Aug. 25, 1820, asking for '60 Copies Assorted of the last & *Best* editions of Washington, Franklin (Hagers-

town edit.) & Marion.' Again he wrote, Dec. 22, 1820: 'M^r Rufus King, wonderfully gracious — all but adores our Life of Washington — will recommend it to the Nation as the best of all Books for their Children.' And on Nov. 21, 1821: 'Mr. Gerardine, much admir'd by M^r Jefferson, as a Linguist, is very desirous of translating for you the Life of the Great Washington — as a School Book for exercise of Classes in *the French* — he says it w^d shine in the French — he will do it in style for 250 Doll^s — And probably, w^d take *it out in books*.' To Henry C. Carey, Apr. 16, 1822: 'Had you ever a correspondence with Mons^r. Gerardine, Teacher of the College [*at*] Balt^o. about translating y^r Washington into French[*?*] Many w^d sell in that dress for scholastic exercises.'

No twenty-fourth edition has been found by me, but it is fair to assume that there was one because, Weems being still alive, it would have been like him to continue to number the editions in order to show the popularity of his work. It is noteworthy that the last numbered edition found was issued in the year following his death, 1826.

NUMBER 37 1823

THE LIFE | OF | GEORGE WASHINGTON; | [*Nine lines*] | Twenty-fifth Edition Greatly improved. | Embellished with Eight Engravings. | BY M. L. WEEMS, | [*Seven lines*] | PHILADELPHIA: |

H. C. CAREY & I. LEA. | 1823. | 12mo. pp. 228. *Port., Plates.* EI., HSP.

1. The only change in the title page from the twenty-second edition 1819, title 35, is in the imprint; frontispiece, unsigned, engraved, with inscription 'TOMB OF WASHINGTON'; portrait, unsigned, after Stuart, face to right, plain stippled border, inscription below 'Gen^l. George Washington.' in script; plates are upright rectangles, unsigned, with paging in italics in upper right or left hand corner above plates, and inscriptions in script below. See also title 36, note 2.

2. Baker's *Bibliotheca Washingtoniana* No. 148. '. . . in the left distance, an encampment indistinctly seen.' [See title 31, note 1, last lines, and note 2.] Baker's *Portraits of Washington* No. 364. Henry Whelen Catalogue No. 404. Hart No. 545. [See also title 54, last lines of note 2.]

NUMBER 38 1824

*THE LIFE | OF | GEORGE WASHINGTON; | [*Nine lines?*] | Twenty-sixth Edition Greatly Improved. | BY M. L. WEEMS | Formerly Rector of Mount Vernon Parish. | PHILADELPHIA: |

H. C. CAREY & I. LEA. | 1824. | 12mo. pp. 228. *8 Plates.*

1. 'In the possession of H. C. Carey, Esq.' *Note* of Paul L. Ford.

2. Baker's *Bibliotheca Washingtoniana* No. 152. 'In 1824, the twenty-sixth edition was printed. This appears to have been the last edition issued by Carey, who about that time sold the plates, the book having been stereotyped in 1818, to Joseph Allen, of Frankford . . . whose descendants, I believe, still derive some revenue from them.' Article [*Anon.*] quoting William S. Baker, *Phil. Inquirer*, Feb. 18, 1894, LC. [See title 19, note 2.] Holden Catalogue No. 3042.

NUMBER 39? 1824?

*The Life of Washington . . . Twenty-seventh Edition . . . Philadelphia. [*n.d. 1824?*]

1. Copyright entries for this date, and the number of the edition to be found in the twenty-ninth edition 1826, title 42. This would be the first of the new copyright editions of H. C. Carey & I. Lea.

2. Holden Catalogue No. 3042.

3. Weems wrote to Carey, Sept. 18, 1824: 'W$^{d}$ God we had a good duod$^{o}$ edition of Washington Moraliz$^{d}$.'

4. *Reviewed:* 'Weams [*sic*], Dr.: — a D.D. perhaps: Rector of Mount Vernon — the seat of George Washington, whom he knew from his boyhood: author of a Washington's Life — not one word of which we believe. It is full of ridiculous exaggerations. [*signed*] X.Y.Z.' *American Writers*, in *Blackwood's Magazine*, Vol. XVII, No. V, 1825, p. 203, LC.

NUMBER 39A 1824?

Geschichte Gg. Washington's . . . Philadelphia . . .

Otto Maasz. [*n.d. 1824?*]
HHL., HSP.

1. See titles 47A and 55.

NUMBER 40? 1825

*The Life of George Washington. . . . Twenty-eighth Edition. . . . Philadelphia . . . 1825.

1. Copyright entries for this edition, see title 39, note 1. Under date of May 12, 1899, Mr. John Edmunds, Librarian of the MLPHIL., wrote to Paul L. Ford that their 'copy of the 1825 edition has disappeared.' In 1925 it was still missing.

Baker, in *Bibliotheca Washingtoniana* No. 161, gives a twenty-ninth edition printed at Frankford by Joseph Allen *in 1825, with a portrait.* Not found.

NUMBER 41 1825?

THE | LIFE OF WASHINGTON, | AND | HISTORY OF THE | AMERICAN REVOLUTION. | [*Cut*] | TOGETHER WITH | WASHINGTON'S FAREWELL ADDRESS. | DECLARATION OF INDEPENDENCE, | CONSTITUTION OF THE UNITED STATES. | NEW YORK: |

J. SLATER, PUBLISHER, *No.* 42 *Division-St.* | [*n.d. 1825?*] | Small 12mo. pp. (1), 2, (1), 1, 6–74, 1, 76–108, (2). *Front., Port., Plates.*
HHL.

1. Cover imprint is similar to title; the cut on the title is of Washington with his horse; other cuts face pp. 7, 23, 35, 55, 63, 67 and 74; some are signed 'Dinwiddie'; the text consists of ten chapters ending at p. 74; addenda follow.

2. 'This is an abridgement of Weems' work, and I think it was published about 1825.' *Private letter of Mr. W. U. Lewisson.*

NUMBER 42 1826

THE LIFE | OF | GEORGE WASHINGTON; | WITH | CURIOUS ANECDOTES, | EQUALLY HONOURABLE TO HIMSELF, | AND | EXEMPLARY TO HIS YOUNG COUNTRYMEN. | [*Four lines of verse*] | Twenty-ninth Edition greatly improved. | EMBELLISHED WITH EIGHT ENGRAVINGS. | BY M. L. WEEMS, | FORMERLY RECTOR OF MOUNT VERNON PARISH. | [*Six lines*] | FRANKFORD NEAR PHILAD. |

PUBLISHED BY JOSEPH ALLEN. | 1826. | 12mo. pp. 5, 2, (1), 3, 4–228. *Front., Port., Plates.*

AAS., BA., HSP., LC., NYPL. [*lacks front.*]

1. This is the last numbered edition found, the year following Weems' death. The title is like the twenty-fifth edition 1823, title 27; on reverse of title is new Penn. copyright, dated 1824, to H. C. Carey & I. Lea, Twenty-seventh edition, with announcement of purchase by Joseph Allen; frontispiece is an unsigned engraving, with inscriptions, below 'TOMB OF WASHINGTON', and above 'FRONTISPIECE'; portrait, after Stuart, stippled, rectangle with plain two-lined border, bust, face to right, no inscription. The NYPL. copy has portrait with inscription 'G. WASHINGTON.' in open letter, signed '*A*' in rectangle; plates, upright, unsigned, like those in the twenty-fifth edition 1823, title 37; some copies have 228 pages, some 216 thus lacking Chapter XVI and Washington's Will. The AAS. and HSP. copies have portrait like tenth edition 1813, title 24, after Stuart, unsigned, bust, face to left, in rectangle, no border, inscription below 'G. WASHINGTON.' in open letter. The differences in the portraits may be explained by the new publisher's using various left-overs from former editions, and by carelessness, due partly, perhaps, to Weems' death in the year preceding.

2. Baker's *Bibliotheca Washingtoniana* No. 164. 'When the transfer was made to Allen the illustrations were from other copper-plates than the original, of which several sets has [*had*] been executed. The new sets were much more artistic and better in workmanship and design than the preceding ones. The

woodcuts replaced the copperplates in 1828, and subsequently, about 1840, new stereotype plates were cast.' Article [*Anon.*] quoting William S. Baker, *Phil. Inquirer*, Feb. 18, 1894, LC. 'This edition is printed from the same forms that Mathew Carey used. [*Plates are*] by Alexander Anderson the first American wood engraver.' [1] *Notes* of Paul S. Ford.

NUMBER 43 1828

THE LIFE | OF | GEORGE WASHINGTON; | [*Nine lines*] | EMBELLISHED WITH SIX ENGRAVINGS. | BY M. L. WEEMS, | [*Seven lines*] | PHILADELPHIA: | PUBLISHED BY JOSEPH ALLEN, | AND SOLD BY J. GRIGG, | No. 9. North Fourth Street. | 1828. | 12mo. pp. (1), 4, 4–228. *Front. port., Plates.*
HSP., VStL.

1. Different title from the twenty-ninth edition 1826, title 42; portrait, unsigned, after Stuart, bust, face to right, stippled, in plain two-lined border, inscription below 'G. WASHINGTON.' in shaded letter; all the five plates are woodcuts, some signed 'A', or 'AA', for Alexander Anderson.

2. *Hawkins Sale*, 1887, No. 1141. 'With this edition, wood-cuts, copies of the upright copper-plates of the editions from 1820, were introduced, and appear in all subsequent editions.' Baker's *Bibliotheca Washingtoniana* No. 168.

[1] Dr. Anderson was born in New York in 1775 and by 1793 was employed by printers and publishers in N. Y., N. J., Philadelphia, and even Charleston to illustrate their books. 'Like other engravers, he began by cutting in type-metal, or engraving upon copper. . . . After 1812 Anderson almost gave up engraving on copper also and devoted himself to satisfying the great demand for his work on wood.' *Forgotten Books of the American Nursery*, Rosalie V. Halsey, Boston, 1911, pp. 166–167. — 'For . . . Matthew [*sic*] Carey, of Philadelphia, Anderson was an engraver, at the beginning of this century.' *A Memorial of Alexander Anderson, M.D., First Engraver on Wood in America*, Benson J. Lossing, 1872, p. 57, LC. [I found no specific mention of his work for Weems' *Washington* or *Marion*.] — 'Mr. Lossing, the historian and engraver, says that when he [*Anderson*] began his work in New York, there were not more than twenty professional wood-engravers in the U. S., and that, when the father of American engraving died [*1870*] there were over four hundred.' *Life and Works of Alexander Anderson, M.D., the first American Wood Engraver*, Frederic M. Burr, 1870, pp. 67–68. [Includes A.A.'s diary for 1795–1798.] See also *History of the Rise and Progress of the Arts of Design in America*, William Dunlap, New York, 1834, Vol. II, pp. 8–9, LC. — Anderson is believed to have copied or engraved after Bewick [*Thomas or John?*]. The first crude efforts in wood engraving by these brothers were introduced to the public by Thomas Saint, in 1770. See *Banbury Chap Books*, Edwin Pearson, London, 1890, p. 126, LC.

NUMBER 44 1830

THE LIFE | OF | GEORGE WASHINGTON; | [*Nine lines*] | EMBELLISHED WITH SIX ENGRAVINGS. | BY M. L. WEEMS, | [*Seven lines*] | PHILADELPHIA: |

PUBLISHED BY JOSEPH ALLEN, | AND SOLD BY J. GRIGG, | No. 9, North Fourth Street. | 1830. | 12mo. pp. (3), 4, 4–228. *Front. port., Plates.*
AAS., HHL., HSP.

1. The title page is slightly different in type from the 1828 edition, title 43, but the line arrangement is the same; portrait, after Stuart, signed '*A*', stippled, bust, face to right, in rectangle with stippled border, inscription below 'G. Washington.' in open letter; plates are upright rectangles, after but not identical with those in the 1826 and the 1828 editions, titles 42 and 43; one is signed 'A' [two in the HSP. copy].

NUMBER 45 1831

THE LIFE | OF | GEORGE WASHINGTON; | [*Nine lines*] | EMBELLISHED WITH SIX ENGRAVINGS. | BY M. L. WEEMS, | [*Seven lines*] | PHILADELPHIA: |

PUBLISHED BY JOSEPH ALLEN, | AND SOLD BY J. GRIGG, | No. 9, North Fourth Street. | 1831. | 12mo. pp. (1), 4, 4–228. *Front. port., Plates.*
AAS., HSP.

1. Title, portrait and plates are identical with those of the 1830 edition preceding.
2. Baker's *Bibliotheca Washingtoniana* No. 173.

NUMBER 46 1832

THE LIFE | OF | GEORGE WASHINGTON; | [*Nine lines*] | EMBELLISHED WITH SIX ENGRAVINGS. | BY M. L. WEEMS, | [*Seven lines*] | PHILADELPHIA: |

PUBLISHED BY JOSEPH ALLEN, | AND SOLD BY J. GRIGG, | No. 9 North Fourth Street. | 1832. | 12mo. pp. (1), 4, 4–228. *Front. port., Plates.*
AAS., HSP., *JCB., *MLCin., *MStL.

1. The portrait, after Stuart, signed '*A*', stippled, bust, face to right, rectangle, in a plain two-lined border, inscription below 'G. WASHINGTON.' in shaded letter; the last three plates are signed 'A'.

2. Baker's *Bibliotheca Washingtoniana* No. 180.

NUMBER 47 1833

THE LIFE | OF | GEORGE WASHINGTON; | [*Nine lines*] | EMBELLISHED WITH SIX ENGRAVINGS. | BY M. L. WEEMS, | [*Seven lines*] | PHILADELPHIA: | PUBLISHED BY JOSEPH ALLEN, | AND SOLD BY GRIGG & ELLIOTT, | No. 9 North Fourth Street. | 1833. | 12mo. pp. 228. *Front. port., Plates.*

BA., EI., HSP.

1. Title, portrait and plates are identical with the 1832 edition, title 46.
2. Baker's *Bibliotheca Washingtoniana* No. 188.

NUMBER 47A 1833?

Geschichte Gg. Washington's. . . . Philadelphia. . . .

Otto Maasz. [*n.d. 1833?*]

1. See titles 39A and 55.

NUMBER 48 1834

THE LIFE | OF | GEORGE WASHINGTON; | [*Nine lines*] | EMBELLISHED WITH SIX ENGRAVINGS. | BY M. L. WEEMS, | [*Seven lines*] | PHILADELPHIA: | PUBLISHED BY JOSEPH ALLEN, | [*Two lines*] | 1834. | 12mo. pp. (1), 4, 4–228, (2). *Front.port., Plates.*

AAS., HSP.

1. Title, portrait and plates are identical with those of the 1832 edition, title 46.

NUMBER 49 1836

THE LIFE | OF | GEORGE WASHINGTON; | [*Nine lines*] | EMBELLISHED WITH SIX ENGRAVINGS. | BY M. L. WEEMS, | [*Seven lines*] | PHILADELPHIA: | PUBLISHED BY JOSEPH ALLEN, | [*Two lines*] | 1836. | 12mo. pp. 228. *Front.port., Plates.*

EI., HHL., HSP.

1. Title, portrait and plates are identical with those in 1832 edition, title 46.
2. Baker's *Bibliotheca Washingtoniana* No. 210.

NUMBER 50 1837

THE LIFE | OF | GEORGE WASHINGTON; | [*Nine lines*] | EMBELLISHED WITH SIX ENGRAVINGS. | BY M. L. WEEMS. | [*Seven lines*] | PHILADELPHIA: | PUBLISHED BY JOSEPH ALLEN, | AND SOLD BY GRIGG & ELLIOTT, | [*One line*] | 1837. | 12mo. pp. (1), 4, 4–228. *Front.port., Plates.*

BA., LCHS.

1. This is identical with the copies of the other 1837 edition which follow, except that there are four first fly leaves of publisher's advertisements, and that the letter 'A' is not missing in the third line from the bottom of the title, as it is in the title following, as well as in that of the 1838 edition. As this letter is somewhat elevated above the line, and as the type throughout is so much clearer than the other issue of this year, I have assumed that in trying to align the 'A,' it was hammered out altogether in error, and therefore I have placed this edition first. Portrait and plates are identical with those in the 1832 and 1834 editions, titles 46 and 48. See also title 80A.

NUMBER 51 1837

THE LIFE | OF | GEORGE WASHINGTON; | [*Nine lines*] | EMBELLISHED WITH SIX ENGRAVINGS. | BY M. L. WEEMS, | [*Seven lines*] | PHILADELPHIA: | PUBLISHED BY JOSEPH ALLEN, | ND [*sic*] SOLD BY GRIGG & ELLIOTT, | [*One line*] | 1837. | 12mo. pp. 228. *Front.port., Plates.*

AAS., HU., NYPL.

1. Identical with preceding edition, except that the letter 'A' is missing from 'And' in the third line from the bottom of the title.

2. Baker's *Bibliotheca Washingtoniana* No. 213.

NUMBER 52 1838

THE LIFE | OF | GEORGE WASHINGTON; | [*Nine lines*] | EMBELLISHED WITH SIX ENGRAVINGS. | BY M. L. WEEMS. | [*Seven lines*] |

PUBLISHED BY JOSEPH ALLEN, | ND [*sic*] SOLD BY GRIGG & ELLIOTT, | [*One line*] | 1838. | 12mo. pp. 228. *Front.port., Plates.*
HSP., *LC., NYPL., VStL.

1. Title identical with the preceding edition, including the missing 'A' in third line from bottom; portrait and plates identical with the 1832 edition, title 46.

2. Baker's *Bibliotheca Washingtoniana* No. 223.

NUMBER 53 1838

Lebensbeschreibung | des | Georg Waschington, | mit | merkwürdigen Anekdoten begleitet, | ehrenvoll für sein Andenken, und der amerikanischen Jugend | zur Nachahmung aufgezeichnet. | [*Four lines of verse*] | Von M. L. Weems, | Ehemaligen Prediger der Mount Vernon Kirche. | Philadelphia. |

gedruckt und verlegt von Edmund Y. Schelly. | 1838. | 12mo. pp. (1), 2, (1), 2, (1), 2, 2–297, 3, (2). *Front.port., Plates.*
AAS., HSP., NYPL.

1. Following the title is the *Vorrede*, as from *Der Herausgeber*, dated Philadelphia, im Juny [*sic*], 1838, which states that the book is given out in the German language for the benefit of the German-American people, and is according to his knowledge ['*Es ist dieses unseres Wissen*'] 'the second German edition' [if this is correct, it would throw the date of the Maasz edition beyond 1838 as I have believed, see titles 39A, 43A, and 55]; on reverse is *Inhalt* listing sixteen chapters in German; the frontispiece portrait, after Stuart, unsigned, stippled, bust, 3/4 face to left, no buttons on coat, in rectangle, in an ornamental border like a frame, height of rectangle within border 8.7 c., width 7.5, inscrip-

tion below 'General Washington'; the first plate, entitled 'Tod des General Montgomery', is different from any other; there are six plates altogether after Anderson, five unsigned, like those in the 1837 edition, title 50, but with inscriptions in German; the plate of Andre at p. 129 is signed 'T.'; at p. 188 of the text is 'Waschington's Farewell'; p. 220, 'Death'; p. 231, 'Character'; p. 252, 'Wohlthätigkeit'; p. 271, 'Fleiss'; p. 284, 'Patriotismus'; p. 295, 'Letzter Wille'; the reverse of the last page and one fly leaf contain five commendations, with 'Brackenridge' misprinted 'Breckenridge.' The HSP. has another copy with neither *Vorrede* nor *Inhalt*.

2. Baker's *Bibliotheca Washingtoniana* No. 224.

NUMBER 54 1840

THE LIFE | OF | GEORGE WASHINGTON; | WITH | CURIOUS ANECDOTES, | EQUALLY HONOURABLE TO HIMSELF, | AND | EXEMPLARY TO HIS YOUNG COUNTRYMEN. | [*Four lines of verse*] | EMBELLISHED WITH SIX ENGRAVINGS. | BY M. L. WEEMS, | FORMERLY RECTOR OF MOUNT VERNON PARISH. | [*Six lines*] | PHILADELPHIA: |

PUBLISHED BY JOSEPH ALLEN, | AND SOLD BY GRIGG AND ELLIOTT, | No. 9. North Fourth Street. | 1840. | 12mo. pp. 1, (1), 3, 6–244, (2). *Front.port., Plates.*

AAS., BM., HHL., HSP., *JHL., LC., MHS., NYPL.

1. New typography of title and text since 1838 edition, title 52; on reverse of title, copyright notice, and 'Philadelphia: King & Baird, Printers, No. 9 George St.'; portrait signed 'A' and plates [three signed 'A'] are by Anderson, like those in the editions between 1832 and 1837. Some copies have eight fly leaves, containing publisher's advertisements, including Weems' *Washington* and *Marion*. The HSP. has an edition with this title page, but undated, with publisher's advertisements on eight front fly leaves, naming books of a somewhat later date — perhaps to be imputed to 1848 or 1850, see title 59, note 1.

2. Brinley No. 4260. 'Printed from the second set of stereotype-plates, referred to in the note of No. 86 [*Tenth edition, 1810*]; the pages, being slightly shorter, will account for the additional number, sixteen.' Baker's *Bibliotheca Washingtoniana* No. 248. 'The cuts are copies of the plates in the twenty-fifth ed. 1823, Phil.' *Ms. note in Baker's copy*, HSP.

NUMBER 55 1841?

Geschichte | Gg. Washington's | von der Wiege bis zum Grabe, | von | M. L. Weems, | einem Zeitgenossen Washington's. | PHILADELPHIA, |

zu haben bei Otto Maasz. | [*n.d. 1841?*] | 12mo. pp. (1), 1, (2), 1, (1), 4, (1), 2, 8–240. *Front.port., Plates.*
HHL., HSP. [*lacks front. and port.*], LC.

1. 'Washington,' printed thus on the title, is spelled 'Waschington' throughout the rest of the book; no copyright notice; portrait, plates and inscriptions are like those in the edition of Schäffer & Maund, Baltimore, 1817, but touched up; between the portrait and the title page are the quotation from Lee and the usual five signed commendations, in German. The HHL. copy had a map when I saw it in Mr. Lewisson's collection. The HSP. copy has cover imprint with 'George' printed thus in full, and a small portrait after Stuart, woodcut, bust, face to left in a square ornamental border like a frame, placed above the word 'Philadelphia'; four front fly leaves contain the usual five undated commendations, but in German, in which 'Breckenridge' and 'Rusch' are printed thus; on the back cover of this copy are Otto Maasz' advertisements of 'T. Paine Schriften Vermischten Inhalts von Thomas Paine. . . . Mlle. Lenormand . . . diese berühmteste Wahrsagerin . . . sie war es, die 1840 als das Todesjahr Friedrich Wilhelm III bezeichnete.' This date is one reason for ascribing this issue to a so much later year than do the experts cited in note 2 following, though of course it is possible that this cover imprint was added later. Also, it might be noted in their support that it is unlikely that two German editions should be issued in Philadelphia so close in time as that of Schelly 1838, title 53, and this in 1841. Yet see title 53.

2. Mr. W. U. Lewisson ascribes this edition to about 1824. The LC. CATALOGUE ascribing it to the same year says 'The text of this edition is a reprint of that of 1817 in German.' [See title 31, note 1; also titles 39A and 47A.] Baker's *Bibliotheca Washingtoniana* No. 189, which spells the publisher's name 'Maaszt,' ascribes it to 1833. A partially illegible note of Paul L. Ford ascribes its issue to between 1830 and 1840, without setting forth his reasons.

NUMBER 56                                                    1842

THE | LIFE OF GEORGE WASHINGTON; | WITH | CURIOUS ANECDOTES, EQUALLY HONORABLE TO HIMSELF, | AND | EXEMPLARY TO HIS YOUNG COUNTRYMEN. | [*Four lines of verse*] | BY M. L. WEEMS, | FORMERLY RECTOR OF MOUNT VERNON PARISH. | KNOXVILLE: |

PRINTED AND PUBLISHED BY JAMES WILLIAMS, | AT THE OFFICE OF THE POST. | 1842. | Sq. 12mo. pp. 1, (1), 1, 4–235, (1).
HSP.

1. Without portrait or illustrations.

2. 'An unauthorized reprint, outside of the regular succession of editions.' Baker's *Bibliotheca Washingtoniana* No. 260.

NUMBER 57                                                    1844

THE LIFE | OF | GEORGE WASHINGTON; | [*Nine lines*] | EMBELLISHED WITH SIX ENGRAVINGS. | BY M. L. WEEMS, | [*Seven lines*] | PHILADELPHIA: |

PUBLISHED BY JOSEPH ALLEN, | AND SOLD BY GRIGG AND ELLIOTT, | [*One line*] | 1844. | 12mo. pp. 244, (8). *Front.port., Plates.*
HSP., LCPhil., NYPL.

1. Portrait, plates, text and typography are identical with those in the 1840 edition, title 54. The HSP. and NYPL. copies have no fly leaves of advertisements.

2. Baker's *Bibliotheca Washingtoniana* No. 272.

NUMBER 58                                                    1847

THE LIFE | OF | GEORGE WASHINGTON; | [*Nine lines*] | EMBELLISHED WITH SIX ENGRAVINGS. | BY M. L. WEEMS, | [*Seven lines*] | PHILADELPHIA: |

PUBLISHED BY JOSEPH ALLEN, | [*Two lines*] | 1847. | 12mo. pp. (1), 4, 6–244, (4). *Front.port., Plates.*
AAS., BPL., HSP., LCPhil.

1. Title, portrait, plates and typography are identical with the 1844 edition preceding; on reverse of title, copyright notice, also 'King and Baird, Printers. . . .'

2. Baker's *Bibliotheca Washingtoniana* No. 282.

NUMBER 59 1848–1850?

THE LIFE | OF | GEORGE WASHINGTON; | [*Nine lines*] | EMBELLISHED WITH SIX ENGRAVINGS. | BY M. L. WEEMS, | [*Seven lines*] | PHILADELPHIA: |
PUBLISHED BY JOSEPH ALLEN, | AND SOLD BY GRIGG AND ELLIOTT, | No. 9, North Fourth Street. | [*n.d. 1848–1850?*] | 12mo. pp. (8), 3, 1, (1), 3, 6–244. *Front., Port., Plates.*
HSP.

1. Title (except for lack of date), text and plates are like those of 1840 and 1844, titles 54 and 57; but eight front fly leaves contain advertisements of books of a later date than those of 1840. Since, judging by preceding titles, it was not the habit of Grigg and Elliott to issue undated editions, whereas Lippincott, who succeeded to that firm in 1848, was responsible for at least one other [see titles succeeding], it seems reasonable to account for the above issue by supposing that Lippincott, upon acceding to Grigg and Elliott's stock and finding the *Life of Washington* to be a good seller, got out an edition shortly after, using the old plates as holdovers, and omitting the date merely as a matter of business expediency. As Grigg and Elliott had issued a dated edition as late as 1847, and as the other undated editions of Lippincott seem to fall more definitely in the period from 1850 to 1854 [see titles 60–63], it seems probable that the above issue came out some time between the two, or between 1848 and 1850.

NUMBER 60 1850–1854?

THE LIFE | OF | GEORGE WASHINGTON; | [*Nine lines*] | EMBELLISHED WITH SIX ENGRAVINGS. | BY M. L. WEEMS, | [*Seven lines*] | PHILADELPHIA: |
PUBLISHED BY JOSEPH ALLEN, | AND SOLD BY LIPPINCOTT, GRAMBO & CO., | No. 14 NORTH FOURTH STREET. | [*n.d. 1850–1854?*] | 12mo. pp. 244, 12. *Plates.*
AAS. [*front. torn out.*]

1. I place this and the three following undated editions between the years 1850 and 1854 primarily because, according to the Philadelphia directories, it was during those years that Lippincott was located at 14 North Fourth Street, the address upon the title pages of all these copies. The fact that the text and plates in each are identical with those of the 1855 dated edition seems further to fix them in this period; while the differences in fly leaves, binding, and occasionally punctuation in the titles, suggest that they came from the press at different, if short, intervals. The above copy I place before the other undated AAS. copy because its plates are fresher, and it is bound like the 1847 edition, title 58, with a larger sheet and more elaborate cover than that of 1855, title 64.

NUMBER 61 1850–1854?

THE LIFE | OF | GEORGE WASHINGTON; | [*Nine lines*] | EMBELLISHED WITH SIX ENGRAVINGS. | BY M. L. WEEMS, | [*Seven lines*] | PHILADELPHIA: |

PUBLISHED BY JOSEPH ALLEN, | AND SOLD BY LIPPINCOTT, GRAMBO & CO., | No. 14 NORTH FOURTH STREET. | [*n.d. 1850–1854?*] | 12mo. pp. (3), 5–244. *Front.port., Plates.*
AAS., HHL.

1. See note to title 60. The AAS. copy is bound like the 1855 dated edition, title 64; on a front fly leaf has been written in pencil 'Robert Eugene Mims from His Mother Febry 1s 1856', which might seem to place the edition later than suggested, were it not for the address on the title page.

NUMBER 62 1850–1854?

THE LIFE | OF | GEORGE WASHINGTON; | [*Nine lines*] | EMBELLISHED WITH SIX ENGRAVINGS. | BY M. L. WEEMS, | [*Seven lines*] | PHILADELPHIA: |

PUBLISHED BY JOSEPH ALLEN, | AND SOLD BY LIPPINCOTT, GRAMBO & CO., | No. 14 NORTH FOURTH STREET. | [*n.d. 1850–1854?*] | 12mo. pp. 244, 46. *Front.port., Plates.*
NYPL.

1. See note to title 60. This copy has 46 back fly leaves containing publisher's advertisements, including Weems' *Marion* and *Washington*, from 20

North Fourth Street, Lippincott's address after 1854, which suggests merely that it was put on the market later than the other undated editions of this period — this despite the fact that the binding itself is again after that of 1847, title 58, with the printing, as in that edition, on a larger sheet.

NUMBER 63 1850–1854?

THE LIFE | OF | GEORGE WASHINGTON; | [*Nine lines*] | EMBELLISHED WITH SIX ENGRAVINGS. | BY M. L. WEEMS [*punctuation destroyed*] | [*Seven lines*] | PHILADELPHIA: |

PUBLISHED BY JOSEPH ALLEN, | AND SOLD BY LIPPINCOTT, GRAMBO & CO., | No. 14 NORTH FOURTH STREET. | [*n.d. 1850–1854?*] | 12mo. pp. 244. *Front.port., Plates.*
NYPL.

1. See note to title 60. This edition has a smaller page again, and is bound like that of 1855, title 64.

NUMBER 64 1855

THE LIFE | OF | GEORGE WASHINGTON; | [*Nine lines*] | EMBELLISHED WITH SIX ENGRAVINGS. | BY M. L. WEEMS, | [*Seven lines*] | PHILADELPHIA: |

PUBLISHED BY JOSEPH ALLEN, | SOLD BY | J. B. LIPPINCOTT & CO. | NO. 20 NORTH FOURTH ST. | 1855. | 12mo. pp. 244. *Front. port., Plates.*
AAS.

NUMBER 65 1856

THE LIFE | OF | GEORGE WASHINGTON; | [*Nine lines*] | Embellished with Six Engravings. | BY M. L. WEEMS, | [*Six lines*] | PHILADELPHIA: |

J. B. LIPPINCOTT & CO. | 1856. | 12mo. pp. 244. *Front.port., Plates.*
AAS., *UNC.

1. A new title page, with the announcement of 'Six Engravings' in Old English type and six lines given to Lee's quotation instead of seven; on reverse of title, copyright notice, undated; portrait and plates like those in preceding editions. In the AAS. copy, p. 134 is printed '4' in error; there are publishers' advertisements on back fly leaves, pp. 13–18, 33, 34.
2. Baker's *Bibliotheca Washingtoniana* No. 355.

NUMBER 66 1857

THE LIFE | OF | GEORGE WASHINGTON; | [*Nine lines*] | Embellished with Six Engravings. | BY M. L. WEEMS, | [*Six lines*] | PHILADELPHIA: |

J. B. LIPPINCOTT & CO. | 1857. | 12mo. pp. 244. *Front.port., Plates.*
HSP.

1. Identical with the 1856 edition, title 65.
2. Baker's *Bibliotheca Washingtoniana* No. 365.

NUMBER 67 1858

THE LIFE | OF | GEORGE WASHINGTON; | [*Nine lines*] | Embellished with Six Engravings. | BY M. L. WEEMS, | [*Six lines*] | PHILADELPHIA: |

J. B. LIPPINCOTT & CO. | 1858. | 12mo. pp. 244, (8). *Front.port., Plates.*
HHL., LC.

1. Plates are identical with the 1857 edition; the last eight pages, numbered 17–23, (1), consist of publishers' advertisements.
2. Baker's *Bibliotheca Washingtoniana* No. 370.

NUMBER 68 1860

THE LIFE | OF | GEORGE WASHINGTON; | [*Nine lines*] | Embellished with Six Engravings. | BY M. L. WEEMS, | [*Six lines*] | PHILADELPHIA: |

J. B. LIPPINCOTT & CO. | 1860. | 12mo. pp. 3, 6–244, (4). *Front. port., Plates.*
BPL., LC., MLPhil., *WisHS.

1. The engraved portrait and plates are after those by Anderson, like the 1858 edition. The LC. copy has four back fly leaves of publishers' advertisements.

2. Baker's *Bibliotheca Washingtoniana* No. 394.

NUMBER 69 1867

THE LIFE | OF | GEORGE WASHINGTON; | [*Nine lines*] | Embellished with Six Engravings. | BY M. L. WEEMS, | [*Six lines*] | PHILADELPHIA: |

J. B. LIPPINCOTT & CO. | 1867. | 12mo. pp. 3, 6–244, (4). *Front.port., Plates.*

*CinPL., HHL.

1. Identical with the 1860 edition.

NUMBER 70 1869

THE LIFE | OF | GEORGE WASHINGTON;| [*Nine lines*] | Embellished with Six Engravings. | BY M. L. WEEMS, | [*Six lines*] | PHILADELPHIA: |

J. B. LIPPINCOTT & CO. | 1869. | 12mo. pp. 244. *Front.port., Plates.*

AAS., *IndPL.

NUMBER 71 1873

THE LIFE | OF | GEORGE WASHINGTON; | [*Nine lines*] | Embellished with Six Engravings. | BY M. L. WEEMS, | [*Six lines*] | PHILADELPHIA: |

J. B. LIPPINCOTT & CO. | 1873. | 12mo. pp. (2), 5–244. *Front.port., Plates.*

*ClPL., HHL.

NUMBER 72 1877

THE LIFE | OF | GEORGE WASHINGTON; | [*Nine lines*] | Embellished with Six Engravings. | BY M. L. WEEMS, | [*Six lines*] | PHILADELPHIA: |

J. B. LIPPINCOTT & CO. | 1877. | 12mo. pp. 244, (8). *Front.port., Plates.*

AAS.

NUMBER 73 1882

THE LIFE | OF | GEORGE WASHINGTON; | [*Nine lines*] | Embellished with Six Engravings, | BY M. L. WEEMS, | [*Six lines*] | PHILADELPHIA: |

J. B. LIPPINCOTT & CO. | 1882. | 12mo. pp. 244, (8). *Front.port., Plates.*

HSP.

1. No copyright notice; the eight back fly leaves contain publishers' advertisements.

2. Baker's *Bibliotheca Washingtoniana* No. 468.

NUMBER 74 1883

The Life of George Washington; | WITH CURIOUS ANECDOTES, EQUALLY HONORABLE TO HIMSELF, AND EXEMPLARY | TO HIS YOUNG COUNTRYMEN. | By M. L. WEEMS, formerly Rector of Mount Vernon Parish. | NEW YORK:

GEORGE MUNRO, PUBLISHER, | [*One line*] | 4to. pp. 3, 4–35, (9). *Port.*

AAS., LC.

1. In unbound paper; caption title 'Seaside Library. Vol. LXXIX. . . . No. 1596.'; portrait is a rude cut. There seems no reason to suppose that this edition was unauthorized.

NUMBER 75 *1885–?*

THE LIFE | OF | GEORGE WASHINGTON; | [*Nine lines*] | Embellished with Six Engravings. | BY M. L. WEEMS, | [*Six lines*] | PHILADELPHIA: |

J. B. LIPPINCOTT COMPANY. | [*n.d. 1885–?*] 12mo. pp. 244. *Front. port.*

AAS.

1. Identical with the 1877 edition except for the publishers' name on title page. As Lippincott changed their firm name thus in 1885, and as the firm write that their records were practically all burned in 1899, I have no data by which to date the above edition except as of some time subsequent to 1884.

NUMBER 76 1891

THE LIFE | OF | GEORGE WASHINGTON; | [*Nine lines*] | Embellished with Six Engravings. | BY M. L. WEEMS, | [*Six lines*] | PHILADELPHIA: |

J. B. LIPPINCOTT COMPANY. | 1891. | 12mo. pp. 244, (8). *Front. port., Plates.*

HSP.

1. Identical with the 1882 edition, except for the publishers' name on the title.

NUMBER 77 1892

THE LIFE | OF | GEORGE WASHINGTON; | [*Nine lines*] | Embellished with Six Engravings. | BY M. L. WEEMS, | [*Six lines*] | PHILADELPHIA: |

J. B. LIPPINCOTT COMPANY. | 1892. | 12mo. pp. 244, (8). *Front. port., Plates.*

HHL.

1. Identical with the 1891 edition.

NUMBER 78 1918

A History of the Life and | Death, Virtues and Exploits of | General George Washington | WITH CURIOUS ANECDOTES | EQUALLY HONOURABLE TO HIMSELF AND | EXEMPLARY TO HIS YOUNG COUNTRYMEN | BY | MASON L. WEEMS | FORMERLY RECTOR OF MOUNT VERNON PARISH | MOUNT VERNON EDITION | WITH 8 ILLUSTRATIONS AND THE OLD WOOD CUTS | [*Four lines*] | PHILADELPHIA: AND LONDON |

J. B. LIPPINCOTT AND COMPANY | 1918 | 12mo. pp (2), 2, (1), 4, 6, 3, 10, 288, (2). *Front.port., Plates.*
BPL., LC., NYPL., VStL.

1. On reverse of title page, copyright notice, dated 1918; frontispiece is of Washington crossing the Delaware; no portrait; besides five of the old woodcuts, there are four new process illustrations.

2. *Ad.* 'The Life and Death, Virtues and Exploits of General George Washington By Mason L. Weems Mount Vernon Edition. Profusely illustrated with new pictures in addition to the interesting old wood cuts from earlier issues. Printed from new type. J. B. Lippincott Company.' *Reviewed:* [*Anon.*, including one quotation] *Nation* (N.Y.), Apr. 18, 1918, NYPL.

NUMBER 79 1921

A History of the Life and | Death, Virtues and Exploits of | General George Washington | [*Three lines*] | BY | MASON L. WEEMS | [*Seven lines*] | PHILADELPHIA: AND LONDON |

J. B. LIPPINCOTT AND COMPANY | 1921 | 12mo. pp. (2), 2, (1), 4, 6, 3, 10, 288, (2). *Front., Plates.*
HHL.

NUMBER 80 *19—?*

A History of the Life and | Death, Virtues and Exploits of | General George Washington | [*Three lines*] | BY | MASON L. WEEMS | [*Seven lines*] | PHILADELPHIA: AND LONDON |

J. B. LIPPINCOTT AND COMPANY | [*n.d. 19—?*] | 12mo. pp. (2), 2, (1), 4, 6, 3, 10, 228, (2). *Front., Plates.*
HHL.

1. Identical with the 1918 edition.

NUMBER 80A 1927

GEORGE WASHINGTON | AND THE | CURIOUS ANEC-DOTE, | EQUALLY HONOURABLE TO HIMSELF | AND | EXEMPLARY TO HIS YOUNG COUNTRYMEN, | OF | HOW HE HACKED THE CHERRY TREE | AND | WHAT CAME OF IT | *The Original Story Extracted from the "Life" by* | M. L. WEEMS, | FORMERLY RECTOR OF MOUNT VERNON PARISH | "EMBELLISHED WITH A PORTRAIT" | *reproduced with all its faults from the Frontispiece of the 1837 Philadelphia edition.* | NEW YORK: 1927.

JAMES A. ANDERSON. 12mo. pp. 3, (1). *Front.port.*

1. Reproduction only of the portrait and reprint of the anecdote, from the 1837 edition.

NUMBER 80B 1927

*AN AMERICAN BOOKSHELF | A HISTORY | of the | LIFE AND DEATH | VIRTUES & EXPLOITS | of | GENERAL GEORGE | WASHINGTON | by | MASON WEEMS |

MACY-MASIUS: PUBLISHERS | 1927 | 12mo. pp. (1), 4, (1), 7-374, (2).
BA.

1. One reprint of a series (consisting thus far of six items) edited by Mark Van Doren. Rubrication on title.

## EDITIONS OF DOUBTFUL DATE OR AUTHENTICITY

[See also titles 1, 2, 3, 4, 6, 7, 8, 9, 23, 39, 39A, 40, 41, 47A, 55, 59, 60, 61, 62, 63, 75 and 80.]

NUMBER 81? 1807?

*Das Leben des Georg Waschington mit sonderbaren anecdoten. Johann Gruber. Hagerstown. [*1807?*]

1. This edition is mentioned in a letter to Paul L. Ford from the late Dr. William H. Egle, formerly State Librarian at Harrisburg, under date of March 25, 1899. I have never been able to find a copy. The present State Librarian has no trace of it. It has been suggested that as Dr. Egle himself owned many rarities, this edition may have been one of them, which he removed when he was displaced by a political appointee. I doubt whether Weems knew of this issue, if indeed it existed, for I have found no mention of it in his letters.

2. 'John Gruber went to Hagerstown in 1795 and started there a German paper called the "German Washington Correspondent," which . . . was not a permanent success. [*Quoting from Scharf's History of Western Maryland, Vol. 2, p. 1141.*] It is possible . . . that the paper referred to by Scharf was established in 1795 and succeeded in 1799 by the "Westliche Correspondenz," . . . published by Johann Gruber. . . . The paper is mentioned frequently in contemporaneous prints from 1804 to 1811.' *Bibliography of American Newspapers*, Clarence S. Brigham, *ProcAAS.*, Vol. XXV, April, 1915, p. 192.

NUMBER 82? 1829

*The Life | of | George Washington | with | Curious Anecdotes | equally honourable to himself | and | exemplary to his young Countrymen | [. . . *poetry*] | embellished with six engravings | By M. L. Weems | formerly rector of Mount Vernon Parish | [. . . a puff, by Gen. Lee] | Philadelphia: |

Published by Joseph Allen, | and sold by J. Grigg, | No. 9, North Fourth Street | . . . | 1829.
Free Library of the General Society of Mechanics and Tradesmen of the City of New York.

1. *Notes* of Paul L. Ford. Not found up to 1925.

NUMBER 83?

## *Das Leben des Georg Waschington. Harrisburg. Benjamin Mayer.

1. The late Dr. William H. Egle, formerly State Librarian of Pennsylvania, in a letter to Paul L. Ford, under date of March 25, 1899, stated: 'There was an edition published by Benjamin Mayer at Harrisburg, which I glean from a notice in his newspaper "Die Morgenröthe" (The Aurora) — but I have never seen it.' This reference not found.

NUMBER 84?

## *The Life of George Washington. York.

1. This edition is mentioned in a letter to Paul L. Ford from the late Dr. William H. Egle, formerly State Librarian at Harrisburg, under date of March 25, 1899, but I have never been able to find such an issue.

NUMBER 85? 1810?

*The Life of Gen. Francis Marion. Robinson? Baltimore? [*n.d. 1810?*]

1. The existence of this edition has been inferred not only from the advertisements and letters which follow — especially the letter of May 3, 1810, and those to Horry — but also from the copyright notice, dated Nov. 20, 1809, in the earliest edition seen by me, that of 1814, as well as by the fact that this latter edition is clearly entitled the 'second,' while that of 1815 follows in proper sequence as the 'third edition improved.' It may be judged by the letter of Nov. 18, 1809, below, that Robinson, of Baltimore, was the printer. It seems possible that this unfound first edition was printed for Weems by the end of 1809, and then delivered, or sent, to Carey, who refusing, or delaying, to bind, when and as Weems expected, the books were another source of contention between the two. Later, when or if sent to the South, probably still unbound, or only 'stitched in blue paper,' they failed to survive in so frail a form to our day.

2. *Ad.* [*M.L.W.?*] 'NOTICE. THE Rev. M. L. Weems will offer for sale, during the week of Commencement, a large assortment of Books: among others a New Work "*The life of General Francis Marion, of South Carolina*"; a work highly interesting to those who look back with pleasure on the heroic men who established our Liberties.' *Ga.Express*, July 25, 1810, UN'YGA. 'The Following valuable Books . . . . Life of Marion. . . .' *Ga.Jour.*, Nov. 1, 1810, UN'YGA. 'Chronicle Office and New Book Store For Sale at this Office, a general & Choice Selection of Books . . . following . . . Weems' . . . Ditto of Marion. . . .' *Aug. Chron.*, Mar. 8, 1811 *et seq.*, UNY'GA. 'M. L. WEEMS begs leave very respectfully to inform the Honourable the Gentlemen of the Legislature, that his FLYING LIBRARY will leave town on Friday morning. Those who mean to procure some good books will please honor him with their attention. . . . Liberal allowance made to those benevolent characters who take several copies of Washington and Marion for Christmas Boxes to their young relations. . . .' *Ga.Jour.*, Nov. 28, 1810, UNY'GA.

3. Weems wrote to Carey, April 20, 1809: '. . . My Life of Marion is done. My friends to whom I have read parts of the work are pleas[d] to say it will do. Had I better get it printed in Philad[a] or Baltimore?' May 20, 1809: 'As to printing Marion. I beg you to be assured I shall never owe you one Doll[r] on any account whatever.' Aug. 23, 1809: 'A M[r] Robinson or Robertson, Printer Calvert Street Balto has agreed to print my Life of Marion, will have it ready for me in the first of October — figure 1500 Copies — half bound like your Washington. . . . The whole (*printing & binding*) about 500 Doll[rs] for the 1500 Copies. Now if you will take upon you to settle with Robinson . . . I will solemnly pledge myself that you shall have the *whole* of the monies raised . . . till the 1[st] day of April 1810. Besides, you may take 300 copies of Marion which in the present indignant state of the public mind against the British, wod I think in 6 weeks, get back one half of your money.' Nov. 7, 1809: 'I beg you to do all you can for Marion.' Nov. 13, 1809, he urged Carey that Marion be 'ready . . . this season at the South. I may lose the sale utterly for a twelvemonth at least, if not sent. . . . I intreat you to *insure Marion* for me.' Nov. 18, 1809: 'Let me most earnestly intreat you to order from M[r] Robinson the Printer, Balt[o] the whole of *Marion* & have them bound & push[d] off for me.' Nov. 27, 1809: 'I know you will not forget nor forsake me in the Affair of Marion. Now or *never* is the season . . . I mean this Winter. . . . I shall go on to send you, not only of your own money but also of Marion liberally. So I pray you let not Robinson ruin me in his delays of that work. Get several Binders to work & push it off.' Dec. 13, 1809: 'I shall from that book [*Marion*] alone be able to remit you a good many hundred dollars.' Dec. 18, 1809: 'I therefore once more intreat you instantly to have Marion bound for me & sent on to New York . . . to some friend of yours who will . . . immediately put them on board the Charleston packet . . . you cou'd easily get my little book [*Marion*] to me by the time I shall want it. I shou'd not think so much about it, but that I am every hour importun'd for Marions Life, & by the greatest Men of the State, to whom he was uncommonly dear.' Dec. 19, 1809: 'While at Balt[o] I agreed to [*get?*] Marion printed even tho' I shou'd do it on money borrowd from my friends, for you had *refus'd* to print it for me. . . . Let me now for the last time intreat you to bind & send me on Marion, . . . If I coud get that book it w[d] . . . keep me from the necessity of touching one dollar of your money.' Dec. 26, 1809: 'I can hardly support my family, cannot give them the education they deserve, and even have not the means to pay for the binding of 10 or 1200 Chap books (I mean Marion). . . . Tell the Binders to *insure*, and to direct to John Hoff, Bookseller Charleston, with orders to receive the money before he delivers the books. I have friends

in Charleston who will *lend* me a little money for that purpose.' Jan. 5, 1810: 'You say had Marion been sent with your books to Richmond I shoud have been there much sooner than I was. . . . that little book (Marion) from which I hop[d] to raise enough to send you (at least the money you had engag'd to pay Robinson & to subsist myself & horse & send a little to my family) most unfeelingly withheld from me. . . . It is my hope that you have, led by a wise & magnanimous policy, accomplish[d] my wishes & bound & sent on to New York my Life of Marion. . . . Only be so good as to beg M[rs]. Bailey or some other *safe* hand, just to stitch them in blue papers (It wont cost perhaps more than *one or two cents apiece*) and send them on to M[r]. John Hoff . . . Charleston, with orders to him to receive the money before delivery of the books.' Jan. 12, 1810: 'Please also to let me know what you have done for *me as to Marion.* I requested you in my last from Columbia, in which I sent you 20 Dolls of my own private small monies, to have them done up for me in the cheap inexpensive style of *blue papers* only, . . . They shall be paid for the moment I get to Charleston & not out of your money . . . you will find it your best policy to hurry me on that little book (*Marion*) especially as it is to cost you nothing in the binding.' Jan. 22, 1810: 'I say you need not even put Marion into blue papers, but send him in sheets to M[r]. John Hoff. . . . what you have done with Marion, I pray you to write instantly.' Jan. 29, 1810: 'And that w[d] you now but send me on a good supply . . . especially Religious books & my Life of Marion, I might yet by the 1[st] of June make you up a noble Collection.' Feb. 3, 1810: 'I pray you write to me at Charleston and send me on my Marion. . . . I told you besides that if you w[d] take on you to pay for Marion, I w[d] not touch a penny of your money till June. You have taken the Book & now won't send it on, tho I have repeatedly told you that all the monies arising from the sales shou'd be sent to you, except a little for my own support & for remittance to my children.' May 3, 1810, from Augusta: 'The Books are arriv[d]. 19 boxes and 2 or 3 with Marion of former shipments.' Oct. 29, 1810: 'Marion sells well.' Further proof is found in the following quotations from *Weems, The Biographer and Historian*, in *Views and Reviews, Second Series*, William Gilmore Simms, 1845. Quoting from a letter of Weems to Horry, dated Dumfries, June 3, 1808: ' "I beg you to indulge no fears that Marion will ever die, *while I can say or write anything to immortalize him. . . .*" It is curious to observe that he answers the doubts of Horry as to the mode of getting means to print the book, with the modest hope that in spite of the embargo, and the scarcity of cash, he should still be able to get enough for the purpose; — and this, with reference to a book, which, for its size, has probably yielded more money to the publishers than any other volume of American manufacture. . . . The probability is that . . . the embargo opposed a greater obstacle to the acquisition of the necessary cash, [*for publishing Marion*] than, . . . he had anticipated.' Writing to Horry from Dumfries, Feb. 5, 1809, Weems says: '". . . *I am happy to tell you, that in a few weeks, I shall put Marion to press.* . . . Many persons, and some of them, perhaps, pretty good judges, have been pleased to commend various pages which were read to them. It is my hope, at least, that it will become a school book in South Carolina, &c. . . ."' From Columbia, Dec. 13, 1809: '". . . It gives me great pleasure to be able to inform you, by our mutual friend Dr. Blythe, *that your ever-honored and beloved Marion lives in history. . . . the history of the great Marion, . . . is finished.* . . . You have no doubt constantly kept in memory, *that I told you I must write it in my own way, and knowing the passion of the times for novels, I have endeavoured to throw your ideas and facts about Gen. Marion into the garb and dress of a military romance.* . . . The Life of Marion will, I hope, be at Charleston in three weeks. But I don't believe that you will have the opportunity to see it earlier than the Races. . . ."' '"Columbia, S. C., Dec. 1810. Dear Sir: — I have lately heard and with infinite astonishment, that you are displeased with the Life of Marion. *Though I have so heard, yet I can hardly believe it. What! is it possible that you can be displeased with a book which places both yourself and your beloved Marion in so conspicuous and exalted a light?* — a book that contains every fact that you yourself gave me — *a book that everywhere meets with unbounded applause — of which, I have orders for 90 copies, in one single county in Georgia — which has, in fact, changed the county of Wilkinson into that of Marion. A book, which, in short, sells better even than the Life of Washington. Now, that you should be displeased with such a book, is to me, very astonishing!* I want very much to see you to procure some additional anecdotes for our 2d edition; and when I see you, if you can point out any errors, or any places where improvement can be made, I shall cheerfully attend to your instructions. My daughter, Fanny, *who has lately turned out poetess*, desired me to give her love to you. She says — *she fears that you are fickle.* God bless you."' From Horry to Weems: '"Georgetown, (S. C.) Feb. 4, 1811. Dear Sir: — Having been very poorly for a long time, and in expectation of seeing you, I deferred writing you. Disappointed in the latter, and feeling myself better, I am enabled to resume my pen and shall freely and candidly give you my sentiments relative to Marion's history. A former letter of yours to me says, — 'You have, no doubt, constantly kept in memory, that I told you I must write the history in my own way.' *This, I do not recollect, but I well recollect that I repeatedly mentioned to you 'not to alter the sense or meaning of my work, lest when it came out I might not know it; and, perverted, it might convey a very different meaning from the truth.'* That officers were alive that well knew Marion's history, and would say, *as (perhaps they have said,*) [*sic*] I wrote what was not true. I requested you would, (if necessary,) so far alter the work as to make it read grammatically, and I gave you leave to embellish the work, — *but entertained not the least idea of what has happened — though several of my friends were under such apprehensions, which caused my being urgent on you not to alter as above mentioned. Do you not recollect my sitting on the ground with you near the Georgetown Printing Office*, and urging you again on the subject of no alterations to the work — That you replied, (*seemingly out of humour,*) That, 'When the work came out, you engaged I would be satisfied.' I replied 'That is enough;' — and I recollect nothing farther passed between us afterwards on the subject. How great was my surprise on reading these words in your letter: 'Knowing the passion of the times for novels, I have endeavoured to throw your ideas and facts about General Marion into the garb and dress of a military romance.' *A history of realities turned into a romance!* The idea alone, militates against the work. The one as a history of real performance, would be always read with pleasure. The other as a fictitious invention of the brain, once read would suffice. Therefore, I think you injured yourself, notwithstanding the quick sales of your book. *Nor have the public received the real history of General Marion. You have carved and mutilated it with so many erroneous statements*, [that] your embellishments, observations and remarks, must necessarily be erroneous as proceeding from false grounds. *Most certainly 'tis not* MY history, but YOUR romance. You say the book sells better than Washington! The price of the one is much less than the other — [that] is the reason. Besides, persons unacquainted with the real history, buy and read your books as authentic. When known to be otherwise, [it] will lie mouldering on the shelves, and no more purchasers [will] be obtained. You have my work; compare [it] with yours, and the difference will appear. Yours is greatly abridged, and the letters contained in mine (which I thought much of,) are excluded from yours. You say, 'you are surprised to hear that I am displeased with your book, particularly as it places Marion and myself in so conspicuous and exalted a light.' *Can you suppose* [that] *I can be pleased with reading particulars* (*though ever so elevated, by you*) *of Marion and myself, when I know* [that] *such never existed.* Your book is out. My dissatisfaction of it is in no ways material. You say you want to see me to procure some additional anecdotes for your 2d edition — and that, if I can point out any errors or places where improvement may be made, that you will cheerfully attend to any instructions. Could such improvement be really made, I fear for its fate — to be disregarded as my first performances were. A second edition would add to your emoluments. I cannot think I can amend my former work in your hands. Much time and deliberation were used to form, correct, and perfect the same. To attempt further, I fear, at this distant day, would detriment, rather than benefit. After having compared my work, — *which I call history, and which you call 'documents'* — with your book, I wish you would send it to me, in order that I may also compare it. I before wrote you for this, but received no answer. I thank your daughter Fanny for [her] remembrance of me. She fears that I am fickle. 'Tis not so. Tell her my numerous friends and acquaintances here know the many encomiums I constantly lavish in her praise. I know not her equal. Sometimes, I think I make Miss B- jealous. I shall ever retain a grateful sense of the favours conferred on me by your most excellent and worthy family. Please to make my love and veneration to them. I am your well-wisher. (Signed,) P. Horry." We have before us a considerable number of Horry's manuscripts, his documents and a portion of a narrative of his own life, which included, with his own, a considerable part of the military career of Marion. The liberties which Weems took with Horry's documents did not, in all probability, except in one or two instances, affect the substantial history.'

4. 'Robinson, Joseph, printer, bookseller and circulating library, 96 Balt. st. dwel, 18 Granby st O T' *Baltimore Directory*, 1814.

5. 'Marion, the Agamemnon of these wars, had already become a kind of legend, thanks to the popular memory and the fantastic ardour of Weems. . . .' Carl Van Doren, in *Cambridge History of American Literature*, Vol. I, p. 315. 'His looseness as an historian, is happily illustrated by an anecdote which he tells in the Life of Marion, of the son of Isaac Hayne . . . [*as having*] studied the small-sword exercise in order to fight Rawdon, and whose intense excitement on this subject brought on a raving madness of which he died. The son in question lived to a good old age and died in 1844.' *Weems, The Biographer and Historian*, William Gilmore Simms, in *Views and Reviews, Second Series*, 1845, p. 131, LC. His *Life of Marion* is also alluded to in *The Life of Marion*, William Gilmore Simms, 1844, and in *A Grandfather's Stories of Our Country*, Edward L. Ellis, 1911, Vol. II, pp. 308–309, LC.

6. 'The stony antipathies of Thomas Carlyle have to answer for many a miscarriage of historic justice; but for none more unfounded than that superior air with which he teaches the nineteenth century to sit in judgment on the eighteenth.'[1] It is easy to scoff at the obviously sensational methods of Weems' so-called biography. But in line with Harrison's comment it may help us to judge ourselves and our own generation more accurately if we admit that history must still be presented as a highly spiced tale, if intended to reach certain kinds of minds. The following was only one of a series, probably quite as

[1] Frederic Harrison, in *A Few Words about the Eighteenth Century*, in *The Nineteenth Century*, 1883.

lively in tone, syndicated throughout 'these United States,' within the last ten years: 'Vivid Vamps of History. By Anne Jordan. Gabrielle D'Estrees, Who Made Henry of Navarre Turn Catholic So She Could Buy Clothes in Paris . . . *she* punched the time clock for her entry into the world in 1576. . . . Henry had done some fancy training for the kingly title. Every now and then he would interrupt a gentlemanly spree at his hangout at Nancy, and dash out, all laced up in aluminum overalls, to fight a battle. . . . But after office hours he had his Royal High Trotter out-trot the best looking corn-fed ballet that ever shone on the front page of the Gazette de Police. With the ladies Henry was a fourteen-toed bear-cat. "Where did you get them eyes?" was all *the Duke of Bellegarde* could say to the coosome Gabrielle. She fixed him with a baby-vamp stare that made the keys rattle in his pocket. . . . Gabrielle served the drinks, and saluted the King with a kiss on his goblet hand. That settled it. The kiss ran up Henry's shoulder and tickled his cerebellum. Thus was the rival pooh-poohed out of the royal sun-parlor. . . . "You're just what I need to brighten up the royal upholstery" said Henry. . . . "I'm strong for you, like a garland of garlic." "Don't get so used to me On-ree," objected Gabrielle, "You know I'm already took." . . . Gabrielle gave way when she saw the love-light in the unwashed royal visage. "You're bad, Hen!" she whispered, "but you've sure got cute ways. . . . Gather me in, kid, I've parked my foot on a banana peeling." . . . Thenceforth Gabrielle ruled the roost. Her clothes had the weather backed off the ironing board as a topic of conversation. . . . But collective vamping was too much for her . . . the poor girl had shimmied too long and too violently at the court balls. . . . She died of convulsions. . . . At that she . . . kept her family in the society columns for generations.'

NUMBER 86 1814

THE LIFE | OF | GEN. FRANCIS MARION, | A CELEBRATED | PARTIZAN OFFICER, | IN | THE REVOLUTIONARY WAR, | against the | BRITISH AND TORIES, | IN | SOUTH-CAROLINA AND GEORGIA. | BY BRIGADIER GENERAL P. HORRY. | Second Edition. | "On VERNON'S Chief, why lavish all our lays? | Come, honest Muse, and sing great Marion's praise." | BALTIMORE: | PRINTED FOR THE REV. M. L. WEEMS, | By W. D. BELL & J. F. COOK. | 1814. | 12mo. pp. (2), 3, 4-6, 1, 8-270, (4).
AAS., LC.

1. On reverse of title, Md. copyright, to Mason L. Weems, dated Nov. 20, 1809 'the thirty-fourth year . . .'; Preface, undated, signed Peter Horry, but this, as well as the text, is unmistakably by Weems, though unsigned.

2. Sabin No. C33044. *Encyclopedia*, Duyckinck, Vol. I, p. 503 [*ed. 1875*]. *Views and Reviews, Second Series*, William Gilmore Simms, 1845, p. 133.

3. *Ad.* [*M.L.W.*] 'COMMUNICATION. BIOGRAPHY OF ANOTHER AMERICAN HERO. "*Immortal may their mem'ry be* "*Who fought and bled for Liberty!*" Letter from colonel Howard [1] of Baltimore; one of the Heroes in the decisive battle at the Cowpens!! "SIR — It gives me pleasure to hear from the papers, that you are about to publish the life of another Hero of the revolution, I mean GENERAL FRANCIS MARION, of South Carolina. I entirely agree with generals Green, Lee, and other excellent judges, that he was an officer of uncommon merit, and one who rendered *great services* to this country during the revolutionary war. One trait in his character, especially, deserves immortal credit; he was not ambitious of command! and when the good of his country required it; he would act in *any station* In the battles at Scot's Lake, Motles' Fort and Friday's ferry, he acted with colonel Lee; and although he was entitled to the command, yet, from *patriotic motives* he permitted Lee, in great measure, to direct the operations! Wishing that you may so succeed in delineating the character of General Marion, as to rouse our youth to the imitation of HIS VALOUR AND VIRTUES. I remain, Sir, your obedient serv't. JOHN E. HOWARD. The Rev. M. L. WEEMS. *Belvidere, Nov.* 25, 1814." "No man" says General Green, "has a better claim to public gratitude and admiration than General Marion. History furnishes no equal to him in the art of partizan warfare." General Henry Lee [2] says — "Marion was virtuous all over — and his history is admirably calculated to shew what wonders may be done, even with slender means, by a brave individual, whose soul is devoted to the good of his country." Lord Cornwallis has been often heard to declare, that "there was no partizan officer in the American army whom he so dreaded as General Marion." How well he deserved such praise will appear by considering the singularly gloomy situation of our country when Marion commenced his military career. When one of our finest armies under Gen. Lincoln was captured at Charleston, and another under General Gates was cut to pieces at Camden, when a choice division under General Sumpter was completely surprized, and that under Beaufort entirely mas-

[1] John Eagar Howard, patriot, soldier and statesman, whose equestrian statue in Baltimore attests to the love and admiration of his compatriots, without succeeding itself in arousing equally agreeable emotions in the observer.

[2] Lee, Henry, 1756–1818, soldier, born at Leesylvania, Westmoreland Co., Va.; Lieut.-Col. under Greene in Revolution. *Twentieth Century Biographical Dictionary*.

sacred; when by such a run of horrible blunders and disasters, the last spark of Liberty seemed to be extinguished in the Southern States, and multitudes of frightened citizens thought of nothing but getting *British protections* — then it was, in that dark and hopeless state of our cause, that Marion came forth. Instead of floating with the coward herd down the stream of despair, he rose upon the wings of Genius and Virtue against the cloud of war, and like the eagle of Heaven seemed to rejoice in the darkening storm. 'Tis known to many of his countrymen now in congress, that at this awful crisis he had but *thirty men!* with only *two rounds* of powder and ball! and *thirty swords!* And yet, with this slender stake he played the game of war with such astonishing skill, that in five weeks he gave the enemy as many signal overthrows! — Britons were captured — tories dispersed — whigs reanimated — crowds flocked to his standard, and battles were fought on a larger scale, and with a success which ultimately accomplished his great wish, the liberties and glory of his country. But splendid as were his accomplishments as a *soldier*, they were all eclipsed by his virtues as a citizen. His foes (the *foes of justice*) who found him a LION while they resisted, found him still more a LAMB when they submitted: And if his friends admired him for the resources of his mind, they all but adored him for the *purity* of his morals. In short, it is hoped, that the reader will find the LIFE OF MARION, a rich assemblage of that *moral and military heroism*, which, while it charms all hearts, has an admirable tendency to multiply in our land, *virtuous youth — soldiers of sentiment*, and *excellent partizan officers!* This interesting work, from the most authentic documents, is now preparing for the public eye — in one volume of near 300 pages, neatly printed and bound, and to be delivered to subscribers for one dollar — to non-subscribers one dollar and a quarter. M. L. Weems, author of the "*Life of Washington*" (in a small volume) that has been so unexpectedly honored by the citizens of Baltimore and the United States, is now receiving subscriptions for the "*Life of Marion*." "There is no reading so proper for American youth as the Biography of American worthies." — GEORGE WASHINGTON.' *Balt. Tel. and Merc. Adv.*, Dec. 10, 1814, NYHS.

NUMBER 87 1815

THE LIFE | OF | GEN. FRANCIS MARION, | A CELEBRATED | PARTIZAN OFFICER, | IN THE | REVOLUTIONARY WAR, | AGAINST THE | BRITISH AND TORIES, | IN SOUTH CAROLINA AND GEORGIA | BY BRIGADIER GENERAL P. HORRY, | of Marion's brigade; | and M. L. WEEMS. | Third edition improved. | "On VERNON'S Chief, why lavish all our lays | "Come, honest Muse, and sing great Marion's pra [*sic*]. | BALTIMORE: |

Published by the Rev. M. L. WEEMS. | J. Hagerty, Printer. | 1815. |
12mo. pp. 3, 4–6, 1, 8–257, (1).
AAS., BPL., HU., LC.

1. On reverse of title Md. copyright, Nov. 9, 1809; Preface; typographically this edition differs from that of 1814; also, abbreviations beginning in Chapter IV are noticeable on p. 41 as distinguished from 1814; p. 43, 'Governour' is spelled thus.

2. John Hagerty, born in Prince George's C'y, Md., 1747. 'In 1779 he entered the itineracy of the M. E. Church and in the following year was appointed to the Berkeley circuit. In 1781 he was sent to Baltimore Circuit; in 1782 to Calvert; in 1783 to Chester; and in 1784 to Frederick. In 1785 he was stationed in New York; and in 1786–7 acted as Presiding Elder. In 1788 he was stationed at Annapolis, in 1789 at Baltimore, in 1790 at Fell's Point and in 1791 and 1792 at Baltimore, where he finally located. Died 4 Sept. 1823.' *Notes of Mr. Louis H. Dielman.* 'A partnership in the printing business commenced on the 6th of this month between John Hagerty & Ralph W. Pomeroy & Co. . . . office at No. 12, Light-Street.' *Fed. Gaz. & Balt. D. Adv.*, Mar. 14, 1815, MDHS. 'Sept 14, 1796 [*Baltimore*] Bought several books of J. Hagerty.' *Ms. Diary of Rev. William Duke*, owned by MDDIO'NL. in PIL. 'John Hagerty Book & Paper Warehouse.' *Baltimore Directory*, 1807, LC. 'Hagerty, John, printer & bookseller, 12 Light st' *Baltimore Directory*, 1814, LC.

3. This is deservedly one of Weems' successful books — given the reader's taste for his assorted condiments: 'The heart is sometimes so *embittered*, that nothing but divine love can *sweeten* it; so *enraged*, that *devotion* only can becalm it; and so broke down, that it takes all the force of heavenly hope to raise it.' [Pp. 249–250]; 'The remarkable resemblance between him [*Marion*] and the great Washington. . . . They were both born in the same year, both lost their fathers in early life; both married excellent and *wealthy* ladies: both left widows: and both died childless.' [P. 251]; 'When he [*Marion*] was near his end, seeing his lady weeping by his bed-side, he gave her a look of great tenderness, and said, "My dear, weep not for me, I am not afraid to die; for, thank God, I can lay my hand on my heart and say, that since I came to man's estate I have never intentionally done wrong to any."' [P. 269.]

NUMBER 88 1816

THE LIFE | OF | GEN. FRANCIS MARION, | A CELEBRATED | PARTIZAN OFFICER | IN THE | REVOLUTIONARY WAR, | AGAINST THE | BRITISH AND TORIES | IN SOUTH CAROLINA AND GEORGIA. | BY BRIGADIER GEN. P. HORRY, | OF MARION'S BRIGADE | AND M. L. WEEMS. | "On VERNON'S Chief, why lavish all our lays? | Come, honest Muse, and sing great Marion's praise." | FOURTH EDITION IMPROVED. | PHILADELPHIA: |
PUBLISHED BY M. CAREY, 121, CHESNUT STREET. | 1816. |
12mo. pp. (2), 3, 4–6, 1, 8–260.
BA.

1. On reverse of title Md. copyright, 1809; slight changes between this edition and those of 1814 and 1815; in 1816 on p. 4 of the Preface, the expression 'Burn Caesar' is used instead of 'Damn' him; on p. 23 'alarm' becomes 'report'; on p. 29 'Harry' becomes 'Horry'; and on p. 33 there is a fling added at 'morning slings and mid-day draughts of strong grog.' See also title 89, note 1.

2. Alibone's *Dictionary*. Sabin No. 33045.

3. Advertised in: *Del. Gaz.*, Aug. 27, 1817, WI. *Frank. Repos.*, Dec. 2, 1817, FROF.

4. Weems wrote to Carey, Mar. 7, 1815, suggesting that as he was to be allowed the *Life of Washington* 'at *12 1/2 pr cent advance on the prime cost* payable say in Philad[a].' that the 4th edition of *Marion* be taken in exchange. 'I have actually sold 1500 of Marion in 3 Months for cash. No one book ever pleas[d] all, for some you know can't bear Ossian, Milton or even the *bible*. But Marion, with some Enemies, has a world of Friends and I declare solemnly, and you know that lying is not on the list of my sins, that I have receiv[d] some of the highest plaudits for Marion that I ever receiv[d] for any book that I had the honor to write. . . . Howard, Scott,[1] Lee, Greene, all blow the trumpet & bend the knee to Marion. The 2[d] edition is all gone & 3 to 400 of the 3[d] exchang[d] & the rest nearly or all bespoke & yet without help of plates. This 4[th] edition will be greatly improv[d]. Now if you were to get

[1] Winfield Scott, appointed brigadier-general in the War of 1812, Mar. 9, 1814. *Twentieth Century Biographical Dictionary*. For other names see 1814 edition, title 86, note 3.

some good plates for it, and take care to interest some of the Leading officers & Hearty Republicans in it, you might distribute 1000s of copies and thus in times of Peace spread over our Country the shield of Minerva against a future war. And besides, in a few months you might make Marion & Washington School books throughout the U. States.' There is a letter from Weems to Thomas Jefferson, written from North Garden, July 31, 1815, presenting him with *The Life of Marion* and asking for data for a *Life of Franklin*, with reply written from Monticello, Aug. 2, 1815, in *Thomas Jefferson Correspondence*, from the Collections of William K. Bixby, Worthington Chauncey Ford, Boston, 1916, pp. 224–226. [See *Letters*, Vol. III.] Weems to Carey, Feb. 14, 1816: 'I have thoughts of printing a 4th edition of Marion with some improvements by the South Carolina Members in Congress. I wish you wd take 1000 of it for Washington in sheets, or bound. As I wd never have parted with Wash. but from expectation of that Grand Book Crusade of ours which has long been knock[*ed*] on the head, I hope you will exchange with me as you do with others. I verily believe that you might sell 5000 copies.' May 31, 1816: 'Tell me when you will put Marion to press. For I have a most gallant act of his which the Members of Congress from that Country beg I will put in the fourth edition. I have also an elegant critique on Marion by Judge Brackinridge [*sic*].' [This latter I have not seen.]

NUMBER 89? 1817–1818?

## *The Life of Gen. Francis Marion. Fifth Edition. Philadelphia. M. Carey & Son [*1817–1818?*]

1. Between the fourth edition of 1816 and the sixth of 1818 no edition has been seen by me. There is evidence, however, that in this interval certainly one, and perhaps two editions were issued. Carey's Catalogue for 1818 lists the following: '653 Weems' (Rev. Mason L.) Life of Gen. Francis Marion, the celebrated Partizan Officer in the Revolutionary War, in South Carolina and Georgia. Fourth edition, with Engravings $1 Philad. 1817.' The point to be stressed here is that this advertisement cannot be made to apply to the fourth edition of 1816, since that has no plates. Weems' letters of May 6th and 15th, 1818 below speak of a '5th' edition as actual. Possibly these two unseen editions are identical, but it would seem to me more likely that the former, as advertised as of 1817 by Carey, was issued in 1817, and the latter later in that year or early in 1818. Weems' agitation for engravings for *Marion* as early as July,

1816 seems to have some bearing upon these two imputed editions. His proposals for issuing by subscription a *Life of Marion* simultaneously with one of Washington and one of Franklin were never carried out, so far as I know. [For this advertisement dated 1817, see title 30, note 3.]

2. Weems wrote to Carey [*n.d. received July 8, 1816*]: 'How goes on Marion? I am inclin$^{d}$ to believe that if you w$^{d}$ give a large folding plate of some one, or two of Marion's Coups de main — in the style of "*Col$^{o}$ Johnson's Mounted Men charging the British Artillerists & Indians,*" with a good edition on thick paper, you might soon do great things with this work. . . . As we never did those great things that I counted on when I sold you the Life of Washington, I do really think that in Equity you ought to allow me a good commission on that book.' Jan. 31, 1817: 'Now there is Marion by numbers of People pronounc$^{d}$ more interesting still than Washington, for 7 months that we have had it as a partnership book it has not even yet got *off the stocks*. Now if it were your own & the profits your own, you w$^{d}$ have better inducement to have it rigg$^{d}$ and put on an extensive & lucrative cruise in a short time. I will sell it to you. You have lying about in Virginia a parcel of old books. Can't we make an exchange? *Tell* me when you think and talk over this.' Feb. 16, 1817: 'I am dying for Marion &c &c.' Apr. 1, 1817: 'Send me *instantly* 50 Marion. This work begins to be in much demand.' July 10, 1817: 'It w$^{d}$ be a great help to us to have a good keen French looking likeness of Marion.' July 20, 1817: 'If I had but a good figure for Marion, I sh$^{d}$ be complete, especially if you w$^{d}$ send me the large show bills that are at the little Bookbinders below the drawbridge. I mean the show bills with the pictures taken from the Looking glasses.'[1] Oct. 9, 1817: 'I w$^{d}$ advise . . . especially, if you cou'd get a good French face, keen, aqueline & intelligent, for Marion.' Nov. 4, 1817: 'If you have not [*yet?*] printed *Marion*, let me know & I'll send you [*a new?*] anecdote of him, which many of the S. Carolinian members of Congress beg sh$^{d}$ be inserted in the next edition. Nov. 29, 1817: 'The demand here [*Hagerstown*] for Marion is very great.' May 6, 1818: 'Paper of Marion 5th ed. miserable.' May 15, 1818: 'I w$^{d}$. indulge a strain of deepest regret that Wash. the 19 & Marion the 5 Ed$^{s}$. are so well calculated to fill me with fear & trembling in the presence of my Sub$^{s}$. So dark a paper & Vol$^{s}$. so compress$^{d}$ & thin and . . . especially so badly bound were hardly ever yet offer$^{d}$ for one Dollar.'

[1] His own tracts issued under that title.

NUMBER 90 1818

THE LIFE | OF | GEN. FRANCIS MARION, | A CELEBRATED | PARTISAN OFFICER | IN THE | REVOLUTIONARY WAR, | AGAINST THE | BRITISH AND TORIES | IN SOUTH CAROLINA AND GEORGIA. | By Brig. Gen. P. HORRY, of Marion's Brigade. | AND | M. L. WEEMS. | "On VERNON'S CHIEF, why lavish all our lays? | "Come, honest Muse, and sing great MARION'S praise." | SIXTH EDITION. | PHILADELPHIA: | PUBLISHED BY M. CAREY & SON, | NO. 126, CHESNUT STREET. | 1818. | 12mo. pp. (2), 3, IV–VI, 1, 8–251, (1). *Front., Plates.* AAS., LC. [*lacks front.*], WL.

1. On reverse of title Md. copyright, 1809; Preface like the 1814 edition; six unsigned woodcuts differing entirely from those in all other editions and not upright; after the frontispiece, they are: '*Sergeant Jasper rescuing the American prisoners*,' and above, '*Page 56*'; '*Cap^t. James, knocking down Captain Ardeisoff with a chair*,' and above, '*Page 115*'; '*British Captain discovered in the Chimney*,' and above, '*Page 118*'; '*Gen^l. Marion, feasting the British Officer on sweet potatoes*,' and above, '*Page 156*'; '*Sergeant M^c.Donald and his party charging into Georgetown*,' and above, '*Page 164*.' The LC. copy is inscribed to 'James Madison 1819.' See note 2.

2. Weems wrote to Carey, Feb. 7, 1818: 'I have intreated you to get a good French face for Gen^l Marion.' [*N.d. received Feb. 19, 1818*]: 'If I had a good French phizz^d. likeness of Marion, sharp, aquiline, & determin^d, to accompany the prospectus of Wash. & Franklin, it wd do well indeed. But I cant get things as I want them.' To James Madison, from Richmond, Jan. 22, 1819 [LC.]: 'Very Dear Sir — I do myself the honor to send you a copy of the Life of Marion. It is already in the Sixth edition, and makes much noise in the Country. If you shou'd be pleased with *the Spirit* of Marion, and think that it ought to be universal among the youth of our Republic, you will do both them & me a great Kindness by giving us a line commendatory of Marion as a School book. My Life of Washington written for that purpose is now in the 21^st edition; and from the demand for Marion I have reason to believe he will not lag far behind him. Please present my very best Respects to M^rs. Madison, to whom I have taken the liberty to send a paper for Doct^r. Hunter's admired work.[1] As

[1] See title 253.

the object of this book is so Divine, and its eclat so very extraordinary I feel confident that Mrs. Madison will not disdain to employ a portion of her great influence to circulate it among her numerous & wealthy friends — especially as it is somewhere prophecied that "*Queens shall become nursing Mothers to the church.*" Wishing you, both, many happy & useful years here yet, before you are calld to your Celestial Patrimony. I remain Your sincere friend M. L. Weems. Compts. to Mr. Todd — cannot but hope that he will peruse with edification "Hymens Recruitg. Serjeant!"'[1] For Madison's reply, see title 92, note 3.

NUMBER 91 1820

THE LIFE | OF | GEN. FRANCIS MARION, | A CELEBRATED | PARTISAN OFFICER | IN THE | REVOLUTIONARY WAR, | AGAINST THE | BRITISH AND TORIES | IN SOUTH CAROLINA AND GEORGIA. | By Brig. Gen. P. HORRY, of Marion's Brigade. | AND | M. L. WEEMS. | [*Two lines of verse*] | SEVENTH EDITION. | PHILADELPHIA: |

M. CAREY & SON. | 1820. | J. M. Gardiner. | 12mo. pp. vi, 251.
*Front., Plates.*
NYPL.

1. Weems wrote to Carey, Mar. 29, [*1820?*]: 'Mr. Madison has sent me a letter highly flattering of our Marion. I will send you an extract that you may print it if you think proper.' [See title 92, note 3.] From Dumfries, Aug. 31, 1820: 'Marion also shd be printed again. I have some *capital additions* to make to it.' Sept. 12, 1820: 'I am happy to tell you that the character of that book is rising wonderfully. . . . I have some noble anecdotes for Marion.' M. Carey & Son to Weems, Sept. 19, 1820: 'We shall probably soon put an edition of Marion to press.' Oct. 25, 1820: 'We are now printing a very handsome Edition of Marion which will be finished in about 3 or 4 weeks. . . .' Weems to Carey, Nov. 14, 1820: 'I have one admirable chapter to add to Marion.' [Never added.] Dec. 22, 1820: 'At 5 oclock waited on Mr Munro[2] — found him with his Fair Lady & Friends at table — was receivd with a general smile. "*They had just been talking of my Life of Marion*" — the conversation happend to turn on a theme fruitful of fine fruits & figures for fancy — mirth & merriment went around.'

[1] See titles 160 *et seq.* [2] President Monroe.

NUMBER 92 1821

THE LIFE | OF | GEN. FRANCIS MARION, | A CELEBRATED | PARTISAN OFFICER | IN THE | REVOLUTIONARY WAR, | AGAINST THE | BRITISH AND TORIES | IN SOUTH CAROLINA AND GEORGIA. | By Brig. Gen. P. HORRY, of Marion's Brigade. | AND | M. L. WEEMS. | [*Two lines of verse*] | SEVENTH EDITION. | PHILADELPHIA: |

PUBLISHED BY M. CAREY AND SON, | NO. 126, CHESNUT STREET. | 1821. | 12mo. pp. (1), 4, IV–VI, 1, 8–251, (2). *Front., Plates.*
AAS.

1. On reverse of title Md. copyright; frontispiece and five plates, unsigned, upright, different from the sixth edition: frontispiece '*Sergeant Jasper rescuing the American prisoners.*'; opp. p. 77 '*M'Donald's trick on the old Tory.*'; opp. p. 86 '*The Author and Marion expostulating with the Innkeeper.*'; opp. p. 114 '*Captain James, knocking down Cap[t] Ardeisoff with a Chair.*'; opp. p. 154 '*General Marion, feasting the British Officer on sweet potatoes*'; opp. p. 205 ' "*Oh my father! my father! I will die with you!!*" '

2. Carey's Catalogue, June, 1821. Sabin No. 33045.

3. [*M.L.W.*] ' Communicated for the Georgian "Not hate, but glory made the Chiefs contend, "For each brave foe was in his heart a friend." Homer. When the battle had [*sic*] ceas'd along the field, and the feeble foe can no longer lift the sword, how passing lovely 'tis to see the victors and the vanquished meet together at the feast, like brothers; and drink a generous oblivion of all their former hostilities! This was seen on the banks of the broad flooded York, when the English army yielded to "Columbia's first and Great son." "The Hero spread his feast, and sent around the shell" of invitation to the conquered chieftain and his officers to share with him in the banquet. Seated together at the same table, Britons, Franks, and Americans, all forget the past and brightening with joy as in the beams of returning peace, they filled the sparkling goblets, and drank to the memory of those who had distinguished themselves in the war. When it came to the turn of Lord Cornwallis, the brave Englishman lifted high a bumper to the "Honor of General Marion" — "Yes, please your Excellency," continued he, looking at Washington, "I honor Marion. Slender as was his force, he yet gave me more alarm than any of your officers. I often

detached my ablest partizans to surprise him; and they as frequently promised me, by express, that they had got within striking distance, and would soon give me a good account of him. But instead of surprising him, it always turned out that he surprised them." The brave antagonist of Cornwallis (I allude to General Green) was often heard to say, that "he never, in any history, ancient or modern, met with a partizan officer that deserved to be compared with Marion." General Henry Lee, writing of Marion, employs the following energetic language: — "Marion was virtuous all over! And his life demonstrates what wonders a brave individial may achieve, whose whole soul is devoted to his country." And hence our poet Paulding exclames — | "Brave Marion! by his country not half known: | Who kept a war alive himself alone! | Who, when the prostrate south defenceless lay | To foreign bands and home bred foes a prey: | Still nurs'd the fainting spirits of the state, | And bravely tripp'd the heels of adverse fate; | Still hung undaunted on the plundering foe | Who thought him distant till he felt the blow. | Or fell upon his flank or broken rear, | And made him buy each inch of ground too dear." | And every American patriot will read with pleasure the following tribute paid to Marion by our ci-devant President, the amiable Mr. Madison: Dear Sir — I have just read your "Life of Marion", and have been much pleased with the rich vein of patriotism running through it; as well as the vivid pictures, and *fine moral lessons*, for which the career of your justly admired hero furnished you the happy occasions. The rapid sale, and repeated editions of the Life of Marion, like that of his great prototype, (Washington) are pleasing proofs in the one as in the other, you have received a sanction from the public suffrage. I tender you my cordial respects and best wishes. James Madison. The Rev. Mason L. Weems. N.B. A few copies of the 7th and best edition, at Schenk's Book Store; also of the Life of Franklin, the 5th edition; and of the Life of Washington, the 23d edition. A part of the profits, sacred to the Sunday Schools, will be deposited with Wm. B. Bullock, Esq., M. L. Weems.' *Georgian*, May 18, 1821, GAHS. Also advertised in: *Ibid.*, May 15, 1821, GAHS. *Car. Cent.*, June 16, 1821, NYHS.

4. Weems wrote to Carey, Jan. 15, 1821: 'Elijah [*Weems*] is eternally writing to me about printing an edition of Marion.' Jan. 19, 1822: 'Dont stereotype Marion yet.' [*N.d. received Feb. 4.*] 1822: 'I intreat you not to stereotype Marion yet. I have two brilliant anecdotes for it.' [The first stereotyped edition found is dated 1826.]

NUMBER 93 1822

THE LIFE | OF | GEN. FRANCIS MARION, | A CELEBRATED | PARTISAN OFFICER | IN THE | REVOLUTIONARY WAR, | AGAINST THE | BRITISH AND TORIES | IN SOUTH CAROLINA AND GEORGIA. | By Brig. Gen. P. HORRY, of Marion's Brigade: and | M. L. WEEMS. | "On VERNON'S CHIEF why lavish all our lays? | "Come, honest Muse, and sing great MARION'S praise." | EIGHTH EDITION. | PHILADELPHIA: |

M. CAREY & SONS — CHESNUT STREET. | 1822. | 12mo. pp. (1), 4, IV–VI, 1, 8–251, (1). *Front.*, *Plates.*
AAS.

1. A new title; the name 'GEN. FRANCIS MARION' is in open letter; the frontispiece and plates are identical with those in the 1821 edition preceding, but worn.

2. Advertised in: *Charles. Cour.*, Feb. 16, 1822, CLS. *Georgian*, Apr. 18, 1822, GAHS.

NUMBER 94 1823

THE LIFE | OF | GEN. FRANCIS MARION, | A CELEBRATED | PARTISAN OFFICER | IN THE | REVOLUTIONARY WAR, | AGAINST THE | BRITISH AND TORIES | IN SOUTH CAROLINA AND GEORGIA. | By Brig. Gen. P. HORRY, of Marion's Brigade: and | M. L. WEEMS. | [*Two lines of verse*] | NINTH EDITION. | PHILADELPHIA: |

H. C. CAREY & I. LEA — CHESTNUT STREET. | 1823. | 12mo. pp. (4), 3, IV–VI, 1, 8–251, (4).
EI.

1. The frontispiece and plates are identical with those in the 1821 edition, title 92; colophon, on p. 251: '*Printed at Doylestown,* | by | ASHER MINER: | May – 1823'

NUMBER 95 1825

THE LIFE | OF | GEN. FRANCIS MARION | [*Seven lines*] | By Brig. Gen. P. HORRY, of Marion's Brigade, and | M. L. WEEMS. | [*Two lines of verse*] | TENTH EDITION. | Philadelphia: |

H. C. Carey & I. Lea - - - [*sic*] Chestnut Street | 1825. | 12mo. pp. 3, IV–VI, 1, 8–251, (2). *Plates.*
BPL.

1. Five plates, unsigned, like but not identical with Anderson's of 1828 and later.

2. Sabin No. 33045 gives the date as '18 .', listing it *after* the Frankford edition of 1826.

3. *Ad.* 'Charleston Apprentice's Library . . . Weems' Life of Marion. . . .' *Charles. Cour.*, Mar. 24, 1825 *et seq.*, CLS.

NUMBER 96 1826

THE LIFE | OF | GEN. FRANCIS MARION, | A CELEBRATED | Partisan Officer | IN THE | REVOLUTIONARY WAR, | AGAINST THE | BRITISH AND TORIES | IN SOUTH CAROLINA AND GEORGIA. | BY BRIG. GEN. P. HORRY, OF MARION'S BRIGADE: | AND M. L. WEEMS. | "On VERNON'S CHIEF, why lavish all our lays? | "Come, honest Muse, and sing great MARION'S praise." | ELEVENTH EDITION. | FRANKFORD, (*near Phil.*) |

PUBLISHED BY JOSEPH ALLEN. | Stereotyped by L. Johnson. | 1826 | 12mo. pp. (1), 4, IV–VI, 1, 8–252, (2). *Front., Plates.*
AAS., HSP.

1. A new title; 'Partisan Officer' in Old English; 'In South Carolina,' 'Georgia,' and 'Frankford,' in italicized capitals. On reverse of title Penn. copyright dated 1824 to H. C. Carey and I. Lea with notice of purchase by Joseph Allen; plates are identical with the 1821 edition, title 92, though much worn.

2. Sabin No. 33045. Catalogue of Library of Guy M. Walker, Anderson Galleries, February, 1925.

NUMBER 97 1828

THE LIFE | OF | GEN. FRANCIS MARION, | A CELEBRATED | Partisan Officer | IN THE | REVOLUTIONARY WAR, | AGAINST THE | BRITISH AND TORIES | IN SOUTH CAROLINA AND GEORGIA. | BY BRIG. GEN. P. HORRY, OF MARION'S BRIGADE; | AND M. L. WEEMS. | [*Two lines of verse*] | STEREOTYPED BY L. JOHNSON. | PHILADELPHIA: |

PUBLISHED BY JOSEPH ALLEN, | AND SOLD BY J. GRIGG, | No. 9 North Fourth Street. | 1828. | 12mo. pp. (1), 4, IV–VI, 1, 8–252. *Front., Plates.*

LC.

1. On reverse of title Penn. copyright, 1824; the six plates are woodcuts, three signed 'A,' or 'A.A.' [*for Alexander Anderson*]; on p. 50 'Joassilin' of the earlier editions becomes 'Josselin' in this.

2. Sabin No. 33045.

NUMBER 98 1829

THE LIFE | OF | GEN. FRANCIS MARION, | [*Seven lines*] | BY BRIG. GEN. P. HORRY, OF MARION'S BRIGADE: | AND M. L. WEEMS. | [*Two lines of verse*] | STEREOTYPED BY L. JOHNSON. | PHILADELPHIA; |

PUBLISHED BY JOSEPH ALLEN, | AND SOLD BY J. GRIGG, | No. 9 North Fourth Street. | 1829 | 12mo. pp. (1), 4, IV–VI, 1, 8–252, (2). *Front., Plates.*

AAS., LC.

1. The six plates are woodcuts, two signed 'A.' or 'A.A.' after but not identical with those of 1828.

2. Sabin No. 33045.

NUMBER 99 1831

THE LIFE | OF | GEN. FRANCIS MARION, | [*Seven lines*] | BY BRIG GEN. P. HORRY, OF MARION'S BRIGADE: | and M. L. WEEMS. | [*Two lines of verse*] | STEREOTYPED BY L. JOHNSON. | PHILADELPHIA: |

PUBLISHED BY JOSEPH ALLEN, | AND SOLD BY J. GRIGG, | No. 4 North Fourth Street. | 1831. | 12mo. pp. (3), 4, IV–VI, 1, 8–252, (2). *Front., Plates.*
AAS., HSP.

1. Frontispiece of Serjeant Jasper; five other plates, two signed '*A.*' or '*A.A.*'; all are after but not identical with those of 1826, title 96.
2. Sabin No. 33045.

NUMBER 100 1833

THE LIFE | OF | GEN. FRANCIS MARION, | [*Seven lines*] | BY BRIG GEN. P. HORRY OF MARION'S BRIGADE: | AND M. L. WEEMS. | [*Two lines of verse*] | STEREOTYPED BY L. JOHNSON. | PHILADELPHIA: |

PUBLISHED BY JOSEPH ALLEN, | AND SOLD BY GRIGG & ELLIOTT | [*One line*] | 1833. | 12mo. pp. (1), 4, IV–VI, 1, 8–252. *Front., Plates.*
AAS., LC.

1. On reverse of title Penn. copyright dated 1824 to H. C. Carey & I. Lea, purchased by Joseph Allen; six plates by Anderson.
2. Sabin No. 33045.

NUMBER 101 1835

THE | LIFE | OF | MAJOR GEN. FRANCIS MARION: | THE MOST | CELEBRATED PARTISAN OFFICER | IN THE | REVOLUTIONARY WAR, | AGAINST THE BRITISH AND TORIES, | IN SOUTH CAROLINA AND GEORGIA. | BY COLONEL HORRY, OF MARION'S

BRIGADE, | AND | M. L. WHEEMS, CHAPLAIN TO WASHINGTON. | On Vernon's Chief why lavish all your lays? | Come honest muse and sing great Marion's praise. | NEW-YORK: |

PUBLISHED BY P. M. DAVIS, LATE OF THE UNITED STATES' ARMY. | 1835. | 12mo. pp. (3), 4, IV–VI, 1, 8–252, (2). *Front., Plates.*
AAS., BPL., LC.

1. On reverse of title page, '(Copy-right secured) W. Applegate, Printer, 257 Hudson-street.'; Preface; five woodcuts, unsigned, after those in the later preceding Johnson and Allen editions.

2. Sabin No. 33045.

NUMBER 102 1835

THE LIFE | OF | GEN. FRANCIS MARION, | A CELEBRATED | PARTISAN OFFICER | IN THE | REVOLUTIONARY WAR, | AGAINST THE | BRITISH AND TORIES, | IN SOUTH CAROLINA AND GEORGIA. | ABRIDGED FROM HORRY AND WEEMS' LIFE | OF MARION. | ["On VERNON'S CHIEF, why lavish all your lays, | Come, honest Muse, and sing great MARION'S praise."] | DEVON: |

PUBLISHED AND SOLD BY S. THORNE, | SHEBBEAR, HATHERLEIGH. | 1835. | 24mo. pp. (3), 2, (1), 1, VI–VIII, 1, 10–324, (2). *Front., Plates.*
AAS., LC.

1. Published in England; the six plates unsigned are woodcuts, after those in Johnson's editions; the frontispiece being the same subject but with a different inscription: '"*It was a fearful odds.*" — Page, 60,' while none of the other plates has an inscription except the last which copies that in Johnson's editions.

2. Sabin, after No. 33045, gives this as from Rich's *Bibliotheca Americana*, Vol. II, p. 272.

NUMBER 103		1837

THE LIFE | OF | GEN. FRANCIS MARION, | A CELEBRATED | Partisan Officer | IN THE | REVOLUTIONARY WAR, | AGAINST THE | BRITISH AND TORIES | IN SOUTH CAROLINA AND GEORGIA | BY BRIG. GEN. P. HORRY, OF MARION'S BRIGADE: | AND M. L. WEEMS. | "On VERNON'S CHIEF, why lavish all our lays; | "Come, honest Muse, and sing great MARION'S praise." | STEREOTYPED BY L. JOHNSON. | PHILADELPHIA: |

PUBLISHED BY JOSEPH ALLEN. | AND SOLD BY GRIGG & ELLIOTT, | No. 9 North Fourth Street. | 1837. | 12mo. pp. 4, (1), 4, IV–VI, 1, 8–252, (2). *Front., Plates.*
LC., LCPhil., MdHS., NYHS., WL.

1. On reverse of title Penn. copyright, 1824 to H. C. Carey and I. Lea; four front fly leaves contain Grigg & Elliott's advertisements; text identical with earlier editions; six plates by or after Anderson, signed 'A.' or 'A.A.'
2. Sabin No. 33045.

NUMBER 104		1839

THE LIFE | OF | GEN. FRANCIS MARION, | [*Seven lines*] | BY BRIG. GEN. P. HORRY, OF MARION'S BRIGADE: | AND M. L. WEEMS. | "On VERNON'S CHIEF, why lavish all our lays; | Come, honest Muse, and sing great MARION'S praise." | STEREOTYPED BY L. JOHNSON. | PHILADELPHIA: |

PUBLISHED BY JOSEPH ALLEN. | AND SOLD BY GRIGG & ELLIOTT, | No. 9 North Fourth Street. | 1839. | 12mo. pp. 4, (1), 4, IV–VI, 1, 8–252, (2). *Front., Plates.*
AAS.

1. Identical with the 1837 edition preceding.
2. Sabin No. 33045.

NUMBER 105 1840

A | REMINISCENCE | OF THE | BOLD AND SUCCESSFUL ADVENTURES | OF | SMALL SCOUTING PARTIES | OF | REVOLUTIONARY PATRIOTS, | AGAINST THE | British and Tories in South Carolina and Georgia, | DURING THE | REVOLUTIONARY WAR, | AS RELATED BY ONE WHO TOOK AN ACTIVE PART IN MANY OF THE SCENES. | Embellished with several beautiful Engravings. | NEW-YORK. |

1840. | 8vo. pp. 1, (1), 1, 4–40. *No plates.*
LC.

1. Consisting of extracts as follow: pp. 1–11 are the same as pp. 28–43 of the 1818 edition, title 90; pp. 12–18 correspond with pp. 46–53; pp. 18–22 with pp. 74–81; pp. 22–27 with pp. 108–114; pp. 27–28 with pp. 115–117; pp. 28–31 with pp. 118–124, with changes; pp. 31–33 with pp. 133–137; pp. 33–35 with pp. 153–156; pp. 36–37 with pp. 160–163; pp. 38–40 with Chapter XX.

NUMBER 106 1841

THE LIFE | OF | GEN. FRANCIS MARION, | [*Seven lines*] | BY BRIG. GEN. P. HORRY, OF MARION'S BRIGADE: | AND M. L. WEEMS. | [*Two lines of verse*] | STEREOTYPED BY L. JOHNSON. | PHILADELPHIA: |

PUBLISHED BY JOSEPH ALLEN. | AND SOLD BY GRIGG & ELLIOTT. | [*One line*] | 1841. | 12mo. pp. 8, (1), 5, IV–VI, 1, 8–251, (1). *Plates.*
BPL., HU.

1. Title identical with the 1837 and 1839 editions, titles 103 and 104; on reverse of title is Penn. copyright, dated 1824 to H. C. Carey & I. Lea, purchased by Joseph Allen; the eight front fly leaves consist of publishers' advertisements; five woodcuts after Anderson.

2. Sabin No. 33045.

NUMBER 107? 1844?

*The Life of Gen. Francis Marion. Philadelphia. Joseph Allen. [*1844?*]

1. A note of Mr. Clarence S. Brigham, who has seen but cannot locate it.
2. Sabin No. 33045.

NUMBER 108 1845

THE LIFE | OF | GEN. FRANCIS MARION, | [*Twelve lines*] | PHILADELPHIA: |

PUBLISHED BY JOSEPH ALLEN. | [*Two lines*] | 1845. | 12mo.
pp. 8, (1), 4, IV–VI, 1, 8–252, 1. *Front., Plates.*
AAS., HSP., LC.

1. The eight front fly leaves consist of publisher's advertisements, including Weems' *Marion* and *Washington;* six woodcuts after Anderson.

NUMBER 109 1847

THE LIFE | OF | GEN. FRANCIS MARION, | [*Twelve lines*] | PHILADELPHIA: |

PUBLISHED BY JOSEPH ALLEN. | [*Two lines*] | 1847. | 12mo.
pp. 252. *Front., Plates.*
YU.

1. Identical with the 1845 edition preceding.

NUMBER 110 1848

THE LIFE | OF | GEN. FRANCIS MARION, | A CELEBRATED | PARTISAN OFFICER | IN THE | REVOLUTIONARY WAR, | AGAINST THE | BRITISH AND TORIES | IN SOUTH CAROLINA AND GEORGIA. | BY | BRIG. GEN. P. HORRY, | OF MARION'S BRIGADE: AND | M. L. WEEMS. | "On VERNON'S CHIEF why lavish all our lays; | Come, honest Muse, and sing great MARION'S praise." | PHILADELPHIA: |

PUBLISHED BY JOSEPH ALLEN. | AND SOLD BY GRIGG, ELLIOTT & CO. | No 14 North Fourth Street. | 1848 | 12mo. pp. (1), 4, IV–VI, 1, 8–252. *Front., Plates.*
AAS., VStL.

1. A new title page; on reverse, besides copyright of 1824, is '*Stereotyped by* R. P. MOGRIDGE — PHILAD'A. *King & Baird, Printers.*'; the twelve front fly leaves consist of publisher's advertisements but without mention of Weems' works; the six plates are the same as in the last preceding Allen editions.

NUMBER 111 1851

THE LIFE | OF | GEN. FRANCIS MARION, | [*Seven lines*] | BY | BRIG. GEN. P. HORRY, | OF MARION'S BRIGADE: AND | M. L. WEEMS. | [*Two lines of verse*] PHILADELPHIA. |
PUBLISHED BY JOSEPH ALLEN, | SOLD BY | LIPPINCOTT, GRAMBO & CO., | No. 14 NORTH FOURTH STREET. | 1851. | 12mo. pp. (1), 4, IV–VI, 1, 8–252. *Front., Plates.*
AAS., NYPL.

1. On reverse of title, besides copyright of 1824, is stereotype notice by R. P. Mogridge, as in preceding title; there are six plates, including frontispiece.

NUMBER 112 1852

THE LIFE | OF | GEN. FRANCIS MARION, | [*Thirteen lines*] | PHILADELPHIA. |
PUBLISHED BY JOSEPH ALLEN, | [*Three lines*] | 1852. | 12mo. pp. (5), 4, IV–VI, 1, 8–252, 23, (5). *Front., Plates.*
AAS., YU.

1. Title and contents are identical with the 1851 edition, title 111, except for the twenty-three back fly leaves of publisher's advertisements added to this one.

NUMBER 113 1854

THE LIFE | OF | GEN. FRANCIS MARION, | [*Thirteen lines*] | PHILADELPHIA: |

PUBLISHED BY JOSEPH ALLEN, | [*Three lines*] | 1854. | 12mo. pp. (1), 4, IV–VI, 1, 8–252, (4). *Front., Plates.*
AAS., HU., LC.

1. Identical with the 1851 edition, title 111; six woodcuts after Anderson. The LC. copy has forty-six back fly leaves of publisher's advertisements, including Weems' *Marion* and *Washington.*

NUMBER 114 1855

THE LIFE | OF | GEN. FRANCIS MARION, | [*Thirteen lines*] | PHILADELPHIA: |

PUBLISHED BY JOSEPH ALLEN, | SOLD BY | J. B. LIPPINCOTT & CO. | NO. 20 NORTH FOURTH ST. | 1855. | 12mo. pp. 3, IV–VI, 1, 8–252, (2). *Front., Plates.*
AAS., BPL. [*lacks front.*]

1. Text and plates identical with 1851 edition, title 111.

NUMBER 115 1856

THE LIFE | OF | GENERAL FRANCIS MARION, | A CELEBRATED PARTISAN OFFICER, | IN THE | Revolutionary War, | AGAINST THE | BRITISH AND TORIES | IN | SOUTH CAROLINA AND GEORGIA. | BY | BRIG. GEN. P. HORRY, | OF MARION'S BRIGADE, AND | M. L. WEEMS, | FORMERLY RECTOR OF MOUNT VERNON PARISH. | [*Two lines of verse*] | PHILADELPHIA: |

J. B. LIPPINCOTT & CO. | 1856. | 12mo. pp. (1), 4, IV–VI, 1, 8–252, 1, 2–48. *Front., Plates.*
AAS.

1. New title page; 'Revolutionary War' is in Old English; frontispiece and five woodcuts after Anderson; last forty-eight pages consist of publishers' advertisements, including Weems' *Washington* and *Marion*, both at 63 cents.

NUMBER 116 1858

THE LIFE | OF | GENERAL FRANCIS MARION, | [*Fourteen lines*] | PHILADELPHIA: |

J. B. LIPPINCOTT & CO. | 1858. | 12mo. pp. 3, IV–VI, 1–252. *Front., Plates.*
AAS., PIL.

NUMBER 117 1859

THE LIFE | OF | GENERAL FRANCIS MARION, | [*Fourteen lines*] | PHILADELPHIA: |

J. B. LIPPINCOTT & CO. | 1859. | 12mo. pp. VI, 252. *Front., Plates.*
AAS.

NUMBER 118 1860

THE LIFE | OF | GENERAL FRANCIS MARION, | [*Fourteen lines*] | PHILADELPHIA: |

J. B. LIPPINCOTT & CO. | 1860. | 12mo. pp. VI, 252. *Front., Plates.*
LC.

NUMBER 119 1863

THE LIFE | OF | GENERAL FRANCIS MARION, | [*Fourteen lines*] | PHILADELPHIA: |

J. B. LIPPINCOTT & CO. | 1863. | 12mo. pp. VI, 252. *Front., Plates.*
AAS.

NUMBER 120 1866

THE LIFE | OF | GENERAL FRANCIS MARION, | [*Fourteen lines*] | PHILADELPHIA: |

J. B. LIPPINCOTT & CO. | 1866. | 12mo. pp. VI, 252. *Front., Plates.*
AAS.

NUMBER 121 1868

THE LIFE | OF | GENERAL FRANCIS MARION, | [*Fourteen lines*] | PHILADELPHIA: |

J. B. LIPPINCOTT & CO. | 1868. | 12mo. pp. VI, 252. *Front., Plates.*
AAS.

NUMBER 122 1879

THE LIFE | OF | GENERAL FRANCIS MARION, | [*Fourteen lines*] | PHILADELPHIA: |

J. B. LIPPINCOTT & CO. | 1879. | 12mo. pp. VI, 252. *Front., Plates.*
AAS.

NUMBER 123 1882?

THE LIFE OF | GEN'L FRANCIS MARION, | A CELEBRATED PARTISAN OFFICER IN THE REVOLUTIONARY WAR AGAINST THE | BRITISH AND TORIES IN SOUTH CAROLINA AND GEORGIA. | BY | BRIGADIER-GENERAL P. HORRY, | *Of Marion's Brigade.* | AND M. L. WEEMS. | [*Two lines of verse*] | NEW YORK |

UNITED STATES BOOK COMPANY | SUCCESSORS TO | JOHN W. LOVELL COMPANY | 142 TO 150 WORTH STREET | [*n.d. 1882?*] 12mo. pp. 1, 2, 1, (1), 1, 4–6, 1, 8–311, (1).
AAS.

1. Title page is of different paper from the rest of the book; on the page following appear the words 'Lovell's Library . . . Vol. 2, No. 36. Oct. 10, 1882.' and above 'Copyright 1882'. The cover title bears the same caption, but with the copyright date given as 1884, which we may assume refers to the copyright of some later numbers in Lovell's Series. The United States Book Company succeeded the John W. Lovell Company about 1890, and according to the New York directories, were located at 150 Worth Street only from 1891 to 1895. With the above facts in mind, I venture to place this issue as by the Lovell Company in 1882, assuming that the United States Book Company, after they had succeeded to the former, added their own title.

NUMBER 124 1883

THE LIFE OF | GEN'L FRANCIS MARION, | A CELEBRATED PARTISAN OFFICER IN THE REVOLUTIONARY WAR AGAINST THE | BRITISH AND TORIES IN SOUTH CAROLINA AND GEORGIA. | BY BRIGADIER-GENERAL P. HORRY, | *Of Marion's Brigade.* | AND | M. L. WEEMS. | [*Two lines*] | NEW YORK: |

JOHN B. ALDEN, PUBLISHER, | 1883. | 12mo. pp. 1, (1), 4–6, 1, 8–311, (1).
BPL.

1. Given complete in *Cyclopedia of Biography*, 1883.

NUMBER 125 1884

THE LIFE | OF | GENERAL FRANCIS MARION, | [*Seven lines*] | BY | BRIG. GEN. P. HORRY, | OF MARION'S BRIGADE, AND | M. L. WEEMS, | [*Three lines*] | PHILADELPHIA: |

J. B. LIPPINCOTT & CO. | 1884. | 12mo. pp. (1), 4, IV–VI, 1, 8–252.
*Front., Plates.*
LC.

1. On the title there are quotation marks only at the close of the two lines of verse; on reverse of title, Penn. copyright, dated 1824; six woodcuts after Anderson, identical with those in the 1854 edition, title 113.

NUMBER 126 1891

THE LIFE | OF | GENERAL FRANCIS MARION, | [*Seven lines*] | BY | BRIG. GEN. P. HORRY, | OF MARION'S BRIGADE, AND | M. L. WEEMS, | FORMERLY RECTOR OF MOUNT VERNON PARISH. | [*Two lines of verse*] | PHILADELPHIA: |

J. B. LIPPINCOTT COMPANY. | 1891. | 12mo. pp. (3), 4, IV–VI, 1, 8–252. *Front., Plates.*
AAS.

1. Of the six woodcuts, the frontispiece is transposed.

## EDITIONS OF DOUBTFUL DATE OR AUTHENTICITY

[See also titles 85, 89, 107 and 123.]

NUMBER 127? 1828?

*The Life of Gen. Francis Marion. Frankford. [*1828?*]

1. *Notes* of Paul L. Ford, but no reference given, and not seen by me.

NUMBER 128? 1829?

*The Life of Gen. Francis Marion. Frankford. [*1829?*]

1. *Notes* of Paul L. Ford, but no reference given, and not seen by me.

NUMBER 129? 1834?

*The Life of Gen. Francis Marion. Frankford. [*1834?*]

1. *Notes* of Paul L. Ford, but no reference given, and not seen by me.

NUMBER 130? 1839?

*The Life of General Francis Marion. Philadelphia. [*1839?*]

1. In J. T. Doonan's catalogue of a sale in Atlanta, Ga., date unknown, there was listed No. '40 Horry and Wheems. [*sic*] Life of General Francis Marion . . . Philadelphia, 1839.' If this was an accurate entry, it would appear to be a reprint of the 1835 New York edition, title 101, but it seems fully as probable that it represents a cataloguer's error for title 104.

NUMBER 131 1815

THE | LIFE | OF | DOCTOR BENJAMIN FRANKLIN, | WRITTEN CHIEFLY BY HIMSELF; | WITH A COLLECTION | Of his finest Essays, | HUMOROUS, MORAL, AND LITERARY. | A new edition, revised and enlarged | BY MASON L. WEEMS, | OF LODGE NO. 50, DUMFRIES. | BALTIMORE: |

PRINTED BY RALPH W. POMEROY, & CO. | No. 12, Light street. | 1815. | 12mo. pp. 3, 4–264. *Front.port. in one copy.*
AAS., HU., MdHS., NYPL.

1. Portrait [found only in NYPL. copy] engraved by Thackera & Vallance, 1794;[1] on reverse of title 'Picture of doctor Franklin, as he rose by the side of Washington, in the first congress, to rouse his countrymen to oppose Lord North's accursed "TAXATION without REPRESENTATION," and when the British armies and navies were darkening all our shores. | "Sage Franklin next arose, in cheerful mien, | And smill'd [*sic*], unruffled, o'er the solemn scene; | High on his locks of age, a wreath was brac'd, | Palm of all arts that e're a mortal grac'd — | Beneath him lies the sceptre kings have borne, | And crowns

[1] James Thackera, partner of John Vallance, 'but inferior to him as an engraver . . . long time keeper of the Pennsylvania Academy of Fine Arts . . . merely having charge of the property . . . a respectable citizen.' *History of the Rise and Progress of the Arts of Design in America*, William Dunlap, 1834, Vol. I, p. 432, LC. See also *American Engravers upon Copper and Steel*, David McNeely Stauffer, Vol. I, Part I, p. 267, NYPL. — John Vallance worked in partnership with James Thackera. *History of the Rise and Progress of the Arts of Design in America*, William Dunlap, 1834, Vol. I, p. 432, LC. — Vallance was an excellent script engraver, and good early bank-notes bear his name. *American Engravers upon Copper and Steel*, David McNeely Stauffer, Vol. I, Part I, p. 281.

and laurels from their temples torn." | *Barlow's Vision of Columbus.'* | ; the text consists of Franklin's *Autobiography* as far as p. 84; thereafter follow excerpts from *Poor Richard's Almanack* to p. 96, prefaced by remarks which may or may not be by Weems, though strongly smacking of him; from p. 96 to p. 205 there are letters and conversations quoted, with comments and other matter by Weems; from p. 206 to p. 264 there are more excerpts from Franklin's writings, without any original matter by Weems. The edition of 1815 is the first one thus far found. Probably it was called a 'New Edition' because it was practically a reprint of parts of Franklin's *Autobiography*, though it may be noted that in others of his works Weems possibly misnumbered his first editions.

2. Ford's *Franklin Bibliography:* 'The fourth "continuation" [*of Franklin's Autobiography*] was printed in 1815 in a chap-book edition of Franklin's works, and was from the lively imagination of Mason Locke Weems.' [Note to No. 382, p. 181.] Weems' Life of Franklin 'though . . . [*varying*] in many respects . . . [*was*] nevertheless based on . . . Works | of the late | Doctor Benjamin Franklin: | Consisting of | His Life Written by Himself, | together with | Essays, Humorous, Moral, & Literary, | Two Volumes. | Vol. I. | . . . | London: | Printed for G. G. J. and J. Robinson, | Paternoster Row | 1793.' [P. 221.] 'This retranslation of the autobiography and the collection of essays has become the "popular" and one might almost say the "chap-book" edition of Franklin's "Life and Writings" . . .' [No. 437, pp. 205, 207.] 'I have included the editions of it [*Weems' Life of Franklin*] in this list. Not satisfied with Stuber's continuation of the autobiography, the editor has added a new one "by one of his, [*Franklin's*] friends," which is about as accurate a description of Mr. Weems as his other title of "Washington's pastor." Having invented half a life of Franklin in this work, the editor printed three editions and then from his imagination wrote the whole life, editions of which are given . . . and which should not be confused with this [*authorized*] edition of the autobiography.' [No. 477, p. 221.] [See title 134 below, note 1.] 'Between the "old school" imaginative biography of Mr. Weems and the "new school" critical biography of Professor McMaster . . .' [P. 371.] '. . . the inventive Mr. Weems, in his *Life of Benjamin Franklin*, gives a stanza from the second [*The Taking of Teach, the Pirate, 1719*] (which fortunately for Franklin, we know to be by another hand). . .' [*F.n.* to title 1, p. 1.] 'Franklin's Life and Miscellaneous Works . . . revised and enlarged by the Rev. M. L. Weems, 12mo. 1 00'. Carey's Catalogue, 1816. 'Thackera & Vallance. Benjamin Franklin. Line. Oval. Bust; profile, right. 4.2 x 3.6. Inscription Engraved by Thackera & Vallance. Philad[a] 1794. | Benjamin Franklin, L.L.D.' Stauffer No. 3146.

3. Weems wrote to Carey [*n.d. 1810?*]: 'Neat cheap editions of . . . Doct[r] Franklins life w[d] do admirably.' In writing to Jefferson, July 31, 1815, for facts for his *Life of Franklin*, he said that Jefferson had 'read a thousand Magazines, Museums and all other publications perfum'd with praises of him by Rousseau, Voltaire, etc., etc., also enrich'd with Bons mots, Anecdotes, Stories, etc., etc., all which, if only tolerably "*cooked up*" wou'd make a savoury dish for Juvenile palates.' *Thomas Jefferson Correspondence, From the collections of William K. Bixby*, Worthington Chauncey Ford, pp. 224–225, LC. [For this letter and Jefferson's reply of Aug. 2, 1815, see *Letters*, Vol. III.] To Carey, Oct. 3, 1815: 'My Life of Franklin is finished, about 265 pages. I am confident you will prefer it to any Biography of his of that size that you have seen. . . . John Hagerty Baltimore will send you Franklin.' Dec. 11, 1815: 'The plates which you gave me for Franklin as also 400 of the impression are in the smallest of the two little trunklike boxes lying at M[r] Biorens.' Dec. 13, 1815: 'I INTREAT you to send me 100 or 200 of the plates of Franklin. They are in one of the *trunklike* boxes, (2 of which are lying at Citizen Bioren's) Shoud they be gone M[r]. W[m]. Woodward [*for Woodhouse*] has a plate of Franklin of which I am certain he w[d] let you strike 3 or 400 impressions.' Dec. 16, 1815: 'Sh[d] like to have all my pictures of Franklin & the plate, if you can get them. Woodhouse [1] has, he told me, a fine likeness of F. with the plate. If Bioren has sent my plate away w[d] it not be well to get Woodhouse's [*?*]' Dec. 28, 1815: 'Can you send on the ballance of the pictures of Franklin, or must I pay 20 Doll[s] (*inconvenient at this time!*) for a new plate [*?*]' Jan. 4, 1816: 'If you have not sent my pictures of Franklin, you can easily send them by some of y[r] numerous friends coming on to Balt[o].'

4. Despite Paul L. Ford's comment [see title 148, note 4], this work, although dealing with one of our public characters most full of flavor, is comparatively flat and tasteless, unlike most of Weems' writings. Perhaps Franklin, whom Lecky calls the epitome of common sense, did not lend himself to the hyperbolic treatment meted out to Washington and Marion, or possibly 'the bead' of Weems' effervescence worked itself off in his tracts at this period. Whatever the cause, it is clear that the author fails to register his hero of the moment in the reader's memory as he does, for praise or blame, for 'laughter or for tears' in the two earlier biographies. That Weems always appreciated

[1] '1766. William Woodhouse . . . was a binder and bookseller . . . died December 28, 1795, and was succeeded by *his son* of the same name.' *The History of Printing in America, with a Biography of Printers and an Account of Newspapers*, Isaiah Thomas, LL.D., in *Trans.&Col.AAS.*, Vol. VI, 1810, p. 238. See also *McCulloch's Additions* to the above in *ProcAAS.*, Vol. XXXI, 1922, p. 106.

Franklin is shown by his inclusion of some of his work as early as in *The Immortal Mentor* of 1793, with its subsequent issues under that or another title [see titles 219 to 225], as well as in *The Maryland & Virginia Almanac* of 1798 [title 236].

5. Weems 'would have made a first rate daily editor. He could alternate between pen, paste, and scissors, with rare felicity.' *Views and Reviews, Second Series*, William Gilmore Simms, p. 137. '. . . FRANKLIN'S KITE ABOVE SUSPICION by DONALD MCNICOL. . . . The reference to Franklin's kite experiments . . . it should be known that Weems's biography was a work mainly of imagination. . . .' *Times* (N.Y.), Jan. 8, 1925.

NUMBER 132 1817

THE | LIFE | OF | BENJAMIN FRANKLIN, | WRITTEN CHIEFLY BY HIMSELF; | WITH A | COLLECTION OF HIS BEST ESSAYS, | HUMOROUS, MORAL, AND LITERARY. | A NEW EDITION, REVISED AND ENLARGED | BY MASON L. WEEMS, | OF LODGE NO. 50, DUMFRIES. | "Sage Franklin next arose, in cheerful mien, | And smil'd, unruffled, o'er the solemn scene; | High on his locks of age, a wreath was brac'd, | Palm of all arts that e'er a mortal grac'd; | Beneath him lies the sceptre kings have borne, | And crowns and laurels from their temples torn." | *Barlow's Vision of Columbus.* | PHILADELPHIA: | PUBLISHED BY M. CAREY. | 1817. | 12mo. pp. (1), 5, 5–264. *Front. port.*

AAS., APhS., HSP., MdDio'nL.

1. The portrait is engraved, signed by Warnicke,[1] profile to left, with inscription below 'Benjamin Franklin | Born Jan$^{y}$. 17$^{th}$. 1706 Died April 17$^{th}$. 1790'; on reverse of title Penn. copyright to Mason L. Weems dated 1817.

2. 'Weems's (Rev. Mason L.) life of Dr. Benjamin Franklin. Written chiefly by himself; with a collection of his Essays, humorous, moral, and literary. A new edition, revised and enlarged, $1.' Carey's Catalogue, 1818. Alibone's

[1] John G. Warnicke. 'Died in Philadelphia Dec. 29, 1818. In 1811–14 and again in 1818, Warnicke was engraving in Phila. His one portrait found by the compiler, that of Franklin, is a very good piece of stipple work.' *American Engravers upon Copper and Steel*, David McNeely Stauffer, Vol. I, Part I, p. 285.

*Dictionary.* Ford's *Franklin Bibliography* No. 483. Brinley No. 3257. 'J. Warnicke Benjamin Franklin. Stip., vign. Bust; profile, left. 2.12 x 1.11. Ins. Warnicke Sc. | Benjamin Franklin | Born Jan$^{y}$ 17$^{th}$, 1706. Died April 17$^{th}$, 1790.' Stauffer No. 3350.

3. *Reviewed:* 'We have but a word or two to say respecting Mason L. Weems' edition of Dr. Franklin's Essays; and indeed, we placed it by the side of the other works [*previously reviewed*] chiefly because it is, in a small way, another example of the editorial abuse which that philosopher has suffered. We had another motive, also, in the character of the editor; who, if we have a correct account of him, has the power of doing considerable good, and considerable mischief, among the lower orders of readers in this country. If he "of Lodge No. 50, Dumfries" be the same that was formerly "Rector of Mount Vernon Parish," he has written a Life of Washington, which has reached the "seventeenth edition — greatly improved"; and, from the manner in which we understand he gets off a book, we suppose his Life of Franklin will go through an equal number of republications. Our readers should know, that he is an author, a pedlar, and a preacher. He writes a book, and carries it about the country; holding forth a goodly sermon in every village, and taking occasion to exhort all manner of persons to open their eyes and read fructifying books. The cart stands ready at the door; and, after a congregation have heard a sermon for nothing, they will seldom be so hard-hearted as not to pay for a book. This is the account we have of the matter. We cannot vouch for its accuracy; and, indeed, until we read his Life of Franklin, we could not ourselves believe, that the part which concerns the preaching had any foundation. The following passage, however, seems to be something like it. "Ye blind parents, who can think hard of laying out a few dollars for *books* [we use his own *italics*,] and education of your children; meanly grumbling all the time, as if it were so much precious money thrown *away*, *and lost forever*, O attend to this story of Dr. Franklin's! That is to say, give me a 'dollar for the book.' God grant it may open your eyes; and convince you that the most profitable pounds, shillings, and pence, which his father ever laid out on him, were laid out on his education and books." &c. &c. P. 138. Now as we take Mr. Weems to be one of those men, who mean no harm, we have a little piece of information for his own especial ear — namely, that, when he re-prints the memoir of a person, written by himself, the critics will not hold him guiltless, if he presumes to add or to omit any thing whatsoever, — and that, when he professes to give himself a continuation of such a memoir, he should be careful to avoid copying too closely, in any instance, a similar continuation by another hand . . . Mr. Weems has made it [*the Continuation by Dr. Stuber*] the substratum of his own article; but he has stuffed it

so full of queer expressions, that it is greatly altered *ab illo*. Sundry passages are entirely omitted; while others, again, have given away [*sic*] to such substitutions as none but a Lodger at 50 Dumfries, could ever have composed. The following Greek passage must suffice: — [*quoted from p. 105*] "To a common kite . . . the approach of her wanton mate . . ."' [*Anon.*] *Analectic Magazine*, Vol. 9, May, 1817, pp. 389–391, AAS. *Ad.* [*M.L.W.*] 'PROPOSALS OF M. L. WEEMS, FOR PRINTING BY SUBSCRIPTION THE LIVES OF *George Washington. Doctor Franklin*, and *General Marion* . . . in three separate volumes. . . .' *Martinsburgh Gaz.*, July 10, 1817, AAS. [For advertisement in full, see title 30, note 3. So far as I know this project was abortive.] Also advertised in *Frank. Repos.*, Nov. 25, 1817, FROF.

4. Weems wrote to Carey [*received July 11, 1816*]: 'You promis[d] to print Franklin & give me 33 1/3. I am not positive that I shall print that work this summer. At any rate I am willing to wave [*sic*] giving you the trouble and expense of printing that book for me if you chuse to give the same profit on Washington, which as the types are standing must cost you much less. . . . I ought to have show bills for Washington, for the sake of Merch[ts]. You give me no aid in these things.' Feb. 11, 1817: 'If Jessy [*sic*] be at hand, give him my manuscripts of Franklin that I sent you & also the two beautiful pictures I sent with them.'

NUMBER 133 1818

THE | LIFE | OF | BENJAMIN FRANKLIN; | WITH | MANY CHOICE ANECDOTES | AND | ADMIRABLE SAYINGS | OF THIS | GREAT MAN, | NEVER BEFORE PUBLISHED BY ANY OF HIS BIOGRA– | PHERS | BY M. L. WEEMS, | AUTHOR OF THE LIFE OF WASHINGTON. | THE THIRD EDITION GREATLY ENLARGED. | "Sage Franklin next arose in cheerful mien, | And smil'd, unruffled, o'er the solemn scene; | High on his locks of age a wreath was brac'd, | Palm of all arts that e'er a mortal grac'd; | Beneath him lay the sceptre kings had borne, | And crowns and laurels from their temples torne." | HAGERS–TOWN: |

PRINTED BY W. D. BELL, FOR THE AUTHOR. | 1818. | 12mo. pp. (2), 3, 4–337, (5).
EI.

1. No portrait.
2. Ford's *Franklin Bibliography* No. 485. Brinley No. 3258.
3. Weems wrote to Carey, July 1, 1817: 'Franklin is by no means in the right sailing trim. I have a small edition printing for you, which will I hope please you a good deal tho' still far short of what the book may be — it will be ready by Christmass.'
4. The *Torch Light* (Hagerstown) was published by William D. Bell in the only issue known of that year, June 15, 1819. *Bibliography of American Newspapers*, Clarence S. Brigham, *ProcAAS.*, Vol. XXV, Part I, p. 191.

No fourth edition found but there are two entitled 'Fifth.' See titles next succeeding.

NUMBER 134 1820

THE | LIFE | OF | BENJAMIN FRANKLIN; | WITH | MANY CHOICE ANECDOTES | AND | ADMIRABLE SAYINGS | OF THIS | GREAT MAN, | NEVER BEFORE PUBLISHED BY ANY OF HIS BIOGRAPHERS. | BY M. L. WEEMS, | AUTHOR OF THE LIFE OF WASHINGTON. | THE FIFTH EDITION, GREATLY ENLARGED. | "Sage Franklin next arose in cheerful mien, | And smil'd, unruffled, o'er the solemn scene; | High on his locks of age a wreath was brac'd, | Palm of all arts that e'er a mortal grac'd, | Beneath him lay the sceptre Kings had borne, | And crowns and laurels from their temples torn." | Baltimore: |
PRINTED BY JOHN D. TOY, FOR THE AUTHOR. | 1820. | 12mo.
pp. (1), 4, 4–264. *Front.port.*
AAS., LC.

1. The frontispiece, signed by Warnicke, is identical with that in the 1817 edition, title 132; on reverse of title Penn. copyright, dated 1817; the text differs from the earlier editions as follows: the Autobiography is eliminated, and the text by Weems is rewritten and enlarged, divided into Chapters I–XLIV, the citations from Franklin being mostly after XXXVII; near the end is given Franklin's own epitaph which, in the earlier editions, came in the body of the book. See also title 131, note 2.

2. 'The later editions [*of the Franklin*] are entirely by Weems, although in the first half he has done little more than turn the "Autobiography" into the narration of a third person.' *Parson Weems*, Lawrence C. Wroth, Baltimore, p. 87.

3. Carey wrote, Aug. 28, 1820: 'We have none of Franklin & very few of Marion.' Weems wrote to Carey, Aug. 31 [*1820*]: 'You have a number of Printers in arrears to you — wou'd it not be well to get one of them to strike off 1000 copies of Franklin according to the Hagerstown copy? Tanner has, from me, one of the best Likenesses of that Great Man I have ever seen.'[1] Sept. 12, 1820: 'The Character of that book is rising wonderfully & also that of Doct$^{r}$ Franklin, the Glorious Patriot of our Country . . . these Great Moralists . . .' From Carey, Sept. 19, 1820: 'There is too much in Franklin to be offer$^{d}$ for a Dollar, & moreover, the sales are not sufficient to warrant the expenditure of so much money as it w$^{d}$ require to print it at a time when money is so valuable. By the 1$^{st}$ Ed$^{n}$ of Franklin we are persuaded we did not make anything worth notice.' To Carey, Oct. 6, 1820: 'That Book [*Franklin*] may do [*more*], by promoting "THE SAVING VIRTUES," to prolong the Independence of this Country, than all the Maps in the World. I am shortening it & altering it prodigiously for the better. Truth is, since you seem so backward to print these Books of mine if you will recommend some Printer who will print them for me, at a profit that will enable me to give a Commanding Commission to Trust Worthy Agents you will do me a great kindness.' This seems to have 'drawn' Carey for on Oct. 25 he wrote: 'We are now printing a very handsome Edition of Marion which will be finished in about 3 or 4 Weeks & we shall then, if you think proper put Franklin to press. Try to curtail it. It is too extravagantly long for a Dollar.' To Carey, Nov. 27, 1820: 'As to *Franklin*, I have not heard twice from you: but will soon have the copy ready for you — that being my chief employment at nights. I wish you wd send me a "PICTURE OF PHILADELPHIA" [2] for my own use in draw$^{g}$ up Franklin & Penn [3] . . . And if there be in y$^{r}$ possession anything new & valuable concerning Franklin, such as the Book lately printed in England, I sh$^{d}$ like to see it — We may, perhaps, in the course of one or two editions more, get that most Exemplary Great Man into a better travelling case than he has yet been. When we think of what we have done with his illustrious Compat[*riot*]. Washington we must keep up our hopes.' Dec. 8, 1820: 'I intreat you forget not M$^{rs}$. Weems. As much friendship as I have for you and

[1] According to note 1 above, evidently Toy, the printer, did not carry out this desire of Weems as expressed to Carey.

[2] *The Picture of Philadelphia*. . . . By James Mease, M.D., Philadelphia: . . . B. & T. Kite. . . . 1811. LC.

[3] Titles 148 *et seq.*

Henry, I will go off by myself to Davies [1] & Franklin & Marion [2] &c. &c. rather than have a woman so deservedly dear to me & her daughters starving in pining solitude. I verily believe that if Mrs. Carey had written such a letter to you as I got from her, you woud print no more Bibles.'

4. 'Toy, John D. printer, office cor. of Baltimore and Light' *Baltimore Directory*, 1819, LC.

NUMBER 135 1821

## THE | LIFE | OF | BENJAMIN FRANKLIN; | WITH | MANY CHOICE ANECDOTES | AND | ADMIRABLE SAYINGS | OF THIS | GREAT MAN, | [*One line*] | BY M. L. WEEMS, | AUTHOR OF THE LIFE OF WASHINGTON. | THE FIFTH EDITION, GREATLY ENLARGED. | [*Six lines of verse*] | Baltimore: |

PRINTED BY JOHN D. TOY, FOR THE AUTHOR. | 1821. | 12mo.
pp. (2), 4, 4–264. *Front.port.*
AAS., APhS., BPL., EI. [*lacks port.*], LC.

1. The frontispiece is identical with that in the 1817 edition; the longer text, as rewritten, see title 131, note 2, and title 134, note 1.

2. Ford's *Franklin Bibliography* No. 989. 'Life of . . . Franklin . . . Rev. M. L. Weems . . .' M. Carey & Son's Catalogue for June, 1821. *Benjamin Franklin, Life and Writings*, Henry Stevens, No. 164, NYPL.

3. *Ad.* 'COMMUNICATION . . . at Schenk's Book Store; also of the Life of Franklin, the 5th edition. A part of the profits, sacred to the Sunday Schools, will be deposited with William B. Bulloch, Esq. M. L. WEEMS.' *Georgian*, May 18, 1821, GAHS. 'Messrs. Pasteur & Watson, You will oblige your friend, the undersigned . . . at the Druggist Store of Dr. E. Hawes . . . may be had, the Biographies of . . . FRANKLIN . . .' *Car. Cent.*, June 16, 1821, NYHS. '. . . Rev. M. L. Weems, who has written the EXEMPLARY LIVES OF . . . Franklin . . .' *Georgian*, Apr. 18, 1822, GAHS. Also advertised in: *Ibid.*, May 15, 1821 *et seq.*, GAHS.; *Charles. Cour.*, Feb. 16, 1822, CLS.

4. Weems wrote to Carey, Nov. 28, 1820: 'Mr. Lovegrove [3] Says he & Mr. Toy, will print a very handsome edition of Franklin — also bind it, and take

[1] Title 239.

[2] Title 91.

[3] 'Lovegrove, James, book binder and stationer, 20 S Calvert, dw. Lovely lane, S side E of Calvert st' *Baltimore Directory*, 1822. LC.

it out in Family Bibles at a *Disct. of 25 pr. cent.* This I promis$^{d}$ them to mention to you for y$^{r}$ consideration. You can note it in your next.' Dec. 8, 1820: 'M$^{r}$. Toy has the Franklin in hand. He wants the *paper* INSTANTLY. O let it be *good.* Toy says he wants to make the work SHINE. I w$^{d}$ God you w$^{d}$ get a better likeness of that greatest of the American Patriots & who has been so *shamefully neglected.* Honest James Lovegrove, the Quaker Bookbinder here [*Baltimore*], says he will bind Franklin, for thee at 20 cents — & handsomely.'

NUMBER 136 1822

THE | LIFE | OF | BENJAMIN FRANKLIN; | WITH | MANY CHOICE ANECDOTES | AND | ADMIRABLE SAYINGS | OF THIS | GREAT MAN, | [*One line*] | BY M. L. WEEMS, | AUTHOR OF THE LIFE OF WASHINGTON. | THE SIXTH EDITION. | [*Six lines of verse*] | *Philadelphia:* |

H. C. CAREY & I. LEA — CHESNUT-STREET. | 1822. | 12mo. pp. (1), 4, 4–264. *Front. port.*
BPL., HSP., LC., MHS., NYHS., PStL.

1. Frontispiece and copyright as in former editions.

2. Ford's *Franklin Bibliography* No. 990. Brinley No. 3259. Alibone's *Dictionary.*

NUMBER 137 1829

THE LIFE | OF | BENJAMIN FRANKLIN; | WITH MANY | CHOICE ANECDOTES | AND | ADMIRABLE SAYINGS OF THIS GREAT MAN, | [*One line*] | BY MASON L. WEEMS, | AUTHOR OF THE LIFE OF WASHINGTON | [*Six lines of verse*] | STEREOTYPED BY L. JOHNSON | Philadelphia: |

PUBLISHED BY URIAH HUNT, No. 147 MARKET STREET, | AND MORTON & CO. LOUISVILLE, (KEN.) | 1829. | 12mo. pp. (1), 3, (2), 1, 6–239, (1). *Front. port., Plates.*
AAS., HSP., LC., NYPL., PIL.

1. The frontispiece, unsigned, is a woodcut, half length, face to left, in an oval set in an upright rectangle with horizontal lines and with lightning, sun's

rays, laurels and bays, plain lined border; height of rectangle, 3 3/16, width 2 7/16; this and the other plates are signed 'F. G. Harrison,' and have no inscriptions; Penn. copyright to Uriah Hunt, dated 1829, on reverse of title; in Chapters I–XLVIII [misprint for XLIII] the text is the same as the 1820 edition. See notes to other 1829 edition succeeding.

2. Ford's *Franklin Bibliography* No. 991.

NUMBER 138 1829

THE LIFE | OF | BENJAMIN FRANKLIN; | WITH MANY | CHOICE ANECDOTES | AND | ADMIRABLE SAYINGS OF THIS GREAT MAN, | [*One line*] | BY MASON L. WEEMS, | AUTHOR OF THE LIFE OF WASHINGTON | [*Six lines of verse*] | STEREOTYPED BY L. JOHNSON | Philadelphia: |

PUBLISHED BY URIAH HUNT, NO. 19 N. THIRD STREET, | AND MORTON & CO. LOUISVILLE, (KEN.) 1829. | 12mo. pp. (1), 5, 6–239, (2). *Front.port.*

BPL., EI., MdHS., YU.

1. Some copies lack portrait; Penn. copyright dated 1829 on reverse of title; is identical but for the change in the publisher's address with the other 1829 edition. The *Philadelphia Directory* for 1828, 1829 and 1830 gives Hunt's address as 147 High St., which was then interchangeable with the name of Market St. I have not seen the 1832 *Directory*. That of 1833 gives Hunt's address as 19 N. Third St., which would make this issue not earlier than 1831 at earliest, yet there is an 1829 edition of the *Life of William Penn*, also stereotyped by Johnson for Hunt, who was then at 19 North Third St., see title 150.

NUMBER 139 1834

THE LIFE | OF | BENJAMIN FRANKLIN; | WITH MANY | CHOICE ANECDOTES | AND | ADMIRABLE SAYINGS OF THIS GREAT MAN, | [*One line*] | BY MASON L. WEEMS, | AUTHOR OF THE LIFE OF WASHINGTON | [*Six lines of verse*] | STEREOTYPED BY L. JOHNSON | Philadelphia: |

PUBLISHED BY URIAH HUNT, NO. 19 N. THIRD STREET, | AND MORTON & CO. LOUISVILLE, (KEN.) 1834. | 12mo. pp. 239. *Front.port., Plates.*
JHL.

1. Identical with the second 1829 edition.
2. Ford's *Franklin Bibliography* No. 992.

NUMBER 140 1835

THE LIFE | OF | BENJAMIN FRANKLIN; | WITH MANY | CHOICE ANECDOTES | AND | ADMIRABLE SAYINGS OF THIS GREAT MAN, | [*One line*] | BY M. L. WEEMS. | AUTHOR OF THE LIFE OF WASHINGTON | [*Six lines of verse*] | STEREOTYPED BY L. JOHNSON. | Philadelphia: |

PUBLISHED BY URIAH HUNT, NO. 101 MARKET STREET | AND SOLD BY ALL THE BOOKSELLERS IN THE UNITED STATES | 1835. | 12mo. pp. (1), 4, 6–239, (1). *Front.port., Plates.*
AAS., BA., BM., BPL., HC., LC., MHS., NYPL., WL.

1. Identical with the second 1829 edition.
2. Alibone's *Dictionary*.

NUMBER 141 1845

THE LIFE | OF | BENJAMIN FRANKLIN; | WITH MANY | CHOICE ANECDOTES | AND | ADMIRABLE SAYINGS OF THIS GREAT MAN, | [*One line*] | BY M. L. WEEMS, | AUTHOR OF THE LIFE OF WASHINGTON. | [*Six lines of verse*] | STEREOTYPED BY L. JOHNSON. | PHILADELPHIA: |

URIAH HUNT & SON, | NO. 44 NORTH FOURTH STREET. | AND FOR SALE BY BOOKSELLERS GENERALLY THROUGHOUT | THE UNITED STATES. | 1845. | 12mo. pp. 239, 1–9. *Front. port., Plates.*
AAS.

1. The portrait and plates are identical with those in the preceding editions of the same publishers; the nine back fly leaves consist of publishers' advertisements.

2. Ford's *Franklin Bibliography* No. 993.

NUMBER 142 1854

THE LIFE | OF | BENJAMIN FRANKLIN; | [*Five lines*] | BY M. L. WEEMS, | AUTHOR OF THE LIFE OF WASHINGTON. | [*Six lines of verse*] | STEREOTYPED BY L. JOHNSON. | PHILADELPHIA: |

URIAH HUNT & SON, | NO. 44 NORTH FOURTH STREET. | CINCINNATI: APPLEGATE & CO. | 1854. | 12mo. pp. (1), 3, 6–239, 3, 2. *Front.port., Plates.*
AAS., CIPL.

1. Contents are identical with the preceding editions of the same publishers; the two back fly leaves consist of publishers' advertisements.

NUMBER 143 1873

THE LIFE | OF | BENJAMIN FRANKLIN; | [*Five lines*] | BY M. L. WEEMS, | AUTHOR OF THE LIFE OF WASHINGTON. | [*Six lines of verse*] | STEREOTYPED BY L. JOHNSON. | PHILADELPHIA: |

URIAH HUNT'S SONS, | NO. 64 NORTH FOURTH ST. | 1873. | 12mo. pp. (3), 4, 6–239, (3). *Front.port., Plates.*
AAS., HSP., LC.

NUMBER 144 1876

THE LIFE | OF | BENJAMIN FRANKLIN; | [*Fourteen lines*] | PHILADELPHIA: |

URIAH HUNT'S SONS, | LIPPINCOTT & CO. NO. 64 NORTH FOURTH ST. | 1876. | 12mo. pp. (3), 4, 6–239, (1). *Front.port., Plates.*

1. Collated by me in Cator's bookshop, Baltimore, 1921. Identical with the preceding editions.

NUMBER 145 1884

*THE LIFE | OF | BENJAMIN FRANKLIN; . . . J. B. Lippincott & Co. | PHILADELPHIA: | 1884 | 12mo. pp. 239. *Plates.*

1. Ford's *Franklin Bibliography* No. 994.

## EDITIONS OF DOUBTFUL DATE OR AUTHENTICITY

NUMBER 146? 1825?

*Life of Benjamin Franklin. Fifth edition. Frankford. [*1825?*]

1. Ford's *Franklin Bibliography*, p. 391, *f.n.:* 'I have also found mention in catalogues of issues dated 1825, 1839 and 1854.' [The 1854 edition is the only one of these which I have found. See title 142.]

NUMBER 147? 1839?

*The Life of Benjamin Franklin. [*1839?*]

1. Not found, but see note to preceding title.

NUMBER 148 1822

THE LIFE | OF | WILLIAM PENN, | THE | SETTLER OF PENNSYLVANIA. | THE | *Founder of Philadelphia, and one of the First Lawgivers* | *in the Colonies, now United States, in* 1682. | CONTAINING ALSO | His celebrated treaty with the Indians — his purchase of their coun- | try — valuable anecdotes of Admiral Penn — also of King Charles | II, King James II, King William, and Queen Anne, in whose | reigns William Penn lived — curious circumstances that | led him to become a Quaker — with a view of the ad- | mirable traits in the character of the People cal- | led FRIENDS or QUAKERS, who have | done so much to meliorate the con- | dition of suffering humanity. | BY M. L. WEEMS, | Author of the Life of Washington, &c. | *Character of William Penn, by Montesquieu.* | "William Penn is a real Lycurgus. And though the former made PEACE his | principal aim, as the latter did WAR; yet they resemble one another in the sin- | gular way of living to which they reduced their people — in the astonishing ascen- | dant they gained over freemen; and in the strong passions which they subdued." | *Character of William Penn, by Edmund Burke.* | "William Penn, as a Legislator, deserves immortal thanks from the whole | world. 'T is pleasing to do honour to these *great men* whose *virtues* and *genero-* | *sity* have contributed to the peopling of the earth, and to the *Freedom* and *happi-* | *ness* of *mankind;* and who have preferred the interest of a remote Posterity and | times unknown, to their own fortune, and to the quiet and security of their own | lives." | PHILADELPHIA: |

H. C. CAREY & I. LEA — CHESNUT STREET. | 1822. | 12mo. pp. (6), 3, 2–219, (5). *Front.port.*
AAS., CLS., LC., MHS., NYHS., NYPL., PStL., YU.

1. The frontispiece, unsigned, is engraved, stippled, in oval, bust length, face to right, with inscription below border 'William Penn. | B. 1644. D. 1718'; on reverse of title, Eastern District of Penn. copyright to H. C. Carey & I. Lea, dated Jan. 10, 1822.

2. *Reviewed:* 'The Rev. Dr. Abercrombie,[1] of Philadelphia, thus eulogizes the "*Life of Penn,*" by the Rev. M. L. Weems, just published. I have just got the life of William Penn, by M. L. Weems, and have perused it with that high degree of satisfaction which I have always experienced from his publications. Indeed, the life of that extraordinary man, who first settled *Philadelphia,* one of the most flourishing of the American colonies — who founded that most regular and beautiful of cities, *Philadelphia* and who accomplished all this by means so honorable to Christianity, and so instructive to all Legislators and Politicians, that the greatest Philosophers have unanimously placed him on a ground still higher than that even of Lycurgus and Solon. The life of such a man could hardly have been so written as not to excite an interest: but from the pen of Mr. Weems, it has come forth with an effect entertaining and interesting in a high degree. Indeed, so fully has he entered into the spirit of his hero (Wm. Penn) that those who do not know the author would suppose him to be a Quaker of the first class, instead of an orthodox Episcopal Clergyman. But still the native gaiety of his genius, and his extraordinary talent for enlivening his pages, and refreshing his reader, shines out, at proper intervals, in streams of humor of the most genuine and fascinating lustre. He has certainly drawn a portrait of the *old Admiral* (father of the great Wm.) in as vivid colors, and as correct costume, as Sterne has that of "*my uncle Toby.*" I only wish he had given us more of it — a *full length* instead of a *bust:* for there is a peculiar vein of wit and raciness, and an originality of thought, in his writings, which are seldom to be met with, and which never

[1] 'Abercrombie James, D.D. senior assistant minister of Christ Church, St. Peter's and St. James', 111 Spruce' *Philadelphia Directory,* 1823, LC. — Rev'd Charles H. Wharton, D.D. and the Rev'd James Abercrombie, D.D. writers of 'The Quarterly Theological Magazine and Religious Repository,' a periodical work. *Lancaster Journal,* Apr. 11, 1817 *et seq.,* LIOF.

fail to seize the hearts of his readers, especially the young, with sentiments the most friendly to Virtue and Happiness. JAMES ABERCROMBIE. Philadelphia, Feb. 25, 1822.' *Charles. Cour.*, April 11, 1822, CLS. *Ad.* [*M.L.W.?*] 'Communicated for The Georgian. Most people have been taught to think highly of William Penn . . . 'Tis a pleasure to us to inform our readers that the Rev. M. L. Weems . . . the Life of Penn. . . . One volume, neatly bound; price one dollar; may be procured at the book stores, Savannah.' *Georgian*, Apr. 18, 1822, GAHS. [Including mentions of Weems' *Washington*, *Franklin* and *Marion.*] Also advertised in *Charles. Cour.*, Mar. 24, 1825, CLS. Mentioned in *Annals of Philadelphia and Pennsylvania*, John F. Watson and Willis P. Hazard, 1877, Vol. I, p. 123, HSP.

3. In a letter to James Madison, dated Feb. 20, 1820, Weems speaks of Penn being 'launch$^{d}$ and, thank Heaven, nearly half seas over — of the 1$^{st}$ edition.' [I have never found an edition of so early a date as this, nor any further evidence that there was one — see also letter of Nov. 27, 1820, in title 134, note 3. Weems sedulously stalked every anecdote which might prove readable or popular, as shown in his letter to Thomas Jefferson of Oct. 14, 1821. See *Letters*, Vol. III. Jefferson's reply, endorsed on the letter, was probably the means of an amiable and picturesque historical myth being lost to the credulous reading public for all time.] To Carey, Nov. 8, 1821: 'These moralizing Biographies especially with Penn in the squadron, & the *Moral* Looking Glasses, will help many a poor child to early wisdom, and Patriotism & honor like Washington &c &c.' Nov. 17, 1821: 'How do you come on with Penn?' Dec. 13, 1821: 'What have you done with W$^{m}$. Penn? I wish you w$^{d}$ make haste & put him in print & send me a couple of Copies, that I may go over his work & get it into better fix.' M. Carey & Son to Weems, Dec. 18, 1821: 'W. Penn will be finished shortly & shall be forwarded shortly.' Weems to Henry C. Carey, Mar. 2, 1822: 'What are you going to do with Penn? It will sell — but you wont say anything about it.' Mar. 14, 1822: 'I reciev$^{d}$, yesterday, a very flattering letter on Penn, from Doct$^{r}$. Abercrombie. If you cou'd think of some person in Philad$^{a}$, perhaps such an one as Doct$^{r}$ Griffith, who wou'd give us an ad captandum *critique* commendatory of it — and have this printed & sent with the Books, it w$^{d}$ be well. In that case, and especially if the critique, like an aurora borealis, threw up some fine streaks of light pointing towards that high Zenith of fame where Montesquieu & Burke & Voltaire & so on, have placed W$^{m}$ Penn, among the First Founders & Legislators of this Country, you might send 25 to Cottom, Richmond. . . . Tell the Rev$^{d}$ M$^{r}$. Abercrombie that I got his letter — & that I wish he w$^{d}$ give you a Critique on PENN — in short I sh$^{d}$ be glad [*if*] the world

were all Penns. There w[d] be no more Wars nor Cruelties among mankind.' Apr. 10, 1822: 'I wish M. Carey w[d] draw up a critique on Penn & have it printed in large letters.'

4. 'In Penn are strong evidences that even Weems' imagination had its limits. In each of his other biographies he had succeeded in coining an anecdote which almost at once took its place in tradition & popular acceptance. George & his "little hatchet" Marion giving the British officer roast corn for dinner: Franklin's requesting his father to say grace over all the pork barrels at once, have, for better or worse, become established in our mythology: In his last biography Weems invented no such bit, & though the work sold well at the time, it is the only one of the four which has ceased to do so.' *Notes* of Paul L. Ford, written before 1900.

NUMBER 149 1829

THE LIFE | OF | WILLIAM PENN, | THE | SETTLER OF PENNSYLVANIA, | THE | FOUNDER OF PHILADELPHIA, AND ONE OF THE FIRST LAWGIVERS | IN THE COLONIES, NOW UNITED STATES, IN 1682. | CONTAINING ALSO, | HIS CELEBRATED TREATY WITH THE INDIANS — HIS PURCHASE OF | THEIR COUNTRY — VALUABLE ANECDOTES OF ADMIRAL PENN — ALSO | OF KING CHARLES II., KING JAMES II., KING WILLIAM, AND QUEEN | ANNE, IN WHOSE REIGNS WILLIAM PENN LIVED — CURIOUS CIRCUM- | STANCES THAT LED HIM TO BECOME A QUAKER — WITH A VIEW OF | THE ADMIRABLE TRAITS IN THE CHARACTER OF THE PEOPLE | CALLED FRIENDS OR QUAKERS, WHO HAVE DONE SO MUCH TO | MELIORATE THE CONDITION OF SUFFERING HUMANITY. | BY M. L. WEEMS, | Author of the Life of Washington, &c. | *Character of William Penn, by Montesquieu.* | *[Four lines]* | *Character of William Penn, by Edmund Burke.* | *[Five lines]* | Philadelphia: |

PUBLISHED BY URIAH HUNT, 147 MARKET STREET, | AND MORTON & Co. LOUISVILLE, (KEN.) | STEREOTYPED BY L. JOHNSON. | 1829. | 12mo. pp. (3), 4, 5–208, (2). *Front.port.*
BPL., EI. [*lacks port.*], LCPhil. [*imp.*], MdHS., NYHS., NYPL., PStL., UTS.

1. The frontispiece is identical with that in the edition of 1822; on reverse of title, 'Eastern District' of Penn. copyright to Uriah Hunt, 1829. The only difference between this and the other 1829 edition which follows lies in the publisher's address. See note to later 1829 edition of the *Life of Franklin*, title 138.
2. Alibone's *Dictionary*.

NUMBER 150 1829

THE LIFE | OF | WILLIAM PENN, | THE | SETTLER OF PENNSYLVANIA, | [*Twelve lines*] | BY M. L. WEEMS, | [*Twelve lines*] | Philadelphia: |

PUBLISHED BY URIAH HUNT, NO. 19 N. THIRD STREET, | AND MORTON & CO. LOUISVILLE, (KEN.) | STEREOTYPED BY L. JOHNSON. | 1829. | 12mo. pp. (3), 4, 5–208, (2). *Front.port.*
AAS. [*lacks port.*], LC., NYHS., NYPL., UTS.

1. The portrait is identical with that in the 1822 edition.

NUMBER 151 1836

THE LIFE | OF | WILLIAM PENN, | THE | SETTLER OF PENNSYLVANIA, | [*Twelve lines*] | BY M. L. WEEMS, | [*Twelve lines*] | Philadelphia: |

PUBLISHED BY URIAH HUNT, No. 101 MARKET ST., | AND SOLD BY THE BOOKSELLERS GENERALLY THROUGHOUT THE UNITED STATES. | *Stereotyped by L. Johnson.* | 1836. | 12mo. pp. (2), 3, 6–208, (2). *Front.port.*
AAS. [*lacks port.*], BA., HU. [*lacks port.*], LC., NYPL., VStL.

NUMBER 152 1845

THE LIFE | OF | WILLIAM PENN, | [*Fourteen lines*] BY M. L. WEEMS, | [*Twelve lines*] | PHILADELPHIA: |

URIAH HUNT & SON. | No. 44 NORTH FOURTH STREET. | AND FOR SALE BY BOOKSELLERS GENERALLY THROUGHOUT THE | UNITED STATES. | 1845. | 12mo. pp. (1), 4, 6–282. *Front.port.*
BPL.

NUMBER 153 1850

THE LIFE | OF | WILLIAM PENN, | [*Fourteen lines*] | BY M. L. WEEMS, | [*Twelve lines*] | PHILADELPHIA: |
URIAH HUNT & SON, | NO. 44 NORTH FOURTH STREET. | AND FOR SALE BY BOOKSELLERS GENERALLY THROUGHOUT THE | UNITED STATES. | 1850. | 12mo. pp. (2), 3, 6–208, (8).
AAS.

1. No portrait; the eight back fly leaves contain publishers' advertisements, including Weems' *Life of Penn*, pp. 282.

NUMBER 154 1854

THE LIFE | OF | WILLIAM PENN, | [*Fourteen lines*] | BY M. L. WEEMS, | [*Twelve lines*] | PHILADELPHIA: |
URIAH HUNT & SON. | [*Three lines*] | 1854. | 12mo. pp. (2), 3, 6–208, 1, 28–100, 1, 2–6, (2).
AAS.

1. No portrait; the last pp. 1, 28–100, consist of 'Reflections and Maxims of William Penn'; the six back fly leaves contain publishers' advertisements, including Weems' *Franklin* and *Penn*, pp. 282.

## EDITION OF DOUBTFUL DATE OR AUTHENTICITY

NUMBER 154A? 1859?

*The Life of William Penn . . . PHILADELPHIA. [*1859?*]

1. *Note* of Paul L. Ford, giving no authority.

# MISCELLANEOUS WORKS BY MASON LOCKE WEEMS

NUMBER 155? 1798–1799?

## *The Lover's Almanac. [*1798–1799?*]

1. Vainly sought, yet from those that follow, as well as other letters, it appears that there actually was such an imprint. As early as Aug. 4, 1797 Weems wrote to Carey of his plan to print 'the Lovers Almanac, the *Devils* Almanac and I dont know what else.' [See title 174, note 2.] By 1798 already he was vending Almanacs, in which he may have had a part proprietary interest if not entire ownership. [See title 236.] For Carey wrote to him as early as Feb. 20th of that year: 'By Guthrie's Geography [1] alone you might have made more in twelve months, than you will clear in five years pedling with shabby almanacs & chap Books.' Weems wrote to him, Sept. 1, 1798: 'I shall go down shortly to sell some of my Almanacs. . . . The moment I get clear of my almanacs. . . .' And again, Nov. 19, 1798: 'You may laugh at it, but we cou'd make (*clear*) 300 Dol. pr. an. by Almanacs, I have just printed 10,000 of the *Lovers Almanac*, containing a beautiful treatise on Love, courtship & matrimony. My first edition (5,000) are more than half sold at 5/7½ pr doz. My last and handsomer edition (5,000) one third sold, at 7/6 per doz. Centaur like, tis half fabulous, half real, half my own, and half borrow'd.' This implies that matter similar to his two *Hymens*, either or both [titles 160 *et seq.* to 171A], and his *Virginia*, and *Virginia and North Carolina Almanacs for 1800* [titles 172 and 172A] was in the issue. See also notes to title succeeding.

[1] See title 242.

NUMBER 155A? 1799–1800?

*The Bachelor's Almanac. [*1799–1800?*]

1. It is, of course, possible that Weems' allusions to this title in his letters below may refer only to either of the two Almanacs for 1800 issued by him in 1799 [titles 172 and 172A] as those contain similar matter of his own. Yet his references over a period of more than a year are so definite that it has seemed expedient to include this title among his works. As those other two Almanacs for 1800 were unearthed only after a search of more than ten years, it may be hoped that this and the preceding title may yet be brought to light. What seems likely is that Weems in 1799 issued this third imprint under the above title, at the same time putting out exactly the same text but with the more restrained titles of *The Virginia* and *The Virginia & North Carolina Almanacs*. In the *Mathew Carey Account Books* [Vol. 16 : 6812, AAS.] Robert Cochran's bill rendered to him, dated July 10, 1798, 'To Sundry Printing on acc[t] of M[r] Weems £16 12 9' is for too large an amount for circulars, etc. An ample edition of an almanac would explain it and this lends further slight credence to this issue above. The only other 1798 imprint found was printed by Green & English [title 236].

2. By Mar. 19, 1799 Weems' sales were in full tide, for he wrote to Carey on that date: 'I have 3000 Doll. worth of Blairs Sermons. I wish you to assist me to get clear of these in a way perfectly easy and highly advantageous to yourself. I can sell this fall between 10 and 20,000 Almanacs, and @ from 50 to 65 cents pr Doz. Can't you print these for me (on one sheet Royal or super royal paper) in [*sic*] such terms as to get Blair's Sermons at nearly one third of their value [*?*] . . . I will obligate myself to remit you *two thirds*, two dollars out of three, *of all that* I sell which will be very fast, for it will be a continuation of the Lover's Alm[c]. w[h] has met with a great run among the young people of this State [*Va.*]. I have sold off (2 gross excepted) the whole of two large editions. . . . At Norfolk . . . delug[d] with Alm[cs]. I sold 6 or 700 in a little time. I suppose that 12,000 Alm[cs]. containing each but one sheet super royal might be printed for *a trifle*. . . . Alm[cs]. will bring the money. And if I were to sell 1 or 2,000 doz. and you get 8 or 900 Doll[s]. 'twoud be a handsome thing on such a small affair as an Alm[c]. w[h] I w[d] manage *in conjunction with better business*. The sooner I can get clear of my stock in hand the sooner shall I be ready to cooperate with you on a large & mutually profitable plan.' Sept. 17, 1799: 'I have . . . just got out my Bachelors Almanac, with an Essay (by myself) entitled "Hymen's Recruiting Serjeant." Much admir[d] by the best Critics in Alexandria where last week I sold 8 gross in one day & an half. Be assur[d] Friend Carey I am in-

capable of doing you intentional wrong. As to your books, in the coming spring, when we can start even, I am your man. Yours with a fervent prayer that I may live to better your fortune to the tune of Cent per Cent.' On Oct. 7, 1799, he alluded to his successful sales [see title 156, note 3] and once more, Oct. 21, 1799: 'I have sold about 8,000 of my Bachelors Alm$^{c}$. already.' See also his letter of Nov. 24, 1799 [title 156, note 3] and the notes to the two *Hymens*, titles 160–171A, and to the *Bachelor's Almanac*, title 186. By 1801, for which year Carey printed his first *Franklin Almanac*, the case is different, for Weems speaks of that as 'our' [titles 174 and 175]. See also title 172, note 2.

3. See also notes to titles 160–171A and 186.

NUMBER 156 1799?

## THE PHILANTHROPIST; | OR, | A GOOD TWELVE CENTS WORTH | OF | POLITICAL LOVE POWDER, | FOR THE FAIR DAUGHTERS | AND | PATRIOTIC SONS OF | VIRGINIA. | ALL MEN ARE EQUAL. | "SOHO! What the plague have we here now? . . ." |

[*n.d. 1799?*] 8vo. pp. 1, (1), 1, 4–28+ [*30*].
MdHS. [*imp.*]

1. Caption title only; on a separate sheet preceding the caption title is 'To his Excellency George Washing- | ton, Esquire, Lieutenant General of | the Armies of the United States. | *Most Honor'd General,* | Scarcely was I delivered of this | young republican Philanthropist, before I began, | according to good Christian *usage*, to look about for | a suitable god-father for it. My thoughts, presump- | tuously enough, I confess, instantly fixed on you — | for *two* reasons.

First, I was desirous of paying to | you, (as being next to God, the *greatest* benefactor | of my dear country) this little mite of grateful & affec- | tionate respect: — and Secondly, because I well know | there exists not on this side of heaven, the man who | will more cordially than *General Washington*, approve of | whatever tends to advance the harmony and happiness | of Columbia. | *God, I pray him, grant!* that you may live to see us | *all*, your *loving* countrymen, catching from your fair | example, that reverence for the Eternal Being; that | veneration for the laws; that infinite concern for the | *National Union;* that un- extinguishable love for our | country; and that insuperable contempt of pleas- ures, | of dangers, and of death itself, in its service and de- | fence, which have raised you to Immortality, and | which alone can exalt us to be a great and happy re- | public. | *On the square of Justice,* | *And on the Scale of Love,* | *I remain, Most Honored General,* | *Your very sincere friend,* | *And Masonic Brother,* | M. L. WEEMS.:' This would seem the first issue of the pamphlet, because, though it lacks a title page, the paging and signatures are complete. Weems probably first printed it thus and sent a copy to Washington with the above printed letter of inscription of his own. After receiving Washington's acknowledgment, so gracious as to make it an endorsement, I believe that he had it printed and added it with a title page to the pamphlet, where the value of the commendation is re- flected in the increase of price over that named in the above caption title — from 12 to 25 cents. [See title next succeeding.] The above copy, at the Mary- land Historical Society, bears out this assumption, for the signatures from A to D run correctly, though the latter has actually but two pages, while the paging would indicate that the letter of inscription *to* Washington was originally in- cluded, being printed on the first page and on the same quality of paper, while the title and Washington's letter are on a different quality. The text is largely taken from the following: *An Essay on the Natural Equality of Men; on The Rights that Result from it, and the Duties which it imposes:* . . . By William Law- rence Brown, D.D. . . . The First American Edition. Philadelphia: Printed for John Ormrod, by William W. Woodward, . . . 1793, APHS., HSP., NYPL. [See letter below.] In this edition 'Maddison's' name is misspelled thus (p. 21), Dr. Goldsmith and 'a little captive fly' are mentioned on p. 6, and 'chearful' is thus misprinted on p. 20. It is possible that Green & English printed this pamphlet, as Weems had given them his *Maryland & Virginia Almanac for 1798*, and later they issued what is believed to be the first edition of his *Washington* over his name. Or they may have printed only the title page which, I contend, was added later, see title succeeding. In any case, their advertisement in note 2 below is the only one of this early issue found by me; they also advertised in the same paper his *Maryland & Virginia Almanac* [title 236].

2. *Ad.* [*M.L.W.?*] 'For sale at this Office, THE PHILANTHROPIST; OR, A GOOD TWELVE CENTS WORTH OF POLITICAL LOVE POWDER FOR THE FAIR DAUGHTERS AND PATRIOTIC SONS OF AMERICA. Dedicated to that great *Lover* and *Love* of his country GEORGE WASHINGTON, Esq. God prosper long . . . If but Columbia to herself be true.' *Cent. Lib.*, Aug. 27, 1799 *et seq.*, LC. *The Philanthropist* was also advertised by Weems on the last page of *Hymen's Recruiting Serjeant* [see notes to titles 160A *et seq.*], at 'Twelve Cents', this helping to prove that he changed its price after its first issuance.

3. Weems wrote to Carey from Dumfries, June 15, 1799, that he was having printed '4000 Copies of (as I think) a very lively and entertaining dissertation on Natural Equality abridgd from the famous Brown, and enrich'd with curious anecdotes, &c &c. . . . This I print in great measure on credit & on w[h] I shall make my large profit.' Again, on Sept. 17, 1799: 'I have just launch[d] a little Political piece entitled "The Philanthropist." (By Myself). Washington has given me his thanks for it which will be printed in the gazzette today. [Letter not found in *Md. Gaz.*] In three days I sold 350 at a dollar per dozen.' [This price tends to prove that the first issue lacked the title page and the letter from Washington.] On Oct. 7, 1799, he wrote to Carey that he sent him $40 'being part of what I clear'd in 3 days by sales of the Bachelors Almanac [title 155A] & the Philanthropist.' That this first edition sold well and rapidly is shown by his writing to Carey, Nov. 24, 1799, that he expected to 'soon be done with the sales of the Almanacs, Philanthropists &c. &c.' Again, May 21, 1800: 'I send you also a copy of the Philanthropist, that you may see that I am not yet quite a Simpleton nor a Sluggard.'

4. The Philanthropist is really a political sermon. On p. 20 Weems holds forth thus on the theme of American taxes: 'Again, you own a heavy wagon and team: with this, Jehu like, you rattle along the high ways, tear up the roads, break down the bridges and set the poor road-menders to cursing and swearing, and after all, what is your tax? Why not even a sharp-shin.[1] But lo! here comes one of the quality in a little gim-crack Phaeton and Lilliputian pair, not a *tithe* the substance of your waggon, a carriage that makes no more impression on the roads than does a cat running over a harpsichord. And yet this gentleman pays a tax of 9 dollars.' In the following Weems showed himself far ahead of most of his generation in his attitude toward the salaries of public officials. 'Few of our public officers, viz. our Judges, members of Assembly, Senate, Congress, &c. are allowed more than they could make by their respective professions, many not so much. And as to our good old President, though his 25.000 dollars have made a great noise, yet 'tis questionable whether it be a sharp shin too

[1] Sharp-shin, a colloquialism for a denomination of paper currency at that time.

much. He is placed in a situation of all others the most public and expensive. His Levee, his table &c. must consume vast sums. It were high treason in him to eat his venison or to drink his wine by himself. He is expected to act the national Publican, to keep open house and to entertain comers from all the winds of heaven. Think of that my Brothers.' Pp. 23–24. 'Despite errors in taste, Weems produced much that is both good and readable. His characterization of heroines of fiction as "goose quill beauties" [1] is both witty and original and the following extract but for the obscurity of its publication would certainly suggest being the original of Sidney Smith's famous paragraph on British taxation: "They tax the air above, the earth beneath, and the waters under the earth. And as if all this was not enough, as if wearied of this little piece-meal kind of work, they have made lately a short apoplectic stroke at once of ten per cent ad valorem . . . in addition to a thousand little hectic taxes besides! If they kindle a fire for the little trembling children, they must pay a tax for the hearth. If they let in a ray of heaven's light they must pay a *tax* for the window. If they keep a mare, horse or gelding, they must pay *tax* for stretching their sinews while living; and a tax also for tanning their hides when dead. Even for the making of coffee; for a dipping of candles; for trying up a pot of lard; or brewing a tub of beer there is a tax."' *Note* of Paul L. Ford. 'He was ingenious in literary hashes; admirable in dove-tailing, in cutting, clipping, fitting, contriving and furbishing, . . .' *Weems, The Biographer and Historian*, William Gilmore Simms, in *Views and Reviews, Second Series*, 1845, p. 137.

NUMBER 157 1799?

THE | PHILANTHROPIST; | OR, | A GOOD TWENTY-FIVE CENTS WORTH | OF | POLITICAL LOVE POWDER, | FOR HONEST ADAMITES AND JEFFERSONIANS: | With the following recommendation by | GEORGE WASHINGTON. | REV. SIR, | MOUNT VERNON, *29th Aug.* 1799. | *I have been duly favored with your letter of the 20th instant* | *accompanying the* "PHILANTHROPIST." | *For your politeness in sending the latter I pray you to receive* | *my best thanks. Much indeed is it to be wished that the Senti-* | *ments contained in your pamphlet, and the doctrine it endeavors* |

[1] Alluding, of course, to the quill pen, at that time the only kind in use.

*to inculcate, were more prevalent* — HAPPY *would it be for* THIS | COUNTRY *at least, if they were so.* | *With respect I am, Rev. Sir,* | *Your most obedient* | *Humble Servant,* | GEO. WASHINGTON. | *The Rev. Mr.* WEEMS. | God prosper long these sister States, | In union, health and peace, | And grant henceforth that quarrels vile, | 'Twixt A's and D's may cease. | Nor Gaul nor Brit, need dear Columbia rue, | If but COLUMBIA to HERSELF *be true!* | *By the Rev.* M. L. WEEMS (OF LODGE NO. 50). | DUMFRIES. |

[*n.d. 1799?*] 8vo. pp. 1, (1), 1, (1), 1, 4–30.
AAS., BPL., HSP., JCB., LC., LCPhil., YU.

1. I believe that this is the same issue as the preceding number, save that its title page, with Washington's letter to Weems, had been printed and pasted into it: the title's paper is of different quality from that of the rest of the pamphlet, while in every other respect all the parts of both pamphlets are identical.

2. Alibone's *Dictionary.* The NYPL. has manuscript letter press copy of Washington's letter.

3. *Ad.* [*M.L.W.?*] '. . . Just Published, and for Sale at this Office, The Philanthropist; or A Good Twelve Cents Worth of Political Love Powder, &c. Dedicated to that great Lover and Love of his Country, George Washington, Esquire. By the Rev. M. L. Weems (of Lodge No. 50) Dumfries, Virginia.' *Unpart. Harris. Morg. Zeit.*, Dec. 30, 1799 *et seq.; Farm. Instruct.*, Jan. 15, 1800 *et seq.*, PStL. 'For Sale At the Printing Office . . . Philanthropist. . . .' *Md. Gaz.* (Annap's), Dec. 4, 1800 *et seq.*, MdStL.

NUMBER 158 1800

THE | PHILANTHROPIST; | OR, | A GOOD TWENTY-FIVE CENTS WORTH | OF | POLITICAL LOVE POWDER, | FOR | HONEST ADAMITES AND JEFFERSONIANS: | with the following recommendation by | GEORGE WASHINGTON.: | MOUNT VERNON, 29th August, 1799. | REV. SIR, | I have been duly favored with your letter of the 20th instant accompanying | the "PHILANTHROPIST." | For your politeness in sending the latter, I pray you to receive my best thanks. | Much indeed is it to be wished that the Sentiments contained in your pamphlet, | and the doctrine it endeavors to inculcate, were more prevalent — HAPPY would | it be for THIS COUNTRY, at least, if they were so. | With respect, I am, Rev. Sir, | Your most obedient | Humble Servant, | GEO. WASHINGTON. | The Rev. Mr. WEEMS. | God prosper long these sister States, | In union, health, and peace, | And grant henceforth that quarrels vile, | 'Twixt A's and D's may cease. | Nor Gaul nor Brit, need dear Columbia rue, | If but COLUMBIA to HERSELF BE TRUE! | BY THE REV. M. L. WEEMS (OF LODGE, NO. 50) | DUMFRIES. | CHARLESTON: |

Re-Printed by W. P. YOUNG, No. 43, Broad-Street. | [*n.d. 1800*] 8vo.
pp. 1, (1), 2, 5–31, (1).
HSP., SCHS.

1. On the page which precedes the text is the undated letter from Weems asking Washington to be godfather to the pamphlet. On p. 24 the word 'groan', correctly printed in earlier editions, here appears '*grone.*'

2. *Ad.* 'PUBLISHED THIS DAY, By *W. P. YOUNG* & the *EDITORS* of the *TIMES* At 43 Broad and 137 Tradd Streets, THE *PHILANTHROPIST;* or A good 24 [*sic*] centsworth of *Political Love-Powder*, for honest Adamites and Jeffersonians: with the following recommendation by *George Washington:* [*Letter quoted in title 157 preceding, followed by the same verses.*] By the Rev. M. L. WEEMS (of Lodge No. 50) Dumfries. October 6.' *Times* (Charles.), Oct. 6, 1800, CLS. 'AUGUSTA, May 13. A pamphlet called the *Philanthropist*, or *political* LOVE POWDER, by the reverend Mr. Weems, of Virginia, has been put into our hands — it was written in the year 1799, and a copy thereof being sent to General Washington, he expressed his opinion of it by the following letter to the author: [*Letter as on title page follows.*] Believing this recommendation to be just, and not having seen many copies of this little work here, we shall take the liberty of presenting it to our readers in *this* and a subsequent paper, and we venture to believe, that the time spent in perusing it *attentively*, will not be unprofitably employed.' *Alex. Adv. and Com. Intel.*, June 19, 1801, NYHS. [The issues of this paper said to contain those reprints have not been seen by me.] *Reprints:* "The Philanthropist, &c. (By the Rev. Mr. Weems, of

Virginia.) All men are equal. "Soho! What the plague have we got here now?" [*Nineteen paragraphs*]' *Sal. Gaz.*, July 28, 1801; 'And besides, what can sink a man more . . . . [*Six paragraphs*]' *Ibid.*, Aug. 14, 1801; 'Since then . . . . [*Six paragraphs*]' *Ibid.*, Aug. 18, 1801, MHS.

3. Weems wrote to Carey, Sept. 28, 1801: 'You have no doubt seen how my little Son of the goosequill has sped; how on the wings of the Newspapers he has travell'd from Augusta to the Province of Maine? I mean my primo *genus* [?] my political Placebo, my aristocratico-Democratico political Anodyne, "*The Philanthropist.*"' [See also title 187, note 3.]

4. 'Mr. Young was a job printer and publisher and for many consecutive years conducted The Palladium of Knowledge, or the Caroline and Georgia Almanac, which was issued from 44 Broad Street. . . .' *The Newspaper Press of Charleston, S.C.*, William L. King, p. 72, LC. W. P. Young was printing Almanacs in Charleston as early as 1776. See *American Almanacs*, Hugh Alexander Morrison, LC. W. P. Young wrote to Carey from Charleston, July 27, 1790 [L.&F.]: '*Money scarce & dunning brisk.*'

NUMBER 159 1809

THE PHILANTHROPIST; | OR | *Political Peace-maker* | BETWEEN | ALL HONEST MEN OF BOTH PARTIES. | WITH THE RECOMMENDATION PREFIXED | BY GEORGE WASHINGTON, | IN HIS OWN HAND-WRITING. | BY M. L. WEEMS, | LODGE NO. 50, DUMFRIES. | [*Six lines of verse*] | THE TENTH EDITION. PRICE 25 CENTS. | PHILADELPHIA: |

PRINTED FOR THE AUTHOR, | BY T. & G. PALMER. | 1809. |
8vo. pp. (1), 4, (1), 1, 6–40.
AAS., APhS., HU., LC., LCPhil., MdHS., NYPL.

1. In this edition Washington's letter is engraved in facsimile by Tanner and faces title page; on reverse of title is Penn. copyright dated Jan. 1, 1809; letter from Weems to Washington is on the following page; there are many changes of text in this edition from that of 1799: 'the amiable Yorick' is cited as an instance of humanity (p. 8) while in the earlier issues Goldsmith is the perpetrator of the ill-advised philanthropy toward flies; there are verses added as well as other alterations on pp. [3], 5, 7, 9, 14 and 22; the note on p. 26 reads 'our good president', having dropped the word 'old', and there are minor changes

throughout, while on p. 27 and after, it is entirely rewritten to the end, and greatly lengthened.

2. Carey's Catalogue, 1816, '8vo. 1 13.' Alibone's *Dictionary*.

3. *Ad.* [*M.L.W.?*] 'The Philanthropist; or, Political Peace maker, between all honest Men of both Parties; — Recommendation prefixed by George Washington, in his own hand writing.' *Intel. & W'kly Adv.*, Feb. 14, 1809, LIOF. Also advertised in *Poulson's American Daily Advertiser*, Jan. 5, 1809 *et seq.*, AAS.

NUMBER 160? 1799?

## *Hymen's Recruiting Serjeant. [*1799?*]

1. There seems a great likelihood that Weems issued, in 1799 or 1800 or in both, the above imprint. Two entirely different texts under this title were written by him, one definitely labelled '(No. 2)' [see titles 171 and 171A], and the above work, bearing no number but always referred to in his letters as 'No. 1.' Though the first *dated* imprints which I have found of this latter are of 1805 [see titles 161 and 162], considerable proof does exist of one and even two earlier editions: (1) One of his letters alludes to the work as early as June 15, 1799 [see note 3 below], and another attests that it had been actually on the market before Aug. 9, 1800, when he was discussing another issue [see title 160A, note 4]. (2) In title 160A — and all subsequent issues — in one set of verses, presumably by Weems, it is stated 'Three pledges of our mutual love, Kind Providence has giv'n,' which indicates their having been originally written — perhaps as a paean of thanksgiving — shortly after the birth of his first son and third child, Jesse, on June 2, 1799. As his fourth child, Charlotte, was born Jan. 7, 1801, those lines must have been written before that date. (3) On Jan. 25, 1805, Weems wrote to C. P. Wayne, urging 'a 3[d] edition' of *Hymen* [see title 161, note 3]. This again would point to there probably having been *two*

issues before the dated editions of 1805. Yet on this point it should also in fairness be mentioned that his *Virginia Almanac* and *Virginia and North Carolina Almanac for 1800*, printed, of course, in 1799 [titles 172 and 172A], contained very similar matter to his *Hymen* No. 1, notwithstanding the fact that they were always alluded to as almanacs in his letters while *Hymen* was given its own name or a synonym. It therefore seems likely that the first issue of *Hymen* had proved so popular as to encourage him in using it for an almanac, with two different titles, and perhaps even in its first year of publication. For these reasons it has seemed expedient to include the above title here. A hitherto undiscovered copy of it is as likely to be eventually found as in the case of the two almanac rarities.

2. Of the size and style of this first assumed edition it is possible to conjecture only that it had no plate, as it is unlikely that another would have been ordered in 1800 [see Weems' letter of Aug. 9th and Tiebout's bills for July and August of that year, succeeding title, notes 4 and 1].

3. Weems wrote to Carey, June 15, 1799: 'I have likewise just sent to press a little piece which I am morally certain will be *in great request.* "Hymen's recruiting Serjeant or the New Matrimonial Yankee Doodle."' [This subtitle as planned was actually used, so far as I have found, only in his *Virginia* and *Virginia and North Carolina Almanacs for 1800*, titles 172 and 172A — yet see bills for printing, etc., in note 1, title succeeding.]

4. The two following bear no relation to Weems' work: 'Matrimony. The Fifteen Comforts of Matrimony. With an addition of Three Comforts more. . . . Worcester, Mass. 1795.' AAS. 'Books Just Published, . . . For Maids and Bachelors! A concise view of the advantages and disadvantages of Matrimony. Price 6 d. . . .' *Republican Citizen* (Fredericksburg, Va.), Sept. 7, 1796 *et seq.*, HU.

NUMBER 160A? 1800–1803?

## Hymen's Recruiting Serjeant. [*1800–1803?*] 8vo. pp. 5–20.

NYPL. [*imp., lacks title, earlier pages and a possible plate.*]

1. Lacking its title, there is furthermore no internal evidence of the date of its publication. If, however, any deductions may be made from Weems' letters, it seems clear that there was a second edition after the first assumed one in 1799, which had probably been sent out in a cheaper dress than this issue [see title 160]. That earlier one, having proved itself a good seller [see letter of Aug. 9, 1800, in note 4 below], Weems was planning as early as July 11, 1800, to issue another [see point 3 herein]. That it was to have a plate (and probably Tiebout's,

for which its size is fit) is proved by his letter of Aug. 9th, as well as the bills at the end of this note. And this is further attested by the second advertisement in note 3 below. Since this NYPL. copy is of a format for that plate, it is a fair inference that both book and plate were printed *after* 1799, during which year no hint is found of a plate. For the further hypothesis that it should be placed *before* those of 1805 [titles 161 and 162], various collateral facts exist: (1) In general, it is much more like those dated editions of 1805 than any of the editions which succeeded them, after a lapse of ten years. If it be urged that perhaps it came directly *after* 1805 rather than *before*, my objection is that there is no evidence in letters or advertisements of an edition actually printed between that date and the next authentic edition found by me, of 1815. For Weems' advertisements in late 1806 and early 1807 [see title 161, note 2] might just as well apply to a stock on hand of one of the two 1805 editions as to a new one which he had desired to have called 'the fifth'; for, although he had been clamoring for such a one in some letters of 1805 and 1806 [see title 161, note 3], as neither of the almanacs in these same advertisements has ever been found by me, 'the fifth edition' of *Hymen* may, like those, be still in limbo or never have been issued. (2) Typographically the above issue differs from the few copies dated 1805 which I have seen, and since, judging from the variations in them, we already have two issues in that year, it would again seem more likely that this NYPL. copy is of another year as well as of an earlier date than they. (3) On the last page of this undated edition, and of the two of 1805, *The Philanthropist* is advertised with its original price of 'Twelve cents' as announced *only* on the caption title of what I believe was its first issue [title 156]. If Weems had been issuing *Hymen* No. 1 later than 1799 or 1800 he would have been more likely to give the second price of 'A good Twenty-Five Cents' Worth [title 157]. As a matter of fact, he did write to Carey from Wilmington, July 11, 1800: 'Suffer the *last sheet* of the old Bachelor to lie unspread and the old scoundrel, trembling and cold, untill I come up.' This, with the foregoing letters, makes it seem clear that a *second* issue of *Hymen* was in question and that possibly Weems intended the price named therein for *The Philanthropist* to be changed from twelve cents to twenty-five. That this was not done was perhaps due to Carey's printer putting the last sheet to press without awaiting Weems' arrival, and thereafter the subsequent issues, even so late as the editions of 1805, merely copied the blunder from the earlier one verbatim. In Weems' roving and distracted life this point might easily have escaped him. Or again, he might even have decided to sell his *Philanthropist*, over which he had entire control, at the lower price *wholesale*. (4) In the early summer of 1804 a few reprints of extracts from *Hymen* appearing after a lapse of time, imply an edition still extant of which this NYPL. copy may possibly be one [see note 3 below]. Also, in July, 1800, H. Maxwell rendered duplicate bills to Carey for 'Composition 36212 Ms Eng. & S Pica @ 40 Cts . . . 14.40' and printing '2000 copies of 5 half sheets — the Matrimonial Tattoo.' He included 'An advertizement of one half sheet 100 copies — 3.00,' which suggests the last page of *Hymen* giving the puff of *The Philanthropist.* See *Mathew Carey Account Books*, Vol. 15 : 5796, AAS. In the same volume [5995 and in Vol. 16 : 6892], in August, 1800, Cornelius Tiebout rendered duplicate bills to Carey for 'Engraving a Plate *Palemon* & *Lavinia* . . . Dol^rs 30.00.' On Nov. 22, 1800, Mary Smith charged Carey '£13.15. For Stitching 989 Copies of the Tatoo at 3/9' *Ibid.*, Vol. 15 : 5987.

2. Without any definite date being ascribed to this copy, it is here compared, for expediency, with the 1805 dated editions: (1) throughout the text no long 's' is used in this NYPL. copy; (2) the numbers at the top of the pages differ in size from each other and from those in the other issues; (3) on p. 13 the last words on each line of the last paragraph agree with those in the HSP. and LC. copies, which differ in this point from that of AAS.; (4) on p. 15, on the last line of paragraph 4, the word 'happines' is misprinted thus; (5) on the last page there are the exclamation point after '*obey!*', the semicolon after the word 'PHILANTHROPIST;' in the advertisement of that book, the hyphen between 'TWELVE-CENTS'' and the apostrophe after the latter, which four points only the AAS. copy lacks; (6) the words 'OR,A' following 'PHILANTHROPIST;' have been partially covered by a stain but the faintest suggestion of print through the mark seems to justify the supposition that in this respect the NYPL. copy again agrees with those in the HSP. and LC., only the AAS. copy lacking the comma between the words; (7) in the body of Washington's letter of recommendation of *The Philanthropist*, three dashes precede the word 'Happy' in the NYPL. copy, the three other copies having only two, and there is no comma after the word 'respect' at the end of the letter; (8) in the abbreviation for George in the signature of that letter, the 'o' is raised and a colon follows, thus, '*G^o:*', this name being printed '*Go.*' in all the other copies; (9) at the bottom of that page the words 'To be had . . . in the City.' are in larger type than in any of the other copies.

3. *Ad.* 'Just received from New York, and for sale at William W. Morse's Bookstore, Hymen's Recruiting Serjeant, Or a new Matrimonial Tat-too for Old Bachelors. Inviting all both great and small, A lovely wife to take; Nor longer lead, — Oh! shameful deed, The life of worthless rake.' *Mess.*, Nov. 13, 1800, YU. [*M.L.W.?*] '. . . ALSO, A beautiful work, entirely new, ENTITLED, *Hymen's Recruiting-Serjeant;* OR, THE New Matrimonial Tat-too for the Batchelors, Inviting all . . . *useless* [*sic*] *rake.* Wherein is shewn, in a manner singularly

satisfactory and sprightly, that the *married life* is, of *all lives*, the most *safe, pleasant, profitable and happy;* and a good *wife*, of all *goods*, the most *precious* and *desirable*. This choice *patriotic treatise* is divided into *eight* chapters, *each* enlivened with lovely songs, and the *whole* ornamented by a fine engraving of Thomson's delicate courting-scene, between the elegant Palemon and his lovely Lavinia.' *Va. Arg.*, Dec. 26, 1800 *et seq.*, LC., VSTL. 'The above pamphlets are for sale at the Office of the . . . Argus . . .' *Ibid.*, Jan. 23, 1801 *et seq.*, VSTL. *Reprints:* 'From Hymen's Recruiting Serjeant, addressed to Old Bachelors. And the Lord said "It is not good for . . . 1. If you are for pleasure — Marry! . . . a fine cat-and-dog concert of it for life."' *Sal. Reg.*, June 25, 1801, AAS., BPL. 'From Hymen's Recruiting Sergeant . . . For. 1. If you are for pleasure . . . cat-and-dog concert of it for life!!' *Guard.*, July 16, 1801, HU. [*M.L.W.?*] 'From the True American . . . From the number of marriages which I weekly see published, it appears as if the Ladies were availing themselves of the privilege which Leap-Year gives them. . . . As a friend to *Matrimony*, however . . . I send you an extract from a celebrated pamphlet called "*The Bachelor's Tattoo*" which I hope will *stimulate* those gentlemen, both old and young, who . . . continue to live *single*, *useless*, and *miserable* lives, . . . [*Signed*] No friend to Celibacy. "If you are for *pleasure* — Marry! If you prize *rosy health* — Marry! And even if *money* be your object — Marry! A good wife is "Heaven's last best gift to Man"; . . . "If you love the *Creator* you ought to *marry*, to raise him up worshippers . . ."' *True Amer.*, May 14, 1804, NJSTL.; *Conn. Cour.*, June 6, 1804, CONNHS.; *Col. Mus. & Sav. Adv.*, June 20, 1804, GAHS.; *Conn. Post & N. H. Vis.*, June 21, 1804, CONNHS., YU.

4. Weems wrote to Carey, Aug. 9, 1800: 'You may thank Washington and the Bachelor for most of the remittances made you. . . . I hope you have got Mr. Tiebout on the other engraving.' [See also letter of Aug. 18, 1806, title 161, note 3.] Nov. 8, 1800: 'The Bachelor sold well [*at Annapolis*]' Nov. 17, 1800: 'Send me not another book except my own, i. e. . . . Washington, Bachelor, Mentor [*titles 219 et seq.*] & Paine [*title 243*]. For the two latter I'll get out subscriptions incontinently, and send you the money.' Nov. 26, 1800: 'Washington, the Bachelor & Surplice fees have done all.' Feb. 16, 1801: 'Of the Bachelor I left up in my room at one end of the Settee, a pyramid 3 or 4 feet high. They've been mislaid.' Feb. [?] 1801: 'I left a pyramid of Bachelors at your house . . . with Mrs. Smith, without the cuts.' [These allusions may possibly apply equally to *Hymen* No. 2, see titles 171 and 171A.] Dec. 3, 1801: 'The Legislature Old & young, married & single, took of No. 1.' Feb. 4, 1804: 'In these warm latitudes [*N.C.*] there is a great call for both Nos But the 1st is unfortunately run out.' [This probably meant that his own supply

in the South had given out, for the book was being pushed in New Jersey and Connecticut a number of months later — see last items in note 3 above.]

5. *The Virginia* and *Virginia & North Carolina Almanac for 1800* also contain similar matter [see titles 172 and 172A]. Extracts from *Hymen* were also printed in *Carey's Franklin Almanack for 1803* and *1805* [see titles 174 and 175].

6. To show that our times present nothing new: 'After Braddock's defeat in order to pay for an increase in the Militia, taxes were laid upon some additional items, among them "batchelors." Every year the Vestry prepared a list of such *delinquents* in the parish who were over twenty-five years old . . . [*which*] was then fastened upon the church door (which was a favorite place for advertising parish business), and, when revised, was sent to the Sheriff. . . . This imposition . . . ceased after eight years. . . . This persecuted class [*had*] sought refuge at church in "bachelor's pews." . . .' [Gov. Sharpe, and Messrs. *Husband* and *Love* were among those taxed.] *Parish Institutions of Maryland*, Edward Ingle, in *Magazine of American History*, April, 1883, p. 270, LC. Weems constituted himself an unofficial matrimonial agent. Throughout his works he stoutly defended and maintained the traditional view of connubial bliss. Thus: 'The truth is, though general Lee was extremely splenetic, (which such a miserable *batchelor* and *infidel* could hardly otherwise than be,) . . .' *Life of Marion*, 1814, p. 103; 'I have related this story, partly to show what a savage man would be without that softening, polishing friend, a good wife.' *Life of Marion*, 1818, pp. 85–86. Note also the following: '"Do you go to Powheek church, Sylvia, tomorrow?" said the enamoured swain. "Who preaches there? If Parson Weems preaches, I wont go. He always preaches up matrimony."' *Travels . . . in the United States, 1798–1802*, John Davis, 1803, p. 228, LC.

NUMBER 161 1805

HYMEN'S RECRUITING-SERJEANT: | OR THE | NEW MATRIMONIAL TAT-TOO, | FOR | THE OLD BACHELORS. | Inviting all, both big and small, | A lovely *wife* to take: | Nor longer lead — Oh! shameful deed! | The life of worthless rake. | WITH SOME ELEGANT SONGS. | 'Tis madness sure, you must agree, | To lodge alone at *thirty-three*! | For writings, penn'd by heav'n, have shewn, | That man can ne'er be blest alone. | FRENEAU. | BY THE REV. M. L. WEEMS, LODGE NO. 50, DUMFRIES. | God prosper long *Columbia dear*, | In plenty, love and peace; | And grant henceforth, that bach'lors old | 'Mongst pretty maids may cease!!! | PHILADELPHIA: |

PRINTED BY JOHN BIOREN, NO. 88, CHESNUT-STREET, FOR THE AUTHOR. | 1805. | (COPY-RIGHT SECURED ACCORDING TO ACT OF CONGRESS.) | 4to. pp. (1), 2, (1), 1, (1), 1, 6–19, 1. *Front.plate.*

HSP., LC.

1. No. 1. Frontispiece engraved, stippled, oval, with plain stippled border, signed 'C. Tiebout Sc.,' inscription below 'PALEMON *and* LAVINIA. . . . . . [*sic*] *Won by the charm* | *Of goodness irresistable, and all* | *In sweet disorder lost she blush'd consent* | *Thompsons Autumn*'; then follows 'TO ALL THE SINGLES, | WHETHER | MASCULINES OR FEMININES, | THROUGHOUT | THE UNITED STATES. | DEAR GENTLES, | I AM very clear that our *Buckskin heroes* are made of, at | least, as *good* stuff as any the *best* of the *beef* or *frog-eating* gentry | on t'other side the water. But neither this, nor all our fine speeches | to our President, nor all his fine speeches to us again, will ever save | us from the British gripe or Carmagnole hug, while they can out-number us, *ten to one!* NO, my friends, 'tis population, 'tis *popu-* | *lation alone*, that can save our bacon. | List, then, ye Bach'lors, and ye Maidens fair, | If truly ye do love your country dear; | O list with rapture to the great decree, | Which *thus* in Genesis, you all may see: | "*Marry, and raise up soldiers might and main,*" | Then laugh you may, at England, France, and Spain. | Wishing you all, the *hearing ear* — the *believing heart* — and a | saving antipathy to *apes*, | I remain your's, dear Gentles, | In the bonds of Love and Matrimony, | M. L. WEEMS.'; then follows, at p. 5, 'GENESIS, CHAP. II. VERSE 18. And the Lord said, "*It is not good for the man to be alone.*" NO, verily, nor for the woman neither. . . . For, 1. If you are for *pleasure* — Marry! . . . THE PLEASURES OF THE MARRIED STATE. . . . THE FIRST BLISS OF MATRIMONY, . . . EIGHTH BLISS. . . .'; there are thirteen songs and seven incidental couplets or quatrains interspersed throughout the text, all of which are presumably by Weems, except one song by Dr. Doddridge; on p. 9 the typography changes slightly, the long 's' being used on that page and thereafter, except in the verses, in italicized words, and as an end letter; on p. 13 the last words on each line of the last paragraph are: 'race, union, bo-, purest, into, tremble, ever, bloom, the, dis-, found, friends, in'; the last page reads as follows: 'DEFINITION OF THE ODIOUS WORD OBEY, IN THE MARRIAGE CEREMONY. | LET none e'er say the fates ordain, | That *man* should bear the sway; | When

reason bids — let woman *reign*, | When reason bids — *obey!* | JUST PUBLISHED, | THE PHILANTHROPIST; | OR, A | GOOD TWELVE-CENTS' WORTH | OF | POLITICAL LOVE-POWDER, | FOR | HONEST ADAMITES AND JEFFERSONIANS. | WITH THE FOLLOWING RECOMMENDATION BY | GEORGE WASHINGTON. | MOUNT VERNON, 29th Aug. 1779. | REV. SIR. | [*Six lines*] | *With respect, I am, Rev. Sir,* | *Your most obedient* | *Humble servant,* | *Go.* WASHINGTON. | *The Rev. Mr.* WEEMS. | To be had of the principal Booksellers in the City.' The AAS. copy [see title 162], though also dated 1805, differs typographically from the above, suggesting more than one edition in that year. See also notes to title 160A. The price here named for *The Philanthropist* has some possible bearing on the date of an earlier edition of *Hymen*, see title 160 A, note 1.

2. *Ad.* 'M.L.W. congratulates his Charleston friends, . . . is still with his friend Dr. Moses [*Moser*] — has still . . . Hymen's Recruiting Sergeant for the Poor Bachelors; . . .' *Times*, July 1, 1806, CLS. [*M.L.W.?*] 'Have an eye here. JUST PUBLISHED. . . . 1st. The Maids and Bachelors Almanac, for 1807 — 2d. The Grand Republican ditto for ditto, both uncommonly large and curious. And immensely entertaining and profitable. ALSO, Some elegant copies of Hymen's Recruiting Serjant — 5th Edition. . . . Please enquire at DR. GEORGE HARRAL'S Medicine Store. Nov. 18.' *Ga. Rep.*, Dec. 5, 16, 1806, UN'YGA.; Dec. 23, 1806 *et seq.*, GAHS. [From Jan. 12–20, 1807, the heading was printed 'Have an Eye hear . . .'] 'The Rev. Mason L. Weems, well known in the Southern States as . . . author of "Hymen's Recruiting Serjeant or a Matrimonial Tattoo for the Bachelors," . . . and several other whimsical publications. . . .' *Star*, Feb. 9, 1809, NCSTL. 'Books . . . for sale cheap. . . . Also, the following pamphlets . . . Hymen's Recruiting Sergeant . . .' *Louisv'l. Gaz.*, May 4, 1810, AAS. [Probably a left-over from the 1805 editions, since I have found no trace of a later issue before 1815.]

3. Weems wrote to Wayne, Jan. 25. 1805: 'You w$^{d}$ find it to your interest to print as a 3$^{d}$ edition, 1000 cop. of Hymen's recruiting Sergeant, & send on 200 to Charleston & 200 to Savanna.'[1] May 14, 1805: 'As you declin$^{d}$ Hymen I desir$^{d}$ Bioren to print me a 1000. I wish you wd ask him how it goes on & let me know all in your next.' May 16, 1805: 'Why wont you send me my . . . (Pamphlets — also Hymens sent to you from Balt$^{o}$?)' Aug. 9, 1805: 'In your next, please to let [*me*] know exactly what is done with my Hymen's re-

1 'To Wayne, Jan. 25, 1805: Can be addressed at Charleston. Wants a 3rd ed. of Hymen's Recruiting Sergeant and to have 300 sent to Charleston and Savannah each! Mr. Carey will furnish the copper-plate of Hymen, that is of Palemon & Lavinia.' Benson J. Lossing in *American Historical Record*, Vol. II, February, 1873, p. 82 [with notes by the editor], LC. [For letter in full, see *Letters*, Vol. II.]

printed by Bioren — tell Bioren all shall be well when I see him.' Sept. 18, 1805, introducing 'my friend John Adams — As he is almost an entire stranger in Phila., any little book that you can throw into his hands will be acceptable to him. Expense will constantly meet us on every tack & turn. This can only be successfully combatted by as constant a sale of little Books, not clashing with the great Work [*Marshall's Washington.*] The most saleable little piece that I know of, is Hymen's Recruiting Serjeant. If you will give the printing of it to Mr. Adams we will as usual divide the profits. 800 or 1000 Copies will do. The plate perhaps may require some little retouching — You have but to furnish Mr. Adams the paper. He will attend to everything else & thereby save you all trouble except that of sending them to D^r Sir Your M. L. Weems. The plate, which is mine, is in Mr. Carey's hands — he will deliver it.' Aug. 18, 1806: I wrote to you 10 days ago begging that you w^d instantly get John Bioren, (if you cou'd not attend to it yourself) to print me 6000 Almanacks, one half of them, containing Hymen's Recruiting Serjeant, and thereby entitled "The Lover's or Bachelors Almanac." . . . I wish you cou'd instantly print me a 1000 cop. of my Hymen's recruit^g Serjeant, on a fine paper. Have the plate retouch^d by Tiebout.' [See titles 155 and 155A; also 186 and 187.] [*N.d. after Aug. 25*] 1806: 'Attend to the edition of Hymen. Be so good as to remember to put it the *5^th. edition.* The different editions have pass^d unnoticed. . . . If you employ Bioren, tell him I conjure him to do his *utmost to have* the Alm^cs. Hymnen's [*sic*] &c. &c. by the 1^st of Octob. at farthest.' Oct. 11, 1806: 'Be so good as to desire Bioren & Adams to send me on immediately my Hymen & Almanacs, INSURED. [*No issue by Adams found.*] I want 600 Hymens sent to Augusta — 400 to Charleston. All the Almanacs to Augusta.' To Websters & Skinners of Albany, Mar. 31, 1814 [BPL.]: '3^d The Way to get married . . . The *two last* have gone thro several editions & have sold, each, to the tune of 30 to 40.000.' [For the letter in full see *Letters*, Vol. II, and title 198, note 2. For other excerpts from letters, see title 160A, note 4.]

4. Pp. 10–11 contain a reprint of one of Solomon's Psalms, with alterations and additions which Weems calls 'a touch or two of an American brush.'

5. See title 160A, note 5.

NUMBER 162 1805

## HYMEN'S RECRUITING-SERJEANT: | OR THE | NEW MATRIMONIAL TAT-TOO, | FOR | THE OLD BACHELORS. | [*Fifteen lines*] | PHILADELPHIA: |

PRINTED BY JOHN BIOREN, NO. 88, CHESNUT-STREET, FOR THE AUTHOR. | 1805. | [*One line*] | 4to. pp. 19. *Front.plate.* AAS.

1. No. 1. The same title page as that of title 161; thereafter, however, this copy differs typographically from those of HSP. and LC. as follows: on p. 13 the last words on each line of the last paragraph are: 'race, cer-, bo-, sa-, into, tremble, ever, bloom, the, dis-, that, were, arms'; on the last page, there is no exclamation point after the word '*obey*,' no semi-colon after the word 'PHILANTHROPIST', no comma between the words 'OR' and 'A' following, no hyphen between the words 'TWELVE' and 'CENTS,' and no apostrophe thereafter. See also notes to titles 160A and 161.

NUMBER 163 1815

HYMEN'S RECRUITING-SERJEANT: | OR THE | NEW MATRIMONIAL TAT-TOO, | FOR | THE OLD BACHELORS. | [*Four lines of verse*] | WITH SOME ELEGANT SONGS. | [*Four lines of verse*] | FRENEAU. | BY THE REV. M. L. WEEMS, LODGE No. 50, DUMFRIES. | [*Four lines of verse*] | MIDDLETOWN: |

PRINTED BY SETH RICHARDS, FOR THE PUBLISHER. | 1815. | 4to. pp. 1, (1), 1, (1), 1, 6–19, (1). BPL., YU.

1. No. 1. This edition differs slightly from that of 1805 in: 'TO ALL THE SINGLES, | WHETHER | MASCULINES OR FEMININES, | THROUGHOUT | THE UNITED STATES. | DEAR GENTLES, | I am very clear that our *Yankee heroes* are made of, at | least, as *good* stuff as any the BEST of the *beef* or *frog-eating* gen- | try on t'other side the water. But neither this, nor all our fine | speeches to our President, nor all his fine speeches to us again, | will ever save us from the British gripe or Carmagnole hug, | while they can out number us, *ten to one!* No, my friends, 'tis population, 'tis *population alone*, that can save our bacon. | List, then, ye Bach'lors, and ye Maidens fair, | If truly ye do love your country dear; | O list with rapture to the great decree, | Which *thus* in Genesis you all may see: | "*Marry, and raise up soldiers, might and main,*" | Then laugh ye may, at England, France, and Spain. | Wishing you all, the *hearing ear* — the *believing heart* — and a | saving antipathy to *apes*, | I remain your's, dear Gentles, | In the bonds of Love and Matrimony | M. L. WEEMS.'

NUMBER 164 1816

HYMEN'S | RECRUITING SERGEANT: | OR THE | NEW MATRIMONIAL TAT-TOO, | FOR | THE OLD BACHELORS. | [*Four lines of verse*] | WITH SOME ELEGANT SONGS. | ADORNED WITH A HANDSOME FRONTISPIECE. | [*Four lines of verse*] | FRENEAU. | BY THE REV. M. L. WEEMS, LODGE NO. 50, DUMFRIES. | [*Four lines of verse*] | SIXTH EDITION. | PHILADELPHIA: |

PRINTED FOR THE AUTHOR. | 1816. | 8vo. pp. (1), 4, (1), 1, 6–40. *Front.plate.*
AAS.

1. No. 1. The frontispiece is a copper plate, unsigned, oval, engraved, stippled, with inscriptions, above '*Engraved for Hymen's Recruiting Sergeant*' and below '*Maternal Love.*'; on reverse of title is Penn. copyright to Mason L. Weems, dated 1816; the text follows the 1805 editions [titles 161 and 162] as far as 'when reason bids — *obey.* | THE END. |'

2. [*M.L.W.?*] 'Old Bachelors Of these unsocial beings, who suffer some of the fairest objects of creation to pine on the virgin throne, a very respectable writer thus expresses himself: — "Their passions are in unison with the frozen regions of the Arctic Circle, and their sympathies with those of timid animals, that are frightened at their own resemblance, and who never think themselves safe in solitude. They eat their morsels alone, and call it happiness."' *Adams Cent.*, Apr. 2, 1817, GTOF. *Reprinted:* '(*From the N. Y. Republican Chronicle.*) "*Marriage is honorable,*" . . . EXTRACT. "If you are for *pleasure* — marry! If you prize *rosy health* — marry! . . . glorious angels to the other."' *Wash. City W'kly Gaz.*, May 10, 1817, LC.

3. Weems wrote to Carey, June 22, 1816: 'Wou'd God you coud make haste with the pamphlets & add Hymen's Recruit[g] Serjeant to them — Much ask[d] for. Can't you choose some most lovely young Lady as a frontispiece for it?' June 28, 1816: 'You neglect me about my *pamphlets*, dreadfully.' Nov. 29, 1817: 'The demand here [*Hagerstown*] . . . is very great . . . and for the Bachelors.' To James Madison, Jan. 22, 1819: 'Compt[s]. to M[r]. Todd — cannot but hope that he will peruse with edification Hymen[s] Recruit[g]. Serjeant!'

NUMBER 165 1821

HYMEN'S | RECRUITING SERGEANT; | OR THE | NEW MATRIMONIAL TAT-TOO, | FOR | THE OLD BACHELORS. | [*Four lines of verse*] | WITH SOME ELEGANT SONGS. | ADORNED WITH A HANDSOME FRONTISPIECE. | [*Four lines of verse*] | FRENEAU. | BY THE REV. M. L. WEEMS, LODGE NO. 50, DUMFRIES. | [*Four lines of verse*] | SEVENTH EDITION. | PHILADELPHIA: |

PRINTED FOR THE AUTHOR. | 1821. | 8vo. pp. (1), 4, (1), 1, 6–40. *Front.plate.*

AAS., CLS., LC. [*lacks front.*], NYPL.

1. No. 1. New title; on reverse of title, copyright 1816; the frontispiece is identical with that of the 1816 edition, title preceding; there are slight changes in typography from the 1805 editions; 'president' is printed thus in the address, 'TO ALL THE SINGLES'; the text ends with the four verses on the 'Definition of the odious word *obey*.' and 'THE END.' There are many changes from the 1815 edition.

2. *Ad.* [*M.L.W.?*] 'To the Editor of the Courier . . . . VI. *Hymen's Recruiting Sergeant*, alias *The Matrimonial Tattoo*, alias *The Old Bachelor's Looking Glass* — Shewing the blisses of a marriage from virtuous love, and the ninety and nine curses of Old Bachelorism.' *Charles. Cour.*, Apr. 14, 1821, CLS. *Reprinted:* '"Pleasures of a Married State." Believe me, citizen bachelor, never yet man received his full allowance *heaped up, and running over*, of this life's joys, until measured out to him by the generous hand of a loving wife. A man, with half an eye, may see that I am not talking here of those droll matches which now and then, throw a whole neighborhood into a wonderation; where scores of good people are called together to eat mince pies, and to hear a blooming nymph of fortune promise to take "for better for worse" an old icicle of four score! or to see the sturdy, blooming youth, lavishing amorous kisses on the shrivelled lips of his *great grand-mother's* [*sic*] *bride!* O cursed lust of proof [*pelf?*] from such matches good Lord, deliver *us* all true hearted souls! For *such matches* have gone a great way to make those *sweetest notes husband and wife*, to sound prodigiously *out'o tunish*. The old husband, after all his honeymoon looks, grunts a jealous *bass*, while young madam, wretched in spite of her coach and *lutestrings*, squeaks a scolding treble; making between them a

fine cat-and-dog concert of it for life! "But I am talking . . . . THE FIRST BLISS OF MATRIMONY. . . . Let the self-scraping Bachelor . . . . "Yes the sweetest drop . . . "Are you poor? . . . "Are you prosperous? . . . with a joy too big for utterance."' *Del. Gaz.*, Mar. 8, 1822, WI. [With minor changes.]

3. Weems wrote to Carey, Dec. 4, 1820: 'If the edition [*of Hymen*] be out, I wish you $w^d$ order an edition (the $7^{th}$) to press.'

NUMBER 166 1823

HYMEN'S | RECRUITING-SERGEANT; | OR THE NEW | MATRIMONIAL TAT-TOO, | FOR | OLD BACHELORS. | [*Four lines of verse*] | BY THE REV. M. L. WEEMS, | LODGE NO. 50, *Dumfries.* | HARTFORD: |

PUBLISHED BY SILAS ANDRUS. | 1823. | 24mo. pp. 1, (1), 3, 6–52.

HSP., NYHS.

1. No. 1.

NUMBER 167 1833

HYMEN'S | RECRUITING-SERGEANT; | OR THE NEW | MATRIMONIAL TAT-TOO, | FOR | OLD BACHELORS. | [*Four lines of verse*] | BY THE REV. M. L. WEEMS, | *Lodge No. 50, Dumfries.* | Hartford, Ct. |

PUBLISHED BY ANDRUS & JUDD. | 1833. | 24mo. pp. 3, IV, 1, 6–52.

AAS., HU., MdHS., NYPL.

1. No. 1. On reverse of title, Penn. copyright dated 1816; Address 'To all the Singles . . .'; text ends with 'Advice to Old Bachelors,' and 'Definition of the odious word . . . *obey.* | FINIS.'

NUMBER 168 1840

HYMEN'S | RECRUITING SERGEANT: | OR THE NEW | MATRIMONIAL TAT–TOO, | FOR | OLD BACHELORS. | [*Four lines of verse*] By Rev. M. L. Weems, | Author of "Life of Marion," &c. | LODGE NO. 50, DUMFRIES. |

PUBLISHED BY | R. L. UNDERHILL & CO. | BATH, N. Y. | HENRY D. SMEAD, PRINTER. | 1840. | Sm. 24mo. pp. (2), 3, IV, 1, 6–52, 1, 54–59, (3).
AAS.

1. No. 1. Text ends with 'Advice to Old Bachelors' and there are verses following the 'Definition of the odious word OBEY . . .' followed by 'TO YOUNG LADIES . . . advice . . . selected from an excellent work, by Mrs. Farran, entitled, "THE YOUNG LADIES FRIEND.["]'

NUMBER 169 1845

HYMEN'S | RECRUITING–SERGEANT; | OR THE NEW | MATRIMONIAL TAT–TOO, | FOR | OLD BACHELORS. | [*Four lines of verse*] | BY THE REV. M. L. WEEMS, | *Lodge No. 50*, Dumfries. | HARTFORD: |

S. ANDRUS AND SON. | *1845*. | 12mo. pp. (4), 1, (1), 3, 6–52, (4).
HU., NYPL.

1. No. 1. Contents end with 'When reason bids obey.' The HU. copy has cover imprint 'OLD | BACHELOR | WEEMS' | [with title following].

NUMBER 170 1851

HYMEN'S | RECRUITING–SERGEANT; | OR THE NEW | MATRIMONIAL TAT–TOO, | FOR | OLD BACHELORS. | [*Four lines of verse*] | BY THE REV. M. L. WEEMS. | *Lodge No. 50, Dumfries.* | HARTFORD: |

SILAS ANDRUS AND SON. | 1851. | 18mo. pp. 1, (1), 1, IV, 1, 6–52, 4.
BPL., LC.

1. No. 1. Cover imprint 'OLD | BACHELOR | WEEMS' | ; Address 'To all the Singles . . .'; the four back fly leaves contain publishers' advertisements, including: '*Weems' Old Bachelor* | By Rev. M. L. Weems.'

2. Duyckinck's *Cyclopedia* states that this work was printed as late as 1875. The latest edition that I have seen is this of 1851; no mention of anything subsequent in *American catalogue of 1876* or index to the *Publishers' trade-list annual for 1875*.

NUMBER 171? 1801?

## *Hymen's Recruiting Serjeant. [*1801?*]

1. No. 2. The only proofs found of such an edition are Weems' letters to Carey, as follow. Sept. 2, 1801: '*Thank God* my two treatises on Marriage (the happiness of) have caus[d] me to be sent for, far and near, the grand Porter at the Hymeneal Vestibule. Their douceurs of gratitude often make a corps de reserve for remittance. This week my fees (grace au dieu) makes [*sic*] nearly 20 Doll[s]' Dec. 3, 1801: 'Had I bro[t] a handsome edition of N[o] 2 of "Hymen's recruiting Serjeant" I might have made my fortune.' [For letters immediately following these, see title succeeding, note 4. There is also a letter of Feb. [?] 1801 which may apply as well to No. 2 as No. 1, see title 160A, note 3. See also advertisements, title 161, note 3.]

NUMBER 171A 1802

(N°. 2!!!) | HYMEN'S RECRUITING-SERJEANT: | OR, THE | MAID'S AND BACHELOR'S FRIEND. | CONTAINING | A VERY SEASONABLE AND SAVOURY DISSERTATION, ON | LOVE, COURTSHIP, AND MATRIMONY. |

WITH A FINE FLOURISH ON TRUE BEAUTY; | Admirably calculated to disclose those two most *delectable* and *desirable Secrets;* FIRST, | How the *Homely* may become *Handsome*, and the *Handsome*, *Angelic:* | AND, SECONDLY, | How the *Single* may become *Married*, and the *Married*, *Happy!* | Exemplified in the History of Miss Delia D——, one of the *brightest* and *loveliest* of all | the bright and lovely Daughters of Columbia. | "Fram'd to give joy, the lovely Sex are seen, | Beauteous their form, and heavenly is their mien. | To noblest ends the glorious passion sways, | By *love* and *honor* bound the youth obeys; | 'Till by his virtues won, the grateful Fair, | *Blushing*, consents to ease her lover's care. | Seals all his hopes, and in the Bridal Kiss, | Gives him a title to *untainted Bliss!!!!* | WITH SOME ELEGANT SONGS. | BY M. L. WEEMS, | LODGE NO. 50, DUMFRIES, VIRGINIA. | PRICE. THREE-EIGHTHS OF A DOLLAR. | PHILADELPHIA: |

PRINTED BY R. COCHRAN, FOR THE AUTHOR. | 1802. | (COPY-RIGHT SECURED ACCORDING TO LAW.) | 4to, pp. (1), 2, (1), 1, 4–20. *Front.plate.*

AAS., BA. [*lacks front.*], BPL., NYHS., NYPL. [*imp.*]

1. The frontispiece is engraved, stippled, signed below '*Tanner. Sc.*' with inscriptions, above '*Engraved for M. L. Weems*', below 'NEST OF LOVE.'; in it two cherubs are caressing one another inside a circle of foliage and a substance which looks to the callous eye like the spun sugar of certain highly decorated sweets; another cherub fondles a demonstrative spaniel which is licking his cheek, while the most obese of the four sits in 'splendid isolation' contemplating the others' endearments; the text of the volume is of the best 'Sarah Matilda' sentiment: 'Chap. I. ON LOVE'; '. . . II. ON BEAUTY'; . . . DELIA'S FIRST GRACE: GOODNESS. . . . GOOD SENSE. . . . INNOCENCE. . . . SENSIBILITY. . . .' etc., to the 'NINTH GRACE: POLITENESS.'; with twenty-one extracts of verse, the last one only without quotation marks, evidently inscribed to his wife Fanny Ewell, as follows: '*A Song for her that's far away.* While some for pleasure pawn their health, | 'Twixt Lais and the Bagni —O | I'll save myself and without stealth, | Kiss and caress my Fanny —

O | She bids more fair t'engage a Jove | Than Leda did or Danae — O. | Where [*sic*] I to paint the queen of love | None else should sit but Fanny — O | How joyfully my spirits rise | When meeting she moves finely — O | I guess what heaven is by her eyes, | Which sparkle so divinely — O. | A titheless Priest is my degree | And few there be that ken me — O; | But what care I how few there be, | I'm welcome ay to Fanny — O.'

2. Brinley No. 8940.

3. *Ad.* 'Extracts from Hymen's Recruiting Serjeant, written by M. L. Weems. . . . "Love's dear delightful fire, . . . Let the poor Gentoo kiss and caress the dried great toe of his dead Saints! . . . and a thousand other little amorous Cupids are then fluttering about the heart. (The work from which the above extracts are taken is for sale at this office.)' *Cent. Freed.*, Sept. 22, 1802, NJSTL.; Sept. 28, 1802, NJHS. [*M.L.W.?*] 'NEW PUBLICATIONS . . . The Maid's & Bachelor's Freind [*sic*]. ALSO, . . . *The* TRUE PATRIOT. . . .' *Bartgis's Repub. Gaz.*, July 1, 1803 *et seq.*, HU. Also advertised in: *Alex'a Expos.*, Dec. 13, 1802, HU. *Amer. Lit. Adv.*, Dec. 16, 1802, HU. *Intel. & W'kly Adv.*, Dec. 20, 1803 *et seq.*, LIOF.

4. Weems wrote to Carey, Nov. 30, 1801: 'When I pass^d thro' this Country 15 months ago, I scarcely left a stall unattempted. . . . When I came to this place [*Trenton*] I made a brave charge on that heavy Democratic Corps, the Assembly, . . . Hymen's Recruiting Serjeant I sold by the armful.' Jan. 12, 1802: 'How comes on the Nid D'Amitie? I mean the engraving you were so good as to let me place in the hands of Tanner for the 2^d N^o. of Hymen's Recruitg Serjeant?' Feb. 28, 1802: 'I have got No. 2 of Hymen &c ready for the press. I hope M^r. Tanner has got the engraving in readiness.' Apr. 7, 1802: 'No. 2 of Hymen has sold to admiration [*in Trenton*]. The *Friends* prodigiously fond of it. . . . Wou'd it not be well for M^rs. Sharpless to keep Hymen in her good keeping? For if brought to 118 they'll strait down into the Cellar; and there's such an eternal Volcanic eruption in the Cellar.' Apr. 9, 1802: 'After all my scolding of Cameron &c &c to have the Cards put on the *bottoms* of the Boxes!! and the 50 elegant Bibles drawn and jolted topsy turvy from Lamberton to Trenton, and the Hymens so ramm^d & jam^d that I'm sure the nests of Love will hardly ever again be got into ship-shape.' Apr. 14, 1802: 'Please *Instantly* to pack 400 Hymens in a box and push them off to me at N. York.' Apr. 16, 1802: 'I begg^d you to send me, via Bordenton 400 Hymen.' Apr. 28, 1802: 'As to Hymen, thank God, that sells [*New York*].' May 4, 1802: 'Had it not been for Hymen I shou'd hardly have done more than pay current expenses.' May 24, 1802: 'I call^d at about 50 houses [*in Wilmington*], and sold 18 Hymens. . . . For a *poor* and *unmanaging* Man, with a helpless Wife & five Children, with

no *cure* (voluntarily renounc[d] on account of your Bible) I have sign[d], seal[d] & deliver[d] to [*you*] payment of a large sum.' Jan. 12, 1804: 'I go to Charleston, S.Carolina — whence I shall write to you relative to . . . and my Maids & Bachelors Friend.' Feb. 4, 1804: 'I left in your store a little box of books that opens in a curious way, in the middle — please to send that box — also my 4 or 500 Hymen's recruit[g] Serjeant No. 2, I mean the "Nest of Love." In these warm latitudes there is a great call for both N[os].' To Wayne, Nov. 30, 1805: 'I have 400 or 500 2[d] No. Hymen & 320 Vol. 2[d] Blair, gather[d] &c in Carey's Lumber Store where he carries on his Bible. I will *forever* thank, & in cash will pay *Mr. Adams* liberally if he will find out the Hymen and the Blair & send on the Former to Charleston or Savanna & set the Blair in his paper room till Spring.' Dec. 6, 1805: 'See good care [*be*] taken of my Books.'

5. 'Robert Cochran printed for Joseph Scott a specimen issue of "The Independent Whig" Mar. 20, 1802.' *ProcAAS.*, Vol. XXXII, 1922, p. 142. He also issued *Cochran's Philadelphia Almanac*, 1809, LC.

NUMBER 172 1799–1800

THE VIRGINIA | ALMANAC, | FOR THE YEAR OF OUR LORD 1800. | *Being the* FOURTH * *after* LEAP-YEAR: | CONTAINING | Besides the necessary Calculations — Lists of Members of | the Council, Senate, Assembly, &c. of this State — | Fine Anecdotes, Songs, &c. | A NEW AND BEAUTIFUL DISSERTATION ON | THE MARRIED LIFE; | worth a JEW'S EYE to all pretty MAIDS and BACHELORS | who would live Healthy, Wealthy, and Happy. | Since writings pen'd by Heav'n have shewn, | That man can ne'er be blest alone; | In *kindness*, sure, *he* far surpasses, | Who teaches all, both lads and lasses, | That *Lads* are seldom worth a fig, | Until they've learn'd old Hymen's jig, | Nor lasses e'er to bliss attain, | Until they've try'd sweet wedlock's chain. | Hurra for Matrimony! that happy state, which gave us Wash- | ington, Jefferson, Adams, Franklin, &c. | *This Year would, in course, have been a Leap-Year, | were it not that adding one Day in four Years occasions an | excess of 18 hours in a Century; therefore Astronomers | and Chronologers have adopted the following rule — Every | *Centurial Year* not divisible by 400, without a remainder, is | a *Common Year.* | FREDERICKSBURG: |

PRINTED BY T. GREEN, | FOR THE REV. MASON L. WEEMS. | [*1799*] 12mo. pp. 36 unnumbered.
AAS.

1. From pp. 19–35 the contents, unsigned, are 'HYMEN'S RECRUITING SERJEANT; | OR, THE | NEW MATRIMONIAL YANKEE DOODLE, [*for the only mention of this subtitle, see title 160, note 3*] | *For the Bachelors.* | Inviting all, both Big and Small, to LOOK SHARP, and with | all convenient speed to take unto themselves | A LOVELY AND A LOVING WIFE, | THE SWEETEST COMFORT OF THIS LIFE. | WITH SOME BEAUTIFUL SONGS. | "'*Tis madness sure, you must agree,* | "*To lodge alone* at TWENTY-THREE; | "*For writings penn'd by Heaven have shewn,* | "*That Man can ne'er be blest alone.*" | "And the Lord said it is not good for Man to be alone." — | No, verily, nor for Woman neither. | But what says the Preacher? — Why "I will (says Paul) that | the young Women marry, and love their Husbands, | and raise up good Children." | Well said most noble patriotic Paul! | MAY the children of Columbia hearken to thy counsel | that there be no more bachelors in our land like scrubby | oaks standing selfishly alone, while our maidens like tender | vines, lacking support, sink to the ground, but that united in | wedlock's blest embraces they may grow up together as the | trees of the Lord, whose summits reach the skies and their | branches over spread the nations, making their country the | pride and glory of the earth! "I will that the young people marry," — Yes | If you prize pleasure, marry, | If you prize wealth, marry, | If you prize health, marry. | Now I set me to prove these delightful truths, draw near | ye bachelors of the willing ear while with the grey quill of | experience I write | The Pleasures of the Married State. | Believe me, citizen bachelor, never man yet . . . set down as | *The first Bliss of Matrimony* . . . . The Eighth Bliss of Matrimony . . . *quiver is full of them.*"' Last page contains a Table giving the value in Virginia Currency; Florio's Song is in the Eighth, and minor verses are in the other 'Blisses.' This is very like *Hymen's Recruiting Serjeant,* No. 1 [titles 160A *et seq.*], parts of it being verbatim, and others merely shorter, the songs especially being extended

in that publication. I believe it to be possibly a reprint, with a different title page, of *The Lovers'*, or *The Bachelor's Almanac*, of which he wrote to Carey, Mar. 19, 1799 [note 2 below]; or it may have been planned by Weems as the first issue of *Hymen* under one of those titles [see letters of 1798 and 1799 in title 155A, note 1] and then diverted to these Almanacs. It will be noted that in this issue he gives ten years' less grace to all bachelors who desire to be in their right minds before making the matrimonial plunge. In *Hymen* the age limit is thirty-three instead of twenty-three. [This title has no connection with *The Maryland & Virginia Almanac . . . 1798*, title 236.]

2. On Mar. 19, 1799, Weems urged Carey to print him an Almanac of which he could 'sell this fall between 10 and 20,000 . . . @ from 50 to 65 cents pr Doz. . . . it will be a continuation of the Lover's Alm[e]. w[h] has met with a great run among the young people of this State [*Va.*]. . . . I have sold off (2 gross excepted) the whole of two large editions. . . . At Norfolk . . . delug[d] with Alm[es]. I sold 6 or 700 in a little time. I suppose that 12,000 Alm[es]. containing each but one sheet super royal might be printed for *a trifle*.' Sept. 17, 1799: 'I have likewise just got out my Bachelors Almanac, with an Essay (by myself) entitled "Hymen's Recruiting Serjeant." . . . in Alexandria . . . last week I sold 8 gross in one day & an half.' Oct. 7, 1799: 'Today I pay unto Mr. Brundige for you 40 dollars (being part of what I clear'd in 3 days by sales of the Bachelors Almanac & the Philanthropist.)' Nov. 24, 1799: 'I shall soon be done with the sales of my Almanacs.' Sept. 15, 1800: 'I . . . hope by the arrival of the Philad[a] imports to be able to give a good account of the 1,000 Alman[s] I brought down. I sold a few doz on the road. What do you think I got for them? 3/3 !!! If you dont shave Bioren the Jew, There'll be bad blood 'twixt I and you.' Sept. 16, 1800: 'You must never hope for absolution if you charge above 2/6 or at farthest 37½ Cents per doz for Almanacs. Put a curb on Bioren & reject the bag of Judas.'

3. 'Green, of Fredericksburg, a descendant of Samuel Green, the second printer of Cambridge, Mass., the first of a distinguished family of printers.' See *American Dictionary of Printing and Bookmaking*, New York, 1894, pp. 244–245, LC.

4. In a generation which erred on the side of free speech and frankness to the point of coarseness in all printed matter except the infantile or the theological, Weems, for all his unexpected candor in his letters, showed himself, to any discerning mind, as exceptionally clean-minded for his day. *De jure*, if not *de facto*, he would have endorsed the following comment on another Almanac: 'The Author . . . sorry . . . in the supplementary pages, replete with such unsavoury, indelicate expressions; and in a style so very dissonant and grating

THE VIRGINIA & NORTH CAROLINA

# ALMANAC,

FOR THE YEAR OF OUR LORD 1800.

*Being the* FOURTH* *after* LEAP-YEAR:

CONTAINING

Beſides the neceſſary Calculations—Liſts of Members of the Council, Senate, Aſſembly, &c. of this State—Fine Anecdotes, Songs, &c.

A NEW AND BEAUTIFUL DISSERTATION ON

THE MARRIED LIFE;

worth a Jew's EYE to all pretty MAIDS and BACHELORS who would live Healthy, Wealthy, and Happy.

—

Sure writings pen'd by Heav'n have ſhewn,
That man can ne'er be bleſt alone;
In *kindneſs*, ſure, *he* far ſurpaſſes,
Who teaches all, both lads and laſſes,
That *Lads* are ſeldom worth a fig,
Until they've learn'd old Hymen's jig,
Nor laſſes e'er to bliſs attain,
Until they've try'd ſweet wedlock's chain.

—

* This Year would, in courſe, have been a Leap-Year, were it not that adding one Day in four Years occaſions an exceſs of 18 hours in a Century; therefore Aſtronomers and Chronologers have adopted the following rule—Every *Centurial Year* not diviſible by 400, without a remainder, is a *Common Year*.

FREDERICKSBURG: PRINTED BY T. GREEN,
FOR THE REV. MASON L. WEEMS.

FACSIMILE TITLE PAGE OF THE 1800
*VIRGINIA & NORTH CAROLINA ALMANAC*

to a modest and delicate ear . . . such low-lived, turpid [*sic*] stuff . . .' *Conn. Jour.*, Feb. 27, 1788, LC. A well-considered *publicity* was part of the game with others as well as our parson, as shown in the following, written by no less a person than Nathaniel Hazard, whose 'respectability' of habit and attainment were above suspicion. In writing to Mathew Carey from 'Newyork' 28 July, 1788 [L.&F.], about copy for the Columbian Museum, he says: 'I have often thought if I was to commence Almanack Maker, I would sell more than any others; for I would have in it every Officer in the State, from the Governor, down to the Constable, in the civil; and the Serjeant Major, in the military Line; every Clergyman, Physician & Attorney. Every Member of every Kind of Society and in short every Man who could be pleased to see his name in Print, in the only way he could ever expect it.'

NUMBER 172A 1799–1800

*THE VIRGINIA & NORTH CAROLINA | ALMANAC, | FOR THE YEAR OF OUR LORD 1800. | [*Seventeen lines*] | *This Year would, in course, have been a Leap-Year, | [*Five lines*] FREDERICKSBURG: |

PRINTED BY T. GREEN, | FOR THE REV. MASON L. WEEMS. |
12mo. pp. 36, unnumbered.
AAS.

1. So far as I have found, this is a unique copy. As may be seen by the facsimile of the preceding title, this title page is identical, except for a slight difference of spacing in the first line and the omission of the two lines 'Hurra for Matrimony! that happy state which gave us Wash- | ington, Jefferson, Adams, Franklin, &c.,' this naturally resulting in a difference in spacing below the lowest line of ornaments across the title. Evidently issued by Weems in order to reach the North Carolina market also. The text varies only in the relative space given to the Courts of Virginia and those of North Carolina and Maryland, which latter are included only in this issue. The excerpts, unsigned, from his own *Hymen's Recruiting Serjeant* are identical. For notes referring to his almanacs of this year, see title 172.

NUMBER 173 1802

THE | TRUE PATRIOT: | OR | An Oration, | ON THE BEAUTIES AND BEATITUDES | OF | A REPUBLIC; | AND | THE ABOMINATIONS AND DESOLATIONS | OF | DESPOTISM. | With an Affectionate Persuasive to the AMERICAN PEOPLE, | TO FEAR GOD, | AND | TO HONOR THEIR RULERS; | TO LOVE ONE ANOTHER, | AND | TO BEWARE OF DISCORD. | Delivered in the State-House, TRENTON, before the Hono- | rable the Governor and Legislature, and printed at their | request. | WITH A DEDICATION | *To His Excellency* JOSEPH BLOOMFIELD, *Governor of the State* | *of New-Jersey.* | BY THE REV. M. L. WEEMS, | LODGE NO. 50, DUMFRIES, VIRGINIA. | PRICE 37½ CENTS. | PHILADELPHIA: |

PRINTED FOR THE AUTHOR, | *By* WILLIAM W. WOODWARD, N°. 52, South Second, corner | of Chesnut Street. | (Copy-Right Secured.)
[*n.d. 1802*] 8vo. pp. 1, (1), 1, (1), 1, 6–56.
BPL., HSP., LC., LCPhil., MdHS., NYPL.

1. The Dedication is dated Trenton, January, 1802. Contents: 'LITTLE CHILDREN *Love one another;* FORMS OF GOVERNMENT; FIRST EXCELLENCE OF A REPUBLIC; . . . EIGHTH [*ditto*]', concluding with 'WASHINGTON'S *Prayer for his Country';* parts were reprinted in *Weems' Washington Almanack for 1804*, title 176.

2. Alibone's *Dictionary.*

3. *Ad.* 'New Publication. We have read, and with much pleasure, an Oration, delivered before the Governor and both Houses . . . by the Rev. M. L. Weems. It is dedicated to his Excellency Joseph Bloomfield . . . and ornamented with an elegant and accurate likeness . . . some idea may be formed . . . from the following extracts . . . [*four paragraphs of citations*]. *The Above Ora-*

*tion for sale at this Office, Price 37 1/2 Cents.' True Amer.*, Feb. 16, 1802, NJSTL. [*M.L.W.*] 'Please look this Way. *Just Published*, and now at the Mercy of the *Good Ladies and Gentlemen of Lancaster* WEEMS'S ORATION, *On the Beauties and Beatitudes of the American Republic.* If the fairest view of the Wisdom and Equity of our Government, and its natural tendency to make Men, Women and Children happy — If to have too much light to be led astray by Jack-a-lantern Demigods; and, at the same time, not such a *glare* as to keep us from *heartily loving* the Constitution; dutifully obeying its Laws; chearfully paying its Taxes; and steadily concurring with its administration — If, in short, to become *Rational Politicians, True Republicans, Hearty Patriots, Honest Men*, and *Happy Citizens*, have any charms; then has this Oration as many charms as any quarter dollar pamphlet ever brought to Lancaster. N.B. The Author will leave town tomorrow. Mar. 17, 1802.' *Intel. & W'kly Adv.*, Mar. 17, 1802, LIOF. '*Pamphlets For Sale at this Office.* . . . The True Patriot: or an Oration on the Beauties and Beatitudes of a Republic. By the Rev. M. L. Weems. . . .' *Intel.*, May 31, 1803 *et seq.*, PSTL. [*M.L.W.*] 'NEW PUBLICATIONS . . . *The* TRUE PATRIOT. Containing 11 Essays, on the following Subjects: . . . Republicans! "Let us have *Light!*" The bipeds in a tyrant's gear can draw in the *dark* — Their drivers will keep them on the turnpike. — But self-governing and self-guided *we*, leaders and followers, shall all soon be in the ditch, *without light.* "Let us have light!" And we shall have "a reason for the faith that is in us." — We shall see and adore the goodness of God, for giving us our excellent republic. We shall cordially love it — bravely defend it — chearfully pay its taxes — honor its officers — and, like little children, love one another, and consequently be great and happy for ever. Ornamented with an elegant copperplate likeness of Governor Bloomfield. Price 37 1-2 cents. May 27, 1803.' *Bartgis's Repub. Gaz.*, July 1, 1803 *et seq.*, HU. [No portrait found in the copies examined. See letter of Jan. 12, 1802, note 4 below.]

4. Weems wrote to Carey, Oct. 21, 1799: 'I have now on the Anvil and pretty well hammer'[d]. out a piece that will sell to admiration. THE TRUE PATRIOT OR BEAUTIES OF WASHINGTON Abundantly Biographical & Anecdotical Curious & Marvellous.' [From what we know of Weems' facile methods as a book maker and seller, it is likely, judging from this quotation, that he used some of the material in the 'piece' above mentioned for his *Life of Washington.* Then, as would be in character, he used this title as planned three years earlier, for another work.] Sept. 28, 1801: 'Were I able to print, I shou'd in 8 weeks have ready for the press a piece that w[d] set on edge the cursed teeth of Tyranny, but sooth[*e*] & comfort the nerves of all honest Republicans. Tis written, "on the Excellencies of a Republican Government." A view is exhibited

of the *Nature* of a Republic, in order you see to guard our beloved Profanum Vulgus against the wiles of our Tavern-table & Cyder cask Demagogues — To attach to it, the affections of the People, its peerless beauties are display[d], and to heighten those Beauties, they are contrasted with the Deformities & Horrors of Monarchy. The Gratitude due for such a Gov[t]. such a Cœlo-descended Governm[t], and the fine Virtues which we shou'd cultivate in order to give it Sempeternal duration, form the rear of this work. What think you of it? May it not do great good?' Dec. 1, 1801: 'This moment I receiv'd their [*the N.J. Legislature's*] approbation on a Motion to deliver before them an Oration tomorrow mor[g] 9 O Clock — Tis now 7 O' Clock P.M. The Oration points at Sydney [*sic*].' Dec. 3, 1801: 'Yesterday morn[g] 9 O Clock, attended at the State house, where according to the Sois-devant [*sic*] promise was waited on by his Excellency — Gov[r] Bloomfield & the honorable House of Legislature to whom I had the honor of address[g] an Oration. "*On the Nature & Excellencies of a Republic*" Their Attentions (I mean, of their aforesaid Honorables & Excellents) in coming; Their attentions in hearing, and their Attentions after hearing, were flattering passing flattering in-deed. Scarcely had I quitted the Rostrum, before I was surrounded by the Members, the Gov'[r] a leur tete. The Gov'[r] press'd my fist — thank[d] me for my performance — insisted I s[d] print it; his Excellency's proposition was seconded, thirded &[c]. &[c]. by the Hon'ble the House. Quid Multis? The Gov[r] without my knowledge got out a Subscription paper, & presented it to the Council who desir[d] 50 Copies. Of the Lower house, some took 12, some 24 Copies apiece. I believe I cou'd easily have gotten 500 Copies engag[d].' Jan 5, 1802: 'The people are tearing me in pieces for my Republican Oration & for the Life of Washington.' Jan 12, 1802. 'Mr. Kollock of this place [*Elizabethtown*] offers to print my Oration for 12 ½ Dol pr sheet for the first 1000 and five Dol[s] for 2[d] 1000. . . . I've reason to believe I cou'd vend 15,00 [*sic*] in this State. Has Mr. Tanner sent up the fine likenesses of Gen[l] Bloomfield? If he have, be so good as to take good care of them.' [No portrait found. See end of note 3 above.] Feb. 19, 1802: 'Thank God the True Patriot goes off manfully — Feds or no Feds they all seem to approve it. . . . [*It*] begins to tell.' Feb. 28, 1802: 'Gov[r] Bloomfield advises me to be at Woodbury (. . . *Jersey side*) on Thursday 4th March. It seems there's to be a great meeting of Republicans.' To 'Th. Jefferson, Dumfries Nov. 22 [*1804*].' [LC.]: 'Very Honord Sir. I beg your acceptance of the enclosed "The True Patriot." 'Tis among the first of my little callow brood, and, throughout, bears too evident marks of the pinfeather but I think I feel the growing strength of my quill, and hope e'er long to send you something better worth perusal.' [For other parts of this letter and for Jefferson's reply, see title 237, notes 3 and 2.]

5. Some of the brochure's choicest bits are as follows: 'In front of this immortal band [*of 'gallant souls who . . . went forth in conquering steel, and saved their trembling country'*] GENERAL BLOOMFIELD acted an early and a distinguished part. The doves of liberty then should coo with peculiar pleasure in the ear of him whose sword so gallantly defended their sacred olive; and to him, the dedication of this Patriotic Oration is at once the duty and delight of his Excellency's Affectionate Countryman, and Masonic Brother, M. L. Weems.' A letter was printed from Gov. Jos. Bloomfield [*dated Dec. 1796*] repudiating attempts made 'to blast my character with Anti-Federalism to serve electioneering purposes. . . .' *Cent. Freed.*, Jan. 4, 1797, NJHS.

NUMBER 174 1802–1803

Carey's | FRANKLIN ALMANACK, | FOR THE YEAR 1803. | PHILADELPHIA: |

Printed by John Adams . . . [*1802*] 12mo. pp. 48 unnumbered. *Port.* AAS., LC., LCPhil.

1. The portrait, on the title page, is of Franklin. Pp. 26–27 contain excerpts, unsigned, from *Hymen's Recruiting Serjeant* [*No. I*]: 'ADDRESS TO OLD BACHELORS. *And the Lord said — It is not good for man to be alone. For,* 1. *If you are for pleasure — Marry!* 2. . . . 3. . . . *Now let's to the point, and prove these precious truths. Draw near, ye Bachelors. . . . The pleasures of the Married State . . . cat and dog concert for life!!'*

2. Carey had issued a *Columbian Almanac for 1798*, printed for him by William and Robert Dickson of Lancaster[1] [LC.], and, so far as I have learned, issued the first of his series of *Franklin Almanacks*, for 1801, running them until 1814. That Carey and Weems had a joint interest in the *Franklin Almanack* is attested both by the excerpts from *Hymen's Recruiting Serjeant* in the issues of 1803 and 1805, and by Weems' letters, though, judging by the latter, it was not continued long. It is possible that Weems suggested the title, and thus

[1] Publishers of the Lancaster *Intelligencer*, 1799–1802, when Robert Dickson died and William became sole publisher. See *Bibliography of American Newspapers*, Clarence S. Brigham, *ProcAAS.*, Vol. XXX, Part I, p. 128.

obtained an interest before anything of his own was inserted. He had projected a *Franklin Almanac* as is shown in the following extract of a letter to Carey, written from Georgetown, Aug. 4, 1797: 'I am getting under way a large edition and a handsome one too, of D[r]. Franklins Almanac, I call it D[r]. Franklins because it will be enrich[d] with his famous *Way to Wealth* &[c]. As a good Patriot, I suppose you will give the undertaking the right hand of fellowship. You may have any number you please in exchange for such little chap books & Pamphlets as I shall approve. Tho considerably larger than the common Almanac it shall be put at the usual Philad[a] price 3/9 per doz. In this low ebb of Money, occasion[d] by the bad steering of our *brave* political pilots, nothing can keep afloat but Almanacs & such little skiffs. Sho[d] this be the case much longer, I mean to have the whole Ocean cover[d] with Almanacs next season. There shall be the Lovers Almanac, the *Devils* Almanac and I dont know what else.' [Neither of these almanacs ever found — for the first see title 155.] There seems little doubt, however, that Weems never got any further in his projected *Franklin Almanac* than in this partial participation in Carey's publication, in his own *The Maryland & Virginia Almanac*, title 236, or in his previous compilation of Franklin and Lewis Cornaro in *The Immortal Mentor*, titles 219 *et seq.* But from the letters in note 4 below, it seems very clear that Weems was pushing *Carey's Franklin Almanack for 1801*, and from the fact that his first letter speaks of it as 'our' Almanac it seems likely that he may have had a proprietary or a part author's interest in it. In this *Franklin Almanack for 1804* there are two pages of citations from Blair's *Sermons*, on 'Industry In Youth,' perhaps supplied by Weems, see titles 229 and 230.

3. *Ad.* ['Just Published Carey's Franklin Almanack for the year 1801. 1. . . . 13. Political and moral reflections. . . .' *Va. Arg.*, Jan. 17, 1801 *et seq.*, VSTL.] 'Carey's Franklin Almanack, 1803.' *Ibid.*, Nov. 28, 1802 *et seq.*, LC.

4. Weems wrote to Carey, Apr. 14, 1800: 'Suppose we print a confounded large edition of our Almanac this year. If I coud have them at Norfolk, Petersburg, Richmond, Fredericksbg & Alexandria, by the 1[st] day of September, I coud sell 20,000. I w[d] engage 15,000, what coud you print that number for? One sheet & one half Royal paper or size Last half sheet Brevier type?' July 10, 1800: 'Put not the definitive touch to any thing that Bioren alias Black-Beard may say about 2/9 the doz. for Almanacs. [*Bioren printed Carey's Franklin Almanack for 1801.*] M[r]. Niles of this place [*Wilmington*] will print us an Almanac 48 pages, Medium, *Beautiful*, &c. &c. for 2/– !!!!!!!!' July 30, 1800: 'Strike me off, but 6,000 Almana[cs].' Oct. 2, 1800, he stated to Carey that he had at Fauquier Court house sold '9 Doz Alm[cs]. . . . Thus all the monies sent you have been rais[d] on Alm[s] & my own little shavers.' Oct. 17, 1800, he

wrote of having sold '14 Dol.' worth of *Washingtons*, *Bachelors* & *Almanacs* in a few hours, and again on Nov. 17, 1800, he wrote of not having sold '20 Dol'' worth of Carey's books 'setting aside' the *Almanac*. Later, Nov. 26, 1800, he wrote that 'of all the monies hitherto sent you, not 20 dol have been rais'd on your books *Alm[cs] excepted*. Washington, the Bachelor & Surplice fees have done all.' Dec. 1, 1800: 'You will not fail to send my Washington, Bachelor, Paine & Mentor. I will do a great deal with those books . . . God prosper me! I need it, for you have put a great many Alm[cs] on me . . . I bespoke, all along, 6.000.' Dec. 4, 1800: 'No more Almanacs — yesterday I sold 400.' Dec. 17, 1800, he wrote of having 'but 1000 of your Almanacs,' and was indignant at being forbidden to obtain more of them from Pollard. On Dec. 18, 1800, Carey wrote: 'I regret that M[r]. Pollard did not allow you to take out the almanacks. There are too many quite to lose totally. . . . I have already lost enough, & suffered sufficient injury by our Connexion — and am desirous to avoid any addition to it.' Weems wrote to Carey, Jan. 27, 1801: 'The people rage about the Alman[c]. No Weather in them!' And again, some time in February of the same year: 'Had your Almanac said a good deal about the *weather*, and hit off nicely the *rising* &c of the Sun it w[d] have cut out all the Almanacs.' Nov. 1, 1803: 'There is a great deficit in the tale of Almanacs.' Dec. 15, 1803: 'I have counted all the Alm[cs] they amount to 1785 w[h] are more than I can safely take at $\frac{50}{100}$.'

5. 'Samuel [*Adams*] died about the year 1802. John, about the same time, removed to Philadelphia, where he opened a printing house, published a vast number of toy books; but did not succeed in money making.' *McCulloch's Additions to Thomas's History of Printing*, *ProcAAS.*, Vol. XXXI, April, 1921, p. 131.

## NUMBER 175 1804–1805

Carey's | FRANKLIN ALMANACK, | FOR THE YEAR 1805. | PHILADELPHIA: |

J. & J. Wilson, Printers. Trenton. . . . [*1804*] 12mo. pp. 48, unnumbered. *Port.*
LC., LCPhil.

1. The portrait is identical with that in 1803. Contains excerpts, unsigned, from *Hymen's Recruiting Serjeant* [*No. I.*]: 'MATRIMONY. *If you are for* pleasure — *Marry! . . . And even if* Money *be your object — Marry!* A GOOD WIFE "Heaven's last best gift to Man" his *angel and minister of graces* innumerable —

his *Sal Polychrestum* or *giver of many virtues* — his *Pandora*, a casket of celestial jewels — her *presence* forms his best company — her *voice*, his sweetest music — her *smiles*, his brightest day — her *kiss*, the guardian of his innocence — her *arms*, the pale of his safety, the balm of his health, the balsam of his life — her *industry*, his surest wealth — her *lips*, his faithfullest councellors — her *bosom*, the softest pillow of his cares — and her prayers the ablest advocates of Heaven's blessings on his head! If you love the *Creator*, you ought to *marry*, to raise him up worshippers . . . good citizens to the one, and glorious angels to the other!' [P. 26.]

2. *Ad.* 'Almanacks. Bates's and Carey's Franklin . . . for 1805 for sale.' *Va. Arg.*, Nov. 21, 1804 *et seq.*, VSTL.

3. Weems wrote to Carey, July 20, 1803: 'Send a good supply of . . . and your *Almanacs.*' Oct. 5, 1810: 'The Almanac cannot be here *too soon.* 3000 perhaps will be enough, I have written to Doct Harall for an Alm[c] for the year 1811, but cannot hope to get one sent to you, for 4 weeks yet. Ca'nt it be done for this latitude [*Augusta*] & entitled the Franklin Georgia Almanac & sent *off at once?*' [No issue found to correspond with this.]

4. James J. Wilson was co-editor of the Trenton *True American*, 1801–1808, after which he became sole publisher. See *Bibliography of American Newspapers*, Clarence S. Brigham, *ProcAAS.*, Vol. XXVI, p. 454.

NUMBER 176 1803–1804

WEEMS'S | WASHINGTON | ALMANACK, | FOR THE YEAR | 1804: | BEING BISSEXTILE OR LEAP YEAR. | CONTAINING, | The rising, setting, places, and eclipses of the Sun and Moon; the | southing, phases, age, and latitude of the Moon; longitude of the | ascending Node, &c. the geocentric places and aspects of the | Planets; the rising, setting, and southing of the most conspicuous | Planets and fixed Stars; the passage of Alioth over the Meridian; | the equation of time, Sun's declenation, and time of high water at | Philadelphia, &c. Also, the increase, decrease, and length of | Days, with the festivals, &c. | Carefully calculated for the latitude and Meridian of Philadelphia. | By ABRAHAM SHOEMAKER, New-York. | PHILADELPHIA: | PRINTED BY JOHN ADAMS. | [*1803*] 12mo. pp. 48 unnumbered. ESPCol., HHL., LC., MdHS., VStL.

1. At p. 17, there is an Introduction to 'a good treatise on a Republic,' quoting Jefferson in praise of Washington, and thereafter extracts from *The True Patriot;* then follows 'I dedicate this Almanack on the nature and excellencies of a Republic . . .'; FIRST EXCELLENCE OF A REPUBLIC. *It is the Government of Reason . . .,*' and so through: 'THE SIXTH EXCELLENCE . . . BROTHERLY LOVE. TO BE CONTINUED IN THE NEXT YEAR'S ALMANACK. BY M. L. WEEMS.' In the LC. copy, following the 'Sixth Excellence of a Republic' are 10 back fly leaves of advertisements of: 'Family Medicines . . . Federal Courts . . . Tables of Values . . . and interest.'

2. *Ad.* [*M.L.W.*] 'FOR SALE AT THIS OFFICE *Price* 10 1–2d. The GEORGE WASHINGTON OR True Republican ALMANAC for 1804 — BEING LADIES YEAR Containing — Besides the risings, settings, eclipses and other important manœuvres of the sun, moon and stars, weather, family medicines, money tables and "a that and a that," a *copious dissertation* on the nature and excellencies of our American Republic, contrasted with a view of the nature and curses of the European Despotisms — Admirably calculated (by making us sensible of our *great political advantages*) to inspire *gratitude to heaven, union among ourselves*, and that cheerful obedience to the laws, which alone can render our peace and prosperity *everlasting*. God prosper long Columbia dear, | In Plenty, Love and Peace, | And grant henceforth that quarrels vile | 'Mongst Fed's and Dem's may cease!!! Of 30,000 of this Political Almanac, there remain but one hundred on hand. The Rev. M. L. Weems leaves town on Thursday morning, but not without the deepest impressions of gratitude to the citizens of Charleston for their truly filial attentions to the memory of their beloved Washington. M. L. Weems puts up at Doctor Moser's.' *City Gaz.*, Mar. 6, 1804 *et seq.*, CLS.

3. Weems wrote to Carey, July 25, 1803: 'I told you that John Adams Esq$^{r}$. had printed for me 5000 Almanacs. You said you w$^{d}$ take them, as our contract will not allow me to sell them for myself — The paper — 21 Reams for 5000 — $39.20. For printing 3000 @ $11 p. 1000 — 33 $72.20. For this you will please to credit me. You have but to settle, with Mr. Adams for *print-*

*ing only* of the other 2000 at 11$ p. 1000. . . . I have no doubt but I shall be able to sell among the *Good Republicans* of the South, at least 10,000 Almanacs for this coming year — *My Alm*$^{c}$ I mean, entitled Weems's Washington Almanac.' Dec. 7, 1803: 'You cannot but recollect that [*as*] soon as I had ratified our last unfortunate contract I told you that the Almanacs which Mr. Adams had been printing for me, sh$^{d}$ be surrender'd to you and thrown into the common current of books on sale for you. This surrender was the natural and necessary consequence of a prómise on my part to sell no books on my own account. You agreed to it & the Almanacs were sent on, but, as I told you in a former letter, not in the quantity (5000) I expected. Mr. Adams will tell you that our contract was, to the best of my recollection, for 5000. But there have been sent only as follows — 1 Trunk — carefully counted — 749. 1 D$^{o}$ of same size and therefore suppos'd (for it was not counted) to contain 749. 1 Large Box twice counted 2333–3831. What have been vended, wholesale, have been vended *constantly* at $\frac{50}{100}$ pr Dozen. There remain on hand between 1000 & 1500. As winter sets in it may throw obstacles or delays in the way of their speedy return to Philad$^{a}$. I think it adviseable not to pack the Almanacs, *for fear of accident.* I am willing to account for the whole, (taking on my *own risk*, the unsold) at $\frac{50}{100}$ per doz.' To Wayne, Jan. 1, 1804: 'I take with me the same young Relative to whom I give the perquisites (for I'm not able to give wages) of 2 or 3 little boxes of Alm$^{cs}$ & chap books &c.' To Carey, Jan. 12, 1804: 'However to take away from you every shadow of complaint, that I have thrown, "*as waste paper on your hands, 70 Doz. of valuable Almanacs,*" I am content, late as it is in the season, to [*take?*] them all on myself in this way. Of the 38,00, [*sic*] and *some odd*, sent me, I have sold somewhat more than 20,00 [*sic*] at $\frac{50}{100}$ universally pr doz. and, generally, at $\frac{6}{100}$ for retail. Of these retails, I made no entries, but they cou'd not, as you may suppose, be very numerous, and sometimes I was oblig$^{d}$ to sacrifice an Almanac to the cravingness of your *Book Buyers.* But this was not often. I am content, I say, if you be satisfied with $\frac{50}{100}$ per doz *on all* (upwards of *160 Doz*) *sold*, to take the rest (upwards of 1700) at my own risk, and at whatever John Adams charges me for them . . . I set out this hour with your carriage & my Almanacs.' Feb. 4, 1804: 'I also inform$^{d}$ [*you*] that, rather than give you any cause for complaint that 1700 or 1800 Almanacs were left as waste paper on your hands, I had embark$^{d}$ them on your little stage to vend or not vend as time and chance might order, and at *prime cost risk.* I mean at my own risk, allowing you for them, sold or unsold, your prime cost charge. This, (the lateness of the season consider'$^{d}$) *appeared* to me *right & reasonable.* . . .' Feb. 11, 1804: 'Many of my almanacs are still on hand, to the tune of 150.' [It would seem possible that Weems issued an almanac for 1805, though the plan may have failed. See letters which follow. In any case, no such issue has been found by me.] May 29, 1804: 'Let me hear from you about the Almanacks. I am certain money may be made on that article. I desir[d] M[r] John Adams to call on you. Cou'd you not instantly procure a Kalendar calculated for N. & S. Carolina & Georgia? They sell their Kalendars, as they do everything else here, as Men who think very little about God or Devil. I beg to tell you once more that Almanacks sell very high in this Country. Print, & *deliver* them *here* and we go halves in the profits. As I travel a great deal, needs must that I shall sell a great many. But, by *all means* confer with Mr. J. Adams, whom you will find worthy of your friendship. . . . Give me a full answer, . . . inform [*me*] . . . that my almanacs are at press . . . I must have the same essay that I had in the last year's Alm[c].' [This *might* apply to the extracts from *Hymen* in *Carey's Franklin Almanack*, 1803 edition, title 174.] Weems wrote to Wayne, June 16, 1804: 'As to my Alm[c] I trust that some sufficient arrangements are made with Mr. Adams.' July 11, 1804: 'Don't forget my Almanacks. I mean, that you sh[d] let me know what you have done in that affair.' In an undated letter which follows Nov. 27, 1804: 'I coud sell 20.000 Alman[cs]. W[d] it be worth while to print one?' Jan. 25, 1805: 'As to the Alm. affair, There, also, you misunderstood me, when I wrote to you, there was not a moiety of them sold. And as you never told me so, I knew not that you considered yourself as a party in the loss or gain of the undertaking. As then 'tis now at your option.' Feb. 14, 1805: 'You wrote about the Al[cs] with a sarcasm as if I wish[d] to have the whole of the emolument in that poor enterprise. Now the truth is, I fear[d] the Alm[cs] w[d] not all be sold — and my fears I believe will prove to have been well founded.' Mar. 10, 1805: 'You say you w[d] cheerfully have undertaken Sydney [*sic*] & the R Serjeant, had it not been for the *Almanacs* — the *prayer books* — and Anquetil. Now 1[st] as to the *Almanacs* — I told you my reasons for asking, whether you meant to be a Party in that, or not. The Alm[cs] were not a *third sold;* the Season was far advanc[d], and I wish[d] but to know whether you meant to be a Partner in their fate *good* or [*bad?*]' May 14, 1805: 'Now that we can do it to mutual understanding, I am willing to join you in an edit. of 8000 elegant alm[cs]. Let me hear from you. . . . Can you get a Kallendar for the lattitude of Savanna.[?]' May 16, 1805: 'Now I'm morally certain that if you cou'd but get Sydney and the Almanacs deliver[d] to me at the very places to which you are to send Washington . . . by the middle of October I cou'd vend to Sub[s] & to the 4 State Legislatures 1000 Cop. of Sydney & 7 or 8000 Almanacs. However if you dont like the trouble of the Almanac I wish you w[d] instantly speak to Mr. John Adams . . . latitude of Georgia & S

Carolina. . . . Let it be done immediately. I will furnish the *matter* &c &c.' Sept. 18, 1805: 'I wd advise also that you let Mr. Adams print us an almanac. 4000 in number — that is, 1000 for each of the southern states of Virg. N. & S. Carol[s] & Georgia. We will divide all the Whole Sales — for it will be impossible to keep account of what few I may give away, or retail.'

4. 'Abraham Shoemaker, was a justice of the Peace for Philadelphia.' *McCulloch's Additions to Thomas's History of Printing, ProcAAS.*, Vol. XXXI, April, 1921, p. 199.

NUMBER 177 1807

GOD'S | REVENGE AGAINST MURDER; | OR, | THE DROWN'D WIFE OF STEPHENS'S CREEK. | A TRAGEDY, | *As lately performed, with unbounded applause,* | (OF THE DEVIL AND HIS COURT) | BY NED FINDLEY, ESQUIRE, | ONE OF THE | GRAND COMPANY OF TRAGEDIANS | IN THE SERVICE OF THE | BLACK PRINCE, | Who was so highly gratified with Mr. Findley's performance, | that he instantly provided him Rooms in one of his own PAL- | ACES; created him a Knight of the most ignoble order of | the Halter; clapped bracelets on his wrists, and an ornament | round his neck; and in a few days promoted him to the ridge | pole of the gallows, at Edgefield Court-House, South Carolina. | BY M. L. WEEMS, OF LODGE NO. 50, DUMFRIES. | SECOND EDITION ENLARGED—PRICE, *25 Cents.* | *O Reader dear, I give you here* | *A book*

*GOD's*

# REVENGE AGAINST MURDER;

*OR,*

## THE DROWN'D WIFE OF STEPHENS'S CREEK.

## A TRAGEDY,

*As lately performed, with unbounded applause,*

(OF THE DEVIL AND HIS COURT)

## BY NED FINDLEY, ESQUIRE,

ONE OF THE

GRAND COMPANY OF TRAGEDIANS

IN THE SERVICE OF THE

*BLACK PRINCE,*

Who was so highly gratified with Mr. Findley's performance, that he instantly provided him Rooms in one of his own PALACES; created him a Knight of the most ignoble order of the Halter; clapped bracelets on his wrists, and an ornament round his neck; and in a few days promoted him to the ridge pole of the gallows, at Edgefield Court-House, South Carolina.

---

*BY* M. L. WEEMS, *OF LODGE No.* 50, *DUMFRIES.*

---

*SECOND EDITION ENLARGED*—PRICE, 25 *Cents.*

---

*O Reader dear, I give you here*
*A book to look upon,*
*That you may pray, both night and day,*
*Nor go, where* NED *has gone.*

---

*AUGUSTA:*

PRINTED BY *HOBBY & BUNCE*, AT THE HERALD-OFFICE.

*COPY RIGHT SECURED.*

1807.

FACSIMILE TITLE PAGE OF THE 1807 EDITION OF
*GOD'S REVENGE AGAINST MURDER*

*to look upon,* | *That you may pray, both night and day,* | *Nor go, where Ned has gone.* | AUGUSTA: |

PRINTED BY HOBBY & BUNCE, AT THE HERALD-OFFICE. | COPY RIGHT SECURED. | 1807. | 8vo. pp. 1, (1), 1, 4-40. BA.

1. Heading to text is 'THE | SORROWFUL LIFE | AND | CRUEL DEATH OF MARY FINDLEY, | *Daughter of Major Hugh Middleton, Edgefield District,* | (South Carolina.) Who after giving a handsome fortune to a most depraved | Husband, was barbarously murdered by him in | eight weeks after Marriage!!! | *The man whose blossom buds in blood,* | *To death shall sure be cast,* | *And from the earth full soon be swept* | *By God's avenging blast.* |' Embellished throughout with other verses of Weems' own, such as '*Reader! if you have nature for a tear,* | *O! look to that gallows, and shed it there.*' or '*Read in the wretched Findley's fate* | *How God such cruel fraud doth hate.*' [Pp. 38 and 39.] This is the first of Weems' tracts found, and from his letter to Wayne [see note 5 below] as well as from the fact that it is printed as a 'SECOND EDITION ENLARGED', I believe that there was an earlier edition; issued, probably, in a cheap and unsubstantial format, the author might have sold it off so promptly that he was encouraged to enlarge and reprint it, as had been the case with his *Life of Washington.* But of that other edition I have found no trace. As will be seen from the titles, the first, third, seventh, and ninth editions are also wanting. The third edition, judging from the advertisements from Dec. 31, 1808 to Mar. 25, 1809, was probably printed in Philadelphia. See notes to the fourth edition, titles 178 and 180.

2. 'It was the last of these works [*God's Revenge against Murder*] that contained the offensive inscription — "Another Murder in Old Edgefield." It was a long time before the Edgefieldians forgave him this indignity.' *Weems, The Biographer and Historian,* William Gilmore Simms, in *Views and Reviews, Second Series,* 1845, p. 130, LC. [As none of the editions seen by me has the sub-title here mentioned, it is possible that the first missing or the successive ones, not found hitherto but noted above, had it.]

3. It can be surmised, without undue severity to Weems, that he took the title of his series of 'God's Revenge' from the books of one John Reynolds: 'The Triumphs of God's Revenge against the Crying and Execrable Sin of Murther;[1]

[1] 'Numerous tracts, under the imposing title, borrowed from Old Reynolds, of his "God's Revenge . . ."' *Views and Reviews,* William Gilmore Simms, *Second Series,* 1845, p. 129 — 'Poor starved souls of these young gentlewomen of the sixteenth century, who

expressed In thirty severall Tragicall Histories, (digested into Six Books) which contein great variety of mournfull and memorable Accidents, Amorous, Morall, and Divine . . . London: 1656', NYPL. Or in another edition, 1670, these tales are announced as '. . . committed in divers Countreys beyond the Seas: never published or imprinted in any other language.' Or in still another issue, 1708, 'Each History Illustrated with curious Cuts.' Or in a 1779 edition the title includes: 'The whole extremely interesting entertaining and instructive! Very necessary to deter and restrain us from giving a Loose to our Passions and irregular Appetites.' The resemblance appears even more striking in the 'Epistle Dedicatory' to 'My Sacred Sovereign Charles King of Great Britain, France, and Ireland, . . .' where the author says: 'These Histories therefore, which may serve as a Looking-glasse to all Nations . . .' adding 'That all this may appear more lively, I have added the several Brazen Cuts. . . .' All of which applies almost equally well to Weems' tracts, for which he used both epithets — God's Revenge, and Looking Glass. When we come to that one of Reynolds: '. . . against . . . Adultery, Expressed in Ten several Tragical Histories. Shewing The Various Strategems, Subtile Practices, and Deluding Oratory, used by many Gentlemen, to seduce *Young Ladies* to their Unlawful Pleasures. To which are Added The Triumphs of Chastity. In some Heroick Examples, and Delightful Histories. The whole Illustrated with several Elegant Epistles, relating to Love and Galantry, and proper Cuts to each History . . .' we are not astonished that the work lacks a dedication to 'the Merrie Monarch.' That, in the vernacular of his British descendants, would have been 'a bit too thick.' Dibdin's comment applies equally well to Weems' works, although written of his predecessor: 'A volume . . . it does well to cling to of wintry nights when the snow is falling, & the wind is whistling, . . .' *Northern Tour*, Vol. II, p. 614, NYPL. From these titles what more natural than to assume that when studying in England, Weems came across them and used them later when he entered the same field? It is no derogation to admit his quick eye for a telling phrase or an apt epithet. In reading his works, the impression is very clear that he was an alert listener, a ready adapter and a prompt outpourer, and part of his value as a mirror of his time is in this all-inclusive assimilation. [See also title 197, note 4.] There is also a coincidence both of names and aims in the works of one John

were recommended, for their entertainment in hours of recreation, to read "God's Revenge against Murther" . . .' *Children's Books and Reading*, Montrose J. Moses, New York, 1907, p. 23. —'Brydges refers to another of this author's curious compilations as an apparent imitation of the amatorious and chivalrous Romances. Even the above reminds one of *Boccaccio* at times, though the moralising is hardly so flippant. "Mournful and Memorable Accidents" are introduced a good deal more frequently too.' Note to advertisement of Reynolds' *Murther* in catalogue of J. & M. L. Tregaskis, London, before 1902.

Weemse, of Lothaquar, Scotland, 1623, 1634–1636, YU.: 'Christian Synagogue. Portraiture of the Image of God in Man. Observations Naturall and Morall; Exposition of the Morall Law; Ceremonial and Judiciall; Exercitations Divine. A Treatise of the foure degenerate Sonnes, the Atheistik Magician, idolator and Jew.' Other possible sources of titles: 'God's Miraculous revenge against murder; being a relation of undoubted truth out of the West, How the skull of a person murdered about thirty yeares agoe in an Inn, was found with a linen capp thereon still whole, with the two letters wherewith 'twas mark't plain to be seen, though it had laid soe many yeares in ye Earth. . . .' *Term Catalogues* (Arber.), p. 316. 'A new yeares gift for Protestants, or a looking glasse displaying the sweet face of Popery . . .' *Benjamin Harris*, Worthington C. Ford, *MHSProc.*, Oct. 1923, p. 59. There is a tale, unrelated to Weems' work, entitled 'God's Revenge against Murder and Adultery' [*Anon.*] in *The American Moral & Sentimental Magazine*, New York, Mar. 26–May 21, 1798, pp. 609, 641, 685, 711, 739, BA., LC. The following caption serves merely as an introduction to a gibe against Talleyrand, Merlin, Barras and Bonaparte: 'God's Revenge against Murder has in no period of time been . . . displayed than during the French revolution. . . .' [*Anon.*], *Gaz. U. S.*, Jan. 5, 1799, HSP.

4. *Ad.* 'Just Published, And For Sale at this Office. God's Revenge against Murder: or, The Drown'd Wife, (Of Stephen's Creek, South Carolina.) A Tragedy, As it was lately performed, with unbounded applause, (of the devil and his court) By Ned Findley, Esq. One of the Grand Company of Tragedians, in the service of the Black Prince. By M. L. Weems. Price 25 Cents. Jan. 3.' *Col. Cent.* (Aug., Ga.), Jan. 17, 1807 *et seq.*, UN'YGA. 'For sale at this Office (Price only 25 Cents.) God's Revenge Against Murder, or the Sorrowful Life and Cruel Death of Mary Findley Daughter of Major Hugh Middleton, (South Carolina,) Who, after bringing a handsome Fortune to a wicked Husband, was most barbarously Drowned by him, in eight weeks after Marriage — for which he was lately hung at Edgefield. The man whose blossom buds in guilt, To death shall sure be cast, And from the earth full soon be swept, By God's avenging blast. (By M. L. Weems. [)]' *Repub.* (Sav'a), Feb. 13, 20, Mar. 21, 1807, UN'YGA.; Feb. 17, 1807, GAHS.; Mar. 21, 1807, HU. *Louisv'l. Gaz.*, Mar. 20, 1807, HU. [*M.L.W.*] 'Just Received And For Sale at this Office, A few copies of a second and improved edition of that very interesting and popular pamphlet, entitled God's Revenge against Murder. . . . This piece is well calculated to plead the cause o' poor little Orphans, & to touch the least sensibilities of the human heart. Price only 25 cents. Communicated [*with additions as follow, by M.L.W.*] Few Tragedies have been read with such avidity as this of poor Mary Findley, which has already run largely into the second edition. May he,

whose "*unsuffering Kingdom* yet shall come" render it a mean of preventing the repetition of such horrid crimes and cruelties. The following *critique* from the pen of the celebrated American Historian, cannot but interest the public. Charleston. Mar. [*sic*] 16, 1807. "Dear Sir — I thank you for your much esteemed Pamphlet 'God's Revenge on Murder.' No man can read it without having his risible faculties often excited — NO man can read it without having both his horror of *evil* and his respect for virtue increased. You have the art of blending instruction with amusement — while you keep your readers in high good humour by the frolicksomeness of your manner, you are inculcating upon them important moral and religious truths, conducing to their present and future happiness. I am very respectfully yours, David Ramsay — The Rev. Mr. Weems" ' *Repub.* (Sav'a), May 14, 1807, UN'YGA., May 28, 1807 *et seq.*, GAHS.

5. Weems wrote to Wayne, May 16, 1805: 'I am getting ready for you another beautiful book which Gen[l] Pinckney says ought to be in the hands of every youth in the U. States. — You shall have it soon.' [The dates of publication of Weems' later works or their character, as well as the evidence of newspaper advertisements, precluding the probability of any of them being here referred to, it seems possible to assume that he is speaking in this letter of the above title. Does this not still further imply the existence of an earlier edition than this of 1807?] To Carey, Mar. 24, 1810: 'I shall settle in a few weeks with Hobby, Merriweather &c. &c. in full. The former printed me a little pamphlet. In paying you *for that,* which sells rapidly, I shall pay you some little part of what they owe U & sooner or as soon perhaps as you w[d] have gotten your *money otherwise.*' June 14, 1811: 'Hobby, I fear, will give trouble. But he is safe *at last.*'

6. 'William J. Hobbey, postmaster, Petersburg, Ga., Jan. 1, 1795 (first return) — July 1, 1795.' *P.O.Rec.Bk. No.1*, pp. 482–483, P.O.Bldg., Washington, D.C. 'Hobby & Bunce (W. J. Hobby and William J. Bunce) published the *Augusta Herald*, Georgia, from 1804 to 1817.' *Bibliography of American Newspapers*, Clarence S. Brigham, *Proc.AAS.*, Vol. XXIII, Part II, Oct. 1913, p. 374. 'In 1805 William J. Hobby was intendant [*of the city of Augusta, Ga.*]. This gentleman was long a resident of Augusta; carried on the business of a stationer and journalist, and was for years editor of the *Herald.*' *Memorial History of Augusta, Georgia*, Charles C. Jones, Jr., LL.D., and Salem Dutcher, Syracuse, 1890, p. 166, LC.

7. This tract on Murder preaches forgiveness toward the fallen woman, which in that day was rare indeed. Credit should also be given Weems for his charity and tolerance in religious questions, his free expression of which bespeaks an open mind as well as considerable courage.

No third edition found.

1. *Ad.* '. . . 3[d] edition was sold in Philadelphia in about one week.' *Mus. Del.*, Dec. 31, 1808 *et seq.*, AAS. See also last lines of advertisement in note 2, title succeeding.

NUMBER 178 1808

GOD'S | REVENGE AGAINST MURDER; | OR | THE DROWN'D WIFE, | A TRAGEDY, | LATELY PERFORMED, WITH UNBOUNDED APPLAUSE, | (OF THE DEVIL AND HIS COURT) | BY NED FINDLEY, ESQUIRE, | ONE OF THE | GRAND COMPANY OF TRAGEDIANS | IN THE SERVICE OF THE | BLACK PRINCE, | Who was so highly gratified with *Ned's* performance, that he instantly | provided him Rooms in one of his own *Palaces;* created him a | Knight of the most ignoble order of the Halter; clapped | bracelets on his wrists, and an ornament round his | neck; and in a few days promoted him to the | ridge pole of the gallows, at Edgefield | Court-House, South-Carolina. | BY M. L. WEEMS, | OF LODGE *No. 50,* DUMFRIES. | FOURTH EDITION — PRICE, 25 CENTS. | *O Reader dear, I give you here | A book to look upon, | That you may pray, both night and day, | Nor go, where* NED *has gone.* | PHILADELPHIA: |

PRINTED FOR THE AUTHOR, | BY JOHN ADAMS. | 1808. | 8vo. pp. (1), 3, 4–40. *Front.plate.*

AAS., ConnHS., HSP., HU., LC., MdHS., NYHS., NYPL., WL.

1. Frontispiece, oval, stippled, with inscription, in script, below 'Mary Finley [*sic*]', signed '*J. Boyd; sc.*'[1]; on reverse of title is 'Criticism . . .' signed 'David Ramsey [*sic*]', dated May [*sic*], 1807, and Penn. copyright to M. L. Weems dated 1808, 'thirty-third year . . .'; caption to the text '*The man whose blossom buds in blood, | To death shall sure be cast | And from the earth full soon be swept | By God's avenging blast.*' The text is much changed from

[1] 'J. Boyd. Mary Findley Reported, but not seen.' Fielding's *Index* to Stauffer's *American Engravers upon Copper and Steel,* No. 252.

the 1807 edition; the type after p. 32 is much smaller and more compressed.

2. *Ad.* [*M.L.W.?*] 'Just published, and for sale at this Office, God's Revenge against Murder: or the Drowned Wife. A faithful history of the beautiful Miss Polly Middleton. who, after bestowing herself, with a fortune of four thousand dollars, on a young husband, Mr. Edward Findley, was drowned by him in the eighth week after marriage!!! with a number of curious incidents, and a fine likeness of the unfortunate lady. The Fourth Edition — Price 25 cents. By M. L. Weems, who was on the spot where Mr. Findley, in the midst of an immense concourse of people, was executed at Edgfield [*sic*] Court-House, South Carolina, on the 27th of April, 1804. O reader dear, . . . Criticism on this work by that celebrated American historian, Dr. David Ramsey, South Carolina, dated, Charleston, May [*sic*] 16, 1807. [*See note 4, second edition, title 177.*] Of this very interesting work, Mr. Carey of Philadelphia, sold an edition in six days!' *Oracle Dauph.*, Nov. 5, 1808 *et seq.*, PSTL. Same advertisement, with slight changes, in *Mus. Del.*, Dec. 31, 1808 *et seq.*, AAS. [See also announcement preceding this title.]

3. Weems wrote to Carey [*received Sept. 29, 1808*]: 'I pray you urge the sale of Mary Findley — that we may have a lovely edition for the South. This you can do the better now that you have suspended your Antimasonic Drastic.' Oct. 7, 1808: 'But who coud have thought the 600 woud not have serv[d] my turn & satisfied the curiosity of so few towns & villages from Wilmington to Laureltown [*Del.*] . . . The miserable paper . . . of this 4[th]. edition of Mary Findley mortifies me dreadfully. Were it not that there is murder in the thing it cou'dn't possibly fly at this rate. But really I'm dying to have it off, that we may have another edition. . . . Indeed I am very certain that it wou'd be worth, *well* worth your while to start William with a trunk of 10 or 12,00 of them to *Trenton, Princeton, Brunswick, Bridgetown, Elizabeth, New Ark &* [*New*] *York.* In this coming mild weather of *October*, — this Indian summer, when the spirits of the People shall be getting gay and bold, let William fall upon them with his popular advertisements & the sweetly mournful Likeness of the Murdered Fair One, & he will certainly put off 1200. There is a time to catch popular feelings as well as young Rabbits & a cold cloudy day is not that time — a warm bright day is the thing.'

4. John Boyd — 'Excellent engraver of portraits in stipple.' *American Engravers upon Copper and Steel*, David McNeely Stauffer, 1907, Vol. I, Part I, p. 28. 'Boyd was an engraver in Philadelphia in 1812.' *History of the Rise and Progress of the Arts of Design in America*, William Dunlap, 1834, New York, Vol. II, p. 254, NYPL.

NUMBER 179　1808

GOD'S | REVENGE AGAINST MURDER; | OR, | THE DROWN'D WIFE, | A TRAGEDY, | LATELY PERFORMED, WITH UNBOUNDED APPLAUSE, | (Of the Devil and his Court) | BY NED FINDLEY, ESQUIRE, | ONE OF THE GRAND COMPANY OF TRAGEDIANS | In the Service of the | BLACK PRINCE, | Who was so highly gratified with *Ned's* performance, that he instantly provided him Rooms | in one of his own *Palaces;* created him a | Knight of the Halter, clapped | bracelets on his wrists, and an ornament round his neck; and | in a few days promoted him to the ridge-pole of the | gallows, at Edgefield Court-House, | South-Carolina. | BY M. L. WEEMS, | OF LODGE, No. 50, DUMFRIES. | FIFTH EDITION — PRICE 25 CENTS. | O Reader dear, I give you here | A book to look upon, | That you may pray, both night and day, | Nor go, where NED has gone. | PHILADELPHIA: |

PRINTED FOR THE AUTHOR, BY A. DICKINSON. | 1808. | 8vo.
pp. 3, 4–40.
NYPL.

1. On reverse of title 'Criticism' signed 'David Ramsey' [*sic*], and Penn. copyright 'thirty-third year . . . 1808.'; the text is headed with the usual verses, and is still without chapters, the first lines being 'Ned Findley, the hero of the following Tragedy . . .'; after p. 32 the type is much smaller, as in the preceding edition; the verses throughout appear to be the same; from the 1807 edition there are elisions, abbreviations, and changes, notably, on p. 1, of one of the judges, and on p. 5, where 'tackies' is changed to 'ponies'; additions, on pp. 30–31, elisions on p. 51, and additions, as well as changes, on pp. 52–54.

2. *Ad.* 'Just received . . . . God's Revenge against Murder, or the Drowned Wife . . .' [with criticism by Dr. Ramsay]. *Intel.*, Dec. 13, 1808; abbreviated, Dec. 27, 1808, LIOF.

3. '(The widow of the late Abel) Dickerson [*Dickinson*], finds it to her advantage to hire a woman for the household affairs, and betake herself to the office.' *McCulloch's Additions to Thomas's History of Printing, ProcAAS.*, Vol. XXXI, April, 1921, p. 217.

NUMBER 180 1809

GOD'S | REVENGE AGAINST MURDER; | OR, | THE DROWN'D WIFE. | A TRAGEDY, | LATELY PERFORMED, WITH UNBOUNDED APPLAUSE, | (Of the Devil and his Court) | BY NED FINDLEY, ESQUIRE, | ONE OF THE GRAND COMPANY OF TRAGEDIANS | In the Service of the | BLACK PRINCE, | Who was so highly gratified with *Ned's* performance, that he instantly provided him Rooms | in one of his own *Palaces;* created him a Knight of the Halter, clapped | bracelets on his wrists, and an ornament round his neck; and | in a few days promoted him to the ridge-pole of the | gallows, at Edgefield Court-House, | South-Carolina. | BY M. L. WEEMS, | OF LODGE, No. 50, DUMFRIES. | SIXTH EDITION — PRICE, 25 CENTS. | O Reader dear, I give you here | A book to look upon, | That you may pray, both night and day, | Nor go where NED has gone. | PHILADELPHIA: |

PUBLISHED BY M. JONES, BY PERMISSION OF THE AUTHOR. | 1809. | Dickinson, Printer. | 12mo. pp. (1), 4, 4–48, (2). *Front.plate.* HU.

1. The frontispiece is an oval portrait, after the fourth edition, 1808, title 178, but unsigned, and different from others, stippled, bust, stippled line border, face to left, with the inscription 'Mary Findley.' in script; on reverse of title are Criticism,' signed, 'David Ramsey [*sic*]', and Penn. copyright, 1808; no heading to text save the few lines of verse; the last page has eight lines of verse 'Could you with ink the ocean fill . . . Tho' stretched from sky to sky!', followed by 'The Travels of Captains Lewis and Clarke. will soon be published by Mithra Jones, and ready to deliver to subscribers, (by the young men who sell this pamphlet) . . .' with a recommendation signed 'Th. Jefferson.' After this edition the text remained practically unchanged, save where noted in title 185, note 1.

2. *Ad.* [*M.L.W.?*] 'The Rev. Mason L. Weems, well known in the Southern States as agent for procuring subscribers for the Life of Washington . . . and several other whimsical and amusing publications, has lately published "The Drown'd Wife . . . eighth week after marriage."' [Ramsay's criticism follows,

for which see title 177, note 4.] *Star*, Feb. 9, 1809, NCSTL. 'Just Published, for sale . . . God's Revenge against Murder; or the Drowned Wife, a faithful history of the beautiful Miss Polly Middleton. . . .' *Mus. & George'n Adv.*, Mar. 8, 1809 *et seq.*, LC. [Almost identical with advertisement in title 178, note 2.]

3. Weems wrote to Carey from Lancaster, Jan. 13, 1809: 'What I send you is the fruit of Washington & Mary Findley, —' Jan. 15, 1809: 'If Dickinson or others sh[d] apply for copy right of Mary Findley, do the best for me you can.' Oct. 19, 1809: 'I pray you to send to Sam[l] Pleasant 500 Findley *immediately*.' Nov. 18, 1809: 'I pray you send him [*Pleasants of Richmond*] 300 of Mary Findley.' Feb. 28, 1810: 'And here now in this very Country, where two years ago I sold a great part of *one edition* of Washington & *two* of M. Findley, I still sell more of them than of any, even *the best School books* that you have sent me, and yet you coud get mad because I offer[d] you the purchase of my little books on *your own terms*.' Mar. 24, 1810: '[*I have sold*] near 800 Dolls and no School books, no Religious books, not even a Pilgrims progress & Washington & Findley all gone — People tearing me to pieces for the *first, and the last*.'

No seventh edition found.

NUMBER 181 1809

GOD'S | REVENGE AGAINST MURDER; | OR, | THE DROWN'D WIFE, | A TRAGEDY, | LATELY PERFORMED, WITH UNBOUNDED APPLAUSE, | (Of the Devil and his Court) | BY NED FINDLEY, ESQUIRE, | ONE OF THE GRAND COMPANY OF TRAGEDIANS | In the Service of the | BLACK PRINCE; | Who was so highly gratified with *Ned's* performance, that he | instantly provided him Rooms in one of his own *Palaces;* | created him a Knight of the Halter, clapped bracelets | on his wrists, and an ornament round his neck; | and in a few days promoted him to the ridge- | pole of the gallows, at Edgefield Court- | House, South-Carolina. | BY M. L. WEEMS, | OF LODGE, NO. 50, DUMFRIES. | EIGHTH EDITION — PRICE 25 CENTS. | *O Reader dear, I give you here,* | *A book to look upon,* | *That you may pray, both night and day,* | *Nor go, where* NED *has gone.* | PHILADELPHIA: |

PRINTED FOR THE AUTHOR. | 1809. | 12mo. pp. (1), 4–47, (1). *Front.plate.*
HU.

1. The frontispiece is like that of the fourth edition, but unsigned.

2. *Ad.* '. . . Also — The History of the beautiful Miss Polly Middleton — . . . eighth week after marriage . . . [Ramsay's criticism follows, for which see title 177, note 4.] *Petersburg Repub.*, Apr. 9, 1810, AAS. 'Books . . . for sale cheap . . . Also, the following pamphlets — God's Revenge against Murder . . .' *Louisv'l. Gaz.*, May 4, 1810, AAS. 'Museum of Elegant Wax-Figures. Just arrived and may be seen . . . at the City Tavern, Richmond . . . a very handsome collection of Wax Figures, as large as Life . . . Miss Charlotte Temple . . . Mary Findley, that was drowned by her Husband only eight weeks after Marriage. William, her beautiful Son, at the age of five years . . .' *Va. Arg.*, Oct. 23, 1810, AAS. Also advertised in: *Am. Watch.*, Nov. 1, 1809 *et seq.*, AAS. *Ga. Express*, Dec. 8, 1810 *et seq.*, UN'YGA. *Mus. & Georg'n Adv.*, Mar. 8, 1809 *et seq.*, LC. *Ga. Arg.*, Jan. 16, 1811, HU.

NUMBER 182 1814

GOD'S | REVENGE AGAINST MURDER; | OR, | THE DROWN'D WIFE, | A Tragedy, | LATELY PERFORMED, WITH UNBOUNDED APPLAUSE, | (Of the Devil and his Court) | BY NED FINDLEY, ESQUIRE, | *One of the Grand Company of Tragedians in the service of the* | *Black Prince*, | who was so highly gratified with *Ned's* performance, that he instantly provided him | Rooms in one of his *Palaces;* created him a Knight of the Halter, clapped | bracelets on his wrists, and an ornament round his neck; and | in a few days promoted him to the ridge-pole of | the gallows, at Edgefield, Court- | House, South-Carolina. | BY M. L. WEEMS, | OF LODGE NO. 50, DUMFRIES. | *Eighth Edition — Price 25 Cents.* | BALTIMORE: |

PRINTED for the AUTHOR, by BELL & COOK. | 1814. | 12mo. pp. (1), 3, 4–54, (2). *Front.plate.*
BA., NYHS.

1. The frontispiece, unsigned, engraved, stippled, face to right, is a half-length likeness of 'Mary Finley [*sic*]'; on reverse of title are Penn. copyright 1808 and 'Criticism by Ramsey'.

2. Weems wrote to Websters & Skinners: 'Dumfries, Mar. 31, 1814. . . . 4 God's revenge against Murder . . . The *two last* have gone thro several editions & have sold, each, to the tune of 30 to 40.000.' [BPL.]

No ninth edition found.

NUMBER 183 1816

GOD'S | REVENGE AGAINST MURDER: | OR | THE DROWN'D WIFE. | A TRAGEDY, | AS LATELY PERFORMED, WITH UNBOUNDED APPLAUSE, | (OF THE DEVIL AND HIS COURT) | BY NED FINDLEY, ESQUIRE, | ONE OF THE GRAND COMPANY OF TRAGEDIANS | IN THE SERVICE OF | THE BLACK PRINCE, | Who was so highly gratified with *Ned's* performance, that he instantly | provided him Rooms in one of his own *Palaces;* created him a Knight | of the most ignoble order of the Halter, clapped bracelets on his wrists, | and an ornament round his neck; and in a few days promoted him to | the ridge pole of the gallows, at Edgefield Court-House, South Carolina. | BY M. L. WEEMS, | OF LODGE NO. 50, DUMFRIES. | TENTH EDITION, ENLARGED — PRICE, 25 CENTS. | *O Reader dear, I give you here | A book to look upon, | That you may pray, both night and day, | Nor go, where* NED *has gone.* | PHILADELPHIA: |
PRINTED FOR THE AUTHOR. | 1816. | (*Copy-right secured, according to Act of Congress.*) | 8vo. pp. (1), 2, (1), 1, 4–40. *Front.plate.*
AAS., LC., NYPL.

1. The frontispiece, unsigned, engraved, is an upright rectangular picture of Findley, striking his wife in the water; inscription below '*The cruel catastrophe of* MARY FINLEY [*sic*]'. The AAS. copy has cover imprint 'GOD'S REVENGE AGAINST MURDER; | OR THE | DROWN'D WIFE: | A TRAGEDY. | AS LATELY PER-

FORMED, WITH UNBOUNDED APPLAUSE, | (OF THE DEVIL AND HIS COURT) | *By Ned Findley*, ESQ. | ONE OF THE GRAND COMPANY OF TRAGEDIANS | IN THE SERVICE OF | THE BLACK PRINCE, | Who was so highly gratified with *Ned's* performance, that he instantly provid- | ed him Rooms in one of his own *Palaces*, created him a Knight of the most | ignoble order of the Halter; clapped bracelets on his wrists, and an ornament | round his neck; and in a few days promoted him to the ridge pole of the | gallows, at Edgefield Court House, South Carolina. | BY M. L. WEEMS, | OF LODGE No. 50, DUMFRIES. | TENTH EDITION, ENLARGED — PRICE 25 CENTS. | O Reader dear, I give you here | A book to look upon, | That you may pray, both night and day, | Nor go, where NED is gone. | PHILADELPHIA: | Printed for the author. | 1816. | (*Copyright secured, according to Act of Congress*).'

2. Weems wrote to Carey, May 24, 1816: 'From numerous experiments that I have made, I am pretty confident that you may raise a great deal of my salary from the Pamphlets. An ad Captandum show bill, such as I gave you — with all the plates arranged in stricking [*sic*] order on the top — a couple of these with 2, 3 or more dozens of each of the pamphlets sent to at least 100 of y^r Booksellg Friends. By sticking them up at the taverns along the roads I have sold them off, frequently, with great success. One tavern keeper sold me 3 parcels. Preachers & Parents will recommend [*them*]. Wyeth had 50 of Mary Finley alone & he p^d me for all t'other day, and is raging to get 50 to 100 of each.' July 31, 1816: 'For the Gambler & Mary Finley, as they [*the plates*] are worn out I pray you have them done anew & in as beautiful a style as you can — for the effect of good things will abundantly pay extra costs.'

NUMBER 184 1818

GOD'S REVENGE | AGAINST | MURDER; | OR, | THE DROWN'D WIFE. | A TRAGEDY, | AS LATELY PERFORMED, WITH UNBOUNDED APPLAUSE, | (OF THE DEVIL AND HIS COURT) | BY NED FINDLEY, ESQUIRE, | ONE OF THE GRAND COMPANY OF TRAGEDIANS | IN THE SERVICE OF | THE BLACK PRINCE, | Who was so highly gratified with *Ned's* performance, that he instantly | provided him Rooms in one of his own *Palaces;* created him a Knight | of the most ignoble order of the Halter, clapped bracelets on his wrists, | and an ornament round his neck; and in a few days promoted him to | the ridge pole of the gallows, at Edgefield Court-House, South Carolina. | Y M. L. WEEMS, | OF LODGE No. 50, DUMFRIES. | ELEVENTH EDITION, ENLARGED — PRICE 25 CENTS. | *O Reader dear, I give you here* | *A book to look upon,* | *That you may pray, both night and day,* | *Nor go, where NED has gone.* | PHILADELPHIA: |

PRINTED FOR THE AUTHOR. | 1818. | (*Copy-right secured, according to Act of Congress.*) | 8vo. pp. (1), 2, (1), 1, 4–40. *Front.plate.*

AAS., CLS., HU.

1. On the title the 'B' in the word 'BY' before Weems' name is missing. The frontispiece, unsigned, engraved, with inscription '*The cruel catastrophe of* MARY FINLEY [*sic*].' is identical with the 1816 edition, title preceding; preceding the usual verses there is a long caption to Chapter I 'THE SORROWFUL LIFE | AND | CRUEL DEATH | OF | MARY FINDLEY, | *Daughter of Major Hugh Middleton. . . .*' The HU. copy has cover imprint 'GOD'S REVENGE AGAINST MURDER; | OR, THE | DROWN'D WIFE. | A TRAGEDY, | AS LATELY PERFORMED WITH UNBOUNDED APPLAUSE, | (OF THE DEVIL AND HIS COURT) | BY NED FINDLEY, Esq. | ONE OF THE GRAND COMPANY OF TRAGEDIANS | IN THE SERVICE OF | THE BLACK PRINCE. | BY M. L. WEEMS, | OF LODGE No. 50, DUMFRIES. | ELEVENTH EDITION, ENLARGED — PRICE 25 CENTS. | PHILADELPHIA: | PRINTED FOR THE AUTHOR. | 1818. | (*Copy-right secured, according to act of Congress.*)'

2. *Ad.* [*M.L.W.*] 'To the Editor of the Courier. . . . V. The Bad Husband's Looking Glass — Presenting a fine melodramatic history of the beautiful Miss Polly Middleton, who, after bestowing herself and a handsome fortune on a young husband, was drowned by him in the eighth week after marriage.' *Charles. Cour.*, Apr. 14, 1821, CLS.; with slight changes, signed, in *Georgian*, May 15, 1821, GAHS. 'Messrs. Pasteur & Watson, You will oblige your friend, the undersigned . . . The Bad Husband's Looking Glass . . . at the Druggist Store of Dr. E. Hawes. . . .' *Car. Cent.*, June 16, 1821, NYHS.

NUMBER 185 1823

GOD'S | REVENGE AGAINST MURDER; | OR | THE DROWN'D WIFE, | A TRAGEDY, | AS LATELY PERFORMED, WITH UNBOUNDED APPLAUSE, | (OF THE DEVIL AND HIS COURT) | BY NED FINDLEY, ESQUIRE, | ONE OF THE GRAND COMPANY OF TRAGEDIANS | IN THE SERVICE OF | THE BLACK PRINCE, | Who was so highly gratified with *Ned's* performance, that he instantly | provided him Rooms in one of his own *Palaces;* created him a Knight | of the most ignoble order of the Halter, clapped bracelets on his wrists, | and an ornament round his neck; and in a few days promoted him to | the ridge pole of the gallows, at Edgefield Court-House, South Carolina. | BY M. L. WEEMS, | OF LODGE No. 50, DUMFRIES. | ELEVENTH EDITION, ENLARGED — PRICE, 25 CENTS. | *O Reader dear, I give you here,* | *A book to look upon,* | *That you may pray, both night and day,* | *Nor go, where* NED *has gone.* | PHILADELPHIA: |

PRINTED FOR THE AUTHOR. | 1823. | (*Copy-right secured, according to Act of Congress.*) | 8vo. pp. (1), 2, (1), 1, 4–40. *Front.plate.*

AAS., BPL., HSP., LC., LCPhil., NYHS., NYPL. [*lacks front.*], PStL.

1. The frontispiece, unsigned, engraved, with inscription below '*The cruel catastrophe of* MARY FINLEY [*sic*]', is identical with the 1816 and 1818 editions, titles 183 and 184; on p. 1 the text is abbreviated from Dickinson's 1808 edition, title 179, and shows minor changes throughout; heading to text 'THE SORROWFUL LIFE | AND | CRUEL DEATH | OF MARY FINDLEY, | (*Daughter* . . . | . . . | Who, after giving a handsome fortune . . . | . . . | . . .' |; the usual verses follow. NYPL. has one copy with a cover imprint identical with the title save that it lacks copyright notice.

2. Brinley Nos. 3163 and 3164.

NUMBER 186? 1806–1807?

## *The Bachelor's Almanac. [*1806–1807?*]

1. Though I have found no such work, both the advertisements which follow and Weems' letters in note 3 partly prove its actuality.

2. *Ad.* [*M.LW.?*] 'Have an eye here. JUST PUBLISHED, 1st The Maids and Bachelor's Almanac, for 1807. . . .' *Ga. Rep.*, Dec. 5, 16, 1806 *et seq.*, UN'YGA. [From Jan. 12–20, 1807, the heading was printed 'Have an Eye hear. . . .]' [*M.L.W.?*] 'For Sale at this Office, By the *unit, ten,* or *hundred.* WEEMS'S *Two Famous* ALMANACS. The 1st, *The Bachelor's Almanac;* . . . The first, demonstrates that, *For Man it surely is not good To live without a Wife,* . . .' *Col. Cent.*, Jan. 31, 1807 *et seq.*, UN'YGA. This implies that Weems may have issued another Almanac with extracts from *Hymen's Recruiting Serjeant.* For another advertisement which possibly bears on this, see note 3 to title 171A. [See also notes to titles 155A and 160 *et seq.* and especially letter of March 31, 1808 in note 3 below.]

3. Weems wrote to Wayne, Aug. 18, 1806: 'I wrote to you 10 days ago begging that you w[d] instantly get John Bioren, (if you cou'd not attend to it yourself) to print me 6000 Almanacks, one half of them, containing Hymen's Recruiting Serjeant, and thereby entitled "The Lover's or Bachelors Almanac." The other containing . . . "The Grand Republican Almanac." [*See titles 155, 155A and 187.*] . . . Urge M[r] B., or whomever you may employ, to make the greatest possible dispatch. The Legislature of this state [*Georgia*] will sit in the beginning of Nov. as also will that of S. Carol[a] during my attendance for distribution of Washington, Sidney, Anquetil &[c] &[c] I may distribute a good many almanacs. . . . Attend to my Almanacs — to Hymen . . . Once more, beg Bioren if you shou[d] employ him, to drive on . . . with all his might. I shall by [*the*] next mail, send the list of Courts &c &c let him push the calculations and the matter for the body of the work. let it be on a good paper.' On Aug. 20, 1806, he urged Wayne to get the calculations for a South Carolina and Georgia Almanac from Abraham Shoemaker of New York and if 'by good natur[d] & *great*

*exertions'* the book should reach him by the 1st day of October he should think himself much indebted. Aug. 25, 1806: 'Please to attend to my Almanac — to Hymen 5th. edition — Hurry on Washington — And as I order'd 50 Sidney, & 100 Montague — & I hope I shall give a good account of them.' [*After Aug. 25, 1806*]: 'I cant dismiss the Subject, without reiterating *my request* that you wd make some exertions to get me this Almanac in Charleston & Savanna, by the 1st. of Octob. & *sooner if possible*. . . . If you employ Bioren, tell him . . . to do his *utmost to have* the Almcs. . . . by the 1st of Octob. at farthest.' Sept. 7, 1806: 'Dont forget my almanacs & 5th Edition of Hymen. They have sold admirably.' Sept. 20, 1806, to Wayne: 'Attend to my Almanacs & Hymen.' Sept. 30, 1806: 'You talk of my following so many plans & books for *Conrad* &c &c. I tell you that I have not gotten 10 Subs & those altogether by accident.' Oct. 11, 1806: 'Be so good as to desire Bioren & Adams to send me on immediately my Hymen & Almanacs, INSURED. I want 600 Hymens sent to Augusta — 400 to Charleston. All the Almanacs to Augusta. It *is now*, and *ever has been* my wish that you shou'd be Jointly concernd in the profits & losses of everything publishd at my request since we were concernd.' The following from a letter of Mar. 31, 1808, may possibly have some bearing on these undiscovered Almanacs. '[*In May 1806?*] . . . I wrote to you for 6000 Almcs. You sent them, but *so late*, that not *one half ever sold!!!*' For other letters see notes to title following, especially that of Dec. 28, 1806.

NUMBER 187? 1806–1807?

## *The Grand Republican Almanac. [*1806–1807?*]

1. It seems probable that Weems printed an Almanac with the title substantially the same as the advertisements below. That it has not been found thus far is not surprising, since of his two almanacs for 1800 [titles 172 and 172A] only one copy of each is accessible, and considering the light esteem in which such ephemeral prints were held and the hard usage given them.

His letters make this issue quite other than any of the four Almanacs which I have seen, printed over his name. Undoubtedly the excerpts were from *The Philanthropist* or *The True Patriot*, titles 156 and 173, more likely the latter, see note 3 below. See also title preceding, note 3.

2. *Ad.* [*M.L.W.?*] 'Have an eye here. JUST PUBLISHED . . . 2d. The Grand Republican ditto [*Almanac*] for ditto [*1807*], both uncommonly large and curious. And immensely entertaining and profitable. ALSO, . . . Please enquire at Dr. George Harral's Medicine Store. Nov. 28'. *Ga. Rep.*, Dec. 5, 16, 1806 *et seq.*, UN'YGA. [From Jan. 12–20, 1807, the heading was printed 'Have an Eye hear. . . .'] [*M.L.W.?*] 'For Sale at this Office, By the *unit, ten*, or *hundred*. WEEMS's *Two famous* ALMANACS. . . . The 2d, The *Grand Republican* do. [*Almanac*] . . . The second [*demonstrates*] *That those who groan beneath a King, Must lead a wretched life.*' *Col. Cent.* (Aug., Ga.), Jan. 31, 1807 *et seq.*, UN'YGA.

3. Weems wrote to Wayne, Aug. 4, 1806: 'If you think it adviseable that I shou'd spend the winter here, you will infinitely oblige me by setting about 5000 or 6000 Almanacs for South Carolina & Georgia. If you have no wish to go in partnership in the matter, you may have them done at *my own risk.* M[r] Bioren (as Johnny Adams is engag[d] at Anquetil) will do them for me. M[r]. Bioren is a man of *energy*, he will *instantly* get some person to *calculate* for the *latitude* of 33 & 32 (being the latitude of Charleston & Savannah) the sooner he sets about it *the better*. . . . I have written to M[r] Bioren to call on you about y[r] mind as to the Almanac. If, (as *I think* will be the best we can do) I sh[d] wait here untill I can wind up all the Washington business so long neglected by Murray &[c] we must have a large assortment in exch[e]. for your books on hand.' Aug. 18, 1806: 'I wrote to you . . . begging that you w[d] instantly get John Bioren . . . to print me 6000 Almanacks, one half . . . The other containing my dissertation on the Excellencies of a Republic, (printed by John Adams & I believe by John Bior [*e*]n in some late Almanacs) and thence call[d] "The Grand Republican Almanac."' [No such issues found.] Dec. 28, 1806, from Augusta: 'By sending those Almanacks so late & to Persons never mention'd . . . I lost I dont know how much. In August last I wrote to you [*about*] an Almanac which I hop[d] w[d] be here in Nov. — but only about one half have yet got to Savannah. I suppose that nearly one half of this edition will, as to the Kalander [*sic*], be lost.' [See also title 186, last lines of note 3.]

NUMBER 188? 1810?

## *God's Revenge against Gambling. [*1810?*]

1. Clear evidence of the existence of such an edition, which I have not seen, seems to lie in the advertisements cited in note 3 below, and in the letters of note 4, as well as in the fact that the 1812 edition was issued as the 'Second Edition.'

2. Probably the source of one of 'these terrible examples' was in 'The Fatal Effects of Gaming, exemplified in the History of Miss Braddock.' [*Anon.*] *Md. Gaz.*, Mar. 10, 1786, MDSTL.; *W'kly Mus.*, Sept. 22, 1792, LC.; *Cent. Freed.*, Dec. 1, 1801, NJHS.; *Phil. Repos.*, Vol. II, Feb. 20, 1802, pp. 117–119, LC. The *Georgia and South Carolina Almanack for 1807*, Augusta, Hobby & Bunce [LC.], also contains 'The Story of Miss Braddock' in the above newspaper version, which consists of fourteen paragraphs and two stanzas and is entirely different from Weems' rendering. Another article unlike that of Weems is as follows 'On Gambling. To wake the soul by tender strokes of art, to raise the genius and to mend the heart. Gambling, may justly be said to be a vice that is pregnant with misery and distress . . . to answer for his crimes at the tribunal of his God.' *Louisv'l. Gaz.*, Mar. 20, 1807, HU.

3. *Ad.* [*M.L.W.*] 'BOOKS. THE following collection . . . in addition to former supplies, is opened at the Printing-Office, and for sale cheap — . . . ALSO, *The following pamphlets* . . . LIKEWISE, *Just Published and for Sale Here*, A Most Extraordinary new Pamphlet, ENTITLED GOD'S REVENGE AGAINST Gambling, Exemplified in the *Miserable Lives & Untimely Deaths* Of a number of persons of both sexes, . . . *With curious Anecdotes on the following Unfortunate Gamblers:* 1. . . . 6. With many other awful cases of young Gamblers, and their untimely ends, well calculated to caution young men against that *cursed sin*, which after wasting their time, spoiling their temper, ruining their morals, and grieving their *fondparents* [*sic*] seldom fails to bring them to Poverty and Disgrace, and often to the Gallows. RECOMMENDATION. *To the Rev. L. M.* [*sic*] *Weems*, SIR, I have read with pleasure your Pamphlet against *Gambling;* — which ought to be placed on the shelf of every citizen. It will produce extensive good; and much more good than if its price had been considerable. I sincerely wish you success in the various efforts which you are making to promote the best

GOD'S

REVENGE AGAINST

# GAMBLING.

EXEMPLIFIED IN THE

MISERABLE LIVES AND UNTIMELY DEATHS

OF A NUMBER OF

PERSONS OF BOTH SEXES,

WHO HAD SACRIFICED THEIR

*HEALTH, WEALTH, AND HONOR AT GAMING TABLES.*

WITH CURIOUS ANECDOTES OF THE FOLLOWING

UNFORTUNATE GAMBLERS:—

I. Miss Fanny Braddock, sister of General Braddock, who, from Gambling, hung herself.
II. Drisden Harwood, Esq. Maryland, who, from Gambling, drowned himself.
III. Jack Gilmore, Esq. Virginia, who, from Gambling, shot himself.
IV. T. Alston, Esq. (N. C.) who, from Gambling, was shot by Capt. Johnson.
V. Maria Antoinette, Queen of France, who, for Gambling, was brought to the Guillotine.
VI. Other awful cases of young Gamblers, and their untimely ends.

*Blest is the* YOUTH *who ne'er consents*
*In* GAMBLERS' *haunts to stray;*
*But hates their games, and shuns the place,*
*Where men* PROFANELY PLAY.

*In* HEALTH *and Wealth, in Peace and Love,*
*Full safe that Youth shall grow,*
*And then with saints shall sing above,*
*Whilst Gamblers weep below.*

*BY M. L. WEEMS,*

FORMERLY RECTOR OF MOUNT VERNON PARISH.

[SECOND EDITION.]

*PHILADELPHIA:*
PRINTED FOR THE AUTHOR
1812.

Facsimile Title Page of the 1812 Edition of *God's Revenge Against Gambling*

interests of our country. I am with esteem and very respectfully yours, J. MEIGS.[1] *Franklin College, Athens, March* 31, 1810.' *Louisv'l. Gaz.*, May 4, 1810, AAS. Also advertised in *Ga. Arg.*, Jan. 16, 1811, HU.

4. Weems wrote to Carey, Mar. 12, 1810: 'My little books "Life of Wash. Mary Findley, Hymen ["] & my late little book "God['*s*] revenge against Gambling" have render<sup>d</sup> me more popular than I deserve. And it is a great thing at these Public times & places, to have the big People take me by the hand & send the Little Fry to me. . . .' See letter, dated Mar. 31, 1814, in note 3 to succeeding title. Weems' dedicatory letter to Jesse therein, dated Jan. 29, 1811, could not have been in the first edition, unless issued later than 1810; also on p. 33 Weems stated that he was writing 'this pamphlet' on Feb. 10, 1811, which seems to suggest that it was a revision of the pamphlet rather than to disprove the issue of this putative edition.

5. Ten years or so before this time, Weems was already animadverting on the sin and dangers of gambling, see his *Washington* [1800? p. 7, titles 2 *et seq.*]. For the need of some check upon gaming in all walks of life there was ample contemporary evidence. [Writing from Annapolis, Md.] 'They Game high, Spend freely, and Dress exceedingly gay, but I observe they seldom show any money, it is all tobacco notes.' *Journal of Nicholas Cresswell*, New York, 1924, pp. 21–22, LC.

NUMBER 189 1812

GOD'S | REVENGE AGAINST | GAMBLING. | EXEMPLIFIED IN THE | MISERABLE LIVES AND UNTIMELY DEATHS | OF A NUMBER OF | PERSONS OF BOTH SEXES, | WHO HAD SACRIFICED THEIR | HEALTH, WEALTH, AND HONOR AT GAMING TABLES. | WITH CURIOUS ANECDOTES OF THE FOLLOWING | UNFORTUNATE GAMBLERS: — | I. Miss FANNY BRADDOCK, sister of ⁝ General Braddock, who, from ⁝ Gambling, hung herself. II. DRISDEN HARWOOD, Esq. Ma- ⁝ ryland, who, from Gambling, ⁝ drowned himself. III. JACK GILMORE, Esq. Virginia, ⁝ who, from Gambling, shot him- ⁝ self ⁝ IV. T. ALSTON, Esq. (N.C.) who, ⁝| from Gambling,

[1] Josiah Meigs, first Land Commissioner of the United States; later President of the College of Georgia at Athens.

was shot by ⁝| Capt. Johnson. ⁝| V. MARIA ANTOINETTE, Queen of ⁝| France, who, for Gambling, was ⁝| brought to the Guillotine. ⁝| VI. Other awful cases of young ⁝| Gamblers, and their untimely ⁝| ends. ⁝| *Blest is the Youth who ne'er consents* | *In* GAMBLERS' *haunts to stray;* | *But hates their games, and shuns the place,* | *Where* men PROFANELY PLAY. | *In* HEALTH *and Wealth, in Peace and Love,* | *Full safe that Youth shall grow,* | *And then with saints shall sing above,* | *Whilst Gamblers weep below.* | BY M. L. WEEMS, | FORMERLY RECTOR OF MOUNT VERNON PARISH. | (SECOND EDITION.) | PHILADELPHIA: |

PRINTED FOR THE AUTHOR. | 1812. | 8vo. pp. (1), 4, IV, 1, 6–51, (1). *Front.plate.*

AAS., BPL., HU., LC.

1. Issued by Carey, according to letters of Weems in note 3 below; on reverse of title are Penn. copyright 'Second Edition,' to Mason L. Weems, dated Feb. 17, 1812, commendation by Jacob Rush, dated Jan. 20, 1812, and letter 'To Master Jesse Ewell Weems' signed 'Your affectionate Father, M. L. Weems, dated 'Augusta, in Georgia January 29, 1811.' [this would imply that the earlier edition was issued without the letter to Jesse]; the frontispiece is unsigned, engraved, stippled, with inscription '*He writhes: he gnashes his teeth. On* | *bended knees, he curses the Authors of* | *his ruin. Page 19.*'; on pp. 14 and 50 there are allusions to Washington's brush with Payne already used in the *Life of Washington;* pp. 26–51 consist of 'DISSUASIVES AGAINST GAMBLING'; on p. 33 Weems states that 'this pamphlet is written . . .' on Feb. 10, 1811 in Augusta. The HU. copy has cover imprint rather similar to title, with advertisements on the reverse 'Books lately published, and for sale at the place where this pamphlet is sold.' Colophon 'PRINTED BY LYDIA R. BAILEY, | No. 10, NORTH ALLEY.' The sign ⁝ means that the title is there broken into two columns, the sign ⁝| indicating the second column. This procedure is adopted from the *Notes* of Paul L. Ford.

2. *Ad.* 'Just Received (Price, 25 Cents) God's Revenge against Gambling. [*Exact title in full follows.*] By M. L. Weems, formerly Rector of Mountvernon [*sic*] Parish. — Second Edition.' *Intel.*, Nov. 23, 1816 *et seq.*, HSP. Also advertised, with no mention of Weems' name, in *Amer. Watch.*, June 13, 1812 *et seq.*, DHS., LCPHIL.; as by the Rev. M. L. Weems, *Va. Arg.*, Mar. 8, 1813 *et seq.*, LC.

3. Weems wrote to Carey, Feb. 13, 1812: 'A thought has often occur[d] to me which you will approve; suppose after the first Chap. of the "*God[s] Revenge against Gambling*," which ends with the bloody fate of the Queen of France, you were to give a few good *verses*, shewing that no *Rank* nor *Power* can save from condign punishment those who abuse these advantages to the ruin of others, Doct[r] Watts in his *psalms* has some fine lines. Your children (sans compliment) if put on the track w[d] soon find them. I need not tell *you* the good effect of such caping [*sic*] to such a chapter. Also at the close of the book — & particularly if ½ a page be wanting, it will do admirably to wind up with some awefully painted verses. In the cheap repository (complete sett) & in other places you will find good matter; or make some.' To President Madison Weems wrote [*n.d. received June 17, 1812*, LC., — see Vol. III] giving him a copy of '*God's Revenge Against Gamblers*.' To 'Websters & Skinners', from Dumfries, Mar. 31, 1814: '. . . 2 The Gamblers Looking Glass. . . . The two first are but of recent date however have gone, *each*, thro' two editions — and large editions too — and I am now getting Mr. John Bioren of Philad[a] to reprint me heavy editions of them both. You may reprint 2.000 of each, if you'll give me 2 cents on every copy. Shou'd you think of it, you w[d] find it worth y[r] while to get some good Engraver in New York to give you a good Caricature for the first, i.e., the Drunkards Looking Glass. There is an admirable one for the Gamblers look[g] Glass, which M. Carey got executed for me. Carey printed me an edition of 4000 the 2[d] edition. . . .' For other allusions see letters in Vol. III.

NUMBER 190 1815

GOD'S REVENGE | AGAINST | GAMBLING. | EXEMPLIFIED IN THE | MISERABLE LIVES AND UNTIMELY DEATHS | OF A NUMBER OF | PERSONS OF BOTH SEXES, | WHO HAD SACRIFICED THEIR | HEALTH, WEALTH, AND HONOUR | AT | GAMING TABLES. | WITH | CURIOUS AND AWFUL ANECDOTES. | BY M. L. WEEMS, | Third edition. | FORMERLY RECTOR OF MOUNT VERNON PARISH. | Blest is the YOUTH who ne'er consents | In GAMBLER'S haunts to stray; | But hates their games, and shuns the place, | Where men PRO–

FANELY PLAY. | In HEALTH and Wealth, in Peace and Love, | Full safe that Youth shall grow, | And then with saints shall sing above, | Whilst GAMBLERS howl below. | BALTIMORE: |

PRINTED FOR THE AUTHOR, | by J. Hagerty. | 1815. | 8vo. pp.(1), 4, IV, 1, 6–48. *Front.plate.*
LC.

1. The frontispiece, unsigned, engraved, stippled, is identical with that in the 1812 edition; on reverse of title Penn. copyright, and commendation by Jacob Rush; pp. 3–4, letter to Jesse Weems; pp. 24–46 consist of: 'CALM DISSUASIVES . . .'; pp. 46–48 contain 'THE TRUE CURE OF GAMBLING.', but where, in the 1812 edition, the text ends, this one contains the following: 'The reader may perhaps say . . . Well then in the following story take The True Cure of Gambling. Captain John Giles . . . colonel John Taylor of the senate . . .'; which is not in the 1816 nor subsequent editions.

NUMBER 191 1816

GOD'S | REVENGE AGAINST GAMBLING. | EXEMPLIFIED IN THE | MISERABLE LIVES AND UNTIMELY DEATHS | OF A NUMBER OF | PERSONS OF BOTH SEXES, | WHO HAD SACRIFICED THEIR | HEALTH, WEALTH, AND HONOR, AT GAMING TABLES. | WITH CURIOUS ANECDOTES OF THE FOLLOWING | UNFORTUNATE GAMBLERS: — | I. Miss FANNY BRADDOCK, sister of General Braddock, who, from Gam- ⁝ bling, hung herself. ⁝ II. DRISDEN HARWOOD, Esq. Mary- ⁝ land, who from Gambling, drowned ⁝ himself. ⁝ III. JACK GILMORE, Esq. Virginia, ⁝ who, from Gambling, shot himself. ⁝ IV. T. ALSTON, Esq. (N.C.) who, ⁝| from Gambling, was shot by Capt. ⁝| Johnson. ⁝| V. MARIA ANTOINETTE, Queen of ⁝| France, who, for Gambling, was ⁝| brought to the Guillotine. ⁝| VI. Other awful cases of young Gam- ⁝| blers, and their untimely ⁝| ends. ⁝| *Blest is the* YOUTH *who ne'er consents* | *In* GAMBLERS' *haunts to stray;* | *But hates their games, and shuns the place,* | *Where men* PROFANELY PLAY. | *In* HEALTH *and Wealth, in Peace and Love,* | *Full safe that Youth shall grow,* | *And then with saints shall sing above,* | *Whilst Gamblers weep below.* | BY M. L. WEEMS, | FORMERLY RECTOR OF MOUNT VERNON PARISH. | (THIRD EDITION.) PHILADELPHIA: |

PRINTED FOR THE AUTHOR. | 1816. | 8vo. pp. 3, IV, 1, 6–47, (1). LC., NYPL.

1. Copyright, commendation by Jacob Rush, and letter to Jesse Weems are identical with the 1812 edition, title 189; pp. 25–47 contain 'Dissuasives against Gambling. After reading what has been already said . . . Hell. The End.' One NYPL. copy has cover imprint with slight changes from the title and at bottom '*Price 25 Cents.*'; colophon '*Printed by J. Bioren,* | 88 *Chesnut Street.*' For the signs ⁝ and ⁝ | see title 189, last part of note 1.

2. I have found a *Note* of Paul L. Ford querying whether there was another 1816 edition, but I have not discovered such. The note is so indefinite that possibly it refers to the next title.

3. Weems wrote to Carey, May 2, 1816: 'The 4 pamphlets sh[d] go *together.*' [Alluding to his own tracts.]

NUMBER 192 1818

GOD'S REVENGE | AGAINST GAMBLING. | EXEMPLIFIED IN THE | MISERABLE LIVES AND UNTIMELY DEATHS | OF A NUMBER OF | PERSONS OF BOTH SEXES, | WHO HAD SACRIFICED THEIR | HEALTH, WEALTH, AND HONOR, AT GAMING TABLES. | WITH CURIOUS ANECDOTES OF THE FOLLOWING | UNFORTUNATE GAMBLERS: — | I. Miss FANNY BRADDOCK, sister of Ge- ⁝ neral Braddock, who, from Gambling, ⁝ hung herself. ⁝ II. DRISDEN HARWOOD, Esq. Ma- ⁝ ryland, who, from Gambling, drowned ⁝ himself. ⁝ III. JACK GILMORE, Esq. Virginia, who, ⁝ from Gambling, shot himself. ⁝ IV. T. ALSTON, Esq. (N.C.) who, ⁝ | from Gambling, was shot by Capt. ⁝| Johnson. ⁝| V. MARIA ANTOINETTE, Queen of ⁝| France, who, from Gambling, was ⁝| brought to the Guillotine. ⁝| VI. Other awful cases of young Gam- ⁝| blers, and their untimely ends. ⁝| *Blest is the* YOUTH *who ne'er consents,* | *In* GAMBLERS' *haunts to stray;* | *But hates their game, and shuns the place,* | *Where men* PROFANELY PLAY. | *In* HEALTH *and Wealth, in Peace and Love,* | *Full safe that Youth shall grow.* | *And then with saints shall sing above,* | *Whilst Gamblers weep below.* | BY M. L. WEEMS, | FORMERLY RECTOR OF MOUNT VERNON PARISH. | (FOURTH EDITION.) | PHILADELPHIA: |

PRINTED FOR THE AUTHOR. | 1818. | 8vo. pp. (1), 4, IV, 1, 6–47, (1). *Front., Plates.*

AAS., MdHS.

1. The frontispiece is identical with that in the 1812 edition, title 189; on reverse of title is Penn. copyright, dated 1812, and Commendation by Jacob Rush; letter of dedication to Jesse Weems follows on another page; at pp. 13, 16, 21 and 27 there are four unsigned cuts; pp. 26–47 contain 'DISSUASIVES AGAINST GAMBLING.' For the signs ⁝ and ⁝| see title 189, last part of note 1.

2. *Ad.* [*M.L.W.*] '*To the Editor of the Courier.* . . . II. The Gambler's Looking Glass — Reflecting 19 likenesses highly tragi-comic, of unfortunate Gamblers, admirably calculated to show the madness of exchanging the safe, sure-card play of honest industry, for the hazardous trumps of "Snap & Battle," "All-Fours," etc.' *Charles. Cour.*, Apr. 14, 1821, CLS.; with some changes, in *Georgian*, May 15, 1821, GAHS.; *Car. Cent.*, June 16, 1821, NYHS.

3. Weems wrote to Carey, Apr. 8, 1817: 'The times require all the Antidot^es to Drunkenness, Gambling &c &c. And I know you wish to do good. . . . Preachers & Parents & Legislators will rise up in behalf of them [*the pamphlets*].' Apr. 12, 1817: 'If you w^d but turn y^r attention more to the Pamph^ts, getting many *good Caricatures*, & I also going over them again & working them up to a good fix, much might be done.' Oct. 9, 1817: 'Inclosed I send you the case of that Elegant Gentleman, a Scots Merchant of Augusta, Georgia, of the name of M^cIntosh, see the page 31, near the bottom. It is sketch^d by the pencil of a youth of this place [*Richmond*], who is deaf but can read, and is astonishingly quick with his pencil to hit off in that strong style which best suits subjects of this nature. I have promis^d to give him 3 dollars *in books*, for every one that he

will do equal to this. Such pieces as these w^d give a wonderful popularity to our pamphlets . . . I w^d advise you *immediately* to put this drawing in good hands — please put the name of the youth who did it, i.e "Young Rob K. Smith. Richmond."[1] Tho we are to cooperate only for 8 or 9 months, yet I think great things might be done in that time by these pamphlets with plates & showbills.' To Henry C. Carey, Nov. 18, 1821: 'In every box send TWO SHOW BILLS, or send no boxes at all — and in y^r note beg them in *one word* to nail the show bill *on a board.* You said that in this contract, you w^d give every thing a *fair trial* — I w^d advise you to follow the excellent idea of yr father — viz. to strike off on a small type — a hand bill of the large show bill & put one *in every pamphlet.* "He saves the Country who checks vice" — and again "A VIRTUOUS PEOPLE WILL BE FREE" and again "*True Self love* & *Social is the Same.*" I dont know how it may turn out but I have a strong hope that Providence will make your Father like Sampson, most useful & glorious at the last.'

NUMBER 193 1822

GOD'S REVENGE | AGAINST GAMBLING. | EXEMPLIFIED IN THE | MISERABLE LIVES AND UNTIMELY DEATHS | OF A NUMBER OF | PERSONS OF BOTH SEXES, | WHO HAD SACRIFICED THEIR | HEALTH, WEALTH, AND HONOUR, AT GAMING TABLES. | WITH CURIOUS ANECDOTES OF THE FOLLOWING | UNFORTUNATE GAMBLERS: | I. Miss FANNY BRADDOCK, sister of ⁝ General Braddock, who, from Gam ⁝ bling, hung herself. ⁝ II. DRISDEN HARWOOD, Esq. Mary- ⁝ land, who, from Gambling, drowned ⁝ himself. ⁝ III. JACK GILMORE, Esq. Virginia, who, ⁝ from Gambling, shot himself. ⁝ IV. T. ALSTON, Esq. (N.C.) who, ⁝| from Gambling, was shot by Capt. ⁝| Johnson. ⁝| V. MARIA ANTOINETTE, Queen of ⁝| France, who, for Gambling, was ⁝| brought to the Guillotine. ⁝| VI. Other awful cases of young Gam- ⁝|

[1] 'R. K. Smith engraved a stippled portrait of Rev. John Flavel published in Richmond, Va., 1824.' *A History of the Rise and Progress of The Arts of Design in the United States*, William Dunlap, Boston, 1918, Vol. III, p 335, LC.

blers, and their untimely ends. ⁞| Blest is the *youth* who ne'er consents | In *Gamblers'* haunts to stray; | But hates their games, and shuns the place, | where men profanely play. | In *Health* and Wealth, in peace and love, | Full safe that youth shall grow, | And then with saints shall sing above, | Whilst gamblers weep below. | BY M. L. WEEMS, | FORMERLY RECTOR OF MOUNT VERNON PARISH. | (FOURTH EDITION.) | PHILADELPHIA: |

PRINTED FOR THE AUTHOR. | 1822. | 8vo. pp. 1, (2), 4, IV, 1, 6–24, [25]–47, (1). *Front.plate.*
AAS., HSP., LC., LCPhil., NYPL., PStL., YU.

1. The frontispiece differs from, but is after that in the 1812 edition, title 189; inscription '*Thrice accurs'd* CARDS *and* DICE! | *You have been my ruin!*'; copyright and Rush's letter on reverse of title; letter to Jesse Weems follows; pp. [25]–47 contain 'DISSUASIVES AGAINST GAMBLING.' The AAS., LC., and NYPL. have each one copy with cover imprint identical with the title. For the signs ⁞ and ⁞| see title 189, last part of note 1.

2. *Ad.* [*M.L.W*] '. . . popular little tracts on Gambling . . . with J. R. Schenck, bookseller . . . [*preceded by a letter of commendation from Bishop Bowen*].' *Charles. Cour.*, Feb. 16, 1822, CLS.

NUMBER 194 1816

ANECDOTES | OF | GAMBLERS, | EXTRACTED FROM A WORK ON GAMBLING. | BY M. L. WEEMS, | FORMERLY RECTOR OF MOUNT VERNON PARISH. | [*Monogram of T.A.F.*] | PHILADELPHIA: |

TO BE HAD OF BENJAMIN & THOMAS KITE, NO. 20, NORTH THIRD | STREET: AND FOR SALE BY SOLOMON W. CONRAD, NO. 87, | KIMBER & SHARPLESS, NO. 93, JOHN RICHARDSON, NO. 31, | and ISAAC PIERCE, NO. 316, MARKET STREET. | 1816. | No. 9. | 12mo. pp. 2, 3–12.
AAS.

1. Colophon 'JOSEPH R. A. SKERRETT, Printer, | No. 135, south Ninth street.'
2. These booksellers are all listed in the *Philadelphia Directory*, 1816.

NUMBER 195 1818

ANECDOTES | OF | GAMBLERS, | EXTRACTED FROM A WORK ON GAMBLING. | BY M. L. WEEMS, | FORMERLY RECTOR OF MOUNT VERNON PARISH. | [*Monogram of T.A.F.*] | PHILADELPHIA: |

TO BE HAD OF BENJAMIN & THOMAS KITE, NO. 20, NORTH THIRD | STREET: AND FOR SALE BY SOLOMON W. CONRAD, NO. 87, KIMBER | & SHARPLESS, NO. 93, AND JOHN RICHARDSON, NO. 8. NORTH THIRD STREET. | 1818. | *No. 9.–2d. ed.*–6000 12mo. pp. 2, 3–8.
AAS., MdHS.

1. Colophon 'J. R. A. SKERRETT, PRINTER.'

NUMBER 196 1878

Anecdotes of Gamblers. | FROM A WORK ON GAMBLING. | BY | M. L. WEEMS, | FORMERLY RECTOR OF MT. VERNON PARISH, AUTHOR OF "THE | LIFE OF WASHINGTON," ETC. | PHILADELPHIA: |

JAMES A. MOORE, | 1220–1224 SANSOM STREET. | 1878. | 16mo. pp. 3, (1), 1, 6–34, (2).
MdHS.

1. Cover title only. On reverse of title is announcement that this was a reprint of the 2nd edition, dated 1818, 'of six thousand copies' under the auspices of the Tract Ass. . . . of Friends, of Phila. . . . The page following contains a short account of Weems. . . . 'Bishop Meade's elder brother knew him well. . . . He had some peculiarities . . . but all who knew him loved him.' [*signed*] C. W. Andrews, dated Shepherdstown, Va., 1870; slight changes from the former editions on p. 3, and, on p. 24, at the end of a Bible quotation; thereafter the contents are not by Weems.

NUMBER 197? 1812?

*The Drunkard's Looking Glass. Philadelphia? Cochran? [*1812?*]

1. There seems clear evidence, in the advertisement and letters following, as well as in the fact that the issue of 1813 was expressly called the 'second edition,' with copyright date of 1812, that Weems did print an earlier one, although I have not been able to find it. [See letter, dated Mar. 31, 1814, note 2 to 1813 edition, title 198.] I have not assumed the first date of publication as before 1812, for even though the growing irritation between England and the United States during the years that preceded the War of 1812, plus the Embargo, so greatly dislocated all business as to discourage any new ventures, is it not possible that he ordered the book from Mrs. Cochran shortly before hostilities commenced? See note 3 below.

2. *Ad.* [*M.L.W.*] 'That which beggars more client [*s*] than *lawyers!* Kills more patients than *physicians;* and ruins more souls than *antichrist.* Just Published, and for sale at Brynberg's Bookstore, the New Drunkard's Looking Glass; reflecting . . . the dogs. This Looking-Glass may be well worth squinting at, even by the oldest veterans in the service — but particularly profitable to young recruits, who are discovering in themselves, a growing appetite for morning slings and 11 o'clock grog. — By M. L. Weems.' *Amer. Watch.*, June 13, 1812 *et seq.*, DHS.

3. Weems wrote to Carey early in 1812: 'M[rs]. C [*ochran*] has already wetted down some of the paper which you sent to finish the pamphlet.' Again, speaking, presumably, of the same pamphlet, May 4, 1812: 'I also pray you to do me the following great services — 1[st]. send to M[rs] Cochran, the letter *post paid*, which accompanies this. 2[d]. procure me a good frontispiece for my pamphlet, against Drunkenness, One of the *funny sort* will be best perhaps. If your designer cou'd consult Hogarth, or go to M[rs]. Cochran's & read some of the Blackguard sins recorded in this pamphlet, his imagination might fall into the right track. I assure you my prospects for this year are squally, and unless I can make something by other People's Gambling & drink, I shall be strongly tempted myself.' [See letters of May 8, 1812, in Vol. III.] June 27, 1812:

'Can't you instantly send me the ballance of the Drunkards Looking Glass to Alexandria? From the little experience that I have had, it will do well by & by when it comes to be polished.' Sept. 29, 1812: 'Can hear nothing of the Maps for this place, nor of the D[s]. looking glass. But for the faint hope it may do some good to Youth I cou[d] almost wish I had never written that illfated pamphlet — tho' it outsells anything I have lately written . . . Had I foreseen that I shou'[d] have lost 10 months time about the Maps & the D[s]. Looking Glass I w[d] have sent my stage as far as Balt[o]. to meet them, or w[d] have had an edition printed at Alexand[a].'

4. Weems was essentially a gleaner, and possibly he took his title from one of the following, of which the text, however, bears no slightest resemblance to his: '. . . The Drunkard's Looking-Glass . . .' [*Anon.*] *Conn. Gaz.*, Nov. 19, 1790, YU.; *Md. Gaz.*, Nov. 27, 1790, LC. 'The Drunkard's Looking Glass. First. Some general effects of Intemperance. . . . Some particular characters of a Drunkard. . . .' [*Anon.*] *Amer. Merc.*, Dec. 13, 1790, AAS.; *Mass. Spy*, Dec. 16, 1790, YU.; reprinted in *The Columbian Almanac for 1796*, Philadelphia, Stewart & Cochran, [LC.]; also, with changes and abbreviations: 'Messrs. Printers. Please to give the following a place in your useful paper. The Drunkard's Looking-Glass. O Thou Monster, if like a man — but O thou wretched wretch if thou be like a woman — deprived of reason, besotted understanding, causes error in judgment, debauches the mind, defiles the conscience, hardens and steels the heart — it is the work of darkness — it is an annoyance to modesty, a gate to debauchery — it is a discloser of secrets, a betrayer of truth, a depriver of honesty, a forerunner of misery, cracks men's hearts and credits, empties their purses, consumes their estates, violates all the rules of temperance, occasions loss of confidence, reverses the order of nature, causes profane, scurrilous and cursed speeches, fightings and murders — it is the mother of mischief and father of all vices, the nurse of riot and fury, the school of lying and slander, an impairer of health, deforms the visage, decays the brain, memory, body and mind, renders the body so filthy, loathsome and odious as to be forbidden to all who behold it — it decays moral virtues, destroys private and public societies — it has its violent ambitions, destroys love and all confidence between those that ought to be mutual friends, and confidence lost from ill rewards can never be regained. The first of blessings are thus destroyed. [*signed*] A Spectator.' *Balt. D. Repos.*, Aug. 10, 1793, LC.

5. Mrs. Cochran was the widow of Robert Cochran, printer, who died in 1811 or shortly thereafter. The *Philadelphia Directory* of that year lists him at '108 Sassafras,' while that of 1813 records 'Cochran widow of Robert, printer' at the same address.

6. Judge E. R. Hoar's report cited that when any young child died at Concord, Mass., a table was set with bottles of rum, whiskey and gin, and each of the young boys who had been selected as pall-bearers freely partook. 'In Randolph's time excessive drinking was common in every part of our country. . . . And Josiah Quincy, Jr. is not picturing Silenus and his purple-faced crew, but the members of one of the blowing Clubs of Harvard in or about the year 1821, when he pens these words: "One of these societies, which is yet in existence, though it is to be hoped that the habits of its members have improved, was wont to have a dinner on exhibition days. After the exercises in the Chapel, the brethren would march to Porter's Tavern, preceded by a full band; and an attempt was made to return in the same way. First, would come the band, the only steady part of the show, whose music attracted a crowd of lookers-on. Then came, reeling and swaying from side to side, a mass of Bacchanals in all stages of intoxication."' *John Randolph of Roanoke*, William Cabell Bruce, Vol. II, pp. 171, 172–173. Leesburg, Loudoun County, Virginia. Wednesday 'Nov. 30, 1774, 'Have been genteely treated and am now going to bed drunk. This is the first time.' Garralland, Loudoun County, Jan. 6, 1776. 'All of us got most feloniously drunk.' Jan. 7. 'Went to bed about two o'clock in the afternoon, stupidly drunk, not been in bed or asleep for two nights. The uneasiness of my mind causes me to drink deeper when in company to elevate my spirits.' Feb. 14, 1776. 'A confounded mad frolic.' *Journal of Nicholas Cresswell*, New York, 1924, LC.

NUMBER 198 1813

THE | *Drunkard's Looking-Glass.* | REFLECTING | A FAITHFUL LIKENESS | OF | THE DRUNKARD, | IN | SUNDRY VERY INTERESTING ATTITUDES; | WITH LIVELY REPRESENTATIONS | OF THE MANY STRANGE CAPERS WHICH HE CUTS | AT DIFFERENT STAGES OF HIS DISEASE; | *As first,* | When he has only "A DROP IN HIS EYE," | *Second,* | WHEN HE IS "HALF SHAVED," | *Third,* | when he is getting "A little on the Staggers or so," | *And fourth and fifth, and so on,* | TILL HE IS "QUITE CAPSIZED," | OR, | "Snug under the Table with the Dogs," | AND | *Can* "*Stick to the* FLOOR *without holding on.*" | BY M. L.

THE

# *Drunkard's Looking-Glass.*

REFLECTING

A FAITHFUL LIKENESS

OF

## THE DRUNKARD,

IN

*SUNDRY VERY INTERESTING ATTITUDES;*

WITH LIVELY REPRESENTATIONS
OF THE MANY STRANGE CAPERS WHICH HE CUTS
AT DIFFERENT STAGES OF HIS DISEASE;

*As first.*
When he has only "A DROP IN HIS EYE,"
*Second,*
WHEN HE IS "HALF SHAVED,"
*Third,*
When he is getting "A little on the Staggers or so,"
*And fourth and fifth, and so on,*
TILL HE IS "QUITE CAPSIZED,"
OR,
"Snug under the Table with the Dogs,"
AND
*Can "stick to the FLOOR without holding on."*

---

BY M. L. WEEMS,
*Author of the Life of Washington, &c.*

---

SECOND EDITION. GREATLY IMPROVED.

[*Price Twenty-five cents.*]

1813.

FACSIMILE TITLE PAGE OF THE 1813 EDITION OF
*THE DRUNKARD'S LOOKING GLASS*

WEEMS, | *Author of the Life of Washington, &c.* | SECOND EDITION, GREATLY IMPROVED. |
(*Price Twenty-five cents.*) | 1813. | 8vo. pp. 3, 4–60.
BA. [*imp.*], NYPL.

1. On reverse of title, in Penn. copyright to M. L. Weems, dated 1812, 'thirty-sixth year', are four lines of verse: [*M.L.W.*] '"God prosper long these noble States.!" | And all therein that dwell; | And grant both Church and State to join, | This monster vice to quell. | By M. L. Weems, (late Rector of General Washington's Parish.)'; followed by '*Golden Receipts against Drunkenness*'; the text begins with the heading '*The Drunkard's Looking Glass.*' and four citations from Proverbs, and is without chapter headings until p. 42, where Chapter IV is headed 'Thus, lips that do with brandy burn,| Shall never prosper long; | God's righteous vengeance, shall consume | The whiskey loving tongue'; some of the other verses may be imputed to Weems, both from their style and the fact that they are printed without quotations: 'His face alas! has lost its red! | His cheeks their burning hue, | Ragged and warty is his nose, | But ah! that nose how blue!—,' [p. 44]; pp. 48–60 contain 'TRUE CURE OF DRUNKENNESS! *A word from the Pulpit. . . .*'

2. In a letter to the Websters, publishers, of Albany, Weems wrote, Mar. 31, 1814 [BPL.]: 'I have lately written & publish[d] with great success two or three pamphlets about the size of Washington's life. 1. The Drunkards Looking Glass. 2 The Gamblers Looking Glass . . . The two first are but of recent date however have gone, *each*, thro' two editions — and large editions too — and I am now getting Mr. John Bioren of Philad[a] to reprint me heavy editions of them both. You may reprint 2.000 of each, if you'll give me 2 cents on every copy. Shou'd you think of it, you w[d] find it worth y[r] while to get some good Engraver in New York to give you a good Caricature for the first, i.e., the Drunkards Looking Glass.'

3. Advertised in *Pol. Exam.*, Aug. 18, 1813 *et seq.*, AAS.

4. That Weems liked a glass of wine himself is shown in passages in his letters, as well as in the 'Golden Receipts of Drunkenness' which preface this pamphlet, in which he advises 'a *little* wine' as well as 'Hot Coffee.' Elsewhere he compared unfavorably his southern contemporaries when he pointed out that 'the dauntless Yankees still drank their Switchel, a mild moralizing malmsey, made of molasses and water, which the prudent Yankees drink to the great benefit of their health, and senses, while their southern neighbors are befooling and bepoisoning themselves with grog.' If the vulgarisms of his pamphlets are compared with other skits of his period on the same subject, he will be

seen not to have erred more than other lampooners. In Sept., 1722, in the *New England Courant* Franklin wrote over the *nom de plume* of *Silence Dogood,* comments upon 'the Manners & Conversation of men' under the influence of spirits. 'It argues some Shame in the Drunkards themselves, so that they have invented numberless Words and Phrases to cover their Folly, whose proper Significations are harmless, or have no signification at all. They are seldom known to be *drunk,* tho they are very often *boozey, cogey, tipsey, fox'd, merry, mellow, fuddl'd, groatable, Confoundedly cut, See two moons,* are *among the Philistines, In a very good Humour, See the Sun,* or, *The Sun has shone upon them; they Clip the King's English,* are *almost froze, Feavourish, In their attitudes, Pretty well enter'd,* &c. In short, every day produces some new Word or Phrase which might be added to the Vocabulary of the *Tiplers:* But I have chose to mention these few, because if at any Time a Man of Sobriety and Temperance happens to *cut himself confoundedly,* or is *almost froze,* or *feavourish,* or accidentally *sees the Sun,* &c. he may escape the Imputation of being *drunk,* when his misfortune comes to be related.' See also the sixth edition, title 202, note 5.

NUMBER 199 1814

THE | Drunkard's Looking Glass; | REFLECTING | A FAITHFUL LIKENESS | OF | THE DRUNKARD, | IN | SUNDRY VERY INTERESTING ATTITUDES; | WITH | LIVELY REPRESENTATIONS OF THE MANY STRANGE CAPERS WHICH HE CUTS | AT DIFFERENT STAGES OF HIS DISEASE; | As First, | WHEN HE HAS ONLY "A DROP IN HIS EYE;" | Second, | WHEN HE IS "HALF-SHAVED;" | Third, | WHEN HE IS GETTING "A LITTLE ON THE STAGGERS OR SO;" | And Fourth and Fifth, and so on, | TILL HE IS "QUITE CAPSIZED;" | OR, "SNUG UNDER THE TABLE WITH THE DOGS," | and | CAN "STICK TO THE FLOOR WITHOUT HOLDING ON." | BY M. L. WEEMS, | AUTHOR OF THE LIFE OF WASHINGTON, &c. | THIRD EDITION, GREATLY IMPROVED. |

(*Price Twenty-five cents.*) | 1814. | 8vo. pp. (1), 4, 4–57. *Front.plate.* LC., MdHS. [*imp.*]

1. Probably printed by John Bioren [see Weems' letter to the Websters, title 198, note 2]. The frontispiece, unsigned, is of a woman with a bottle, labelled 'Gin,' and a glass; inscriptions, above 'Half Shav'd!! "A *drap* of the *Real* for *them that loves* a dram!"' below '"Och the sweet crature! if I could but always get a *drap* of you, my honey, I should *live forever!*"' [see title 202, note 1 and letter of Nov. 15, 1819, note 4]; the second, third and fourth words of title are in Old English; on reverse of title are Penn. copyright, dated 1812, and 'Golden Receipts against Drunkenness.'

NUMBER 200 1816

THE | DRUNKARD'S LOOKING GLASS: | REFLECTING | A FAITHFUL LIKENESS | OF | THE DRUNKARD, | IN | SUNDRY VERY INTERESTING ATTITUDES; | WITH | LIVELY REPRESENTATIONS OF THE MANY STRANGE CAPERS WHICH | HE CUTS AT DIFFERENT STAGES OF HIS DISEASE; | AS FIRST, | WHEN HE HAS ONLY "A DROP IN HIS EYE;" | SECOND, | WHEN HE IS "HALF SHAVED;" | THIRD, | WHEN HE IS GETTING "A LITTLE ON THE STAGGERS OR SO;" | AND FOURTH AND FIFTH, AND SO ON, | TILL HE IS "QUITE CAPSIZED;" | OR | "SNUG UNDER THE TABLE WITH THE DOGS," | AND | CAN "STICK TO THE FLOOR WITHOUT HOLDING ON." | BY M. L. WEEMS, | AUTHOR OF THE LIFE OF WASHINGTON, &C. | FOURTH EDITION, GREATLY IMPROVED. |

PRINTED FOR THE AUTHOR. | 1816. | (*Price Twenty-five Cents.*) |
8vo. pp. (1), 1, (2), 3, 4–55, (1). *Front.plate.*
AAS., LCPhil.

1. Frontispiece, unsigned, is of a drunkard being knocked off his horse by a tree, with inscription below 'DRUNKARDS BEWARE!' [perhaps by William Charles, see title 202, notes 1 and 4]; on reverse of title, Penn. copyright to Weems, dated June 2, 1812, followed by '*Golden Receipts against Drunkenness.*'; the text

ends with 'BLESS MANKIND. | THE END.'; pp. 32-38 of both the editions of 1816 were reprinted as *Narrative of Peter and John Hay*, 1816 and 1818, titles 206 and 207; also as *Effects of Drunkenness*, 1823, title 208.

2. Alibone's *Dictionary*.

3. Advertised, with title in full, *Intel.*, Aug. 3, 1816, HSP.

NUMBER 201 1816

THE | DRUNKARD'S LOOKING GLASS: | REFLECTING A FAITHFUL | *Likeness of the Drunkard*, | IN | SUNDRY VERY INTERESTING ATTITUDES, | WITH | Lively Representations of the many strange Capers which he | cuts at different Stages of his Disease; | AS FIRST, | WHEN HE HAS ONLY "A DROP IN HIS EYE;" | SECOND, | WHEN HE IS "HALF SHAVED;" | THIRD | WHEN HE IS GETTING "A LITTLE ON THE STAGGERS OR SO;" | AND FOURTH AND FIFTH, AND SO ON, | TILL HE IS "QUITE CAPSIZED;" | OR | "SNUG UNDER THE TABLE WITH THE DOGS," | AND | CAN "STICK TO THE FLOOR WITHOUT HOLDING ON." | BY M. L. WEEMS, | AUTHOR OF THE LIFE OF WASHINGTON, &c. | FIFTH EDITION, GREATLY IMPROVED. |

PRINTED FOR THE AUTHOR. | 1816. | (*Price Twenty-five Cents.*) | 8vo.
pp. (1), 1, (2), 3, 4–55, (1). *Plate.*
AAS., MdDio'nL.

1. The copyright, 'Golden Receipts,' and the plate are the same as in the fourth edition, 1816, except that the last is placed opposite p. 8; this edition is printed on larger sheets than those preceding but the text ends identically.

2. Weems wrote to Carey, May 24, 1816: 'I have certificates of the most complete Cures wrought by a single peep at the Drunkards Looking Glass. And if my correspondents keep going on at this rate I shall be obliged to come out presently in the Katiefelto style and publish what wonders I am doing among the Swine. With y[r] resources you cou'd have them all out in 10 days, lathering away

among the Gamblers, Drunkards, Adulterers, & Sinners at a most heroic rate. Mess$^{rs}$. Law, Herbert, Key [1] and thousands of great men every where, tell me that you can't multiply too many copies of these books, which they say, form the most successful mode of attacking those vices (among our Youth) which by swallowing up National Morals will assuredly swallow up National Liberty. The Subjects & Titles are all important and Interesting — and if we cou'd but get (for subsequent impressions corrected) good Caricatures there is no doubt, with the advantages you possess, you cou'd distribute myriads annually to great profit.' May 28, 1816: 'Every hour the People are telling of the Great Good that you & I may do by putting into the hands of the young "who know not their right hand from the left," our moral looking glasses. If you think you give me too much (40 pr. Cent) give less. So they be well done & speedily sent to me that's all I care for, with show bills perhaps on a Folio paper & the caricatures *pasted* on the head.'

NUMBER 202 1818

THE | DRUNKARD'S LOOKING GLASS: | REFLECTING A FAITHFUL | LIKENESS OF THE DRUNKARD, | IN | SUNDRY VERY INTERESTING ATTITUDES, | WITH | *Lively Representations of the many strange Capers which he cuts at* | *different Stages of his Disease;* | AS FIRST, | WHEN HE HAS ONLY "A DROP IN HIS EYE;" | SECOND, | WHEN HE IS "HALF SHAVED;" | THIRD, | WHEN HE IS GETTING "A LITTLE ON THE STAGGERS OR SO;" | AND FOURTH AND FIFTH AND SO ON, | TILL HE IS "QUITE CAPSIZED;" | OR | "SNUG UNDER THE TABLE WITH THE DOGS," | AND | CAN "STICK TO THE FLOOR WITHOUT HOLDING ON." | BY M. L. WEEMS, | Author of the Life of Washington, &c. | SIXTH EDITION, GREATLY IMPROVED. |

[1] 'Philip Key, born in St. Mary's Co., Md. in 1750; served in State House of Representatives; representative from Maryland in second Congress, 1791–93; died on his estate, St. Mary's Co., 1820.' *The Political Register and Congressional Directory . . . of the United States of America, 1776–1878*, compiled by Ben. Perley Poore, Boston, 1878, LC.

PRINTED FOR THE AUTHOR. | 1818. | (*Price Twenty-five Cents.*) |
8vo. pp. (1), 4, 4–63, (1). *Front.plates, Cuts.*
AAS., CLS., HSP., LC., LCPhil., NYHS., NYPL., PStL.

1. The frontispiece, unsigned, is like that of the 1816 editions, and is probably by the well-known caricaturist, William Charles [1] [see note 4 below]; the twelve unsigned cuts probably by William Mason [2] [see note 4 below] are at pp. 4, 6, 12, 15, 22, 27, 30, 32, 35, 39, 46 and 58; on reverse of title, beneath Penn. copyright notice, 1812, are '*Golden Receipts against Drunkenness,*'; pp. 37–44 contain 'Case XXV Of Peter and John Hay, South Carolina'; pp. 50–63 'TRUE CURE OF DRUNKENNESS.' with examples. The AAS. and HSP. copies have a cover imprint with an unsigned woodcut of a woman with a bottle labelled 'Gin,' and inscription above 'THE DRUNKARD'S | LOOKING GLASS. | [*Cut*] | BY M. L. WEEMS, | AUTHOR OF THE LIFE OF WASHINGTON, &C. | SIXTH EDITION, GREATLY IMPROVED. | PRINTED FOR THE AUTHOR. | 1818. | (*Price 25 Cents.*)' This is first found in title 199.

[1] 'Charles William, copper plate engraver, book-seller, publisher and stationer 32 S. Third' *Philadelphia Directory*, 1817, LC. — 'William Charles, engraver and caricaturist, native of Scotland; died in Phil., in 1820. He was a prolific engraver and publisher of caricatures and juvenile literature, both in a style similar to contemporary English productions. He worked in line, stipple and aquatint.' *A History of the Rise and Progress of The Arts of Design in the United States*, William Dunlap, Boston, 1918, Vol. III, p. 289, LC. — 'Mr. Lossing says that William Charles was a Scotchman who was compelled to hastily depart from Edinburgh to escape prosecution for caricaturing some of the dignitaries of that city.' *American Engravers upon Copper and Steel*, David McNeely Stauffer, Vol. I, Part I, p. 45. — 'Wm. Charles engraved the drawings by H. Bunbury for *Lessons in Horsemanship* by Geoffrey Gambado.' Fielding's *Index* to Stauffer's *American Engravers upon Copper and Steel*, p. 81. — 'But of the copper-plate engravers, perhaps none did more work for children's books than William Charles of Philadelphia, who is best known by his series of caricatures of the events of the War of 1812 and of local politics . . . [*His*] method of coloring the pictures engraved with the text was a slight advance, perhaps, upon the illustrations inserted separately, but it is doubtful whether [*they*] afforded as much entertainment to little readers as the separate figures similar to paper dolls which Belcher, and somewhat later Charles also, used in a few of their publications. . . . Later, when engraving had become more general in use, William Charles cut for an advertisement, as frontispiece to some of his imprints, an interior scene containing a shelf of books labelled "W. Charles' Library for Little Folks."' *Forgotten Books of the American Nursery*, Rosalie V. Halsey, pp. 170–171, 183. See also letter dated July 1, 1814, *God's Revenge against Adultery*, title 210, note 2.

[2] 'Mason William, wood engraver 2 Norris's Alley' *Philadelphia Directory*, 1814, LC. — 'Mason Wm. & A. engravers in brass &c. 11 S. 4th' *Ibid.*, 1817, LC. — William Mason began to practice in Philadelphia in 1810 but 'during the last war with Gr. Britain Mr. Mason entered into other employments, and relinquished his wood engraving to his pupil, Mr. George Gilbert.' *A History of the Rise and Progress of The Arts of Design in the United States*, William Dunlap, Boston, 1918, Vol. II, pp. 383–384, LC.

2. Brinley No. 3164.

3. *Ad.* [*M.L.W.*] 'Messrs. Pasteur & Watson, You will oblige your friend, the undersigned . . . "I was amusing my family last night, sir," — so said to me lately a Virginia Sage of the very first class, — "with counting up those who were the Grandees . . . MORAL LOOKING GLASSES FOR YOUTH." I. *The Drunkard's Looking Glass* — . . . N.B. The . . . above are in handsome pamphlets, about 50 pages each, with plates; & though costing only 25 cents, may, as preventives or restoratives of innocence . . . sympathising friends. M. L. Weems These pamphlets may be had in Newbern, at the Druggist Store of Dr. E. Hawes, corner. . . .' *Car. Cent.*, June 16, 1821, NYHS. The same advertisement, with appropriate changes, had been printed in *Charles. Cour.*, Apr. 14, 1821, CLS., and in *Georgian*, May 15, 1821, GAHS. [*M.L.W.*] '. . . popular little tracts on . . . Drunkenness . . . with J. R. Schenck, bookseller . . .' [Preceded by a letter of commendation from Bishop Bowen.] *Charles. Cour.*, Feb. 16, 1822, CLS. The following extracts, with changes, preceded by an editorial introduction, are after pp. 52–56 of this edition: '*On the Importance of a Good Education* . . . The preceding remarks were occasioned by reading a late publication of the Rev. M. L. WEEMS from which we have made the following extract . . . he thus facetiously but emphatically expresses himself: "Every man should set off with recollecting that his son is, by birth, a nobleman, or, as the Asiatics term it, 'a bashaw of three tails,' or natures. The 1st, is a mere ANIMAL NATURE, . . . The 2d, is a RATIONAL NATURE, . . . The 3d, is a DIVINE NATURE, which *loves!* . . . These are the three natures . . . Many a silly mother, . . . Is not this enough to show you . . . directed his course."' *Hillsb'ro. Rec.*, Feb. 13, 1822, UNC.

4. Weems wrote to Carey, July 14, 1816: 'If you have any show bills for the Drunkard &c. please send a copy or two.' Feb. 11, 1817: 'I intreat you to send for Charles and desire him to make the faces of his drunken characters look as whiskey always makes them, i.e. haggard & distemperd — It must strike everyone that a pure healthy rouge is unnatural in Dead Subjects & may do harm to the Living. Let their carbuncles show disease and disgrace.' Feb. 16, 1817: '[*I*] am surprised that our large drunken Caricature does not solicit Purchasers in all Beholders. All gaze & laugh, but only one yet has bought. . . . I wonder you & I did not *Americanize the labels*. "Purl & bitters" for ex[*ample*] ought to be *alterd*, being obsolete — also others. Please cast yr. eye over them. The letters on the plate are wretchedly cut. I wish Mr. Charles cou'd do them better. Give this thing fair play & I verily believe that I shall sell a great many for you yet.' Apr. 5, 1817: 'If you cou'd get Mr. Charles to erase those miserable inscriptions on the grand Caricature & put *some handsome* [*ones*] in their places, also

add "Choice accompaniment for the Drunkard's Looking Glass," or "Weems's Drunkards Looking," we might sell a number.' [*N.d. after May 6, 1817*]: Mason, the wood Engraver in Norris alley is retouch[g] one of the plates for the Drunkard. Pray look at it — I know you will do all you can to give the pamphlets an ad captandum — Some curious dashes on the outsides.' Jan. 9, 1818: 'I sent you a design yesterday. I now send you two. The Designers in Philad[a]. charged me 5 Doll[s] These cost but 3. Good Judges pronounce them well done for fright'ning. The Legislatures here [*Richmond*] are going to take up the subject of drunkenness & lay heavy hands upon it. By proper management we might do much good to the world & its morals.' Nov. 15, 1819: 'Please then send Elijah [*Weems*] 150 each of the *aforesaid 4 varieties* [*the pamphlets' frontispieces*] & 200 of the Drunkards (The OLD LADY I prefer).' [Used apparently in this edition on the cover imprint, see end of note 1 above.] To Henry C. Carey, Feb. 28, 1822: 'I am frequently, even daily receiv[g] thanks from the Bishop & Clergy of all Churches as well as from Patriots & Philanthropists of all Professions & Ranks, for our Moral Looking Glasses. Woud it not be well as y[r] father once hinted, to take some of the *best* of these Recommendations, & printing them in a 1/4 sheet, place them in the Pamphlets a sheet to each?' May 29, 1822: 'I told you tho I don't suppose you will see any necessity for it, that if you w[d] allow me an hour or so in the day, to make a short oration to the crowd on the great good they might do their children by sett[g] before them the advantages of such virtues as those of Washington &[c]. &[c]. &[c]. and the curses of yielding to such base and cowardly vices as Drunkenness, Duelling, &[c]. &[c]. &[c]. I might sell a good deal for you.'

5. Even the most extreme teetotaler might find this pamphlet amusing. Perhaps it is the raciest of all Weems' four tracts, though *Duelling* is a close competitor. Possibly this is due to our inherited attitude toward bibulousness, which from the Restoration in England on was viewed by most Anglo-Saxon nationals as, at worst, an amusing weakness, whereas both Murder and Adultery were counted amongst the seven deadly sins. The change in attitude amongst us was registered, as well as reinforced, by the Volstead amendment, and within the next two generations it is possible that most sensible people will feel as unperturbed by that enactment as we of the twentieth century feel toward the practice of duelling or the laws passed to prevent it. In the less squeamish generation of 1800 even Massachusetts did not dodge vulgarisms which have sometimes been imputed to Weems for his unrighteousness: 'A witty writer in a late Salem Gazette says: To express the condition of an honest fellow and no flincher, under the effects of good fellowship, it is said that he is *drunk;* intoxicated; fuddled; flustered; rockey, tipsey merry; half-boozy; top-heavy; chuckfull hocky; hickins

(probably from hiccuping); cup stricken; cropsick; cup sprung; . . . switchery; pot-valiant; maudlin (probably from Magdalen the penitent, who is always represented by those who drink till the liquor flows out of their eyes); a little how came you so groggy (this is a West Indian phrase) rum and water without sugar being called grog; in drink; in his cups; . . . high (used at Harvard University); sewed up in nubibus; . . . under the table; snuffy; not the same man afternoon [*sic*]; mopsey; tipsey; slewed; crank (this is a sea phrase; a ship is said to be crank, when by excess of lading she is liable to be overset); cut; cheery chery [*sic*] merry; overtaken; elevated; . . . cast away (a phrase for being dead drunk); . . . bosky in altitudes; half-cocked; tiperary (probably from being likely to tip or fall down); topsey; friisey [*sic*]; exhilerated [*sic*]; on a merry pin; a little in the suds; in a quandary; pigeon-wing'd; snuffy; as wise as Solomon; Business on both sides of the way; got his little hat on; bung'd his eye; been in the sun; soaked his face; got aps ur [*?*] in his head (this is said by brother jockies of each other); got a crumb in his beard; had a little; had enough; got more than he can carry; . . . got glass eyes; . . . been amongst the philistines; lost his legs; been in a storm (a sea phrase for being less than dead drunk); got his cap on; got his skin full; had a cup too much; has his cold tea; a red eye; got his dose; taken drops; taking a lunar; a pinch of snuff in his wig; had too much coffee; his wig askew; tar on his keel; sugar in his eye; his wig oil'd; catch'd a turkey; he clips the king's English; sees double; reels; heels a little; heels and sets (as a boat in a rough sea); shews his hob nails; looks as if he could'nt help it; crooks his elbow; goes over the tops of trees; it is after eleven o'clock with him; he makes a Virginia fence; takes an observation; takes a lunar; chases geese; loves a drop; takes it by the word of mouth; cannot sport a right line; he is drunk as [*a*] piper; drunk as an owl; drunk as David's sow; drunk as a lord; fuddled as an ape; merry as a grigg; happy as a king.' [*Anon.*] *City Wash. Gaz.*, July 21, 1818, LC.

NUMBER 203 1827

THE | DRUNKARD'S LOOKING GLASS, | REFLECTING A FAITHFUL | LIKENESS OF THE DRUNKARD, | IN | SUNDRY VERY INTERESTING ATTITUDES, | WITH | *Lively Representations of the many strange Capers which he cuts* | *at different Stages of his Disease;* | AS FIRST, | WHEN HE HAS ONLY "A DROP IN HIS EYE;" | SECOND, | WHEN HE IS "HALF SHAVED;" | THIRD, |

WHEN HE IS GETTING "A LITTLE ON THE | STAGGERS OR SO;" | AND FOURTH, AND FIFTH, AND SO ON, | TILL HE IS "QUITE CAPSIZED;" | OR | "SNUG UNDER THE TABLE WITH THE DOGS," | AND | CAN "STICK TO THE FLOOR WITHOUT HOLDING ON." | BY MASON L. WEEMS, | AUTHOR OF THE LIFE OF WASHINGTON, &C. | *Seventh Edition, greatly Improved.* | PHILADELPHIA: | PUBLISHED BY JOSEPH ALLEN. | Sold by John Grigg, North Fourth street. | 1827. | 24mo. pp. (5), 4, 4–120, (2). *Front.*
AAS., NYPL.

1. The frontispiece, unsigned, is like that in the 1818 edition, title preceding, folded twice to fit the small size of the page, with the same inscription; on reverse of title Penn. copyright dated 1827 to Joseph Allen.

NUMBER 204 1838

THE | DRUNKARD'S | LOOKING GLASS: | REFLECTING | A Faithful Likeness of the Drunkard | IN SUNDRY VERY INTERESTING ATTITUDES, | *With lively representations of the many strange Capers which* | *he cuts at different Stages of his Disease;* | AS FIRST, | WHEN HE HAS ONLY "A DROP IN HIS EYE;" | SECOND, | WHEN HE IS "HALF SHAVED;" | THIRD, | WHEN HE IS GETTING "A LITTLE ON THE STAGGERS OR SO;" | AND FOURTH AND FIFTH, AND SO ON, | TILL HE IS "QUITE CAPSIZED;" | OR | "SNUG UNDER THE TABLE WITH THE DOGS;" | AND | CAN "STICK TO THE FLOOR WITHOUT HOLDING ON;" | BY M. L. WEEMS, | AUTHOR OF THE LIFE OF WASHINGTON, ETC. | SEVENTH EDITION, GREATLY IMPROVED. | PHILADELPHIA: |

PRINTED FOR MRS. F. M. WEEMS, (WIDOW OF THE AUTHOR.) *June*, 1838. | PRICE TWENTY-FIVE CENTS. | 8vo. pp. 3, 4–67, (1). *Cuts.*
LC., NYPL.

1. No frontispiece; the cuts are on pages 5, 6, 13, 16, 28, 32, 37, 42, 49, and 62.

NUMBER 205 1843

THE | DRUNKARD'S LOOKING GLASS: | REFLECTING A | FAITHFUL LIKENESS OF THE DRUNKARD | IN SUNDRY VERY INTERESTING ATTITUDES, | *With lively representations of the many strange Capers which* | *he cuts at different Stages of his Disease;* | AS FIRST, | WHEN HE HAS ONLY "A DROP IN HIS EYE;" | SECOND, | WHEN HE IS "HALF SHAVED;" | THIRD, | WHEN HE IS GETTING "A LITTLE ON THE STAGGERS OR SO;' | AND FOURTH AND FIFTH, AND SO ON, | TILL HE IS "QUITE CAPSIZED;" | OR | "SNUG UNDER THE TABLE WITH THE DOGS;" | AND | CAN "STICK TO THE FLOOR WITHOUT HOLDING ON;" | BY M. L. WEEMS, | AUTHOR OF THE LIFE OF WASHINGTON, ETC. | EIGHTH EDITION. | Baltimore: |
PRINTED FOR MRS. F. M. WEEMS, (WIDOW OF THE AUTHOR,) | 1843. | PRICE TWENTY-FIVE CENTS. | 8vo. pp. 3, 4–63, (1).
NYPL.

1. The single quotation mark on line thirteen of the title is thus misprinted; on reverse of title Penn. copyright 'eastern district' to Mrs. F. M. Weems, and 'PRINTED BY ROBERT NEILSON, . . .'; the text is divided into Cases III–XXV; on p. 45 'CHAPTER IV' appears as the first heading of this sort; this chapter includes 'TRUE CURE OF DRUNKENNESS.'

NUMBER 206 1816

NARRATIVE | OF | PETER AND JOHN HAY, | EXTRACTED FROM THE | DRUNKARD'S LOOKING GLASS, | By M. L. WEEMS, | AUTHOR OF THE LIFE OF WASHINGTON, &C. | [*Monogram of T.A.F.*] | PHILADELPHIA: |

TO BE HAD OF BENJAMIN & THOMAS KITE, NO. 20, NORTH THIRD | STREET: AND FOR SALE BY SOLOMON W. CONRAD, NO. 87, | KIMBER & SHARPLESS, NO. 93, JOHN RICHARDSON, NO. 31, AND | ISAAC PIERCE, NO. 316, MARKET STREET. | 1816. | 12mo. pp. 1, (1), 1, 4–12.
AAS.

1. The text is taken from pp. 32–38 of both 1816 editions of *The Drunkard's Looking Glass*, titles 200 and 201.

2. Weems wrote to Carey [*n.d. received Feb. 19, 1818*]: 'That [*design*] which mnrks the combustion of Peter & John Hays, whose case the Tract Societies have so widely diffus[d], is admirably done. Have you put them into hands yet. I am prodigiously afraid you will neglect these things.'

3. All the booksellers on the title are listed in the *Philadelphia Directory*, 1816, HSP.

NUMBER 207 1818

NARRATIVE | OF | PETER AND JOHN HAY, | EXTRACTED FROM THE | DRUNKARD'S LOOKING GLASS, | BY M. L. WEEMS, | AUTHOR OF THE LIFE OF WASHINGTON, &C. | [*Monogram of T.A.F.*] | PHILADELPHIA: |

TO BE HAD OF BENJAMIN & THOMAS KITE, NO. 20, NORTH THIRD | STREET: AND FOR SALE BY SOLOMON W. CONRAD, NO. 87, KIMBER | & SHARPLESS, NO. 93, AND JOHN RICHARDSON, NO. 31, MARKET- | STREET; ALSO, CALEB RICHARDSON, NO. 8, NORTH THIRD STREET. | 1818. | *No.* 10. — *2d. ed.* — 6000. | 12mo. pp. 2, 3–8.
AAS.

1. Colophon 'J. R. A. SKERRETT, PRINTER.' The text is identical with that of title 206.

2. Weems wrote to Carey, Jan. 8, 1818: 'I send you the case of poor Peter & John Hays [*sic*] — which has made some noise. Mason will engrave it well. Who will do it the best & cheapest . . . Did you get the last engrav[d].' [Mason was spoken of as retouching for *The Drunkard* (*n.d. after May 6, 1817*), see title 202, note 4.] Mar. 2, 1818: 'I sent you 5 designs for the Drunkards Looking Glass — all of them bold Caricatures, especially that for Peter & John Hays who were burnt to death. Have you put them into hands?'

NUMBER 208 1822

## EFFECTS | OF | DRUNKENNESS, | ILLUSTRATED IN THE HISTORY OF | PETER AND JOHN HAY. |

[*n.d.*] 12mo. pp. 1, 2–12.
AAS.

1. Caption title only, being tract '[No. 112.' in Vol. VI of the publications of The New England Tract Society. Colophon at end of pamphlet on p. 12 reads 'ANDOVER: | PRINTED FOR THE NEW ENGLAND TRACT SOCIETY | BY FLAGG AND GOULD. | 1822. [2d. edit. 6000.' There is no mention of Weems but the text of this work is identical with that of *The Narrative of Peter and John Hay* in the two titles preceding, with the addition of comments on the narrative from p. 10 to p. 12.

NUMBER 208A 1828–1832?

## HISTORY | OF | PETER AND JOHN HAY. | [*Cut*] | Pale and silent with anguish, he got up and went to the door. | *See page* 6. |

PUBLISHED BY THE | AMERICAN TRACT SOCIETY, | AND SOLD AT THEIR DEPOSITION, NO. 144 NASSAU-STREET,

NEAR | THE CITY-HALL, NEW-YORK; AND BY AGENTS OF THE | SOCIETY, ITS BRANCHES, AND AUXILIARIES, IN | THE PRINCIPAL CITIES AND TOWNS | IN THE UNITED STATES. [*n.d. 1828–1832?*] 12mo. pp. 2, 3–12.
AAS.

1. Tract 'NO. 112' in Vol. IV of the publications of the American Tract Society. The text is substantially that of the three preceding titles, but differs slightly throughout in phrasing; comments on the narrative close the text as in title 208. No date is given, but since, according to the New York directories, the American Tract Society was located at 144 Nassau Street from 1828 to 1832, I assume the pamphlet to have been issued within that period.

NUMBER 209? 1812?

## *The Devil Done Over. [*1812?*]

1. *Ad.* 'Just received and for sale At S. Hall's Book-Store, Price 25 Cents, THE DEVIL DONE OVER; or the Grand Revival in Old Edgefield in 1809, wherein seven hundred souls were added to the Baptist Church in nine Months.—Taken chiefly from the Minutes of the Rev'd Daniel Marsh, Robert Marsh, John Landrum, and Samuel Cartledge,[1] who were the Honored Instruments of

[1] Revs. Samuel and Robert Marsh, John Landrum and Samuel Cartledge, prominent Baptists of Edgefield, in records sometimes called 'elder,' sometimes 'Rev.' 'Constituted,' with others, several Baptist churches in Edgefield, to wit: Dry Creek — Samuel Marsh, also Rev. John Landrum; Bethany — Robert Marsh; Red Hill — Samuel Cartledge; Red Oak Grove — Samuel Marsh and Samuel Cartledge; Chestnut or Chestnut Ridge — Robert and Samuel Marsh. Rev. John Landrum was minister of Red Bank Baptist Church (Edgefield), 1812–1816. It would seem that the 'Rev'd Daniel Marsh' is mentioned in the above advertisement in error for 'Samuel,' who is again referred to in Weems' *Bad Wife's Looking Glass*, title 218.

the Glorious Work. By M. L. Weems, Formerly Rector of General Washington's Parish . . .' *Car. Fed. Repub.*, Jan. 4, Mar 21, 1812 *et seq.*, LC. Of this work, presumably a small pamphlet, I have not been able to find any trace, unless it be connected with the following: THE | DEVIL LET LOOSE; | OR, | A WONDERFUL INSTANCE | OF THE | GOODNESS OF GOD. | IN | A LETTER | FROM A GENTLEMAN IN SOUTH CAROLINA, TO HIS FRIEND | IN ANNAPOLIS. | Philadelphia: | Printed for the purchasers. | 1807. Sq. 12mo. pp. 1, (1), 4–24, HSP. 'A Letter, . . . Dear Friend, Though the dark age of miracles is long past, and the gloomy understanding of the human mind has gradually become enlightened by the benign influence of the Sun of Reason, before whose glittering rays the mists of superstition and tyranny flee, like the shades of night before Aurora's dawn; yet there now and then happens, even in this enlightened one, such a concurrence of strange phenomena, as often excites our just surprise and wonder. A marvelous circumstance of this kind has lately transpired here, the particulars of which I shall give you as fully as the limits of a letter will admit, and leave you to determine, whether it was brought about by chance or ordered by the immediate finger of heaven. . . . lived a Mr. W—— K——. . . . Thus you see how easy it is for God to bring good out of evil. The wickedness of this K. perhaps was the means of converting his sinful companions to God. This is certainly a wonderful instance of the power and goodness of God. But least I should tire your patience with this long letter, farewell. [*Signed*] L.M.' This little skit, while not having all the ear marks of Weems, is sufficiently related to him both in style and subject to suggest his being partially its author; also in the incidents described of a man 'good yet wicked' — because *only* of his detestation of religion — frightening his pious neighbors at their camp meetings in the disguise of a devil, from which finally transpired his own complete conversion (*and death!*) as well as that of many others of that ilk. Then too, there is a very slight coincidence in the letter being written from South Carolina to a friend in Annapolis and signed by two of his initials. I believe, if this imprint does have any connection with the pamphlet advertised as above, that Weems had merely edited and touched up the work of another hand, in the same way as, though in a lesser degree than, he edited Horry's *Life of Marion*.

2. This pamphlet has no connection with the book widely read at that period, *History of the Devil*, nor with the following title 'THE DEVIL LET LOOSE, OF THE WO occasioned to the Inhabitants of the Earth by his wrathful Appearance among them, ILLUSTRATED IN A DISCOURSE DELIVERED ON THE DAY OF THE NATIONAL FAST, APRIL 25, 1799. Boston, 1799,' 8vo., pp. 16, AAS.

3. The following shows Weems' acquaintance with Edgefield and with some of the clergymen mentioned in the advertisement above: 'This, I'm told, was

*old Edgefield*, some five and twenty years ago!! But blessed be God for sending such *judges* as Trazevant and Johnson, Grimke and Brevard — and blessed be God for such preachers as Marsh and Lendrum, and Marshall! for in no place have the labours of judges and preachers been crown'd with more singular success. Edgefield, with but *few exceptions*, is now quite a *decent place!* a district of gentlemen and Christians —' From *God's Revenge against Murder*, p. 5.

NUMBER 210 1815

GOD'S REVENGE | AGAINST | ADULTERY, | AWFULLY EXEMPLIFIED IN THE FOLLOWING CASES | OF | AMERICAN CRIM. *Con.* | I. THE ACCOMPLISHED DR. THEODORE WILSON, (DELAWARE,) WHO | FOR SEDUCING MRS. NANCY WILEY, HAD HIS BRAINS | BLOWN OUT BY HER HUSBAND. | II. THE ELEGANT JAMES ONEALE, ESQ. (NORTH CAROLINA,) WHO, | FOR SEDUCING THE BEAUTIFUL MISS MATILDA LES | -TRANGE, WAS KILLED BY HER BROTHER. | BY MASON L. WEEMS, | AUTHOR OF THE LIFE OF WASHINGTON. | BALTIMORE: |

PRINTED by RALPH W. POMEROY & CO. | 1815. | 8vo. pp. (1), 4, 4–48. *Front.*
AAS.

1. The frontispiece, unsigned, engraved, has inscription below *'There! G–d d—n you take that!'* [perhaps by William Charles, see note 2 below]; on reverse of title are Md. copyright to Mason L. Weems, dated 1815 'thirty-ninth year . . .', with two stanzas from Burns.

2. Weems wrote to Carey, July 1, 1814: 'I am now parleying with Mr. Wm. Charles the Caricaturist for the aid of his pencil to render my little Serio comical melo dramatical pamphlets more interesting. He speaks of reference to you as a

"*mutual friend.*" If he sh[d] call, I trust you'll give me thro' him the aid of y[r] counsel. I am prodigiously in want of the frontispiece that he is to give me. I tell him that as I have already launched 7 or 8 pamphlets, & *2* books, with several others of various rates on the stocks, all requiring the Squibs & Rockets & Long Toms of his Fancy, if he can but contrive ways & means to mould me them cheap I may throw a good deal of work in his way. . . . All I want is *strong expression.* I care not how coarse.' Dec. 28, 1814: 'I send you a little affair which I have just got, *rough out of the stock* — hardly worth your reading & M[rs] Carey's but if I live, I'll put the chizel to it.'

3. In this pamphlet Weems pictures the guilty Dr. Wilson, when presaging his own death, taking 'down the Age of Reason' and throwing it 'into the fire, saying at the same time, cursed book! it was you that helped to undo me.' Weems having sold Paine's works over a period of years, this apparent inconsistency needs an explanation. But it will be seen by his letters on those works [see title 243, note 3] that he emphasized the sale of Watson's reply to *The Age of Reason* rather than that work itself and that he stipulated for Paine's political works rather than for the famous free-thinking pamphlet. Moreover, from many statements in his letters, it can be clearly seen that his moralizing bent increased with his years, and that in later life he stressed more than ever his wish to sell only such works as had an ethical value. So it is fair to assume that by 1815 he had come to believe that books encouraging free-thinking led to personal license.

4. 'Pomroy, Ralph, printer, Liberty st O T,' *Baltimore Directory*, 1814, LC.

NUMBER 211　1816

GOD'S REVENGE | AGAINST | ADULTERY, | AWFULLY EXEMPLIFIED IN THE FOLLOWING CASES | OF | AMERICAN CRIM. CON. | I. THE ACCOMPLISHED DR. THEODORE WILSON, (DELAWARE,) WHO FOR SEDUCING | MRS. NANCY WILEY, HAD HIS BRAINS BLOWN OUT BY HER | HUSBAND. | II. THE ELEGANT JAMES O'NEALE, ESQ. (NORTH CAROLINA,) WHO FOR SEDUCING THE | BEAUTIFUL MISS MATILDA L'ESTRANGE, WAS KILLED BY HER | BROTHER. | BY MASON L. WEEMS, | AUTHOR OF THE LIFE OF WASHINGTON. | SECOND EDITION. | PHILADELPHIA: |

PRINTED FOR THE AUTHOR. | PRICE 25 CENTS. | 1816. | 8vo. pp. (3), 4, 4–48. *Front.*
AAS., HU., NYPL. [*lacks front.*]

1. After, but not identical with, the 1815 edition; frontispiece and reverse of title the same. The HU. copy has cover imprint, somewhat similar to the title; on reverse of it Md. copyright, dated 1816, and two stanzas from Burns.

2. *Ad.* 'Just Received (Price, 25 Cents) God's Revenge against Adultery, Awfully exemplified in the following cases of American Crim. Con. 1. The accomplished Dr. Theodore Wilson (Delaware) who, for seducing Mrs. Nancy Wiley, had his brains blown out by her Husband. 2. The elegant James Oneale, Esq. (N-Carolina) who, for seducing the beautiful Miss Matilda Lestrange, was killed by her brother. By Mason L. Weems Author of the life of Washington.' *Intel.*, Aug. 3, 1816, HSP.

3. Weems wrote to Carey, May 24, 1816: 'Bioren has some of the plates (in the Adulterers pamphlet) that are good I mean *fresh.* Wou'd it not be well to have it cut *over* again? or send to Mr. Pomroy of Balt° to hurry that on by *my order*, by some person in the steam boat[*?*]'

NUMBER 212 1818

GOD'S REVENGE | AGAINST | ADULTERY, | AWFULLY EXEMPLIFIED IN THE FOLLOWING CASES | OF | AMERICAN CRIM. CON. | I. THE ACCOMPLISHED DR. THEODORE WILSON, (DELAWARE,) WHO FOR SEDUCING | MRS. NANCY WILEY, HAD HIS BRAINS BLOWN OUT | BY HER HUSBAND. | II. THE ELEGANT JAMES O'NEALE, ESQ. (NORTH CAROLINA,) WHO FOR SEDUCING | THE BEAUTIFUL MISS MATILDA L'ESTRANGE, WAS KILLED | BY HER BROTHER. | BY MASON L. WEEMS, | AUTHOR OF THE LIFE OF WASHINGTON. | THIRD EDITION. | PHILADELPHIA: |

PRINTED FOR THE AUTHOR — PRICE 25 CENTS. | 1818. | GRIGGS & CO. PRINTERS. | 8vo. pp. (1), 4, 4–48. *Front.*
AAS., CLS., HSP., LC., LCPhil., MdHS., NYHS., NYPL., PStL.

1. Frontispiece and reverse of title the same as the 1815 and 1816 editions.

2. Brinley Nos. 3163, 3164.

3. *Ad.* [*M.L.W.*] '*To the Editor of the Courier.* . . . III. The Adulterer's Looking Glass — Wherein men who can dispise [*sic*] marriage and marriage purity, may see something at once most curious and instructive.' *Charles. Cour.*, Apr. 14, 1821, CLS. 'COMMUNICATION. . . . III. The Adulterer's Looking-Glass — wherein those, who can laugh at marriage, and marriage loves and purity, may see, that though they dread not the devil, there is yet something to be dreaded from jealous husbands.' *Georgian*, May 15, 1821, GAHS. 'Messrs. Pasteur & Watson, You will oblige your friend, the undersigned . . . The Adulterer's Looking Glass . . . at the Druggist Store of Dr. E. Hawes . . .' *Car. Cent.*, June 16, 1821, NYHS.

4. 'John Grigg came to Philadelphia in 1816 and formed a partnership with Benjamin Warner, a bookseller, after whose death, soon after 1825, a new firm was formed of Grigg, Elliott & Co., which continued until 1850, after which the firm became Lippincott, Grambo & Co. and then J. B. Lippincott & Co.' *History of Philadelphia*, Scharf & Westcott, Vol. III, p. 2329, LC. Although the name is spelled with an 's' in the above imprint, since the next edition seen by me, that of 1828, was sold by John Grigg, the assumption is borne out that this man was one of that firm of Griggs & Co.

5. Here Weems gives an early instance of the sentimental sympathy with a criminal. For young George L'Estrange having killed his sister's seducer, 'his prison chamber was scoured and *furnished* as for the reception of the great Washington. It was perfumed with odours and garnished with fairest flowers: and every day his board was spread with dainties, and every night his bed with down . . . the ladies despatched a courier with a petition . . . for a pardon . . . [*and*] then repaired to the prison and brought him forth in great triumph.' P. 47.

NUMBER 213 1828

GOD'S REVENGE | AGAINST | ADULTERY, | AWFULLY EXEMPLIFIED IN THE FOLLOWING CASES | OF | AMERICAN CRIM. CON. | I. THE ACCOMPLISHED DR. THEODORE WILSON, (DELAWARE,) | WHO FOR SEDUCING MRS. NANCY WILEY, HAD HIS BRAINS | BLOWN OUT BY HER HUSBAND. | II. THE ELEGANT JAMES O'NEALE, ESQ. (NORTH

CAROLINA,) WHO | FOR SEDUCING THE BEAUTIFUL MISS MATILDA L'ESTRANGE, | WAS KILLED BY HER BROTHER. | BY MASON L. WEEMS, | AUTHOR OF THE LIFE OF WASHINGTON. | PHILADELPHIA: |

PUBLISHED BY JOSEPH ALLEN. | Sold by John Grigg, North Fourth street. | 1828. | 16mo. pp. 3, 4–71, (1). *Front.plate.*
HSP., NYPL. [*lacks front.*]

1. Reverse of title identical with former editions; HSP. has the large engraved, unsigned plate, folded twice.
2. Catalogue of Hawkins sale, 1887, No. 1155.

NUMBER 214 1820

GOD'S REVENGE | AGAINST | DUELLING, | OR | THE DUELLIST'S LOOKING GLASS; | EXHIBITING THAT | GENTLEMANLY MODE | OF | TURNING THE CORNER, | IN | FEATURES ALTOGETHER NOVEL, AND ADMIRABLY | CALCULATED TO | ENTERTAIN AND INSTRUCT THE AMERICAN YOUTH. | BY M. L. WEEMS, | AUTHOR OF THE LIVES OF WASHINGTON, MARION, | DRUNKARD'S LOOKING GLASS, &C. | "*Ridiculum acri melius et fortius, magnas plerumque, secat res.*" — Horace. | "For ridicule shall frequently prevail | To cut the knot, when graver reasons fail." | GEORGETOWN, D.C. |

PUBLISHED BY ELIJAH WEEMS, FOR THE AUTHOR. | GIDEON, PRINT. WASHINGTON. | 1820. | 8vo. pp. 3, 4–54.
AAS., LC., NYPL.

GOD'S REVENGE

AGAINST

DUELLING,

OR

THE DUELLISTS LOOKING GLASS;

EXHIBITING THAT

GENTLEMANLY MODE

OF

TURNING THE CORNER,

IN

FEATURES ALTOGETHER NOVEL, AND ADMIRABLY

CALCULATED TO

ENTERTAIN AND INSTRUCT THE AMERICAN YOUTH.

---

BY M. L. WEEMS,

AUTHOR OF THE LIVES OF WASHINGTON, MARION, DRUNKARDS LOOKING GLASS, &c.

---

" *Ridiculum acri melius et fortius, magnas plerumque, secat res.*"—*Horace.*

" For ridicule shall frequently prevail
" To cut the knot, when graver reasons fail."

---

GEORGETOWN, D. C.

PUBLISHED BY ELIJAH WEEMS, FOR THE AUTHOR.

GIDEON, PRINT. WASHINGTON.

1820.

FACSIMILE TITLE PAGE OF THE 1820 EDITION OF
*GOD'S REVENGE AGAINST DUELLING*

1. On reverse of title is D. C. copyright to M. L. Weems, dated 1819 — 'forty-fourth year.' The AAS. and LC. copies have an advertisement of Elijah Weems on back cover. The AAS. copy has cover imprint identical with title.

2. Weems wrote to Carey, Nov. 15, 1819: 'Elijah is printing only 1000 Copies of my Duell[*ist's*] *Looking Glass*. I hope that after due setting up of its rigging it will fall into its proper place in the *line*. I have begged Mr. Rob. Smith New York to send you a fair specimen of the *Frontispiece*, two of the Sable Sons of Ham, with stormy brows, looks of murderers, and hard gritted teeth drawing their triggers at each other like Devils & letting fly like h—ll. [*Apparently not used in this edition; possibly this is the same as the frontispiece of the 1821 edition, which might originally have been drawn by Rob. Smith, later engraved by Clay, but not being ready in time for the 1820 edition might have been used in that of 1821.*] . . . Elijah is printing me 200 show bills.' Jan. 19, 1820: 'But, a few hours, antecedently, it struck me that I w[d] run up to Georgetown to see how Elijah (no scholar & no Printer, but the best, or as good as this vile country can afford) came on with my "GOD'S REVENGE AGAINST DUELLING" which, as *you remember*, you told me, you w[d] rather sh[d] be printed here to the South than in Philad[a].' Feb. 19, 1820: '5 days ago [*I*] left home again for this place to see the winding up of the "*Duellist*" which I told you was printing here [*Georgetown*]. Owing to some horrible blunders by the Printer I have been detain'd a couple of days longer than I expected. . . . I send you a copy of the Duellist, tis horribly printed — our next edition may be much better — 'tis at present only in the block — an unfinished slab — a mere Promethean figure — not full limb[d] nor of right dimensions — nor hard featured — nor Devil painted — nor indeed anything as it ought to be.' Feb. 24, 1820: 'The Duellist was printed, as all the rest, for you[1] . . . I know it is utterly unfinished, but I see how it is to be finish'd . . . If you w[d] get good Caricatures, you w[d] aid the cause you have so long advocated—The Good of Man.' Mar. 29, 1820: 'The Rev[d] M[r] Abercrombie informs me that you have two or three very ad Captandum Caricatures for the Duellist. Were it not adviseable to order the pamph[ts]. from Elijah Weems's Georgetown, to Phil[a] that the engravings may be inserted. . . . The sooner that this edition can be sent away the better.' May 16, 1820: 'Mr. Clay has executed the designs for the Duellist, so much in the style of Bunbury, that you w[d] do well to let him try his hand on some few of the cases in the Drunkard's Looking Glass that best kindle his fancy.'

[1] Elijah Weems to Messrs. Carey & Son: 'Geo Town April 20, 1820. Gentlemen, . . . I would be thankful for a statement of my a/c, with all of the *separate* Items. There are 500 of the Duellist which parson Weems wish[d] me to send to you. . . .'

May 18, 1820: 'But still [*I*] think & shall forever think that the *Moralizing* & *Popular Biographies* & *Pamphlets,* put into safe hands & well-chosen places, w[d] afford to M.C. & M.L.W. the exceeding advantage to be derived from adding the gains of 500 Sellers to those of *one* Subscriptioneerer. . . . Woud it not be well to put Clay's Caricatures into the "Duellist" & send them on to different places[?]' Oct. 19, 1820: 'My nephew Elijah did not treat me so honorably in Georgetown as he ought to have done.'

3. Even in a state notoriously given to the fire-eating bravado of the *code duello*, the trend of legislation was already markedly against this exercise of the prerogative of arbitrary settlement of personal grievances. 'A law against DUELLING was passed by the Legislature of South Carolina at their late session . . . any persons . . . resident of that State, [*that*] shall fight a duel, or shall send or accept a challenge . . . or shall cause any such challenge to be sent, given or accepted within the limits of the U. S., such person . . . seconds or . . . persons indirectly concerned, their councillors, aidors [*sic*] and abettors shall upon being thereof convicted, be severally imprisoned for 12 months, . . . pay a fine of two thousand dollars . . . and . . . be forever disqualified from holding office of profit or trust . . . State, or from practising of law, physic, or divinity within the State, or . . . any other trade or profession or calling whatever.' *Ral. Reg.*, Jan. 15, 1813, NCStL. As one would expect Dr. Johnson to be an advocate of the unbloodthirsty settlement of disputes, and choleric John Randolph to have upheld the traditions of his caste, the two following extracts are of interest: 'Duelling: A man may shoot him who invades his character as he may shoot him who breaks into his house.' Boswell's *Life of Johnson.* 'In nine cases out of ten, both parties are entirely wrong — foolhardy, perhaps: or cowards, at heart, trying to get a name as fighting men.' Diary, *John Randolph of Roanoke*, William Cabell Bruce, Vol. II, p. 382, LC.

4. Weems cites one of his idols' — Marion's — example against duelling in this pamphlet, p. 34.

NUMBER 215 1821

## GOD'S REVENGE | AGAINST | DUELLING: | OR, | THE DUELLIST'S LOOKING GLASS; | EXHIBITING THAT | GENTLEMANLY MODE | OF | TURNING THE CORNER, | IN | FEATURES ALTOGETHER NOVEL, AND ADMIRABLY | CALCULATED TO | ENTERTAIN AND INSTRUCT THE AMERICAN

YOUTH. | *Second Edition . . . . . [sic] Revised and greatly improved.* | BY M. L. WEEMS, | AUTHOR OF THE LIVES OF WASHINGTON, MARION, DRUNKARD'S LOOKING | GLASS, &C. | "*Ridiculum acri melius et fortius, magnas plerumque secat res.*" — Horace. | "For ridicule shall frequently prevail | "To cut the knot, when graver reasons fail." | PHILADELPHIA: |

*Printed for M. L. Weems.* | J. BIOREN, PRINTER. | 1821. | 8vo. pp. (1), 3, 1, 4–48. *Front., Plates.*
AAS., BPL., HSP., LC., NYHS., NYPL.

1. On reverse of title is Penn. copyright, dated 1816 to Mason L. Weems. Most copies have but one plate [p. 16], of a Frenchman in a highly indignant attitude, with the face of an outraged Punch or Quilp,[1] expostulating with a handsome, debonair American who leans smilingly upon a picket fence, while the trouble-seeker struts toward him, indignantly exclaiming '"Jaun foutre de Shicken! Vat I care for de Shicken."'; the text differs radically from the first edition before p. 8 and after p. 12; on p. 46 there is an allusion to the oft-printed tale of Col. Payne's quarrel with Washington, used always by Weems in his *Life*. The AAS. and HSP. copies have a frontispiece of a negro duel, engraved, stippled, signed 'E. W. Clay del.',[2] 'C. P. Harrison Printer.' with an inscription 'Like master like man.' The AAS., HSP. and NYPL. copies have opposite p. 12 or 14 an unsigned engraving with the inscription '"Arrah now, my Honey! and that Shot you!"' and opposite p. 43 another, unsigned, with the inscription '["] Ah you black rascal I'll Duel you."'

2. Brinley No. 3163.

3. *Ad.* [*M.L.W.*] '*To the Editor of the Courier. . . .* IV. *The Duellist's Looking Glass* — with 30 cases, or "Demonstrations", that anything except true courage and real honor, may betray young men into that worse than savage

[1] Weems seemed to have but one standard of a French face. See his letter of Oct. 9, 1817, *Life of Marion*, title 89, note 2, letters of July, 1817, and others.

[2] Edward W. Clay, engraver and lithographer, born Philadelphia, 1792; died New York, December 31, 1857. He produced many caricatures. See *A History of the Rise and Progress of The Arts of Design in the United States*, William Dunlap, 1918, Vol. III, p. 290, LC. Clay 'was a merciless caricaturist and some of his lampoons of his fellow-citizens are said to have caused him much personal inconvenience.' *American Engravers upon Copper and Steel*, David McNeely Stauffer, 1907, Vol. I, Part I, p. 50. — 'J. Clay. Negro Duel.' Entered in AAS. index to *Fielding's List* #309. [See also letters of Nov. 15, 1819, and of May 16 and 18, 1820, title 214, note 2 and *f.n.*]

practice.' *Charles. Cour.*, Apr. 14, 1821, CLS. [*M.L.W.*] 'COMMUNICATION. . . . V. *The Duelist's Looking Glass* — containing 30 striking cases, or "*demonstrations*", that any thing short of *good sense*, *true courage*, and *real honor*, can make a duelist of the first chop.' *Georgian*, May 15, 1821, GAHS. [*M.L.W.*] '. . . You will oblige your friend, the undersigned . . . *The Duellist's Looking Glass* . . . at the Druggist Store of Dr. E. Hawes . . .' *Car. Cent.*, June 16, 1821, NYHS. [*M.L.W.*] '. . . popular little tracts on . . . Duelling . . . with J. R. Schenck, bookseller . . .' [Preceded by a letter of commendation from Bishop Bowen.] *Charles. Cour.*, Feb. 16, 1822, CLS.

4. In a letter to Carey [*n.d.received Sept. 25, 1821*] Weems alluded to desiring 'a Show bill for the Looking glasses &c.' Nov. 8, 1821, he asked Carey to send to him at Charleston, whither he was shortly starting, the *Duellist* as soon as it should be finished. 'I wish to get Gen[l] C. C. Pinckney [1] & other great men there to turn the attention of the Public to them.'

NUMBER 216 1821–1822

## GOD'S REVENGE | AGAINST | DUELLING: | [*Eleven lines*] | BY M. L. WEEMS, | [*Five lines*] | PHILADELPHIA: | *Printed for M. L. Weems.* | J. BIOREN, PRINTER. | 1821. | 8vo. pp. (1), 3, 1, 4–48. *Front.*, *Plates.*

AAS.

1. Cover imprint 'GOD'S REVENGE | AGAINST | DUELLING; | OR, | THE DUELLIST'S LOOKING GLASS; | EXHIBITING THAT | GENTLEMANLY MODE | OF | TURNING THE CORNER, | IN | FEATURES ALTOGETHER NOVEL, AND ADMIRA- | BLY CALCULATED TO | ENTERTAIN AND INSTRUCT THE AMERICAN YOUTH. | *Third Edition.* . . .

[1] 'Charles Cotesworth Pinckney, 1756–1825; attorney general; delegate to first provincial congress in 1775; member of South Carolina senate in 1779; member of the constitutional convention in 1787, and of the state convention that ratified the constitution, 1790. "Millions for defence but not one cent for tribute," a remark made while on his mission as Minister to France in 1796, from which he was requested to withdraw by the French. On his return to the United States was commissioned major-general. Federalist candidate for Vice-President in 1800 and for President in 1804 and 1808. Died in Charleston.' *Twentieth Century Biographical Dictionary*. See also *Diary of Edward Hooker, 1805–1808*, reprinted in *Annual Report of the American Historical Association for the year 1896*, Washington, Govt. Printing Office, 1897, Vol. I, pp. 859, 885, *f.n.*, LC.

[*sic*] *Revised and greatly improved. . . .* [*sic*] *Embellished* | *with several Engravings.* | BY MASON L. WEEMS, | Author of the lives of Washington, Marion, Drunkard's Looking Glass, &c. | "*Ridiculum acri melius et fortius, magnas plerumque secat res.*" — Horace. | "For ridilcule [*sic*] shall frequently prevail | "To cut the knot, when graver reasons fail." | PHILADELPHIA: | PRINTED FOR MASON L. WEEMS. | 1822. |' Title, plates and contents are identical with the 1821 edition, including date.

2. See notes to 1821 edition, which apply equally to this. It will be noted that this is probably only nominally a third edition, due to its cover imprint. As Weems wrote resentfully of Bioren, perhaps he himself obtained the types of the 1821 edition and issued it, with a cover title without Bioren's name, thus making it, only apparently, another edition.

NUMBER 217 1827

GOD'S REVENGE | AGAINST | DUELLING, | OR | THE DUELLIST'S LOOKING GLASS; | EXHIBITING THAT | GENTLEMANLY MODE | OF | TURNING THE CORNER, | IN | FEATURES ALTOGETHER NOVEL, AND ADMIRABLY | CALCULATED TO ENTERTAIN AND INSTRUCT THE | AMERICAN YOUTH. | *Third Edition — Revised and greatly Improved.* | BY M. L. WEEMS, | AUTHOR OF THE LIVES OF WASHINGTON, MARION, DRUNKARD'S | LOOKING GLASS, &C. | "*Ridiculum acri melius et fortius, magnas plerumque secat res.*" — *Horace.* | "For ridicule shall frequently prevail | to cut the knot, when graver reasons fail." | PHILADELPHIA: |

PUBLISHED BY JOSEPH ALLEN. | *Sold by John Grigg, North Fourth street.* | 1827. | 16mo. pp. (1), 4, 4–96, (2). *Front.plate.*
AAS., *MdDio'nL., NYPL.

1. The frontispiece, folded twice, is identical with that in the 1821 edition, title 215; on reverse of title is Penn. copyright to Joseph Allen, dated 1827, 'fifty-second year . . .'; the text is the same as the 1821 edition.

NUMBER 218 1823

THE | BAD WIFE'S | LOOKING GLASS. | OR, | GOD'S REVENGE AGAINST | CRUELTY TO HUSBANDS. | EXEMPLIFIED IN THE AWFUL HISTORY OF | THE BEAUTIFUL, BUT DEPRAVED | MRS. REBECCA COTTON, | WHO MOST INHUMANLY MURDERED HER HUSBAND | JOHN COTTON, ESQ. | FOR WHICH HORRID ACT GOD PERMITTED HER, IN | THE PRIME OF LIFE AND BLOOM OF BEAUTY, | TO BE CUT OFF BY HER BROTHER | STEPHEN KANNADY, | May, 5th 1807. | WITH A NUMBER OF INCIDENTS AND | ANECDOTES, MOST EXTRAORDINARY AND | INSTRUCTIVE. | BY M. L. WEEMS. | SECOND EDITION IMPROVED. | CHARLESTON: |

PRINTED FOR THE AUTHOR | 1823. | *Price, 25 cents.* | 8vo. pp. 1, (1), 1–44.

AAS., CLS., HSP., LC., NYPL.

1. The HSP. copy has cover imprint 'THE | BAD WIFE'S | LOOKING GLASS. | WELL WORTH | LOOKING INTO, BY EVERY | YOUNG MARRIED MAN AND WOMAN, | IN THE WORLD.' The anecdote of Archbishop Secker earlier printed in the newspapers [see note 3 below] is on pp. 37–38; on pp. 42–44 appears 'In New York, . . . three wealthy citizens who though not yet sots . . . One night, as they boasted of their wives . . . should be the best wife . . . *divine friendship* that is to last forever.' Although, in the letter of Mar. 15, 1823, given in note 4 below, Weems asked only that Henry Carey should have a frontispiece made for this

pamphlet, it is possible that he hoped the firm might take it up and print it for him. Which would explain his numbering the above title 'a second edition.' In the light of his preceding relations with the Careys, one can understand his diffidence about asking them definitely to print it for him. There is still another possible supposition. Weems may have believed that to label a book 'second edition' implied that a first had already gone off successfully. The fact that the first *Marion* edition found is thus labelled, as well as those of *God's Revenge against Murder*, *God's Revenge against Gambling*, *The Drunkard's Looking Glass*, and the above title, is at least a possible explanation of the various missing first editions. Moreover, the first edition of *Franklin* found is also called 'a new edition.' In his *Franklin Bibliography* Paul L. Ford explained this very cogently as due to Weems' having cribbed a large part of the material in the earlier section of his volume from Franklin's *Autobiography*, but the repetition of this would seem to me to point plausibly to Weems' keen realization of the value of such a ruse in advertising.

2. Brinley No. 3163.

3. *Ad.* [*M.L.W.*] 'A HINT TO THE MARRIED. THE good old Secker, Archbishop of Canterbury . . . kindle into never ceasing transports.' *Pub. Intel.*, June 4, 1807, AAS. [*M.L.W?*] '[By Request], Extract from a small work by the Rev. M. L. Weems, just published, entitled, "The Bad Wife's Looking Glass, or God's Revenge against Cruelty to Husbands."' *Charles. Cour.*, Apr. 9, 1823, CLS.

4. Weems wrote to Henry C. Carey, from Charleston, Mar. 15, 1823: 'I sent [*you?*] part of a pamphlet which I shall alter & call it the Bad Wife's Looking Glass, or Gods Revenge against cruelty to the Lords of the Creation. I begg'd you to put it, *instantly* into the hands of some Artist good *at design* who wd give us at once the likeness of a very beautiful woman distorted or convulsed with Diabolical passion, in the act of murdering, with up-lifted axe, her husband in sleep. There is a *poor man* here who has just commenc[d] printing it for me in five half sheet for 63 Doll[s]. for the 10 pamphlts stitch[d] & find the paper. This is some little above the Philad[a] price, but I thought you w[d] prefer [*it?*] to be done here rather than be saddled with the trouble & risks & the Dear knows what other penalties of sending it to Philad[a]. You have therefore *only to send on* the 1000 frontispieces, good bold ad captandum caricatures. Y[r] Artist can design it *in a day*, *engrave* & *knock it off & have it here in 3 weeks*. It is *now at press as I said.*' [No frontispiece found.]

# WORKS EDITED BY, OR PRINTED FOR, MASON LOCKE WEEMS

NUMBER 219 1793

SURE AND CERTAIN | METHODS | OF | ATTAINING | A | LONG AND HEALTHY LIFE, | WITH MEANS OF CORRECTING A | BAD CONSTITUTION. | WRITTEN BY | LEWIS CORNARO, | An Italian Nobleman, when he was near an | HUNDRED Years of Age. | WITH A | RECOMMENDATORY PREFACE, | BY THE | HON. JOSEPH ADDISON, ESQ. | The First American Edition. | PHILADELPHIA: |

REPRINTED FOR THE REV. M. L. WEEMS, | BY PARRY HALL, CHESNUT STREET. | M,DCC,XCIII. | 24mo. pp. XVII, (19)–156.

AAS., LC., NYPL.

1. Chapters I–IV consist of Cornaro; pp. 137–156 consist of an Appendix: 'GOLDEN RULES | OF HEALTH, | SELECTED FROM HIPPOCRATES, PLU- | TARCH, AND SEVERAL OTHER EMI- | NENT PHYSICIANS AND | PHILOSOPHERS.' The Appendix was probably compiled by Weems, and the two footnotes have his unmistakable tincture, for the hortatory is combined with the medical and the altruistic. See note 5 below.

2. Evans No. 25349. *Bibliographica Catholica Americana*, J. M. Finotti, p. 95. Weems was mentioned as the first American editor of Cornaro's 'little treatise' in a notice in the *Nation* of an edition of this work issued by Crowell. See 1815 edition, title 225, note 4. 'Besides the lives of . . . he [*Weems*] wrote or edited a number of other books and pamphlets, viz. . . . "The Life of Cornaro, a

converted Italian" . . .' [*Hayden's Genealogies*, p. 351, LC.] This is a mistaken reference to this title.

3. *Ad.* [*M.L.W.?*] 'JUST PUBLISHED, *And to be sold by the printer hereof,* That celebrated little book, entitled — *Sure and certain methods of attaining a long and* HEALTHY LIFE, written by Lewis Cornaro. . . . N. B. The London edition . . . sold at 6/6. The American edition on a good paper, large type, handsomely bound, lettered and filletted with gold, for 3/3 only.' *Del. Gaz.*, June 15, 1793, LC.; *Md. Jour.*, July 5, 1793 *et seq.*, LC.; July 25, 1793, MDHS. Also advertised in *Nat'l Gaz.*, Aug. 3, 1793 *et seq.*, LCPHIL.

4. There is an excellent though uninspired portrait of Cornaro by Titian in the Pitti gallery — showing him as already far advanced in years, with a delicately featured face, bearded, and lacking the rubicund tints or rotund outlines so often seen in the portraits of that day.

5. Very early Weems had developed a style. So, on p. 140 we find this footnote (or foot-print) indubitably his. 'I saw (says an American officer) thirteen grenadiers lying dead by a spring, in consequence of drinking too freely of the cold water, while dripping with sweat in a hard day's march in summer. And many a charming girl, worthy of a tenderer husband, has sunk into the icy embraces of death, by suddenly exposing her delicate frame, warm from the ball-room, to the cold air. And since "the universal cause acts not by partial, but by general laws," many a good soul, with more piety than prudence, turning out quite warm from a crowded preaching into the cold air without cloak or surtout, has gone off in a galloping consumption to that happy world, where pain and sickness are unknown. What a melancholy thing it is, that people cannot take care of their souls, without neglecting their bodies, nor seek their salvation without ruining their health.' And again a footnote on p. 147: 'Would to God, all ministers of religion (I mention *them* because they are generally most wanting in this great article of prudence) would but attend to the advice of this eminent Philosopher. They would, many of them, live much longer, and consequently stand a good chance to be more useful men here on earth, and brighter saints in heaven. What can give greater pain to a man who has the prosperity of religion at heart, than to see an *amiable, pious, young divine,* (who promised great services to the world) spitting up his lungs, and dying of a consumption brought on by preaching ten times louder than he had need! Since the world began, no man ever spoke with *half* the energy which the interests of eternal souls deserve, but there is a wide difference betwixt an *instructive, moving, melting eloquence*, and a loud unmeaning monotony.' Yet see a reference, possibly to Weems as a preacher, in Duke's *Diary*, Aug. 9, 1789, *Appendix XV*.

NUMBER 220 1796

THE | IMMORTAL MENTOR: | OR | MAN'S UNERRING GUIDE | TO A | HEALTHY, WEALTHY, AND | HAPPY LIFE. | In three Parts. | BY | LEWIS CORNARO, DR. FRANKLIN, AND | DR. SCOTT. | "Reason's whole pleasure, all the joys of sense, | "Lie in three words — health, peace and competence. | "Blest health consists with temperance alone, | "And peace, O virtue! peace is all thy own." | POPE. | PHILADELPHIA: |

PRINTED FOR THE REV. MASON L. WEEMS, | BY FRANCIS AND ROBERT BAILEY, | NO. 116, HIGH-STREET. | 1796. | 12mo. pp. (3), 2, (1), 1, (1), 1, IV, 1, 2–80, 1, 82–94, 1, (1), 1, 98–130, 1, (1), 1, 134–321, (1).

AAS., BPL., HSP., *JCB., LC., NYPL.

1. On the page opposite the title is a printed letter: 'Mount-Vernon, July, 3^d^. 1799. Rev. Sir, | For your kind compliment — "The IMMORTAL MENTOR", | I beg you to accept my best thanks. I have perused it | with singular satisfaction; and hesitate not to say that it | is, *in my opinion at least*, an *invaluable compilation*. I cannot | but hope that a book whose *contents* do such *credit* to its *title*, | will meet a very generous patronage. | Should that patronage equal my wishes, you will have no | reason to regret that you ever printed the Immortal Men- | tor. | With respect I am Rev. Sir, | Your most obedient | Humble Servant, | George Washington. | The Rev. Mr. Weems.' This letter being *pasted* on the opposite page from the title shows that it was an addition after the first issuance of the book. [This would tend to prove the same contention concerning *The Philanthropist.*] Among Weems' letters may be found allusions to just such expedients to stimulate sales, the insertion of letters from prominent persons being one of his forms of the modern 'blurb.' A quotation from 'The Great Addison' follows the title. Part I consists of four chapters by Cornaro; notes, presumably inserted by Weems, on pp. 11–12, 84, 85 and 89; the Appendix, pp. 81–94, is the same as that in the 1793 issue, which was differently entitled [see title preceding]; Part II, Introduction, also presumably by the editor, pp. [*97*]–105, to 'The Way to Wealth', pp. [*107*]–125; 'Advice to a Young Tradesman,' pp. 126–130; Part III, Chapter I. 'A Sure Guide to Happiness, By Doctor Scott', pp. [*133*]–321; Chapter II. 'On Social Love'.

2. Ford's *Franklin Bibliography* No. 137. Brinley No. 3264.

3. *Ad.* [*M.L.W.?*] 'Proposals for re-printing by subscription, that excellent book, entitled, The Immortal Mentor; or, Man's unerring Guide to a Healthy, and Happy Life. In three Parts. Recommended by the Hon. Joseph Addison, Author of the Spectator. Conditions. This valuable Book, containing 3 Vols. bound in one, shall be printed on a fair paper, large type, neatly bound and lettered, and delivered to subscribers at One Dollar only; nor is that required till the book is delivered. Sept. 23.' *Del. & East. Shore Adv.*, Oct. 10, 1795, LC. Also advertised in: *Va. Gaz. & Petersburg Intel.*, Nov. 1, 1796 *et seq.*, NYPL. *Va. Arg.*, July 12, 1799, Oct. 28, 1800 *et seq.*, LC. *Md. Gaz.* (Annap's), Dec. 4, 1800 *et seq.*, MDSTL. *Va. Arg.*, Jan. 16, 1801, NYPL. *Times & D. C. D. Adv.*, July 9, 1801, AAS.

4. On July 28, 1796, Weems wrote to Carey that their binder, Mr. James Wilson, had bound some '*little* books chiefly,' for him and that he was drained of money by his old Friends, Messrs. Adams. Again, Sept. 20, 1796: 'If you will be so good as to let your Neighbour Bailey have 30 Dol. and beg him to send on (as I desir[d] him) to Fredericksburg, Virginia 200 copies of the Mentor, you will oblige me much, and perhaps not lose anything in the long run.' Oct. 12, 1796: 'I was here about to enter a complaint against our Friend Bailey for neglecting me so in the affair of the Mentor . . . If I had the Mentor, I coud, in six months time make 1,000 Dol. clear profit for the good of our concern . . . If [*he*] sh[d] be slack in stays about the Mentor, be pleas[d] to get 400 copies in sheets have them boun[d] & send on . . .' July 13, 1798: 'I have now in the hands of Citizen Bailey 2 or 3 and twenty hundred copies of the Immortal Mentor, a book very saleable. For that work I have paid M[r]. Bailey and his paper Maker M[r]. Steel, 964 Dol. . . . I w[d] not wish more than *one half* of my Mentors to be dispos[d] of in this way [*by exchange for*] little histories &c. &c. . . .' On July 20, 1798, Carey wrote to Weems: 'I have a number of small books, pamphlets, Maps, prints, magazines, &c which I should willingly exchange for the Mentor.' Weems wrote to Carey, June 15, 1799: 'I wish you w'd be so good as to ask M[r]. Bailey how many of my Immortal Mentors are now on hand. Wou'd it not be well for me to open a subscription paper for the Immortal Mentor stitch[d] in Marble paper for 4/6 Virg[*inia*] money. I cou'd sell immense numbers.' Aug. 4, 1800: 'I wish you w[d] overhall my old papers — you may lay hand on my subscription paper for Immortal Mentor for New York.' Aug. 8, 1800, he wrote concerning 'the little box that brings the Mentors to New York.' He was disappointed in the disposal of the Mentor, writing on Aug. 9, 1800, to Carey that 'the great revolutions among my subscribers . . . (during the six years since they touch[d] the paper) have operated against me. Deaths,

removals, insolvencies & villainies have prov[d] pernicious to me.' Sept. 16, 1800: 'If I had Paine & the Immortal Mentor I think I coud metamorphose them into good bank notes, by spring.' Oct. 14, 1800: 'In the little closet upstairs You will find a large bundle of Subscription papers for . . . Mentor.' Nov. 26, 1800: 'I might as soon borrow a ton of brimstone from the Devil as get my Washingtons, Bachelors & other books (Mentor & Paine) from you.' Feb. [?] 1801: 'Beg Robinson [1] to bind me 100 Mentor . . . From the Mentor . . . I can send you much money this year.' May 8, 1801: 'Now I beg your advice Don't you think I had better instantly, turn my Mentors . . . now lying with you & Robertson [1] and the Binder, into an assortment of *readily whole sale* books? . . . I mean to make a great sacrifice for *cash*. You saw me offer my Mentors (to the little French Jew [*John Bioren*]) for 5/.' Sept. 2, 1801: 'M[r] Robertson the Binder inform[d] me last week that I had engag[d] him to bind me the whole of my Mentors 1000 Copies for the payment whereof, I was to make arrangements with you. It *may* be so, but I remember it not. He has it seems bound nearly 50£ worth, and with great conciseness threatens to take a very summary way of paying himself. I wish you w[d] be so good as to tell him that I shall be up in Philad[a] about the middle of the next month and shall bring money in purse for him.' Oct. 15, 1801: 'Dont forget to tell Robinson. Why sh[d] he without my orders bind my books & then without orders sell them? especially when I have the money.' Dec. 8, 1801: 'I w[d] God you coud get from (Wallace I think you call[d] him) successor to Robinson, some of my Immortal Mentor and convert them into some saleable books such as Charlotte Temple, Watts Psalms &c &c by the sale of which I may cover my expences in this Crusade.' Dec. 9, 1801: 'If you can, send me some little *popular pieces* in exchange for the Immortal Mentor. The choice is left to you.'

5. 'Francis Bailey was bred a carpenter . . . and obtained some smattering of instruction in the art of printing at Ephrata, in Lancaster County. I do not positively deny, for I have not correct information, but I very much doubt whether he ever published a newspaper at Lancaster.[8] [*f.n. 8.* 'Bailey published "Das Pennsylvanische Zeitungs-Blat" at Lancaster from Feb. 4 to June 24, 1778. He began printing in Philadelphia in 1779, and established "The Freeman's Journal," April 25, 1781.'] . . . He possessed an office at Lancaster two or three years, with which he removed to Philadelphia in the fall of 1778, and the following year, 1779, commenced the Freeman's Journal, . . . The United States Magazine, which Bailey published in 1779, was continued to the 9th

[1] 'Robertson Duncan bookbinder next 103 North Sixth st' *Philadelphia Directory*, 1800, LC. It may be assumed that these two names apply to the same man, since the *Philadelphia Directory*, 1801, gives 'Duncan Robinson, book binder' as at 'North Sixth Street . . . 105'.

number only. It was edited by H. H. Brackenridge.[1] ['Francis Bailey was the publisher who had the courage to undertake another monthly magazine in the midst of the war, and with Brackenridge as editor, which insured some pungent writing, he issued . . . 1779, . . . "*The United States Magazine*."' *Philadelphia Magazines*, A. H. Smyth, pp. 53–54.] 'In religion, Bailey attached himself to the Swedenborg sect. Bailey continued in Philadelphia till the legislature removed their sittings to Lancaster, in 1799, when, as he had a share of the public work, he removed with part of his office to that place, and left his son Robert in the city with the residue. Robert did not continue long in the office at Philadelphia. . . . Robert died in 1807. His widow, Lydia R. Bailey, has since that carried on the printing business with success and reputation.' *William McCulloch's Additions to Thomas's History of Printing*, in *ProcAAS.*, Vol. XXXI, April, 1921, pp. 103 and 98.

6. In Robert Bailey's Letter Books [HSP.], between Oct. 20 and 24, 1796, after Francis Bailey had joined him, occurs the following entry: 'Printed for the Rev[d] M. L. Weems 3000 Copies of The Immortal Mentor @ 2/ Pd. £300.'

NUMBER 221 1802

THE | IMMORTAL MENTOR: | OR, MAN'S UNERRING GUIDE | TO A | HEALTHY, WEALTHY, AND | HAPPY LIFE. | *In three parts.* | BY | LEWIS CORNARO, DR. FRANKLIN, | AND DR. SCOTT. | "Reason's whole pleasure, all the joys of sense, | "Lie in three word's — health, peace and competence. | "Blest health consists with temperance alone, | "And peace, O virtue! peace is all thy own." | POPE. | PHILADELPHIA: |

PRINTED FOR THE REV. MASON L. WEEMS. | 1802. | 12mo.
pp. 3, (1), IV, 1, 2–80, 1, 82–94, 1, (1), 1, 98–105, (1), 1, 108–130, 1, (1), 1, 134–321.
HSP.

1. The contents are identical with those of the 1796 edition, preceding title, except that the letter from Washington is incorporated in the text.

2. Paul L. Ford's *Franklin Bibliography*, 1889, No. 144.

3. *Ad.* 'Books and Stationary, For sale by the subscriber, opposite Doctor

[1] For the relations between Brackenridge and Weems, see commendations of his *Life of Washington*, 1809, title 14, *et seq.*

Hill's in Market-street. . . . The Immortal Mentor. . . .' *Wilm. Gaz.*, May 13, 1802 *et seq.*, HU.

4. Weems wrote to Carey, Apr. 28, 1802: 'You know, my Mentors (which you take in exchange [*for Prayer Books*], are ready for you.' May 24, 1802: 'As to the *Mentor*, you well know I told you they are not full bound, — Yea, I show[d] you a copy of one. Wallace & Coghlan have them & will bind for you. If an order be necessary I'll cheerfully give it. *Charge* the binding to me, as *an additional favor* to your M. L. Weems.' [See also letter of Feb. [?] 1801, title 241, note 4.]

NUMBER 222 1803

THE | IMMORTAL MENTOR: | OR, | MAN'S UNERRING GUIDE | TO A | HEALTHY, WEALTHY, AND | HAPPY LIFE, | *In three Parts.* | BY | LEWIS CORNARO, DR. FRANKLIN, | AND DR. SCOTT. | "Reason's whole pleasure, all the joys of sense, | "Lie in three words — health, peace and competence. | "Blest health consists with temperance alone, | "And peace, O virtue! peace is all thy own." | POPE. | PHILADELPHIA: |

PRINTED FOR THE REV. MASON L. WEEMS. | 1803. | 12mo. pp. (2), 3, 2–80, 1, 82–94, 1, (1), 1, 98–105, (1), 1, 108–130, 1, (1), 1, 134. BPL.

1. Contents the same as the 1796 and the 1802 editions, titles 220 and 221; Washington's letter of commendation on reverse of title; no table of contents.

2. Advertised in: *Wilm. Gaz.* (N.C.), Jan. 22, 1804 *et seq.*, HU.; Jan. 15, 1805, AAS. Fly leaves of Johnson's *Pennsylvania & New Jersey Almanac*, Philadelphia, 1807, LC. [This suggests that Johnson might have been the printer.]

NUMBER 223 1809

MEANS | OF OBTAINING A LONG | AND | HEALTHY LIFE. | BY LEWIS CORNARO. | With Notes | BY MASON L. WEEMS. | To which is added, | THE | WAY TO WEALTH. | BY DOCTOR FRANKLIN. | PHILADELPHIA: |

PRINTED AND SOLD BY BENJAMIN JOHNSON. | No. 249, Market-Street. | 1809. | 24mo. pp. 1, (1), 1, (1), 1, 6–64, 1, 66–75, (1), 1, 78–90, (2).

BPL., LC. [*imp.*], LCPhil., NYPL.

1. The quotation from Addison follows title; same notes as in the former editions on pp. 12–13, 67, 68 and 71; between Cornaro's and Franklin's work are the 'Golden Rules of Health'; Dr. Scott is not included in this edition; lacks Washington's letter of commendation; slight changes from Cornaro's text of the 1796 edition; no table of contents; there is no Introduction to 'The Way to Wealth'; it also lacks everything thereafter which was in the 1793 and 1796 editions.

2. Cornaro was 'a new edition of the greater part of a compilation by Weems published in 1796 under the title: The Immortal Mentor. 1. Hygiene. 2. Longevity.' LC. CATALOGUE.

3. *Ad.* 'Just Published and for sale By Benjamin Johnson, No. 249 Market Street, Philadelphia: Means of obtaining a long and healthy life. By Lewis Cornaro. With notes by Mason L. Weems. To which is added, The Way to Wealth. By Doctor Franklin. Price 25 cents. . . .' Back cover of *Johnson's Almanac*, Philadelphia, 1810, LC. Also advertised in: *Va. Arg.*, May 29, 1810; Sept. 26, 1811, AAS. *Va. Gaz.*, Oct. 7, 1811, VSTL.

4. Benjamin Johnson kept a bookshop on Market Street, Philadelphia, in the concluding quarter of the eighteenth century. Sold it to Benjamin Warner, and he sold it to Grigg. See *History of Philadelphia*, Scharf & Westcott, Vol. III, p. 2231, LC. Grigg was followed by Grigg & Elliott, to whom Lippincott succeeded in 1848.

NUMBER 224 1810

THE | IMMORTAL MENTOR: | OR | MAN'S UNERRING GUIDE | TO A | HEALTHY, WEALTHY, & HAPPY LIFE. | IN THREE PARTS. | BY LEWIS CORNARO, DR. FRANKLIN, | AND DR. SCOTT. | [*Four lines of verse*] | POPE. | PUBLISHED BY DANIEL FENTON, | MILL-HILL, NEAR TRENTON. |

Printed by Brown and Merritt, Philadelphia. | 1810. | 12mo. pp. 1, (1), 3, 2–80, 1, 82–94, 1, (1), 1, 98–105, (1), 1, 108–125, 1, 127–130, 1, (1), 1, 134–235, 236–323, (1), 8.

BM., BPL., NYPL.

1. Without Weems' name on the title; it has the letter of commendation addressed to him from George Washington, and quotation from 'The Great Addison' on the sheet following title; table of Contents; text identical with the 1796 and 1802 editions, titles 220 and 221; back fly leaves contain a list of subscribers and publishers' advertisements.

NUMBER 225 1815

THE | IMMORTAL MENTOR, | OR, | MAN'S UNERRING GUIDE | TO A | HEALTHY, WEALTHY, AND | HAPPY LIFE. | *In Three Parts,* | BY | LEWIS CORNARO, DR. FRANKLIN, AND | DR. SCOTT. | [*Four lines of verse*] | POPE. | CARLISLE, PA. | PUBLISHED BY ALEXANDER MAGEE AND JOHN SCOTT. |

*Printed at the Volunteer Office,* | 1815. | 12mo. pp. (2), 1, (1), 1, (1), 1, 6–61, (1), 1, 64–72, 1, (1), 1, 76–85, (1), 1, 88–99, (1), 1, 102–104, 1, (1), 1, 108–175, (1), 1, 178-234, 6, (2).
BPL.

1. Without Weems' name on the title; has table of Contents; the text is identical with the 1796 and 1802 editions, with list of subscribers on the back fly leaves; Washington's letter is *pasted* on the reverse of front cover, as in the edition of 1796.

2. Carey's Catalogue, 1816; 1818, No. 1000.

3. Advertised in *Frank. Repos.*, Nov. 25, 1817 *et seq.*, FROF.

4. 'Luigi Cornaro's "Discorsi della vita sobria" . . . first translated by George Herbert, highly praised by Addison, and "perused with singular satisfaction" by George Washington (according to a letter of his, written in 1799 to the Rev. Mr. Weems, the first American editor of the little treatise.) . . . The book is full of eminent good-sense. . . . At eighty-three he wrote a comedy "abounding with innocent mirth and pleasant jests," . . . or because ten years later his voice had grown "so strong and sonorous that I cannot help chanting aloud my prayers," as because of his patriarchal delight in family and in estates, and his sincere piety towards human and divine. "I really never knew," he says, "till I grew old, that the world was so beautiful." Cornaro urges the avoidance of extreme heat and cold, over-exertion, bad air, melancholy, and hatred.' Review [*Anon.*] of an edition by Crowell Publishing Co. in the *Nation* (New York), July 13, 1916.

NUMBER 226 1794

AN ACCOUNT | OF THE | PELEW ISLANDS, | SITUATED IN THE | GREAT SOUTH SEA. | COMPOSED FROM THE JOURNALS OF | *Capt.* HENRY WILSON, *and his* OFFICERS; | WHO, IN AUGUST, *1783*, | WERE THERE SHIPWRECKED | IN THE | ANTELOPE PACKET. | *Nothing can be more interesting to Man, than the History of Man.* | KEATE. | WILMINGTON: |

PRINTED FOR THE REV. M. L. WEEMS, BY SAMUEL AND | JOHN ADAMS, CORNER OF KING AND HIGH-STREETS. | *1794.* | *Sm.*12mo. pp. I, (I), III–IV, I, 2–96.
LC., NYPL.

1. The Introduction to the original edition of London, 1788, is here omitted, while a table of Contents has been added; the abridgment consists of the entire omission of passages rather than the condensation of the book as a whole.

2. Evans No. 27177. 'An abridged account from the original edition, edited probably by M. L. Weems.' LC.CATALOGUE.

3. *Ad.* 'Just Published. . . . An Account of the Pelew Islands . . . to which is added, Anecdotes of the Young Prince, Lee Boo. . . .' *Del. & East. Shore Adv.*, May 14, 1794; with changes May 24 *et seq.*, HSP. 'A HISTORY OF THE PELEWITES, A NEW NATION, Lately discovered . . . by Captain WILSON. . . . PRICE 1/6 only. . . .' *Va. Gaz.* (Rich'd), Feb. 28, 1795; Aug. 1, 1795, HU. 'For Sale, At M. Bartgis' Printing Office . . . Account of the Pelew Islands . . .' *Bartgis's Fed. Gaz.*, Sept. 22, 1796, MDHS. 'J. Gales . . . Keate's Account of the Pelew Islands . . .' *Ral. Reg.*, May 27, 1805, NCSTL. 'A Catalogue of Books for sale at Joseph Gales's Store . . . Keate's Account of the Pelew Islands . . .' *Ral. Reg.*, Nov. 23, 1809, NCSTL. Also advertised in: *Va. Gaz. & W'kly Adv.*, Feb. 28, 1795, May 9, 1795, IIU. *Lanc. Jour.*, Jan. 15, 1796 *et seq.*, LIOF. *Bartgis's Fed. Gaz.*, May 26, 1796 *et seq.*, HU. *Repub. Cit.*,

Sept. 7, 1796 *et seq.*, HU. *Kline's Carl. W'kly Gaz.*, Sept. 14, 1796 *et seq.*, DCHS. *Va. Gaz. & Petersburg Intel.*, Nov. 1, 1796 *et seq.;* Jan. 31, 1797, HU. *Guard.*, June 27, 1797 *et seq.*, CHDESHCOL. *Newark Gaz.*, Dec. 19, 1797, AAS. *Repub. Arg. & County Adv.*, May 18, 1804, HU. *Gen. Lib.*, July 25, 1805, HU. *Guard.*, Mar. 13, 1806 *et seq.*, RUTGERSCL. *Oracle Dauph.*, Feb. 4, 1809, PSTL.

4. Keate, George, born Wiltshire, 1729, died 1797. Called to the bar, 1753, but never practised. Lived abroad for some years, and was an intimate acquaintance of Voltaire. 'Was in turn poet, naturalist, antiquary, and artist. . . . Wrote for pleasure, not for profit.'

5. Samuel & John Adams, sons of James, an Irish immigrant who set up the first printing press in Delaware in 1762, and who started his first newspaper, *The Wilmington Courant*, a year later. His son Samuel joined him, and later another son, John. They first removed their business to New Castle, Del., and about 1800, to Baltimore, where they apparently had had one as early as 1789. See *History of the State of Delaware*, Henry C. Conrad, Wilmington, 1908, pp. 1085–1087, LC.; also *Md. Gaz.*, Aug. 27, 1789 *et seq.*, MDHS. S. & J. Adams established *The Delaware Courant*, Wilmington, in 1786, which ran only a year, and in 1794, they, with W. C. Smyth, established *The Delaware & Eastern Shore Advertiser*, which was discontinued in 1799. See *McCulloch's Additions to Thomas's History of Printing, ProcAAS.*, Vol. XXXI, April, 1921. 'Printing, Samuel and John Adams Return their unfeigned thanks . . . Printing Office is still continued . . . superintendance of Mr. Thomas E. Clayland . . .' *Balt. D. Intel.*, May 29, 1794 *et seq.*, LC. Carey wrote with acrimony Nov. 15, 1800, of advancing 'in favour of Adams' two notes for Weems' works.

6. There had been an earlier American edition advertised: 'Just Published and to be sold by Berry & Rogers . . . An American Edition . . . neatly bound & lettered (Price six shillings) An Account of the Pelew Islands. . . .' *Morn. Post*, Nov. 23, 1791, LC.

NUMBER 227 1791

SERMONS, | ON | Different important Subjects. | By ROBERT RUSSEL, | at *Wardhurst*, in *Sussex*. | BALTIMORE: | Printed by SAMUEL and JOHN ADAMS, in MAR- | KET-STREET, for M. L. WEEMS. | M.DCC.XCI. | *Sm.*12mo. pp. 1, (1), 1, 4-112. AAS.

1. Seven in number, with two prayers. With no apparent trace of Weems' editing.

2. This seems to be the first imprint of Weems thus far found. Had the title which follows this been earlier, it is likely that the Rev. William Duke[1]

[1] 'Duke, William, A.M., a native of St. Paul's, Baltimore Co. — brought up in the Church — ordained by Bishop Seabury in 1785, and became Rector of Queen Caroline, Ann Arundel — in 1787, of St. Paul's, Prince George's — in 1791 of St. Paul's Chapel, Baltimore Co. — in 1792 of North Elk, Cecil — in 1796 of Westminster, Ann Arundel — in 1803, Professor of Languages in St. John's College, and along therewith, in 1804, Rector of St. Ann's, Annapolis — in 1806, in charge of the Academy at Elkton, Cecil Co. — in 1812, Principal of the Charlotte Hall School — in 1815, returned to the Academy in Elkton. He was the Convention Preacher of 1797, and often in the Standing Committee. He published volumes of Hymns, of Defence of Christianity, on Maryland History, and sundry small treatises — died in 1843, aet. 83.' *Clergy of Maryland of the Protestant Episcopal Church*, Ethan Allen, 1860, p. 17, PIL. — 'This movement [*to travel to the west to assist, so far as he might, in planting and spreading religion and learning*], it is believed, was the first ever made in the Episcopal Church in Domestic Missions, to our Western Country.' Sketch of William Duke by Ethan Allen in *Annals of the American Pulpit*, William B. Sprague, 1861, Vol. V, pp. 310-311, LC. — Duke began to preach at 15. Had been licensed at that age as an 'exhorter' by the Society of Methodists, rode on circuit in Pennsylvania, New Jersey, Delaware and Virginia. Wrote that in 1774-1784, a circuit rider at that time, 'before he entered [*a town*] calculated upon being ducked, mobbed, or ludicrously set at naught.' When the Wesleyans showed signs of schism he turned to the regular ministry of the Church. His second charge was conferred after opposition because he 'preached without a manuscript.' Dr. Claggett warned him against this unusual method of address but Duke persevered. — Duke's portrait, reproduced in *The Church Standard*, June 20, 1908, shows him to be very much what his own words in his *Diary* depict him; a serious, sad-faced gentleman, of dignified dress and demeanor, with an anxious cast of countenance which may be well explained by his ever recurrent

would have mentioned this one in his *Diary* or might have shown in his allusions that Weems had been selling it for some time, who by 1792 was already embarked in book publishing and selling: 'June 1, 1792. *At the Convention at Annapolis.* . . . Walked into the country and lodged with M^r. Weems and M^r. Coleman. Subscribed Weems's proposals for 2 books and paid 1/10. . . . Received 5. little books of M^r. Weems . . . came out again to lodge with Weems. . . . Sept. 12, 1792. Went to Church and preached. the Rev^d. M^r. Weems came in the meantime. . . . Was sorry to see Weems's pedling [*sic*] way of life but God knows best by what methods we can most directly answer to designations of his Providence.' *Ms. Diary of Rev. William Duke*, owned by MDDIO'NL. in PIL.

3. Carey's Catalogue, 1795, AAS.

4. *Ad.* 'A new, correct, and improved Edition of that very valuable little Book called RUSSELL'S [*sic*] Seven Sermons, For Sale by S. & J. Adams, and the Printer.' *Balt. D. Repos.*, Feb. 28, 1792 *et seq.*, HSP. 'Books published by M. Carey . . . Russell's [*sic*] Seven Sermons. (Price 20 Cents.)' In back fly leaves of *Letters from an American Farmer*, M. Carey, 1793, LC. 'Dickson & Pescud, have just received, (On consignment) 20 boxes of books; Each box containing the following: viz. . . . 6 Russell's [*sic*] 7 Sermons, &c. &c. . . . August 6, 1805.' *Petersburg Intel.*, Aug. 30, 1805, HU. 'Catalogue . . . Carey (*Price* 50 *cents*) Seven Sermons, By Russell [*sic*] . . .' In back fly leaves of *Life of Washington*, tenth edition, title 19, NYPL. 'Just received And for sale at the Post-Office Milledgeville a collection of choice books, which will be sold at the Philadelphia prices . . . Russels Seven Sermons . . .' *Ga. Arg.*, Jan. 16, 1811, HU. The price varies: advertised at 25 cents, *Oracle Dauph.*, Apr. 13, May 23, 1803, LC.; Oct. 13, 1804, PSTL.; at 20 cents, *Ibid.*, Feb. 4, 1809, PSTL. Also advertised in: *Lanc. Jour.*, June 3, 1796, LIOF. *Kline's Carl. W'kly Gaz.*, Sept. 14, 1796 *et seq.*, DCHS. *Va. Gaz. & Petersburg Intel.*, Nov. 1, 1796 *et seq.*, HU. *Va. Arg.*, Mar. 21, 1797, HU.; Dec. 26, 1800 *et seq.*, VSTL. *Alex'a Expos.*, Dec. 13, 1802, HU. *Amer. Lit. Adv.*, Dec. 16, 1802, HU. *Bartgis's Repub. Gaz.*, Nov. 5, 1802 *et seq.*, HU.; Jan. 21, 1803 *et seq.*, AAS. *Wilm. Gaz.*, Jan. 22, 1804 *et seq.*, HU.; Jan. 15, 1805, AAS.

5. Writing to Carey, Mar. 25, 1809, Weems asked, among other books, for Russell's [*sic*] Sermons.

6. 'Russell's [*sic*] Seven Sermons advertised by Thomas Bradford.' *Forgotten Books of the American Nursery*, Rosalie V. Halsey, p. 90, LC.

ill-health. [See also *Appendix XV.*] That a man who ever lived and thought so circumspectly should have little direct censure for his colleague and apparent friend goes to show that Weems did not err so far from the standard of his time as many would make out.

NUMBER 228? 1791–1792?

*Onania. [*1791–1792?*]

1. Of this work few traces have been found. Of its almost certain issuance by Weems proof is furnished in the written testimony of his friend, the Rev. William Duke, given below. From that it seems clear that Weems did actually bring out an edition himself rather than merely vend one. This latter action alone on the part of a clergyman would have sufficiently stirred any community on this side of the Atlantic in 1791 or 1792, but to have gone to the length of printing such a book or pamphlet, and thereafter offering it for sale would in itself adequately explain Weems' so soon after finding himself without an incumbency — probably in 1792 or 1793. Two entries in Duke's *Diary*, as noted in *Parson Weems* by Lawrence C. Wroth, are as follow: 'June 29, 1792. I see Weems' publication of Onania is in a good many hands. I am afraid rather as a matter of diversion than serious consideration.' 'June 30, 1792. Weems has incurred a good deal of ridicule as well as serious blame by his odd publication.' P. 59. It is characteristic of the Parson, to have ignored the prejudices of others less enlightened, or less zealous than himself.

2. It seems likely that, with misdirected zeal, Weems reprinted, or purchased for resale, one of the translations on this subject, probably from the German. Of English works which suggest themselves as a possible source, I find, in the British Museum Catalogue, 'ONANIA, or the heinous sin of self-pollution, and all its frightful consequences in both sexes, considered. With spiritual and physical advice,' etc. London [*1710?*], with numerous succeeding editions. Books or pamphlets dealing with the same matter are noted in Watt's *Bibliotheca Britannica*, but with differing titles. With this particular title, the first issue known in this country is a small 12mo dated 1724, Boston, called the Tenth pamphlet edition, probably from its predecessors in Great Britain. Of this issue it is stated on the cover title that 'above Fifteen Thousand of the former editions have been sold.' This was reprinted in 1726, and again in 1742, both in Boston. I am told that the pamphlet is written entirely from the moral rather than the physiological viewpoint, which explains Weems' taking it up. For some earlier reprints see *American Bibliography*, Charles Evans, Nos. 2573, 2795 and 5026.

NUMBER 229 1792

SERMONS, | BY | HUGH BLAIR, D.D. | One of the MINISTERS of the HIGH CHURCH, | AND | PROFESSOR of RHETORIC and BELLES LETTRES in the | UNIVERSITY, of EDINBURGH. | To which is prefixed, that admired Tract | ON THE | INTERNAL EVIDENCE | OF THE | CHRISTIAN RELIGION. | BY SOAME JENYNS, | of the British Parliament. | VOLUME THE FIRST. | THE SIXTEENTH EDITION. |

LONDON, Printed: — | BALTIMORE: Re-printed, for the Rev. M. L. WEEMS, | by SAMUEL and JOHN ADAMS, Book-Printers, in | *Market-street*, between *South* and *Gay-streets*. | M DCC XCII. | 8vo. pp. 1, (1), 1, 4–41, (1), 1, XLIV–XLVI, 1, 48–285.

AAS., BPL., NYPL.

1. This and Volume II, title 230, contain together fifty sermons. Pp. 1, 4–41 consist of Soame Jenyns' 'A VIEW OF THE INTERNAL EVIDENCE . . .'; pp. 1, XLIV–XLVI give 'THE CONTENTS'. No trace of Weems' editing found.

2. Evans No. 24120.

3. *Ad.* [*M.L.W.?*] 'PROPOSALS For reprinting by subscription THE CELEBRATED *Dr. Blair's Sermons*, These sermons are so generally read and admired as to render any encomium altogether unnecessary. They are unquestionably among the most rational and elegant sermons in our language. — In justice, however, to these valuable discourses, we find ourselves constrained to relate the following memorable anecdote. — They made their appearance at a time when her present Britannic Majesty, *Charlotte*, was considerably indisposed. Lord *Mansfield*, a great favourite at Court, usually visited his sovereign every day, with a volume of these sermons in his pocket, one of which he daily read in her hearing. The Queen, who has the reputation of a pious woman, was so highly pleased with them, that she immediately settled a pension of £.200 sterling on the worthy author, as a token of her gratitude for the service he had rendered the interests of piety and virtue. CONDITIONS. These sermons will be com-

prised in two handsome volumes, printed with a new type on the best paper, neatly bound, lettered and filletted and delivered to subscribers at TWO DOLLARS; ONE HALF to be paid at subscribing, and the OTHER on delivery of the book. Those ladies and Gentlemen who patronise this valuable work (by their subscriptions) shall have their names prefixed to it. N. B. The editor of this work, the Rev. *Mason L. Weems*, will deposit in the hands of those gentlemen, who take in subscriptions, at a distance, the books subscribed for, as soon as completed. Subscriptions are also taken in by messrs. Samuel and John Adams, in Baltimore, who are to be the printers of the work, and Mr. James Adams, in Wilmington, Delaware State. *The accomplishment of this work will be attended with considerable expense, which renders it necessary that a part of the cost should be defrayed at the time of subscribing — but the subscribers may rest assured, that the editor will adopt such measures as shall, in case of any disaster, effectually secure them from loss. Baltimore*, January 18, 1792.' *Del. Gaz.*, May 5, 1792, LC. Reprinted, almost verbatim, up to the following: '*Subscriptions* are taken in by Rev. Mr. Bend [1]; Rev. Mr. Ralph [2]; Rev. Mr. Richards; Doctor Stevenson; Mr. Jacob Killen;

[1] 'Joseph Grove John Bend, D.D., a native of New York — brought up in the Church — ordained 1787 by Bishop Provost, New York — came from Pennsylvania to Maryland in 1791, and became Rector of St. Paul's Parish, Baltimore Co. He was Convention Preacher in 1808, and was always, Secretary to the Convention, member of the Standing Committee, and Delegate to the General Convention — he published three Occasional Sermons, and edited a number of works for distribution. He died in 1812, aet. 53.' *Clergy of Maryland of the Protestant Episcopal Church*, Ethan Allen, 1860, p. 20, PIL. — 'June 19, 1791 [*At the convention at Baltimore.*] . . . Heard Mr. Bassett preach in the forenoon and Mr. Bend in the afternoon. . . . May 12, 1792 . . . stopped in Town [*en route from Annapolis*] long enough to visit Mr. Bend. . . . Sept. 10, 1793 . . . Rode to the Landing and received the proceedings &c. from Mr. Bend.' *Ms. Diary of Rev. William Duke*, owned by MDDIO'NL. in PIL.

[2] 'George Ralph, a native of England — brought up in the Church — in 1790 he had a school in Baltimore — was ordained by Bishop White in 1791, and in connection with his School, officiated in Baltimore. In 1793 he was Rector of North Sassafras, Cecil and South Sassafras, Kent, and had a school — in 1795, Rector of Washington Parish, D. C., with a School — in 1797, of Queen Anne, Prince George County, with a School — in 1800, Principal of Charlotte Hall, and Rector of Trinity, Charles, and in 1801, of All Faith's, St. Mary's. In 1809, he established an Academy in Baltimore County, and in 1810, in connection with it, was Rector of Trinity Church, Baltimore City, which he resigned in two years — was four times on the Standing Committee — died 1813.' *Clergy of Maryland of the Protestant Episcopal Church*, Ethan Allen, 1860, p. 21, PIL. — 'Aug. 3, 1792 Spent an hour or two [*in Town*] with Mr. Bend. The dispute between him and Mr. Ralph still goes on . . . Aug. 5, 1792. Mr. Ralph met us at the Chapel and gave us a sermon. He mounts the pulpit late in life, and I'm afraid if he had known his talent he would have deferred it longer. Sept. 2, 1792. We went to Chapel where Mr. Ralph met us. He seemed surprised and disturbed upon being informed (reminded) of the erroneous manner in which he had mentioned the proceedings of our Congregation. He delivered a decent discourse tho' not in a handsome manner.' *Ms. Diary*

Mrs. Phill Rogers; Mrs. Rebecca Ridgely; and Messrs. Graham, S. and J. Adams, Printers, Baltimore. . . .' *Balt. D. Repos.*, Feb. 29, 1792; *Del. Gaz.*, May 5, 1792, LC. For advertisements after 1792, see succeeding title.

NUMBER 230 1793

SERMONS, | BY | HUGH BLAIR, D.D. | One of the MINISTERS of the HIGH CHURCH, | AND | PROFESSOR of RHETORIC and BELLES LETTRES in the | UNIVERSITY of EDINBURGH. | VOLUME THE SECOND. | THE THIRTEENTH EDITION. |

LONDON | Printed: | BALTIMORE: Re-printed for the Rev. M. L. WEEMS, | by SAMUEL and JOHN ADAMS, Book-Printers, | in *Gay*, the Corner of *Second-Street.* | M DCC XCIII. | 8vo. pp. (2), I, (I), I, IV–VII, I, 9–329, (I).
MdHS.

1. Pp. I, IV–VII give 'THE CONTENTS'.
2. Evans No. 24120.
3. *Ad.* 'Books, Just Published, And for Sale, at this Printing-Office, . . . Sermons, (in two volumes) By Hugh Blair, D.D. . . . To which is prefixed that admired Tract, on the Internal Evidence of the Christian Religion. By Soame Jenyns. The Sixteenth Edition. . . . [*apparently the Sixteenth Edition all told, including the British editions*]' *Del. & East. Shore Adv.*, May 14, 1794, HSP. [On May 24 there were changes introduced in this advertisement and its insertion was continued. At that time S. & J. Adams & W. C. Smyth were the printers of this newspaper.] 'Mr. Pleasants. The following is an extract from Blair's Sermon "on our imperfect knowledge of a future state." The reader must be sensible that any passage, taken from the place in which it stands, and unconnected with the preceding, and subsequent parts of the discourse, must lose much of their original force and beauty. The whole sermon is a masterly piece of composition, and most ably justifies the ways of God to men. [*Signed*] A Customer. . . . The longer that our thoughts dwell on this subject . . . that

*of Rev. William Duke*, owned by MDDIO'NL. in PIL. — 'Baltimore Academy. Mr. Ralph respectfully informs the Public, that he has fitted up a very convenient SCHOOL-ROOM . . . receive Children. . . .' *Balt. D. Repos.*, Mar. 6, 1792 *et seq.*, HSP. — 'Charlotte-Hall School. On the 25 Oct. 1802, The Trustees . . . [*elected*] Rev. George Ralph . . . for the ensuing year . . .' *Wash. Fed.*, Dec. 6, 1802, LC.

which is in part, shall be done away.' *Rich'd and Manch'r Adv.*, Aug. 22, 1795, HU. 'New Books, for sale at this office. Blair's Sermons. (Likewise a few of the 2[d] Vol. For those subscribers who have received but the first Vol.) . . .' *Va. Gaz. & Petersburg Intel.*, Nov. 1, 1796 *et seq.*, NYPL. Also advertised in: *Col. Chron.*, Aug. 22, 1794, AAS. *Md. Her.* (Easton), May 19, 1795, HU. *Lanc. Jour.*, Jan. 15, 1796 *et seq.*, LIOF. *Del. Gaz.*, June 7, 1796, LC. *Kline's Carl. W'kly Gaz.*, Sept. 14, 1796 *et seq.*, DCHS. *Va. Arg.*, Apr. 18, 1800, LC. *Va.Fed.*, July 12, 1800 *et seq.*, HU. *Va. Arg.*, Oct. 28, 1800 *et seq.*, LC.; Dec. 26, 1800 *et seq.*, VSTL.; Jan. 16, 1801, NYPL. *Times & D. C. D. Adv.*, Dec. 2, 1801 *et seq.*, HU. *Col. Adv.* (Alex'a), Aug. 2, 1802, HU. *Alex'a Expos.*, Dec. 13, 1802, HU. *Amer. Lit. Adv.*, Dec. 16, 1802, HU. *Intel.*, Mar. 22, 1803 *et seq.*, LIOF.; Apr. 5, 1803, PSTL. *Wilm. Gaz.*, June 9, 1803 *et seq.*, HU. *Alex'a Expos.*, Jan. 7, 1804, HU. *Intel.*, Feb. 28, 1804, LIOF. *Wilm. Gaz.*, June 19, 1804 *et seq.*, HU. *Guard.*, Mar. 13, 1806 *et seq.*, RUTGERSCL. Fly leaves of Johnson's *Pennsylvania & New Jersey Almanac*, Philadelphia, 1807, LC. *Oracle Dauph.*, Jan. 28, 1809, PSTL. *Va. Her.*, Sept. 9, 1809, LC. *Aug. Chron.*, Mar. 8, 1811 *et seq.*, UN'YGA. *Alex'a Gaz.*, June 12, 1813 *et seq.*, AAS. *Frank. Repos.*, Dec. 2, 1817, FROF. *Va. Pat.*, Jan. 1, 1819 *et seq.*, VSTL. *Enquirer*, Mar. 6, 1819, VSTL. *Charles. Cour.*, Feb. 13, 1822 *et seq.*, CLS. [Later William Warner advertised 'the only *complete* edition ever published in America — 2 vols. 8vo. . . .' *Balt. Pat.*, Dec. 7, 1814 *et seq.*, BA.]

4. Weems wrote to Carey, July 28, 1796, that he had sent him 'two trunks of Blairs Sermons folded & stitched.' Oct. 12, 1796, he mentioned that he had sent from Baltimore 'perhaps ten weeks ago, two trunks of Blairs Sermons folded and stitch[d].' Oct. 24, 1796: 'I now intreat that thou woudst, as a token of thy gratitude, desire Friend Jacob Johnson to send me 10 of the 2 vol. of Blair's Sermons. . . .' Mar. 19, 1799: 'I have 3000 Dol. worth of Blairs Sermons', and he suggested that as, by printing an almanac he could sell between 10 to 20,000 'and @ from 50 to 65 cents pr Doz.', an exchange could be made for Blair. June 15, 1799, that he was 'just about opening a subscription paper for my Blair's sermons, of which I hope to sell a great many copies in the western counties.' He also proposed to Carey to take some of his *Columbian Museums* in exchange for Blair, and thought that he could sell 200 of them, and added that the money should be paid to Mr. Brundige. Carey wrote to Weems, Nov. 28, 1800: 'To send you any Mentors or Phil[*anthropists*] or Blairs is out of the question. I cannot afford to pay your Bookbinders. . . . I am constantly assailed by paper-makers, printers, engravers, binders, &[c]. who have concocted your works.' And again, Dec. 11, 1800: 'You must certainly have meant a new mockery on my folly, when you hinted your expectations that I

should make any further payment to Mess$^{rs}$. Adams or advance any money to M$^{rs}$. Campbell. . . . I have paid Adams already 100 — & for your Bookbinding &$^{c}$. some hundreds more, yet you have the modesty to expect me to make further advances . . . You have repeatedly desired to have your Washington, Batchelor, &$^{c}$. forwarded to you. . . . Of Washington, there were a few in the hands of M$^{rs}$. Smith, which I have kept, & credited you for. Of the Bachelor, I have not a copy belonging to you.' Weems wrote to Jefferson [*n.d. June 6, 1801?*] [LC.]: 'Highly honor'd Sir. Herewith I send your Copy of the American Edition of Blairs Sermons, which you were so good as to patronize; and for which you *paid*. I have taken upon me to circulate moral and Religious books among the People, with which I know that your Excellency as the Father of the People, is not displeased — Bishop Maddison [*sic*], M$^{r}$. John Dickinson and Doctor Wharton have set me on a good work I. E. to reprint, if possible, a large and cheap American Edition of the Good Old Bishop Wilson's Works — I am not ignorant of the services which your Excellency has had the happiness to render to my Country, and hope you will not be angry with me for saying that I have gratitude enough earnestly to wish to make your Excellency a present of an Elegant Copy of the above very valuable work — Your Excellency's name will greatly help our Undertaking, and so render a real Blessing to our Country as well as a lasting obligation on Your Excellency's sincere well wisher Mason L. Weems. I am not very superstitious, but have this work so much at heart, that if your Excellency sh$^{d}$. frown on it, it may make me unhappy at times, as I sh$^{d}$. be afraid that God Almighty does not think me worthy of such an honor.' To which Jefferson replied [*Letter press copy, partly illegible*] [LC.]: 'June 12, 1801. I have duly recieved your favor of the 6th inst. it happened that at an early period of life, when I had time to read, & was in the habit of acquiring books, D$^{r}$. Blair's sermons becoming a subject of conversation in society, I mistook them for the sermons of a Mr. Blair, of the Virginia family published some 50 or 60 years ago, which I possessed & thought little of. I was not sensible of my misapprehension till some [*time after*] I had become so immersed in public business as to have no [*leisure*] for [*books*] hence it has happened that I have never read, or even seen, D$^{r}$. Blair's sermons; and consequently am unable to attest their merit myself. I have heard them generally commended and from my knowledge of [*other*] work of his, I have no doubt of their excellence, that they are worthy of [*being put*] on a line with [*Sterne*] & Enfield [. . . *moral* . . .] same character. I believe firmly with you in the . . . [*?*] connection between virtue & happiness; that the . . . [*?*] and that virtuous hearts are produced by [*exercising*] the mind . . . [*?*] and contemplating good moral writings. the publication of these [*sermons*] cannot therefore but be publicly useful: and

I regret that I can bear witness to it only in the ordinary way of subscription. the work . . . [?] has too much celebrity to need the commendations of any individual. Its character is not unknown to any who will be disposed to reading of that kind. wishing you . . . [?] sincerely & therefore success in your undertaking I tender you assurances of my consideration from: Th. Jefferson' Weems wrote to Carey, Aug. 1, 1801: 'I am pushing the sale of the Remainder of Blair's Sermons. Mr. Jefferson is my Patron, & Subscriber for several Copies.' To Wayne, May 16, 1805: 'Therefore if you love me, or yourself, send, send of *Blair* (my Blair now *lying dead* in your town!) send as follows — in red sheep. *neat* . . . these books have been *lying dead* a great many years!!! Push them off.' Aug. 9, 1805: 'I beg you to send no more *Blairs* to any place *North* of *N. Carolina.*' Nov. 18, 1805: 'Carpenter,[1] the Book binder, drinks too hard — I must have Blair out of such company. I shall thank Mr. Adams to count & take them away. Carpenter shall have them again in the Spring.' He suggested [*n.d. after Aug. 25, 1806*] that Wayne induce 'Carey & the Johnson's to take a good many of my Blairs & send me the amount in Rippon's hymns . . . Davies Sermons . . .' [This would seem to show that he was already vending an edition of Davies not his own.] To Carey, Oct. 19, 1811: 'Mr. Wayne wrote me a good while ago a request that I wd let him know what he shd do with my *poor* little *cargo* of *books* in his hands. I wrote to you begging you wd take care of them for me. I hope you have taken good care of them. If you cou'd be so exceedingly good as to have 100 Copies of my old Blair bound & sent to me with the books to Edenton you wd infinitely oblige . . .' Nov. 17, 1821: 'Please have my Blairs laid by & send me 4 or 5 copies in each box that you may send to my orders.' For another allusion to Blair and his Sermons, see letter of July 22, 1813, title 253, note 4.

1 'Carpenter John, jun. bookbinder 19 Carters Alley', *Philadelphia Directory*, 1805, LC.

NUMBER 231 1793?

AN | ESTIMATE | OF THE | RELIGION | OF THE | FASHIONABLE WORLD. | BY ONE OF THE LAITY. | There never was found, in any age of the world, | either Philosophy, or Sect, or Religion, or Law, | or Discipline which did so highly exalt the public | good as the Christian Faith. LORD BACON. | THE FIRST AMERICAN EDITION. | PHILADELPHIA: |

PRINTED FOR AND SOLD BY THE REVD. M. L. | WEEMS AND H. WILLIS. | [*n.d. 1793?*] *Sm.*24mo. pp. (2), 1, (1), 5, (1), 1, 2–163, (1). AAS., NYPL.

1. By Hannah More. As the Fourth Edition was issued by William Young, Philadelphia, M, DCC, XCV [HSP.], it might be surmised that this one was printed even as early as 1792; Henry Willis is entered in the *Philadelphia Directory*, 1793, as a book binder; the first edition was issued in 1790, the fifth in 1793, both in London. The above reprint for Weems and Willis is identical with the London edition of 1791, whereas Young's and later American editions show changes.

2. Evans No. 25845. Carey's Catalogue, 1818, '50 c.', No. 3986.

3. *Ad.* 'Just Published, And for Sale at this Printing-Office, A Book, which lately made is [*sic*] appearance in England, under the title of "An Estimate of the Religion of the Fashionable World." By Miss Hannah Moore [*sic*] . . . American edition, neatly bound and lettered, at 3/9.' *Md. Gaz.*, Dec. 5, 1793 *et seq.*, MDHS.; Dec. 12 *et seq.*, AAS.

4. Weems' early interest in Hannah More has an odd connection with the mode of life he was adopting, for she wrote several tracts, '*The History of John Cheap, the Chapman*, *Parley the Porter*, *Stephen of Salisbury Plain*, which were first

published in broadsides.' *Banbury Chap Books*, Edwin Pearson, London, 1890, p. 5, LC. 'Miss More had started the stream of goody-goody books . . . .' *Forgotten Books of the American Nursery*, Rosalie V. Halsey, p. 188. 'Hannah More's social work is to be considered from the year (1789) that Mr. Wilberforce, one of her close friends, discovered the deplorable conditions existing in the districts around Cheddarcliff. Her long intercourse with the Garricks, and her various literary endeavours which took form during 1782 in her "Sacred Dramas" for the young have no bearing upon her connection with the religious movement . . . with Robert Raikes and Mrs. Trimmer.' *Children's Books and Reading*, Montrose J. Moses, p. 113. There is a four-page article on the Memoirs of Miss Hannah More in *Month. Mag. & Amer. Rev.*, December, 1800, Vol. 3, p. 465, LC.

NUMBER 232 1795

THE HISTORY OF | LOUISA, | THE LOVELY ORPHAN; | OR THE | COTTAGE ON THE MOOR. | TWO VOLUMES IN ONE. | [*Seven lines of verse*] | BY MRS. HELME. | VOL. I. | THE EIGHTH EDITION. | WILMINGTON: |

PRINTED FOR THE REV. M. L. WEEMS, BY SAMUEL AND | JOHN ADAMS, | CORNER OF KING AND HIGH-STREETS. | 1795. |
*Sm.*12mo. pp. (3), 2, (1), 1, IV, 3, 8–71, (1), 1 [*title page to Vol. II*], (2), 2, 76–153, (1). *Plates.*
NYPL.

1. Two volumes, with separate title pages, bound together; each has as a frontispiece a stippled engraving, signed '*Barlow sc.*' from the London edition; Preface to the reader signed 'THE EDITOR. *This edition is divided into chapters, mottos added to each, and the whole carefully revised.*'
2. Carey's Catalogue 1816, 'boards, 50 [*cents*]'.
3. *Ad.* 'In the Press, and will be published in a few days The History of Louisa, the Lovely Orphan; or, The Cottage on the Moor.' *Del. & East.*

*Shore Adv.*, Nov. 15, 1794 *et seq.*, HSP. 'Just Published, and for Sale . . . Louisa . . .' *Ibid.*, Dec. 27, 1794 *et seq.*, HSP. [*M.L.W.?*] 'Just Published, and For Sale here, The History of Louisa, The Lovely Orphan, or the Cottage on the Moor. If the basest plot devised against Virtuous Love and Conjugal Felicity; a plot arising from the malice of disappointment, conducted by the darkest intrigue, but so overruled by a kindly vigilant Providence, as at once to disgrace the malevolence of persecution, and shew female innocence and virtue splendidly triumphant and happy; — If such a picture drawn by a very masterly hand, can interest the heart or convey entertainment and instruction to the mind, Louisa, the lovely Orphan, merits our attention. But the judicious reader will require no higher recommendation of this elegant work, than to be informed that it has in a short time passed through no fewer than seven editions. The British Edition of this elegant sentimental and truly pathetic Novel has sold for Nine Shillings — this American Copy sells at Three Shillings only.' *Va. Gaz. & W'kly Adv.*, Feb. 28, 1795, HU. 'Just Published, and For Sale, by the Printers hereof, The History of Louisa, the lovely orphan; or, The Cottage on the Moor.' *Del. & East. Shore Adv.*, Apr. 25, 1795 *et seq.*, HU. 'George Keatinge . . . New Publications . . . Louisa, or the Cottage of the Moor . . .' *Telegraphe* (Balt.), June 22, 1795 *et seq.*, AAS. 'American Literature, published by T. Stephens, No. 60, South Second-Street, Philadelphia . . . VIII Louisa, the Lovely Orphan; or the Cottage, on the Moor — 2 Volumes in one. Price 2 s 9 . . . Sept. 11.' *Del. & East. Shore Adv.*, Jan. 9, 1796, HU. 'Novels, Romances, &c. For Sale at S. Pleasants Printing-Office . . . Louisa . . .' *Va. Arg.*, July 26, 1799; with changes, Oct. 11 *et seq.*, LC. Also advertised in: *Va. Gaz.* (Rich'd), May 9, 1795, HU. *Va. Gaz. & Petersburg Intel.*, Jan. 31, 1797, HU. *W'kly Mus.* (N.Y.), Dec. 16, 1797 *et seq.*, LC. *Va. Arg.*, Apr. 18, 1800, LC. *Va. Fed.*, July 12, 1800 *et seq.*, HU. *Va. Arg.*, Aug. 4, 1802 *et seq.*, Aug. 27, 1803, LC. *Petersburg Repub.*, Mar. 1, 1803 *et seq.*, HU. *Wilm. Gaz.*, Feb. 14, 1804, HU.; Jan. 15, 1805, AAS. Reprinted serially in *The Centinel of Freedom*, Newark, 1805, HU. The earliest issues have not been seen by me, but Chapter III is in the issue of Aug. 13, 1805, and several chapters in succeeding numbers of the file.

4. On Dec. 31, 1794 Weems wrote to Carey that he had 'desir'd Mess[rs]. Adams to deliver (on your acc[t]) to Mess[rs]. Lea & Wilson 250' of *Louisa*. On Jan. 1, 1795 he asked that Carey send him half a ream of paper, directing it to Messrs. Samuel & John Adams, Wilmington. In an undated letter [*Feb., 1796?*] Weems wrote to Carey that he might let Major Martin 'have 50 or an 100 or 200 L[*ouisas?*] . . . [*at an additional*] 5 pr cent on the Philad[a]. prices.' Oct. 27, 1800: 'I have not sent one dollar to M[rs]. Campbell nor to Adams, nor to any

other Creditor.' And again, on Dec. 4, 1800: 'Dont forget the man who never forgets you. I allude to M$^{rs}$. Campbell and Sam & J. Adams.' Dec. 9, 1800, 'I wish you w$^{d}$ do something in the affair of Campbell & Adams.' [What transaction it was with Campbell, which so troubled Weems concerning his widow, I have not been able to ascertain, unless it had to do with Weems' selling Hume, of whose works Campbell had issued an edition. On Dec. 11, 1800 Carey wrote in great indignation over Weems' request that he pay something for him to Messrs. Adams and to M$^{rs}$. Campbell, refusing any further advances, having 'paid Adams already 100 — & for your Bookbinding, &$^{c}$. some hundreds more . . . I w$^{d}$. as soon have thrown the money into the fire, as have given you the notes for Adams. Would to heaven, I had known the miserable termination of my hopes from you.' On Jan. 22, 1801 Weems still seemed worried over what might be done about his debt. Feb. 16, 1801: 'And again here's M$^{rs}$. Campbell to whom I am pay$^{g}$ interest for 500 Dol.' Mar. 27, 1802: 'Poor Sam$^{l}$ Adams who is at my elbow and most troublesomely drunk, will not allow me to give this idea so good a dress as it deserves.'

NUMBER 233 1795

THE | HISTORY | OF A | REPROBATE; | OR, | THE VERY INTERESTING AND SURPRISING ADVENTURES OF | DAVID DOUBTFUL. | BY MR. BROOKE. | SECOND AMERICAN EDITION. | PHILADELPHIA: |

PRINTED FOR THE REV. M. L. WEEMS, | BY JACOB JOHNSON & CO. 147, MARKET-STREET. | 1795. | 12mo. pp. 1, (1), 1, 4–71, (1). LC.

1. Taken from *The Fool of Quality; or the history of Henry, Earl of Moreland*, by Henry Brooke (1703–1783), published in London, 1766 [LC.], being a reprint,

verbatim, from the third volume, of Chapter XVI, entitled 'The History of a REPROBATE', from p. 113 to the end of the first paragraph on p. 219, which does not, however, give the tale complete as printed in the original book; though I have never found an earlier issue of this title, the fact that Samuel Campbell advertised *The History of a Reprobate* in Philadelphia in 1787 seems to me a probable explanation of Weems' designation of his edition as the 'second American edition.' *The Fool of Quality* had also been abridged in another form, under the title of *The History of Henry Earl of Moreland*, published in 1780 by John Wesley, who had some relations with Brooke's friends.

2. *Ad.* 'For Sale at this Office . . . History of a Reprobate . . .' *Bartgis's Repub. Gaz.*, Nov. 5, 1802 *et seq.*, AAS.

3. Weems wrote to Carey, June 17, 1795: 'M[r]. BenjaminJohnson will give you the 400 Reprobates as soon as they are bound. I have just written to M[r]. Johnson by the Wilmington Packet & sent him some books, which with the books he has of mine will amply indemnify him for the 400 Reprobates I wish him to furnish to you.'

4. 'Johnson, Jacob & Co. Printers, Booksellers & Stationers, 147 Market St.' *Philadelphia Directory*, 1796, LC. See also an account in the *History of Philadelphia*, Scharf & Westcott, Vol. I, p. 512, LC. Weems wrote to Carey Nov. 17, 1802: 'Be so good as to send over to Jacob Johnson for my books, and stow them, with the Gross of Columbian Spell[g] books, in my large trunk . . .' And on Mar. 25, 1803: 'Please tell Mr. Jacob Johnson that I left his Bibles with Pritchard in Richmond, owing to a vile cross grain[d] accident.' Jacob Johnson won the $50 gold medal offered by the American Company of Booksellers in 1803, 'for the best specimen of [*printers'*] ink of American manufacture. . . . [*His was*] pronounced superior to London ink.' *American Book-Trade Bibliography in the XIXth Century*, A. Growoll, New York, 1898, pp. III–IV, LC. *Ad.* 'To Printers. Having seen, in the Philadelphia Papers, a Resolve of the Society of Booksellers, . . . awarded a Medal to Mr. Jacob Johnson, for having made the best Printing-ink; feel it my duty to inform Printers, generally, that I lately purchased a keg of Printing-ink, marked as having been made by said Johnson, and will certify I never saw or used worse: So that "all is not Gold that glitters." George Helmbold, jun. Lancaster, Jan. 23, 1804.' *Intel. & W'kly Adv.* Jan. 24, 1804, LIOF. 'Knowledge offered within a small compass seems to have been a novelty introduced in Philadelphia by Jacob Johnson, who had a juvenile library in High Street.' *Forgotten Books of the American Nursery*, Rosalie V. Halsey, p. 173.

NUMBER 234 1795–1796?

THE | AMERICAN FARMER'S | GUIDE: | OR | A NEW AND EXCELLENT TREA- | TISE ON | AGRICUL- TURE. | WHEREIN THE PLANTER AND FARMER WILL | SEE SUCH A JUDICIOUS METHOD FOR THE | MANAGEMENT OF STOCK-RASIING MA- | NURE-ENRICHING AND IMPROVING | HIS LANDS THAT THEY SHALL PRO- | DUCE THE MOST PLENTIFUL CROPS, | AND | IN A FEW YEARS BE- COME AS VALUABLE | AS THOSE OF | ENGLAND OR FRANCE. | PHILADELPHIA: |

Reprinted for the Rev. Mason L. Weems, | by JACOB JOHNSON & CO. | (*Price one quarter of a dollar.*) | [*n.d. 1795–1796?*] 12mo. pp. 1, (1), 1, 4–83.

APhS., HSP., LC.

1. The LC. copy lacks Table of Contents; in the HSP. copy it is misplaced at p. 11.

2. The reference on p. 63 to the source of the succeeding six pages, 'Observations on the best Methods of restoring worn-out soils, without manures', is to the Bath and West of England Society's *Letters and Papers*, Vol. II, Third Edition, 1792, pp. 270–275, LC. See note 3 below. This is a reprint from what may be an earlier issue of the Society's papers; hence the date may be only a partial index to the imprint of Weems. Such of these papers in this volume as are dated are between 1778 and 1783. A part of the section on bees, pp. 72–73, is quoted, abbreviated, from THE | COMPLETE | ENGLISH FARMER; OR | Whole Body of Husbandry, | MADE PLAIN AND EASY. | . . . [*George Cooke*] . . . London: | [*n.d. 177–?*], 12mo. pp. 132, LC., the parts quoted being found on pp. 91–92. Quoting from the book: 'On these several articles I shall make some notes, which are chiefly collected from Mr. Arthur Young's Farmer's Tour through England, published in 1771.' Finding no similarity in Young's *Six Months Tour*, 1770, *An Abridgement of the Six Weeks and Six Months Tours*, Dublin, 1771,

and *Rural Economy, or Essays on the Practical Parts of Husbandry*, Burlington, 1792, I believe that Weems reprinted this little treatise from some undiscovered sources, perhaps the newspapers, or else compiled it himself. I do not believe that he wrote it. As he had shown his intense desire to meliorate human nature in what was, presumably, his first venture in printing [see title 228], so his interest in agriculture might find expression in this imprint. In a vain effort to trace other sources, I have examined the following: *Essays upon Field-Husbandry in New England*, Jared Eliot, Boston, 1760, AAS.; *The Complete English Farmer*, [*David Henry*], London, 1771, LC.; *Ellis's Husbandry*, London, 1772, NYPL.; *A New System of Husbandry*, C. Varlo, Philadelphia, 1785, AAS.; *A Treatise on Agriculture and Practical Husbandry*, Metcalf Bowler, Providence, 1786, AAS., LC.; *Essay on Agriculture*, F. C. H. B. Poellnitz, New York, 1790, BA.; *The New-England Farmer; or, Georgical Dictionary*, Samuel Deane, Worcester, 1790, AAS.; *Fourteen Experiments on Agriculture*, George Logan, Philadelphia, 1791, BA.; *Sketches on Rotations of Crops*, [*John Beale Bordley*], Philadelphia, 1792, BA.; *Letters and Papers on Agriculture, Planting, &c. Selected from the Correspondence of the Bath and West of England Society for the Encouragement of Arts, Manufactures, and Commerce*, Bath, 1792, LC.; *Transactions of the Society Instituted at London for the Encouragement of Arts, Manufactures, and Commerce*, London, 1792, BA.; *The Practical Farmer*, John Spurrier, Wilmington, 1793, NYPL.; *A Treatise on Cattle*, John Mills, Boston, 1795; *The Gentlemen Farmer*, [*Lord Kames*], Edinburgh, 1798, VSTL.; *General View of the Agriculture of the West Riding of Yorkshire*, Robert Brown, Edinburgh, 1799, LC.

3. Carey's Catalogue, 1795: 'Farmer. (*Price 13½ cents*)'. Brinley No. 6601.

4. *Ad.* 'From the American Farmers' Guide. (For sale at this Office.) Observations on the best method . . . from the 2d vol. of the Correspondence Book of the Society . . . at Bath, in England. . . .' *Repub. Cit.*, Sept. 14, 1796, HU. [This is the original letter printed in the Society's proceedings and is not taken, as stated, from *The American Farmer's Guide.*] [*M.L.W.?*] 'BOOKS, *Just Published, for Sale here.* THE American Farmer's Guide: OR, A New and Excellent TREATISE ON AGRICULTURE. Wherein the Planter and Farmer will see such a judicious method for the management of Stock-raising Manure, enriching and improving his lands that they shall produce the most plentiful CROPS, and in a few years become as valuable as those of *England* or *France*. CONTENTS. Means for collecting manure, and the management of a farm yard — the change and course of crops — a method practiced to destroy the turnip fly — clover, haymaking, Indian corn, potatoes, oats, pumpkins, cabbage. — The application of the foregoing crops in feeding. — St. Foine; or

Sanfoine — liming land — the choice and management of stock — Respecting the orchard and its produce — the best method of restoring worn-out soils — a method of preventing the destruction of apple trees by canker worms — on the management of bees. — Price 2 s.' *Va. Gaz. & W'kly Adv.*, Oct. 29, 1796 *et seq.*, HU. Also advertised [at '1s. 6d.'] in: *Repub. Cit.*, Sept. 7, 1796 *et seq.*, HU. *Va. Gaz. & Gen'l Adv.*, Nov. 1, 1796 *et seq.*, HU. *Repub. Jour. & Dumf. W'kly Adv.*, Nov. 3, 1796, HU. *Va. Arg.*, Mar. 16, 1798, AAS. Coupled with other imprints of Weems, in *Ibid.*, Oct. 28, 1800 *et seq.*, LC.

NUMBER 235 1797

SACRED DRAMAS, | WRITTEN IN FRENCH, | BY | MADAME LA COMTESSE DE GENLIS. | TRANSLATED INTO ENGLISH, | BY | THOMAS HOLCROFT. | CONTENTS. | THE DEATH OF ADAM, ⁝ HAGAR IN THE WILDER- ⁝ NESS, ⁝ THE SACRIFICE OF ISAAC, ⁝ JOSEPH MADE KNOWN ⁝| TO HIS BRETHREN. ⁝| RUTH AND NAOMI. ⁝| WIDOW OF SAREPTA, ⁝| RETURN OF TOBIAS. ⁝| FREDERICKSBURG: |

PRINTED BY L. A. MULLIN, FOR | THE REV. MASON L. WEEMS. | 1797. | 16mo [*in 12's*]. pp. 1, (1), 1, (1), 1, VI, 1, VIII, 1, 2–136.

HU., LC., NYPL. [*imp.*], VStL.

1. A comparison of this edition with the original translation from which it is taken reveals the fact that though Weems included the 'Widow of Sarepta' on his title page, he omitted that section from his reprint; he also omitted an

advertisement which, in the original, appears just before the section, the 'Return of Tobias.' The NYPL. copy lacks pp. after 132 [added in photostat]. For the signs ⁝ and ⁝ | see title 189, last part of note 1.

2. *Ad.* 'Books, Just received, at the office of the Enquirer . . . to be sold at the Philadelphia prices . . . Sacred Dramas, by Madame de Genlis, 1.75. . . .' *Enquirer*, Jan. 1, 1805, NYPL. 'Books for Sale by Benjamin Johnson . . . Jacob Johnson . . . Robert Johnson . . . Sacred Dramas . . .' In the fly leaves of Johnson's *Pennsylvania & New Jersey Almanac*, Philadelphia, 1807, LC.

3. Weems wrote to Carey, June 15, 1799: 'I am now getting folded & stitch[d] in flower[d] paper Madame Genlis Sacred Dramas printed by Mullen. I have got out a subscription paper rating their price at 3/9. 1350 of these will bring me at least 500 Dol.' June 19, 1807: 'Constantly lecturing on philanthropy I came to think too favorably of others; and an early Liberator of my Slaves, I, instinctively felt attached to Republicans. Hence I became the easy Dupe of honest weaknesses, It never once occur'd to me, that a Printer Who bawl[d] and bawl[d] for *Liberty*, like a Mullen, or a Prentiss, cou'd be a Rascal. And the man who "smil'd & smil'd" and invited me to dine appear'd far too good to be capable of cheating me. But those days & delusions are all gone.'

4. Mme. de Genlis (Stéphanie-Félicité du Crest de Saint-Aubin, Comtesse de) was born near Autun, 1746, died 1830. She was precocious in her gifts; educated the children of the Duke de Chartres, Louis-Philippe among them. She was a voluminous writer of novels, on education, moral or so-called historical tales and memoirs. See *La Grande Encyclopédie*, LC. 'Besides tales by English authors, there was a Frenchwoman, Madame de Genlis, whose books many educated people regarded as particularly suitable for their daughters, both in the original text and in the English translations.' *Forgotten Books of the American Nursery*, Rosalie V. Halsey, p. 132. 'Mme. de Genlis is represented upon the library shelves by nearly a hundred volumes.' *Children's Books and Reading*, Montrose J. Moses, p. 66.

5. Thomas Holcroft also translated de Genlis' *Tales of the Castle de Genlis*, 3rd edition, London, 1787, G. G. J. & J. Robinson. His merits as a linguist and disingenuousness as a translator are discussed by Captain Elbridge Colby, U. S. A., in *The Papers of the Bibliographical Society of America*, Vol. XVII, Part I, January, 1925. This article was severely reviewed [*Anon.*] at some length in the *Times* (N.Y.), Jan. 18, 1925.

6. Lancelot A. Mullin had been publisher of the *Fayetteville Gazette* of North Carolina, 1793–1794, before going to Fredericksburg.

NUMBER 236 1797-1798

THE | *Maryland & Virginia* | ALMANAC; | OR | WASHINGTON EPHEMERIS: | FOR THE YEAR OF OUR LORD, | 1798; | BEING THE SECOND AFTER LEAP-YEAR. | *Adapted to the Latitude and Meridian of* | *Washington; and consequently to the* | *States above mentioned.* | CONTAINING | *The rising, setting, places,* ⁞ *and eclipses of the sun and* ⁞ *moon, the phases; place of* ⁞ *the ascending node, latitude* ⁞ *and southing of the moon;* ⁞ *the places and aspects of the* ⁞ *planets; (including the late-* ⁞ *ly discovered planet, Georgi-* ⁞ *an): the rising, setting,* ⁞ *and southing of the planets,* ⁞ *and of the most conspicu-* ⁞ *ous fixed stars; conjuncti-* ⁞ *ons of the planets with fixed* ⁞ *stars; all the visible eclipses of Jupiter's first satel-* ⁞ *lite; the conjunctions of the* ⁞ *moon with all stars not less* ⁞| *than the fourth magnitude,* ⁞| *which can be occultations* ⁞| *any where in America; the* ⁞| *equation of time, true with-* ⁞| *in half a second, for the* ⁞| *noon of every day in the* ⁞| *year; and (in the preface)* ⁞| *rules for finding the rising,* ⁞| *setting, and southing of any* ⁞| *fixed star, for any day in* ⁞| *the year, not set down in the* ⁞| *calendar; and for finding* ⁞| *the length, increase or de-* ⁞| *crease of any day in the* ⁞| *year.* ⁞| LIKEWISE, | The Way to Wealth, Advice to Young Tradesmen | and several useful Tables. | GEORGE-TOWN: | PRINTED BY GREEN, ENGLISH, & CO. FOR THE | REV. MASON L. WEEMS. | [1797] 12mo. pp. 32 unnumbered.
LC.

1. An ornamental border surrounds the title; on pp. [*2-4*] 'PREFACE. *The* AUTHOR *to the* READER,' signed 'ISAAC BRIGGS. Sharon, Montgomery county (Maryland) 7th of Second Month, 1797.' There does not seem to be one word of Weems' own writing throughout, but as the Preface is (except for abbrevi-

ations in the second and third paragraphs) absolutely identical with that in *Briggs's Maryland, Pennsylvania & Virginia Almanac*, of the same year, even to the date, I believe that Weems purchased the rights for the book from Briggs and then issued it for his own sales. Given the matter by Franklin, which may have been added by Weems, it is quite possible that it is this which he called, in his letters, *his* Franklin Almanac, of which I have been unable to find any more definite trace. [See letters in notes to titles 174 and 175.] Except for the technical parts and the tables, where there are also some trifling changes, all the additional matter is totally different from Briggs' *Almanac*, his having been culled from varied sources. His Preface gives 'Nor shall that have any place | At which a virgin hides her face.', which, with its context, was deleted from Weems' imprint. For the signs ⋮ and ⋮| see title 189, last part of note 1.

2. A later edition was advertised as follows, but not having found it, I have no means of ascertaining whether or not Weems issued it: 'NOW IN THE PRESS, AND WILL SOON BE READY FOR SALE, AT THIS OFFICE, *The Maryland & Virginia* ALMANAC, FOR THE YEAR OF OUR LORD, 1800; *Being one of the Centennial Years, and therefore not a Leap Year;* CONTAINING Besides the Astronomical Calculations, &c. Table of interest at six per cent, Table of the weight and value of coins, Times of holding federal courts and State courts in Maryland, List of the principal executive officers of the Government of the United States, with their respective salaries. List of the members of Congress. Rates of postage of letters. ALSO, A VARIETY OF *Instructive & Entertaining Matter*, IN PROSE AND VERSE. George-Town, October 11, 1799.' *Cent. Lib.*, Oct. 11, 1799 *et seq.*, LC.

3. Weems wrote to Carey, Mar. 10, 1798: 'I consider it as a great misfortune that a man of my industry & spirits sh$^{d}$ have no better materials to work with than Almanacs.' [For further data possibly bearing on this almanac, see title 174, note 1.]

4. Green, English & Co. (Charles D. Green and David English) published the *Centinel of Liberty* (Georgetown), 1796–1800, with its country edition, the *Centinel, & Country Gazette*, 1796–1798; and its continuation as the *Museum*, 1800–1801. See *Bibliography of American Newspapers*, 1690–1820, Clarence S. Brigham, *ProcAAS.*, Vol. XXIII, pp. 343, 348. See also title 2, and title 156, last part of note 1.

NUMBER 237 1805

DISCOURSES | CONCERNING | GOVERNMENT. | BY ALGERNON SIDNEY, | SON TO ROBERT EARL OF LEICESTER, | AND AMBASSADOR FROM THE COMMONWEALTH OF ENGLAND TO | CHARLES GUSTAVUS KING OF SWEDEN. | TO WHICH IS ADDED, | A SHORT ACCOUNT OF THE AUTHOR'S LIFE, | AND | A COPIOUS INDEX. | IN TWO VOLUMES. | VOL. I. | PHILADELPHIA: |

PRINTED AND PUBLISHED BY C. P. WAYNE. | FOR THE REV. M. L. WEEMS. | 1805. | 8vo. pp. (2), 1, (1), 1, IV–VI, 1, VIII–XXII, 1, XXIV–XXVI, 1, XXVIII–XXXI, (1), 1, 2–446, (2). Vol. II., pp. (2), 1, IV–VII, (1), 1, 2–384, 59 unnumbered, (1).
AAS.

1. In Vol. I the last 59 pages contain 'An Alphabetical Table.' It is apparent that Weems instigated Wayne to print this edition, which evidently Weems prepared for the press. See letters of Jan. 1, May 7 and 16, and June 8, 1805 in note 3 below. As will be seen by letters of 1801, he was already at that time soliciting subscriptions for it.

2. *Ad.* [*M.L.W.*] 'Proposals, of M. L. Weems, for printing by subscription that immortal work, entitled SIDNEY ON GOVERNMENT. Gentlemen who have never read this celebrated performance may form some idea of its intrinsic worth and importance to our country, by perusing the following extract of a letter (to the editor) from his excellency the President of the United States. "Washington Dec. 13, 1804 Sir — . . . the world has so long and so generally sounded the praises of his Discourses on government, that it seems superfluous, and even presumptuous for an individual to add his feeble breath to the gale. They are in truth a rich treasure of republican principles, supported by copious and cogent arguments, and adorned with the finest flowers of science. It is

probably the best elementary book of the principles of government, as founded in natural right which has ever been published in any language: and it is much to be desired in such a government as ours that it should be put into the hands of our youth as soon as their minds are sufficiently matured for that branch of study. in publishing it, I think his life, trial and letters should be thrown into one volume and the Discourses into another. the latter is the most important, and many purses can reach one volume which could not conveniently extend to the other. Should you proceed to the publication, be so good as to consider me a subscriber: and accept my salutations and assurances of great esteem and respect. Th. Jefferson" Conditions of this so entertaining and interesting work — The London editions sell at seven and eight dollars. This American edition (prefaced with a history of the life, trial and death of the author) shall be beautifully printed, and as handsomely bound, in two octavo volumes for five dollars only — nothing to be paid until the books are delivered. Mr. W. owes *much* to the Honorable the Legislature for their liberal patronage — hopes they will increase his debt of gratitude before he leaves town on Monday.' *Va. Arg.*, Jan. 5, 1805, VSTL.; reprinted, without the last sentence, and with 'Sydney' thus misspelled, in *Aug. Chron.*, June 22, 29, Aug. 24, 1805, UN'YGA. [The original of the above letter from Jefferson is at LC. and its first sentence, deleted by Weems in reprinting the letter, reads 'I thank you for the pamphlet you were so kind (*as*) to send me, which I have read with great satisfaction.' (*The True Patriot.*)] 'Lately Published, and for sale at this office, Discourses Concerning Government. By Algernon Sidney. With a short account of the Author's Life, and copious Index. Subscribers who entered with the Rev. M. L. Weems, will be supplied on application as above.' *Va. Arg.*, May 6, 1806, AAS. 'M.L.W. congratulates his Charleston friends, . . . is still with his friend Dr. Moses [*Moser?*], — has . . . the great Algernon Sidney for Politicians . . .' *Times* (Charles.), July 1, 1806, CLS. [*M.L.W.?*] 'Just received, And for sale at the office of the Times, that immortal work entitled, Sidney On Government. Gentlemen who have never read . . .' *Times* (Charles.), Oct. 4, 1806 *et seq.*, CLS. [identical after 'Entitled' with subscription advertisement in *Aug. Chron.*, June 22, 1805 *et seq.*, UN'YGA.]; *Col. Cent.* (Aug., Ga.), Oct. 4, 18, 25, 1806, UN'YGA. [*M.L.W.?*] 'Subscribers to Sidney on Government, Are informed that the work is ready for delivery at this office. — . . . Gentlemen who have never read . . . [*Letter from Jefferson follows* ]' *Va. Arg.*, Jan. 9, 1807, AAS. [*M.L.W.*] 'OUR friends will recollect that in the Intelligencer of the 21st instant,[1] we presented

[1] Alluding to a column and a half of anecdotes on Sidney's death from the Trenton *True American* in the Savannah *Public Intelligencer* of May 21, 1807, not by Weems but perhaps inserted in the *Intelligencer* at his instigation.

them with several remarkable anecdotes of the Great ALGERNON SIDNEY, the ardent lover of man, and the most eloquent and undaunted champion of human Liberty. 'Tis unnecessary to tell Gentlemen of reading that the fame of Sidney has gone throughout the earth. Mr. Thompson, a favorite bard of Nature and of Scotland, calls him the "*British Brutus*." The famous Gordon, says "*Sidney wrote better on politics than any other man that ever lived — was brave as Ceasar [sic] and eloquent as Cicero.*" General Charles C. Pinckney us'd always to put Sidney, as a first book, into the hands of his students. Washington, Jefferson, Franklin, Maddison [*sic*], &c. received from Sidney those clear views of our *Rights*, which bore them up so gloriously against Lord North's encroachments. And there can be no doubt, had we but the spirit of Sidney, we should forever continue a *Great* and *Happy People*, ungalled by foreign chains, *unblooded* by domestic faction — and blest in the precious power of acting perhaps on some future day, the enviable part of Joseph towards his necessitous brethren. We mean, in the event of Bonaparte's triumph, secure and abounding ourselves we should be able to look over to the Old Canaan (Britain) where our Fathers dwelt, and invite our Brothers to make haste and fly, they and their little ones, and all come and enjoy with us the Peace and Plenty of our happy Goshen. Gentlemen who have never read this celebrated work of ALGERNON SIDNEY's may form some idea of its exceeding importance to our young countrymen by perusing the following letter (to the Editor) from his Excellency the President of the United States: — [*letter from Jefferson follows*] A few copies of this valuable work are just received and For Sale at this Office at the subscription price — two handsome volumes at Five Dollars only. The Subscribers to General D. B. Mitchell, for the above work are respectfully informed, that their copies are now in his possession, Also, for sale at this office, . . . and at Dr. Harral's Medicine store.' *Pub. Intel.*, May 30, 1807 *et seq.*, AAS.; June 16, 1807 *et seq.*, HU. Also advertised in: *Oracle Dauph.*, Jan. 28, 1809, PSTL. *Va. Arg.*, May 29, July 6, 1810, AAS.; Aug. 22, 1811 *et seq.*, VSTL.; Apr. 1, 1813 *et seq.*, LC. *Col. Cent.* (Aug., Ga.), Feb. 7, 1807 *et seq.*, UNY'GA.

3. Weems wrote to Carey, Nov. 26, 1801: 'Imposition or no imposition I shall keep Sydney [*sic*] at five dollars. If I cou'd vend Sidnies as fast as you vend goose quills, I w[d] put them at four dollars, but as things now stand they must go at five dollars or not go at all. Your name shall not be seen on any subscription paper save that in my portfolio, nor there any longer than I can get to Philadelphia to have it exchang'd for my own.' [See Carey's letters of Nov. 25 and 27, 1801, Vol. II.] To Thomas Jefferson, Nov. 22, [*1804*]: 'I had the hardiness to ask of you a line somewhat recommendatory of "Sidney's Republic," a work much extolld by *Taylor*, Rush & Dickinson. But these, tho

Great men & True, are, comparatively, but stars of feeble light, and seen, only by the Few. — But your Excellency's Wisdom, Humanity, and Rank, have made you as a Sun in our land; and one beam of your approbation thrown on Sidneys Liberty pleading Vol. w$^{d}$. render it the dazzling desideratum of thousands. This w$^{d}$ be cutting out good work for an honest Ambition that has learned its right aim "the increased Happiness of Man," and covets but little more, now, at middle life, than to be doing something that may cheer the fireside of old age. That God may Continue your Excellency, a Great Blessing to our Nation, is both the Sabbath & Week day prayer of your very Obt. M. L. Weems.' [For first part of this letter see title 173, note 3.] To Wayne, evidently in enclosing the letter about Sidney from Jefferson, Jan. 1, 1805: 'You see it is written in Mr. Jefferson's *first* style — it gives unbounded satisfaction to every body to whom I've shewn it; and I trust you are not the last to appreciate its importance to us. Tis the general opinion that I shall get as many sub$^{s}$. for this work as for the Life of Washington [*Marshall's*]. Be pleas$^{d}$ to hear my words, and you have the better reason, as they are the words of one who is independent. . . . But with respect to Algernon Sydney the case is somewhat tho' very trivially, different. This is my book; I shall have some trouble in vising & revising, in modernizing the obsolete & in turning Latinisms into Anglicisms. . . . On Sydney — one half the profits, with 5 pr Cent only, of extra allow[*an*]$^{ce}$.' Jan. 9, 1805: 'In 18 hours subscriptioneering [*at Richmond*] I obtain$^{d}$ from the Legislature 100 sub$^{s}$. to Sydney. Pleasants talks of sub$^{g}$ for *100 Copies*. I have put that work pretty high 5$!!! 2 Vol$^{s}$.' Jan. 25, 1805: 'And moreover I can, with W[*ashington*]. & A[*nquetil*]. carry Sydney, of which last work I think I could insure to you the sale of 1000 copies, even before the last vol. of W[*ashington*]. shall be at press. . . . On the above plan relative to W. Anq. & Syd. I have no doubt that judge W[*ashington*]. and general M[*arshall*]. w$^{d}$ if consulted, concur in my opinion as much the best for us both . . . if you do not approve . . . [*and*] cannot assist in Sydney I should be glad to know.' Feb. 14, 1805: 'Sydney does not seem to possess on [*sic*] your mind, that Great Importance to which he is most justly entitled. Mr Jefferson is very much thought of throughout the Continent; and if we cou'd get his letter handsomely *engraven in fact* [*sic*] *simile* (which I beg you w$^{d}$ let me know) I have not a doubt but that you might print *3 editions* of it of 1000 each.' Feb. 25, 1805: 'I begg$^{d}$ you to write me, when Anq. in *full* will be [*ready?*] whether you will spiritedly Cooperate with Sydney whether you can get Mr. Jefferson's letter done in fac simile.' May 7, 1805: 'As to Sydney, agreably to your wishes, I now will say something. Numerous will be the Sub$^{s}$. to that work, but I hate large editions. We must have 1000 copies ready for delivery by the *1st day of October* in order to get the work off our hands, (I mean the 1st edit.) . . . As I shall have a good deal of vexation in Anglifying, modernizing &c &c. I thought 5 pr cent ought to be allowd me. However give me a dozen copies of the work and I'm satisfied, to *divide* &c as you propos'd. As to *proposals* you need print none — the type must be the same as that usd in printing Washington's Life and the paper shd be as *fair* and good, *perhaps* not quite so thick as that of yr best edition . . . I shall send you on the 1st Vol. in a fortnight.' May 14, 1805: 'Sydney ready for press comes with them. I beg you to do great justice to Sydney & credit to yourself — in the *impression* I mean.' May 16, 1805: 'The 1st Vol [*of Sidney* ] is corrected & will be on the way by water to you by the time *you get this*. The 2d will soon follow There are but two Vols of about 400 pages 8°.' June 8, 1805: 'Captn Pope is so very good as to bring on the 2d Vol. of Sydney — You can hardly be sufficiently attentive to this Book. I must have it out at Savanna & Augusta by the middle of Octob. . . . From Charleston I sent you the 1st Vol. of Algernon. I must have the work beautifully printed etc. by the next Legislative sessions in these States. Great success may crown my exertions for our mutual good — I entreat you to do something for John Adams.' July 21, 1805: 'Let me also know whether . . . you have got the 1 & 2 Vols Sydney: for sweet heaven's sake push that work — that Good work.' July 31, 1805: 'Put Sydney to press.' To Wayne, June 5, 1806, he stated that Somerville had 34 Subscribers for Algernon Sidney, but he had feared to leave any of the books with him. [This was the same Somerville of whom he suspected dishonesty, and slackness.] Again Aug. 20, 1806, he wrote, concerning an order for books from the College of Athens, that perhaps Wayne could get 'a great part or the whole of them in exchange for Anquetil Sidney and Montague.' Sept. 2, 1806: 'Sidney goes off admirably.' Oct. 11, 1806: 'It *is now* and *ever has been* my wish that you shou'd be Jointly concernd in the profits & losses of everything publishd at my request since we were concernd. I had no other idea with respect to Alg. Sidney.'

4. The pseudonym of Algernon Sidney had been assumed for some publications in the American press by Gideon Grainger, later Jefferson's Postmaster-General, see many issues of the press, 1788.

NUMBER 238? 1813?

*Dream Book. Georgetown. W. Rind, Jr. [*1813?*]

[*Front.?*]

1. I can offer no evidence of the existence of this issue except the following from Weems to Carey: 'Gates C. house N. Carola, [*n.d. received Apr. 15, 1813*]. . . . Mr. Rind of Georgetown is printing 2000 of my Dreamlands books. Glass shou'd be glad if any time 3 weeks hence 2000 of the frontispieces cou'd be sent him. Yours M. L. Weems.' One still finds these compilations, which seem to be comic precursors of Freud, in the cheap drug shops throughout the South where they can make an appeal only to the most illiterate and superstitious folk. That Weems sold these books as early as 1803, before he ever attempted to have one printed for himself, is shown in his letter below. Like almanacs, such a slight publication would stand small chance of surviving domestic usage.

2. [*?*] Carey's Catalogue, 1816: 'Dream Book, 18 mo. 25.'

3. Weems wrote to Carey, Aug. 27, 1803: 'In my last I gave you a list of a few books which I am sure will sell well; to that list you may add . . . Some dream books, dreaming Dictionaries . . .' Two dream books had been advertised, with other books that Weems was selling constantly, in *Bartgis's Repub. Gaz.*, Jan. 21, 1803 *et seq.*, AAS. Mar. 25, 1809, Weems asked, among other books, for '6 dream book[*s*]'. On July 23, 1809, he wrote to Carey: 'If I had some good materials such as you command, I think I coud draw up a most ad captandum book *on Dreams*.' [There is a possible connection between this title and No. 242A, for the sub-title of that suggests that both books were of the same general character.]

4. In 1809 William Rind, Jr., established *The Museum and Georgetown Advertiser*, issued for only a part of that year, 'under the sanction of his father, late proprietor of *The Washington Federalist*.' He joined with James C. Dunn in issuing *The National Messenger* (Georgetown) in 1817, but withdrew in 1818. *Bibliography of American Newspapers, ProcAAS*. It was probably the son who printed the missing '2.000 Little Dreamland's Books.'

NUMBER 239 1816

SERMONS | ON IMPORTANT SUBJECTS; | BY THE LATE REVEREND AND PIOUS | SAMUEL DAVIES, A.M. | SOMETIME PRESIDENT OF THE COLLEGE OF NEW JERSEY. | IN FIVE VOLUMES. | VOLUME I. | BALTIMORE: |

PRINTED FOR MASON L. WEEMS, | By Pomeroy & Toy. | 1816. |
12mo. pp. (4), 1, (1), 1, IV–V, (1), 1, 2–290, (4).
Presb'nHS.

1. Of the five, Vols. I and III only were issued over Weems' name, with identical title pages. Vol. I contains Sermons Nos. I–XII; Vol. III, pp. 4, 1, (1), IV–VII, 1, 2–290, (2), contains Sermons Nos. XXV–XXXVII; though both volumes are dated 1816, owing probably to a contract with Pomeroy & Toy, undoubtedly Vol. III was printed after Vol. II, which was issued by Carey, without mention of Weems on the title page: '. . . PHILADELPHIA: | PUBLISHED BY M. CAREY AND SON, | AT THE SOUTH-EAST CORNER OF CHESNUT AND FOURTH STREETS. | 1818.' pp. (4), 1, (1), 1, VI–VIII, 1, 2–307, (3), containing Sermons Nos. XIII–XXIV. Vol. IV, containing Sermons Nos. XXXVIII–LI, pp. (4), 1, (1), 1, IV, 1, 2–287, (3); and Vol. V, containing Sermons Nos. LII–LXVII, pp. (2), 1, (1), 1, VI–VIII, 1, 2–373, (4), were also published by Carey in 1818, with the same title page omitting mention of Weems.

2. [*M.L.W.*] [Printed Subscription Paper, *n.d. follows Feb. 2, 1818*][L.&F.]: 'Dumfries, Virginia. Dear Sir — I send you a subscription paper for the most *popular* and *useful* Sermons ever composed. For every nine subscribers (you distributing the books which shall be sent at my cost) you shall receive one copy *gratis*, or some other handsome books of the same price. On ascertaining the amount of *your* subscription be so good as to drop me a line by mail, at my expense, and the books shall be sent *immediately*. . . . Proposals For publishing by Subscription, Davies's Sermons. These sermons, *sixty-three* in number, [*actually*

*sixty-seven*] so justly admired, not only in America, but throughout Great Britain, as MASTER PIECES of pulpit eloquence, and the most POWERFUL PLEADERS with our families to every GRACE and VIRTUE, that can render them AMIABLE and HAPPY, will be printed in five handsome volumes, on a good type and paper, neatly bound and delivered to subscribers for five dollars; not paid until delivered. God has brought us safely through a second most dangerous war, and granted us another breathing time to consolidate and immortalize the LAST REPUBLIC. And now is the precious season for every true patriot to do all in his power to promote that "RIGHTEOUSNESS WHICH EXALTETH NATIONS;" and which alone can make the Americans a UNITED and GREAT PEOPLE, and also recommend their FREE CONSTITUTION to other nations. Among the best human means to that end, we may fairly set down these admirable Lectures of Dr. Davies on the importance of PIETY and MORALS. Subscriber's Names, residence, number of copies'

3. *Ad.* [*M.L.W.*] 'Communication. Dr. Samuel Davies, the Pulpit Henry of Virginia. This great Divine originally a poor boy of Hanover, but for his extraordinary talents and piety, early advanced to the professorship of Princeton College, crossed the Atlantic to solicit the means of completing that noble institution. His fame as a mighty man of God had arrived long before him. He was, of course, speedily invited up into the pulpit. From a soul at once blazing with Gospel Light and burning with divine love, his style of speaking was so strikingly superior to that of the cold sermon readers of the British Metropolis, that the town was presently running after him. There was no getting into the churches where he was to preach. The coaches of the nobility stood in glittering ranks around the long-neglected walls of Zion; and even *George the Third* with his Royal Consort, borne away by the holy epidemic, became humble hearers of the American orator. Blest with a clear glassy voice sweet as the notes of the Harmonica, and loud as the battle-kindling trumpet, he poured forth the pious ardor of his soul with such force that the honest monarch could not repress his emotions; but starting from his seat with rolling eyes and agitated manner, at every burning period he would exclaim, loud enough to be heard half way over the church, — "*Fine! fine! fine Preacher! faith, a fine Preacher! Why — why — Charlotte! Why Charlotte! This beats our Archbishop!!* ["] The people stared at the king. The man of God made a full stop, and fixing his eyes on him, as would a tender parent on a giddy child, cried aloud, "*When the Lion roars, the beasts of the forest tremble; and when the Almighty speaks, let the Kings of the earth keep silence.*" The monarch shrunk back into his seat, behaved during the rest of the discourse, with the most respectful attention. The next day he sent for Dr. Davies, and after complimenting him highly for an "*honest Preacher*" ordered him a check on his banker for a hundred guineas for his college. We understand that the Rev. L.

M. [*sic*] Weems, who has circulated so many useful books through our country, is now publishing the very popular and eloquent sermons of this great divine, and in a far more convenient form than usual. Instead of two octavo vols. which must be heavy and oppressive, especially to young readers, he means to give them in five duodecimos, as not only much more portable but also affording to more persons in the family the pleasure of reading them at the same time. The price the same as the old edition, — *i,e*, the five Vols. on good paper and type, neatly bound and lettered, only five dollars. *Quere to parents* — might not a present of these divine discourses prove a great blessing to a child about to marry and encounter the troubles of life [*?*]' *Va. Pat.*, Feb. 16, 1818, VSTL.; reprinted partially in *Nat'l Mess.*, Feb. 18, 1818 (From *Rich'd Daily Compiler*), LC. 'To the Rev. M. L. Weems. Richmond, Feb. 12, 1818. Sir, You were pleased to ask our opinion of Davies's Sermons . . . [*Signed*] John D. Blair. J. H. Rice. John Bryce. John Courtney. Bishop Moore. whose learning and piety have, very meritoriously placed him at the head of the Episcopal Church in Virginia has been frequently heard to say that in his opinion, Davies's Sermons are among the most eloquent in our language . . . I subscribe most cordially . . . [*Signed*] John Buchanan. These Sermons, *sixty-three* in number, printed in five neat duodecimo volumes, on good plain paper, type and binding, will be delivered to subscribers for five dollars, not to be paid until delivered, A subscription paper is left at the office of the Patriot.' *Va. Pat.*, Feb. 19, 1818, VSTL. [See letter, *n.d. received Feb. 19, 1818*, in note 4 below.] [Perhaps the edition here advertised is the same as that listed in Carey's Catalogue, 1816.] Weems had formerly sold other editions of Davies' Sermons, of which there are advertisements in: *W'kly Mus.* (N.Y.), July 4, 1795, LC. *Va. Arg.*, Jan. 18–July 12, 1799, LC.; Dec. 26, 1800, VSTL. *Times & D. C. D. Adv.*, Dec. 2, 1801 *et seq.*, HU. *Intel.*, Apr. 5, 1803, PSTL. *Va. Arg.*, Oct. 29, 1803, AAS. *Ral. Reg.*, Aug. 20, 1804, NCSTL.; Dec. 17, 1812, VSTL. *Va. Arg.*, Sept. 16, 1811, AAS. Wm. F. Grady advertised 'to The Religious Public . . . the *entire collection* of eighty-two Sermons of Dr. Samuel Davies . . . [*f.n.*] NINETEEN more than are contained in Weems's *cheap* Edition.' *Va. Her.*, Feb. 13, 1819 *et seq.*, LC.

4. Weems wrote to Carey [*n.d. received July 26, 1811*]: 'I am just going to strike off, also, Davies's Sermons, I mean *Proposals for*. This is a book of great demand in all these S[*outhern*]. States.' Apr. 14, 1815: 'Six months ago I got out a sub$^{n}$ paper for Davies's Sermons the original 63 in 2 Vol$^{s}$ — but now to be bound in 5 duod$^{os}$. at 5$. I have a good many sub[*scriber*]$^{s}$. for it. Mr. Hagerty & other Balt$^{o}$. Printers offer to print it for me a[*t*] the usual price 50 Cents all around and 6 months. But I fear they will be too slow for me. You have strong handed Printers in Philad$^{a}$ who will be idle this summer.

If you can speak of me to them "nothing extenuating nor setting down aught in malice" you will oblige me & perhaps not do them any wrong; for nothing but my death will stop me from paying them as fast as I get the monies on the books. I want but 1,000 copies. . . . To diminish the chances against me the Undertaker need send me but 100 or 200 as I remit for them — and his monies will be coming in soon after they are sent. . . . Please Let me know what wou'd be the amount of 1.000 copies Davis [*sic*] in 5 Duod°. Vol. paper & binding like y^r^ Washington.' To Pomeroy & Toy: 'Phila^d^. Octob. 24, 1816 D^r^. Sirs, M^r^. Carey, to whom I am engag^d^, is willing to take Davies' Sermons off my hands, provided you will be content to be paid in 3, 6, & 9 months.' Jan. 3, 1817, he wrote to Carey that Pomeroy & Toy were calling upon him to pay for the printing of Davies' Sermons which he had supposed settled long ago by Carey's buying them from him at cost. 'Now all I want of you is immediately to put my mind at rest in this affair of Davies. . . . Let me not in my old age be taught, and by you to speak of human Virtue as did Brutus.' Jan. 11, 1817: 'It grieves me to the Soul that a Gentleman in most things so magnanimous shou'd for such a Trifle (to you) as Davies Sermons — & a small edition too, keep me in such pain and subject me to such hard thoughts from a couple of poor young Printers.' On the 17th he again repeated his regrets on this subject. Feb. 8, 1817: 'As to Davies, My dear Sir, why sh^d^ there be a dead fly in such a pot of Arabian spices!! I hope you have written to Pomeroy, & that the vile ghost is laid forever.' Mar. 21, 1817: 'Davies, to the amount of 4,000 ought to be all turn'd into money by Christmass.' Apr. 20, 1817: 'As to Davies, I have a great many subscrib^d^ for in 2 or 3 of the Counties of Virginia that trade to PETERSBURG. If you cou'd send on, 60 or 70 Copies . . . directed to the Rev^d^ M^r^. Campbell or to John Grammar, Petersburg, I shou'd soon convert them into cash.' After Apr. 24, 1817, in an undated letter, he wrote to Carey: 'As to DAVIES, I was never made more unhappy about such a trifle. Pomeroy wrote to me 4 weeks ago & expects an answer. I pray you write to him this moment [*and*] tell him that you will take the work at 90 days. Deo Judice I thought, untill he wrote to me, that all that little matter was settled.' Oct. 17, 1817: 'As to Davies y^r^. letter menacing a close of the connexion at NEW YEAR, produc^d^. a similar paralasysis [*sic*]. But in the morning I shall place, perhaps, 30 of the Sub^n^. papers in as many hands of the popular Presbyterian Preachers, now here in session.' Oct. 20, 1817: 'At 9 o'clock this morning I am to meet the Synod of Divines who have promis^d^ all their support of Davies' Sermons.' Jan. 12, 1818: 'At Norfolk I begin with Coxe & Davies.' Jan. 22, 1818: 'Shall in my next, make proposition to take back Davies.' Feb. 7, 1818: 'God willing shall return on the 3^d^ day & commence the sub^n^ for Davies. &c.'

[*N.d. received Feb. 19, 1818*] 'Just this morning began Davies. Hope, from 3 hours trial, to get Davies off by 1st of July. Begged you to sketch a plan of my operations twixt now & that time. . . . I send you a Paper of this town. You will see something in it about Davies.' Feb. 21, 1818: 'In 7 days I have receivd to the amount of 400 Vols. i.e. 80 copies — & all in the best hands.' Feb. 25, 1818: 'I have now a *moral certainty* that Richmond alone will want 200 copies of Davies.' Mar. 2, 1818: 'I have done little more than start the Gazette Typesetters on our edition of Davies Sermons. Did I not do wonders at such a place as Richmond, in getting as good as one thousand vols of Davies's Sermons there? I lament that the paper is not something better. I intreat you to attend to the binding. Let that be very neat & *fresh* & it may help us out a little. I am going on here & at Norfolk as under the conclusion that "*Davies delendus est*" or Davies fuit.' Mar. 13, 1818: 'In 5 days I have receivd subs. [*for Davies*] to the amount of 605 Vols. or Dolls. . . . James River alone, I have good reason to believe, will take more than half your edition of Davies.' Apr. 9, 1818: 'Having been very busy in getting the names of those Divines whose commendations of Davies wd stand me in best stead. The Bishop & some other Eminent Revds & right Revds. "the De'il stick their Kingshood in a spleuchan!" — will not put their shoulders to the wheel at all.' May 6, 1818: 'Davies paper so much complaind of that I am glad in the highest that I got them off so well.' May 14, 1818, he spoke of Davies 'with his 63 Sermons.' May 8, 1820, he stated that on the James River 'alone in 6 weeks I got near 2000$ subd to the Sermons of Doctr. Davies.' May 16, 1820: 'Remember that the Atlas & Vesey are only for the Few, Wealthy, Learned &c. the Bibles, Hunter & Davies & my own Little Affairs are for the Million. ergo ponder on these *two latter* articles. And as to Davies give him not up for the World — he is the Idol of the Nation, . . .' [*Dec.*] 4, 1820: 'I have found a copy of Davies's Sermons. 3 Vol 8o.' [*Ad.* 'Just received from Philadelphia . . . Davies's Sermons, 3 vols . . .' *Enquirer*, Mar. 6, 1819, VSTL.]

5. See notes concerning Davies' prophecy under *Life of Washington*, title 2, note 6. 'Until the age of twelve, he represents himself as living carelessly, and utterly negligent of religion.' *Memoir of the Rev. Samuel Davies*, Boston, 1832, p. 7, LC. There is an interesting account of him by J. G. Hughes in *Historical Papers, Randolph-Macon College*, June, 1914, Vol. IV, No. 2, pp. 657–659, BA. 'South-side Virginia, under the influence of Samuel Davies, of Delaware, who seemed, as one said of him on seeing him pass through a courtyard, "an embassador of some mighty king," and who was as great as he looked, and other Presbyterian missionaries, only less famous, early became one of the strongholds in America of . . . Presbyterianism. . . . In a letter to the So-

ciety in London for Promoting Religious Knowledge among the Poor, dated Mar. 1755, Samuel Davies says that to some of the many houses in Virginia which lacked good books he had distributed, in addition to other works, Baxter's Call, etc . . .' *John Randolph of Roanoke*, William Cabell Bruce, 1922, Vol. I, pp. 62–63, LC. 'A collection of poems came from distant Virginia from the pen of Mr. Samuel Davies . . . the dissenting minister in Hanover County, Virginia, who made use of the pseudonym "Virginianus Hanoverensis."' *Philadelphia Magazines*, Albert Henry Smyth, p. 45, NYPL. Davies was appointed President of the College of New Jersey and died in 1761.

6. 'Besides the lives of . . . he [*Weems*] wrote or edited a number of other books and pamphlets, viz . . . "Davies' Sermons".' Hayden's *Genealogies*, 1891, p. 351, LC.

NUMBER 240 1816

A | CALM DISSUASIVE | AGAINST | INTEMPERANCE; | OR, | AN AWFUL VIEW OF THE HORRORS AND MISERIES | OF | DRUNKENNESS. | ORIGINALLY PUBLISHED IN CONNECTICUT. | PHILADELPHIA: | PRINTED FOR MASON L. WEEMS. | 1816. | 8vo. pp. 3, 4–44. AAS.

1. Cover imprint is identical with the title, save for the addition at the end, '(*Price twenty-five cents.*)' On reverse of title are 'EXTRACTS From the Report of the Committee of Association of Fairfield County, Connecticut . . . 1812.' There is nothing by Weems in the text, so far as one may judge from its style and its solid regimentation of facts.

2. Weems wrote to Carey, Apr. 8, 1817: 'People wont buy the Dissuasives. I am rather sorry you put my name to 'em.' [Perhaps his protest arose from a consciousness that a disappointed purchaser, after reading such heavy matter, would be little likely to buy anything else with his name on the title.]

# BOOKS PURCHASED, SOLD BY, OR SUBSCRIBED FOR THROUGH MASON LOCKE WEEMS

NUMBER 241 1764 (1794?)

THE | DEATH | OF | ABEL | IN | FIVE BOOKS. | ATTEMPTED FROM THE | GERMAN *of Mr.* GESSNER. | BY MARY COLLYER. | NEW-YORK: |
PRINTED AND SOLD BY S. CAMPBELL, | NO. 37, HANOVER-SQUARE. | 1764. [*1794?*] | *Sm.*12mo. pp. 237. *Front.plate.*
NYHS.

1. Dr. Eames, of NYPL., and Mr. Wall, of NYHS., believe that this date was a misprint, really intended to be 1794. This would fit into Samuel Campbell's career, and would make this the edition probably sold by Weems. He was in New York in 1795, and may have purchased copies from this printer, to whom he alluded at times in his letters. [In *Sketches of Printers and Printing in Colonial New York*, Charles R. Hildeburn, 1895, p. 70, this title is reproduced in facsimile, but the probable error of date on the title page is not noted.] Then, again, it may have been Spotswood's issue, Philadelphia, 1791, 24mo [HSP.], but from Weems' letters this does not seem so likely. John Tiebout printed for E. Duyckinck & Co., 1797, a 16mo edition [AAS., NYPL.] but this has no frontispiece, of which Weems wrote. See letters below.

2. Evans No. 27049. Carey's Catalogue, 1816, '12mo. with plates 100.'

3. *Ad.* 'Books Just Published, and for Sale at the Office of the Republican Citizen. . . . The Death of Abel (in V. Books) Translated from the German. Price — 1s6.' *Repub. Cit.*, Sept. 7, 1796 *et seq.*, HU. 'Amusing and Entertain-

ing New Books . . . Death of Abel, with plates. . . .' *Telegraphe* (Balt.), Jan. 5, 1798 *et seq.*, PIL. Advertised as 'Gessner's Idylls' in *Va. Arg.*, July 31, 1802 *et seq.*, VSTL.; Jan. 8, Sept. 21, 1803, LC. Also advertised in: *Kline's Carl. W'kly Gaz.*, Sept. 14, 1796 *et seq.*, DCHS. *Va. Gaz.* (Rich'd), Oct. 29, 1796 *et seq.*, HU. *Ral. Reg.*, May 27, 1805, NCSTL. As 'Cain and Abel' in *Va. Gaz. & Petersburg Intel.*, Jan. 31, 1797, HU. *Bartgis's Repub. Gaz.*, Jan. 21, 1803 *et seq.*, AAS. *Intel.*, Mar. 22, 1803 *et seq.*, LIOF. *Alex'a Expos.*, Dec. 13, 1802, HU. *Amer. Lit. Adv.*, Dec. 16, 1802, HU. *Oracle Dauph.*, May 23, 1803, LC.

4. Weems wrote to Carey, May 5, 1797: 'I sent on the other day from Alexand[a]. a large trunk of the Death of Abel in sheets.' To Mrs. Carey, July 13, 1797: 'The good widow Carey will be pleased to take care of my books (Blair & Death of Abel) in her custody.' To Carey, Dec. 31, 1799: 'I have about a thousand of the Death of Abel (most of them in your hands) what will you give me in exchange for them[?] They are doing neither of us any good. Whereas the monies that might be obtain[d] by the sale of whatever you w[d] give me in lieu, might do us some good . . . I'll give you the 1000 Death of Abel large type and frontispiece for 21 cop. Goldsmith.' Sept. 16, 1800: 'Of those two boxes which Brundige sent you last, one contains the odd sheets of my Death of Abel. W[d] it not be well to put them into a cheap but flashy dress and send them on?' Feb. [?] 1801: 'Beg Robinson to bind me 100 Mentor & 100 Death of Abel . . . From the Mentor & Death of Abel . . . I can send you much money this year.' May 8, 1801: 'Now, I beg your advice. Don't you think I had better instantly, turn my . . . Death of Abel now lying with you & Robertson and the Binder into an assortment of *readily whole sale* books? . . . I mean to make a great sacrifice *for cash*.'

5. Samuel Campbell, New York, was Vice President of the American Company of Booksellers. See *Mir. Times* (*Wilm'n*), July 16, 1803, AAS.

NUMBER 242    1794–1795

A NEW | SYSTEM | OF | MODERN GEOGRAPHY: | [*Five lines*] | SEVERAL NATIONS OF THE WORLD. | [*Twenty-three lines*] | BY WILLIAM GUTHRIE, ESQ. | [*One line*] | IN TWO VOLUMES. | [*Two lines*] | THE FIRST AMERICAN EDITION | [*One line*] | PHILADELPHIA: |

PRINTED BY MATHEW CAREY | FEB. 1, M.DCC.XCIV., M.DCC. XCV. | Large 8vo. pp. 572. Vol. II, pp. 704, 42, 1, VI–XI, 1. AAS., BA., HU., JCB., LC., NYPL.

1. Guthrie's *Geography* was advertised over a wide region of country during the early 1800's, but judging by the internal evidence of Weems' letters, he seems to have ceased pushing Carey's edition before that date.

2. Evans No. 27077. Listed in Carey's Catalogues.

3. It is possible that some of the following references are to some other editions than Carey's: *Ad.* 'Geography. Mathew Carey Respectfully submits to the Citizens of the United States Proposals for publishing by Subscription, An American Edition of Guthrie's Geography Improved . . . the terms . . . .' *Gaz. U. S.*, Nov. 7, 1791 *et seq.*, NYPL. 'Just Published, by Mathew Carey . . . A New System of Modern Geography. . . . By William Guthrie, Esq. . . . The First American Edition: . . . Phil. August 19.' *Del. & East. Shore Adv.*, Jan. 9, 1796 *et seq.*, HU. Reviewed and criticized as being a plagiarized compilation in an article signed 'Criticus' in the *City Gaz.*, Mar. 17, 1797, CLS. Also advertised in: *Lanc. Jour.*, Aug. 12, 1797 *et seq.*, LIOF. [with atlas]. *N.J. Jour.*, Nov. 8, 1797, NJHS. [with atlas]. *Va. Arg.*, Jan. 16, 1801, NYPL. *Times & D. C. D. Adv.*, Dec. 2, 1801 *et seq.*, HU. [with atlas]. *Md. Gaz.*, Oct. 14, 1802 *et seq.*, MDSTL. *Intel.*, Mar. 22, 1803 *et seq.*, LIOF. *Wilm. Gaz.*, June

19, 1804 *et seq.*, HU., Jan. 15, 1805, AAS. [with atlas]. *Ral. Reg.*, Aug. 20, 1804, NCSTL. [with atlas]. *Repub. Arg.*, Sept. 28, 1804 *et seq.*, HU. [with atlas]. *Va. Arg.*, Aug. 22, 1811 *et seq.*, VSTL. *Enquirer*, Mar. 6, 1819, VSTL.

4. Carey wrote to Weems, May 27, 1796: 'A project of considerable importance, with respect to Guthrie's Geography, which might be carried into immediate operation, makes me desirous of seeing you, as soon as convenience will allow you to direct your peregrinations hither.' Weems wrote to Carey, June 6, 1796: 'I am well pleas[d] with the idea of undertaking a book which having pass[d] through its puny stages of embryo foetus and infant will so soon enable me to give a perfect Man to the World. In brief, I am your Man for the *present edition* of Guthrie. . . . if anything is to be done in this affair of Guthrie it *sh[d] be done while I am* distributing Goldsmith. . . . Allons donc. Draw me up 300 elegant subscription papers — no man more capable than yourself. I sh[d] like to see an eloquent little preamble on the pleasures and advantages which a Gentleman may promise himself from so complete a system of Geography. I see you have pass[d] over the pretty little history of the revolution contained in your edition of Guthrie. I think it were well to mention it in your proposals.' June 22, 1796: 'I am sorry that you have so hastily dismiss[d] the affair of Guthrie. I cou'd soon have gotten you 3 or 500 subscribers for that work at 16 Dollars, and shoud have been satisfied with a fourth, on condition of having had the books delivered to me in Virginia. Perhaps it were better, not loosing [*sic*] sight of our goose, to resume that work. It may be eggs of gold in your pocket, and of silver in mine.' Carey to Weems, June 27, 1796: 'With respect to Guthrie, I am very irresolute. I am afraid we should have too many Irons in the fire, if that were added to our other objects. I regret exceedingly that you have not pilgrimaged hither, agreeably to my earnest request. We should have been able to digest some extensive & profitable plans, were we face to face, & probably Guthrie might then come in play.' June 29, 1798: 'For you I reprinted Guthrie.'

5. 'I printed a large edition of Guthrie's Geography, in 4to., two thousand five hundred copies . . . which, though at present of an ordinary character, was regarded as respectable at that early stage of the arts in this country.' *Letters*, Mathew Carey, *New England Magazine*, Vol. VI, Mar., 1834, p. 229, LC.

NUMBER 242A? 1794–1795?

## *Twelve Cents Worth of Wit. [*1794–1795?*]

1. Presumably this was an American edition of the English Chap-book entitled '*Six Penny-worth of Wit For a Penny, or, Dreams Interpreted.* By John Booker. . . . Printed for W. Thackeray, at the sign of the Angel in Duck-Lane [*n.d. 177–?*]', LC. The first American edition found by me is: '*Twelve Cents Worth of Wit, or, Little Stories For little folks of all denominations.* Adorned with Cuts. . . . Philadelphia: Printed for John Curtis, Bookbinder and Stationer, North 4th street No. 43 [*n.d. 1795?*]', AAS. This was probably the very issue of which Weems spoke in his letters to Carey in note 3 below.

2. Advertised with other books which were sold by Weems, including his own edition of *Louisa*, 'Sept. 11. [*1795*]' in *Del. & East. Shore Adv.*, Jan. 9, 1796, HU. Possibly referred to as 'Dream Book' in an advertisement of several other books sold by Weems in *Bartgis's Repub. Gaz.*, Jan. 21, 1803 *et seq.*, AAS.

3. Weems wrote to Carey Nov. 1, 1796: 'While you were to the Northward I desird your good Lady to pacify M[r]. James Wilson Book binder Wilmington, who was about that time very outrageous with me on account of some little children's books (12 cents worth of wit) which he had bound for me and for which my poverty at that period w[d] not allow me to pay him. If M[rs]. Cary's many perplexities at that widow[d] season did not allow her to attend to it, I shall greatly thank you to quiet M[r]. Wilson on that head and to keep the little books (between 7 and 800) for D[r]. Sir, your . . .' [Whether or no, he was permitted by Wilson to take these books out of pawn, he evidently felt a keen enough interest in them to offer them for sale out of his own pocket, judging by the other work of which he wrote to Carey, see title 238, and letter of July 23, 1809 in *Letters*, Vol. II. The sub-title of the English Chap-book above suggests a possible connection between the two works.] Jan. 25, 1798: 'I beg[d] you a thousand times to get my little books from Wilson. About 700 of the 12 cents worth of Wit a very saleable little thing.' May 11, 1798: 'Have you gotten my little books (12 cents of wit) from M[r]. Wilson?' July 13, 1798: 'You have never told me whether M[r]. Wilson, of Wilmington, had sent you up my little books (12 cents of Wit).' See also letter of Oct. 29, 1810, Vol. III.

NUMBER 242B 1794

EXPOSITORY NOTES, | WITH | PRACTICAL OBSERVATIONS | UPON THE | NEW TESTAMENT | OF | OUR LORD AND SAVIOUR | JESUS CHRIST. | WHEREIN THE WHOLE OF THE | SACRED TEXT IS RECITED, THE SENSE EXPLAINED, | AND THE | INSTRUCTIVE EXAMPLE OF THE BLESSED JESUS, AND HIS APOSTLES, | TO OUR IMITATION RECOMMENDED. | BY WILLIAM BURKITT, M.A. | LATE VICAR AND LECTURER OF DEDHAM, IN ESSEX. | NEW-HAVEN: | PRINTED by ABEL MORSE, for the REV. DAVID AUSTIN of ELIZABETH-TOWN. | M, DCC, XCIV. | 4to. pp. 1168.
AAS.

1. As recorded in Rev. William Duke's *Diary*, Dec. 10, 1793, 'In the afternoon offered M^r^. Weems's subscription paper for reprinting Burket [*sic*] to several people.' Of the actual existence of an issue for Weems, there is small probability, nor do his letters throw any side light on such. On the contrary, their frequent allusions to Burkitt, some of which are given below, suggest only that he vended the book from time to time like any other work of salable value, and quite probably in different issues, though the citation of Nov. 11, 1796, points to the above edition quite definitely. [See *Appendix XV* and *Index* to Vol. III under BURKITT.] Note also the following: Michael Conrad rendered an account to Weems in December, 1798, 'To folding gethering colating 50 Burkett 161 Sheets each . . . Beating 7 placeing the frontispiece of d°. . . . Sewing . . . These were delivered to M^r^ Campbell.' *Mathew Carey Account Books*, Vol. 14 : 4922, AAS. The book was so popular that in England alone between 1700 and 1814 thirty-four editions with variations were issued, while in America there were editions in 1788, 1795, New York, and in 1794, 1796, Philadelphia. It is probable that in 1793 Weems was pushing the sales of an English or the earlier New York edition, rather than a projected one of his own.

2. Widely advertised throughout the regions and the earlier years of Weems' book-selling activity.

3. Carey wrote to Weems, Mar. 13, 1796: 'Burkett I shall keep on hand for the Benefit of the Snuff men of the rising generation rather than deliver them a shilling under six dollars. They cost me 5. I am willing to *divide* the profit with you but not as you wish. . . . I wish an *equal division.*' Nov. 11, 1796: 'M[r]. Austin offers me 70 copies of Burket at a liberal Credit. I feel pretty much disposed to take them, do you advise, or dissuade me?' Dec. 5, 1796: 'I bought . . . 150 Burket on the Testament, wholly & entirely for you. . . . Burket I expect hourly, ready bound. They sell at 7 dollars. I have them for 5 — and will charge them to you at 6. I have an offer of 150 More, on the same terms, — ought I to accept them? Where, when the first parcel arrives shall I forward them?' Weems wrote to Carey, Dec. 21, 1796: 'I w[d] not advise you to purchase any more of Burkit.' Carey wrote to Weems, Dec. 30, 1796: 'have I been guilty of Folly in purchasing for you . . . 150 Burket . . .?' Weems to Carey, Jan. 20th, 1797: 'Don't trouble [*about*] Burkitt.' Jan. 31, 1797: 'If you can get the *folio* edition of Burkit I cou'd sell 100 Copies for you. I have a good many subscribers for that work all of whom prefer the folio edition. What cou'd you get 100 copies for? Be pleas[d]. to ask Woodward.' Feb. 21, 1797: 'As to Burkit my subscribers here give as I told you, a decided preference to the Folio form. Nor do I know what abatement w[d] reconcile them to what their Rustic humour might call a-bobtail[d] quarto. . . . send 30 copies. . . .' Carey to Weems, Jan. 3, 1798: 'Monday next I must pay 817 Dollars for Burkit, about which I wrote you repeatedly, previous to the purchase.' June 10, 1799: 'The amt. which I have paid for Two Books alone The Laws & Burket, purchased wholly for you, would extricate me.' Weems to Carey, Aug. 24, 1801: 'But still u go on to assert that I have near hand min'd u, and actually carry the Joke so far as to cite Burkitt, the Laws, and the Dear knows what, in proof!! And yet . . . I never desir'[d] nor advis'[d] such purchases.'

NUMBER 243 1797

THE | WORKS | OF | THOMAS PAINE, | SECRETARY FOR FOREIGN AFFAIRS, | TO THE | CONGRESS OF THE UNITED STATES, | IN THE LATE WAR. | IN TWO VOLUMES. | VOL. I. | PHILADELPHIA: |

PRINTED BY JAMES CAREY, | *No.* 83, NORTH SECOND-STREET. | 1797. | 8vo. Vol. I, pp. 391. Vol. II, pp. 368, and 80 *or* 148.
LC., NYPL.

1. The NYPL. copy contains, bound with the second volume at the end, and with separate paginations, THE | AGE OF REASON. | BEING AN | INVESTIGATION | OF | TRUE AND OF FABULOUS | THEOLOGY. | BY THOMAS PAINE, | [*Four lines*] | PHILADELPHIA: | PRINTED BY JAMES CAREY, No. 83, North Second-Street. | [*n.d.*] pp. 1, (1), 1, (1), 1, 6–148. The 'Advertisement' following the title page of this second volume reads as follows: ' THE Editor thinks it necessary to say a few words relative to this second volume, before he sends it forth to the public. He has here inserted many articles not to be found in any other edition of Mr. Paine's works; some of which were with difficulty procured. . . . Several subscribers, and others, expressing a wish to have THE AGE OF REASON omitted in their volumes, the work has been printed so as to accomodate them: — to this end it was necessary to page that treatise distinctly from the body of the work, so that it may be bound up at the end of the volume, or wholly omitted. . . . Philadelphia, April 20, 1797.' The LC. copy of these works contains, similarly bound at the end of the second volume, and with separate pagination, AN | APOLOGY | FOR THE | BIBLE, | IN A | SERIES OF LETTERS, | ADDRESSED TO | THOMAS PAINE, | *Author of a Book entitled,* | THE AGE OF REASON, PART THE SECOND, | BEING AN INVESTIGATION | OF TRUE AND OF FABULOUS THEOLOGY. | BY R. WATSON, D.D.F.R.S. | [*Two lines*] | CAREY'S THIRD PHILADELPHIA EDITION. | PHILADELPHIA: | Printed by JAMES CAREY, No. 83, North Second-Street. | 1797. | [*One line*] | pp. (2), 80. *The Age of Reason* does not appear in this copy, though it is listed at the end of the table of contents of the second volume, with numericals indicating a separate pagination, as follows: 'The Age of Reason, Part 1, . . . 1 | Part II, . . . 55.' See also *Addenda*.

2. Weems was too good a book-seller not to perceive the popular quality of Paine's controversial work. The excerpts from his letters given below imply very clearly that it was he who early suggested to and urged James Carey so to print these works as to include by turns *either* the author's *Age of Reason* or Watson's reply. The latter alone he had asked Carey to print in 1796. His letters also imply that he had taken a certain measure of proprietorship in these issues. For therein he links them with his own imprints, as well as in many of the advertisements which filled the newspapers of the day and which are too numerous to give here. The country had been set aflame by the *Age of Reason*, the first Philadelphia edition of which, so far as I have found, was in 1796 [By the Booksellers]. Its wide-spread publicity tempted him to push it,

even where he saw the impropriety of openly coupling his name with that of the trenchant pamphleteer. The *Age of Reason* set people by the ears both in Great Britain and America, and on all sides it elicited replies, criticisms, refutations and denunciations, chiefly consisting of sound and fury. In the light of our present liberalism, most of these deserve the oblivion which has buried them as effectually as if their own fulminations had been hurled boomerang-wise. Time has its revenges and Paine's cottage on Long Island Sound is being made into a memorial to which admirers may make pilgrimages. There may consort the shades of that courageous spokesman and of those who condemned his 'bold and impious libels against government; against religion and the holy scriptures themselves. . . . In these writings were concentrated all the malignity . . . shrewdness . . . sophistry . . . brevity . . . vulgar ribaldry, and artful misrepresentations' and so *ad infinitum*.[1]

3. Weems wrote to Mathew Carey, Sept. 16, 1796: 'Watson's answer to Paine is much in demand — but the extravagant price ask$^{d}$ for it must retard its sale — if you coud *instantly* get off an edition of 2,000 Copies, and set them low, you w$^{d}$ be doing a great service to the interests of Religion and you w$^{d}$ have put much money into your coffers — for I think I cou$^{d}$ sell a great many for you.' Nov. 11, 1796, Carey replied to Weems: 'I am unable to ascertain which of Watsons apologies was sent you. Will [*you*] let me know.' Weems to Carey, Nov. 17, 1796: 'Give my best wishes to your type setting and good Brother, [*James Carey*] & tell him that I will assist him in the affair of Master Tommy Pain provided he will print them with Watson's reply.' Jan. 20, 1797: 'Present my good wishes to y$^{r}$ Brother, James, tell him that I have receiv$^{d}$ his letter, read his propositions and am content to subscribe them, on condition that the books shall be shipp$^{d}$ at his risque; the freight and trunks (at prime cost) payable by *me*. And that in case I dispose of one or two hundred copies of M$^{r}$. Paine's works for him he shall defray the trifling expence of a flashy Prospectus or Proposals which I have just sent to the press.' May 5, 1797: 'Tell your Brother I have got subscribers for Paine.' On July 13, 1797, he desired Paine without the *Age of Reason* but with Watson. June 11, 1798, he spoke of Paine's works '(his *infidelity* excepted)'. Mathew Carey wrote, June 15, 1798: 'Is it not absurd to bind up Watson's Apology, without the Age of reason?' Weems again mentioned Paine, June 25, 1798, and on Sept. 1 he wrote: '13 or, 12 of the cop[*ies*] of Paine have no defense of Christianity (by Watson) The Bishop & Lords spiritual here w$^{d}$ tear me to pieces if I sold them. Shall return them to Brundige.' Sept. 9, 1798: 'If your Brother w$^{d}$ let me have Paine's Works

[1] Citation from one of the *Lectures* of Rt. Rev. Beilby Porteus, D.D., Bishop of London, in *Wash. Fed.*, Apr. 4, 1804 [LC.], where it was used as a political weapon against Jefferson.

*without* the age of reason & *with* Watson, I coud[d] sell him a great many copies. I'll answer for the *Absurdity* of the *thing*.' Sept. 16, 1800: 'If I had Paine & the Immortal Mentor I think I coud metamorphose them into good bank notes, by spring.' Oct. 14, 1800, he wrote to Carey asking him to send on to him 'the Alman[c] and ballance of Washington with M[rs]. Smith [*evidently in her custody*] & Tattoo & Mentor & Paine.' Oct. 22, 1800, he asked for '*some Mentors*, Paine, Bachelors, Washington & Alm[cs].' He again coupled these books as if they were all of his ownership or at least partially so, on Oct. 27, 1800: 'I wish to receive no more books (the Mentors, Bachelors, Washingtons Paine's Almanacs, & if you think proper 1,000 Columbian Spell[g] books *excepted*.' [Here again he brackets Paine with his own works exclusively, the spelling book being under another category.] Nov. 17, 1800: 'Send me not another book except my own, i.e. the residue of Washington, Bachelor, Mentor & Paine. For the two latter I'll get out subscriptions incontinently, and send you the money. . . . The greatest part of the monies sent you have been from my own little stock. Send me *my* books & I'll do all that can be done.' Nov. 26, 1800: 'I might as soon borrow a ton of brimstone from the Devil as get my Washingtons, Bachelors & other books (Mentor & Paine) from you. If I had Mentor & Paine I w'd instantly open subscrip. papers and try to push them off this winter. But I can't get 'em!! Nor can I get Washington & Bachelor tho they be the best ammunition I ever had in my cartouch box yet.' Dec. 1, 1800: 'You will not fail to send my Washington, Bachelor, Paine & Mentor. I will do a great deal with those books.' [Perhaps he made himself responsible by purchase, or called Paine's books *his* merely because he had them bound. See letters, Nov., 1803, 1805 and (*n.d. after Aug. 25, 1806*).]

4. 'James Carey and John Markland established "The Daily Advertiser," Philadelphia, Feb. 7, 1797. . . . With the issue of July 3, 1797, the partnership was dissolved, and James Carey became sole publisher, changing the title with the issue of July 5, 1797, to "Carey's Daily Advertiser." The last issue located is that of Sept. 12, 1797, . . .' *Bibliography of American Newspapers*, Clarence S. Brigham, *ProcAAS.*, Vol. XXXII, April, 1922. Later published *Carey's United States' Recorder*, which ran from Jan. 23 to Aug. 30, 1798.

5. Weems' opinion of Thomas Paine underwent a marked change after this time when in his *Washington* [1800, title 2], he said of him: '. . . (if common report be true) [*he*] has no other church but the alehouse, and [*his*] palsied legs can scarce bear him to that sink of vomitting and filth.' P. 70.

NUMBER 244 1795

AN | HISTORY | OF THE | EARTH, | AND | ANIMATED NATURE. | BY OLIVER GOLDSMITH. | IN FOUR VOLUMES. | VOL. I. | PHILADELPHIA: |

PRINTED FOR MATHEW CAREY, | NO. 118, MARKET-STREET. | MAY 12, M,DCC,XCV. | 8vo. pp. (1), 2, (1), 1, IV–IX, (1), 1, 12–469, (1), 1–472. *Plates*. Vol. II. August 5, M,DCC,XCV. pp. 1, (1), 1, 4–437, 1, 439–440. *Plates*. Vol. III. Sept. 3, M,DCC,XCV. pp. (2), 1, (1), 1, 4–432, 1, 434–436. *Plates*. Vol. IV. Nov. 5, M,DCC,XCV. pp. (2), 1, (1), 1, 4–322, 1, 62 unnumbered [*giving Index*], 1, II–XIII, 3 unnumbered, (2). *Plates*.
AAS.

1. This work was sold by Weems under the following conditions: [*Printed*] '1796, April 1st. Memorandum of an agreement between Mason L. Weems & Mathew Carey. 1. Mathew Carey engages to furnish M. L. Weems, with as many copies of Goldsmith's animated nature as he can procure Subscribers for, at four dollars & three quarters each, neatly b'd; of the American and general Atlas, at one fourth deduction from the retail price; and of Hervey's Meditations, at two thirds of a dollar each, neatly bound. 2. All the books shipped by Mathew Carey for M. L. Weems, are to be insured by the former at the expense of the latter. 3. M. L. Weems engages to make remittances as speedily as possible after the receipt of the Books, through the hands of John Grammar, at Petersburg, & of Timothy Brundige at Dumfries, whose receipts respectively are to be valid against Mathew Carey. Should W. B. Magruder, of Georgetown, undertake to remit any part of the Money to Mathew Carey, his receipts are to be equally valid. Mason Locke Weems.' [L.&F.]

2. Listed in Carey's Catalogues.

3. *Ad.* 'Proposals By Mathew Carey, for publishing by subscription The History of the Earth and Animated Nature. By Oliver Goldsmith. . . .' *Amer.*

*D. Adv.*, Mar. 19, 1795 *et seq.*, NYPL. [*M.L.W.*] 'Books. Just now received at the Office of the Republican Journal, a neat American edition of Doctor Goldsmith s Natural History of this Great World, The Earth, Sea, and Air. With its curiosities, and wonderful properties — together with a History of All the living creatures, that fly the air, swim the seas, or walk the earth — embellished with fifty five copper plate engravings In Four large Octavo Volumes — the American *edition sells* at eight *dollars.*' *Repub. Jour. & Dumf. W'kly Adv.*, Nov. 3, 1796, HU. 'For sale at this Office. Goldsmith's Animated Nature, in 4 vols. with plates, price 8 Dollars.' *Amer. Staats.*, Nov. 21, 1804, NYHS.

4. Weems wrote to Carey, June 6, 1796: 'My earliest and very numerous Patrons of Goldsmith are now wondering what the D——l is become of me and of the books from which I taught them to expect so much pleasure. Hope defer[d] maketh the heart sick — and when once the heart becomes sick the animal spirits must flag of course, and then all the heroic *ardours for subscribing are no more!* . . . You were generous to me in this business of Goldsmith. . . .' [*June, 1796?*]: 'I have a great many more subscriptions to Goldsmith and all good.' Mar. 24, 1801: 'You saw what I did with Goldsmith, of which I sold for you nearly 1,000 copies in a twelve month.'

5. 'Nature stories were attempted . . . written after Oliver Goldsmith's "Animated Nature" had won its way into great popularity.' *Forgotten Books of the American Nursery*, Rosalie V. Halsey, p. 108.

NUMBER 245 1795

CAREY'S | AMERICAN ATLAS: | [*Fourteen lines*] | PHILADELPHIA: |
ENGRAVED FOR, AND PUBLISHED BY, MATHEW CAREY. | . . . | M.DCC.XCV. | . . . | Sm.folio. pp. unnumbered 21 Maps. LC.

1. For the conditions under which Weems sold this work, see title 244, note 1. This work, like the *Bible*, went through many editions by Carey and was sold by Weems throughout the period of his connection with the firm.

2. Widely advertised in the press of the day.

3. As late as Jan. 10, 1822, Weems wrote to Carey: 'It is regretted here [*S.C.*] that in the Specimen of the Am$^{n}$ Atlas, you have not given a map of this state or of Virginia or Georgia. The little states of Connecticut, Maine, &c. are rather too remote & unimportant to excite Curiosity in the first degree.'

4. Besides the larger atlases, there are frequent references in Weems' letters to *Carey's American Pocket Atlas* and Melish's Maps. Of the former LC. has the first edition, as well as several subsequent issues; of the latter it seems likely that the works most handled by Weems were: *A Military and Topographical Atlas of the United States; including the British Possessions & Florida* . . . by John Melish, Philadelphia, printed by G. Palmer, 1813, [LC.], and *Travels in the United States of America, in the Years 1806 & 1807, and 1809, 1810, & 1811*, by John Melish, Printed for the Author in 1812 by T. & G. Palmer, illustrated by eight maps, MDHS.

5. In Mathew Carey's LETTER BOOK, 1793–1794 [L.&F.], is a list of 28 maps sent by Geo. Washington (retained) and others returned by Carey.

NUMBER 246 1795

THE | GENERAL ATLAS | For CAREY's EDITION OF | Guthrie's Geography improved. | — Containing: — | [*45 items listed*] | [*One line*] | PHILADELPHIA: |

PUBLISHED BY MATHEW CAREY. | *May* 1, 1795. | Sm.folio. pp. unnumbered 45 Maps.
APhS.

1. Judging by advertisements, a few of which are cited in note 3, Carey issued his 'General Atlas' in several forms, of which the above seems likely to be the one referred to in the agreement of April 1, 1796 [see title 244, note 1], both because of its date and because of the fact that Weems was also handling for Carey at this time Goldsmith's *Animated Nature*. It is quite likely, however, that later he sold whatever editions of the General Atlas were current at the time. The earliest edition of his 'General Atlas' seen by me is 'A | GENERAL ATLAS | FOR THE | PRESENT WAR | CONTAINING, | SIX MAPS AND ONE CHART. | [*Ten lines*] | INCLUDING EVERY PLACE | IN EUROPE AND THE WEST-INDIES, | IN

WHICH | THE WAR HAS BEEN CARRIED ON. | Philadelphia: | PRINTED BY MATHEW CAREY. | January 28, 1794. | (PRICE TWO DOLLARS.)' LC.

2. *Ad.* 'Just received and for sale at S. Pleasants Richmond, . . . Carey's general atlas (the best collection of Maps yet made in this country). . . .' *Va. Arg.*, July 21, 1809 *et seq.*, AAS. [*M.L.W.*] 'Mr. Mathew Carey . . . proposals . . . General Atlas, to contain fifty-seven maps . . . agent now in this city who will speedily wait upon the citizens to solicit their patronage . . .' *Nat'l Intel.*, Dec. 25, 1813, UN'YGA. Also advertised in: *Wilm. Gaz.*, Feb. 14, 1804 *et seq.*, HU. *City Gaz.*, Mar. 8, 9, 1804, CLS. *Va. Arg.*, Nov. 10, 1809 *et seq.*, LC. *Charles. Cour.*, Feb. 1, 1810 *et seq.*, CLS. *Louisv'l. Gaz.*, May 4, 1810, AAS. *Va. Pat.*, Jan. 1, 1819 *et seq.*, VSTL. *Enquirer*, Mar. 6, 1819, VSTL. *Petersburg Repub.*, June 21, 1822, AAS.

NUMBER 247 1795

MEDITATIONS | AND | CONTEMPLATIONS: | IN TWO VOLUMES. | CONTAINING, | VOL. I. Meditations among ⁝ the Tombs; ⁝ Reflections on a Flower-gar- ⁝ den; and, ⁝ A Descant upon Creation. ⁝ VOL. II. Contemplations on ⁝ | the Night; ⁝ | Contemplations on the Starry ⁝ | Heavens; and, ⁝ | A Winter-Piece. ⁝ | BY JAMES HERVEY, A.M. | LATE RECTOR OF WESTON-FAVELL, NORTHAMP- | TONSHIRE. | VOLUME I. | PHILADELPHIA: | PRINTED BY JACOB JOHNSON & CO. NO. 147, | MARKET-STREET. | M DCC XCV. | 8vo. Vol. I. pp. 189. Vol. II. pp. 354. BPL.

1. According to his friend, the Rev. William Duke's *Diary* [see *Appendix XV*], as early as July, 1791, Weems was seeking subscriptions for Hervey's *Meditations* though at that date it was probably for either Isaiah Thomas' edition [Worcester, Mass., 1789], or for an English edition, unless for one which he hoped to reprint himself. Of this last I have found no trace. Robert Campbell issued an edition in Philadelphia in 1794, and again in 1796 (printed for him

by V. Bonsal, Wilmington, 1796), so it was probably one of these or the above Johnson edition which was sold by Weems for Carey, according to their contract of Apr. 1, 1796. It is difficult to decide which edition it actually was, as both parties to that contract had continuing dealings with Campbell and Johnson. Yet I have selected the latter, because no disagreements with the Johnson firm are recorded in Weems' letters. Also it seems evident that the 1794 edition of Campbell must have been exhausted by 1796 else he would not have issued another in that year, while Johnson's 1795 imprint would have been ready and on the market for Carey's and Weems' plan in early 1796. Moreover, Johnson printed *The American Farmer's Guide* for Weems [*n.d. 1794–1795?*] and what more natural than for both men to make terms for payment by some other book-deals — possibly Hervey? No other editions found fit so neatly into the dates and circumstances mentioned by Weems.

2. The following excerpts from Weems' letters throw a somewhat confusing light on the above question. To Carey, May 16, 1796: 'I coud wish you w$^{d}$ not dispose of any of our [*Herveys?*]. I hope before I see you to cover the whole 800, — I have got my subscription papers.' Sept. 24, 1803: 'I am often ask$^{d}$ for . . . Hervey's Meditations.' Nov. 18, 1803: '. . . make up . . . a box . . . of the following . . . your London Edition of Harvey's Meditations.' Only one other letter mentions Hervey at all and that is to Wayne [*n.d. after August 25$^{th}$, 1806*] where he asks Wayne to 'get Carey & the Johnson's to take a good many of my Blairs & send me the amount in [*a long list of books, including*] Herveys Works'.

NUMBER 248 1801

THE | HOLY BIBLE | CONTAINING THE OLD AND NEW TESTAMENTS: | together with the APOCRYPHA: | . . . MAP OF PALESTINE, and NINE HISTORICAL ENGRAVINGS. | PHILADELPHIA: |

PRINTED FOR MATHEW CAREY . . . | BY JOSEPH CHARLESS. | October 20th, 1801. | 4to. pp. 972 unnumbered.
NYPL.

1. Contains, among the articles and tables in the appendix, 'PORTRAIT OF AN APOSTOLIC PREACHER, from COWPER. The pulpit therefore . . . truth and soberness assail'd in vain.'; 'A CLERGYMAN'S ADDRESS TO MARRIED PERSONS AT THE ALTAR. The duties between man and wife . . . mutual portion both in this world and in the next.'; 'THE OLD AND NEW TESTAMENT DISSECTED.' and 'JUDEA, PALESTINE, OR THE HOLY LAND.'

2. As early as 1790 the firm of Carey, Stewart & Co. had issued the first American edition of the Douay *Bible*,[1] in quarto [LCPHIL., NYPL.]; also '*A Brief Concordance to the Holy Scriptures, of the Old and New Testaments;* . . . Philadelphia, By John Brown. . . . Printed . . . Mathew Carey . . . M. DCCC.X.', pp. 72. [HSP.] But as will be seen from Weems' letters below, he was the prime cause of Carey's issuing later the above successful edition of the *Bible*, — taking a hand in its make-up as well as in that of subsequent editions, in 4to and 12mo, and in a wide range of qualities and prices.

3. Carey's Catalogue, 1816, contains a list of 62 different issues of the Bible; 1818, pp. 149–152, contains a long list of Bibles of every description and grade, and ranging in price from $3.75 to $20. An ample list of Carey's Bibles, with detailed descriptions, in *A List of Editions of the Holy Scriptures, Printed in America Previous to 1860*, E. B. O'Callaghan, Albany, 1861, LC. See also list in Growoll's *Book-Trade Bibliography*, New York, 1898, LC.

4. *Ad.* 'Elegant Family Bible. Proposals of Mathew Carey, for publishing by subscription, An elegant Edition of the Bible, In Quarto . . . besides a map of Palestine, it shall contain nine Historical Engravings . . . The work is now very considerably advanced and will be finished about the Middle of October. . . .' *Adams Cent.*, Sept. 30, 1801, AAS. 'Philadelphia, November 20, 1801. Elegant Family Bible. (Price Seven Dollars.) Just Published, By Mathew Carey, . . . In large quarto. This edition contains . . . 11. Portrait of an Apostolic Preacher, from Cowper . . . 13. A Clergyman's Address to married persons, containing a seasonable and judicious sketch of the requisites to happiness in the married state.' . . . half sheet map of Palestine and 9 historical engravings.' *Pa. Gaz.*, Dec. 16, 1801, AAS. 'M.L.W. congratulates his Charleston friends, . . . is still with his friend Dr. Moses [*Moser*], — has still a few elegant red morocco Family Bibles, with Cuts; . . .' *Times*, July 1, 1806, CLS. All of Carey's Bibles were extensively advertised in Weems' territory, and in his period of bookselling there. From a group of such references too numerous to list, the following only is quoted, as representing, possibly,

[1] 'First Douay Bible in America Printed at Phil. by Carey, Stewart & Co. 1790. Besides being the first American edition of the Douay Bible, it is also the first quarto edition of an English Bible printed in America.' NYPL. CARD CATALOGUE.

a project for issuing his own Bible, or, at least, one to be so-called by a special arrangement with Carey: '*A Card to the Ladies of Charleston*. The Rev. M. L. Weems, begs leave, in this way, to salute the patriotic and pious fair ones of this wealthy city; and, with the profoundest respect, tender to their patronage, an elegant edition of that best of all books — the BIBLE. He should deem himself very culpably deficient in his duty, indeed, if he did not give *them* the first call, in every case where an effort in favor of that Divine Book required aid. Gratitude is the virtue of Women; and certainly none, like them, are under such obligations to the Bible, without whose sublime hopes and consolations, as the Apostle well observes, "their condition would, of all others, be the most miserable." Is there a portion of the earth, as in all Mahometan countries, where the feeble sex, denied the honors of rationality, are cooped up, by hundreds, in a gloomy seraglio? Let the pure light of the Gospel but beam on that vile sink of pining discontent and jealousy, instantly it is demolished; and the joyful sparklers, freed from the hated thraldom, spring again to their native equality, and, arm in arm, each with her beloved husband, tread the gay walks of dear connubial affection. Is there a portion of the globe, as among most savage nations, where helpless Woman, still worse oppressed, is doomed the weeping drudge of tyrant man, and, when worn down by unequal toils, is often burnt alive on his funeral pile? Let the sun of Gospel love but rise in that land of death, and, straitway, those diabolical delusions disappear; the oppressed female is recognized as dearer than a sister; "All tears are wiped from her eyes" and, in the amiable spirit of true Christian gallantry, "the winds of Heaven are not permitted too rudely to visit her beloved face." But all this is still but a small part of what this divine book does for Woman. Her tender bosom is the seat of a sympathy with those she loves, which subjects her to pangs far beyond the bitterness of personal degradation. How often, for example, as a maiden sister, is she distressed with her fears, lest a beloved brother should be betrayed into a duel, and brought home a bleeding corpse! Well, this is the blessed book to throw over that brother the mantle of such meek and modest merit, that not even a demon can find the heart to injure him. How often, as a widowed mother, does she feel the gushing tear, as looking around on her tender cheek'd babes, she anxiously asks "what shall they eat? — or, what shall they drink? — or wherewithal shall they be clothed?" Well, this is the book to dissipate her fears — It points her to the unfailing table which Heaven spreads for the *ploughless birds*, and to those bright robes which adorn the *unspinning lilly*, far beyond the pride of Kings — and "Shall God so feed the sparrows, and clothe the grass of the field, shall He not much more clothe her infant cherubs?" And even when the grave has opened its insatiate jaws, and, in a beloved child or husband, swallowed the dearest of all her earthly comforts, yet even there this Heaven-sent book can supply a cordial equal to the occasion. It points her tear-streaming eyes to that Eternal Power, who does all things right — in whose great plan, her child or husband was not truly born until he died; and where, from his short and sickly slumbers, as an embryo, he is now waked up to the real life of a vigorous immortal, forever beyond the reach of sin and sorrow. And, besides all this, what eternal thanks does not Woman owe to the Bible, that "Grand Cosmeticon," (or *beautifier* of angels,) [*which*] gives to the ministering spirits above, all their charms; and which, in proportion as their fair sisters here below practice its divine prescriptions (Purity and Love) will assimilate them to the same bright originals? Yes, for if there be anything on earth that can aid our conceptions of angelic loveliness, it is a pious woman — one whose face, ever shining from the heavenly loves and joys within, is never darkened by clouds of passion; and who, in all her duties as daughter, sister, wife, mother, or mistress mingles so much of suavity and endearment, as to elucidate the Gospel in its living form, and make even infidels sigh for that society above, where all are good and lovely like her. But, divine as this book confessedly is, it has seldom been printed, in this country, at least, in a style worthily expressive of the gratitude due for so inestimable a gift. Truly, we may all here say, in the excellent language of the church, "We have left undone those things that we ought to have done." — "The children of this world are wiser in their generation than the children of light." To insure the reading of them, their books, though of mere momentary amusement, are often decked in the most splendid and alluring style; while this blessed book, though it has God for its author, and even for its end, is often sent out in mean apparel. It is true, the devout would not, on that account, be withheld from reading their Bibles — no, even though it were printed on oak leaves, they would read it. But only think, ye tender parents, of the danger of your young daughter, who has, all the week, been reading Shakespeare and Walter Scott in silk wove and gold, but is sent Sunday morning to read Christ and His Apostles in common foolscap and sheep! "The bliss of man, and pride that blessing find, Is not to hope or look beyond mankind." POPE. And many a young creature, long familiarized to the silks and splendors of high life, though on the *charity* of some wealthy cousin has been known to hide her blushing cheeks at the sight of her own father in *homespun*. To remove from the young and fashionable, such a serious obstacle to their reading the books of God, the Rev. M. L. Weems now respectfully invites the Ladies of Charleston to aid him in reprinting it in a style of beauty and elegance that shall no longer risk giving offence to the amiable young persons aforesaid, but rather furnish a chance to elicit their more frequent glances over its sublime pages. He does not mean to press them with an argument in favor of the Bible. He would only ask, in the pathetic language of the Prophet — "Our fathers, where are they? And our wise men, do they still live?" No; they are, as "with the years beyond the flood." We too must soon follow them. And now where is the question more natural to a parent's bosom than this: "In what present can I invest a little of my wealth, (while it is yet in my hands,) that may most benefit my child, and cause him most tenderly to cherish my memory?" Here, all eyes are turned to the Bible: "this book," every father is ready to say — "this book, printed in this attractive form, and especially presented to him by me, may arrest my son in the commencement of his folly. — From this book my daughter, if treated unkindly by an earthly husband, may come to the knowledge of that heavenly husband, who will never prove inconstant." Or, ["?] in the pages of the sacred volume my poor orphans may find a father who will never leave nor forsake them.["?] This splendid edition of the Bible will be printed in one royal quarto volume, on a silk wove paper, from new sterotype plates, superbly bound in red Morocco, and illustrated with between 30 and 40 exquisite engravings, from Westal's celebrated British edition.[1] The price of the British copies, now for sale in this town is 56 [*sic*] dollars; this American edition, though confessedly equal if not superior, will come to subscribers at but 30 dollars; and two percent from the sales, given to the Sunday Schools of this place. A list of patrons will be printed in the Bible; and every subscriber for two copies or more, shall have stamp'd on the front lid in gold capitals, the names of those beloved friends to whom he presents them. If not equal to promise, the subscribers shall be at full liberty to refuse them. The following critique will shew what degree of confidence the public may repose in this undertaking: "Having been requested by the Rev. M. L. Weems to examine the paper, binding, and especially the engravings of a splendid edition of the Bible, proposed to be printed in this country, we do not hesitate to pronounce that they are more elegant than any we have seen done in the U. States. It affords us great pleasure to see the Fine Arts lending their aid to clothe the best of all books in a dress that might happily allure the young to a more frequent perusal of its divine contents. We cannot otherwise than wish Mr. Weems much success in this laudable undertaking, especially as the work is afforded on terms comparatively so cheap; and as it is intended to appropriate a portion of the profits to the religious education of our own poor. [*Signed*] N. BOWEN. Bishop of the Pro. Ep. Church So. Ca. C. H. HANCKEL. Rec. of St. Pauls. C. E. GADSDEN. R. of St Philips. RICHARD FURMAN. Pastor

[1] 'Holy Bible, embellished with 30 engravings by Charles Heath, from Designs by Richard Westall, R.A. 3 vols. Imperial 8vo. boards, $36 [*sic*]' Carey's Catalogue, 1818, No. 8; the NYPL. CARD CATALOGUE lists what is evidently this edition as of London, 1815.

of the Baptist Church. P. DALCHO. Asst. M. of St. Michaels. A. GIBBS. Asst. Min. of St. Philips." ' *Charles. Cour.*, Feb. 6, 1822, CLS. Same letter of commendation in an advertisement in the *Georgian*, Mar. 16, 1822, GAHS. For other puffs, see reprints of Feb. 14 and Mar. 21, 1822, in *Letters*, Vol. III.

5. Weems wrote to Carey, Aug. 18, 1800, suggesting that he use extracts from Locke, Milton, Penn, &c. 'instead of notes' in his edition of the Bible. I have never discovered, however, that this suggestion was carried out. To Carey, Nov. 17, 1800: 'I tell you as I have told you already a thousand times, that the *Quarto Bible business* (I allude not to *this first little spurt*) duly attended to w[d] make a handsome fortune for *one at* least of your little Daughters.' Carey wrote to Weems, Aug. 21, 1801: 'Among the articles promised to be added to the Bible are two or three, which you were to furnish. As the Index is in hands, I shall very soon want those things which are to follow it immediately. I therefore request you to without delay dispatch them.' And again on Sept. 23, he urged Weems to send him the 'articles assuredly promised in the proposals. N[os]. 8, 9, & 13, I neither have nor do I know where to find them.' Weems replied, Sept. 28, 1801: 'I am surpris[d] that tables N[o] 8 & 9, sh[d] have given you a moments uneasiness. They are in some one or more of that grand caucus of Bibles which you caus[d] to be held at No 118 when you contemplated this Bible crusade. I don't know that N[o]. 8 bears, in your bible, the title which we chose to give it "*a curious analytical &c.*" but you may easily apprehend it by these marks; it is a mere bobtail'[d] thing, and its fort lies in telling "how many *chapters*, *verses*, *words*, *syllables*, *and letters* there are in the Bible; which is the *shortest*, which the *longest*, and which the *middle chapter* in D[o]. And all such goodly discoveries as are fit to make Old Women & Children wonder." However as many of our Readers are of that sort, insert it by all means. To have it said that Carey's bible contains more Curious things than were ever seen in any other bible wou'd be a great Matter. As to N[o] 13 I sh[d] have thought myself uncommonly happy in an opportunity to prepare something on that head. The present wretched state of that Country which was once emphatically call[d] "the Land of promise," — "the land flow[g] with milk & honey" furnishes ample matter of the most infuriated Declamation against the curses of Despotism, — as also a precious hint to the People of America. Had I, like you, Leisure evening[*s*] & evenings at home, I shoud rejoice in writing on this subject. But you can do it much better, and have access to more and better materials than I possess, and besides I am constantly travel[g]. But were I to advise I w[d] advise that it sh[d] be very short.' [1] From Trenton, Nov. 27, 1801: 'Yesterday I sent you 90 Dol. Today I send you 35. Tomorrow

[1] 'The Old and New Testament Dissected' in the appendix to the 1801 edition corresponds exactly to the description of 'No. 8' in this letter. Moreover, if one omits the Index, the

I shall send more. When you first mentiond the advance of price on the Bible, I suggested a difficulty — viz. the indignation which the people wd feel on seeing all their Neighbours possess'd of the *same bible* at *six* dollars for which, they, by subscrib[g] a flying advertisement, had given *seven*.[1] But to leave that — The propos[d] advance may do any where better than in Trenton or perhaps in New Jersey. Isaac Collins [2] a few years ago printed a Bible which for *correctness* & *beauty*, was hardly ever surpass[d] by Oxford or Cambridge. His cost but 4 Dollars. Well mark the Consequence — "What do you have for your Bible?" says the Man to whom I make a leg with Book & hat: *"Only six dollars Sir"* "Hoot, hoot" quoth he, "why Isaac Collins gives us a Bible for 4"!! "But please to observe, Sir, the style in which this is done: M[r] Collins's was a plain unvarnish[d] edition, Sir; but be so good as to note the valuable improvements w[h] M[r] Carey has made on this — here, Sir, you see is a fine map on Copper plate of the holy land; here, Sir, is Nazareth where Christ was born, here is Cana of Gallilee, where he wrought his first miracle; *here* is a view of the country immortaliz[d] by his travels, labours, &[c]. &[c]. &[c]. And here, Sir, (skipping nimbly from the *Map* to the midst of the psalms) here you see is David the sweet singer of Israel, in the house of God, before the sacred lamps, celebrat[g] the praises of his God, while his applaud[g] courtiers & exulting Angels join their voices Symphonious with his swelling harp — And here, Sir, here at the end of the Apocrypha, is a neat card on which to inscribe your name — And here, Sir, the family Register, and the charm[g] scene of the Nativity, from the celebrated Angelica Kauff-

article from Cowper, and 'A Clergyman's Address,' which are in a different category, this table is the eighth in sequence. The article immediately following, actually the ninth by the above reckoning, is probably the one referred to in the letter as 'No. 13,' being a description, largely geographical, of 'Judea, Palestine, or the Holy Land.', not quite two pages long, and decidedly more in Carey's than Weems' style. Evidently the appendix was not made as full as originally planned, since all told there are not thirteen articles in the edition as finally issued.

[1] *Ad.* 'Now printing by Mathew Carey, Philadelphia, and to be published in September next, an elegant quarto Family Bible, containing many elegant engravings, at six dollars each' *Cent. Freed.*, Aug. 4, 1801, NYHS. — 'Elegant Family Bible. Subscriptions are received at the office of the Intelligencer, for Carey's Quarto Edition of the Bible. Price, to Subscribers, 6 Dollars. To others, it will be raised.' *Intel.*, Oct. 28, 1801, LCHS. — Subscribers were also warned to pay for their copies before the middle of Jan., 1802 or they 'will have to pay $7.' *Oracle Dauph.*, Dec. 7, 1801 *et seq.*, LC.; *Intel.*, Dec. 23, 1801 *et seq.*, LIOF.

[2] 'Collins, Isaac, printer 189 Pearl' *Longworth's American Almanac, New York Register, and City Directory*, 1801, LC. — There is a biographical sketch of him in *American Dictionary of Printing and Bookmaking*, New York, 1894, p. 101, LC. — 'Isaac Collins . . . apprenticed to James Adams printer, in Wilmington, Delaware, and at his request, in his twentieth year [*1766*] entered the office of William Rind at Williamsburg, Va.' *New Jersey Printers of the 18th Century*, William Nelson, *ProcAAS.*, Vol. XXI, April–Oct. 1911, pp. 29–30.

mann," and so on, and so on. Well what is my dole for all this? Why he replies, "All this is clever, yes, 'tis clever enough indeed, but I w[d]n't give a fig the more for all that, for it only sarves to make the Children spoil the book, however tho Isaac Collins ax[d] but 4 dol[s] for his'n, here's five doll[s] for your'n." . . . let me beg you not to lay a veto on my exertions to give as [*wide a*] circulation as possible to this edition, this *your* first edition, and let me add after *you*, this *miserable*, this *garbled* edition, but that's between you & I only. If I am not honest why trust me? And in the name of God, what motive can I have but your interest & that of M.L.W. The Bibles you sent (44) are arriv[d] but some of them much rubb[d].' Jan. 15, 1802: 'If You had a neat Quart[o] at 6 Dol. which you cou[d] print at 3.75 and put to me at 5 — and retail at 7, I sh[d] not fear to make great sales to the Northward. Such a bible in the hands of one who cou[d] at once expatiate, preach, and press among the People w[d] (Deo adjuvant) cut its way maugre the odds (one dollar) between that and the 5 dol[s] New York Bible.' Jan. 20, 1802 Weems believed that Carey would agree 'that our Engravers have not yet come up to the mark of Sentimentalism. And, afore God, I'd as lieve look to catch devotion from speering at fancy form[d] figures on a sooty chimney back, as on the generality of Bible engravings done in our country.' On Apr. 28, 1802 his description of New York sounds a trifle eccentric in 1927: 'The town is delug[d] with Bibles & Deism. 'Tis astonishing! I meet with smiles and compliments in profusion, but no money—I mean for the Bible.' July 29, 1802: 'My heart is set upon having it to say that I sold off one half of your whole edition — 68 more will make up the half.' Oct. 1, 1802: 'Say no more about "The Evidences."[1] They shall be forth coming and earlier than the 14th.' Oct. 2, 1802: 'Now for the "Evidences;" Send one of your little Shavers up to N[o] 118 North fourth S[t], to that man of God the Rev[d] Ezekiel Cooper:[2]

[1] '*A Concise View of the Evidences of the Christian Religion*,' by J. Fletcher. '1. The sacred pen-men the Prophets and Apostles . . .', being a quotation, with slight changes, from pp. 134–150 of his '*Appeal to Matter of Fact & Common Sense*,' of which BA. has a London, 1803 edition and NYPL. a Baltimore 1814 edition. This article was included in Carey's second Philadelphia edition of the Bible of October 27, 1802, and in most of his subsequent 4to editions. —John W. Fletcher [*De La Flechière*], A.M., was born in Nyon, Switzerland, 1729. After settling in England and taking orders in 1757, he requested permission to preach to many French prisoners in their own language. This petition the Bishop of London rejected. 'A few months after, his Lordship died with a cancer in his mouth. Mr. Wesley, in reference to this event, says, "I do not think it any breach of charity to suppose that an action so unworthy of a Christian bishop had its punishment in this world."' Served the Church and the Methodists until 1781. Died 1785. His biography was written by one of the Wesleys. See *Lives of Eminent Methodist Ministers*, Peter Douglas Gerrie, 1859, pp. 50–69, BA.

[2] 'Cooper Rev Ezekiel, 118 N. Fourth' *Philadelphia Directory*, 1802, LC. — Letter of commendation for *Carey's Family Bible*, signed: 'Ezekiel Cooper, one of the Ministers, and

lo, he hath just printed or rather, reprinted an holy Book, entitled "An Appeal to Fact & Common Sense &c." 'Tis generally call[d] "*Fletcher's* Appeal." You, who have recently printed Priestl[*e*]y's Biographico Chrononhotonthological Synopsis, need not to be told that this Fletcher was a famous Divine of the last century. A native of Geneva, but a Labourer in Britain. His mind's eye was beyond that of his Countryman, our Gallatin, and his pen, like the sword of Fingal prostrated all his Foes. Get, I say, this Appeal, turn to page, 136; there you will find a Summary of "*the Evidences*," clear, concise and energetic, to your Mind. NB. at page 149, line 2[d] Ducian sh[d] begin with an L. But Cooper is not, like you, a Scholar nor a man of taste. Read it, and perhaps you may detect some other errors. . . . Observe this Apology will make one sheet. On a small type, perhaps not half a sheet.' At one moment, Apr. 2, 1803, in the excitement of his bookseller's zest he wrote: 'My Bibles are, now, nearly all thrown overboard'; at another, June 30, 1803, when cautioning Carey to watch the binders, he wrote fervently: 'People revere the Bible'. To Wayne, Nov. 13, 1806: 'I promis[d] you that the whole of my Negociations with M[r] Carey in this affair of the bible, sh[d] be committed to black & white. That mode had been agreed on by M[r] Carey & Myself, and correspondently with that compact I rec[d] the inclos[d] from M[r] Carey, to which I instantly responded verbatim & literatim as follows.' [A quotation from this response, dated Nov. 13, 1805, follows: 'I understand, i.e. intelligo, that M[r]. Carey is to furnish M[r]. [*Weems*] with Bibles of such paper, print, price &c, &c. as agreed on by Mess[rs] Carey & Weems — II. From the retail price of the Bibles aforesaid, M[r]. C. is to *deduct 25* pr Cent. III. They are to be deliver[d] to M[r]. Weems, free of all loss & cost, at such ports as he shall direct — 4[th]. Mr. Wayne is to pay for them in ninety days after shipment.'] To Carey, July 3, 1809: 'Religious books ought to be made as *beautiful* as possible to captivate the more.' [*July 26?*] 1811: 'I am at this moment printing a subscription paper for a Bible at 6.00. This I do because there are no subscription papers for bibles, & because in my travels home I shall pass over a great deal of Country and consequently have many opportunities of putting papers into good hands. I contemplate a noble addition to the Bible. Kingly Governments you know are the curse of the Human Race. The Bible, you also know, is point blank against Kingly governments. The People of America enjoy a REPUBLIC, which, next to a Theocracy, must be the most perfect form that can be. But they don't know its value. And therefore like Esau

Superintendent of the Book-concern for the Methodist Episcopal Church, in the United States.' *True Amer.* [*Dec., 1803?*], HU. — Rev. Ezekiel Cooper republished a pamphlet published in Europe containing letters from Irish missionaries. See *Surprising Accounts of the Revival of Religion, in the United States of America*, William W. Woodward [*Philadelphia*], 1802, p. 75, LC.

they may sell it for a song. To set their own form of Government before them in all its Amplitude & brightness of Blessings must in my opinion at least be one of the most patriotic services that any man can do to this Country. Now what book so proper as a vehicle (to *print it in*) as the book which in consequence of the universal veneration attach[d] to it, finds a ready admission into every house? And what book so proper to accompany it as that which in every Chapter, in every verse, and indeed in its *whole Spirit* condemns the aggarandisments [*sic*] of Aristocrats; & enjoins that fervent Charity which w[d], if common, make one Commonwealth of the whole world? I have got a synopsis, for the tract must be in that way only, nearly ready for the purpose.' [As far as I have investigated, I have found no such tract used in any of Carey's Bibles.] Sept. 10, 1812: 'For the political [*tract?*] which I am determine[d] to have in the *Bible, even if I am to get you* to print an edition for *myself* & in *my name*, I pray you again & again to send me all the little tracts on the abuses of Kingly Governments in the way of taxes, excises, Tythings &c. Would not Mr. Duane's Politics for farmers,[1] & the Livre rouge of France [2] &c. &c. do service [*?*] M[r]. Madison & thousands say that such a thing in a popular manner w[d] do infinite service.' Dec. 6, 1812: 'I wrote to you also to send some Bibles at 4.50 (my edition I mean). Many of these are bespoke.' [Although, in his letters, Weems is continually referring to this apparent edition of his own of the Bible, I have never been able to identify it. See also advertisement of Feb. 6, 1822 in note 4 above.] Mar. 25, 1814: 'You see that Sword & others are printing Bibles.[3] . . . I tell you once for all that I do not wish to be engaged in a bible against you. And I do not wish to have any trouble with you about my little Book, (Washington). But there is one thing I wish, which is that you w[d] confer calmly on this matter, with the two best friends you have in this world, Conscience & M[rs]. Carey.' Aug. 31, 1815: 'I want to see you, greatly, because of your Doctor[g] me up 2 or 3 varieties of y[r] Bible to which I mean to turn much of my labours & attention during the rest of my life.' Feb. 8, 1816: 'I want to sketch a Prospectus that I may sell a good many [*Bibles*] for you.' Feb. 14, 1816: 'There is an infinite difference between a man running red hot to a store to buy a bible, and another getting a bible on subscription to which he had

[1] *Politics for American Farmers;* Washington City: Printed for W. Duane, Philadelphia, 1807, LC.

[2] *Le livre rouge, or Red book . . . being a list of private pensions paid from the public treasury of France* . . . New-York . . . 1794, LC.

[3] For T. & J. Swords' bibles, see *Early Bibles of America*, Rev. John Wright, New York, 1894, LC. — In 1814, according to O'Callaghan, Bibles were printing by Collins, New York; Dodge & Sayre, New York; W. W. Woodward; Hudson & Goodwin; Thomas & Andrews. — See also the NYPL. CARD CATALOGUE.

been overpersuaded & had blam[d] himself afterwards. The eagerness of the one makes him overlook scars & patches — The peevishness of the other makes him boggle & find fault.' Feb. 15, 1816: 'I w[d] . . . most earnestly advise you to drop all the maps but that of Palestine & the neighbouring Countries — & the travels of the Apostles . . . I wish you to give *Me* a 7 Dollar Bible of *my own* with the above two maps, perhaps the Journeyings of the Israelites may be added to this & the former — but with the 7 Dollar Bible give 22 historical engravings.[1] . . . And if the Concordance coud be dropp[d] out of the 20$ Bible & the price put to me at 19$ it w[d] be a good thing for them.[2] I cou'd put it at a copy for every 6, & by getting me a handsome gigg I might do great things for you.' Feb. 27, 1816: 'The young Gentleman of Collins, mention[d] in my last, as getting sub[s]. here, is making a noise about his *finer plates*. And some almost laugh at me about mine. But this only makes me more ingenious & eloquent.' Aug. 10, 1819: 'Whenever I turn my thoughts retrospectively, I smell his [*the Devil's*] brimstone. When Collins, in evil hour for *him*, gave up the Fam[*ily*]. Bible — when there was no acknowledg[d] Fam. Bible Printer in all N. Am[a]. — and when I intreated you to grapple that Inestimable Galeon, what but Infernal influence cou'd have kept you deaf to all my Enchantments, for TWO FULL YEARS?' May 16, 1820: 'Remember that the Atlas & Vesey are only for the Few, Wealthy, Learned &c. . . . the Bibles are for the Million.' Jan. 10, 1822: 'Please set one of your BEST artists on the "*Mother of Moses* ["] turning her back on that sweet infant as he sleeps near the Crocodiles of the Nile! . . . Also beg M[r]. Heath to look at the Holy Mother & Son in the "*Angel warning to flee into Egypt*" [3] and try if he cant make their blessed faces a little more *soft* & *delicate*, & send me 6 or 8. These are not *small matters*, but will greatly aid me when expatiating on the Beauties of this Bible in [*the*] presence of the Great People of this Country [*South Carolina*].' To Henry C. Carey, Feb. 19, 1822: 'The town [*Charleston*] is chockfull of Bibles — Westall's Bibles from London — Collins's Ditt[o] from New-York [4] — some fair sales —

[1] 'Old and New Testaments, Apocrypha, Concordance, 25 Plates, and Ostervald's Notes - - - 7 00.' Carey's Catalogue, 1818, No. 2225.—'The Holy Bible: . . . twenty-five maps and historical engravings . . . M. Carey & Son . . . 1819.' 4to, NYPL.

[2] 'Old and New Testaments, Apocrypha, Concordance, and 100 Plates, Morocco gilt, and gilt edges - - 20 00' Carey's Catalogue, 1818, No. 2266. NYPL. has such an 1818 edition.

[3] In the 1819 4to edition of Carey's Bible, plate 16, facing p. 836 and there called plate 17, shows Joseph, Mary and the child departing with an ass. No signature to plate, which carries only a reference to Matthew, Chap. 2, verse 13; this verse will be found to describe the Angel appearing to Joseph to warn him to flee from Pharaoh.

[4] According to O'Callaghan, in *a List of Editions of the Holy Scriptures*, pp. 152 *et seq.*, Collins published two editions of the Bible in 1821 and the early part of 1822.

some, whipping the Devil round the stump by *raffles* — But by launching a number of Congress rockets, I have, thank God, put some of the Citizens into the humour to subscribe. All good as Ben Burton.'

6. Mathew Carey wrote: 'In 1801, I published a quarto edition of the Bible, (of three thousand copies,) with various additional references, for which I paid a clergyman one thousand dollars. . . . I had eighteen various editions to collate in the reading of the proof sheets. . . . Soon after the publication of this edition, the success of which fully equalled my most sanguine expectations, I ventured on the publication of a standing edition of the Quarto Bible. . . . About the time when I had the Quarto Bible set up, I purchased of Hugh Gaine of New York the School Bible, for as far as I can recollect, seven thousand dollars. . . .' *Letters*, Mathew Carey, in *New England Magazine*, Vol. VI, March, 1834, pp. 230, 233, LC. 'Mathew Carey bought the standing types of the Hugh Gaine Bible of 1792 (previously imported from Scotland, set up in pages) for $7,000 in 1803.' *A List of Editions of the Holy Scriptures*, E. B. O'Callaghan, pp. XXXVIII, 70. 'The Holy Bible, containing the old and new testaments: together with the apocrypha: 1803. 12 mo. Eighth Phil. ed. "Mr. Carey purchased the standing types of the Hugh Gaine Bible of 1792, which this edition mainly resembles."' NYPL. CARD CATALOGUE. M. Carey 'for many years printed his quarto edition of the Bible in standing separate types, being the first and only instance of so great a collection of standing type in the world!' *Annals of Philadelphia*, John F. Watson, revised by Willis P. Hazard, 1898, Vol. II, p. 399, LC. Weems wrote 'I forewarn all my friends from thinking me capable of charging this vile persecuting spirit on the "*Old W- - - e of Rome*" exclusively. No, thank God, I have not so learned human nature. And they who are yet to learn, may, by reading the "Catholic Layman," soon get satisfied that the *priests* are as apt to abuse *power* as the *people*, and that, when "*clad with a little brief authority*," protestants as well as papists have committed these cruelties which make milder devils blush. By way of a note on a note, I would observe, that the "*Catholic Layman*," is a very sensible and spirited pamphlet; the production, it is said, of Mathew Carey, Esq. of Philadelphia, who though a Roman Catholic, has printed more protestant bibles and testaments than half the preachers and printers in America, put together.' *Life of Marion*, 1814 edition, p. 9, *f.n.*

NUMBER 249 1804–1807

THE | LIFE | OF GEORGE WASHINGTON, | COMMANDER IN CHIEF | OF THE | AMERICAN FORCES, | DURING THE WAR WHICH ESTABLISHED THE INDEPENDENCE | OF HIS COUNTRY, | AND | FIRST PRESIDENT | OF THE | UNITED STATES. | COMPILED | UNDER THE INSPECTION OF | THE HONOURABLE BUSHROD WASHINGTON, | FROM | ORIGINAL PAPERS | BEQUEATHED TO HIM BY HIS DECEASED RELATIVE, AND NOW IN POSSESSION | OF THE AUTHOR. | TO WHICH IS PREFIXED, | AN INTRODUCTION, | CONTAINING | A COMPENDIOUS VIEW OF THE COLONIES PLANTED BY THE ENGLISH | ON THE | CONTINENT OF NORTH AMERICA, | FROM THEIR SETTLEMENT | TO THE COMMENCEMENT OF THAT WAR WHICH TERMINATED IN THEIR | INDEPENDENCE. | BY JOHN MARSHALL. | VOL. I. | PHILADELPHIA: |

PRINTED AND PUBLISHED BY C. P. WAYNE. | 1804. | 8vo. pp. 488, 45. *Front.port.* Vol. II. pp. 560, 72. Vol. III. pp. 580, 28. Vol. IV. pp. 626, 16. Vol. V. pp. 779, 36.
BPL., VStL.

1. Title pages are identical save for their dates, which run to 1807; Vol. V contains an Atlas.

2. Wayne at first attempted to obtain subscribers to this work himself. Later he placed subscription papers in the hands of 1200 postmasters, but was disappointed in the results. The subscriptions lagged, partly because of the delayed issues of the book and the disappointing prolixity of the earlier volumes, but also because of Marshall's well-known Federalism, many of the postmasters being Democratic partisans and appointees. John Adams, in writing to Marshall, July 17, 1806, said: 'If you have detailed the events of the last years of General Washington's Life, you must have run the Gauntlet between two infuriated factions, armed with scorpions.' *John Marshall*, Albert J. Beveridge, Vol. III, p. 258, *f.n.;* see also pp. 229–233. Weems' letters below reflect this situation. See also others in Vol. II.

3. Carey's Catalogue, 1816, p. 26; 1818, p. 41, No. 436.

4. *Ad.* 'Mr. C. P. Wayne, of Philadelphia, has issued proposals for publishing by subscription, the History of the Life of General Washington. . . . The publisher intending to visit many of the large towns in the U. S., for the purpose of obtaining subscribers, declines at present, employing agents for that purpose. Subscriptions will be received by him self alone, at No. 36 Market street, Phil., where all letters must be post paid.' *Fred'kt'n Her.*, Oct. 16, 1802, AAS. 'A report having circulated in remote parts of the country, as well as in this city, that the *Manuscript copy of the History of the late General Washington* was destroyed by the fire of Saturday the 26th ultimo, the subscriber is happy to inform . . . report is wholly destitute of truth . . . [*Signed*] C. P. Wayne.' *Va. Arg.*, Apr. 23, 1803, LC. 'From the Boston Gazette. Washington . . . Judge Marshall is the biographer . . . Ten thousand subscribers already . . .' *Va. Arg.*, July 30, 1803, LC. 'We are happy to announce, that the Life of Washington . . . two of the volumes are now ready for the press . . . Mr. Ormrod of that city [*Philadelphia*] is now in this town collecting subscriptions . . . (From Boston Gaz.)' *Ral. Reg.*, Aug. 8, 1803, NCSTL. [*M.L.W.*] 'ANECDOTE OF WASHINGTON. In 1754, he was stationed at Alexandria. . . . The history of this Illustrious American, from his own papers, compiled by the Chief Justice of the United States, is now at press. For terms, please apply to Mr. L. Weems at Doctor Moser's Broad-street.' *Times*, Feb. 24, 1804, CLS. [Containing the anecdote of Payne, which had been used still earlier by Weems in his *Life of Washington;* see also title 1, note 1, *f.n.* 1]; see also *City Gaz.*, Mar. 5, 1804, CLS. [*M.L.W.*] 'From the Charleston City Gazette. Communication. Anecdote of Washington. 'Tis said by the wise that "*there was never a truly great* man without religion." . . . N.B. The story of this great man (from his own papers) is now at the press. Terms. 5 octavo volumes . . . 15 dollars. . . .' *Wash. Fed.*, Mar. 12, 1804, NYHS.; *Petersburg Intel.*, Aug. 10, 1804, CLS., HU. [Re-

counting the story by Potts of Washington at prayer near Valley Forge, first introduced in the Cochran 1808, sixth edition of Weems' *Life of Washington*, title 11.] [*M.L.W.*] 'Life of Washington!!! The Rev'd M. L. Weems, rector of Mount-Vernon parish, intends to preach a sermon at Brunswick courthouse on Wednesday the 15th — at Lunenbury courthouse on Friday the 17th — and at Amelia courthouse on Sunday the 19th of August, at eleven o'clock. After sermon a very pleasureable opportunity will be afforded at our place, to gentlemen present to subscribe for a complete History (from his own papers) of General George Washington, whose history will be the purest history of his country, and his life the best example to our youth.' *Petersburg Repub.*, Aug. 3, 1804 *et seq.*, HU. [This is the first time Weems made this claim, so far as I have found. In his books he did not make it until the sixth edition of his *Life of Washington*, 1808, title 11. See also second item below.] [*M.L.W.*] 'LIFE OF WASHINGTON . . . THE SUBSCRIBERS to that valuable Work, whose names are on the Proposals, and Book held by the Rev. M. L. Weems, are respectfully informed that the *First Volume* is received . . .' *City Gaz.*, Aug. 23, 1804, CLS. [*M.L.W.*] '*To the subscribers to Washington's Life. On the Rev. Mr. Weems' Book. Gentlemen.* Whereas some person in a spirit utterly unworthy of civilised man has reported that I am not authorised to act in this affair of Washington's Biography; — your perusal of the following will, I trust, at once satisfy you and highly gratify, gentlemen, your most obliged friend M.L.W. "The Rev'd M. L. Weems, late of Mount Vernon Parish, Virginia, is hereby authorised to obtain subscriptions for the same in all the states south of the river Delaware. Mr. W. was warmly recommended to me by the honorable Judge Washington, of Mount Vernon, whose very favorable opinion of him has proved to be perfectly correct; for Mr. Weems alone, has collected as many subscriptions as have been obtained for me by all my friends, the booksellers and postmasters throughout the United States. And his fidelity has kept pace with his industry, for of the large sums collected for me he does not owe one single cent to C. P. Wayne. Proprietor of the copy-right. N.B. Mr. W. is now in town with the first and second volumes to wait on subscribers."' *Tel & D. Adv.*, Oct. 4, 6, 1804, PIL.; *Fed. Gaz.*, Oct. 5, 6, 1804, PIL. [See letters of Sept. 21, 1804 in note 5 below, and of Oct. 3, 1804, *Letters*, Vol. II.] [*M.L.W.?*] 'Life of Washington. Subscribers . . . entered their names at this office with the Rev. Mr. Weems. . . .' *Va. Arg.*, Nov. 24, 1804, VSTL. [*M.L.W.*] 'LIFE OF WASHINGTON. FROM HIS OWN PAPERS. *Compiled by Chief Justice Marshall . . . The Rev. Mr. James Stevenson* . . . has just received the two first volumes . . . As the work is not yet finished, the subscription paper . . . is still invitingly open to those who wish in this LAST, BEST way, to honor the Man whose history will be to THEM, the best history of their country, and his LIFE the best lesson to their Souls . . . *Va. Her.*, Dec. 18, 1804, LC. 'Life of Washington. (*From his own papers.*) . . . M. L. Weems is happy to inform the right honorable the gentlemen of the Legislature, and the right worthy the citizens of Richmond, that he shall exhibit this forenoon, at the Capitol, the *two first* vols . . . As the work is not yet finished the subscription book is still open . . . Mr. W. leaves town this afternoon.' *Va. Arg.*, Dec. 22, 1804, VSTL. [*M.L.W.*] '*Life of Washington.* The FOURTH VOLUME of this Work, is received, and ready for delivery to Subscribers on the list, at the POST-OFFICE . . . and . . . at No. 124 BROAD-STREET, next door to the corner of Church-street, (as before). All orders for BOOKS, must be accompanied with the *Cash*, without which, they will not be delivered. The numerous subscribers on Mr. *Ween's* [*sic*] *List*, who have omitted to call for their preceding Volumes, are respectfully Notified, all Books of that description remaining on hand (1st, 2d, and 3d Vols) on the 5th of November next, will immediately after be re-shipped to C. P. Wayne, in Philadelphia — to whom they will be necessitated to apply for their copies.' *Times*, Oct. 5, 1805, CLS. 'M.L.W. congratulates his Charleston friends, subscribers to Washington, for the *immortal* HONOUR done, as well to their own morals as to the memory of that Hero. — Of 350 subscribers, there remain scarcely a dozen without their books. . . . It may not injure [*the*] flavour of the *sparkling Pintard*, to say on the glorious 4th "I owe nothing now but *Love* to the memory of him HIM [*sic*] who like the flaming Cherubim (by the tree of life) stood firm, where millions where [*were*] firm by that blessed tree of Political life, planted 30 years ago by our Father." M.L.W. is still with his friend Dr. Moses [*Moser?*]. . . .' *Times*, July 1, 1806, CLS. [*M.L.W.*] 'Of the History (in five vols. and an Atlas) of this great man, the first *four* vols. elegantly finished, are now at my friend Doctor Murray's, . . . ruin of a *very valuable citizen and his young family.*' *Col. Cent.* (Aug., Ga.), Oct. 25, 1806, UN'YGA. [Preceded by the anecdote in full of Governor Johnson, first introduced into Weems' *Washington* in the Augusta 1806 edition, title 10.] [*M.L.W.?*] '*Better Late than Never; Life of Washington.* THE 5th Volume, with Atlas . . . John Murray.' *Col. Cent.* (Aug., Ga.), Apr. 25, 1807 *et seq.*, UN'YGA.; *Aug. Chron.*, May 2, 1807 *et seq.*, DER. [*M.L.W.*] 'COMMUNICATION. CURIOUS DREAM OF MRS. MARY WASHINGTON, (THE HONORED MOTHER OF THE ILLUSTRIOUS GEORGE.) . . . A complete and elegant history of this great man, compiled from his own papers, by Chief Justice Marshall . . . Caterpillars and Tornado.' *Col. Mus. & Sav. Adv.*, June 12, 1807, GAHS. [This anecdote of Washington's mother was first included in Weems' *Life* in the Cochran 1808 sixth edition, titles 11 and 12. See also letter of Dec. 22, 1802, note 5 below.] '*The Rev. Mason L. Weems, well known in the Southern States as agent for procuring subscribers for the Life of Washington . . .*' *Star*, Feb. 9, 1809,

NCSTL. Advertisements and reviews found from 1802 to 1811, with the widest advertising from 1804 to 1806, both in America and Great Britain.

5. Weems wrote to Carey, Oct. 22, 1800: 'Judge Washington spoke to me, t'other day, about co-operating with him in that Great work his Uncle's Memoirs.' July 4, 1801: 'I have a letter from B[*ushrod*]. Washington (ali[*a*]s Judge W) begging me to assist him in that *great work* of his Uncle, the Immortal George. I shall try to get it into your hands, it may make our fortunes & also furnish a good field for us to figure on.' Aug. 1, 1801: 'I lost the last week in waiting for a sight of Judge Washington, on the score of his Uncles Memoirs. That Great Work will not be ready earlier than the Spring.' Aug. 10, 1801: 'The Memoirs of Washington are going on under the hands of the Chief Justice.' To Wayne, Dec. 22, 1802: 'Patriotic Orations — Gazette Puffs — Washingtonian Anecdotes sentimental, moral, military & wonderful — All sh[d] be tried and every exertion made to push into every family, into every hand so very interesting & highly moralizing a work as Yours but alass! I am not able to do it on my present allowance.' Apr. 22, 1803: 'Sixteen have already scatter'd their dollars on the tomb of Washington.' Sept. 21, 1804, in asking Wayne for better terms as his agent, he stated that in Annapolis, Mr. Geo. Hill had given out that he, Weems, was not authorized to receive subscriptions for Marshall's *Washington* 'and, yet for lack of allowance I cou'd not venture into the Newspapers to scourge the Invidious Non-Natural!' [See, however, advertisement, Oct. 4, 1804, note 4 above.] For a discussion of the method of printing Marshall's *Washington* etc., see a long letter to Wayne, of Jan. 25, 1805, in *Letters*, Vol. II. To Wayne, Feb. 25, 1805: 'Wou'd God you cou'd send the 2[d] edit. to Ormrod & the Puritans of the North. 'Tis their profession . . . to do good for evil. The People in the South are Infidels. They will run horn mad if you vex 'em in the Life of Wash.' To Carey, Sept. 2, 1805: 'Since the receipt of yours, I've been so hurried with the Biography of Washington, as to lack leisure, to answer it, till now.' Oct. 20, 1806: 'Thro' my *own* & the hands of my Co-Adjutants, M[r]. Wayne has reciev'd about 40,000$ in the course of two years.' May 24, 1807: 'I am not disengag[d] from M[r]. Wayne but tis likely I shall be on winding up this heavy Washingtonian affair which probably will be soon. I am not in my element, tis chiefly the best Religious Work Moral & Political (i.e. Republican) Books that I wish to circulate. ergo in this History of Washington I *feel* no great interest. It is not half so moralizing & Republican as my own of which by the by I publish[d] here this winter and have nearly sold off the whole impression 1500 copies (of a 5th edition improv[d]. without frontispiece) at half a do[llr]. Wayne has no stock — and has met with such disappointments in this affair of Washington — gave so much for it — got so few sub[s]. in comparison of

what he expected. I obtained more than Ormrod & all his Post Masters & Aids throughout the Continent, put together, and yet my muster roll made short of 4000 — such vexatious delays from mismatchings — defalcations of Subscribers &[c] &[c] that I don't think he will do much more at the printing business.' To Wayne, Mar. 29, 1808: 'I feel no uneasiness about any of the numerous Persons into whose hands this book [*Marshall's Washington*] has been put, but Mr. Somerville of Petersb'[g] Virginia.' To Carey, Dec. 19, 1809: 'In July 1808 I arriv[d] in Philad[a] to see M[r]. Wayne &c. You invited me to co-operate with you. I replied that I believ[d] I cou'd do better with my own little Books. However finding Wayne gone & having reason to believe that his Life of Washington was perhaps done with, and you talking with me frequently at your own table of hospitality, I at length agreed to join you.' May 31, 1810: 'I w[d] gladly stay till the Autumnal Courts were all over which w[d] afford a grand harvest (coud I but get the books I send for) but you know I owe a debt of winding up his business to M[r]. W[*ayne*]. I am at a loss what to do till I hear from that Gentleman to whom I have written.' Oct. 5, 1810: 'Cou'd I but get exoneration, or properly speaking separation from M[r]. Wayne, I shou'd be happy. Not but I cordially love him — but because he is done with books all but Washington and that book may divert my attention e're long from your Business. Cou'd you but make a bargain with M[r]. Wayne, which I am pretty confident *you easily might* for the residue of his edition of Washington, at *long instalments* I am confident Deo adjuvant, that I cou'd with your present stock . . . make *treble* the money to meet your engagements with him.' [Weems, however, was still attending to Wayne's business as late as Sept. 24, 1811 — see *Letters*, Vol. III.] Nov. 23, 1811: 'Wayne has been a noble fellow in his behaviour to me, not in any *great* allowance that he ever gave me of his Book, for it was not in his power, but he has at any rate, been exceedingly gentle & generous in his requisitions.' Jan. 17, 1817: 'M[r]. Wayne is an amiable man, but I fear he will never do me Justice. I told him over & over, again & again, that I cou'd not be answerable for the numerous agents he chose that I sh[d] place his books with. But I fear he will. And in that event I shall be most *cruelly wrong*[d].'

NUMBER 250 1805–1809

A SUMMARY | OF | UNIVERSAL HISTORY; | IN NINE VOLUMES. | EXHIBITING | THE RISE, DECLINE, AND REVOLUTIONS OF THE | DIFFERENT NATIONS OF THE WORLD, | FROM THE CREATION TO THE PRESENT TIME. | TRANSLATED FROM THE FRENCH OF | M. ANQUETIL, | [*Three lines*] | VOL. I. | PHILADELPHIA: |

PRINTED AND PUBLISHED BY C. P. WAYNE. | 1805. | 8vo. pp. 528. Vol. II. pp. 551. Vol. III. pp. 534. Vol. IV. pp. 535. Vol. V. pp. 555. Vol. VI. pp. 461. Vol. VII. pp. 561. Vol. VIII. pp. 545. Vol. IX. pp. 603.

AAS., BPL., WIFL.

1. Title pages are identical save for their dates, which run to 1809.
2. Carey's Catalogue, 1816, '9 vols. 8vo. 24 00.'
3. *Ad.* 'Anquetil's Universal history . . . is now publishing by C. P. Wayne . . . Four volumes have been published, the fifth will soon be ready. . . .' *Monthly Register*, Vol. II, April, 1807, p. 403, LC. 'A Proposal for publishing by Subscription, Anquetil's Universal History, . . . Subscriptions received by Birch and Small, Philadelphia.' *Pub. Intel.*, Apr. 23, 1807 *et seq.*, HU. 'Universal History. A new and much admired work. A Proposal For publishing by Subscription, Anquetil's Universal History, . . . Conditions. . . .' *Pub. Intel.*, Sept. 8, 1807 *et seq.*, GAHS. 'For Sale By J. W. Campbell . . . Anquetil's Universal History, 7 vols . . .' *Petersburg Intel.*, Mar. 16, 1810, AAS.
4. Weems wrote to Wayne, June 16, 1804: 'As to your 2[d] edition, Great numbers of subscribers wou'd come forward, provided the Proposals requird *no advance*. I cou'd get much patronage to the Books alluded to in the *proposals sent me*, but I have done nothing yet merely because I do not like to get Sub[s]. one, two or three years before the books can come forward, which I apprehend may be the case, as your powers are all so engaged in the Biography of Washington.'

Jan. 1, 1805: 'You said of Moore & Anquetil that you w$^{d}$ print and I dispense, and that half and half sh$^{d}$ reward our mutual toil.' Jan. 25, 1805: 'You have a very heavy work at press, Auguetil [*Anquetil*].[1] Perhaps you have not one half of it cover'd by subscriptions. Now, is it sound policy, for the sake of saving 1 1/2 or 2 per cent., to keep me trudging about the streets, distributing single vols of a work already secured, rather than give my whole time and exertions to another & larger undertaking? But you'll ask, "Cant W. be distributed and Auguetil subscribed for at same time, and by the same person?" No, by no means so *successfully*. A demand for *money* creates an ill humor that forbids all *immediate* demands for more favors. . . . Thus when your 9000 vols. of Aug. are bro$^{t}$ to bed, 3 or 4000 of them perhaps, will have to lie still in your lumber rooms or to go out into the world in exchange for bad books, and these, in turn, to be hawk'd off at vendue for half price. . . . In your letter to me, at Charleston please to say when you expect Aug. will be ready for distribution; I mean the whole 9 vols.' Dec. 31, 1805: 'Dont be uneasy about Anquetil, I trust I shall do all I promis$^{d}$ for you.' Aug. 4, 1806: 'If you cou'd get Judge Washington, who you say is highly pleas$^{d}$ with Anquetil, to say *something handsome* in favor of that work, and recommending it to all his Friends in this Country, as a valuable thing to be put in the hands of their *Sons*, I may, if I spend the winter here [*Savannah*], do good things for you.' Aug. 5, 1806: 'If I spend the winter in this Country *completing the Washington* business & *getting* Sub$^{s}$ for *Anquetil*, it will be adviseable to send me on a capital assortment of books, exchanges for Sidney & Montague [*sic*].' Aug. 17, 1806: 'I wish to know when Anquetil will be ready.' Oct. 26, 1806: 'Numbers will not subscribe for Anquetil unless they see Washington Complete. They rip & tear prodigiously. 'Tis well that I can talk a little.'

[1] These misspellings are copied verbatim from Benson J. Lossing's article giving this letter, in *Am. Hist. Record*, Vol. II, February, 1873, p. 82, LC. This is the only source found for this letter which is given in full in *Letters*, Vol. II.

NUMBER 251 1806

REFLECTIONS | ON THE | RISE AND FALL | OF THE | ANCIENT REPUBLICKS. | ADAPTED TO THE | PRESENT STATE | OF | GREAT BRITAIN. | [*Three lines*] | BY EDWARD W. MONTAGU, JUN. | PHILA-DELPHIA: |

PRINTED AND PUBLISHED BY C. P. WAYNE. | 1806. | 12mo.
pp. 1, (1), 1, (1), XII, 335, (1).
LC., LCPhil.

1. Carey's Catalogue, 1818, No. 1041.

2. *Ad.* 'M.L.W. congratulates his Charleston friends, . . . is still with his friend Dr. Moses [*Moser?*], — has still . . . Montague [*sic*] on the Fates and Fortunes of all the ancient Republics, a very interesting and valuable work, just reprinted and beautifully bound, price One Dollar.' *Times* (Charles.), July 1, 1806, CLS. [*M.L.W.*] 'PROPOSALS for PUBLISHING BY M. L. WEEMS MONTAGUE'S [*sic*] VIEW OF THE ANCIENT REPUBLICS: VIZ. Sparta, Athens, Thebes, Carthage and Rome. THE people of the United States compose perhaps the only pure Republic; the only *equal* and cheap government now on earth. As such, it is envied and hated by the tyrants of Europe, who are seeking to injure us abroad and to divide and ruin us at home. Under God our salvation now depends wholly on ourselves. Great, therefore, is our need of light. But what light can equal that of experience, the constant experience of all the great republics that have gone before us? their experience is *on record.* And in this *beautiful history* we are given to see how they rose to glory; and *why* they are fallen back *to ruin* — why Greece, once the nurse of arts and mother of *heroes,* now lies prostrate under the iron yoke of *ignorance* and *barbarism!* Why, *Carthage,* once the queen of the ocean, and center of universal trade and wealth,

now puzzles the traveller to tell *where she stood!* And why, Rome, formerly the mistress of the world, is now become the abhorred sink of *poverty* and *wretchedness!* This most interesting and instructive book; this fine politico-historical mirror for Americans, handsomely printed and bound, will be presented to subscribers, for one dollar and a quarter. The SUBSCRIPTIONS for the above work are received at this Office — where a few COPIES are FOR SALE.' *Pub. Intel.*, June 16, 1807 *et seq.*, HU. [*M.L.W.?*] 'Our friends will recollect that in the Intelligencer of the 21st instant [*see title 237, note 2, f.n. 1*] we presented them with several remarkable anecdotes of the great ALGERNON SIDNEY etc. . . . they and their little ones, and come and enjoy with us the Peace and Plenty of our happy Goshen. Gentlemen who have never read this celebrated work of ALGERNON SIDNEY's may form some idea of its exceeding importance to our young countrymen by perusing the following letter (to the editor) from his Excellency the President of the United States: [*letter from Jefferson of Dec. 13, 1804 follows, see title 237, note 2.*]' *Pub. Intel.*, June 18, 1807 *et seq.*, HU. Also advertised in: *Col. Cent.* (Aug., Ga.), Jan. 31, 1807, UN'YGA. *Louisv'l. Gaz.*, May 4, 1810, AAS.

3. Weems wrote Mar. 23, 1807: 'Please tell [*M^r^. Wayne*] that I am dunn'^d^ every day by Sub^s^ for "Montague on the Ancient Republics".'

NUMBER 252 1817

A VIEW | OF THE | CULTIVATION | OF | FRUIT TREES, | AND THE | *Management of Orchards and Cider;* | [*Two lines*] | NATIVE AND FOREIGN | APPLES, PEARS, PEACHES, PLUMS, | AND CHERRIES, | CULTIVATED IN THE MIDDLE STATES OF AMERICA: | [*Ten lines*] | BY WILLIAM COXE, Esq., | [*One line*] | PHILADELPHIA: |

PUBLISHED BY M. CAREY AND SON. | *Nov.* 1, 1817. | D. Allinson, Printer. | 8vo. pp. 3, IV, 1, 6–253, 15 unnumbered.
AAS., VStL.

1. Carey's Catalogue, 1818, No. 3914.

2. In spite of Weems' hopes and plans, Carey seems to have issued the book without his having any part in it. Weems wrote to him in May, 1816: 'It is *infinitely* well worth y[r] while to write to M[r]. Cox [*sic*], of Burlington, on the noble Fruit book he has so long & so ably prepar[d]. The blessings of thousands of little children feasting on sweet wholesome dulce acid fruits — as also the myriads of Adults sav[d] by y[r] giv[g] them good substitutes to [*sic*] cursed Tear brain whiskey — & then thousands of money for yourself — for *the Book will take* & besides you need not print but on the sure card way of supplying subscribers obtain[d] by y[r] old friend M. L. Weems. Write to Cox [*sic*] or I shall be hurt.' Feb. 21, 1817: 'I must get letters from great Men recommending to the People of the U. Stat[*e*]s *more, much more* attention to rich luscious fruits to counteract the morbid appetite excited by the Devil in Whiskey &c &c. . . . I long to be doing something handsome on Hunter, Coxe &c &c.' Apr. 5, 1817: 'I am all impatient to know in what forewardness, Coxe, Hunter &c. are for my starting.' July 10, 1817: 'With the different Bibles, Coxe, Hunter, sports magazine, Davies, Melish, I feel confident that Great things may be done. . . . As to Coxe, but little has been done in it yet, owing to the chilling nudity of the Prospectus. This Department of Rural Economy is not thought of in this Tobacco & Corn Country [*Dumfries*]. An high colour'd prospectus of the advantages with a recommendation by some greatly popular characters wd, I thought be necessary. Judge Washington has given me one, which I shall print.' July 20, 1817: 'As to Coxe I have gotten from Judge Washington & Gen[l] John Mason & shortly from M[r]. Jefferson & M[r] Madison expect those commendations that will greatly aid that work.' [*Not found by me. See, however, letter of Oct. 20, 1817 below.*] July 22, 1817: 'As to Hunter & Coxe, little has yet been done for them, and all owing to their being issued upon the world, as young Females into Company, without any Respectable Character saying one solitary word in their favor. I shall soon get the proper Patronage in the way of High Authorities assuring the American People that Coxe is the very man to teach them the blessed art to enrich their Gardens & orchards with the finest fruits on earth. This will go a great way to a quick and extensive circulation of his book' Aug. 8, 1817: 'On our first acquaintance . . . People knew nothing of the A[*nimated*]. Nature & had done nothing to so simple a Sub[n]. paper. At your own instance, I sketch[d]. out a Prospectus that gave the People

to expect that "Worlds on Worlds inclos[d] were to burst upon their Senses," if they w[d] but seize the precious moment to subscribe. . . . I wanted something in this way in favor of Hunter & Coxe. You say I ought to have had those Commendations. There we differ. You certainly are the All in All. I am but y[r]. Agent. However thro' the Commendations not coming — nothing has yet been done with Hunter & Coxe. . . . I say now . . . as I have said all along, that the moment I get out the ad Captandum Prospectus of those works I am ready to bend to them as to a grand harvest.' Sept. 15, 1817: 'I will dash . . . having now the Commendations I have been waiting for.' Oct. 20, 1817: 'If in one of the boxes to Norfolk you cou'd send . . . 100 of the Fruits (Coxe) . . . I will make a good use of them. . . . The hour I get to Norfolk I shall print Judge Washington's letter & Gen[l] Mason's in favor of Coxe.' Nov. 2, 1817: '8 days ago I got to Norfolk, found no letter relative to . . . Coxe, as I begg[d]. you to send, ergo, I did not print my recommendations.' Feb. 21, 1818: 'Coxe is printing & I shall directly do all I can with him.' June 13, 1818, he stated that Coxe had been 'bro't forward' at his instance.

NUMBER 253? 1818

SACRED | BIOGRAPHY: | OR THE | HISTORY OF THE | PATRIARCHS. | TO WHICH IS ADDED, | THE HISTORY OF DEBORAH, RUTH, AND HANNAH. | BEING | A COURSE OF LECTURES | DELIVERED AT THE SCOTTS CHURCH, LONDON WALL. | BY HENRY HUNTER, D.D. | THE THIRD AMERICAN EDITION. | COMPLETE IN FOUR VOLUMES. | *Vol. I.* | [*Four lines of quotations*] | PHILADELPHIA: |

PUBLISHED BY EDWARD EARLE. | . . . | 1818. | 8vo. pp. 444. Vol. II. pp. 484. Vol. III. pp. 440. Vol. IV. pp. 362.
AAS., BPL., NYPL.

1. In Weems' letters there are many allusions to a projected issue of this work [see also note 2 to title preceding]. By 1807 he was selling it and as early as 1809 he was exercised to have the work reprinted, though apparently he was obliged to wait nearly four years before actually beginning to solicit subscriptions for an issue with which he should have direct connection. [See July 22, 1813, in note 4 below.] In spite of the abundant evidence given in their letters that such an edition was planned by Carey, as urged by Weems — the former even sending him a prospectus with specimen plates and pages — I have never found any trace of it. It seems clear, on the contrary, that Carey, having heard in Philadelphia of the projected edition of Earle (as given above) before its actual issue in 1818, renounced his own. [See Weems' letter of Oct. 17, 1817, in Vol. III.] Since Weems apparently sold the work after Carey had changed his intention of reprinting it, may it not be assumed that he dealt, from 1818 on, in the Earle edition? That Carey had planned for an edition after Weems' heart is shown not only in the letters which follow, but also in his *Account Books* [AAS.]. There under date probably of 1816, 1817 or 1818, 'Alex Rider' [1] rendered an account for 'the following for Hunts [*sic*] Sacred Biography Abraham Sending hagar away the Deluge Adam and Eve praying over the death of Abel Ruth and Boaz Birth of Christ Marriage of Cana Temtation of Satan. Making the Total of $90. Dol' [Vol. 30.] As two of the six plates named by Rider match in title two of the four to be found in J. J. Woodward's Philadelphia, 1832, edition of Hunter [complete in one volume, same issued again in 1834, AAS.], it seems plausible that, by arrangement with Carey or the engraver the plates, or some of them, ordered by Carey for his own edition of this work were transferred to the later publisher. The plates are all signed 'Alexander Rider, del' and 'Alexander Lawson'.[2] *Ruth Gleaning* and *The Marriage of Cana* are the two which match in their descriptions. The editions sold by Weems in earlier years may have been some of the following: 1st American Edition, Vols. 1–4, Boston, 1794; Vols. 5–6 in Boston, 1795: Vol. 7, Walpole, N. H., 1803. [AAS., NYPL.] Second Edition Walpole, 1803; 'Second Edition', New York, 1806. [NYPL.] London editions were issued in 1783, 1792–1795 (called the Fourth edition), 1802 the Fifth edition, and 1820. BM.

2. Carey's Catalogue, 1816: 'Hunter's Biography, 4 vols. 8vo. 5 00'

[1] Alexander Rider 'made miniatures and historical compositions in Philadelphia between 1818 and 1825.' Dunlap's *History of The Arts of Design*.

[2] Alexander Lawson's career is sketched in *American Engravers* . . . by Stauffer, pp. 56, 58. There it is stated that a paper on him was read before the Historical Society of Pennsylvania in 1878 by Townsend Ward, from which the sketch was compiled. See also *Index* to *American Engravers* . . ., Mantle Fielding, Nos. 911, 919, 931, 938, AAS.

3. 'Hunters Sacred Biography' was advertised, along with numerous works known to be issued by Mathew Carey, in *Va. Arg.*, Aug. 13, 1814, AAS. *Ad.* [*M.L.W.*] 'AN INTERESTING CRITICISM, *on a very interesting Author and Work.* "Few authors have been more successful in attracting the attention of the public to their publications than Dr. *Hunter*. . . ." Parents who wish to see their children enriched and adorned with all the angelic and happy, that celestial spirits created in the similitude of God are capable [*sic*], will no doubt be gratified to learn that a work so singularly calculated to do good, is now printing in this country, in the 16th edition. N.B. Mrs. Madison, Bishop Moore,[1] the Rev. Messrs. Wilmer,[2] Norris, Muir, and Andrews, of this town, with many of the most distinguished Preachers in all the Protestant churches in our country, have recommended it in the strongest terms. A subscription paper is left at this Office. Those who procure nine subscribers, and become responsible, shall have the [*c*]loth copy gratis. Any friend to the morals and happiness of mankind, who thinks he can obtain 9 subscribers, will oblige by calling on M. L. WEEMS, at the dwelling of Mr. HENRY SLADE.' *Alex'a Gaz.*, May 12, 1820, AAS. Also advertised in: *Mess.* (George'n), June 28, 1820, LC. *Nat'l Mess.*, July 14, 1820, LC. *Charles. Cour.*, Feb. 13, 1822 *et seq.*, CLS.

4. Weems wrote to Carey, Dec. 2, 1806: 'I begg[d] you to send me to Augusta . . . 20 Copies Sacred Biography. . . . With . . . Sacred Biography (Hunters) . . . I coud do *great things.*' Jan. 31, 1807: 'The Hunters Biography you sent, was snatch[d] at in a moment, but on opening, it was found disfigur[d] with *proof sheet pages!!!* & some pages hardly touch[d] with ink at all at all!!!' June 22, 1809: '*My mind is fix*[d] on "*Hunters sacred biography.*" Let me know instantly, to *Dumfries*, what you can print 2000 copies for on a *good, thick, fine* paper & neat binding. I have a notion I can do more for this book than you are aware of — Can't you get a *short striking preamble to it* [*in*] the subscription paper?' July 3, 1809: '2[d] point. Hunters Sacred Biography is a Divine Work. Such Learning, Piety, & Imagination hardly ever yet met together — and certainly a subject so popular & interesting was never before stumbled upon — I mean the painting of the Sacred Characters. As to myself, I am enchanted with it. And I am happy to find that the Clergy think & speak of it as I do. If I err not most egregiously, Great things may be done with this Book. One or two of the editions that I have

[1] Moore, Richard Channing, born 1762, second bishop of Virginia (elected bishop 1814 and served until death, 1841), and fourteenth in succession in the American Episcopate. See *The Twentieth Century Biographical Dictionary of Notable Americans.*

[2] *Ad.* 'Now ready for the Press, and the Publisher engages its appearance on the 20th September next, a new publication, entitled, The Rock; or, Support under Trials; . . . By James Jones Wilmer, Author of Consolation, &c. . . . July 11.' *Del. & East. Shore Adv.*, Aug. 5, 1795, HU.

seen are abominable. Both the Ladies and the Clergy will exert themselves for this most popular work — but they want a handsome edition. What can you print a handsome edition for? . . . how w[d] it do in 8 Vol[s] duod[o] and [*on*] a *lovely paper* & Lackington, i.e., *showy*, binding, at ten Doll[s]. [*?*] Religious books ought to be made as *beautiful* as possible to captivate the more.' [*July 26?*] 1811: 'My heart is much set upon "*Hunter's* SACRED BIOGRAPHY" but more of that at another time.' July 22, 1813 [LC.], Weems wrote from Dumfries to Mrs. James Madison: 'I beg leave, in this way, to inform M[rs]. Madison that I have it very much at heart to reprint a book which I firmly believe will do great good. As I know of no Lady who has so large an interest at stake *in this Country* as M[rs] Madison has, nor any who holds so distinguished a place in it, I don't know to whom, in equity, I ought so properly to look for patronage to my book as to herself. It is certainly no adulation, Honor'd Madam to say that you are one of the "*Favor'd Few*" who to do good need but to will it. The elevation of your Rank, together with the charm of your benevolent spirit & polish'd manners diffus[d] so widely as they are by the Members of the National Legislature & the brilliant Crowds that attend your Levees give you an Influence which no other Lady can pretend to especially among the Fair Sex of our Country. And this forms another reason why I solicit your patronage to this Book; tis a book peculiarly apt to please & profit the Ladies. Many of the finest delineations of character in it are taken from persons of their sex; the Graces which render them so singularly amiable & beneficent are painted in colours uncommonly correct & captivating; and to crown all, the style is admirably suited to the Sentiments and subjects — at once elegantly rounded & musically sweet. The book I allude to is "*Hunter's Sacred Biography*" — or a delineation of sundry of the most distinguish[d] Characters recorded in the Holy Scriptures. Tho' an European work it has gone thro' several editions in America; and is spoken of in terms little short of rapture, by all who read it. The patronage of this excellent book which I solicit of M[rs]. Madison is a *Recommendation of* it. A recommendation of it, Honor[d] Madam from your pen w[d] insure it a wide Circulation among your Fair Country women; and mingled as it w[d] be by maternal Love, with the milk of a thousand nurseries it wou'd contribute to raise up myriads of Angelic Characters to adorn & bless the rising Generation. Knowing how very dear such a result w[d] be to you — to You Honor[d] Madam who have been nurtur'd in the bosom of a Society remarkable for their Christian Philanthropy, I cannot but assure myself that you will with pleasure give me the powerful aid of your Recommendation to this highly moralizing work. Hundreds of the clergy are ready to give me their recommendations, but as it is chiefly on the Ladies that I count for the Circulation of it, I had rather have a few lines from M$^{rs}$. Madison than from a whole Bench of Bishops. You will please observe that Doctor Blair was much indebted for the wide circulation of his Sermons, to Queen Charlotte. As you may not have seen this Book I send you a borrowed Volume [*evidently not his own edition, see title 253*]; at the 68$^{th}$ page of which, part the 2$^{d}$, you will find the commencement of the Biography of Ruth from which I flatter myself you will find sufficient matter to elicit the approbation I request, & which I believe all important to its wide Success. I pray you accept my heartiest Congratulations for the returning health of His Excellency — to whom I herewith send a Vol of "*Doct*$^{r}$*. Hunter*." If in the lucid intervals of Public Care, his Excellency shou'd honor this vol. with a coup d'œil he will perhaps discover in it the marks of a Genius & Spirit which I think will please him. With sentiments of the Highest Respect, I remain, Honor$^{d}$ Madam Your very hum$^{b}$ Serv$^{t}$ M. L. Weems.' To Carey, Feb. 19, 1814: 'Mrs. Madison has patronized me in a good work which I am just about to undertake — applications are made to me by numbers to cooperate with them. But my impression is that I can do better by myself.' Jan. 31, 1817: 'Formerly I intreated you to reserve y$^{r}$ fire for the old Man of War the Family Bible. Now I intreat you to lay another Manilla ship on board, I mean HUNTER'S SACRED BIOGRAPHY. . . . Of all parts of this blessed book, [*the Bible*] the Biographical (as belongs to man) are the most attractive. And when so elegantly delineated — so elegantly dress$^{d}$, & so elegantly recommended as this most popular Work it cannot possibly fail. But to be short I do not wish you to appear in it. Only let me have 4 engravings *well done* and if I don't sell you 1000 copies (at 10$) i.e. 10,000 Dollars worth in 15 months & without any or but little interruption to our Bibles, I shall be more mistaken than I ever was in my life.' Feb. 8, 1817: 'As to Hunter I repeat my request that you have the Engravings such as to cause you to be *talk*$^{d}$ *of*. Give me 4 or 6 Elegant engravings, and allow me as I said 14 months from the time of starting and I feel a good hope I shall sell of that one *work* 10.000 Doll$^{s}$. . . . How come on the Designs &c for Hunter?' Feb. 21, 1817: 'I must get Recommendations of Hunter from those Divines who stand highest in their respective churches. Staughton among the Baptists,[1] Bishop White, among the Episcopalians [2] &$^{c}$. &$^{c}$.' Apr. 12, 1817: 'I begg$^{d}$ you to get from D$^{r}$. Abercrombie, D$^{r}$. Staughton, & D$^{r}$ Ja, Wilson,

[1] Rev. William Staughton, D.D., 1770–1829; Principal of the Baptist Theological Institution, Washington, D. C.; first President of Columbian College, D.C., etc. See *Memoir of the Rev. William Staughton, D.D.*, Rev. S. W. Lynd, A.M., Boston, 1834, LC. Also *The Twentieth Century Biographical Dictionary of Notable Americans.*

[2] Rev. William White, 1748–1836; Bishop of Pennsylvania, 1787–1836. See *Account of the Meeting of the Descendants of Colonel Thomas White of Maryland*, Philadelphia, 1879, LC. — Listed in *A List of Emigrant Ministers to America 1690–1811*, Gerald Fothergill, London, 1904, LC.

a short pithy commendation of Hunter, I have a fine one from M[rs]. Maddison & from Doct[r] Holcombe & from a famous Quaker here [*Baltimore*]. . . . My hopes of Hunter are very sanguine.' Apr. 24, 1817: '16 of the Specimens for Hunter are almost this hour arrived. The first engraving is beautiful. The 2[d] but so so. Rachel walking in her sleep! I don't wonder that Jacob stares as he does. The artist may afford, I think, to mend that *gratis*. . . . Shall I come on to Balt[o]. & subscriptioneer like a Hero for Hunter, Coxe & Davies (the Bible is there done over) and taking the steamboat dash on to Norfolk . . .? In 10 days there will be a grand meeting of the Episcopal Clergy, with Bishop Moore at their head. If I had but specimens [*of Hunter*] sufficient I cou'd do great things.' And again, in an undated letter, immediately following: 'As to Hunter, I count on good things from it. Much depends on touching the feelings of the Public. You will agree with me that the 4 plates you give me to start with shou'd be *elegant*. All, all, depends on this. by giving 50 or 60$ apiece M[r]. Designer & Engraver will give you something that will ensure a splendid Success.' Apr. 25, 1817: 'I think you put more print in the Specimen for Hunter than need be. 8 pages I sh[d] have thought enough.' Oct. 17, 1817: 'You want to know whether I have done anything with Hunter. I have y[r] letter expressing a determination *not to print it*.' Again he wrote of 'Specimens', commendations, etc., Ap. 30, July 10, 20, Sept. 15, Oct. 17, 20, Nov. 2, 1817, and June 3, 1818. To James Madison, Jan. 22, 1819: 'Please present my very best Respects to M[rs]. Madison, to whom I have taken the liberty to send a paper for Doct[r]. Hunter's admired work.' [For letter in full, see *Life of Marion*, 1818, title 90, note 2. For other allusions to Mr. and Mrs. Madison's interest in his Hunter subscriptions, see under date of Feb. 19 and Mar. 14, 1820, Vol. III.] To Carey, Jan. 15, 1820: As to Hunter about which you ask me, I have put a number of papers into some of the best hands in our Country — and within this hour I have reciev[d] a paper with many names on it — that was plac[d] in the hands of M[rs]. Madison.' In a letter to Madison, Feb. 20, 1820, he asked for payment of Mrs. Madison's subscription to Hunter. May 14, 1820: 'I send you this mornings Gazette; because it contains a little flourish concerning one of y[r] books, Hunter's Biography.' [See note 3 above.]

5. Rev. Henry Hunter, born, Perthshire, 1741, died 1802. Besides writing this 'History of the Patriarchs' (first edition 1783–1792) he 'began the publication in parts of . . . "a careless History of London and its environs" which he did not live to complete. The publisher, John Stockdale, with the assistance of other hacks, issued the discreditable compilation . . . 1811.' Hunter also translated various works on physics from the French.

NUMBER 254 1820

A COMPLETE | GENEALOGICAL, HISTORICAL, CHRONOLOGICAL, AND GEOGRAPHICAL ATLAS; | BEING | A GENERAL GUIDE TO HISTORY, | [*Nine lines*] | ACCORDING TO THE PLAN OF LE SAGE, | [*Three lines*] BY M. LAVOISNE. | [*Two lines*] | SECOND AMERICAN EDITION | [*Five lines*] | PHILADELPHIA: | PUBLISHED BY M. CAREY & SON. | September 1, 1820. | [*Three lines*] | Folio. pp. unnumbered. 71 Maps.
LC.

1. After title and copyright leaf follow Wm. H. Crawford's letter to Weems, dated July 18, 1820 [see note 3 below], 'THE ADVERTISEMENT TO THE FIRST AMERICAN EDITION' and the 'PREFACE.' See also *Addenda*.

2. Carey's Catalogue, June, 1821.

3. *Ad.* 'Messrs. Seymour & Williams are in possession of "Proposals for publishing by subscription, a translation from the French, of A. Le Sage's Historical, Genealogical . . . Atlas:" . . . Gentlemen of the first learning in the United States, have patronised it. . . . A perusal of the proposals will induce every reader to become a subscriber.' *Repub.*, Apr. 11, 1811, LC. [*M.L.W.*] 'Mr. Snowden. I beg leave, on the wings of your "flying folios" to convey to the parents of youth aspiring to literary pleasures . . . Miss Ann Smith . . . Mrs. James Taylor. . . . Having thus performed our part, — dropping "a word to the wise," now for the letter. Sir. You . . . ask my opinion of Le Sage's Atlas . . . [*signed*] *A. H.* . . . Numbers of our first rate critics, such as Drs. Mitchell [*sic*], Barnes, Patterson, Wiley, Corre and Anderson, . . . to be without it.' *Alex'a Gaz.*, July 8, 1820, AAS. [For articles very like this, including a letter signed A. W. S., but actually written by Weems, see *Letters*, Vol. III, following June 20, 1820.] [*M.L.W.?*] 'LE SAGE'S HISTORICAL ATLAS. This

important work, in an English dress, is now republishing in Philadelphia by the enterprizing Messrs. CAREY & SON, Booksellers, of Philadelphia, at so moderate a price as puts it within the reach of most persons who can afford to buy books at all. The following letter, on the subject of this work, from one of out distinguished fellow citizens, is so interesting, that we have pleasure in publishing it. The letter is in reply to a letter from the Rev. Mr. Weems, the Agent of Messrs. Carey, requesting the writer's opinion of the merits of the work. *Washington*, 18th July, 1820 Dear Sir: In reply to your letter of this date, requesting my opinion of the general merits of Le Sage's Historical Atlas and of the propriety of publishing in this country a correct translation of it, I take great pleasure in assuring you that I consider it the most successful effort of the age to facilitate the acquisition of historical, genealogical, chronological and geographical information. In this admirable work the great events which, from the earliest ages, have changed the civil and political condition of man, and ultimately led to the existing state of human society are not only described in strong and appropriate language, but so clearly and distinctly delineated upon maps, that the mind of the student without an effort, comprehends, at a single glance, their cause, the means employed in their accomplishment and their remote effects. By this happy device the senses are, in a degree unknown to any other work of the same general nature, employed in aid of the understanding and memory, and greatly advances the progress of the student. I have, for several years, ardently wished that some enterprising individual would furnish the American youth with the means of profiting by this able work, and am happy that it has at last been undertaken by one whose talents and perseverance cannot fail to command the most complete success. I remain, with sentiments of the highest respect, your most obedient servant, WM. H. CRAWFORD.[1] The Rev. Mr. Weems.' *D. Nat'l Intel.*, July 20, 1820, LC. [*M.L.W.?*] 'Le Sage's Historical Atlas. Persuaded as we are . . . the following letter . . . in answer to one from the Rev. M. L. Weems . . . the patriotic and enterprising M. Carey & Son . . . [*Crawford's letter follows, see above.*] N.B. The price of the American edition . . . the London edition.' *Alex'a Gaz.*, Sept. 13, 1820, AAS. 'LE SAGE'S ATLAS, GREATLY IMPROVED. M. CAREY & SON . . . have nearly ready for publication, the second American edition of . . . Atlas according to the plan of Le Sage . . . by M. Lavoisne. . . .' *Fed. Gaz. & Balt. D. Adv.*, Nov. 17, 1820 *et seq.*, MDHS. Letter of commendation of the *Atlas* and approval of M. Carey's proposal for issuing

[1] W. H. Crawford, of Georgia, was Secretary of State under Monroe. Gallatin, writing to Jean Badollet, July 29, 1824: 'One man at last appeared who filled my expectations. This man was Mr. Crawford, who united to a powerful mind a most correct judgment, and an inflexible integrity.' *The Life of Albert Gallatin*, Henry Adams, Philadelphia, 1879, p. 598, LC.

it in an improved translation, signed Wm. Wirt [1] and addressed to The Rev. Mr. Weems, who printed below it an 'interesting testimony of approbation, from the Presidents of St Mary's College, Mess. Dampheux and Tessier.' *Fed. Gaz. & Balt. D. Adv.*, Nov. 23, 1820, MDHS. [See *Letters*, Vol. III, following Nov. 23, 1820.] 'LAVOISNE'S ATLAS. Persons desirous of possessing this valuable work, are respectfully requested to call at the store of the subscriber, and leave their names before the first day of December, as the publishers, Messrs. M. Carey & Son, will raise the price after that time to thirty dollars — present price twenty-five dollars. F. LUCAS, JR. No. 138 Market St.' *Amer. & Com. D. Adv.*, Nov. 23, 1820 *et seq.*, with slight changes, LC. [*M.L.W.*] 'MEMOIR OF A FINE GIRL. Mr. Willington . . . Ann Smith of Ann-Arundel county, Maryland . . . M. L. Weems. N.B. As the following letter has a very friendly bearing . . . Mar. 7, 1821. Lavoisne's Atlas . . . [*signed*] S. Elliott.' *Charles. Cour.*, Mar. 23, 1821, CLS.; with changes, in *Georgian*, May 16, 1821, GAHS. [See *Letters*, Vol. III, May 16, 1821.] [*M.L.W.?*] 'To the Editor . . . Sir — You have . . . rapid progress. . . . Now for the letter. . . . "Dec. 23, 1820 . . . Mr. Carey's new ed. improved by Lavoisne . . . Le Sage's Historical Atlas . . . [*signed*] H. G. Otis" . . . The Rev. M. L. Weems. N.B. M.L.W. is still receiving the patronage of the friends of useful learning.' *Charles. Cour.*, Mar. 30, 1821, CLS. [*M.L.W.*] '. . . The public has of late . . . elegant letters . . . distinguished citizens, commending . . . a modern French publication . . . LE SAGE'S ATLAS improved by LAVOISNE. CONTENTS . . . (*Candid Criticisms.*) Mar. 31, 1821. "Dear Sir . . . [*signed*] John J. Pringle. Mar. 17, 1821. Sir . . . [*signed*] Thos. Bee. Rev. M. L. Weems." ' *Charles. Cour.*, Apr. 4, 1821, CLS. [*M.L.W.*] '*Printing in the U. States — A Curiosity.* Our readers will be struck with an astonishment of the most agreeable sort, when they learn that the "Historical Atlas," by Lavoisne. . . . A part of the profits to be given to the Sunday Schools of Charleston.' *Charles. Cour.*, July 14, 1821, CLS. [For advertisement in full, see *Letters*, Vol. III, after July 14, 1821.] [*M.L.W.*] 'Dont let the Spark go out. . . .' *Charles. Cour.*, Feb. 14, 1822, CLS. [*M.L.W.*] 'A Letter from the Rt. Rev. Bishop Bowen. . . . Note on the above . . . noble discount.' *Charles. Cour.*, Feb. 16, 1822, CLS. [*M.L.W.*] 'I don't know anything, Mr. Willington. . . . The following letter cannot fail to aid the good cause. [*Letter of commendation follows.*]' *Ibid.*, Feb. 21, 1822, CLS. [For article in full, see *Letters*, Vol. III.] [*M.L.W.*] 'Valuable National Work, *Entirely New*, HENRY C. CAREY & I. LEA, Philadelphia, pro-

[1] William Wirt, born in Maryland, 1772; district-attorney of Virginia, 1816–1817, and attorney-general of the United States in the cabinets of James Monroe and of John Quincy Adams, 1817–1829; died 1834. See *Twentieth Century Biographical Dictionary*.

pose to publish on the plan of the celebrated LAVOISNE, an AMERICAN ATLAS. . . . This work is intended for a companion of the celebrated Lavoisne's . . . Atlas . . . M. L. WEEMS is now receiving subscribers for this work; and while he cordially thanks his numerous Southern friends for their liberal patronage of Lavoisne's General Atlas, he hopes, that, from what they have seen above of the plan of this American Atlas in particular, they will be struck with the idea of its exceeding utility, both for their sons and daughters as an excellent aid of [*sic*] education; and to themselves as a rich source of reference to innumerable important notices relative to the history of their own continent and country. March 15.' *Georgian*, July 6, 1822 *et seq.*, UN'YGA.; *Charles. Cour.*, Feb. 8, 1822 *et seq.*, CLS.; Mar. 15, 1822, GAHS. 'COMMUNICATED. TO THE REV. M. L. WEEMS, SIR — We have examined your *specimen* of the American Atlas, proposed to be printed by Messrs. Carey & Co., on the same luminous plan of Lavoisne's admired work, and to contain maps of all the American *States* and *Territories*. . . . We entirely approve of this undertaking. . . . But exclusive of all these important considerations . . . we feel it a pleasing kind of duty, required of us, to patronize an undertaking by the same spirited Gentleman, who lately gave us a better American edition of the celebrated Lavoisne, than any of the European and at *half* the cost. [*signed*] W. B. Bullock. James M. Wayne. Alexander Telfair. William Law.' *Georgian*, Mar. 22, 1822, GAHS. [*M.L.W.*] 'Literary. . . . He is the best. . . . We stated a twelvemonth ago . . . Rev. Mr. Weems . . . subscription for a Grand Atlas . . .' *Charles. Cour.*, Feb. 14, 1823, LC. [With a commendation signed Moses Waddell.] [See also *Letters*, Vol. III, Feb. 14, 1823.] [*M.L.W.?*] 'We are pleased to learn that the first edition . . . engaged and . . . Mr. Weems . . . receiving subscriptions for the second' *Charles. Cour.*, Feb. 14, 1823, LC. See also advertisements in: *Va. Arg.*, Sept. 3, 1812, NYPL. *Nat'l Intel.*, Oct. 21, 1813, UN'YGA. *Nat'l Mess.*, July 21, 1820, LC. *Balt. Pat.*, Nov. 15, 1820, BA. *Times* (Charles.), Feb. 5, 1821 *et seq.*, CLS. *Georgian*, Mar. 14, 1822, GAHS. *Charles. Cour.*, Apr. 11, 1822, CLS.

4. Weems wrote to Carey, June 12, 1817: 'Were this affair conducted as it ought to be, i, e one or two Super Royal show bills given me to set up at Court houses & to put into the hands of Lawyers &c &c notifying that Maps of every description, Atlasses, Globes, Law books, Medical, Theological, Novels, Histories &c &c w[d] be furnish[d] at such a court day, we might do a great deal.' May 16, 1820: 'Remember that the Atlas . . . [*is*] only for the Few, Wealthy, Learned &c. . . .' July 20, 1820: 'I send you the Nat. Intelligen[r] of this morning. It contains an Elegant Critique by the great W[m]. H. Crawford.' And he added, July 21, 1820: 'Will you notice it to the Honorable Writer of it?'

Aug. 2, 1820, he spoke of 'the prejudice [*against*] subscrib$^{g}$ compell$^{g}$ me to long speeches for Lavoisne,' throwing him back a good deal. Aug. 17, 1820: 'For the very active part taken in my favor by the Honorable W$^{m}$. H. Crawford I believe I signified to him that y$^{r}$ grateful [*p*]resentments of the same w$^{d}$ be manifested in presenting him a copy.' Nov. 30, 1820: 'I am thinking that it wd be well, for the purpose of suspending Subscription lists at *Banks*, Coffee houses, Reading Rooms &c &c, to strike off a half sheet with Crawford's & the Attorney Gen$^{ls}$ Letters on a type LARGE & fascinating with the *conditions*.' Dec. 22, 1820: 'M$^{r}$. Rufus King . . . coud not possibly recommend Lavoisne. He knew *nothing* of it. [I] next waited on M$^{r}$. Otis — who treated me elegantly — promis$^{d}$ to recommend y$^{r}$ Book altho', he said, you had handled him & his friends rather roughly in yr. Ol[*ive*]. branch. In the Countenance of Mr. LOWNDES, I met a most affectionate welcome.' [Followed by the letter of H. G. Otis commending and suggesting corrections to the Atlas, to which Weems evidently added the date when printing the letter. See advertisement of Mar. 30, 1821 in note 3 above.] Dec. 28, 1820: 'From Mr. Munroe's [*sic*] conversation on the subject [*of Lavoisne's Atlas*] I have collected materials which I mean to put together & get him to subscribe to it — for a RECOMMENDATION. Having 3 most Excellent names, Crawford, Wirt & Otis, I have thought of dashing to Annapolis, thence, rapidly thro' Balt$^{o}$. there get an armful of *Circulars* of the *above trio*, with additions of one or two more, i.e. from the PRESIDENT, CALHOUN, &c. hasten on to this place, give a boy a trifle to place them in the hands of all the Members [*of Congress*] (who will by that time be got back from their Christmass holliday) — thus doing all I can by the 20$^{th}$. Jan$^{y}$, set out for Charleston.' To Messrs. Teft & Finn, of Charleston, Apr. 10, 1821 [HSP.]: 'By the "Courier" of today you will receive some printed papers [1] from which you will discover that I am engaged, *in endeavoring*, at least, to accomplish what all, I hope, who command the heavy artillery of the Press have, more or less, in view, i,e to enlighten the Public mind & thereby exalt the Moral & Political Character especially of the rising Generation. M$^{r}$. Millington [*sic*], of the "Courier" tells me that there is some conflict among the Printers of y$^{r}$ City, as generally in all Cities, but that you have acquir$^{d}$ an ascendancy which I am willing to ascribe partly at least to y$^{r}$ superior obligingness & Liberality. Under this supposition I feel a disposition to give you the preference to print for me the "*Prospectus* & *Letters recommendatory*" (as pr the Courier package) of the Historical Atlas alluded to above. My mind, to be explicit & honest, is this — to print letters from Great Public Characters, also essays on Subjects of high public utility as Education &$^{c}$. is what is readily done, in the way of Communications by all Newspaper

[1] *The Charleston Courier* of Apr. 4, 1821, see note 3 above.

Printers — but to print a Prospectus of a Book no matter how publicly useful, yet as for Individual benefit, no Editor can be expected, unless paid for it. So far we are agreed. But still I w[d] not wish that such a Prospectus sh[d] be so *strictly* dealt with as by the *square*. If however you choose to print it, as M[r]. Millington [*sic*], Gale, Ritchie & all others do in a liberal way, and take *a handsome copy in return*, I shall be glad you w[d] immediately insert the Prospectus, sent you with the 3 letters subjoin[d]. 1 from the Secretary of the Treasury. 2[d]. from the Attorney General 3[d] from Senator H. G. Otis. I wish the work to appear in y[r] paper soon as possible, as I am now just setting out for y[r] City & w[d] like to avail myself of that advantage at once, without loss of time. The rest shall be discuss[d] when I see you.' From Carey & Lea to Weems, Nov. 2, 1821: '3[d]. When you arrive in S. C. make every effort to push Lavoisne in preference to everything else. We have that ready and can deliver it immediately.'

5. A. Le Sage was a pseudonym used by Las Cases, Emmanuel, *comte* de, 1766, who compiled this atlas, later 'improved' by C. V. Lavoisne.

6. The third edition of Carey's issue of Lavoisne's Atlas (1821) contains the ADVERTISEMENT TO THE FIRST AMERICAN EDITION; and PREFACE TO THE THIRD EDITION, followed by letters of commendation [some of which had been already printed in newspaper advertisements, see note 3 above] from William H. Crawford [*undated*], William Wirt, Nov. 22, 1820, Robert Goodloe Harper, Nov. 25, 1820, Harrison Gray Otis [*undated*], Rev. E. Damphoux, Rev. John Tessier, Baltimore, Nov. 23, 1820, Charles C. Pinckney, Charleston, March 13, 1821, Winfield Scott, Philadelphia, March 1821, S. Elliott, Charleston, March 7, 1821, John J. Pringle, Charleston, March 17, 1821, Philip Moser, Charleston. March 14, 1821, Richard Furman, Charleston, March 13, 1821, Samuel B. Wiley [*undated*], and D. H. Barnes, New York, October 12, 1819, all addressed to Weems, except Scott's, Wiley's and Barnes', which are to M. Carey & Son.

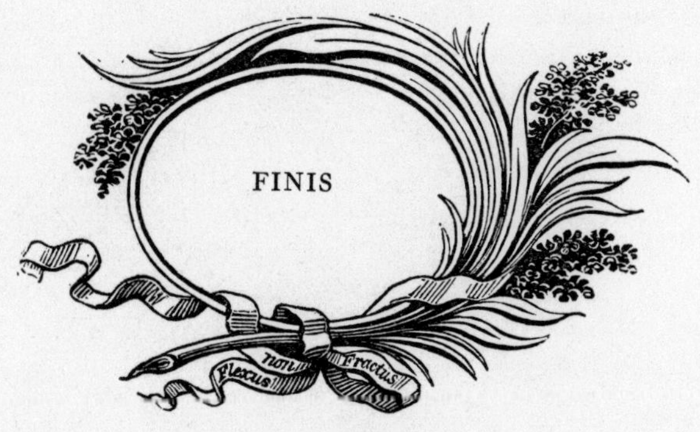

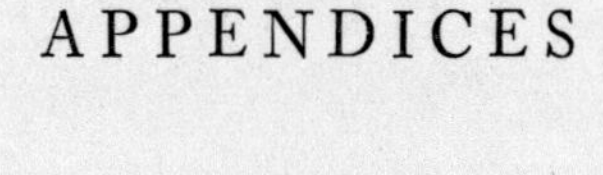

# APPENDICES

# PRINTERS, PUBLISHERS AND BOOKSELLERS NAMED IN BOOKS LISTED

| | |
|---|---|
| DAVIS, P. M. | Title 101. |
| DICKINSON, ABEL | Titles 179, 180. |
| EARLE, EDWARD | Title 253. |
| ELLIOTT. See GRIGG & ELLIOTT | |
| ENGLISH, DAVID. See GREEN & ENGLISH | |
| FENTON, DANIEL | Title 224. |
| FLAGG AND GOULD | Title 208. |
| GARDINER, J. M. | Title 91. |
| GIDEON | Title 214. |
| GOULD. See FLAGG AND GOULD | |
| GRAMBO. See LIPPINCOTT, GRAMBO & CO. | |
| GREEN, CHARLES D. See GREEN & ENGLISH | |
| GREEN, T. | Titles 172, 172A. |
| GREEN & ENGLISH | Title 2. |
| GREEN, ENGLISH & CO. | Title 236. |
| GRIGG, J. | Titles 43–46, 82, 97–99. |
| GRIGG, JOHN | Titles 203, 213, 217. |
| GRIGG & ELLIOTT | Titles 47–52, 54, 57, 58, 59, 100, 103, 104, 106. |
| GRIGG, ELLIOTT & CO. | Title 110. |
| GRIGGS & CO. | Title 212. |
| GRUBER, JOHANN | Title 81. |
| HAGERTY, JOHN | Titles 87, 190. |
| HALL, PARRY | Title 219. |
| HOBBY & BUNCE | Title 177. |
| HUNT, URIAH | Titles 137–140, 149–151. |
| HUNT, URIAH, & SON | Titles 141, 142, 152–154. |
| HUNT'S SONS, URIAH | Titles 143, 144. |
| JOHNSON, BENJAMIN | Title 223. |
| JOHNSON, JACOB, & CO. | Titles 233, 234. |
| JOHNSON, L. | Titles 96, 103, 104, 106, 141, 149–151. |
| JONES, MITHRA | Title 180. |
| JUDD. See ANDRUS & JUDD | |

# BOOKS CONSULTED

Arranged alphabetically, usually according to author or editor, where known or imputed; anonymous works are listed alphabetically according to the salient word of the title. Those containing mentions of Weems or his works are marked with the sign †. Citations merely of titles found in the *Letters* are not here given. The editor regrets that in some instances the title is incomplete, lacking date, place or library, but these omissions cannot now be supplied, as the book goes to press while she is in Europe.


*Account of the Meeting of the Descendants of Colonel Thomas White of Maryland*, Philadelphia, 1879, LC.

ADAM, JAMES. *Practical Essays on Agriculture*, 1789, LC.

†ADAMS, CHARLES FRANCIS. *Works of John Adams*, Boston, 1853, Vol. VIII, pp. 180–186, 349–350, LC.

ADAMS, CHARLES FRANCIS, JR. *A Cycle of Adams Letters*, Boston, 1920, LC.

ADAMS, HENRY. *Life of Albert Gallatin*, Philadelphia, 1879, LC.

†ADAMS, HERBERT BAXTER. *Life and Writings of Jared Sparks*, 1893, Vol. II, pp. 39, 517–519, LC.

†*Adams, Correspondence of the late President John*, Boston, 1809, pp. 52, 53, LC.

AGNEW, J. L. See Lee, F. D.

ALLEN, REV. ETHAN, D.D. *Annals of the American Pulpit*, edited by William B. Sprague, Baltimore, 1861, Vol. V, LC.

——— *Clergy of Maryland of the Protestant Episcopal Church*, Baltimore, 1860, PIL., MDHS.

——— *Historical Notices of St. Ann's Parish in Ann-Arundel County*, Baltimore, 1857, MDHS.

†——— *Ms. Report as Historiographer of the Diocess, May 1783*, MDDIO'NL. in PIL.

——— *Who Were the Early Settlers of Maryland*, Baltimore, 1866, NYPL.

*American Archives*, edited by Peter Force, Washington, 1837–1853, LC.

*American Dictionary of Printing and Bookmaking*, New York, 1894, LC.

*American Jest Book*, Harrisburg, 1796, LC.

†ASBURY, REV. FRANCIS. *Journal*, New York, 1852, p. 485, BA.

*Bailey's Pocket Almanac, 1794*, Philadelphia, HSP.

BAKER, JOHN WYNN. *Abridgment of the Six Weeks and Six Months Tours of Arthur Young*, Dublin, 1771, LC.

†BAKER, WILLIAM SPOHN. *Bibliotheca Washingtoniana*, Philadelphia, 1889, No. 32, HSP.

——— *Character Portraits of Washington*, Philadelphia, 1887, LC.

——— *Early Sketches of George Washington*, Philadelphia, 1894, HSP.

†——— *Engraved Portraits of Washington*, Philadelphia, 1880, LC.

†BAKER, WILLIAM SPOHN. *Opening Paragraphs to Some Biographies and Biographical Sketches of George Washington*, HSP. [*Ms.*]

†—— *Washington after the Revolution*, Philadelphia, 1898, p. 70, LC.

—— *William Sharp, Engraver*, Philadelphia, 1875, LC.

BARBER, JOHN WARNER, and HOWE, HENRY. *Our Whole Country*, Cincinnati, 1861, LC.

BARROW, ELFRIDA DE RENNE, and BELL, LAURA PALMER. *Anchored Yesterdays*, Savannah, 1923, LC.

BARTLETT, JOHN. *Familiar Quotations*, Boston, 1922, LC.

†BASSETT, JOHN SPENCER. *Writers on American History, 1783–1850*, in *Cambridge History of American Literature*, New York, 1918, Vol. II, p. 104, NYPL.

BELL. *Who is John Bell?*, 1860, LC.

BELL, LAURA PALMER. See Barrow, Elfrida De Renne.

†BEVERIDGE, ALBERT JONAH. *Life of John Marshall*, 1916–1919, Vol. II, p. 225, *f.n.*; Vol. III, pp. 231–234, 252 and *f.n.*, 253 and *f.n.*, LC.

BIGELOW, JOHN. See Franklin, Benjamin.

*Bioren's Town and Country Almanack, 1814–1820*, Philadelphia, NYHS.

[BORDLEY, JOHN BEALE.] *Sketches on Rotations of Crops*, Philadelphia, 1792, BA.

BOWLER, METCALF. *Agriculture and Practical Husbandry*, Providence, 1786, LC.

BOYD, T. H. S. *History of Montgomery County, Maryland from . . . 1650 to 1879*, Clarksburg, Montgomery County, Maryland, 1879, LC.

BOZMAN, JOHN LEEDS. *Sketch of the History of Maryland, during the first three years after Its Settlement*, Baltimore, 1811, LC.

†BRADSHER, EARL L. *Mathew Carey, Author, Editor, Publisher*, New York, 1912, pp. 17, 112–113, AAS., LC.

BREWER, E. COBHAM, LL.D. *Dictionary of Phrase and Fable*, Philadelphia, LC.

BRIDGERS, JNO. L., JR. See Turner, J. Kelly.

BRINLEY, GEORGE. *Catalogue*, Hartford, 1878–1893, LC., NYPL.

BROOKE, HENRY. *Fool of Quality; or the History of Henry, Earl of Moreland*, London, 1766, LC.

BROOKS, HENRY M. *Olden-Time Music*, Boston, 1888, LC.

BROWN, JOHN. *A Brief Concordance to the Holy Scriptures*, Philadelphia, 1810, HSP.

BROWN, ROBERT. *General View of the Agriculture of the West Riding of Yorkshire*, Edinburgh, 1799, LC.

BROWN, WILLIAM LAWRENCE, D.D. *Essay on the Natural Equality of Men*, Philadelphia, 1793, NYPL.

BRUCE, WILLIAM CABELL. *Benjamin Franklin Self-Revealed*, New York, 1917, LC.

—— *John Randolph of Roanoke*, New York, 1922, LC.

†BRUMBAUGH, GAIUS MARCUS, M.S., M.D. *Maryland Records Colonial, Revolutionary, County and Church from Original Sources*, Baltimore, 1915, MDHS.

BURR, FREDERIC M. *Life and Works of Alexander Anderson, the first American Wood Engraver*, New York, 1893, BA.

BURTON, H. W. *History of Norfolk, Va.*, Norfolk, 1877, LC.

# BOOKS CONSULTED

*Cambridge History of American Literature*, see Bassett; Tassin; Van Doren.
CAMPBELL, ROBERT. *Catalogues for 1796, 1797*, Philadelphia, AAS.
CAMPBELL, SAMUEL. *Catalogue for 1794*, New York, AAS.
†CAREY, MATHEW. *Catalogues for 1795–1821*, Philadelphia, AAS.
——— *Miscellaneous Essays*, 1834, HSP.; Philadelphia, 1830, LC.
CARSON, JAMES PETIGRU. *Life, Letters and Speeches of James Louis Petigru*, Washington, D. C., 1920, LC.
†*Catalogue of J. T. Doonan*, Atlanta, Ga.
CHRISTIAN, WILLIAM ASBURY, D.D. *Richmond, Her Past and Present*, Richmond, Va., 1912, LC.
†CLARK, ALLEN G. *Life and Letters of Dolly Madison*, Washington, D. C., 1914, pp. 154–156, LC.
CLARK, WALTER, editor. See *North Carolina State Records*, LC.
*Columbian Almanac, 1798*, Philadelphia, NYHS.
[CONDIE, THOMAS.] See Washington, George.
CONRAD, HENRY C. *History of the State of Delaware*, Wilmington, 1908, LC.
†COOKE, JOHN ESTEN. *A History of the People of Virginia*, Boston and New York, 1903, p. 491, LC.
†COOKE, JOSEPH J. *Catalogue*, New York, 1883, Part III, No. 2680, AAS., LC.
COON, CHARLES L. *North Carolina Schools and Academies, 1790–1840*, Raleigh, 1915, LC.
CORDOZO, J. N. *Reminiscences of Charleston*, Charleston, 1866, LC.
*Cresswell, Nicholas, Journal of*, New York, 1924, LC.
†CROCKETT, COL. DAVID. *Exploits and Adventures in Texas*, Philadelphia, 1836, pp. 41–48 [account of an itinerant vender, naming *God's Revenge Against Drunkenness*, without giving Weems' name], BA.
†CROSS, ARTHUR LYON. *Anglican Episcopate and the American Colonies*, in *Harvard Historical Studies*, New York, 1902, Vol. IX, p. 262, LC.
CROZIER, WILLIAM ARMSTRONG, editor. See *Virginia County Records*, LC.

DAVIES, SAMUEL. *Religion and Patriotism, A Sermon*, Aug. 17, 1755, Philadelphia, 1756, LC.
†DAVIS, JOHN. *Travels of Four Years and a Half in the United States of America, 1798–1802*, London, New York, 1803, pp. 228, 237, 305–308, LC.
DEANE, SAMUEL. *New-England Farmer, or, Georgical Dictionary*, Worcester, 1790, AAS.
*Devil Let Loose, or The Wo . . . to the Inhabitants of the Earth* . . . Boston, 1799, AAS.
DIBDIN, CHARLES. *Northern Tour*, Philadelphia, 1825, LC.
*Directories:*
Baltimore 1802, LC.
1810, LC.
1814, LC.
1819, LC.

*Directories* (*continued*):

Baltimore 1822, LC.
1823, LC.
New York 1801, NYPL.
1812, LC.
Philadelphia 1793, LC.
1796, LC.
1797–1801, LC.
1802, LC.
1805, HSP.
1810, LC.
1814, LC.
1816, LC.
1817, HSP.
1823, HSP.

DOANE, GEORGE WASHINGTON. *Remains of C. H. Wharton*, Philadelphia, 1834, LC.

DOUGLAS, SIR ROBERT. *Peerage of Scotland*, Edinburgh, 1813, LC.

DREWRY, P. H. *Story of a Church, A History of Washington Street Church . . . at Petersburg, Virginia, 1773–1923*, Petersburg, 1923, LC.

DU BELLET, LOUISE PECQUET. *Some Prominent Virginia Families*, Lynchburg, 1907, AAS.

†DUKE, REV. WILLIAM. *Ms. Diary*, MDDIO'NL. in PIL.

*Dulany's History of Maryland from 1632 to 1881*, by a Marylander, Baltimore, 1881, LC.

DUNLAP, WILLIAM. *History of the Rise and Progress of the Arts of Design in America*, New York, 1834, LC.

DUTCHER, SALEM. See Jones, Charles C., Jr.

EBERLEIN, HAROLD DONALDSON. *Architecture of Colonial America*, Boston, 1915, NYPL., LC.

EDDIS, WILLIAM. *Letters from America, Historical and Descriptive, 1769–1777*, London, 1792, NYPL.

EGLE, WILLIAM HENRY, M.D., M.A. *Pennsylvania Genealogies; Scotch-Irish and German*, Harrisburg, 1886, LC.

ELIOT, JARED, M.A. *Essays upon Field-Husbandry in New England*, Boston, 1760, AAS.

†ELLIS, EDWARD S. *Grandfather's Historic Stories of Our Country*, New York, 1911, Vol. II, pp. 308–309, LC.

ELLIS, WILLIAM. *Ellis's Husbandry*, London, 1762, NYPL.

——— *Modern Husbandman*, London, 1750, LC.

——— *Practice of Farming and Husbandry in All Sorts of Soils*, Dublin, 1735, LC.

†ELLSWORTH, WILLIAM WEBSTER. *Personal Washington*, 1914–[?], [*Lecture, unpublished*].

ELSON, LOUIS C. *History of American Music*, New York, 1915, LC.

# BOOKS CONSULTED

*Encyclopedias:*

†*Cyclopedia of Biography*, 1883, LC.

†*Duyckinck's Cyclopedia of American Literature*, New York, 1886, Vol. I, pp. 484–492, NYPL.

†*Encyclopedia Americana*, 1904, 1922, Vol. XXIX, p. 158, LC.

*Harper's Encyclopaedia of United States History*, Benson J. Lossing, New York and London, LC.

†*Johnson's Universal Cyclopedia*, 1878, 1890, 1894, 1897, NYPL.

*La Grande Encyclopédie*, LC.

†*Nelson's Encyclopedia*, LC.

†*Nelson's Perpetual Loose Leaf Cyclopedia*, LC.

†*New American Cyclopedia*, 1863, NYPL.

†*New Americanised Encyclopedia Britannica*, 1892–1904, LC.

†*New International Cyclopedia*, 1904, 1905, 1907, 1916, 1917, LC.

*Twentieth Century Biographical Dictionary of Notable Americans*, Boston, 1904, LC.

†*United Editor's Perpetual Encyclopedia*, 1911, LC.

*Watts' Bibliotheca Britannica*, LC.

EVANS, CHARLES. American Bibliography, Chicago, 1903–1925, Vols. I–IX, NYPL.

FIELDING, MANTLE. *Index* to Stauffer's *American Engravers upon Copper and Steel*, Philadelphia, 1917, LC., NYPL.

†FINOTTI, JOSEPH M. *Bibliographica Catholica Americana*, New York, 1872, p. 95, LC.

†FISHER, SYDNEY G. *Legendary and Myth-making Process in Histories of the American Revolution*, Reprinted from *APhSProc.*, Philadelphia, Vol. LI, pp. 56, 64–69, NYPL.

FISKE, JOHN. *Critical Period of American History*, Cambridge, 1888, LC.

——— *Old Virginia and Her Neighbours*, Cambridge, 1898, AAS., LC.

FLETCHER, JOHN. *Fletcher's Appeal to Matter of Fact & Common Sense*, Baltimore, 1814, NYPL.

FOOTE, WILLIAM H. *Sketches of Virginia*, 1st Series, Philadelphia, 1850, AAS.

†FORD, PAUL LEICESTER. See Franklin, Benjamin.

——— *Journals of Hugh Gaine, Printer*, New York, 1902, AAS.

†FORD, WORTHINGTON CHAUNCEY, editor. See Jefferson, Thomas, and Washington, George.

FORREST, WILLIAM S. *Historical and Descriptive Sketches of Norfolk and Vicinity*, Philadelphia, 1853, LC.

†FOSTER, JOHN WATSON. *Century of American Diplomacy*, Boston, 1902, pp. 91–92, NYPL.

FOTHERGILL, GERALD. *American Emigrants, How to Trace Their English Ancestry*, in *Some Special Studies in Genealogy*, Walton-on-Thames, 1908, BA.

——— *List of Emigrant Ministers to America, 1690–1811*, London, 1904, LC.

FRANCIS, JOHN W. *Reminiscences of Samuel L. Mitchell*, New York, 1859, NYPL.

*Franklin, Benjamin, Autobiography of.*

†——— *Bibliography of*, Paul Leicester Ford, Brooklyn, 1889, NYPL.

†*Franklin Bi-Centennial Celebration*, Philadelphia, 1908, LC.

——— *Life and Writings of*, Henry Stevens, London, 1881, Vol. II, pp. 396–409, AAS., NYPL.

†——— *Life of*, John Bigelow, New York, 1899, LC.

†——— *Papers, Calendar of*, 1908, Vol. II, p. 460, and Vol. III, p. 202; Vol. XXXVIII, p. 96, APHS.

†——— *Works of*, John Bigelow, New York, 1888, LC.

†——— *Writings of*, Albert Henry Smyth, Philadelphia, 1906, Vol. IX, pp. 238–240 and *f.n.*, LC.

FRASER, SIR WILLIAM. *Memorials of the Family of Wemyss*, Edinburgh, 1888, LC.

GAMBLE, THOMAS. *Savannah Duels and Duellists, 1733–1877*, Savannah, 1923, LC.

GAMBRALL, THEODORE C. *Church Life in Colonial Maryland*, Baltimore, 1885, MDHS.

German Society, *Catalogue* of, Philadelphia.

GERRIE, PETER DOUGLAS. *Lives of Eminent Methodist Ministers*, 1859, BA.

GOODWIN, EDWARD LEWIS. *The Colonial Church in the Original Colony of Virginia*, 1908, Reprinted from *American Churchman*, LC.

GREEN, RALEIGH TRAVERS. *Genealogical and Historical Notes on Culpeper County, Va.*, Culpeper, 1900, AAS.

GRIFFIN, APPLETON PRENTISS CLARK. *A Catalogue of the Washington Collection in the Boston Athenaeum*, Boston, 1897, HSP., LC.

†GRIFFIN, GRACE GARDNER. *Writings on American History*, New York, 1906–1920, LC.

GRIFFITH, THOMAS W. *Annals of Baltimore*, Baltimore, 1833, LC.

GROWOLL, ADOLF. *Book-Trade Bibliography in the United States in the XIXth Century*, New York, 1898, LC.

HALL, DAVID MOORE. *Six Centuries of the Moores of Fawley*, Richmond, 1904, HSP.

†HALSEY, ROSALIE V. *Forgotten Books of the American Nursery*, Boston, 1911, pp. 179–180, AAS.

†HALSEY, R. T. HAINES. *Pictures of Early New York on Dark Blue Staffordshire Pottery*, New York, 1899, Frontispiece, Appendix B, pp. 302–306, NYPL.

HARRIS, THOMAS, JR., and M'HENRY, JOHN. *Maryland Reports*, New York, 1809, Vols. I, II, AAS.

†HARRISON, FAIRFAX. *Landmarks of Old Prince William*, Richmond, 1924, pp. 387 *et seq.*, AAS., LC.

†HART, ALBERT BUSHNELL. *Historical Liars* [Lecture, unpublished].

†HART, CHARLES HENRY. *Catalogue of the Engraved Portraits of Washington*, New York, 1904, AAS.

†HAWKINS, ERNEST. *Historical Notices of the Missions of the Church of England*, London, 1845, p. 402, AAS., LC.

†HAWKINS, RUSH G. *Catalogue of the Library of*, New York, 1887, No. 1141, AAS.

HAWKS, FRANCIS LISTER. *Contributions to the Ecclesiastical History of the United States*, New York, 1836–1839, AAS., LC.

†HAYDEN, GEN. HORACE EDWIN. *Virginia Genealogies*, Wilkes-Barre, 1891, pp. 350–351, AAS., LC.

†HAZARD, WILLIS P., and WATSON, JOHN F. *Annals of Philadelphia and Pennsylvania*, 1877 and 1898, Vol. I, p. 123, HSP.

HENDERSON, ARCHIBALD. *Washington's Southern Tour, 1791*, Boston, 1923, LC.

†HENNING, HELEN KOHN. *Rare South Caroliniana*, Columbia, 1922, p. 17, NYPL.

HENNING, WILLIAM W. *Statutes at Large of Virginia*, New York, 1819–1823, Vols. VII, XVI, LC.

[HENRY, DAVID.] *Complete English Farmer, by a Practical Farmer*, London, 1771, LC.

†HERNDON, WILLIAM HENRY, and WEIK, J. W. *The True Story of a Great Life*, New York, 1909, Vol. I, p. 37, NYPL.

HILDEBURN, CHARLES R. *Century of Printing, The Issues of the Press in Pennsylvania 1685–1784*, Philadelphia, 1885, AAS., LC.

——— *Sketches of Printers and Printing in Colonial New York*, New York, 1895, LC.

†HILL, JOHN WESLEY. *Abraham Lincoln, Man of God*, New York, 1920, pp. 33, 63, LC.

*Historical Collections of the Joseph Habersham Chapter, Daughters of the American Revolution*, Atlanta, 1902, LC.

*History of the Baptist Denomination in Georgia*, Compiled for the *Christian Index*, Atlanta, 1881, LC.

*Holden Catalogue*, AAS.

HOME, HENRY, see [Kames].

†HOUGH, FRANKLIN B. *Washingtoniana; or, Memorials of the Death of George Washington*, Roxbury, Mass., 1865, Vol. II, p. 274, AAS., LC.

*House of Representatives, List of the Members of . . . at the Second Session of the 16th Congress*, Washington, 1821, LC.

†HOWE, HENRY. *Historical Collections of Virginia*, Charleston, S. C., 1845, pp. 255–257, 543–544, LC.

HOYT, WILLIAM HENRY, editor. See *Murphey*.

HULL, AUGUSTUS L. *Historical Sketch of the University of Georgia*, Atlanta, 1894, LC.

——— *Annals of Athens, Georgia, 1801–1901*, Athens, 1906, GAHS.

*Index to the Journals of the Senate and House of Delegates of the State of Maryland . . . 1794–1800*, Annapolis, 1857, LC.

INGLE, EDWARD. *Parish Institutions of Maryland*, in *Johns Hopkins Studies in Historical and Political Science*, First Series, Baltimore, 1882, AAS.

JACKSON, RICHARD P. *Chronicles of Georgetown*, Washington, 1878, LC.

JAMES, WILLIAM DOBEIN. *Sketch of the Life of Brig. Gen. Francis Marion*, Charleston, S. C., 1821, LC.

†JAMIESON, J. FRANKLIN, editor. *Dictionary of United States History*, Boston, 1894, p. 701, AAS.

*Jefferson, Thomas, Correspondence*, edited by Worthington Chauncey Ford, from the Collections of William K. Bixby, Boston, 1916, pp. 224–225, LC.

†*Johnson's Almanac, 1810*, Philadelphia, back cover, LC.

JOHNSTON, FREDERICK. *Memorials of Old Virginia Clerks*, Lynchburg, 1888, LC.

JONES, CHARLES C., JR. *Dead Towns of Georgia*, Savannah, 1878, LC.

JONES, CHARLES C., JR., and DUTCHER, SALEM. *Memorial History of Augusta, Georgia*, Syracuse, 1890, LC.

*Journal of the House of Representatives of the United States for the 7th and 8th Congresses*, Washington, D. C., 1826, LC.

[KAMES, LORD HENRY.] *Gentleman Farmer*, Edinburgh, 1798, VSTL.

†KELLOCK, HAROLD. *Parson Weems of the Cherry Tree*, New York, 1928, NYPL.

KING, WILLIAM L. *Newspaper Press of Charleston, S. C.*, LC.

KIRKLAND, THOMAS J., and KENNEDY, ROBERT M. *Historic Camden*, Columbia, 1905, LC.

KNIGHT, LUCIAN LAMAR. *Georgia's Landmarks, Memorials and Legends*, Atlanta, 1914, LC.

KONKLE, BURTON ALVA. *John Motley Morehead and the Development of North Carolina, 1796–1866*, Philadelphia, 1922, LC.

LEE, F. D., and AGNEW, J. L. *Historical Record of the City of Savannah*, Savannah, 1869, LC.

LICHTENSTEIN, GASTON. *Early History of Tarboro, North Carolina*, Richmond, 1908, LC.

——— *When Tarboro Was Incorporated*, Richmond, 1910, LC.

LINTON, W. JAMES. *History of Wood Engraving in America*, Boston, 1882, BA.

LIPPINCOTT'S *Gazetteer of the World*, Philadelphia, 1905, AAS, LC.

LIPPINCOTT, HORACE MATHER. *Early Philadelphia*, Philadelphia, 1917, AAS.

*Livre rouge, or Red Book*, New York, 1794, LC.

†LODGE, HENRY CABOT. *George Washington*, Boston and New York, 1891, Vol. I, pp. 10, 39–45, LC.

LOGAN, GEORGE. *Fourteen Experiments on Agriculture*, Philadelphia, 1791, AAS., BA.

†LOSSING, BENSON J. *Eminent Americans*, New York, 1857, pp. 112–113, AAS., NYPL.

†——— *Lives of Celebrated Americans*, Hartford, 1869, p. 301, LC.

——— *Memorial of Alexander Anderson, M.D. First Engraver on Wood in America*, New York, 1872, AAS., LC.

†——— *Pictorial Field Book of the Revolution*, New York, 1855, Vol. II, pp. 213–216, LC.

†——— *The Home of Washington*, Hartford, Conn., and Chicago, 1870, pp. 89–90, LC.

LYND, SAMUEL W. *Memoir of the Rev. William Staughton, D.D.*, Boston, 1834, LC.

†MACMASTER, JOHN BACH. *History of the People of the United States*, New York, 1883, Vol. I, pp. 230–231, LC.

*Madison, Memoirs and Letters of Dolly*, edited by her grand-niece, Boston and New York, 1886, LC.

*Maryland Archives*, MDHS.

*Maryland Land Records*, MDRECOF.

*Maryland Probate Office Records*, for Wills.

## BOOKS CONSULTED

†MASSIE, ROBERT K. *Mason Locke Weems, 1759–1825*, in *Library of Southern Literature*, New Orleans, Atlanta, etc., 1910, Vol. XIII, pp. 5731–5737, BPL., VSTL.

[MATHIAS, THOMAS J.] *Pursuits of Literature*, Philadelphia, 1800, LC.

†MCGUFFEY, W. H. *Eclectic Second Reader*, Cincinnati, 1836, pp. 107–109, AAS.

†MEADE, WILLIAM. *Old Churches, Ministers and Families of Virginia*, Philadelphia, 1878, Vol. II, pp. 233–236, 259, AAS., NYPL.

MEASE, JAMES. *Picture of Philadelphia*, Philadelphia, 1811, AAS., LC.

MEMES, JOHN S. *Works of William Cowper, with a Life and Notes*, Edinburgh, 1835, LC.

MILLS, JOHN. *Treatise on Cattle*, Boston, 1795, AAS.

MILLS, ROBERT. *Statistics of South Carolina*, Charleston, 1826, LC.

MONTGOMERY, ELIZABETH. *Reminiscences of Wilmington, in familiar village tales, ancient and new*, Wilmington, 1872, LC.

MONTGOMERY, THOMAS LYNCH, editor. See *Pennsylvania Archives*.

[MORDECAI, SAMUEL.] *Richmond in By-Gone Days; being Reminiscences of An Old Citizen*, Richmond, 1856, LC.

MOREAU, CHARLES L. *Collection of One Hundred and Fifty Engravings by Alexander Anderson, M.D.*, New York, 1873, LC.

MORLEY, JOHN. *Rousseau*, London, 1873, NYPL.

MORRIS, CHARLES, editor. *Makers of Philadelphia*, Philadelphia, 1894, LC.

MORRISON, COL. E. M. *Isle of Wight County [Norfolk? Va., 1907], 1608–1907*, LC. Compiled for distribution at the Jamestown Tercentenary Exposition.

†MORRISON, HUGH ALEXANDER. *American Almanacs*, LC. See also Toner, J. M.

MOSES, MONTROSE J. *Children's Books and Reading*, New York, 1907, LC.

*Murphey, The Papers of Archibald D.*, edited by William Henry Hoyt, Raleigh, N. C., 1914, LC.

NELSON, WILLIAM. *Controversy over the American Episcopate, 1767–1774*, Paterson, N. J., 1909, AAS., LC.

*New-England Almanack, 1781*, Edmund Freebetter, New London, AAS.

NICHOLS, CHARLES LEMUEL. *Isaiah Thomas, Printer, Writer and Collector*, Boston, 1912, AAS.

*North Carolina, State Records of*, edited by Walter Clark, Goldsboro, N. C., 1907, LC.

†OBERHOLTZER, ELLIS PAXSON. *Literary History of Philadelphia*, Philadelphia, 1906, pp. 343–344, AAS.

O'CALLAGHAN, E. B. *List of Editions of the Holy Scriptures . . . Printed in America Previous to 1860*, Albany, 1861, AAS., LC.

†*One Hundred Years of Publishing, 1785–1885*, Philadelphia, 1885, p. 8, NYHS.

†PAGE, ROSEWELL. *Thomas Nelson Page*, New York, 1923, p. 26, AAS., LC.

PARKINSON, RICHARD. *Experienced Farmer*, London, 1807, NYPL.

——— *Tour in America in 1798, 1799 and 1800*, London, 1805, AAS., NYPL.

PEARSON, EDWIN. *Banbury Chap Books*, London, 1890, LC.

*Pennsylvania Archives*, edited by Thomas Lynch Montgomery, 1894–1914, Fifth Series, Harrisburg, PSTL.

PERRY, WILLIAM STEVENS. *History of the American Episcopal Church, 1587–1883*, Boston, 1885, AAS., NYPL.

——— *Papers Relating to the History of the Church in Virginia, A.D. 1650–1776*, Hartford, 1870, NYPL.

*Pictures of the Passions: or Interesting Narratives*, by the Author of *The Adulteress*, Washington, 1802, AAS., LC.

POELLNITZ, F. C. H. B. *Essay on Agriculture*, New York, 1790, BA.

POORE, BEN PERLEY, compiler. *Political Register and Congressional Directory of the United States of America, 1776–1878*, Boston, 1878, AAS., LC.

†POTTER, ELIPHALET NOTT. *Washington, a Model in His Library and Life*, New York, 1895, pp. 100, 123, AAS., MDHS.

QUINN, SILVANUS JACKSON. *History of the City of Fredericksburg, Va.*, Richmond, Va., 1908, AAS., LC.

*Record Book No. 1. All States and Territories 1720–1820*, in P. O. Building, Washington, D. C.

REYNOLDS, JOHN. *Triumphs of God's Revenge against the Crying and Execrable Sin of Murther*, London, 1656, NYPL. [Also editions of 1670, 1708 and 1779.]

RICE, JOHN A. *Sale Catalogue*, AAS.

†RICH, OBADIAH. *Bibliotheca Americana*, Nova London, 1846, Vol. II, p. 272, AAS., LC.

RIDGELEY, DAVID. *Annals of Annapolis*, Baltimore, 1841, AAS., LC.

RIDGELEY, HELEN WEST. *The Old Brick Churches of Maryland*, New York, 1894, MDHS.

RILEY, BENJAMIN F. *History of the Baptists in the Southern States East of the Mississippi*, Philadelphia, 1898, LC.

†RILEY, ELIHU S. *The Ancient City, A History of Annapolis, in Maryland 1640–1887*, Annapolis, 1887, p. 225, AAS., LC.

——— *History of Anne Arundel County*, Annapolis, 1905, AAS., MDHS.

ROBINSON, JAMES HERVEY. *The Humanising of Knowledge*, New York, 1923, LC.

†ROWLAND, KATE MASON. *Life of George Mason*, New York, 1892, Vol. II, p. 115, AAS., LC.

RUSH, RICHARD. *Washington in Domestic Life*, Philadelphia, 1857, LC.

SABIN, JOSEPH. *Bibliotheca Americana: Dictionary of Books Relating to America: 1492–1892*, New York, 1868–1892, HSP.

†SALLEY, ALEXANDER S., JR. *South Carolina Genealogies*, Columbia, 1910, SCHS.

SCHARF, J. THOMAS. *Chronicles of Baltimore*, Baltimore, 1874, LC.

——— *History of Western Maryland*, Philadelphia, 1882, AAS., MDHS.

†——— & WESTCOTT, THOMAS. *History of Philadelphia*, Philadelphia, 1884, Vol. II, p. 1141, AAS., LC.

## BOOKS CONSULTED

SCHAW, JANET. *Journal of a Lady of Quality.* Edited by Evangeline Walker Andrews, Charles McLean Andrews, New Haven, 1921, LC.

†SEIDENSTUCKER, OSWALD. *First Century of German Printing in America*, Philadelphia, 1893, pp. VII, VIII, IX, 143, 175, 179, AAS.

SEMPLE, ROBERT B. *History of the Rise and Progress of the Baptists in Virginia*, Richmond, 1810, AAS., LC.

†SIMMS, WILLIAM GILMORE. *Weems, The Biographer and Historian*, in *Views and Reviews*, Second Series, 1845, pp. 123–141, NYPL.

SIMPSON, HENRY. *Eminent Philadelphians*, Philadelphia, 1859, LC.

SINCLAIR, SIR JOHN. *Scotland*, 1794, AAS.

SKEAT, WALTER W. *An Etymological Dictionary of the English Language*, New York, 1882, LC.

SKIRVEN, PERCY G. *First Parishes of the Province of Maryland*, Baltimore [1923], AAS., LC., MDHS.

SLAUGHTER, PHILIP. *Brief Sketch of the Life of William Green, LL.D.*, Richmond, 1883, LC.

——— *History of Truro Parish in Virginia*, Philadelphia, 1908, LC.

SLOSSON, EDWIN EMERY. *Great American Universities*, New York, 1910, LC.

SMITH, GEORGE GILMAN. *Story of Georgia and the Georgia People, 1732 to 1860*, Macon, 1900, LC.

SMYTH, ALBERT HENRY. *Philadelphia Magazines and Their Contributors*, Philadelphia, 1892, AAS., LC.

†SMYTH, ALBERT HENRY, editor. See Franklin, Benjamin.

SMYTH, SAMUEL GORDON. *Thomas Leiper, Patriot and Financier in the Revolution*, Conshohocken, 1900, HSP.

SONNECK, OSCAR G. *Bibliography of Early Secular American Music*, Washington, D. C., 1905, AAS., LC.

SOTHERAN, HENRY, *Catalogue of*, London, before 1902, NYPL.

†*South in the Building of the Nation, The*, Richmond, 1909, pp. 537–539, LC.

SPRAGUE, WILLIAM B. See Allen, *Annals*.

SPURRIER, JOHN. *Practical Farmer*, Wilmington, 1793, NYPL.

STACY, JAMES. *History of Midway Congregational Church*, Newnan, Ga., 1903, LC.

STANARD, MARY NEWTON. *Richmond, Its People and Its Story*, Philadelphia and London, 1923, AAS., LC.

STAUFFER, DAVID MCNEELY. *American Engravers upon Copper and Steel*, New York, 1907, AAS., NYPL.

†*Steele, John, Papers of*, edited by H. M. Wagstaff, North Carolina Historical Commission, Raleigh, 1924, Vol. I, pp. 435, 448 and *Index*, AAS.

STEVENS, HENRY. See Franklin, Benjamin.

*St. James' Parish Register* [*Ms.*], MDDIO'NL. in PIL.

TASSIN, ALGERNON. *Books for Children*, in *Cambridge History of American Literature*, New York, 1918, LC.

THOMAS, ISAIAH. *History of Printing in America*, Worcester, 1810, in *Trans&ColAAS.*, Vol. VI, 1810, LC.

†TONER, J. M., M.D. *Index to Bishop Meade's Old Churches, etc.*, Washington, 1898, LC.

†TRENT, WILLIAM P. *William Gilmore Simms*, in *American Men of Letters Series*, Boston and New York, 1892, p. 137, AAS., LC., NYPL.

†TURNER, CHARLES HENRY BLACK. *Some Records of Sussex County, Delaware*, Philadelphia, 1909, pp. 241–246, 269, LC.

TURNER, J. KELLY, and BRIDGERS, JNO. L., JR. *History of Edgecombe County, North Carolina*, Raleigh, 1920, LC.

TYLER, LYON GARDINER, editor. *Encyclopedia of Virginia Biography*, New York, 1915, AAS, LC.

†——— *History of Virginia*, Vol. II, American Historical Society, Chicago and New York, 1924, pp. 436, 512, LC.

TYLER, MOSES COIT. *Literary History of the American Revolution*, New York, 1897, LC.

*U. S. Census, 1790, Maryland, Frederick County*, LC.

†VAN DOREN, CARL. *Fiction II. Contemporaries of Cooper*, in *Cambridge History of American Literature*, Vol. I, p. 315, New York, 1918, LC.

VARLO, CHARLES. *New System of Husbandry*, Philadelphia, 1785, AAS.

*Virginia Archives*, LC.

*Virginia County Records, Spotsylvania County, 1721–1800*, edited by William Armstrong Crozier, F.R.S., published for The Genealogical Association, New York, 1905, LC.

*Votes and Proceedings of the Lower House of Assembly* (Maryland), Vol. II, MDSTL.

WADDELL, ALFRED MOORE. *History of New Hanover County, 1723–1800*, Wilmington, 1909, AAS., LC.

WADLEY, MARY C. *Memorial . . . First Presbyterian Church of Augusta, Ga.*, Philadelphia, 1904, LC.

WALKER, GUY M. *Catalogue of Library*, Anderson Galleries, New York, 1925, AAS.

†WALLACE, JERRY. *A Parson at Large*, Springfield, Ill., 1927.

†WALLIS, REV. SAMUEL A. *Colonial Churches in the original colony of Virginia. Pohick Church, Truro Parish, Fairfax County, Virginia*, Richmond, 1908, pp. 295–301, LC.

WARE, WILLIAM ROTCH. *Georgian Period*, New York, 1923, LC.

WARFIELD, JOSHUAH D. *Founders of Anne Arundel and Howard Counties*, Baltimore, 1905, AAS., MDHS.

*Washington, George, Biographical Memoirs of the Illustrious . . . Also Sketch of His Private Life* [Thomas Condie], Philadelphia, 1800, AAS., LC.

*Biography of Gen. . . . and The Liverpool Tragedy*, CHS.

——— *A Poetical Epistle to His Excellency*, Charles Henry Wharton, London, 1780, LC.

——— *Washington's Diary, or Where and How My Time is Spent* [*Ms.*], LC.

——— *Letters of Jonathan Boucher to*, edited by Worthington Chauncey Ford, Brooklyn, 1899, AAS., LC.

*A Short Sketch of George Washington's Life and Character*, by a Gentleman of Maryland [*later ascribed to John Bell*], London, 1780, LC.

†WATSON, JOHN F. See Hazard.

†*Webster's Calendar: or, the Albany Almanack, 1815*, Albany, AAS., LCPHIL.

WEEMSE, JOHN. *Works*, Scotland, 1623, 1634–1636, YU.

WEGELIN, OSCAR. *Early American Fiction, 1774–1830*, Stamford, Conn., 1902, LC.

——— *Early American Plays, 1714–1830*, New York, 1905, LC.

——— *Early American Poetry*, New York, 1903–1907, LC.

WELLER, EMIL. *Falschen und fingirten Druckorte*, Leipzig, 1858, HSP., LC.

WHARTON, ANNE H. *Social Life in the Early Republic*, Philadelphia, 1902, LC.

WHARTON, CHARLES HENRY. See Washington, George.

WHELEN, HENRY. *Sale Catalogue of the important collection of engraved portraits of Washington*, Philadelphia, 1909, AAS., LC.

WILLIAMS, THOMAS J. C. *History of Frederick County, Maryland*, Hagerstown, 1910, LC.

——— *History of Washington County, Maryland*, Hagerstown, 1906, MDHS.

WILSON, ADELAIDE. *Historic and Picturesque Savannah*, Boston, 1889, LC.

WINBORNE, BENJAMIN B. *Colonial and State Political History of Hertford County, N. C.*, Murfreesboro, 1906, LC.

WINGFIELD, MARSHALL. *History of Caroline County, Virginia*, Richmond, 1924, LC.

WOODS, REV. EDGAR. *Albemarle County in Virginia*, Charlottesville, 1901, LC.

WOODWARD, WILLIAM W. *Surprising Accounts of the Revival of Religion, in the United States of America*, Philadelphia, 1802, LC.

WRIGHT, REV. JOHN. *Early Bibles of America*, New York, 1894, LC.

†WROTH, LAWRENCE COUNSELMAN. *Parson Weems, A Biographical and Critical Study*, Baltimore, 1911, LC.

YOUNG, ARTHUR. *Rural Economy, or Essays on the Practical Parts of Husbandry*, Burlington, 1776, HSP.; 1792, AAS.

——— *Six Months Tour in France*, 1770, LC.

YOUNG, W. P. *Palladium of Knowledge; or, the Carolina and Georgia Almanac*, Charleston, 1807, BPL.

# MAGAZINES, PERIODICALS, TRANSACTIONS, ETC., CONSULTED

Arranged alphabetically; appended thereto is a list of special articles, also arranged alphabetically according to author, with anonymous articles heading that list in the alphabetical order of their magazines; those articles mentioning Weems or his works are marked throughout with the sign †.

*Agriculture, Arts, and Manufactures, Transactions of the Society for*, New York, 1792, Part I, AAS., BA.

*All Hallow's Parish Record* [*Ms.*] and copies, MDHS.

*American Monthly Magazine*, Boston, April, 1829 – April, 1830; January – June, 1838, LC.

*American Monthly Review, or Literary Journal*, Philadelphia, Vols. I, III, January – April, September – December, 1795, LC.

*American Moral and Sentimental Magazine*, New York, March 26 – May 21, 1798, BA., LC.

*American Museum; or, Annual Register*, Philadelphia, Vol. I, 1798, NYPL.

*American Universal Magazine*, Philadelphia, Vols. I–IV, January, 1797 – March, 1798, LC.

†*Analectic Magazine*, Vols. I *et seq.*, AAS.

*Arts, Manufactures, and Commerce, Transactions of the Society Instituted at London for the Encouragement of*, London, 1792, BA.

*Baltimore Weekly Magazine*, Maryland, April 26, 1800 – May 27, 1801, LC.

*Bath and West of England Society, Letters and Papers of*, Bath, Vol. II, 1792, LC.

*Bibliographical Society of America, Papers of the*, New York, Vol. XVII, Part I, January, 1925, AAS., NYPL.

*Experienced Christian's Magazine*, New York, May, 1796 – April, 1797, HSP.

*General Magazine, and Impartial Review*, Baltimore, June, 1798, AAS., HSP.

*Journals of the Protestant Episcopal Conventions . . . Maryland*, Baltimore, 1784–1795, MDHS.

*Key*, Frederick Town, Md., 1798, LC.

*Knickerbocker: or New-York Monthly Magazine*, New York, 1833–June, 1835, LC.

†*Library of Southern Literature*, Richmond, Va., 1921–1923, Vol. VIII, 5737, LC.

*Literary Miscellany*, Philadelphia, Vol. I, Nos. 1–8, 1795, LC.

*Literary Museum*, West-Chester, Pa., Vol. I, January – June, 1797, LC.

*Literary World*, New York, Vol. IV, LC.

*London Chronicle*, London, July, 1780, AAS.

†*Magazine of History*, New York, 1907, Vol. VI, p. 100, AAS.

*Magnolia*, January, 1842 – June, 1843, Charleston, S. C., 1842, LC.

## MAGAZINES, PERIODICALS, TRANSACTIONS

*Manassas Journal, Anniversary Edition*, Virginia, May 19, 1911, VStL.
*Massachusetts Magazine*, Boston, Vol. III, March, 1791, AAS.
*Methodist Magazine*, Philadelphia, 1797, 1798, HSP.
†*Monthly Anthology*, Boston, 1804–1811, Vols. I *et seq.*, AAS., LC.
*Monthly Magazine, or British Register*, London, 1822, Vol. LII, NYPL.
†*Monthly Magazine and American Review*, New York, Vols. I, II, III; 1799, 1800, AAS., LC., NYPL.
*New Annual Register*, London, 1780, AAS., NYPL. †Vol. III, September, 1800, p. 210, LC., NYPL.
*New York Genealogical and Biographical Record*, New York, Vols. XXVIII, XXIX, 1897, 1898, NYPL.
*New-York Magazine; or Literary Repository*, New York, 1793–1797, HSP.
*Norton's Literary Gazette*, New York, Vol. I, 1851–1855, AAS.
*Orion*, Penfield, Ga., 1842–1844, LC.
†*Panoplist and Missionary Magazine*, New York, 1810, Vol. II, pp. 525–532, NYPL.
*Philadelphia Minerva*, Philadelphia, February 11, 1797 – January 27, 1798, HU.
*Philadelphia Repository, and Weekly Register*, Philadelphia, November 15, 1800, HSP.
*Portfolio*, Philadelphia, 1807, 1808, AAS.
*Rural Magazine: or, Vermont Repository*, Rutland, 1795, 1796, HSP.
*Southern Quarterly Review*, Charleston, January – October, 1845, LC.
*St. James' Parish Record*, Baltimore, 1784–1796 [*Ms. and typewritten copies*], MdHS.
*St. Margaret's Parish Register, 1784–1786*, Baltimore, MdHS.
*Thespian Oracle*, Philadelphia, 1798, HU.
*United States Magazine*, Philadelphia, February – September, 1779, HSP.
*Universal Magazine*, London, May, 1800, LC.
*Virginia Magazine of History and Biography*, Richmond, July, 1898, Vol. VI, No. 1, LC.
*Western Monthly Review*, Cincinnati, May, 1827 – July, 1830, LC.
*Westminster Magazine*, London, August, 1780; January, 1784, LC.
*William and Mary College Quarterly*, Williamsburgh, Vol. IV; Vol. XXV, LC.

† — [*Anon.*] *Analectic Magazine*, Vol. IX, May, 1817, pp. 389–391, AAS.
† — " *Blackwood's Magazine*, Vol. XVII, No. 5, 1825, p. 203, *American Writers* [*Signed X.Y.Z.*], LC.
† — " *Magazine of American History, Notes and Queries*, Vol. IV, 1880, p. 222; Vol. IX, 1887, pp. 137, 158–159, LC.
† — " *Maryland Historical Magazine*, Vol. VI, 1911, p. 75, Review of *Parson Weems*, by Lawrence C. Wroth, MdHS.
† — " *Monthly Anthology*, Boston, Vol. VI, March, 1809, p. 215, LC.; Vol. IX, 1810, pp. 414–419, AAS.
† — " *Nation*, July 13, 1916; April 18, 1918; September 9, Dec. 9, 1925; Oct 13, 1926, NYPL.
† — " *Notes and Queries*, Series VII, Vol. VIII, article by *Razzle-Dazil*, p. 248, LC.; Oct. 13, 1926.

## MASON LOCKE WEEMS

†Adams, Charles Francis. *Weems Dispensation*, in *MHSProc.*, Vol. XLIV, 1910, pp. 233–253, MHS.

Adams, Charles Kendall. *Some Neglected Aspects of the Revolutionary War*, in *Atlantic Monthly*, Vol. LXXXII, August, 1898, LC.

†*Biblios*. See *Magazine of American History*, Vol. IV, 1880, p. 222, LC.

Brigham, Clarence S. *Bibliography of American Newspapers, 1690–1820*, in *ProcAAS*.

Bristow, Weston. *William Grayson*, in *Richmond College Historical Papers*, June, 1917, Vol. II, No. I, pp. 74–117, VStL.

*Carey, Letters of Mathew*, in *New England Magazine*, March, 1834, Vol. VI, LC.

†Childs, Allen. In *Southern Churchman*, June 11, 1910, p. 19, LC.

†Coleman, Charles Washington. *Humanizing of Washington*, Review of *The True George Washington*, by Paul Leicester Ford, in *The Book Buyer*, March, 1897, LC.

Condie, Thomas. In *Philadelphia Monthly Magazine*, 1798, HSP.

†Daniel, Frederick. *In An Old Virginia Town*, in *Harper's New Monthly Magazine*, No. 418, March, 1885, pp. 603–606, *Illus.*, NYPL.

†Dubb, Jos[*eph*]. Henry. *Notes and Queries*, in *Magazine of American History*, August, 1881, p. 146, LC.

†'*The Drifter*,' in *The Nation*, December 9, 1925, NYPL.

†Ellsworth, William Webster. *Parson Weems, and His Life of Washington*, in the *Outlook*, Vol. VI, No. 8, February, 1899, pp. 452–456, NYPL.

Ford, Worthington Chauncey. *First Map of Pennsylvania*, in *MHSProc.*, Vol. LVII, November, 1923, NYPL.

——— editor, *A new yeares gift for Protestants*, by Benjamin Harris, in *MHSProc.*, October, 1923, p. 59, NYPL.

†——— Review of Lawrence C. Wroth's *Parson Weems* in *American Historical Review*, Vol. XVII, p. 195, MdHS.

†Gantt, M. S. *Parson Weems*, in *Southern Churchman*, May 21, 1910, p. 20, LC.

†Gray, Arthur P. In *Southern Churchman*, 1888, LC.

†Hale, Edward Everett. *Memoir of Hon. Lorenzo Sabine*, in *MHSProc.*, Vol. XVII, 1880, p. 372, AAS.

Harrison, Frederic. *A Few Words about the Eighteenth Century*, in *The Nineteenth Century*, 1883, NYPL.

†Hart, Albert Bushnell. *American Historical Liars*, in *Harper's Magazine*, Vol. CXXXI, 1915, pp. 732–734, NYPL.

†——— *Imagination in History*, in *American Historical Review*, Vol. XV, p. 242, MdHS.

*Hooker, Diary of Edward, 1805–1808*, in *Annual Report of the American Historical Association for the year 1896*, Washington, 1897, LC.

†Howe, M. A. DeWolfe. *Journal of the Anthology Society*, Boston, p. 244, MHS.

Ingle, Edward. *Concerning Parish Institutions in Maryland*, in *Magazine of American History*, Vol. IX, April, 1883, pp. 262–267, LC.

†Jacoby, John E. Review of *George Washington*, by William Roscoe Thayer, in *The Nation*, January 8, 1923, p. 19, NYPL.

## MAGAZINES, PERIODICALS, TRANSACTIONS

†LOSSING, BENSON J. In *American Historical Record*, Vol. II, February, 1873, p. 82, *Portrait*, LC.

MAXWELL, ARCHIBALD MONTGOMERY. *A Run through the United States during the Autumn of 1840*, in *Southern Literary Messenger*, Vol. III, 1837, VStL.

MCCULLOCH, WILLIAM. *Additions to Thomas's History of Printing*, in *ProcAAS.*, Vol. XXXI, April, 1921, AAS.

NELSON, WILLIAM. *New Jersey Printers of the 18th Century*, in *ProcAAS.*, New Series, Vol. XXI, April – October, 1911, pp. 32–33, AAS.

†NEVINS, ALLEN. Review of two *Lives* of Washington by W. E. Woodward and Rupert Hughes, in *The Saturday Review of Literature*, Dec. 11, 1926, NYPL.

†NORRIS, WALTER B. In *The Nation*, Feb. 29, 1912, pp. 207–208, LC.

——— *Historian of the Cherry Tree. Parson Weems and His Life of Washington*, in *National Magazine*, Vol. XXXI, February, 1910, pp. 495–501, *Portrait*, LC.

†*Razzle-Dazil.* See [*Anon.*], *Notes and Queries.*

†SEINFEL, RUTH. *Textbooks for Moderns*, in *The Nation*, May 25, 1927.

SLOSSON, EDWIN EMERY. *Journalism as an Aid to History Teaching*, in *School and Society*, Vol. III, Jan. 1, 1916, pp. 8–14, LC.

STEINER, BERNARD C. *Maryland Privateers in the Revolution*, in *Maryland Historical Magazine*, 1908, Vol. XXXV, MdHS.

THOMAS, ISAIAH, LL.D. *History of Printing in America, with a Biography of Printers and an account of Newspapers*, in *Trans&ColAAS.*, Vol. VI, AAS.

WROTH, LAWRENCE COUNSELMAN. *William Duke: A Story of a Long Ministry*, in *Church Standard*, June 20, 1908, pp. 239–240, LC.

†——— In *Southern Churchman*, March 19, 1910, LC.

†——— In *Annual Report of the Clements Library*, Ann Arbor, Michigan, January, 1925.

†*X.Y.Z.* See [*Anon.*], *Blackwood's Magazine.*

†YEADON, RICHARD. *The Marion Family*, in *Southern & Western Monthly Magazine*, Vol. I, 1845, pp. 209, 270, 317, 412; II, 50, 121, 200, 265, 333, CLS.

YELLOWLY, HENRY. *Heraldry in America*, in *Americana*, Vol. XII, January, 1918, LC.

# NEWSPAPERS CONSULTED

Arranged alphabetically according to state and town; prefacing is a partial list of articles mentioning Weems or his works, which are marked with the sign †. These are listed alphabetically according to author, where known, with anonymous articles heading the list in the order of their newspapers.


†[*Anon.*] *Globe and Commercial Advertiser*, New York, Mar. 17, 1923, *Famous Men Book Agents.*

†——— News clipping, 1732 — G. W. — 1886, NYPL. [*Unidentified.*]

†——— *New York Times.* Review of *David the Son of Jesse*, by Marjorie Strachey.

†——— ——————— [*Signed: R. J. C.*], Feb. 18, 1923.

†——— ——————— Apr. 29, 1923.

†——— ——————— Dec. 14, 1924.

†——— ——————— Apr. 24, 1927.

†ABBOTT, SAMUEL. *Not Historical Authority. New York Sun*, May 16, 1922.

†BAKER, WILLIAM S. *Weems' Washington. Philadelphia Inquirer*, Feb. 18, 1894.

†BARTON, WILLIAM E. *Lincoln and Weems — A Strange Link. New York Times*, Jan. 2, 1927.

†——— *Defends Story of Cherry Tree. New York Times*, Jan. 13, 1927.

†——— *Cherry Tree Story May Be True. Herald* (Boston), Feb. 13, 1927.

†——— *Washington Cherry Tree Tale Held Not Disproved. Post* (Washington, D. C.), Feb. 13, 1927.

†——— *Weems on Franklin. Herald* (Boston), Feb. 16, 1927.

†BEIRNE, FRANCIS F. *In the year 1800 . . .* Review of the Macy-Masius reprint of *The Life of Washington*, Mark Van Doren, editor, 1927, in *Balt. Eve. Sun*, Feb. 18, 1928, JCBL. Replied to and questioned in following numbers.

†BRANCH, R. S. Notice of a paper read before a meeting of Subscription book sellers at Chicago. *New York Globe*, Mar. 17, 1923.

†DUFFUS, R. L. *New York Times*, Feb. 21, 1926.

†FOX, FONTAINE. Illustration. *New York Globe*, Feb. 22, 1923.

†GILL, MABEL SPICER. *New York Times*, Dec. 6, 1925.

†GOOLRICK, CHESTER B. *New York Times*, Feb. 17, 1924.

†HOPPIN, C. A. *New York Times*, Jan. 10, 1926.

†HYNDMAN, JAMES P. B. *Faith of Washington. New York Sun*, May 11, 1922, NYPL.

†HYNDMAN, JAMES F[*sic*]. B. *A Washington Biography. New York Sun*, May 19, 1922.

†"JOSLYN, JEFF." *Revised History. Tid Bits*, Feb. 20, 1886; reprinted, *New York Morning Journal*, Feb. 22, 1886.

## NEWSPAPERS CONSULTED

†"KESSLER." Illustration. *New York Globe*, Feb. 22, 1923.

†LEWISOHN, LUDWIG. *Strange Career and Surprisingly Clever Literary Work of the Notorious Parson Mason L. Weems. News & Courier*, Charleston, S. C., Aug. 30, 1903.

†MCNICOL, DONALD. *Franklin's Kite Above Suspicion. New York Times*, Jan. 8, 1925.

†MOSHER, O. W., JR. *New York Times Magazine*, Feb. 18, 1923.

†[*Norris, Walter B.?*] *The Truth About the Cherry Tree. New York Herald*, Feb. 19, 1911, *Magazine Section.*

†[*Norris, Walter B.?*] *George Washington's "Billy Sunday" and His Boyhood Love Affairs. Boston Evening Transcript*, Feb. 21, 1917.

†ROUND, GEORGE C. In newspaper clipping dated Oct. 2, 1885, Minnieville Post-Office. *Toner Collection of Clippings*, LC.

SKEEL, EMILY E. F. *Error Enshrined. Saturday Review of Literature*, Feb., 1928.

†TELLER, WOOLSEY. *Tales of Washington. Two Biographers as they are Judged Today. New York Sun*, May 18, 1922.

†VAN NESTE, LAURA LOUISE JORDAN. *Chicago Daily News*, Feb. 21, 1925.

†WROTH, LAWRENCE COUNSELMAN. *Parson Weems, Biographer of Heroes and Moral Pamphleteer*, Address before Rhode Island Historical Society, May 4, 1924, noticed in *Providence Journal*, May 5, 1924.

Other unidentified articles in the press of 1927 and 1928 such as: 'Parson Weems Ran a Bill, Old Ledger shows . . . closed the accounts . . .' Henry M. Hyde. (Probably in a Baltimore paper.) 'Weems on Franklin' and 'Parson Weems,' William E. Barton. ('From the Commonweal'. Probably in Boston papers in February, 1927.) Followed by replies and comments.

### DELAWARE

*Dover*

*Constitutionalist* (; or the Defender of the People's Rights). Sept. 6, 27, 1804; Jan. 17, 24, Feb. 7, Apr. 15, July 11, 1805, AAS.

*Federal Ark.* Sept. 17, 1802, AAS.

*Newcastle*

*Argus and Delaware Advertiser* (Newcastle Argus). May 11, 15, 21, June 4, 1805, HU.

*Wilmington*

*American Watchman* (; and Delaware Republican). Jan. 24, 1810; Dec. 7, 1816; Apr. 5, 1822, BA. Jan. 1 – July 29, 1812; Apr. 20 – July 31, 1816, LCPHIL. Dec. 24, 1814; Dec. 9, 1815, NYHS. July 18, 1820 – Dec. 18, 1821, HSP. Jan. 5 – Apr. 1, 1820; 1821, LC.

*Apollo.* Feb. 12 – July 20, 1805, LC., HSP.

*Ark.* Dec. 31, 1803; May 30, 1804, HU.

*Delaware and Eastern-Shore Advertiser*. May 14, 1794 – May 13, 1795, HSP. Jan. 2, Feb. 2, July 11, Oct. 20, 1796; Apr. 2, May 3, 1798; Mar. 1, 4, 1799, AAS. Mar. 4 – July 4, 1795 (scat'g); Jan. 9 – Dec. 29, 1796 (a few missing); Jan. 19, 26, Feb. 2–27, Nov. 2, 13, Dec. 12, 1797; Aug. 1, 1799, HU. Jan. 21, Mar. 21, June 13, Oct. 10, 1795. LC.

*Delaware Courant* (, and Wilmington Advertiser). May 5, 12, 26, June 2, July 7, 14, 21, Aug 4, 11, 18, Sept. 1, 8, 1787, AAS.

*Delaware Gazette* (; or, the Faithful Centinel; State Gazette; Delaware Gazette or the Faithful Centinel; same, and General Advertiser). June 28, 1795, NYHS. July 5, Aug. 16, Nov. 22, 1786; 1787, 1789, 1790 (a few); June 16, 1792 – Aug. 15, 1795 (scat'g); Jan. 2, Feb. 22, July 11, Oct. 20, 1796; Apr. 2, May 3, 1798; Mar. 1, 4, 1799, AAS. Mar. 7 – Aug. 15, 1795 (scat'g); Mar. 8 – Dec. 31, 1796 (scat'g); Jan. 7 – Apr. 25, 1797 (a few missing), HU. Mar. 18, 1787; July 16, Aug. 27, 1791; May 5, Dec. 1, 1792; June 15, 1793; Feb. 21, Aug. 22, 1795; June 7, 1796; Feb. 4, 8, May 27, 1797; Feb. 20, 1799, LC.

*Delaware Gazette*. Aug. 2, 1809 – Apr. 25, 1810 (scat'g), AAS.

*Delaware Gazette* (and Peninsula Advertiser). Apr. 16, 1816 – Dec. 31, 1817; Jan. 2 – Dec. 30, 1818; Feb. 16, 1820 – Feb. 27, 1824; Mar. 2 – Dec. 31, 1824; Feb. 1 – June 20, 1825, WIL. 1819 – Sept. 18, 1820, LC.

*Delaware Statesman*. Oct. 16, 1811, NYHS.

*Mirror of the Times* (, & General Advertiser). Feb. 12, 19, 1800, BA. Feb. 26, 1800 – Oct. 1, 1805, AAS. Nov. 19, 1800 – Dec. 26, 1801; June 2, 1802 – June 1, 1803, DHS. June 25, 29, July 9, 1803, NYHS. June 10, 1805 – Aug. 5, 1806, HU.

*Monitor*. Oct. 7, 1800, NYHS.

*Museum of Delaware* (, & General Advertiser). Sept. 8, 1804; Sept. 14, 1805; Feb. 14, Apr. 18, Dec. 1, 1807; Dec. 17, 31, 1808; Jan. 14, Feb. 11, 25, Mar. 6, 13 (4, 18 logically), 25, Apr. 24, May 8, June 17, 1809, AAS. June 29, 1805, HU. Jan. 17, 1807, BA.

## DISTRICT OF COLUMBIA

*Georgetown*

*Centinel, & Country Gazette*. Oct. 10, 1797 – Feb. 20, 1798, HU.

*Centinel of Liberty* (and Georgetown Advertiser). Apr. 11, 25, May 2, 16, July 11, Aug. 18, Sept. 1, 12, 19, 1797, AAS. Jan. 4 – Nov. 14, 1799, 1800, LC.

*Columbian Chronicle*. May 20, July 15, Aug. 22, 1794; Jan. 23, June 23, 1795, AAS. Feb. 3, Mar. 3, 6, May 12, 22, June 2, 12, 19, 26, 30, July 3, 7, 17, 21, 28, Aug. 4, 1795, HU.

*Daily Federal Republican*. 1814–1815 (a few), LC.

*Federal Republican* (, and Commercial Gazette). Aug. 11, Dec. 22, 1813; Apr. 30, 1812–1813 (a few); Oct. 7 – Dec. 30, 1814, LC.

*Georgetown Weekly Ledger*. Feb. 18, Mar. 31, Sept. 22, 1792; Feb. 16, Oct. 5, 1793, LC. Aug. 24, Dec. 3, 1793, AAS.

## NEWSPAPERS CONSULTED

*Independent American.* Jan. 16 – Oct. 17, 1810 (some missing), AAS.

*Messenger.* Apr. 17, 1816 – Dec. 30, 1818; Jan. 1 – Dec. 31, 1819; Aug. 1 – Sept. 18, 1820, LC.

*Metropolitan.* Feb. 5 – 29, June 29, July 1–29, Nov. 2 – Dec. 30, 1820; Jan. 1821, LC.

*Museum* (and Washington and George-town Daily Advertiser). Nov. 18 – Dec. 31, 1801, LC.

*Museum and Georgetown Advertiser.* Jan. 21 – Oct. 10, 1809, LC.

*National Messenger.* Oct. 27, 1817 – Feb. 27, 1818, June 1 – Dec. 30, 1818 (scat'g); Dec. 12–31, 1819; Jan. 21 – Mar. 6, June 19 – Aug. 2, Oct. 27 – Nov. 27, Dec. 1–29, 1820, LC.

*Olio.* Sept. 2, Nov. 4, 18, 25, Dec. 23, 30, 1802; Jan. 7, 14, 21, 28, Feb. 3, 17, 1803, NYPL. Feb. 3 – July 28, 1803, CONNHS.

*Spirit of Seventy-Six.* Feb. 26, Apr. 16, May 3, 21, 1811; Dec. 4, 18, 22, 1812; Jan. 1, 12, July 20, 1813, AAS.

*Washington Federalist.* Jan. 1 – June 1 (scat'g), Dec. (scat'g), 1801; June 23–31, 1802 (scat'g); Jan. 3 – Apr. 1, 1803; Oct. 31, 1807, LC. Feb. 3, 1801 – Jan. 13, 1804 (scat'g), HU. Nov. 28, Dec. 10, 17, 19, 22, 28, 31, 1800; Jan. 2, 1804 – Jan. 30, 1805 (scat'g), NYHS.

### *Washington*

*American Literary Advertiser.* Mar. 27, 1802 – Sept. 9, 1803 (scat'g), AAS. Sept. 24 – Dec. 24, 1802, HU.

*Apollo.* May 1, 1802, AAS.

*City of Washington Gazette.* Dec. 4, 1817 – July 31, 1818; Nov. 13, 1819 – June 30, 1820, LC. July 1 – Aug. 31, 1820; Jan. 1821, AAS.

*Columbian Star.* Apr. 5 – Nov. 29, 1803; 1822–1824, LC.

*Colvins' Weekly Register.* Jan. 16 – Apr. 30, 1808, LC.

*Daily National Intelligencer.* Jan. 1 – July 25, 1813; Feb. 1 – Apr. 19, 1814; Aug. 10 – Sept. 21, 1815; Feb. 20 – Mar. 15, May 1 – June 10, 1816; Aug. 1 – 20, Dec. 16 – 30, 1820; Jan., 1821, LC.

*National Intelligencer* (and Washington Advertiser). Aug. 2, Dec., 1802; 1803; 1804; Jan. 1 – Mar. 31, 1806; Mar. 10 – July 30, 1809; June 5 – Dec. 30, 1813; Jan. 11 – Dec. 24, 1814; July 4 – Oct. 31, 1815; Jan. 31 – May 30, 1818 (scat'g); Jan. – Mar., June 27 – Aug. 30, Nov., Dec., 1820; Jan. 1 – June 30, 1826; 1829; Jan. 1, 1840–1842; June 1, 1843, LC. Feb. 2 – Mar. 2, 1815; Feb. 3 – Mar. 12, May 2 – June 1, Aug. 3 – Sept. 3, 1816; July 1 – Sept. 4, 1817; Nov. 3 – Dec. 30, 1819, AAS. Aug. 10 – Nov. 1, 1842, HSP.

*Spirit of Seventy Six.* Jan. 16, Mar. 2, May 29, Aug. 14, 28, Oct. 23, 1810, AAS.

*Universal Gazette.* Nov. 20, Dec. 18, 1800; Feb. 12 – Dec. 24, 1801 (a few); Jan. 21 – Dec. 30, 1802 (a few); Feb. 25 – Apr. 1, 1814 (a few), AAS. Aug. 27 – Oct. 29, 1801 (a few missing); July 8 – Dec. 16, 1802 (a few); Jan. 20 – July 21, 1803 (scat'g); July 4 – Aug. 29, Nov. 28, Dec. 5 – 26, 1805; Sept. 24 – Dec. 31, 1807 (two missing); Sept. 21, 28, Oct. 5, 12, 26, Nov. 2, 1809, LC. Apr. 1 – Oct. 21, 1802 (scat'g), HU.

*Washington City Gazette.* Jan. 19 – Sept. 2, Nov. 12–19, Dec. 10, 17, 1814, AAS.

*Washington City Weekly Gazette.* Nov. 25, 1815 – Oct. 18, 1817, LC. May 24, 31, 1817, AAS.

*Washington Expositor.* Jan. 2, 1808 – Jan. 6, 1809, LC.

*Washington Gazette.* June 6 – Dec. 31, 1796; Jan. 4 – Dec. 23, 1797, LC.

## GEORGIA

### *Athens*

*Georgia Express* (Foreign Correspondent and same). Aug. 6, 1808 – Aug. 19, 1809 (scat'g); Jan. 6 – Dec. 22, 1810; Jan. 3, 1812 – July 23, 1813, UN'YGA.

### *Augusta*

*Augusta Chronicle* (and Gazette of the State; same and Georgia Gazette). Dec., 1793 – Aug. 30, 1800; Oct. 15, 1821 – Apr. 11, 1822, GAHS. Jan. 31, Feb. 7, May 30, July 11, 18, 1795, HU. Mar. 20 – Dec. 19, 1795, LC. Jan. 28, 1804 – Aug., 1807; Aug. 27, 1808 – Jan. 7, 1809; June 10, 1809 – Nov. 11, 1809; Mar. 31, 1810 – Sept. 1, 1811, UN'YGA. (some at DER.). Jan. 3, 1820 – Apr. 11, 1822; Jan. 12 – Apr. 2, 1825, AUGCHRONOF., DER.

*Augusta Herald.* 1799, 1801–1806, 1812, UN'YGA. July 21, 1802 – June 29, 1803; Nov. 3, 1808 – June 28, 1810; Oct. 1, 1819 – June 27, 1802, AUGCHRONOF. Apr. 3, 1806, Feb. 8, 15, Mar. 29, Nov. 8, Dec. 6, 1810; Apr. 25, 1811, AAS. Sept. 1 – Nov. 17, 1814, DER.

*Columbian Centinel.* Aug. 2, 1806 – Dec. 3, 1809, UN'YGA. Nov. 1, 1806; Aug. 1, 1807; June 25, 1808; Feb. 10, Aug. 10, Dec. 7, 1810; June 18, July 2, 22, 29, Aug. 5, 12, 19, Oct. 14, 1811, AAS.

*Georgia Gazette* (and General Advertiser). Feb. 5, 12, 19, Mar. 11, 1816, AAS.

*Mirror of the Times.* Nov. 28, 1808; May 22, 29, June 19, July 3, 1809; Dec. 3, 1810, AAS.

*Southern Centinel* (, and Universal Gazette; same and Gazette of the State). June 6, 1793 – Nov. 7, 1799 (scat'g), GAHS. Oct. 1, 1795, AAS. Oct. 20, 1796 – Apr. 13, 1797 (scat'g), HU.

### *Darien*

*Darien Gazette.* Jan. 4, 1819; Jan. 24, 1820; Apr. 25, May 16, June 6, 27, July 4, 11, 25, Aug. 17, 24, Sept. 14, 19, 26, Oct. 3, 10, 31, Nov. 7, 14, 21, 28, Dec. 5, 1822; May 18, 1824, AAS.

### *Louisville*

*American Advocate.* Feb. 22 – Nov. 28, 1816, GAHS.

*Louisville Gazette* (and Republican Trumpet). May 12, 1802; Dec. 21, 28, 1803; Mar. 20, May 15, 22, 1807; May 4, Sept. 11, Nov. 20, Dec. 4, 11, 1810; Jan. 26, Feb. 2, 16, Mar. 2, 1811, AAS. Sept. 21, Oct. 14, Nov. 26, Dec. 28, 1803; Jan. 4, Feb. 15, Mar. 21, 28, Apr. 25, May 2, 23, 30, June 20, 27, July 11, 23, Aug. 1, 8, 15, 22, 29, Oct. 10, 17, 1804; Jan. 16, 23, 1805, HU.

# NEWSPAPERS CONSULTED

*Milledgeville*

*Georgia Argus.* Apr. 10, 1810 – June 12, 1811 (a few), AAS. Jan. 16, 1811 – Nov. 8, 1814 (scat'g), HU.

*Georgia Journal.* Dec. 12, 1809 – Dec. 26, 1810; Jan. 1 – Apr. 29, 1812, UN'YGA. Jan. 30, 1811 – Jan. 15, 1812; Oct. 23, 1821; Oct. 1 – Nov. 19, 1822 (scat'g); July 1, Nov. 11, Dec. 23, 1823; Mar. 9, May 4, May 11, July 27, Dec. 14, 1824; Mar. 29, Apr. 26, Dec. 27, 1825, AAS. May 29, 1811 – Sept. 29, 1813 (scat'g), HU. Sept. 18, 1820 – June 28, 1825 (scat'g), LC. Jan. 2 – Feb. 21, Apr. 1, 1821; Apr. 10 – Sept. 15, 1822, DER. Nov. 27, 1821; Jan. 23, Dec. 12, 15, 1823, BA.

*Georgia Patriot.* Jan. 6 – Dec. 28, 1824; Jan. 4 – May 3, 1825, GAHS.

*Savannah*

*American Patriot.* Apr. 14 – June 5, 1812, GAHS.

*Columbian Museum* (& Savannah Advertiser). Mar. 4, 1796 – Feb. 27, 1798; Mar. 20, 1801 – Dec. 28, 1802; 1804; Mar. 5, 1806 – Feb. 28, 1807; Mar. 4, 1807 — Feb., 1808; Mar., 1809 – May 28, 1810 (scat'g); Feb. 28, 1811 – Sept. 14, 1812, GAHS. (A few at DER.) Aug. 13, 1799 – July 6, 1803, AAS. 1803, SAVNEWSOF. Oct. 20, 1807, HU.

*Federal Republican Advocate* (and Commercial Advertiser). Sept. 21, 1807, AAS. Oct. 5, 22, 1807, GAHS. Oct. 8 – Dec. 31, 1807; Jan. 4, Feb. 1, 1808, UN'YGA.

*Georgia Gazette.* Jan. 1, 1785 – Nov. 18, 1802 (scat'g), GAHS. Apr. 28, 1785, Oct. 14, 1786 – June 23, 1787 (scat'g), Nov. 6, 1798, DER. Jan. 29, Feb. 5, 19, Apr. 9, 16, May 28, June 4, 11, 25, July 9, 1795; Oct. 20 – Nov. 24, 1796, HU.

*Georgia Journal* (; and Independent Federal Register). Dec. 4, 1793 – Feb. 19, 1794 (a few), GAHS.

*Georgia Republican* (& State Intelligencer). Dec. 15, 1802, Jan. 1 – Dec. 18, 1803 (very few); Jan. 3 – Dec. 24, 1804 (scat'g); Jan. 10 – May 13 (scat'g), Oct. 25, Dec. 17, 1805; Jan. 3 – Dec. 30, 1806; Jan. 2, 12, 20, Feb. 6 – Mar. 6, 1807, GAHS. Jan. 3 – Apr., Oct. – Dec., 1804; Oct. – Nov. 1, 5, 8, 19, Dec. 3, 20, 24, 31, 1805; Jan. 3 – 31, Sept. 5 – Oct. 24, Dec. 2, 5, 16, 1806; Jan. 6 – Feb. 20, 1807, UN'YGA.

*Georgian* (Daily Georgian). May 1 – Aug. 14, 1821; Mar. 10 – Aug. 31, 1822; Nov. 25, 1822 – Feb. 1, 1823; Mar. 1 – Apr. 10, Nov. 23 – Dec. 31, 1823; Jan. 1 – June 1, 1824; May 2 – June 10, 1825, GAHS.

*Georgian for the Country.* July 6 – Dec. 31, 1822, UN'YGA.

*Public Intelligencer.* Apr. 9 – Nov. 10, 1807, HU. Apr. 18, 21, 23, 25; May 7, 9, 12, 21, 30, June 2, 4, 6, 16, 20, 30, July 7, 14, 24, 28, Aug. 7, 11, 21, Sept. 8, Nov. 27, 1807; Mar. 15, 22, 26, July 12, 22, 29, Aug. 23, Sept. 2, 9, 27, Oct. 7, 18, AAS. Aug. 14, 1807 – Feb. 3, 1809, GAHS.

*Republican and Savannah Evening Ledger* (Savannah Republican; Daily Savannah Republican; Savannah Daily Republican). Mar. 10 – Dec. 26, 1807; Jan. 2 – Dec. 31, 1808; Jan. 5 – Dec. 30, 1809; Jan. 2 – Dec. 29, 1810; Jan. 1 – Aug. 3, 1811; Mar. 12 – Dec. 31, 1822; Apr. 1 – May 1, Nov. 29, Dec. 22, 1823, UN'YGA.

Mar. 19 - Dec. 15, 1807 (scat'g), HU. 1807–1810; Jan. 2, 1812 – Mar. 4, 1813, GAHS. Jan. 15 – July 13, 1811; Jan. – Aug. 10, 1812, July 3 – Aug. 30, 1821; Jan. 1 – Mar. 12, 1822, LC.

*Southern Patriot* (Patriot and Commercial Advertiser). 1804–1807 (scat'g), HU. Jan. 31, Feb. 6, Mar. 10, 24, 1806; May 6, 20, 1818, AAS. Jan. 28, Feb. 24, July 21, Aug. 4, 1806 – July 20, 1807, GAHS.

*Sparta*

*Farmer's Gazette*. June 3, 1803 – Nov. 2, 1806 (scat'g); May 2, 1807, HU. June 17, Sept. 16, Oct. 28, 1803; Aug. 16, 1806; Mar. 7, May 23, 1807, AAS. Aug. 16, 1806 – Aug. 31, 1807 (scat'g), UN'YGA.

*Washington*

*Friend and Monitor*. Jan. 13 – Dec. 22, 1815, GAHS.

*Monitor*. Sept. 28, 1805, HU. Dec. 30, 1809 – Dec. 8, 1810, GAHS. July 3, Aug. 4, Dec. 8, 15, 1810; Jan. 26, Mar. 2, Apr. 13, 20, 1811; Apr. 3, Oct. 9, 1813; Mar. 5, May 21, July 2, Aug. 6, 1814; Feb. 23, 1816; Apr. 4, 1817; Apr. 9, 1819, AAS.

## MARYLAND

*Annapolis*

*Maryland Gazette*. Jan. 5, 1769 – Dec. 30, 1790; May 17, 1798 – May 1, Oct. 30 – Dec. 25, 1800; Dec. 9, 1802 – Jan. 20, 1803; Dec. 14, 1815 – Jan. 25, 1816; 1820, MDSTL. May 19, 1785 – Dec. 27, 1787 (scat'g); Jan. 22, 1789 – Sept. 18, 1794 (scat'g), AAS. Jan. 7 – Dec. 30 (a few missing), 1790; Jan. 7 – Dec. 28, 1797; Jan. – May 10, 1798, LC. Jan. 13, 1791; Mar. 15, 1792; Jan. 2, 1794; Jan., 1796, MDHS. Sept. 19, 26, 1793, LCPHIL. Mar. 5, 12, May 28, June 11, 18, 25, July 2, 16, Aug. 13, 1795 – Sept. 21, 1796 (scat'g); Oct. 19, 1797 – Feb. 28, 1799 (scat'g), HU.

*Maryland Republican* (Same and Political and Agricultural Museum). June 22 – Aug. 5, Dec., 1809; Oct. 12 – Dec. 6, 1811; June 10 – Sept. 30, 1812; July 3 – Dec. 25, 1813; Feb. 12 – Apr. 2, June 18 – July 16, 1814; May 1 – Oct. 7, Nov. 18, 1815 – Mar. 2, 1816; Jan. 4 – Sept. 23, Nov. 1 – Dec. 30, 1817; 1818 and 1819 (parts), MDHS.

*Baltimore*

*American* (and Daily Advertiser; same, and Commercial Daily Advertiser). May 18, 1799 – Dec. 30, 1810 (scat'g); Nov. 12, and an undated issue, 1813; Dec. 14, 15, 1814; July 10, Dec. 29, 30, 1815; Nov. 22, 1819, AAS. Oct. 1, 6, 20, 22, 27, 1804; July 2, 1805, HU. Apr. 8 – 14, 1818; Oct. 26 – Nov. 16, 1819; Nov. 20 – Dec. 29, 1820, LC.

*American Farmer*. 1819–1825 (a few missing), LC.

## NEWSPAPERS CONSULTED

*American Patriot.* Nov. 20, 27, 1802, AAS.

*Baltimore Daily Intelligencer.* Oct. 28, 1793 – Feb. 28, 1794, NYHS. Oct. 28, 1793 – Oct. 29, 1794, LC. Oct. 30 – Dec. 30, 1794, PIL. Oct. 31, 1798 – Jan. 26, 1799, HU.

*Baltimore Daily Repository.* Oct. 25, 1791 – June 30, 1792; Apr. 29 – Oct. 19, 1793, LC. Feb. 17 – Dec. 19, 1792, HSP. July 3 – Dec. 31, 1792; Jan. 1 – June 8, 1793 (all scat'g), AAS. Sept. 16 – Oct. 1, 1793, LCPHIL.

*Baltimore Evening Post* (: and Daily Advertiser). Sept. 27, Oct. 3, Dec. 15, 1792; Jan. 11, 12, 14, Mar. 2, Apr. 25, 27, July 18, 19, 20, 1793, AAS. Sept. 17, 18, 19, 21, 24, 26, 28, 30, 1793, LCPHIL.

*Baltimore Evening Post* (Mercantile Daily Advertiser). June 25 – Dec. 26, 1805 (scat'g), HU. Feb. 14, 1810, AAS.

*Baltimore Telegraph* (and Mercantile Advertiser). June 23, July 30, Oct. 20, 22, 26, 31, Nov. 3–30 (scat'g); Dec. 1–31, 1814 (scat'g); Jan. 25, Apr. 18, 1815, NYHS.

*Baltimore Telegraphe* (City Gazette and Daily Telegraphe; Telegraphe and Daily Advertiser). May 14, 1795 – Dec. 29, 1802 (scat'g), AAS. July, 1797 – June 30, 1798, PIL. Nov. 2 – Dec. 24, 1802; Oct. 4–30, 1804; June 11 – Dec. 31, 1805; Sept. 7, 1806, HU.

*Dunlap's Maryland Gazette* (; or the Baltimore General Advertiser). May 2, 1775 – July 16, 1776, MDHS.

*Edwards's Baltimore Daily Advertiser.* Oct. 21, 1793, LCPHIL. Oct. 29, 31, Nov. 14, Dec. 24, 30, 31, 1793; Jan. 8, 9, 29, 30, Feb. 25, Apr. 21, 24, 30, May 1, July 16, 18, Aug. 18, 19, Oct. 3, 4, 1794, AAS.

*Federal Gazette* (& Baltimore Daily Advertiser). Jan. 1, 1796 – Dec., 1800, LC. Jan. – June, 1796; Sept. 25 – Dec. 29, 1797, NYHS. Jan. 1 – May 16, 1801 (a few); Feb. 8, Aug. 21, Nov. 11, 1806, AAS. Sept. 16 – 20, 1799, AAS. Dec. 26, 1814; Jan. 25, July 18, 1815; Aug. 28, 1818, AAS. 1815, MDHS.

*Federal Intelligencer* (Same and Baltimore Daily Gazette). Oct. 30, 1794 – Sept. 30, 1795, LC.

*Federal Republican* (& Commercial Gazette; same and Baltimore Telegraph). Mar. 24 – May 29, 1809; (for the country) 1810 – 1812; Feb. 21 – Mar. 13, 1817; Apr. 4 – May 3, 1818 (some few missing), LC.

*Fell's-Point Telegraphe.* Mar. 6, 9, May 13, 1795, HU.

*Maryland Censor.* Aug. 19, 1818 – Jan. 20, 1819 (scat'g), AAS.

*Maryland Gazette* (, and Baltimore General Advertiser). Apr. 29, 1785; Jan. 31, Mar. 24, 1786 – Aug. 17, 1787 (scat'g), AAS. May 24, 1785 – May 19, 1786, NYPL. 1787 (scat'g), LC.

*Maryland Journal* (, and the Baltimore Advertiser; same and Baltimore Universal Daily Advertiser; same & Baltimore Daily Advertiser). Aug. 20, 1773 – Aug. 23, 1775; Feb. 10, 1778 – Dec. 15, 1779 (scat'g); Jan. 4 – Apr. 29, 1785 – 1789 (some); 1793 – May 16, July 22 – Aug. 5, 1796; Feb. 8–16, 1797, MDHS. Jan. 24 – Dec. 29, 1786; Jan. 2 – Dec. 28, 1787; Jan. 1 – Dec. 30, 1788; Jan. 6 – Dec. 29, 1789; Jan. 1 – Dec. 31, 1790; Jan. 4, 1791 – Dec. 25, 1792; Jan. 1 – Dec. 18, 1793; Jan. 29 –

Nov. 25, 1794; Jan. 15, Oct. 13, 1795, LC. Jan. 13, 1792 – Dec. 27, 1793 – Jan. 10, 1797 (scat'g), AAS.

*Mechanics' Gazette, and Merchants' Daily Advertiser.* Mar. 14, 29, Apr. 27, May 17, 18, July 12, 1815, AAS.

*Morning Chronicle & Baltimore Advertiser.* Apr. 8, May 19, 1819; Nov. 16, 1820, AAS.

*Patriot* (Baltimore . . . & Evening Advertiser; same & Mercantile Advertiser). June 1–30, Nov. 19, 1814 – Jan. 16, May 1 – 22, June 20 – 28, 1815; Mar. 27, Apr. 7, 19, 21, May 1, 18, 19, 20, 24, 25, 27, 29, June 2, 3, 26, July 9, 1817; Apr. 1–16, 1818; Oct. 11 – Nov. 14, 1819; Nov. 18 – Dec. 19, 1820, MDHS.

*Political Examiner & Public Advertiser.* Oct. 13 – Dec. 8, 1819; Aug. 2, 24, 31, Sept. 6 – Dec. 20, 1820 (some missing); 1821–1823, LC.

*Republican* (; or, Anti-Democrat). May 17–26 – Oct. 1, 4–20, 1802; Feb. 14 – Nov. 9, 1803 (scat'g), AAS. Apr. 13 – June 25, 1802, HU.

*Whig* (, or Political Telescope; Baltimore Whig). Nov. 23, 1812 – Jan. 15, 1813, LC. Feb. 13, July 24, Oct. 28, Nov. 16, 18, Dec. 8, 1813, AAS.

*Easton*

*Easton General Advertiser.* Jan. 15, 1819 – Mar. 7, Aug. 22 – Sept. 26, Oct. 10, Nov. 21, 1820, LC.

*Maryland Herald* (, and Eastern Shore Intelligencer; Herald and Eastern Shore Intelligencer). May 18, 1790 – July 16, 1793 (scat'g), AAS.

*People's Monitor.* 1809 – 1815 (scat'g), HU.

*Republican Star* (or Eastern Shore General Advertiser; same or [and] General Advertiser). Sept. 7, 1802 – May 17, 1803; Sept. 2, 1806 – Jan. 27, 1807, MDHS.

*Elizabethtown*

*Maryland Herald* (, and Elizabeth-Town Advertiser; same, and Elizabeth-town Weekly Advertiser). Mar. 2, 1797 – Mar. 29, 1798–1799, MDHS. Apr. 5, 1798 – Feb. 19, 1801 – 1805 (scat'g), HU.

*Washington Spy.* Aug. 26, 1790 – Jan. 18, 1797, MDHS. Mar. 10, 1795, HU.

*Fredericktown*

*Bartgis's Federal Gazette* (, or the Frederick-Town and County, Weekly Advertiser; same, or the Frederick County Weekly Advertiser). Feb. 26, Mar. 12, June 11, 1795; Jan. 7 – Aug. 4, 1796 (a few); Aug. 28, 1799; Feb. 12, Apr. 23, 1800, HU. Jan. 23, 1799, AAS.

*Bartgis's Republican Gazette* (, and General Advertiser; Republican Gazette and General Advertiser). June 17, 1801; Jan. 21, Feb. 18, 25, Mar. 18, Oct. 28, Nov. 18, Dec. 9, 1803; Mar. 2, Aug. 10, 1804; Jan. 18, Feb. 1, 1805; Mar. 7, July 1, 1806; Mar. 4, 1809; May 26, 1810; Apr. 10, 1813; Dec. 31, 1814; Feb. 13, May 22, 1819, AAS.

Oct. 29, Nov. 5, 12, 19, Dec. 3, 17, 24, 31, 1802; Jan. 7 – Oct. 28, 1803; Apr. 1 – Dec. 28, 1804 (scat'g); June 14, 1805 – Apr. 24, 1807, HU. Jan. 7, 1807 – June 23, 1810 (scat'g); Aug. 11 – Dec. 28, 1811; 1819, 1820, beginning and end of 1821, MDHS.

*Frederick-Town Herald.* June 19 – Dec. 25, 1802; Mar. 19 – Apr. 30, Sept. 3 – Dec. 31, 1803 (a few missing); Mar. 10, 1804 – Apr. 11, 1807 (a few), AAS. Nov. 29, 1806 – Jan. 3, 1807, BA. Apr. 7, Nov. 10, 1804, HU.

*Hornet* (; or, Republican Advocate). June 29, Nov. 9, 1802; Mar. 15, June 21, July 5, Sept. 13, Oct. 4, Nov. 22, 1803; Mar. 6, 1804; Apr. 9, Dec. 3, 1805; July 12, 1809; Jan. 17, July 4, Nov. 14, 1810; Dec. 22, 1813; Mar. 23, Apr. 5, 27, 29, 1814, AAS. Oct. 12, 1802; Dec. 13, 1803; Jan. 17, Feb. 7, Apr. 24, May 1, 15, 29, June 19, 26, July 3, 10, 17, 24, 31, Aug. 7, 21, 28, Sept. 4, 25, Nov. 6, 13, 20, Dec. 11, 18, 1804; Jan. 1, July 11, 1805, HU. Jan. 13, 1807, BA. July 21, 1813 – July 6, 1814, LC.

*Independent American Volunteer.* July 8, 15, Aug. 19, 26, 1807, AAS.

*Maryland Chronicle* (, or the Universal Advertiser). June 17, 1787 – May 28, 1788, AAS.

*Maryland Gazette* (, and Frederick Weekly Advertiser). Dec. 11, 18, 25, 1790, AAS.

*Plain Dealer* (& Political Intelligencer). May 25, 1814, HU. July 29, Aug. 9, 19, Sept. 30, 1813, AAS.

*Political Examiner.* Aug. 9, 18, Oct. 15, 1813, HU. Aug. 9, 1813 – Dec. 27, 1815, AAS.

*Republican Advocate.* Dec. 6, 1802 – Dec. 30, 1803; 1804, LC. June 14 – Dec. 27, 1805 (scat'g), HU.

*Rights of Man.* Mar. 4, May 13, 27, June 3, 10, 17, July 1, 29, Aug. 5, 1795, HU.

*Star of Federalism.* June 26, 1818 – Aug. 27, 1819 (scat'g), MDHS.

## NEW JERSEY

### *Bridgetown*

*Apollo, and Bridgetown Weekly Miscellany.* June 21 – Nov. 20, 1804, HU.

### *Chatham*

*New Jersey Journal.* July 30 – Oct. 23, 1782, NJHS. Feb. 27, Mar. 20, Apr. 10, Aug. 28, Sept. 11, 18, Nov. 27, 1782; Jan. 1, Mar. 12, 26, 1783, LC.

### *Elizabeth Town*

*New Jersey Journal* (, and Political Intelligencer). Mar. 8, Nov. 8, 1786; May 26, June 9, 1790; June 5, 1793; Jan. 1 – Dec. 26, 1794; Jan. 7, 1795 – Dec. 26, 1797; Jan. 2, 1798 – Dec. 30, 1800; Jan. 6, 1801 – Oct. 28, 1802, NJHS. Oct. 18, Nov. 22, 1786 – Jan., 1787; Jan. 6 – Mar. 17, 1790, NJSTL. 1789 (some missing); 1791 – Jan. 2 – Dec. 25, 1793 (scat'g), LC. June 1, 29, Nov. 2, 9, 16, 23, 30, Dec. 7, 14, 21, 28, 1796; Jan. 4, 11, 18, 25, Feb. 1, 8, 15, 22, Mar. 1, 8, 15, 22, 29, Apr. 12, 19, 26, May 3, 1797; Dec. 20, 1803 – Dec. 3, 1805 (scat'g); Jan. 21 – Nov. 18, 1806 (a few); Nov. 3, 1807; Sept. 27, 1808, HU.

*Morristown*

*Genius of Liberty* (, and Morris Advertiser). Feb. 28, Mar. 14, 1799; Oct. 9, 23, Dec. 11 – 25, 1800; Jan. 1, 1801, NJHS. Oct. 14, 1803 – Mar. 28, 1805 (scat'g); July 25, 1805, HU.

*Newark*

*Centinel of Freedom.* Oct. 5, 1796 – Dec. 30, 1800 (scat'g); Aug. 18, 1801 – Aug. 30, 1802, NJHS. Mar. 6, 20, Apr. 17 (supplement), 1798; Mar. 19, 26, Apr. 16, 23, 30, May 14, 21, 28, June 4, 11, July 9, 16, 23, 30, Aug. 20, Sept. 10, Dec. 31, 1799, May 13, 1800, AAS. Jan. 7, 1800 – Sept. 22, 1801, NYHS. Aug. – Dec., 1802, NYPL. May 8 – June 11, July 2 – Dec. 31, 1805; Jan. 7 – July 29, 1806, HU.

*Newark Gazette* (and New-Jersey Advertiser; Woods's same). Oct. 2, 1793 – May, 1796; Dec. 7, 1796 – Nov. 1, 1797; Nov. 28, 1797 – Aug. 6, 1798 – 1801, NJHS. Mar. 12 – Sept. 3, Oct. 29, 1794; May 11 – Dec. 7, 1796, LC. July 12, 1798, NJSTL. Apr. 19, Oct. 25, Dec. 5, 26, 1797, Jan. 15, 29, Feb. 5, 19, 1799; Jan. 2 – May 27, 1800 (a few missing); Mar. 20, 1804, AAS.

*New Jersey Telescope.* Nov. 8, 1808 – May 23, 1809, NJHS. Nov. 18, 1808, HU.

*New Brunswick*

*Fredonian.* June 26, 1811 – Mar. 27, 1817; Apr. 16, 1817 – Sept. 24, 1818, RUTGERSCL.

*Guardian* (; or, New-Brunswick Advertiser). Jan. 5, 1796 – Oct. 23, 1798 (two missing); Oct. 25, 1804 – Dec. 26, 1805; Jan. 2, 1806 – Nov. 26, 1807, RUTGERSCL. Nov. 8, 22, 29, Dec. 6, 13, 20, 1796; Jan. 10, 17, 24, 31, Feb. 7, 14, 21, 28, Mar. 14, 21, 28, Apr. 4, 11, 18, 25, May 3, 1797; Jan. 14 – Dec. 17, 1800 (a few); Jan. 22 – Dec. 31, 1801 (scat'g); May 31 – Oct. 18, 1804 (a few); Aug. 6, Sept. 3, 1807, HU. Jan. 8, 1799 – Dec. 24, 1800, LC. May 4, 1803; Aug. 21, 28, Nov. 6, 13, 20, 1806; Jan. 8, Feb. 5, 1807, AAS.

*New Brunswick Gazette* (, and Weekly Monitor). Oct. 5, 1786; July 10, 1787 – Apr. 14, 1789, NJHS. June 21 – Dec. 27, 1791 (a few); Jan. 3 – Apr. 24, 1792, LC.

*Trenton*

*Federalist* (, New-Jersey Gazette; same & New-Jersey State Gazette; Trenton Federalist). July 9, 1798 – Mar. 10, June 16, 1801; Jan. 5 – Mar. 16, Apr. 20 – May 11, Sept. 6 – Dec. 27, 1802, NJSTL.

*Federal Post.* Aug. 5, 1788 – Jan. 27, 1789 (scat'g), NJSTL.

*New Jersey Gazette.* May 29 – Oct. 2, 1782; Jan. 1 – July 2, 1783; Aug. 9, 1784 – Sept. 26, Oct., 1785 – Nov. 27, 1786 (scat'g), LC. July 10 – Dec. 16, 1783 – Dec. 5, 1785; Dec. 12, 1785 – Nov. 27, 1786, YU. Dec. 16, 1783 – Dec. 5, 1785; Dec. 12, 1785 – Nov. 27, 1786, NYHS.

*New Jersey State Gazette* (State Gazette; State Gazette, & New Jersey Advertiser). May 31, 1792 – Mar. 13, 1793; June 4, 1794 – Dec. 26, 1798, NJHS. Feb. 17, Apr. 12, May 12, 26 – Aug. 11, Oct. 13, 1795; Jan. 19 – May 17, June 7 – July 5, Aug. 2 – 30, Sept. 27, 1796; Jan. 3 – 7, 24 – July 3, 1798 (scat'g), LC.

*True American.* Mar. 10, 1801 – Dec. 27, 1802; Jan. 3, 1803 – Dec. 31, 1804; Jan. 7 – Dec. 30, 1805, NJStL. Feb. 6, 1804 – Dec. 30, 1805; Jan. 13 – Dec. 22, 1806; Mar. 9 – Dec. 14, 1807; Oct. 3, Nov. 7, 21, Dec. 12, 19, 1808, HU.

## NEW YORK

### *Albany*

*Albany Register.* 1798–1799, NYPL.

## NORTH CAROLINA

### *Edenton*

*Edenton Gazette* (, and North-Carolina Advertiser; same, and North-Carolina General Advertiser). Nov. 5, 1807 – Mar. 30, 1808; Nov. 3, 1809 – Mar. 23, 1810; Dec. 21, 1810 – Mar. 15, 1811; Dec. 22, 1812 – Mar. 16, 1813, NCStL.

*Edenton Intelligencer.* Apr. 9 – June 4, 1788, LC.

*Herald of Freedom.* Mar. 27, May 1, 1799, HU.

*Post-Angel* (, or Universal Entertainment). Nov. 12, 1800, LC.

*State Gazette of North-Carolina.* Sept. 8, 1788; June 10 – Nov. 11, 1791 (scat'g); Mar. 30, 1792; May 11, 25, June 1, Aug. 17, Sept. 21, Oct. 12, 1793; Jan. 4, 31, Feb. 7, May 2, 1794; Feb. 19 – Dec. 24, 1795 (scat'g); Jan. 14 – Dec. 29, 1796 (some missing); Jan. 5 – Dec. 21, 1797 (some missing); Jan. 18 – Aug. 29 (scat'g), Oct. 31, Dec. 26, 1798; Jan. 2, 23, 30, Feb. 6, 20, 1799, AAS. Oct. 20, 27, Nov. 3, 10, 17, Dec. 1, 22, 29, 1796; Jan. 5, 12, 19, 26, Feb. 16, 23, Mar. 9, 16, 23, 30, Apr. 13, 20, 1797, HU.

### *Fayetteville*

*Fayetteville Gazette.* Aug. 7, Sept. 25 – Nov. 6, 27, Dec. 11, 1792; Jan. 1, Mar. 5, 12, May 21, 28, June 4, Nov. 19, 1793, AAS.

*North-Carolina Centinel.* July 25 – Aug. 15, 29, 1795, LC. Aug. 8, 15, 29, Dec., 1795; Apr. 30 – Oct. 1, 1796 (scat'g), HU.

*North-Carolina Chronicle.* Feb. 1, May 10, 24, 31, June 7, July 19, 1790, AAS.

*North-Carolina Minerva* (, and Fayetteville Advertiser). Mar. 31, 1796 – Dec. 15, 1798 (a few), HU. Nov. 17, 1798, AAS.

### *Halifax*

*North-Carolina Journal.* Aug. 1, 1792 – Dec. 7, 1795; Jan. 4, 1796 – May 6, 1799, LC. Jan. 7, 1805 – Dec. 29, 1806, U'YNC.

### *Hillsborough*

*Hillsborough Recorder.* Jan. 2 – Mar. 27, 1822, U'YNC.

# MASON LOCKE WEEMS

*Newbern*

*Carolina Centinel.* Mar. 28, 1818 – Mar. 6, 1819; Jan. 13 – Sept. 29, 1821, LC.

*Carolina Federal Republican.* Jan. 4, 1812 – Dec. 25, 1813, LC.

*Newbern Gazette* (and Political and Miscellaneous Register). Nov. 24, Dec. 1, 15, 22, 29, 1798; Jan. 12, 26, Feb. 2, 9, 16, 23, July 2, 1799; May 23, Aug. 15, 1800, LC.

*North Carolina Circular* (, and Newbern Weekly Advertiser). Oct. 28, Dec. 16, 1803; Aug. 10, 24, Sept. 28, Oct. 3, Nov. 23, Dec. 7, 21, 1804; Mar. 8, 15, 1805, HU.

*North-Carolina Gazette* (Martin's same). Jan. 4, 1794, AAS. Oct. 22 – Dec. 31, 1796 (scat'g); Jan. 7 – Apr. 15, 1797 (scat'g), HU. July 11, Aug. 15, Dec. 19, 1787; Apr. 1, 15, 1790, AAS.

*True Republican* (and Newbern Weekly Advertiser). Apr. 2, 1810 – Aug. 7, 1811 (scat'g), AAS.

*Raleigh*

*Minerva* (; or, Anti-Jacobin; Raleigh Minerva). Jan. 4, 1803 – Dec. 31, 1804, LC. May 2, 1803 – Mar. 26, 1804 (scat'g), HU. Oct. 26, 1809 – Mar. 1, 1810, NCStL.

*North-Carolina Minerva* (, and Raleigh Advertiser). Dec. 17, 1799; Jan. 5, 1802 – Apr. 18, 1803, HU.

*Raleigh Register* (, and North-Carolina Weekly Advertiser; same, and North-Carolina State Gazette; same, and North-Carolina Gazette). Jan. 5 – Nov. 30, 1802 (some missing); Jan. 4 – Dec. 26, 1803; Jan. 9 – Apr. 23, 1804; Jan. 7 – June 10, 1805 (scat'g), HU. Jan. 25 – Sept. 7, 1803; Jan. 23 – Aug. 27, 1804; Jan. 7, 1805 – Dec. 29, 1806; Sept. 3, 1807 – Mar. 31, 1808; Jan. 5, 1809 – May 31, 1810; Jan. 3 – May 17, 1811; Dec. 25, 1812 – Mar. 5, 1813; Jan. 4 – Mar. 25, 1822, NCStL. Jan. 4 – Feb. 22, 1822; May 27 – July 12, 1823, LC.

*Star* (, and North-Carolina State Gazette). Feb. 2, 1809 – May 10, 1810 (scat'g); July 5 – Nov. 29, 1811; Apr. 16 – May 21, 1813. Indices, 1809, 1810, NCStL.

*Salisbury*

*North-Carolina Mercury* (, and Salisbury Advertiser). Jan. 29, 1801, LC.

*Washington*

*American Recorder.* June 2, 1815; Aug. 23, Sept. 13, Dec. 13, 1816; 1824 and 1825 (very few), LC.

*Wilmington*

*Hall's Wilmington Gazette.* Feb. 9, 16, Mar. 2, 23 – Apr. 6, 20, June 8, Sept. 7, 28 – Oct. 12, 26 – Nov. 3, 1797; Feb. 8, 22, Mar. 8, 29, Apr. 12, May 31, June 21, Aug. 30, Oct. 11, Nov. 15, 29, 1798, HU.

*True Republican* (, or American Whig). June 20, July 4, Nov. 7, 1809, AAS.

*Wilmington Centinel* (, and General Advertiser). June 18, 1788, AAS.

*Wilmington Chronicle* (, and North-Carolina Weekly Advertiser). July 3, 10, 17, 31, Sept. 24, Oct. 22, 1795; Feb. 4, Apr. 14, Aug. 4, 1796, HU.

NEWSPAPERS CONSULTED

*Wilmington Gazette* (; Commercial and Political). May 29 – Aug. 14, 1800; Feb. 4, 1802 – Feb. 3, 1803 (some missing); Feb. 10 – Dec. 27, 1803; Jan. 10 – Dec. 25, 1804 (scat'g); Jan. 1 – Dec. 17, 1805 (scat'g), HU. Feb. 7, 28, Mar. 6, 1804; Apr. 15, 22, 29, June 3, July 8, 1806, AAS.

## PENNSYLVANIA

### *Carlisle*

*American Volunteer*. Apr. 4 – July 3, 1816; Feb. 6 – May 1, 1817, HU.

*Carlisle Gazette* (and the Western Repository of Knowledge; Kline's Carlisle Weekly Gazette). Jan. 2 – Dec. 25, 1793, NYHS. Apr. 1 – Aug. 31, 1803; Aug. 9, 1805 – Jan. 31, 1806, HU. Jan., 1809; Apr. 3 – Sept. 25, 1816; Jan. 1 – May 5, 1817, HSDC.

*Carlisle Herald*. Aug. 11, 1802 – Aug. 22, 1822 (a few), AAS. 1816, HL.

*Cumberland Register*. Sept. 20, 1805 – Feb., 1806, HU. Sept. 20, 1805 – Mar. 4, 1806–1813, LC. July 11, 18, 1810, AAS.

*Telegraphe*. Feb. 10, 17, Mar. 3, 10, 24, June 2, 16, 20, July 14, 28, 1795, HU.

### *Chambersburg*

*Chambersburg Gazette*. June 18, July 30, Aug. 20, Sept. 3, Nov. 19, 1795; Feb. 18, Mar. 17, 24, 31, Apr. 7, 1796, HU.

*Democratic Republican* (and Pennsylvania Advertiser). Nov. 7, 14, 21 – Dec. 26, 1815; 1816; 1817, AAS.

*Franklin Repository*. Feb. 18, Apr. 1, 8, June 10, 1817, FROF.

### *Easton*

*American Eagle*. May 17, June 14, 21, Aug. 2, 1799, HU.

### *Gettysburg*

*Adams Centinel*. Sept. 9, 30, 1801, AAS. Apr. 6 – June 15, 1803; Sept., 1805 – Dec., 1806; July 3 – Sept., 1816; Jan. 1 – May 28, 1817, GTOF. Feb. 9, Apr. 26, May 3, July 5, Dec. 13, 1820; Feb. 7, 1821, NJHS.

*Republican Compiler*. Dec. 16, 1818; July 21, 28, Sept. 1, 29, Oct. 13, Nov. 3, Dec. 15, 22, 1819; Feb. 9, Mar. 8, 22, Apr. 26, May 3, July 5, Dec. 13, 1820; Feb. 7, 1821, NJHS.

*Sprig of Liberty*. Aug. 31, 1804, HU.

### *Harrisburg*

*Chronicle* (or Harrisburgh Visitor; Harrisburg Chronicle). July 1 – Nov. 4, 1816; Jan. 6 – May 19, Nov. 10 – Dec. 1, 1817; Jan. 6 – May 12, 1821, PStL. Feb. 17, Mar. 10, 31, Apr. 14, 21, May 12, 1817, NYHS.

*Dauphin Guardian.* Apr. 19, May 3, 1808; Jan. 10, Aug. 15, Oct. 10, Dec. 12, 1809; Feb. 20, May 29, Sept. 4, 1810; Mar. 5, 12, 26, Oct. 22, 1811, NYHS. Dec. 3, 1808 – Feb. 28, 1809, PStL.

*Farmers Instructor* (and Harrisburgh Courant). Jan. 8 – Apr. 30, 1800; Mar. 3 – May 5, 1802, PStL.

*Harrisburger Morgenröthe* (Unpartheyische Harrisburg Morgenröthe Zeitung; Die Harrisburger Morgenröthe Zeitung). Mar. 12, 1799 – Dec. 26, 1801; Apr. 3, 1802; Jan. 1 – Dec. 31, 1803; Jan. 7 – Feb. 18, Sept. 29 – Nov. 10, 1804; Sept. 7 – Dec. 28, 1805; Jan. 4, 1806 – Dec. 10, 1808; Dec. 17, 1811 – Feb. 25, 1812, PStL. Feb. 6 – Nov. 20, 1802, LC.

*Harrisburg Republican.* Dec. 17, 1816 – Jan. 30, 1818, NYHS. Sept. 29 – Nov. 3, 1820. PStL.

*Oracle of Dauphin* (and Harrisburgh Advertiser). Dec. 20, 1802 – Feb. 28, 1803; Nov. 24, 1804 – Mar. 28, 1805, NYHS. Nov. 16, 1801 – Apr. 26, 1802; Mar. 7 – July 18, 1803 – Aug. 3 (some missing), 1805, LC. Sept. 19 – Oct. 3, 1803; Jan. 14 – Feb. 4, Sept. 2 – Oct. 13, 1804; Dec. 31, 1808 – Feb. 11, 1809, PStL. Dec. 4, 1813; Nov. 11, 18, 1815; June 1, 1816; Mar. 2, 1822; Apr. 10, 1824, NJHS.

*Pennsylvania Republican.* Mar. 5 – Oct. 29, 1816, PStL.

### *Lancaster*

*Americanische Staatsbothe* (und Lancaster Anzeigs-Nachrichten; same, und Lancaster Wochenschrift). Jan. 29, 1800 – Dec. 30, 1801; Jan. 6 – Dec. 29, 1802; Feb. 23 – Oct. 26, 1803; Jan. 4 – Dec. 26, 1804; Jan. 1 – Dec. 31, 1806, LCHS. May 10, Nov. 18, 1801; Apr. 14, June 16, 1802; Apr. 6, June 1, Nov. 16, Dec. 7, 1803; Mar. 21, Apr. 25, Nov. 21, 1804; May 29, 1805; June 9, Aug. 18, 1813; Nov. 30, 1814; Sept. 20, Feb. 1, May 3, July 19, Dec. 20, 1815; Jan. 31, May 29, 1816; Apr. 30, June 25, Dec. 3, 31, 1817; Jan. 7, Mar. 18, July 22, Aug. 12, 1818; Mar. 17, May 19, Sept. 1, 1819, NYHS. Feb. 17, Mar. 24, Sept. 29, Nov. 17, 1802; Jan. 19, 26, Feb. 16, 23, Apr. 20, 27, May 4, July 6, 27, Sept. 28, 1803; Jan. 4, 11, Aug. 22, Oct. 24, Dec. 26, 1804; Jan. 16, Feb. 20, July 3, Sept. 18, 1805; Feb. 28, Apr. 24, July 3, Aug. 7, Nov. 13, Dec. 18, 1816; Feb. 5, May 22, June 11, Dec. 10, 1817, AAS. Sept. 4 – Nov. 27, 1805, LC. Jan. 1 – Feb. 12, 1806, HSP.

*Constitutional Democrat.* July 23, 1805; July 15, Aug. 5, 1806; Nov. 10, Dec. 1, 1807, AAS.

*Deutsche Porcupein.* Aug. 15, Dec. 26, 1798, NYHS.

*Free Press.* June 29 – Dec. 28, 1820, HSP. Oct. 5 – Nov. 2, 1820, HSDC.

*Hive.* May 31, 1797 – May 23, 1798, LCHS. June 22, 29, July 6, 20, Aug. 3, 10, Dec. 21, 1803; Jan. 4, 11, 18, Feb. 1, 8, 15, 22, May 2, 16, 23, 30, June 6, July 4, 11, Aug. 1, 8, 22, 29, Oct. 10, 17, 21, 28, Dec. 5, 7, 12, 26, 1804; Jan. 2, 16, 23, Feb. 20, May 22, 29, 1805, NYHS. June 22, 1803 – May 15, 1805; May 26 – Oct. 23, 1810, LC.

## NEWSPAPERS CONSULTED

*Intelligencer* (& Weekly Advertiser). July 31, 1799 – Nov. 1, 1803; Dec. 20, 1803 – July 8, 1815; Feb. 10, 1816 – Jan. 24, 1818 (scat'g); July 10, 1819 – Feb. 15, 1823, LIOF. Sept. 23 – Dec. 30, 1802; Apr. 5 – July 26, 1803, PStL. 1803–1805 (a few), LCHS. Sept. 10 – Dec. 17, 1805, HSP. Sept. 10 – Nov. 26, 1805 (scat'g), HU.

*Lancaster Correspondent.* Mar. 5 – Sept. 6, 1803, LCHS.

*Lancaster Journal.* June 17, 1795 – June 10, 1796; Mar. 10 – June 10, Aug. 12 – Oct. 28, 1797; Mar. 12 – Oct. 8, 1803; Aug. 23 – Nov. 29, 1805; Dec. 9, 1808 – Mar. 5, 1809; July 1 – Nov. 1, 1816; Jan. 3 – May 2, Oct. 27 – Dec. 8, 1817; Sept. 8 – Nov. 10, 1820, LIOF.

*Pennsylvania Gazette.* Aug. 12 – Dec. 31, 1817, LCHS.

*Times.* Dec. 27, 1808 – Feb. 14, 1809, PStL.

*Marietta*

*Marietta Pilot.* Mar. 15 – May 31, 1816, LCHS.

*Northumberland*

*Republican Argus* (and County Advertiser; same and Weekly Advertiser). May 18, 25, June 22 – Dec. 28, 1804; June 21 – Oct. 11, 1805, HU.

*Philadelphia*

*American Centinel* (and Mercantile Advertiser). Apr. 7, 1817 – Dec. 14, 1822 (scat'g), NJHS.

*Aurora* (General Advertiser; Philadelphia Aurora; Aurora Weekly). Nov. 7 – Dec. 31, 1794; Jan. 1 – June 31, 1795; 1796; 1797; Jan. – Nov., 1798, HSP. 1794; Dec., 1798; 1799, 1800; 1801; 1802 – Mar. 16, 1803, LC.

*Claypoole's American Daily Advertiser.* Jan. – Apr., Oct. – Nov., 1799, LC. Jan. 24, 27, 1800, YU.

*Democratic Press.* Jan. 2 – Feb. 1, 1809; Oct. 5 – Nov. 7, 1816, HSP.

*Dunlap and Claypoole's American Daily Advertiser.* Dec., 1793 – Mar. 31, 1794, LC. July – Oct., 1794; 1795 (April missing), NYPL.

*Federal Gazette* (and Philadelphia Evening Post; same and Philadelphia Daily Advertiser). Dec. 31, 1791; Jan. 2, 10, 14, 16, Apr. 28, 1792; Jan. 23, Feb. 25, June 25, July 16, Aug. 1, 5, 6, 10, 13, 17, 24, Sept. 7, 12, 20, 24, 30, Oct. 1 – Dec. 31, 1793 (scat'g), LC.

*Freeman's Journal* (or, the North-American Intelligencer). Jan. 4 – Dec. 27, 1786; Apr. 18 – Dec. 19, 1787, NYPL. Jan. 2, 1788 – May 2, 1792, LC.

*Freeman's Journal* (and Philadelphia Daily Advertiser; same and Philadelphia Mercantile Advertiser). Oct. 1 – Nov. 30, 1805; Jan. 2 – Feb. 1, 1809; Apr. 29 – July 3, 1812, HSP. Dec. 1, 1809 – Mar. 15, 1810, WIL.

*Gale's Independent Gazetteer.* Sept. 27 – Dec. 23, 1796, LC.

*Gazette of the United States* (& Evening Advertiser; same and Daily Evening Advertiser; same & Philadelphia Daily Advertiser; same & Daily Advertiser; Country Gazette of the United States; Gazette of the United States, for the Country; United States Gazette). [Before Nov. 3, 1790, published at New York.] Apr. 15, 1789 – Nov., 1794 (scat'g); Jan. – July, 1795; Jan., 1797 – Dec., 1798 (scat'g), NYPL. Nov. – Dec., 1790; 1793 to Sept. 18, 1794; July 5 – Dec. 30, 1797 (scat'g); Jan. – Sept. 30, 1799; Jan., Feb., July 1 – 30, 1800: (for the Country) Jan. 1, 1802 – Aug. 19, 1803 (some missing); Jan. 1, 1804 – Dec. 4, 1806 (scat'g), LC. 1793; 1794; 1795; Jan. – June, 1796, AAS. 1795; Jan. – Apr., 1799, HSP. Jan. 1 – Apr. 1, 1799 (Feb. 25, Mar. 6 missing), BA.

*General Advertiser.* 1794, LC.

*Independent Gazetteer* (or, the Chronicle of Freedom; same and Agricultural Repository). Aug 30 – Dec. 27, 1783; 1784, HSP. June, 1784 – Dec., 1785; Oct. 7 – Dec. 30, 1786; Jan. 2 – June 30, 1787, LC. Aug. 22, Nov. 28, 1788, YU. Aug. 17 – Nov. 16, 1793 (a few), LCPhil.

*Library* (or, Philadelphia Literary Reporter). Feb. 25, Mar. 10, May 5, 19, June 16, 30, Aug. 11, 1804; Jan. 5, Feb. 16, Mar. 30, June 22, 1805, NYHS.

*Literary Reporter.* Jan., Mar., Aug., 1809, NYHS.

*Merchants' Daily Advertiser.* Jan. 16 – Dec. 30, 1797; Jan. 1 – June 30, 1798, HSP.

*National Gazette* (and Literary Register). Aug. 3 – Oct. 23, 1793, LCPhil. Dec., 1826 – Jan., 1827, LC.

*Pelican.* Jan. 6, 13, 29, Feb. 3, 17, 21, 1807, HU.

*Pennsylvania Evening Herald* (Carey's Pennsylvania Evening Herald; same, and the American Monitor; Pennsylvania Evening Herald, and the American Monitor; Pennsylvania Herald, and General Advertiser). May 7 – June 15, 1785; 1786 (a few); Jan. 3 – Dec. 29, 1787, LC. Jan. 4, 1786 – Dec. 29, 1787, NYPL.

*Pennsylvania Gazette.* Jan. 4 – Dec. 20, 1786; Jan. 2 – Dec. 31, 1788; Jan. 6 – Dec 29, 1790; Jan. 5 – Dec. 28, 1791; Jan. 1 – Mar. 5, 1794, LC. Jan. 3 – Dec. 27, 1787, 1788–1795 (Jan. 1–7, 1789; June 18, July 9, 1788; Jan. 1–6, 1790 missing), NYPL. Jan. 3, 1798, AAS.

*Pennsylvania Journal.* Sept. 3 – Dec. 31, 1783, HSP. May 4, June, 1785; July – Dec., 1788; Jan. 7. – Dec. 30, 1789, LC. 1786, 1787, NYPL.

*Pennsylvania Packet* (and General Advertiser; same, and Daily Advertiser). Aug. 15 – Dec. 31, 1782; Dec. 1–31, 1785; 1789, LC. Aug. 26 – Dec. 30, 1783, HSP. Jan. 1, 1788 – June 29, 1789, YU., NYPL.

*Philadelphia Evening Post.* May 16 – June 4, 1804, HU.

*Philadelphia Gazette* (and Universal Daily Advertiser; same & Daily Advertiser). Jan. 2 – Dec. 31, 1794, LC. Jan. 1 – Dec. 18, 1795, NYPL. Mar. 30, 31, Apr. 8, May 2 – 31, 1796 – Aug. 1 – Sept. 30, 1800, HSP.

*Philadelphia Minerva.* Feb. 11, 1797 – Jan. 27, 1798, HU. Feb. 18 – Aug. 5, 1797, NJHS.

*Philadelphia Repository* (and Weekly Register). July 2–30, 1803, HSP.

*Porcupine's Gazette* (and United States Daily Advertiser). Mar. 4 – Sept. 2, 1797, HSP. Nov., 1797 – Dec., 1798, NYPL. Jan. – Oct. 4, 1799, LC.

## NEWSPAPERS CONSULTED

*Poulson's American Daily Advertiser.* May 16 – June 2, 1804, HU. July 1, 1807 – Dec. 30, 1808, LC.

*Relfs Philadelphia Gazette* (and Daily Advertiser). Feb. 13 – Dec. 31, 1804 (scat'g), HU.

*Tickler.* Jan. 4 – Feb. 1, 1809, HSP.

*True American* (and Commercial Advertiser). May 16 – Dec. 31, 1804 (scat'g), HU.

*United States' Gazette.* Oct. 1 – Nov. 30, 1805; Oct. 1 – Nov. 30, 1816, HSP.

*Universal Gazette.* Jan. 3 – Dec. 26, 1799; Jan. 1 – Sept. 11, 1800 (scat'g), LC.

*Reading*

*Weekly Advertiser.* Oct. 6, 1798; Jan. 5 – June 15, July 13, Sept. 7 – Dec. 31, 1799 (scat'g), HSP.

*Union*

*Fayette Gazette.* July 12, 1799; Feb. 28, 1800, NYHS.

*York*

*Expositor.* May 17, June 14, 1810, AAS.

*Pennsylvania Herald* (and York General Advertiser). Oct. 2, 1793 – Jan. 20, 1796 (a few), AAS.

*York Gazette* (& Public Advertiser). July 27, 1815; July 11, Nov. 7, 1816, AAS.

*York Recorder.* June 9, 1810; May 18, 1811; Apr. 18, 1812 – Sept. 2, 1828 (a few), AAS.

### SOUTH CAROLINA

*Charleston*

*Carolina Gazette.* Dec. 8, 1803 – July 20, 1804; June 26, 1813, HU. Jan. 4 – Dec. 27, 1805; Jan. 6 – Dec. 26, 1809, MDHS.

*Carolina Weekly Messenger.* Jan. 16, 1810, AAS.

*Charleston Courier* (Courier). Oct. 3, 1803 – Apr. 28, 1804; June 10 – July 1, 1805, HU. June 2–30, Sept. 1 – Oct. 15, 1804; Jan., 1805; Mar. 2, 11, Apr. 23, 26, 1811, AAS. Jan. 2 – June 1, July 2, 14, Aug. 20 – Sept. 1, Oct. 9 – Dec. 31, 1804; Jan. – Dec. 31, 1806; Nov. 27, 1809 – Feb. 10, 1810; Nov. 25 – Dec. 10, 1817; Jan. 5 – June 30, July 2–31, 1821; Jan. 1 – Dec. 31, 1822; Jan. 1 – Dec. 31, 1823; Jan. 1 – July 1, 1825, CLS. 1822; Jan. 1 – Dec. 31, 1823, LC.

*Charleston Evening Gazette.* July 11 – Sept. 3, 1785, CLS.

*City Gazette* (& Daily Advertiser; same and Commercial Advertiser). July 1 – Dec. 31, 1794; Jan. 1 – June 30, Oct. 1, 1795 – Apr. 21, 1796; Oct. 15, 1796 – Dec. 31, 1797; Jan. 1 – June 30, 1798; Jan. 1 – June 29, 1799; July 1 – Dec. 31, 1800; Feb. 21 – Dec. 31, 1804; Nov. 25 – Dec. 10, 1817, CLS. Dec. 14, 25, 1809; Feb. 1, 3, 1810; May 6, 1811, AAS.

*Columbian Herald.* July 4 – Aug. 31, 1785; July 2, 1794 – June 29, 1795; Oct. 7, 1795 – June 29, 1796, CLS.

*South-Carolina Gazette and Public Advertiser.* July 2 – Aug. 31, 1785, CLS.

*South-Carolina State Gazette and Daily Advertiser.* July 8–26, 1785, CLS.

*South-Carolina State Gazette* (& Timothy & Mason's Daily Advertiser; same, and Timothy's Daily Advertiser). July 10 – Dec. 31, 1794; Jan. 1 – June 30, 1795; Apr. 21 – Oct. 14, 1796; Mar. 1 – Dec 30, 1797; July 1 – Dec. 31, 1799; Jan. 1 – Dec. 31, 1800; Jan. 1 – June 30, 1801, CLS.

*Southern Patriot* (and Commercial Advertiser). July 10, 13, 1821, AAS.

*State Gazette of South-Carolina.* July 11 – Sept. 1, 1785, CLS.

*Times.* Oct 1, 1801 – Sept. 10, 1802; Jan. 16, 1803 – July 20, 1804, HU. Oct. 6, 1800; Jan. 3 – Oct. 1, Dec. 31, 1804; Jan. 2, 1805 – Mar. 31, 1806; Oct. 1, 1806 – Mar. 31, 1807; Apr. 1–20, 1811; Nov. 25 – Dec. 10, 1817; Jan. 2 – July 24, 1821, CLS.

*Columbia*

*South-Carolina State Gazette, and Columbian Advertiser.* July 15, 1803; Jan 20, 27, Feb. 3, 10, Mar. 2 – Apr. 20, 1804 (a few); June 15, 29, 1805, HU.

*Edgefield Court-House*

*Anti-Monarchist* (and South-Carolina Advertiser). Sept. 21, 28, Nov. 2, 1811, AAS.

*Georgetown*

*Georgetown Chronicle* (and South-Carolina Weekly Advertiser). Jan. 19, 1797, HU.

*Georgetown Gazette* (and Commercial Advertiser; same, and Mercantile Advertiser). May 15, 1798 – Dec. 24, 1800, CLS. May 8, 22, 1798; Jan. 23, 1799; Feb. 15, 1800; Dec. 1, 1802; May 30, 1804; Nov. 29, 1806; June 27, 1807; Feb. 24, Mar. 19, Apr. 2, June 15, 25, July 6, 9, 13, 20, Aug. 6, 1808; Dec. 12, 1810; Apr. 27, 1814; Sept. 14, 21, 1816, AAS.

*Winyaw*

*Winyaw Intelligencer.* Apr. 4, 1818; Jan. 20, June 12, 26, Aug. 4, 1819; Apr. 9, 20, May 11, 1825, AAS.

## VIRGINIA

*Alexandria*

*Alexandrian.* Nov. 16, 21, 28 – Dec. 30, 1820, LC.

*Alexandria Advertiser.* Feb. 4, 1799, NYPL. Dec. 11, 1800, LC.

*Alexandria Advertiser and Commercial Intelligencer.* Sept. 2–25, 1801; Jan. 1 – Feb. 11, Mar. 16 – Apr. 1, 1803, AAS. Jan. 1 – Dec. 22, 1802; Mar. 8, 1804, HU.

*Alexandria Daily Advertiser.* June 29 – Dec. 27, 1805; Jan. 1, 1805 – Feb. 1, 1806 (a few), HU. Apr. 11 – 30, 1808, AAS.

*Alexandria Expositor* (and the Columbian Advertiser; The Expositor). Nov. 26 – Dec. 24, 1802; Dec. 15–22, 1803; Jan. 9 – May 3, Dec. 22, 24, 26, 1804; Jan. 2 –

Nov. 11, 1805 (scat'g); Nov. 21, 1805 – Jan. 2, 1806, HU. Sept. 14, 1803, NYHS. Jan. 23, 1806, AAS.

*Alexandria Gazette* (Commercial and Political). Jan. 10, 1803, NYHS. June 19 – Dec. 7, 1809; Sept. 10 – Dec. 7, 1811; July 1 – 29, 1813; Mar. 10 – Apr. 2, 1814; Sept. 1–15, 1815; Apr. 30 – June 1, 1816; Dec. 31, 1816 – Jan. 15, 1817; May 1 – 31, Sept. 1–20, July 1 – Aug. 30, 1817, AAS.

*Alexandria Gazette & Daily Advertiser.* Oct. 1–20, 1818; May 1–31, June 21 – July 4 1820; Nov. 1–20, 1821, AAS.

*Alexandria Herald.* Feb. 13, July 24, Oct. 28, Nov. 16, 18, Dec. 8, 1813; Oct. 2, 1816 – Jan. 31, 1817, AAS. May 24 – June 25, 1816; May 1 – 20, July 7 – Nov. 20, 1820; May 16 – June 29, 1825, LC. May 25 – July 8, 1818, LCPHIL.

*Columbian Advertiser* (and Commercial, Mechanic, and Agricultural Gazette). Aug. 2 – Nov. 22, 1802, HU.

*Columbian Mirror.* Nov. 28, 1792 – Dec. 29, 1793, LC. 1792–1793, PStL.

*Columbian Mirror and Alexandria Advertiser.* Apr. 19, May 24, June 19, Aug. 21, Oct. 7, 1794; Apr. 30, June 16, Aug. 6, 1795; Mar. 12, June 7, 1796; 1797; Jan. 13, Mar. 13, June 16, 1798; May 7, 1799; Feb. 27, Mar. 4, June 3, Oct. 11, 18, 23, 30, Nov. 4, 18, 25, Dec. 6, 1800, AAS.

*Columbian Mirror and Alexandria Gazette.* Mar. 20, 27, Apr. 6, 10, May 4, 18, 1793, NYHS. Feb. 27, Mar. 12, 17, May 7 – July 16, 1795 (scat'g); Aug. 15, 1795 – Oct. 20, 1796 (scat'g); Oct. 31, 1799, HU. Apr. 16, 1796, NYPL.

*Columbian Telescope* (& Literary Compiler). June 19, Aug. 7, 1819, AAS.

*Times and Alexandria Advertiser.* Apr. 14, May 19, 1797; Apr. 24, 1798; Mar. 4, 1800; July 9, 1801, AAS. July 31 – Sept. 30, Oct. 28 – Dec. 29, 1797; Jan. 1 – Sept. 29, 1798; Jan. 1, 1799 – Dec. 11, 1800; Jan. 1 – June 15, 1801 (a few missing), LC.

*The Times; and District of Columbia Daily Advertiser.* Oct. 26, 1799 – Apr. 14, 1800, LC. July 9, Dec. 2, 1801 – July 31, 1802, HU.

### *Charlestown*

*Charlestown Gazette.* Apr. 1, 1814, AAS.

*Farmer's Repository.* July 15 – Aug. 5, 1808, HU.

### *Clarksburg*

*Bye-Stander.* Feb. 1, 1814, AAS.

### *Danville*

*Danville Courier.* June 20, 1818, AAS.

### *Dumfries*

*Republican Journal; and Dumfries Advertiser* (Same and Dumfries Weekly Advertiser). May 22, June 12, 19, July 3, 17, 31, 1795; June 30 – Nov. 3, 1796 (a few), HU.

*Virginia Gazette and Agricultural Repository.* Oct. 13, 1791; June 14, July 12, Dec. 13, 1792; Apr. 11, Dec. 19, 1793, AAS.

*Fincastle*

*Fincastle Weekly Advertiser.* May 29, June 12, July 10, 1801, AAS.

*Fredericksburg*

*Apollo.* Sept. 21, 23, Oct. 22, 26, 29, Nov. 9, Dec. 10, 1803; Jan. 14, 18, Feb. 2, 4, 11, 12, 1804, HU. Sept. 7, 17, Oct. 8, 1803, AAS.

*Fredericksburg News-Letter.* Mar. 25, 1801, HU.

*Republican Citizen, and Farmer and Planters' Chronicle.* June 6 – Oct. 12, 1796 (scat'g), HU.

*Virginia Express.* Nov. 17, 1803 – July 12, 1804 (a few), AAS. Jan. 5, Feb. 2, 13, Mar. 13, 15, May 3, June 1, 25, 28, July 2, 12, 16, 19, 23, Aug. 2, 6, 20, Sept. 6, 10, 24, Oct. 4, 8, 13, Nov. 1, 19, Dec. 19, 1803, HU.

*Virginia Herald* (and Fredericksburg Advertiser; same, and Fredericksburg & Falmouth Advertiser). Feb. 2, Nov. 1, 1792; Aug. 10, 1804, NYHS. Feb. 26, Mar. 5, 12, May 12, 26, June 5 – 30, July 7, 1795; Nov. 4, 1796; Apr. 14, 1797, HU. Aug. 16, 1796 – Jan. 31, 1798 (a few), AAS. Oct. 23, 1798, NYPL. Jan. 11 – Dec. 10, 1799; Jan. 21 – Oct. 24, 1800; Feb. 23, 1802 – Dec. 24, 1804 (scat'g); Jan. 6 – Feb. 13, 1807; Oct. 23, 1807 – Mar. 29, 1808; Sept. 2, 1808 – May 27, Sept. 6 – Dec. 30, 1809; Jan. 18 – Feb. 19, June 6, 1812 – Dec. 29, 1813; May 29 – Sept. 28, 1816 – May 30, 1818; Jan. 2 – June 30, 1819; Jan. 1, Feb. 26, 1820, LC.

*Leesburg*

*Genius of Liberty.* Jan. 27, Feb. 4, 1817, AAS.

*Washingtonian.* Feb. 6, 20, 1810, AAS.

*Lexington*

*Rockbridge Repository.* Jan. 5, Mar. 13, Apr. 3, Oct. 2, 1804, HU.

*Virginia Telegraphe; or, Rockbridge Courier.* Dec. 13, 20, 1803; Jan. 3, 10, 24, 31, Feb. 11, 24, Mar. 3, 10, 24, Apr. 7, May 5, 12, June 9, July 7, 27, Aug. 3, 17, Oct. 5, 1804, HU.

*Lynchburg*

*Echo.* July – Aug., 1816 (a few), AAS.

*Lynchburg and Farmer's Gazette.* Apr. 5, 1794 – Nov. 27, 1795 (scat'g), AAS. Feb. 14, 21, Mar. 7, May 2, 16, June 13, 20, Aug. 1, 8, 1795, HU.

*Lynchburg Star.* Feb. 27, June 19, 1806; Jan. 8, 1812, AAS.

*Lynchburg Weekly Gazette.* Oct. 13, 1798; July 13, 20, 1799, AAS. June 29, 1799, NYPL.

*Lynchburg Weekly Museum.* Aug. 21, 1797; Jan. 15, May 19, 1798, AAS.

*Press.* May 13, 1809 – May 2, 1817 (a few), AAS.

# NEWSPAPERS CONSULTED

*Martinsburgh*

*Martinsburgh Gazette.* June 5, July 10, 1817, AAS.

*Potowmack Guardian, and Berkeley Advertiser.* Feb. 18 (?), Sept. 16, 30, 1793; Apr. 14, July 28, Sept. 1, 8, 1794; Jan. 12, 19, 1795; Nov. 21, 1798, AAS. Dec. 28, 1795 – Sept. 22, 1796, LC. Feb. 23, Mar. 2, May 9, 23, June 20, July 4, 1795, HU.

*Norfolk*

*American Gazette & General Advertiser.* May 20, 24, June 24, 28, July 19, Aug. 2, 5, Sept. 6, 13, 23, 1794; Mar. 17, Apr. 7, May 8, Sept. 29, 1795 – Oct. 18, 1796 (scat'g), HU.

*American Gazette & Norfolk & Portsmouth Weekly Advertiser.* Sept. 1, 1795 – Apr. 29, 1796; Mar. 17, May 8, 29, June 2, 30, July 14, 1795, HU.

*Commercial Register.* Aug. 30 – Dec. 13, 1802, HU.

*Epitome of the Times.* July 24, 1800 – Mar. 31, 1801 (scat'g); May 8, 1801, HU.

*Herald, and Norfolk and Portsmouth Advertiser.* Jan. 7 – Dec. 18, 1795 (scat'g), LC. June 17, 1795, HU.

*Norfolk Gazette.* July 17, 1804 – Mar. 29, 1805, NorPL. July 31, 1807; Nov. 30, 1812 – July 16, 1814, LC. Apr. 20, 1808 – Feb. 2, 1809, NYHS.

*Norfolk Gazette and Publick Ledger.* July 17 – Nov. 30, 1812, VStL.

*Norfolk Herald.* Jan. 2 – Dec. 31, 1796; Jan. 4 – Dec. 29, 1798; Jan. 2 – Dec. 29, 1800; Jan. 5, Dec. 29, 1802, LC. Jan. 7 – Sept. 9, 1802 (scat'g), HU.

*Virginia Chronicle & Norfolk & Portsmouth General Advertiser.* Feb. 1 – Dec. 19, 1794 (scat'g), LC.

*Petersburg*

*Petersburg Daily Courier.* Sept. 21, 29, Oct. 3, 1814, AAS.

*Petersburg Intelligencer.* June 17, 1800, NYHS. Aug. 4, Sept. 4, Oct. 2, 1801; Jan. 6, 31, Feb. 17, 28, Mar. 2, 16, 23, Apr. 6, 17, 24, 27, May 1, 15, June 22, 26, July 3, 6, 17, 20, 24, 27, 31, Aug. 7, 17, 21, 24, 28, Sept. 7, 11, 14, 25, Oct. 2, 5, 16, Nov. 2, 6, 9, 16, 20, 23, Dec. 11, 1804 – Dec. 31, 1805 (scat'g); Feb. 12 – Dec. 23, 1808, HU. July 31, Aug. 3, Sept. 24, Nov. 22, 1810; Feb. 12, 1813, AAS.

*Republican* (Petersburg Republican). Apr. 30, May 4, 7, 11, 21, 25, June 4, 8, 18, 22, July 20, Aug. 3, 10, 17, 24, Sept. 14, 17, 24, Oct. 5, 9, 15, 26, Nov. 5, 23, Dec. 3, 7, 10, 21, 1801; Dec. 31, 1802; Mar. 1 – Nov. 11, 1803 (a few); Jan. 31, Mar. 2, Apr. 7, 10, 24, 29, July 3, 6, 13, 20, 27, Aug. 3, 7, 10, 17, 21, 24, 28, 31, Sept. 7, 11, 14, 21, 23, Oct. 2, 5, 12, Nov. 2, 9, 16, 20, 1804; Jan. 1 – Mar. 22, Apr. 2, 23, June 21, 1805 – Feb. 26, 1806 (scat'g); July 27 – Dec. 31, 1808, HU. Apr. 23, 1807; Apr. 9, June 5, 25, July 23, 30, 1810 – Jan. 12, 1813 (a few); May 17 – Dec. 24, 1822, AAS.

*Virginia Apollo.* Apr. 8, 18, 25, May 2, 9, 30, 1807, AAS.

*Virginia Gazette & Petersburg Intelligencer.* Jan. 31, 1793 – Sept. 22, 1815, AAS.

Feb. 27, Mar. 13, May 26, 29, June 5, 9, 12, 16, 19, 23, 30, 1795; Oct. 28, Nov. 1, 4, 1796 – Mar. 31 – Apr. 28, 1797 (scat'g); May 7, June 17, 20, 1799, NYPL.

*Virginia Mercury.* May 20, June 10, 1807; Feb. 10, 1808, AAS.

*Virginia Star and Petersburg Weekly Advertiser.* June 25, 1795, AAS. Apr. 30, June 4, 11, July 2, 1795, HU.

*Richmond*

*Daily Compiler.* June 1, 1813; July 19, 1816, NYPL.

*Enquirer.* Mar. 9 – Dec. 29, 1804; Jan. 1 – Dec. 31, 1805; Jan. 5 – Dec. 31, 1808; Jan. 3 – Dec. 30, 1815; Feb. 29 – Mar. 31; May 2 – June 6, 1820, LC. May 9, 1804 – Jan. 1, 1805; Oct. 14, 1807 – Feb. 9, 1808; Oct. 11 – Dec. 5, 1811; Aug. 28 – Oct. 16, 1812; Jan. 5 – Mar. 12, 1813; Sept. 9 – Oct. 31, Dec. 30, 1817 – Feb. 26, May 5 – June 19, 1818; Feb. 24 – Apr. 5, June 18, 22, July 5 – 13, 1819; Mar. – June (a few), 1820, VStL. Sept. 8, 12, 15, Oct. 10, 13, 17, 20, 31, Nov. 7, 21, Dec. 1, 6, 8, 11, 15, 18, 29, 1804; Jan. 1 – Mar. 21, 1805 (a few); Jan. 14 – Sept. 30, 1808 (scat'g), HU. Jan. 1, 1805; July 1 – Aug. 9, 1808; Dec. 1–30, 1809; Sept. 4–25, 1812, NYPL. Nov. 3 – Dec. 1, 1809; Feb. 3 – Mar. 10, June 2–26, 1818, AAS.

*Examiner.* June 4, 13, 17, 24, July 4, 8, 18, 22, Sept. 5, 12, 16, 19, 23, 30, Oct. 7, 10, 17, 21, 24, 28, Nov. 4, 18, 21, Dec. 10, 1799, NYHS. Oct. 29, Nov. 1, Dec. 3–28, 1799; Jan. 7 – Apr. 1, 1800 (scat'g); Jan. 2 – Mar. 20, 1801; Mar. 30 – May 1, Sept. 3, 6, 10, 17, Oct. 5, Nov. 9, 12, 1802, VStL. Apr. 29 – May 16, 1800; Jan. 1 – Dec. 4, 1802 (scat'g); Mar. 2, 1803, HU.

*Impartial Observer.* May 31, 1806; May 2, 1807, HU.

*Recorder.* Jan. 19, 1803, BA. July 5 – Sept. 10, Dec. 1, 1802 – Mar. 2, 1803, VStL.

*Richmond Chronicle.* May 26, 30, June 6, 9, 16, 23, 30, July 14, 18, 25, Aug. 1, 1795, HU. Jan. 15, 19, 26, Feb. 5, 9, 12, 16, 26, Mar. 1, May 3, 10, 17, 24, June 7, 1796, NYPL.

*Richmond Compiler.* Sept. 10 – Oct. 31, 1817; Jan. 10, June 1 – July 31, 1818, AAS.

*Richmond and Manchester Advertiser.* Apr. 30 – Dec. 26, 1795; Jan. 6 – June 22, 1796, LC. May 9, 23, 30, June 4, 6, 11, 18, July 2, Aug. 22, 1795 – Oct. 22, 1796 (scat'g), HU.

*Richmond and Virginia Argus.* Jan. 18 – Dec. 31, 1799 (scat'g); Jan. 3 – Dec. 30, 1800; Jan. 2 – Dec. 29, 1801; Jan. 8 – Dec. 29, 1802; Jan. 1 – Dec. 31, 1803, LC.

*Spirit of 'Seventy-Six.* Sept 16 – Oct. 3, 1808, HU. Nov. 18, 21, 29, Dec. 9, 12, 16, 20, 23, 27, 30, 1808; Jan. 3, 10, 13, 17, 20, 24, Sept. 8, 15, 1809, VStL.

*Virginia Argus.* Dec. 2, 1796 – Apr. 28, 1797; Dec. 15, 1801; Dec. 29, 1804 – June 12, 1805 (scat'g), HU. Dec. 29, 1797 – Oct. 3 1800 (scat'g); Feb. 6 – Dec. 31, 1803; Mar. 9, 1805 – Dec. 29, 1807 (scat'g); Jan. 1 – Feb. 2, 1808 (a few); Feb. 17 – Aug. 22, 1809 (scat'g); Feb. 16 – Dec. 25, 1810; Jan. 1 – Sept. 30, 1811; Jan. 13 – Aug. 27, 1812 (scat'g); May 3, 1813 – July 8, 1815, AAS. Oct. 9 – Dec. 30, 1800; Feb. 11, 1804 – Mar. 2, 1805; Feb. 12 – Dec. 30, 1808; Oct. 1 – Dec. 23, 1811; Aug. 3, 1812 – Mar. 8, 1813, VStL. Mar. 6, 10, 20 – Apr. 10, 1801 (scat'g); Jan. 1 – Apr.

30, Aug 1 – Sept 28, 1803; Jan 4 – Feb 29, 1804 (a few); Jan 3 – Feb. 10, Oct. 6 – Dec. 29, 1809; Jan. 2 – Feb. 13, 1810; Aug. 31 – Dec. 31, 1812; Jan. 7 – Apr. 29, 1813, NYPL. Jan. 3, 1806, Dec. 14, 1812, BA. Feb. 2, Mar. 9, 1810, NYHS.

*Virginia Federalist.* Aug. 3, 14, 17, 24, 28, Sept. 4, 7, 11, 14, 18, Oct. 5, 9, 12, 16, 19, 23, 26, Nov. 2, 23, Dec. 11, 18, 21, 1799; Jan. 8, 11, 18, Feb. 8, Mar. 5, 29, Apr. 12, 19, 26, 30, May 6, 14, 21, 28, 31, June 7 – Aug. 2, 1800, HU.

*Virginia Gazette and General Advertiser.* June 17, 1795; Oct. 12, 1796 – Apr. 12, 1797 (scat'g), HU. Nov. 6, 1798; Feb. 12, 1799; June 13, 1807, NYHS. Feb. 5, 19, 1799, NYPL. Jan. 1, 1806, BA.

*Virginia Gazette and Richmond Chronicle.* Jan. 24, Feb. 21, Mar. 7, July 1, Aug. 1, Oct. 10, Nov. 11, 14, 18, 25, 28, Dec. 5, 1794; Mar. 10, 13, 24, Apr. 3, 11, 14, 18, 25, May 5, 9, 12, 19, 23, 26, 1795, NYPL. Mar. 3, 10, 13, May 9, 1795, HU.

*Virginia Gazette and Richmond and Manchester Advertiser.* Jan. 1 – Apr. 25, 1795; Jan. 5, 1802 – Feb. 26, July 30 – Oct. 8, 1803; Feb. 26 – Apr. 8, 1808, LC. Mar. 2, 9, 1795, HU. May 28 – Aug. 5, 1795, NJHS.

*Virginia Gazette and Weekly Advertiser.* Feb. 28, May 9, 23, June 6, 20, 27, July 4, 1795; Oct. 29, 1796 – Apr. 22, 1797 (a few), HU.

*Virginia Patriot.* Dec. 26, 1809, Oct. 30, 1810; Aug. 14, 1816 – May 26, 1817, LC. Oct. 1 – Dec. 10, 1811; Sept. 1 – Oct. 16, 1812; Jan. 8 – Mar. 12, 1813; Sept. 21–30, Oct. 4–15, 1817; Jan. 1 – Mar. 2, May 1 – June 15, 1819; Apr. 1–18, June 10 – July 15, 1819; Mar. 1–31, May 12 – June 20, 1820, VStL.

*Snow-Hill Messenger and Worcester County Advertiser.* May 14, 1832, AAS.

*Staunton*

*Phenix.* June 27, Aug. 22, Sept. 5, 1804, HU.

*Staunton Eagle.* Jan. 1 – Dec. 15, 1808 (a few), HU.

*Virginia Gazette.* Feb. 14, June 20, 1795; 1796 (scat'g), HU.

*Warrenton*

*Virginia Gazette.* Oct. 11, 1828.

*Winchester*

*Bowen's Virginia Gazette; and the Winchester Centinel.* Oct. 28, 1796 – Apr. 28, 1797, HU.

*Independent Register.* Oct. 2, 9, 23, Nov. 6, 20, 1804, HU.

*Virginia Centinel.* Jan. 6 – Dec. 29, 1794, LC.

*Virginia Centinel and Gazette or, the Winchester Repository.* July 29, 1793, NYHS. Feb. 23, Mar. 2, May 11, 25, June 8, 22, July 20, 1795, HU.

*Virginia Gazette.* June 28 – Aug. 12, 1808; Oct. 10 – Nov. 28, 1809.

*Virginia Gazette & Independent Chronicle.* Aug. 6, 1785, Oct. 28, 1786, LC.

*Virginian.* Jan. 1, Sept. 16, 1808, VStL.

*Visitor.* Feb. 11, 1809; Feb. 17, 1810, VStL.

# ABBREVIATIONS OF PERIODICALS AND NEWSPAPERS CONSULTED

## PERIODICALS

| | |
|---|---|
| *AmPhSTrans.* | Transactions of the American Philosophical Society |
| *MHSProc.* | Massachusetts Historical Society Proceedings |
| *NYHSCol.* | New York Historical Society Collections |
| *ProcAAS.* | Proceedings of the American Antiquarian Society |
| *Trans&Col.AAS.* | Transactions and Collections of the American Antiquarian Society |

## NEWSPAPERS

| | |
|---|---|
| *Adams Cent.* | Adams Centinel, Gettysburg, Pa. |
| *Alb. Gaz.* | Albany Gazette, N. Y. |
| *Alex'a Adv.* | Alexandria Advertiser, Va. |
| *Alex'a Adv. & Com. Intel.* | Alexandria Advertiser & Commercial Intelligencer, Va. |
| *Alex'a D. Adv.* | Alexandria Daily Advertiser, Va. |
| *Alex'a Expos.* | Alexandria Expositor, Va. |
| *Alex'a Gaz.* | Alexandria Gazette, Va. |
| *Amer. & Balt. Gaz.* | American & Baltimore Gazette, Md. |
| *Amer. & Com. D. Adv.* | American & Commercial Daily Advertiser, Baltimore, Md. |
| *Amer. & D. Adv.* | American & Daily Advertiser, Baltimore, Md. |
| *Amer. Gaz. & Norf'k & Ports. Adv.* | American Gazette & Norfolk & Portsmouth Advertiser, Va. |
| *Amer. Lit. Adv.* | American Literary Advertiser, Washington, D. C. |
| *Amer. Merc.* | American Mercury, Hartford, Conn. |
| *Amer. Staats.* | Americanische Staatsbothe, Lancaster, Pa. |
| *Amer. Vol.* | American Volunteer, Carlisle, Pa. |
| *Amer. Watch.* | American Watchman, Wilmington, Del. |
| *Arg. & N. J. Cent.* | Argus & New Jersey Centinel, Bridge-Town, N. J. |
| *Aug. Chron.* | Augusta Chronicle, Ga. |
| *Aug. Her.* | Augusta Herald, Ga. |
| *Balt. D. Intel.* | Baltimore Daily Intelligencer, Md. |
| *Balt. D. Repos.* | Baltimore Daily Repository, Md. |
| *Balt. Pat.* | Patriot. Baltimore Patriot & Evening Advertiser; same & Mercantile Advertiser, Md. |
| *Balt. Tel. and Merc. Adv.* | Baltimore Telegraph and Mercantile Advertiser, Md. |
| *Balt. Whig* | Baltimore Whig, Md. |

## ABBREVIATIONS OF PERIODICALS

| | |
|---|---|
| *Bartgis's Fed. Gaz.* | Bartgis's Federal Gazette, Fredericktown, Md. |
| *Bartgis's Repub. Gaz.* | Bartgis's Republican Gazette, Fredericktown, Md. |
| *Bost. D. Adv.* | Boston Daily Advertiser, Mass. |
| *Car. Cent.* | Carolina Centinel, Newbern, N. C. |
| *Car. Fed. Repub.* | Carolina Federal Republican, Newbern, N. C. |
| *Cent.* | Centinel, Gettysburg, Pa. |
| *Cent. Freed.* | Centinel of Freedom, Newark, N. J. |
| *Cent. Lib.* | Centinel of Liberty, Georgetown, D. C. |
| *Charles. Cour.* | Charleston Courier, S. C. |
| *Chron. or Harris. Vis.* | Chronicle, or Harrisburg Visitor, Pa. |
| *City Gaz.* | City Gazette, Charleston, S. C. |
| *City of Wash. Gaz.* | City of Washington Gazette, D. C. |
| *Col. Adv. & Com'l Mech. & Agric. Gaz.* | Columbian Advertiser; and Commercial, Mechanic, and Agricultural Gazette, Alexandria, Va. |
| *Col. Cent. (Aug., Ga.)* | Columbian Centinel, Augusta, Ga. |
| *Col. Chron.* | Columbian Chronicle, Georgetown, D. C. |
| *Col. Mir. and Alex'a Gaz.* | Columbian Mirror and Alexandria Gazette, Va. |
| *Col. Mus. & Sav. Adv.* | Columbian Museum & Savannah Advertiser, Ga. |
| *Com. Adv.* | Commercial Advertiser, New York, N. Y. |
| *Conn. Cour.* | Connecticut Courant, Hartford, Conn. |
| *Conn. Gaz.* | Connecticut Gazette, New London, Conn. |
| *Conn. Jour.* | Connecticut Journal, New Haven, Conn. |
| *Conn. Post & N. H. Vis.* | Connecticut Post & New Haven Visitor, Conn. |
| *Cumb. Reg.* | Cumberland Register, Carlisle, Pa. |
| *Del. & East. Shore Adv.* | Delaware and Eastern-Shore Advertiser, Wilmington, Del. |
| *Del. Gaz.* | Delaware Gazette, Wilmington, Del. |
| *Democrat* | Democrat, Boston, Mass. |
| *D. Nat'l. Intel.* | Daily National Intelligencer, Washington, D. C. |
| *East. Shore Gen'l Adv.* | Republican Star or Eastern Shore General Advertiser, Easton, Md. |
| *Edwards's Balt. D. Adv.* | Edwards's Baltimore Daily Advertiser, Md. |
| *Enquirer.* | Enquirer, Richmond, Va. |
| *Ep. of the Times* | Epitome of the Times, Norfolk, Va. |
| *Expos.* | Expositor, Alexandria, Va. |
| *Farm. Instruct.* | Farmers Instructor, Harrisburg, Pa. |
| *Farmer's Repos.* | Farmer's Repository, Charlestown, Va. |
| *Fed. Gaz. & Balt. D. Adv.* | Federal Gazette & Baltimore Daily Advertiser, Md. |
| *Frank. Repos.* | Franklin Repository, Chambersburg, Pa. |
| *Fred'kt'n Her.* | Fredericktown Herald, Md. |

| | |
|---|---|
| *Gaz. U. S.* | Gazette of the United States, Philadelphia, Pa. |
| *Gen. Lib.* | Genius of Liberty, Morristown, N. J. |
| *Ga. Arg.* | Georgia Argus, Milledgeville, Ga. |
| *Ga. Express* | Georgia Express, Athens, Ga. |
| *Ga. Gaz.* | Georgia Gazette, Augusta, Ga. |
| *Ga. Jour.* | Georgia Journal, Milledgeville, Ga. |
| *Georgian* | Georgian, Savannah, Ga. |
| *Ga. Rep.* | Georgia Republican, Savannah, Ga. |
| *Guard.* | Guardian, New Brunswick, N. J. |
| | |
| *Hall's Wilm. Gaz.* | Hall's Wilmington Gazette, Del. |
| *Harris. Repub.* | Harrisburg Republican, Pa. |
| *Hillsb'ro. Rec.* | Hillsborough Recorder, N. C. |
| *Hive* | Hive, Lancaster, Pa. |
| *Hornet* | Hornet, Fredericktown, Md. |
| | |
| *Indep. Amer.* | Independent American, Georgetown, D. C. |
| *Intel.* | Intelligencer & Weekly Advertiser, Lancaster, Pa. |
| | |
| *Kline's Carl. W'kly Gaz.* | Kline's Carlisle Weekly Gazette, Pa. |
| | |
| *Lanc. Jour.* | Lancaster Journal, Pa. |
| *Library* | Library; or, Philadelphia Literary Reporter, Pa. |
| *Lit. Mus.* | Literary Museum, Westchester, Pa. |
| *Louisv'l. Gaz.* | Louisville Gazette & Republican Trumpet, Ga. |
| *Lynchburg and Farmer's Gaz.* | Lynchburg and Farmer's Gazette, Va. |
| *Lynchburg W'kly Gaz.* | Lynchburg Weekly Gazette, Va. |
| | |
| *Martinsb'g Gaz.* | Martinsburgh Gazette, Va. |
| *Mass. Spy* | Massachusetts Spy, Boston, Mass. |
| *Md. Gaz. (Annap's)* | Maryland Gazette, Annapolis, Md. |
| *Md. Her. & Eliz.-Town W'kly Adv.* | Maryland Herald and Elizabeth-Town Weekly Advertiser, Elizabeth (Hager's) town, Md. |
| *Md. Her.* | Maryland Herald, Easton, Md. |
| *Md. Jour.* | Maryland Journal, Baltimore, Md. |
| *Merch. D. Adv.* | Merchants Daily Advertiser, Philadelphia, Pa. |
| *Mess.* | Messenger, New Haven, Conn. |
| *Mess. (George'n)* | Messenger, Georgetown, D. C. |
| *Mir. Times (Wilm'n)* | Mirror of the Times, Wilmington, Del. |
| *Morg. or Morgen* | Harrisburger Morgenröthe, Harrisburg, Pa. |
| *Morn. Post* | New York Morning Post, N. Y. |

## ABBREVIATIONS OF PERIODICALS

| | |
|---|---|
| *Museum* | Museum, Georgetown, D. C. |
| *Mus. & George'n Adv.* | Museum and Georgetown Advertiser, D. C. |
| *Mus. Del.* | Museum of Delaware, Wilmington, Del. |
| *Nat'l. Gaz.* | National Gazette, Philadelphia, Pa. |
| *Nat'l. Intel.* | National Intelligencer, Washington, D. C. |
| *Nat'l. Mess.* | National Messenger, Georgetown, D. C. |
| *N. C. Min. and Fay'l. Adv.* | North Carolina Minerva and Fayetteville Advertiser, Raleigh, N. C. |
| *Newark Gaz.* | Newark Gazette, N. J. |
| *Newbern Her.* | Newbern Herald, Newbern, N. C. |
| *N. J. Jour.* | New Jersey Journal, Elizabethtown, N. J. |
| *N. Amer.* | North American and Mercantile Daily Advertiser, Baltimore, Md. |
| *Olio* | Olio, Georgetown, D. C. |
| *Oracle Dauph.* | Oracle of Dauphin, Harrisburgh, Pa. |
| *Pa. Gaz.* | Pennsylvania Gazette, Lancaster, Pa. |
| *Pa. Her. & York Gen'l Adv.* | Pennsylvania Herald, and York General Advertiser, Pa. |
| *Petersburg Repub.* | Petersburg Republican, Va. |
| *Phil. Min.* | Philadelphia Minerva, Pa. |
| *Phil. Repos.* | Philadelphia Repository, and Weekly Register, Pa. |
| *Plaindealer* | Plaindealer, Fredericktown, Md. |
| *Pol. Exam.* | Political Examiner, Fredericktown, Md. |
| *Poto'ma'k Guard. & Berk'l'y Adv.* | Potomack Guardian, and Berkeley Advertiser, Martinsburgh, Va. |
| *Pub. Intel.* | Public Intelligencer, Savannah, Ga. |
| *Ral. Reg.* | Raleigh Register & N. C. State Gazette, N. C. |
| *Republican* | Republican, Petersburg, Va. |
| *Repub. (Balt.)* | Republican; or, Anti-Democrat, Baltimore, Md. |
| *Repub. (Sav'a)* | Republican, Savannah, Ga. |
| *Repub. Arg.* | Republican Argus, and County Advertiser, Northumberland, Pa. |
| *Repub. Cit.* | Republican Citizen, and Farmers' and Planters' Chronicle, Fredericksburg, Va. |
| *Repub. Jour. & Dumf. W'kly Adv.* | Republican Journal and Dumfries Weekly Advertiser, Va. |
| *Rich'd and Manch'r Adv.* | Richmond and Manchester Advertiser, Va. |

| | |
|---|---|
| *Sal. Reg.* | Salem Register, Salem, Mass. |
| *S. C. St. Gaz.* | South Carolina State Gazette, Charleston, S. C. |
| *S. C. St. Gaz. & Col. Adv.* | South-Carolina State Gazette, and Columbian Advertiser, Columbia, S. C. |
| *South. Pat.* | Southern Patriot, Savannah, Ga. |
| *Spectator* | Spectator, New York, N. Y. |
| *Star* | Star, Raleigh, N. C. |
| *Telegraphe* | Telegraphe, Carlisle, Pa. |
| *Tel. & D. Adv.* | Telegraphe and Daily Advertiser, Baltimore, Md. |
| *Times* | Times, Charleston, S. C. |
| *Times & Alex'a Adv.* | Times and Alexandria Advertiser, Va. |
| *Times & D.C.D. Adv.* | Times; and District of Columbia Daily Advertiser, Alexandria, Va. |
| *True Amer.* | True American, Trenton, N. J. |
| *Va. Arg.* | Virginia Argus, Richmond, Va. |
| *Va. Exp.* | Virginia Express, Fredericksburg, Va. |
| *Va. Fed.* | Virginia Federalist, Richmond, Va. |
| *Va. Gaz. (Rich'd)* | Virginia Gazette and Weekly Advertiser, Richmond, Va. |
| *Va. Gaz. & Agric. Repos.* | Virginia Gazette and Agricultural Repository, Dumfries, Va. |
| *Va. Gaz. & Gen'l Adv.* | Virginia Gazette and General Advertiser, Richmond, Va. |
| *Va. Gaz. & Petersburg Intel.* | Virginia Gazette & Petersburg Intelligencer, Va. |
| *Va. Gaz. & Rich'd and Manch'r Adv.* | Virginia Gazette and Richmond and Manchester Advertiser, Richmond, Va. |
| *Va. Gaz. & Winch. Cent.* | Bowen's Virginia Gazette; and the Winchester Centinel, Va. |
| *Va. Her. & Fred'ksb'g Adv.* | Virginia Herald, and Fredericksburg Advertiser, Va. |
| *Va. Her. & F. & F. Adv.* | Virginia Herald, and Fredericksburg & Falmouth Advertiser, Va. |
| *Va. Pat.* | Virginia Patriot, Richmond, Va. |
| *Unpart. Harris. Morg. Zeit.* | Unpartheyische Harrisburg Morgenröthe Zeitung, Pa. |
| *Wash. City W'kly Gaz.* | Washington City Weekly Gazette, Washington, D. C. |
| *Wash. Fed.* | Washington Federalist, Georgetown, D. C. |
| *Wash. Gaz.* | Washington Gazette, Washington, D. C. |
| *Wilm. Gaz.* | Wilmington Gazette, N. C. |
| *W'kly Mus. (N. Y.)* | Weekly Museum, New York, N. Y. |
| *York Rec.* | York Recorder, Pa. |

# ADDENDA

The following items, all in the *Mathew Carey Account Books* [AAS.], came to light too late to be incorporated with the notes following each title. The editor has ventured to impute a connection between them and certain editions, but in only a few cases does the relationship seem infallible — the others being tentative.

## Life of Washington

Title 2.

'Matthew Carey to Mary Smith......Dr. Nov. 22d. 1800......For Stitching plates & blue paper on the 1st. Edition [*of Washington*] 140 Copies......4.10'. Vol. 15 : 5987.

Title 3.

Three bills from Peter Stewart charge Carey for the following item, as of June 20, 1800: 'To composing sig. C. & E. Life of Washington 29328 m's a 3/ per......£4—7—0 28 token press-work......3/9 per......5—5—0'. Vol. 14 : 5345; Vol. 15 : 5890; Vol. 21 : 1023. Carey was indebted to Benjamin Tanner, as of June 21, 1800, 'To engraving small Portrait of Washington......$10'. Vol. 15 : 5870, 5871. A statement of John Bioren to Carey, commencing in 1797, contains the following items: June 26, 1800, 'To [*printing*] 4 half sheets Life of Washington......20.11', and, July 17th, 'life of Washington......15.10.6'. Vol. 30 : 4740. [John Bioren was of the firm, in 1795, of Bioren and Madan. Vol. 1 : 31; Vol. 3 : 941; Vol. 7 : 2377. He had frequent relations with Carey from that time on. He printed *Télémaque* in French for him. Vol. 21 : 544.] 'Matthew Carey to Mary Smith......Dr. Nov. 22d. 1800 For Stitching 3000 Life of 2d. Edition of Washington £10.10'. Vol. 15 : 5987.

Title 4.

Benjamin Tanner charged Mathew Carey, July 16, 1800, for 'Portrait of Washington ......[$]25'. Another bill prices this item at $30. Vol. 15 : 5870, 5871. An undated bill from John Bioren to Carey, bound concurrently with others of September, 1800, includes the following item, which also appears in more abbreviated form on a bill of September 4: '4 half sheets Life of Washington 1323 ems in a page......20. 8. 0' and 6 half sheets of the same '1372 ems in a page......14.19.3'. Carey was indebted to Robertson & Coghlan, Sept. 6, 1800, for '1214 Life of Washington'. Vol. 15 : 5843.

Title 6.

On April 2, 1802, Cornelius Tiebout rendered a bill to Carey for '1000 impressions likeness of Washington'. Vol. 16 : 6692. An undated, unsigned memorandum in Joseph Charless' handwriting and filed with his receipts for 1802, contains an item 'To 118 Washington @ 13......15.34'. Vol. 17 : 7095.

Title 8.

On April 28, 1803, Robert Cochran charged Carey 'To [*printing*] 10 quires Proposals for Biography......2'. Vol. 21 : 836.

Title 11.

William Spotswood, whose name appears on the portrait in that edition, is referred to frequently as selling books to Carey, one statement of account being dated at the bottom, 'W. Spotswood Boston 19th August 1796'. Vol. 8 : 2646. A long gap comes in his bills between 1796 and 1806, when there is a bill in October to 'The Estate of Wm. Spotswood (Deceased)'. Vol. 20 : 477. See also title 241, note 1.

Titles 11 and 12.

Robert Cochran charged Carey, as of Nov. 12, 1808, for 'Compos 216 Pages Life of Washington 216000 m's......[$]108. To Press Do 9 Sheet — 2000 Copies...... [$]72'. Vol. 7 : 2640; Vol. 23 : 1577.

Titles 13–15.

About the year 1808 John Boyd engraved for Carey a Plate of Washington. Vol. 22 : 1098. On Nov. 11, 1808, T. S. Manning charged Carey for 'Composition 4 half sheets Washington at 5.50......22.00 — 5000 copies or 20 tokens per half sheet......40.00' Vol. 24 : 2375. On Dec. 20, 1808, Frey & Kammerer charged Carey for printing '10 half sheets life of Washington $80.' Vol. 23 : 1446. On Dec. 26, 1808, T. & G. Palmer charged Carey for printing 'Life of Washington 72.' Vol. 23 : 1481.

Titles 16 and 17.

'Mr Mathew Carey To H. B. Cochran Feb. 18 To Half Binding 971 Life of Washington with Roan Backs 97.10'. Vol. 23 : 1431. Robert Cochran charged Carey, April 3, 1809, 'To Composition Life of Washington 216000 m's $97.20 To Press Do. 3000 Copies @ 45/100 102.60 199 80'. Vol. 23 : 1432. Two bills of Robert Cochran to Carey contain the items: 'April 10, 1809, To Balance Printing Life of Washington $35 7 April 17, To 12 pages Criticism on Life of Washington 5 40'. Vol. 23 : 1579; Vol. 24 : 2053. In September, 1810, the 'Estate of R. Cochran' billed Carey for the same items. Vol. 25 : 2468. George Wilson's bill to Carey for 1809 contains an item for binding, on Apr. 22nd, '6 Weems' Life of Washington 12mo. morocco backs a 14c 84'. On Apr. 27th he charged for 44 more, and from May 1st through December 30th he apparently bound nearly 4000 copies, some 'in sheep'. Vol. 23 : 1919–1929. On May 1, 1809, D. Humphreys charged Carey for reading 19 proofs of 'Washington's Life, at 28 cts – 5 32½' Vol. 23 : 1457. In 1809 John Kneass charged Carey, May 6th, 'For Printing 1000 large plate Life of Washington $10 — For Printing 1000 small [*plate*] life of Washington 6', and on July 1st, for '2000 large plate life of Washington 20 — 2000 Head of Washington 12'. Vol. 23 : 1465, 1466. On Sept. 8th, 1809, Benjamin Scott charged Carey for printing '100 Washington 1.00'. Vol. 23 : 1499. In the same month Carey paid Scott for printing '250 Small head of washington 1.25'. Vol. 23 : 1851. In 1809 Peter Thompson bound for Carey 'Twelve Life of Washinton 1/2 bs. in red — 7 — 8 — — 96'. Vol. 23 : 1865–1871. In August, 1809, Lydia Bailey rendered account to Carey for printing '150 Washington each 7......10.50'. Vol. 23 : 1563. Carey was debtor to Henry Charles '1809. Dec. 21 — printing 300 Washington's head — 62½......1.87½'. Vol. 23 : 1425.

# ADDENDA

Title 19.

An item of Nov. 8th, 1796, from William Barker to Carey, is for engraving 'Small Map of United States......£15 0 0'. Vol. 8 : 2732. Bills of George Wilson to Carey throughout 1810 contain items for binding nearly 3000 'Life of Washington' at from 18 to 20 cents a copy. Vol. 24 : 2214–2226. A bill of W. H. Morgan to Carey contains an item, under date of March, 1809 or 1810, 'to Printing 56 Washington......5.70 — to papers for Dit......5.60.' Vol. 24 : 2152. Asher Miner rendered an account to Carey in 1810 on which was the following: 'July Composing 120 pages Life of Washington 924 ms. in a page, 110,880 ms. at .50 per 1000......55.25 —— Printing ten forms, 8 tokens in each, at .50 — 40.00 —— $95.25.' Again 'Composing first form of W's Life, 11,088 ms. at 50 Ch. —— 5.50 — Press-work of do: 21 Tokens, @ 50 cts......10.50.' Vol. 24 : 2150. On a statement from George Wilson to Carey beginning Jan. 4, 1810, there are items for binding as follow: 'Feby. 27, 500 Life of Washington — a 18c......90 — Mar. 30, 300 Life of Washington 18c' — while on May 1 there are 500 apparently in English; on Sept. 26 there are 50 and on the 29th, 213 more both at 20c. On Oct. 24 we find 200 more at that price and on the 26th and 30th, 200 more each; Nov. 1, 150 at 20 cents and on the 6th, 146 more; on the 14th, 204 and the 24th, 50, and the 29th, 250. Vol. 24 : 2214–2226. In 1810 John Kneass rendered a bill to Carey for '985 life of Washington ......9.85 (Feby. 1)'; and on the 8th of the same month '875 Head of Washington — 55 ......4.81'; March 3 '1000 Heads of Washington — 55......5.50' and '750 long plate washington......7.50'; and March 17, '12 Washingtons — 10......1.20'. Vol. 23 : 1687–1688. In May, 1810, John Kneas rendered an account to Carey containing, among many other items, 'For Printing 100 Head of Washington small $55, 150 small Head of Washington $77'. Vol. 24 : 2080.

Title 20.

Mathew Carey to Conrad Zentler Dr March 19, 1810: 'To printing 500 proposal for publishing the Life of Washington, in Germ. 7.50'. Vol. 23 : 1517. On Apr. 18, 1810, George Wilson charged Carey for binding '50 Life of Washington German 18c......9', with another item of May 1 for 132 in German. On a statement rendered to Carey by Hellings & Aitken under date of Mar. 2 [*1811–1812*] there is an item, 'to 149 Das Leben Washington Sheep Leter'd......29.80.' Vol. 25 : 2493. George Wilson bound for Carey [*1812–1813*] '50 Life of Washington (German) @ 20......$10.' Vol. 26 : 2937.

Title 21.

In 1811 John Kneass rendered an account to Carey containing an item of June 24th for '425 Head of Washington fine 70......2.90', and another of July 13th for '430 Heads of Washington 55......2 25'. In 1811 Henry Charles printed for Carey, under date of Nov. 15th, '1000 Washington Head a 75 per 100......7.50', and as of Nov. 20th, '500 Washington Head a 75......3.75.' Vol. 25 : 2461. Carey's accounts with John Martin in 1811 show various items for binding *Washington*, ranging from 1 to 100 copies. Vol. 25 : 2519–2521. In 1811 Daniel Fenton rendered a bill to Carey for binding, amongst many other items, '50 Washington' at 20 cents. Other similar items total 383 copies at the same price. Vol. 26.

Title 22.

Bills of Henry Charles to Carey in 1812 contain items in January, March and May for printing heads of Washington, always at 75¢ a hundred. Vol. 25 : 2462. In 1812 statements of account between John Kneass and Carey give the following items: 'Jan. 30, 288 Washington life 4 designs — 75......2.16. 280 — D° — 2 D° [*designs*] — 50...... 1.40. Sept. 1, 350 Washington 4 designs — 75......2.622. 640 Head of Washington — a 50......3.20. Sept. 8, 200 Washington 4 designs — 75......1.50. 200 D°......2 — D°. [*designs*] — 50......1. 210 Head Washington — 70......1.47. 50 Washington 4 designs — 75......372, 50 D°. — 2 — 50......25. May 6 100 Life of Washington ......75. 100 D°. — D°. — (small plates)......50. . . . June 22, 45 Life of Washington.' Vol. 25 : 2505–2507. On April 20th, 1812, Moore & Lake charged Carey for binding '100 Weems' Washington 20 cts $20.00', and on May 28th a similar item amounted to $12.30. Vol. 26 : 2876. An account to Carey from John Dainty, undated but bound with other bills of 1811 and 1812, contains an item of May 29th for '1000 Life of Washington at 1......10.00. — To do 1000 do small at 50 cts per H<sup>d</sup>......5.00 — To do 550 Washingtons Head at 75 cts......4.12'; another item of June 3rd, 'To 1000 Washingtons Head at 75 cts......7.50'; and another of June 16th for 'Washingtons head'. Vol. 25 : 2473. In 1812 Samuel Lewis rendered an account to Carey including, on Aug. 27, 'To reading 14 Sig. printed by Dickinson of Weems's Life of Washington ......3.50, Reading 2 d°. printed by Aitken (O. P.) —.50......4.00.' Vol. 25 : 2605. William McCulloch in a statement of 1812 put down as owing him from M. Carey 'Sept. 28 [*To*] Engraving Plates Weems Washington by W<sup>m</sup>. Charles......50.00. Oct. 10 [*To*] Printing 5,000 sig B & C Weems Washington......32.12½.' Vol. 25 : 2536. In an undated bill, bound with others of 1812, William C. Charles charged Carey $8.00 for a 'Plate for Life of Washington' and $10.00 for 'Retouching Life of Washington'. Vol 26 : 2788. In 1812 J. B. Reynolds rendered a statement for 'Printing 1000 half Sheet "Washington Life"......10 —'. Vol. 25 : [*unnumbered.*] During 1812 George Wilson bound *Washington* for Carey (with differences noted between 'sheep 7 calf Gilt in 2 copies') to the extent of 2768 copies, exclusive of the 1940 noted as folded or gathered. An item of Oct. 9th reads: '1000 Sheets Washington Folded @ 4<sup>c</sup> P. 100'. Vol. 25 : 2597–2602; Vol. 26 : 3118.

Titles 22–26.

In 1812–1814 Samuel Wakeling of Frankford bound *Washington* for Carey. Vol. 26 : 3109–3115; Vol. 27 : 3376, 3377.

Title 24.

Griggs & Dickinson, on July 17th, 1813, charged Carey for 'Printing Life of Washington 2.500 Copies, 6 Signatures C.D.E.K,M.R. containing 73.000 ms — a 50/o......36 00. To 60 Tokens on Ditto — a 50/o......30.00'. Vol. 26 : 2822. In 1813 John Dainty printed for Carey many books, among which are found 1900 'small' life of Washington and 2300 'small' Heads of the same. Similar items occur in August, 1813. Vol. 26 : 2999–3003. George W. Mentz rendered an account in November, 1813, for 'binding 100. Washington......$20.00'. Vol. 26 : 2872. [There is a note payable after ninety days to George W. Mentz from M. L. Weems for '30 dollars eighty cents', dated Feb. 12, 1812.

# ADDENDA

Vol. 26 : 2934.] In 1813 Robert Porter bound *Washington* for Carey. Vol. 27 : 3546. Samuel Lewis in 1813 asked 1.50 for 'Reading 6 proofs, of Life of Washington Sig: M,K,E,D,C,R,......a 25 Cents ea'. Vol. 26 : 2860.

Titles 25 and 26.[1]

On Feb. 21, 1814, J. B. Reynolds charged Carey $13 'To printing 1300 heads of Washington, discount .65.' Vol. 27 : 3352. Another item of his in 1814 is for printing '365 Washingtons'. Vol. 27 : 3570. On April 28th, 1814, Joseph Brown charged Carey as follows: 'March 26th To Do. [*printing*] 1000 Washington at $1......10.00 Do. Do. Do. Do. at 50 cents......5.00.' April 20th, 'To Do 1000 Washington at $1.25......12.50'. Vol. 27 : 3438. In 1814 John Dainty rendered a statement to Carey on 'June 28th To printing 500 Life of Washington [*possibly not Weems' work*]', and on July 11th, 1250 the same. Vol. 27 : 3168. In 1814 Washington was often bound, according to statements to Carey, by S. & J. Taylor. Vol. 27 : 3367–3369.

Title 27.

On May 20th, 1815, Joseph Brown charged Carey for printing, May 6th, '50 Wash[n]. ......37½' cents. Vol. 28 : 161. Dainty & Duffee charged Carey for printing, on June 9, 1815, '676 Washingtons life' for 45 cents and '150 head of Washington' for $1.87½. Vol. 28 : 4159. On July 23rd, 1815, Robert Thompson charged Mathew Carey for binding '35 Washington......7.00'. Vol. 28 : 4210. A bill to Carey of Thomas DeSilver, undated, but bound with other bills of 1815, included an item of Sept. 9th for binding 100 *Washington* for $20. Vol. 28 : 4175. 'To folding 100 Life of Washington ......76 [*cents*]. . . To folding Gethering & colating 32 Life of Washington...... 25 [*cents*] . . . Benj[n] Hinchman'. Vol. 28 : 4055.

Titles 28–31.

An undated list signed Alex[a] Rider [*1816–1817?*] of 'Drawing done for Mr Mathew Carey at six Dollar a piece' gives the following: 'Defeat of *Bradock*', 'for the life of Washinton for [*page?*] 49 a Maroding party of Endians. page 78 defence of fort Sulivan. page 92 atack on Red Bank. 86 defeat of the Heasian near trenton. 108 death of Colonel Williams. 114 Surrender of Cornwallis. 71 Batle of lexinton. 82 Surender of Sarotoga.' Vol. 30 : 4975, 4976. John Kneass printed in 1816 many heads of Washington, even 'doubleheaded Washington', but probably not those for Weems. Vol. 29 : 4469, 4470. A bill of Lydia R. Bailey to Carey for printing has as one item Oct. 16, 1816, 'Proposal Life of Washington 4000 ms. 1 token 2.50'. Vol. 29 : 4320. John G. Warnicke charged Carey, on a statement of March 10, 1817, for 'retouching two plates Likenesses of Gen. Washington......12.00.' Vol. 30 : 5097.

[1] The following items, pertaining to the engravers of the map and plates in these editions, were obtained too late for entry in their proper place in the text. 'John Bower, engraver, made plates of inferior execution in Philadelphia about 1810.' *History of The Arts of Design*, William Dunlap, Vol. III, p. 284, AAS. 'Robinson. This name, without initials, appears on some very badly engraved plates in Weems' "Life of Washington," Philadelphia, 1815.' *Ibid.*, Vol. III, p. 331, AAS.

Titles 32–34.

'August 4th. 1818. Mr. Mathew Carey & Son To J. R. A. Skerrett, Dr. To . . . 6th Printing proposals for Lives of Washington. Franklin. and Marion. 500 copies 2.50. . . .' Vol. 15 : 5495. A bill of Joseph Yeager[1] for Oct. 27, 1818, has as one of its items, 'Portraits Washington . . . Life of Washington — plates. . . .' Vol. 31 : 5587. A bill of Tanner, Vallance, Kearny & Co. for 1818 includes one item of Nov. 26, 1818, for 'Battle of Lexington & Surrender of Cornwallis' at $50.00 for the engraving. Vol. 31 : 5518.

Title 33.

A statement of account between M. Carey & Son and William Fry includes the following item: in 1818, July 29, 'To Printing 1.000 Copies Life of Washington 20 Edition. . . . . $38.' Vol. 33 : 6013.

Title 35.

On February 20, 1819, William Fry charged M. Carey & Son 'To Printing 22nd Edition of Washington Life . . . $76.' Vol. 33 : 6013. A bill of William Fennell, Jr., to M. Carey & Son, dated Philadelphia, April 19, 1819, includes an item of Jan. 27th for printing '1000 Washington @ 1 50/100. . . . . .15.00', also '500 Heads of Washn. 75/100. . . . . .3.75'; on Feb. 16, similar items for Washington; April 6, 1100 Washingtons and 550 heads of Washington, all at prices first quoted. Vol. 33 : 6040. A bill of Wm. Charles to Messrs. Carey & Son, dated Philadelphia, Aug. 22, 181[*9?*], has items: 'To printing . . . 100 Washington 1.50. . . . . .1.50. . . . 100 Do portraits. . . . . . 90. . . . Retouching Long plate Washington 25.00. . . .' Vol. 32 : 5705.

Titles 35 and 36.

D. Allinson bound *Washington* in 1819 and 1820. Vol. 34 : 6803.

Title 36.

D. Allinson charged Carey, Oct. 24, 1820, 'To bindg. 44 Washingtons life [@] 20 Cts . . . . . .' Vol. 32 : 5606.

Title 37.

On October 13, 1818, William Fry charged M. Carey & Son 'To Printing 25 Edition of Washingtons Life . . . $95.' Vol. 33 : 6013.

### Life of Marion

Title 85.

Hunter & Robinson of Baltimore rendered a bill to Mathew Carey dated Nov. 22, 1809, with the item, 'To printing Weem's Life of Marion 189. — Binders Bill for folding

[1] 'Yeager Joseph engraver 103 Sassafras.' *Philadelphia Directory*, 1816, 1817, AAS. Joseph Yeager was engraving and etching in Philadelphia 1816–1845. He made copies of etchings by Cruikshank and other English artists, for American reprints of books illustrated by them. See *History of The Arts of Design*, William Dunlap, Vol. III, p. 343, AAS.

Ditto 5 sig[n]. 5. — 3 boxes 3. — 1 trunk 4. — $201.' Vol. 23 : 1662. 'M[r]. Mathew Carey D[r] To De Silver & Davis 1810 Jan[y]. 6 To D[o]. [*Binding*] 200 Life of Marion (Ms. Bks) 12......25.' Vol. 23 : 1595. Peter Thompson rendered an account to Carey on which under date of Jan. 11, 1810, he charged eleven dollars for binding 'One Hundred Life of Marion 1/2 b[s]. in red a 11 cts.' and again on Feb. 5, 'Two hundred & fifty Life of Marion a 11 [*cents*] 27.50.' Vol. 24 : 2183.

Title 88.

'Philadelphia Nov[r]. 7[th]. 1816 M[r]. M. Carey To Joseph Yeager D[r]. . . . To Engraving Plates Life Marion......80.00 Copper for D[o].......6.40. . . .' Vol. 29 : 4714.

Titles 88 and 89.

Griggs & Co. rendered a statement to Carey for printing, on which is the following: 'Sep. 7 — Life of Marion......277', and again, 'To printing Life of Marion 22 forms 12.000 ms each at 50 cts......132. 12 tok on each form at 55 cts......145.' Vol. 30 : 4824, 4825.

Title 90.

On Aug. 4, 1818, J. R. A. Skerrett charged Carey for 'Printing proposals for Lives of Washington. Franklin. and Marion. 500 copies 2.50.' Vol. 15 : 5495. A bill of Joseph Yeager for Oct. 27, 1818, contains the item, 'Gen[l]. Marion, plates'. Vol. 31 : 5587. A bill of William Fennell, Jr., to M. Carey & Son dated Philadelphia, April 19, 1819, includes an item of Feb. 16, 1819, for printing '1000 Marions'. Vol. 33 : 6040.

Titles 90 and 91.

A bill of William Charles to Carey, dated at Philadelphia, Aug. 22, 181[*9?*], contains the item: 'To printing 350 Marion 1.50......5.25'. Vol. 32 : 5705. On Sept. 24, 1819, D. Allinson charged Carey 'To binding 212 Marions Life $42.40', and there are similar items on Sept. 14th and Oct. 24th. Vol. 32 : 5606. Similar items occur in 1820. Vol. 34 : 6803.

Titles 91 and 92.

'In ten minutes after sight, pay unto Friend Ben. Warner or order . . . Seventy five of the 7[th] ed. Marion, for value receiv[d]. Feb. 19. 1821. M. L. Weems'. Vol. 34 : 6777.

Title 94.

Concerning the printer of this edition: 'Philadelphia, June 13, 1801. This day received of Mathew Carey, Esq. Books and Stationary to the am[t]. of Thirty-four Dollars Thirteen Cents; for which I am to make payment in printing, at the rate of Fifty Cents per Token and Forty Cents per Thousand; the said Carey to pay the paper-maker's price for paper, which will be procured as reasonably as possible. — Asher Miner.' Vol. 16 : 6451. There is also an accounting from 1801 to 1805 of work done as above, particularly on the *Merry Fellow's Companion*. Vol. 20 : 432.

## MASON LOCKE WEEMS

### Life of Franklin

Title 131.

S. & J. Taylor charged Carey $4.80 for binding 24 *Franklin's Life*. No date. Vol. 26 : 2926. Pomeroy, printer of this edition, signed a release to Mathew Carey for four Hundred Thirty six dollars, and twenty cents 'which when paid [*at four months*] will be in full for all demands against Mason L. Weems [*the note dated Feb. 14, 1817*]'. Vol. 30 : 4943.

Title 132.

'Decemb[r] 18[th] 1816 M[r]. M. Carey to John G. Warnicke D[r]. . . . For Engraving Likeness of B. Franklin......10.00. . . .' Vol. 29 : 4706. On Aug. 6, 1818, J. R. A. Skerrett charged Carey for 'Printing proposals for Lives of Washington. Franklin. and Marion. 500 copies 2.50.' Vol. 15 : 5495.

Title 133.

A bill of Lovegrove, Dell & Co. of 1818 to M. Carey & Son contains an item of Jan. 1, 1819, for 'Bindg 150 Life of Franklin — 20c......30.' Similar items through March, 1819, bring the number bound by him to 953. Vol. 33 : 6174.

Title 135.

'In ten minutes after sight, pay unto Friend Ben. Warner or order twenty five of the 5[th] ed. Franklin . . . for value receiv[d]. Feb. 19, 1821. M. L. Weems.' Vol. 34 : 6777. A bill of James Lovegrove to Matthew Carey & Son in 1821 contains the items, '3 M[o] 24 To Printing Franklin $209.70 . . . Binding 200 d[o] @ 20 c[s] 40 . . . 4 M[o] 14 To Binding 351 Franklin @ 20 70.20', and other items of binding Franklin totalling about 1320 altogether. Vol. 34.

### Philanthropist

Title 159.

T. & G. Palmer rendered a bill for $30.50 to Carey, dated Jan. 3, 1809, for printing the *Philanthropist*. Vol. 23 : 1481. Several other references show printing work done for Carey. There are also numerous receipts for payment by Carey for various numbers, in 1807 mostly, of *The Literary Magazine*. All these receipts are on printed forms 'For John Conrad & Co.', but this inscription is crossed out and the Palmers' names written in. Vol. 21 : 577, 578; Vol. 22 : 1163.

### Hymen's Recruiting Serjeant

Title 164.

J. R. A. Skerrett rendered a bill to Carey, Dec. 20, 1816, 'To composition of Hymen's Sergeant; to wit: 32 page pica at 44 cts pr page......14.08 8 long primer at 67½ cts pr page.' Vol. 15 : 5496. In 1817 Joseph Hermstad charged Carey & Son for folding and stitching '1100 Recruiting Sergeant......6.87½'. Vol. 15 : 5267.

## ADDENDA

Title 165.

In June, 1821, Bioren included in a bill, 'Composition of 5 half sheets Recruiting Sergeant, Pica and long primer — 1000 ems. each page 40. and 45 cts......25.00'. Vol. 34 : 6499.

Title 171.

The following may apply, since it was R. Cochran who printed the 1802 edition of *Hymen No. 2:* 'M[r] M. Carey To Robert Cochran D[r] . . . 1800. . . . July 10 — Sundry Printing fore M[r] Weems......16. 12 9.' Vol. 15 : 5936.

Title 171A.

On Apr. 2, 1802, Cornelius Tiebout rendered a bill to Carey for printing '1815 impressions from a plate intitled the nest of love' for $18.5. Vol. 16 : 6992.

### True Patriot

Title 173.

That there was a portrait in some of the issues of this pamphlet is clearly proved by the following bills: 'M[r]. Weems To B. Tanner D[r]. To Printing 10000 Bloomfield...... [$]6.67 — 4 Quire Paper at 37½ Cents......1.50.' Vol. 16 : 6689. [*In autograph*] 'March 6, 1802 Please to pay unto M[r] Benj[n] Tanner or order the sum of forty seven Dollars and oblige your Mason L. Weems, Mathew Carey Esq[r].' Vol. 16 : 6709.

### Carey's Franklin Almanack

Title 174.

'New York 6 m° 24[th]. 1801 Matthew Carey To Abraham Shoemaker Dr To Astron[l]. Calculations for an Almanac for 1802......14 Doll[s]. Received payment in New York 7 m°. 20[th]. 1801 Abr[m]. Shoemaker.' Vol. 16 : 6619. John Adams' bills for printing *Franklin Almanacks* for 1803 are to be found in Vol. 17 : 6914, 6916, 6917, and a 'second edition', *Ibid.* : 7606, 7607.

### Weems's Washington Almanack

Title 176.

In July, 1803, John Adams charged Carey for 'printing 2,000. Weems's Washington Almanacks, @ $11......$22.0', and for 'folding & stitching 3.000 . . . @ $3...... $9.0'. Vol. 18 : 7719.

### God's Revenge Against Murder

Title 178.

'M[r]. M. Carey To John Adams 1808 Sep. To Composition . . . [*illegible*] 1/2 Sheets Ned Finley 7,226 m's in the Sheet @ 45 bts......$6.50 — To thirty-two tokens — 4000 N°. a 45 bts......14.40 — Rec[d]. of M[r]. Carey Twenty Dollars Ninety Cents in full for printing 4000 N°. of two half sheets of the Drowned Wife Jn° Adams Sep[r]. 29,

1808.' Vol. 22 : 1077. 'Philad[a]. Sept. 16[th]. 1808 M[r] Carey To W[m]. Charles D[r] To Copying Caricature......15.00 — plate for Do 13 by 10 at 4 Cts......5.20.' Vol. 22 : 1102. John Boyd charged Carey, for 'Re-engraving the Plate of Mary Finley', $9. Vol. 22 : 1098.

Titles 178 and 179.

William McCulloch, on Sept. 7, 1808, rendered a statement to Carey with an item for binding '1250 Ned Findley — 5 tokens × 50 = 2.50 22 × 42 = 924 × 8 = 7,392 = 50 — 3.70 —— 6.20.' Vol. 24 : 2384. '1808 Mr. M. Carey To Robert Cochran Sept 12 To composing 32 Pages Mary Findley 39000 m's......$19.50 — To Press D[o]. 1250 Copies ......10. — Oct 20 To compos. 16 pages M. Findley......10 — To press D[o] 4000...... 16.' Vol. 7 : 2640. 'D[r]. M[r]. Matthew Carey in Acc[t] Current with Hastings Etheridge & Bliss Cr. 1808 Octr. 3, By 200 Gods Revenge......33 33' Vol. 24 : 2071. 'M[r]. M, Carey, Bought of Lydia R, Bailey 1000 Almanac's @ $\frac{8}{2}$ p[r] Doz $22.22 Decb[r] 8 1808' 'M[r]. M Carey To Lydia R Bailey......D[r]. To foulding and stiching 12 hun[d]. and fifty pamphlets life of Maroy Finly @ 37½ p[r]. hin[d],......$4..68 — 13 quires blue paper @ 18 c[t] p[r]. q[r].......2..44 . . . Received the above in full Lydia R, Bailey 1808 Sept 17.' Vol. 22 : 1084. 'M[r]. M Carey To Lydia R, Bailey D[r]. To faulding and seawing 17 hundred and 40 life Marey finly @ 39½ cent p[r]. hundred $6..51½ — 8 quires bluw paper @ 19 p[r]. 1..50 . . . Received 283 faulded @ 3 cent p[r]. 9 Received the above in full 1808 Octo 14 Lydia R. Bailey.' Vol. 22 : 1212. 'M[r]. M. C. To B. Graves D[r]. 1808 Oct[r] 5. To printing 1 half sheet of M[rs]. Finlay's pamp[t]. composition — 3.53 Press work 4000 number — 8.00......11.53.' Vol. 23 : 1446. On Nov. 4, 1808, David Longworth rendered to Carey a bill for 'Ned Findley' at 1.15. Vol. 23 : 1115.

Seventh edition, undiscovered, between Titles 180 and 181.

Dec. 17 [*1808?*], Abel Dickinson charged Carey for 'printing 5 half sheets Ned Findley, 8000 ms & 4 tokens @ 45 & 50 — $5 60......$27 00.' Vol. 22 : 1119. Two separate bills rendered Carey by Abel Dickinson, with items dated respectively Jan. 6 and Jan. 26, 1809, for printing 'Mary Findley, 7[th]. Edition, 16 tok[*ens*] @ 50 cts......8.0 — To Impos'[g] Sig. B. & turning letters Ditto 0 62½', together with a third item of Dec. 28, 1808, mentioning the same edition, seem to prove very clearly that there was such an issue. Vol. 23 : 2060; Vol. 27 : 3484; Vol. 24 : 2061.

Title 181.

On Jan. 25, 1809, H. Charles charged Carey 'To printing 50 Mary Finley...... 0,,31'. Vol. 23 : 1559. Robert Cochran rendered a bill to Carey in 1809, containing an item of Nov. 3 'To Composition 38 pages Mary Findley 28,000 m's 50 40 To Press D[o] 2000 — 4 sheet 28 80'. Vol. 24 : 2053. The 'Estate of R. Cochran' rendered a bill to Carey with an item of the same date, as follows: 'To Composition 36 pages Mary Findly 28,000 ms......12.60 — To press work of D[o]. 2000......10.80'. Vol. 25 : 2468. 'M. Carey to Lydia Bailey 1809 Nov. 4 Printing one half Sheet Mary Finley Composition 10,000 M's a 45 4 50.' Vol. 23 : 1535. On Dec. 21, 1809, Henry Charles charged Carey for printing '1000 Mary finley 62½......6.25.' Vol. 23 : 1425. In 1809 Peter Thompson bound for Carey several items for 'Looking Glasses'. Vol. 23 : 1865–1888. In May, 1810, John Kneas rendered an account to Carey containing, among other items, one 'For

## ADDENDA

Printing . . . 640 Mary finley [*June 1*] $55.' Vol. 24 : 2080. Another bill of John Kneas in 1810 bears the items '975 Mary finley — 55......5.36 . . . March 16 880 Mary finly......4.84'. Vol. 23 : 1787–1788. Joseph Hermstad bound in 1810 for Carey '218 Mary Finley' for 1.09. Vol. 24 : 1974. In 1812 John Kneass rendered statements to Carey, giving the following items: 'Mar. 13, 86 Mary Finley.....[*no price given*]; . . . May 30. 100 God's Revenge 65.......65'; and 300 on the same date; and on June 3rd, 525. Vol. 25 : 2505–2507.

Title 182.

'Mr Mathew Carey D^r^ To Stiching 385 Ned Finley $2.92 . . . Benj^n^ Hinchman.' Vol. 28 : 4055.

Title 183.

A bill of Lydia R. Bailey to Carey contains an item of July 29, 1816, for printing '2500 Copies Drownd Wife viz Composition 38.000 ms......19,00 Press work 50 token ......25.' Vol. 29 : 4321. 'M^r^ Carey, To M^rs^. Bailey D^r^ to folding and stitching twelve hundred and fifty Copies of the Drown'd wife at 46 Cts. per hundred 5.75 . . . Reciev'd of M^r^ Carey the above in full — Eleanor Bailey — October 14^th^ 1816 —' Vol. 29 : 4297. 'Philadelphia Nov^r^. 7^th^. 1816 M^r^. M. Carey To Joseph Yeager D^r^. . . . To Engraving Plate Mary Finley......15.00.' Vol. 29 : 4714.

Title 184.

A bill of David Dickinson to Carey dated July 2, 1818, and containing an item 'To printing Drowned Wife 40000 M^s^ at 50 Cents per 1000...... 0.00. To 40 Token on D^o^ at 50 Cents per token 20.00. . . .' Vol. 15 : 5223.

### God's Revenge Against Gambling

Title 188.

On March 10, 1811, Mrs. Lydia Bailey printed for Carey *God's Revenge Against Gambling* for '80'. Vol. 26 : 2960. This item seems to prove the existence of one earlier edition, at least, than the 1812.

Title 191.

On Sept. 8, 1816, Joseph Yeager charged Carey 'To Engraving Plate Gambler...... $15.00'. Vol. 29 : 4714. Sept. 18, 1816, John Bioren, in a statement rendered to Carey, gave the item '[*To*] Composition of 6 half sheets pica God's Revenge against Gambling ......24. Press work of the same & token — 30......54.' Vol. 30 : 4746. On Oct. 14, 1816, Mrs. Eleanor Bailey received payment from Carey 'To folding three hundred copies of the Gamblers at fifty four Cts. per hundred......1.62'. Vol. 29 : 4297. A bill of Mrs. E. Bailey to Carey of Dec. 28, 1816, includes an item: 'To folding and stitching 400 Gamblers at 44 per 100 $2.16'. Vol. 28 : 4297.

Title 192.

A bill of Joseph Hermstad to Messrs. M. Carey & Son has an item of April 13, 1808 [*1818?*], for folding and stitching 1000 Gamblers. The next bill on the page has an item of April 25, 1818, for folding, and stitching 1000 Gamblers. Vol. 15 : 5267.

## MASON LOCKE WEEMS

### Anecdotes of Gamblers

Titles 194 and 195.

'M[r] Mathew Carey[s]. Estate in Chesnut Ward D[r] for the following taxes for 1802 Joseph Skerrett Coll[r] . . . personal tax . . . County . . . City . . . poor . . . health. . . .' Vol. 17 : 7527. Benjamin & Thomas Kite also appear many times in these books as booksellers.

### Drunkard's Looking Glass

Title 197.

John Dainty rendered an account to Carey without the year's date (but bound with 1811 and 1812) on which there are items as follow: June 3, 'To 500 Drunkenness at 75 cts......3.75'; June 4, 'To 500 D°......3.75'; with another item of '500 Drunkenness' on June 16. Vol. 25 : 2473. Ann Cochran charged Carey on June 6, 1812, 'To printing God's Revenge against Drunkenness, containing 62 Pages, at 62 cents per page ......$38.44 Press-work of the same 48 tokens......24.00'. Vol. 26 : [*2791*].

Titles 200 and 201.

In a bill of Lydia R. Bailey to Carey, there is an item, on June 22, 1816, for printing 'Drunkards Looking Glass viz Composition 56 pages 1590 m[s] each......44.50 Press 56 token.....28.' Vol. 29 : 4321. A bill of Fennell & Tiller, dated Philadelphia, Nov. 4, 1816, to Carey, contains an item, on Oct. 25, 'To Printing 835 Drunkard's at 75 cts $6 25'. Vol. 29 : 4409.

Title 202.

'Philadelphia January 17[th]. 1819 Mess[rs]. M. Carey & Son To David Dickinson To printing Drunkards Lookg-Glass of three thousand Copies 8½ Sheets at $12.85 pr 1/2 Sheet......$102.80 By Covers for ditto 30.00......007.10 Setting up 6 pages Do in Pica. — 1.50 . . .' Vol. 32 : 5720. A bill of William Fennell, Jr., to M. Carey & Son contains an item of March 9, 1819, for printing '500 Drunkards', and another of April 6, 1819, for printing '1000 Drunkards'. Vol. 33 : 6040.

### God's Revenge Against Adultery

Titles 210–212.

On Sept. 15, 1816, Joseph Yeager charged Carey 'To [*Engraving*] Plate There g , d d , , n you take that 20.00'. Vol. 29 : 4714.

Title 211.

A bill of J. R. A. Skerrett, dated July 1, 1816, contains the item: 'July, 15, 1816, Gods Revenge against Adultery. [$] 53.4 . . . 48 pages at 48 cts pr page.....$23.04 Press-work, 6 forms at $5.00 each......30.00. . . .' There is a similar bill of July 15. Vol. 29 : 4620, 4621.

# ADDENDA

Title 212.

A bill of Joseph Hermstad to Messrs. M. Carey & Son contains the items, of April 13, 1808, for folding and stitching 2000 *Adultery;* and of April 25, 1818, for 2000 *Adultery*. Vol. 15 : 5267.

## God's Revenge Against Duelling

Title 215.

'Philadelphia February 21: 1820 M$^{r}$. M. L. Weems To Edw W Clay D$^{r}$. To Designing & engraving Caricature......$15. Rec$^{d}$. payment in full Edw W. Clay.' Vol. 32 : 5712. A bill from John Bioren contains an item of Nov. 29, 1801 [*1821?*] 'To Composition of 6 half sheets Duellists . . . Looking glass Containing 66900 ems @ 45.....$30.15 Press work of 6 half sheets 12 Token each 72 Token @ 45......32.40. . . .' Vol. 34 : 6500.

## Immortal Mentor

Title 219.

References to Parry Hall, the printer of this edition, cover bills, mostly for medical books, around 1792–1795, and seem to indicate that he died about 1793.

Title 220.

In a statement from John Bioren to Carey commencing in 1797, under date of June 30, there is the entry, '2000 Cards for I. Mentor......2.12.6.' Vol. 30 : 4740. 'Rev$^{d}$. Mason L Weems D$^{r}$. To Michael Conrad 1798 Dec$^{r}$. . . . folding 1024 Immortal Mentor each 28 Sheets 28.672 Sheets 3$^{d}$. 3[£] 1[*s*] 8[*d*]' as well as for 'gethering' and 'folding with papers' and for 'sewing' same. The same bill states that, in 1797, 248 'Immortal Mentor tool'd, & Edg Rolled', left with Mr. Robertson, cost 20.13.4. Vol. 14 : 4922. 'M$^{r}$ Mathew Carey D$^{r}$ for M$^{r}$. M. L. Weems To Robertson & Coghlan July 18 [*1800?*] 200 Immortal Mentor Lett$^{d}$ & Tooled @ 1/8 £16.13.4 . . . Aug. 7. 151 Immortal Mentor @ 1/8 12.11.8'. Vol. 15 : 5843.

Title 221.

'M$^{r}$. Mathew Carey To Joseph Charless [*1800–*]1802 . . . [*March*] 8 Proposals for Immortal Mentor . . . 3700 *M's*'. Vol. 17 : 7634.

Title 222.

Robert Cochran charged Carey 'To D$^{o}$ [*printing*] 1803 June 13 . . . 750 title page Immortal Mentor......[*$*]2 . . . To Catalogue for Mr. Weems......3.' Vol. 21 : 836. William Duane, of the *Aurora*, rendered a bill to Carey, including items for advertising the *Immortal Mentor*, in 1803 and 1804. Vol. 23 : 1606. May 16, 1808, C. A. LeBreton charged Carey for binding 30 *Immortal Mentors*. Vol. 23: 1702.

Title 223.

In 1809 Peter Thompson bound for Carey '18 Immortal Mentors a 15......2.70.' Vol. 23 : 1888. On Jan. 10th, 1812, William W. Potter charged Carey, for binding 'Immortal Mentor @ 18......6.48'. Vol. 25 : [*unnumbered*].

# MASON LOCKE WEEMS

### Russel's Sermons

Title 227.

Stewart & Cochran printed 3,000 for Carey, on Feb. 18, 1795. Vol. 4 : 1456. A similar item is found in Vol. 7 : 2597. In 1809 Peter Thompson bound for Carey, 'Ninety nine Russels Sermons 1/2 b^s^. in red — 7......6.93'. Vol. 23 : 1865–1871.

### Blair's Sermons

Titles 229 and 230.

'D^r^. M^r^. Mathew Carey To John Curtis 1792 Decem^r^. 18 To Binding 99 Blair ... 1/......4 19 —' Vol. 7 : 2410. In 1809 Peter Thompson bound for Carey 'one Blair's Sermons 2 V. 12^mo^. 1/2 B^s^......16.' Vol. 23 : 1865–1871. In 1812 William W. Potter rendered statements to Carey, including the item: 'Jan^y^. 5th To Binding 98 Blairs Sermons 2 v @ 34......66.64 . . . 12 Blairs Sermons 2 v......8.16.' Vol. 25 [*unnumbered*].

### Maryland & Virginia Almanac

Title 236.

Isaac Briggs was evidently a stationer and bookseller in Georgetown. Vol. 1 : 21–23.

### Discourses Concerning Government

Title 237.

In a bill of 1816 from George Wilson to Carey there is an item for binding '4 Sidney on Government [2 *vols.*] 2.40'. Vol. 30 : 5097.

### Davies' Sermons

Title 239.

David Dickinson charged Carey, on Oct. 14, 1818, 'To printing proposals for D^r^ Davies's Sermons . . .' Vol. 15 : 5223. 'Philadelphia Society For the Promotion of National Industry, To J. R. A. Skerrett, Dr. . . . 1819 . . . Oct^r^. 26th . . . To printing two proposals . . . Davie's Sermons, 9000 ms......4.50. . . .' Vol. 33 : 6349.

Title 241, see title 11.

### Guthrie's Geography

Title 242.

William Barker is referred to many times, once as the engraver of a map for that work.

### Works of Thomas Paine

Title 243.

An account from Mathew to James Carey for $232.38, dated Dec. 19, 1798, contains the items: '6 Apology for the Bible $1.87½' and '70 ditto bound up with Paine's Works by M^r^. Grant 21.00'.

# ADDENDA

## Holy Bible

Title 248.

Bills of 1806 for 'printing Proposals for Splendid Family Bible' were rendered to Carey by Abel Dickinson, who apparently also did considerable printing of the Bibles and Testaments themselves. Vol. 20 : 333; Vol. 21 : 879–880, and many other references. A bill of William Charles to Carey of Sept. 16, 1808, includes the item: 'Repairing Bible plate N 1......8.00'. Vol. 22 : 1102. Proposals, dated 1813, for 'A Cheap Family Bible' at six dollars are in Vol. 26 : 2892. In a statement to Carey from William W. Potter the first item, Feb. 1, 1814, is: 'To Binding 25 Bibles for M^r. Weems......21.87½.' Vol. 27 : 3329. An account between Carey and Joseph Charless, the printer of this edition, dated Jan. 4, 1801, contains items for printing: 'Boy found under a Hay-Cock, Goody two Shoes, Giant Grumbo, Whittington and Cat', etc. Credits on this bill include a silver watch and coloured paper for covers. Vol. 15 : 5947.

## View of the Cultivation of Fruit Trees

Title 252.

On May 10th, 1817, D. Allinson charged Carey 'To Press Work of 20 formd Woodcuts for Coxe's Book on fruit — Cider &c — 1000 Copies making 80 token at 75 Cts. Com^n. includ^d......60$.' Vol. 30 : 4729. Sundry other items of Allinson from 1813 to 1818 are for binding, folding, gathering and sewing Coxe on fruits. A footnote to one item records: 'I have delivered to W^m Coxe five copies — on Fruits &c. & kept on my own account sixteen copies.' Vol. 32 : 5710. A bill of D. & E. Fenton for books bought of Carey in 1820 deducts an item to their credit for binding, including 37 copies of 'Cox on fruit'. Vol. 33 : 6045, 6046.

## Hunter's Sacred Biography

Title 253.

'Mathew Carey & son To Isaac Pierce [*1818?*] — For 50 copies Hunters' Sacred Biography — @ 3......$150 — folding & collating —'. Vol. 15 : 5468. 'Philadelphia Society For the Promotion of National Industry, To J. R. A. Skerrett, Dr. . . . 1819 . . . Oct^r. 26th . . . To printing two proposals — Hunters Sacred Biography, . . . 9000 ms ...... 4.50. . . .' Vol. 33 : 6349.

## Lavoisne's Atlas

Title 254.

Items in 1820 show William W. Potter binding *Lavoisne's Atlas* for Carey. Several bills of Benjamin Gaskill appear in 1820 for binding the same. Vol. 32 : 5754–5756, 5758. A bill of Kneass & Saurman, dated Philadelphia, Sept. 23, 1820, is for 'printing 773 Maps whole sheet Lavoisnes atlas......$17 00'. Other similar bills appear. Vol. 32 : 5780–5783.

## Miscellaneous

Frederick Brown & Co. receipted a bill to Rev. M. L. Weems on July 19, 1800, 'To printing 3500 prints at 5/ per H^d......8.15 — By cash Received 5 doll^s......1.17.6 By d^o. — do^o. — 8 d^o. — 3......4.17.6 Balance due £3.17.6'. Vol. 14 : 4886.

# INDEX

Throughout this Index the sign § indicates those works with which, it is believed, Weems was more than indirectly concerned.

# INDEX

# INDEX

# INDEX

# INDEX

THIS BOOK WAS LEFT INCOMPLETE BY

PAUL LEICESTER FORD

WAS EDITED BY MRS. ROSWELL SKEEL JUNIOR

AND PRINTED BY RICHMOND MAYO-SMITH

— INCEPTOR — SISTER — NEPHEW —

*The cuts are taken from the work of* ALEXANDER ANDERSON, *the color print is reproduced by* THE MAX JAFFÉ COMPANY *of Vienna, Austria, the paper is made by* THE WORTHY COMPANY *of Springfield, and the composition, presswork and binding are by* THE PLIMPTON PRESS *of Norwood, Massachusetts*